THE ENCYCLÖPEDIA ÖF

HEAVY METAL

COMPLETELY REVISED AND UPDATED

THE ENCYCLÖPEDIA ÖF
HEAVY METAL

DANIEL BUKSZPAN
FOREWORD BY RONNIE JAMES DIO

STERLING
New York

STERLING
New York

An Imprint of Sterling Publishing
387 Park Avenue South
New York, NY 10016

STERLING and the distinctive Sterling logo are registered trademarks of Sterling Publishing Co., Inc.

© 2012 by Daniel Bukszpan
First edition published by Sterling Publishing Co., Inc. in 2003
Illustration by Rob Dobi

ISBN 978-1-4027-9230-4

Library of Congress Cataloging-in-Publication Data

Bukszpan, Daniel.
  The encyclopedia of heavy metal/ Daniel Bukszpan.
    p. cm.
  Includes bibliographical references (p.), discography, and index.
  ISBN 0-7607-4218-9 (alk. paper)
  1. Heavy metal (Music)—Bio-bibliography—Dictionaries. I. Title.
  ML102.R6B84 2003
  7 81.66—dc21

                                                      2003004944

Distributed in Canada by Sterling Publishing
c/o Canadian Manda Group, 165 Dufferin Street
Toronto, Ontario, Canada M6K 3H6
Distributed in the United Kingdom by GMC Distribution Services
Castle Place, 166 High Street, Lewes, East Sussex, England BN7 1XU
Distributed in Australia by Capricorn Link (Australia) Pty. Ltd.
P.O. Box 704, Windsor, NSW 2756, Australia

For information about custom editions, special sales, and premium and corporate purchases,
please contact Sterling Special Sales at 800-805-5489 or specialsales@sterlingpublishing.com.

Manufactured in China

2 4 6 8 10 9 7 5 3 1

www.sterlingpublishing.com

PAGE 2: The unmistakable tongue that launched thousands of urban legends belonged to KISS' Gene Simmons.
PAGE 4: Guitarist James Hetfield is ready for an athletic Metallica performance.
PAGE 5: The boys of Venom welcome you to the exciting and glamorous world of faux-Satanic proto-black metal.
Left to right: Tony "Abaddon" Bray, Conrad "Cronos" Lant, and Jeff "Mantas" Dunn.
PAGE 6: Contrary to popular opinion, cocaine did not keep Aerosmith singer Steven Tyler looking so skinny;
rather it was the slimming effects of his vertically striped ensemble.
PAGE 7: Pantera guitarist "Diamond" Darrell Abbott plays a power chord that is totally heavy in every respect.
PAGE 9: The members of Accept sing about the woeful conditions inside the Federal Prison System.
PAGE 10: Mötley Crüe guitarist Mick Mars (right) will just have to wait his turn until the groupie is done with bassist Nikki Sixx.
PAGE 11: Front man Lemmy Kilmister delights the many ladies in Motörhead's fan base with this provocative pose.

To my wife, Asia, and my son, Roman. I love you both more than anything.

I'd like to thank Rosy Ngo at Barnes & Noble for letting me write this book. You started me down a new path in my life when I desperately needed one. I'd also like to thank Afarin Majidi, David Shure, and Jeff Witte—all of whom were among the first to take a chance on me before I had ever published so much as a single sentence anywhere.

As far as stylistic inspiration and influence, I must give credit to Chuck Eddy, who opened the door for all serious academic discussion of heavy metal music. I must also give credit to my personal favorite writer, Jim Goad, for the inspiration he has given me with the example of his excellent work. Despite your best efforts, Mr. Goad, you have influenced a new generation of writers, myself included. You have my sincerest apologies.

Within my personal life, I'd like to thank Leah Wang and Kathleen O'Malley for encouraging me to take risks and to do what I needed to do. Thanks to my parents, Albert and Joanna Bukszpan, for going above and beyond, many, many times over, to allow me to pursue this path in my life; André Aciman, for being the first published author in my family so that I didn't have to be; my drummer, Scott Sanfratello, for letting me blow off rehearsals so that I could finish this monster of a book; Dr. Adele Tutter, for keeping me sane through the wonders of modern chemistry; my sister and brother-in-law, Claudia and Jeff Rutherford, for inviting me up to their house in Massachusetts to chill out and write—next time I'll actually do it, since it probably would be good for me to get out of my Brooklyn apartment from time to time and avoid becoming the unshaven, nocturnal, cave-dwelling vampire that the author's lifestyle has rendered me; Jeff Marshall, my lifelong friend, for showing me that it's possible to pursue your art and live very badly at the same time; Morgan Woolverton, who turned me on to metal in the first place and without whom this book would be very short indeed; and Tim, Valborg, and Hjordis Linn, for providing additional familial support. Thanks also to Jessica Dorfman Jones for working 35-hour days to make the second edition happen; and Nathaniel Marunas for keeping this book out there for the last ten years and developing a plan for the next ten.

CONTENTS

FOREWORD

I have some dim recollections of being taught my ABC's as a lad. These were the building blocks of the words that have allowed us to rise so dramatically above the other animals on this planet, and thanks to those lessons we hated, but learned out of necessity, you'll be able to discover more than you ever imagined about the genesis and guts of heavy metal music.

We seem to have an overwhelming genetic need to chronicle all the events of our passage through life's triumphs and tragedies. So take heart all of you who worship at the feet of the Great God Information: Daniel Bukszpan presents for your viewing and reading pleasure, *The Encyclopedia of Heavy Metal*. From Abdullah to Zebra and everyone in between, it's the most thorough and informative publication on metal that I've ever read. The photos are historical and extensive. From Gene's tongue to Lemmy's mic stand, Blackmore on stage, Steven Tyler off stage, and Rob Halford on his bike, the pics are great. The book rings with facts and statistics but is never overshadowed by either. Daniel Bukszpan's knowledge and obvious love of the music is evident in the care with which he has assembled this wonderful book of reference.

I see my own life reflected in the pages of the *Encyclopedia*. We all wanted to be bigger than life, but never as big as our heroes. Who could be better than Robert Plant, Paul Rodgers, Jimmy Page, John Bonham, or any of the others I listened to until the grooves in the vinyl collapsed from the constant pounding I gave it. Yes, there really were records, and I had to be the first to have them. I would rush home to examine the back and front of the album sleeve for an eternity before even removing the plastic wrapping. The art work was innovative, free of restrictions, and best of all, HUGE! A portrait suitable for framing and very often framed. The info on the backside was invaluable: Who played what? Who wrote what, and in what exotic place did they do all that? Then came the grand opening. Should I save the plastic? No, that's too silly. Well, I'll just put it aside for now. Then, the rules:

1. Don't put your fingers on the surface of the record.
2. Handle the record only by the outer rim.
3. Check the stylus (the needle for those who don't remember).
4. Be sure the rpm speed is properly adjusted (very antiquated).
5. Lower the stylus.
6. BLAST OFF!

We've come so far since then. Aside from a glitch or two, the new generation of musical storage devices is approaching indestructibility and offers options we could only hope for. But one thing remains constant despite the upswing in technology. The music still stirs the imagination, and Daniel Bukszpan's *Encyclopedia of Heavy Metal* takes you on a journey through the minds and times of those musicians who have affected our thoughts, and even our lives, in so many ways. So let the images you see and the images you create flood the senses with memories of what was and always will be, MAGIC METAL.

RONNIE JAMES DIO
2003

Being asked to write the foreword for the second edition of *The Encyclopedia of Heavy Metal* brings fond memories of Ronnie back to me. I remember Ronnie being very proud and honored to be part of this incredible book, which was so packed with facts and wonderful photos of all of our heavy metal heroes, like Gene and Lemmy and Rob.

I was wondering if Daniel could top his own book, but he did it. Now there are bands who didn't get their due last time, like Girlschool and Mountain, and new bands like Wolfmother and Mastodon. So get ready to feast your eyes on yet another masterpiece. You won't be disappointed.

WENDY DIO
2012

INTRODUCTION

When I originally wrote this book in 2002, I believed that I was correcting an injustice. Chuck Eddy's book *Stairway to Hell* ranked the top 500 heavy metal albums of all time, according to him, and even though it's one of my favorite books, I felt like he left out some essential bands, like Iron Maiden, Judas Priest, Dio, Candlemass, and so on. He described himself in the book's introduction as a "seventies snob," which is reflected in his choices. But as someone who was a teenager in the 1980s, and hence an "eighties snob," I felt that it was worthwhile to establish criteria for what heavy metal meant to people my age, or close to it.

For the most part, I feel like I did all right. But of course, when the final manuscript went to press, I thought of all the bands I'd forgotten. I thought of all the bands I'd considered, passed over, and then regretted leaving out. I thought about the bands I wished I hadn't included. And there were also the bands I just didn't know about until after the book came out. So I knew I'd have to take care of all of that. Or hoped I'd be able to.

Then there were the fans. According to most of them, I had betrayed them and their favorite bands by leaving out artist X or artist Y, and the fact that I had included artist Z was conclusive proof that I had zero credibility whatsoever.

One such person e-mailed me a list of problems that he had with the book, and then mailed a hard copy of the e-mail to my house, just to make sure I'd gotten it. So say what you want about heavy metal fans, you can't accuse them of failing to exercise due diligence.

Now that ten years have gone by, I'm very glad that the opportunity has come around to address some of the issues that bothered me and readers of the first edition of this book, and to bring things up to date. And believe me, I certainly did listen to some of the suggestions that I got from readers and fans—there was no band that I caught more shit for leaving out than Dream Theater, so by popular demand, I've included them. I've also included a few others that I had to concede were pretty glaring omissions. And then I included some bands that I thought were very important to the history of heavy metal, even if they didn't fit the strict definition. Finally, I took out a few bands that never should have been included in the first place.

Of course, I couldn't include everybody this time around either. There were some bands that I'd heard since the first edition, like San Francisco's excellent Jex Thoth, that I would have loved to include, but there just wasn't enough space. I'm also sure that I've left stuff out that I'll hear about from newly outraged fans. That's okay. This music is by the fans, for the fans, and it continues to exist today because the fans make noise about it, so it's appropriate that I should hear opinions about who should have been included and who should have gotten the axe. I'm always happy to hear your opinion. Please just don't show up at my door.

As far as my methodology this time around, which I know will be an issue for serious readers of this tome, only musicians who appear on an official recording are listed in band personnel. As for discographies, when an album was issued under different imprints, I chose the label that originally released the album, but if there was a discrepancy between the U.S. label and one from somewhere else I chose the U.S. label.

Reissues aren't listed unless they deviate significantly from the original release, like Metallica's *Garage, Inc.*, which contains *Garage Days Re-Revisited* in its entirety, as well as a disc and a half of other stuff that they recorded years later, so it's a lot more than just a straight reissue. I didn't include greatest hits compilations, but compilations of rarities and previously unreleased material are included.

OPPOSITE: It's obvious to see why Iron Maiden is *Stairway to Hell* author Chuck Eddy's favorite heavy metal band. Left to right: Dave Murray, Adrian Smith, Bruce Dickinson, and Steve Harris.

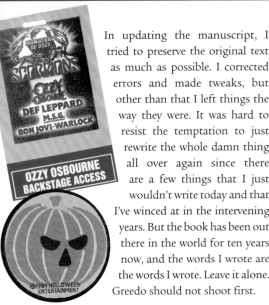

In updating the manuscript, I tried to preserve the original text as much as possible. I corrected errors and made tweaks, but other than that I left things the way they were. It was hard to resist the temptation to just rewrite the whole damn thing all over again since there are a few things that I just wouldn't write today and that I've winced at in the intervening years. But the book has been out there in the world for ten years now, and the words I wrote are the words I wrote. Leave it alone. Greedo should not shoot first.

The hardest part was writing about all the artists who have passed away since the book was originally written. Some of them were among my all-time favorite musicians, people who influenced my own playing and songwriting, such as Peter Steele of Carnivore and Type O Negative, and Denis D'Amour of Voivod. And of course, the mighty Ronnie James Dio. Besides being my favorite singer, he wrote the original foreword. I will never, ever forget the day that I was told that he had read the manuscript and liked it. That meant more to me than I can express, and I'm glad he felt like I did it right.

When Rosy Ngo originally approached me about writing this, it was April 2002. I had done some freelance writing here and there, but this was the first time anyone had ever asked me to write an entire book. I accepted the offer immediately, because I felt like if I didn't do it, I would regret it for the rest of my life. I had no idea what the reaction would be, if anyone would like it, or if it would sell even one copy. But it did well, it stayed in print for ten years and my life is very different today because of it. I'm very grateful to you for buying it, whether this is your first time with it or if you already bought the first edition. Either way, I hope that this new edition lives up to your expectations and incites the same excitement and lively debates that the first edition did. Enjoy.

Death to false metal,
Daniel Bukszpan
February 7, 2012

HOW TO READ THE SYMBOLS

As in the first edition, the band entries feature helpful dingbats to assist you in quick identification of a band's notable attributes. There are two kinds—one that applies to band members and one that applies to song lyrics. These are outlined in the key below.

PERTAINS TO BAND MEMBERS:

 outrageous alcohol consumption

 notorious drug use

 death

elaborate stage show

PERTAINS TO BAND'S LYRICS:

 fantasy-related

 political

 religious

 satanic

 sexual

violent

I'm sure that, despite my in-depth explanations, there will be plenty of you out there who will still feel that I have erred in my judgment. In any event, would-be complainers can certainly take some comfort in the fact that between the bands I omitted and whatever smart-ass comments I've made about those who do appear, I will probably receive hate mail for the rest of my life. Before I even got started writing, I found myself under siege from people, some of whom claimed to be my friends, who could not believe the shocking audacity and ignorance I displayed in my decision to write about, say, Venom but not Bathory. In short, there simply can never be a book of this kind that makes everyone happy—so keep your damn smart comments to yourself!

ABDULLAH

YEARS ACTIVE: 1998–2008

Abdullah's melodic gloom-and-doom sound was the brainchild of Jeff Shirilla (drummer and vocalist) and Alan Seibert (guitarist and bassist). When the Ohio duo's exhaustive efforts to fill their ranks turned up only musicians who were incompetent, drunk, stupid, or some combination thereof, in 2000, the two recorded their debut EP, *Snake Lore*, on a four-track, overdubbing the sounds of the missing members. Although the recording's production values could be said to be in short supply (one gets the impression that the greatest recording-related expense was

a ten-pack of Maxell ninety-minute cassettes), it made the rounds in stoner rock and doom metal circles anyway. The band had come through with the necessary doom metal attributes of stunted tempos and down-tuned guitars, but they steered clear of the genre's Cookie Monster–style growling, opting for a clean vocal style instead. This, combined with Seibert's melodic guitar, added up to a package that was impressive enough to compensate for the EP's technical shortcomings and roaring tape hiss. Among those who were impressed by the debut was the stoner rock label Meteor City, which released the band's first full-length album in 2001. The dark, moody self-titled album, like its predecessor, was well received by fans and critics alike. It even featured rerecorded versions of a few songs from *Snake Lore*, this time not only hiss-free but also mastered, as a special bonus to the discerning customer. Realizing that they would need a whole band to take their show on the road, Shirilla and Seibert recruited drummer Jim Simonian and bassist Ed Stephens and started playing the live circuit. This lineup recorded *Graveyard Poetry*, the band's sophomore outing. They released a split single with the

Argentine band Dragonauta on the Dias de Garage label in 2005, but the band went quiet after that. They officially broke up in 2008.

Jeff Shirilla: vocals/drums; Alan Seibert: guitars/bass; Jim Simonian: drums (*Graveyard Poetry*); Ed Stephens: bass (*Graveyard Poetry*)

Discography: *Snake Lore* (Rage of Achilles, 2000); *Abdullah* (Meteor City, 2001); *Graveyard Poetry* (Meteor City, 2002); *Abdullah/Dragonauta* (Dias de Garage, 2005)

ACCEPT

YEARS ACTIVE: 1979–PRESENT

Accept was formed by vocalist Udo Dirkschneider in Germany in the late 1970s. A few years, a few lineups, and a few albums had to go by before the band hit their stride with the 1981 album *Breaker*. Produced by Michael Wagener of Mötley Crüe and Dokken fame, the album contained all the ingredients that would become Accept trademarks, including brutally fast guitar riffing, an extraordinarily tight rhythm section, and the vocals of Dirkschneider, whose tinnitus-

Accept poses for a 1980 publicity photograph for Passport Records. Left to right: Peter Baltes, Udo Dirkschneider, Wolf Hoffman, Stefan Kaufmann, and Jörg Fischer.

inducing screech presaged black metal by more than a decade. *Restless and Wild*, released in 1982, furthered their success, particularly on the opening cut, "Fast as a Shark." The song's lightning-fast double-bass drumming and lockstep guitars were a blueprint for the thrash metal bands that emerged in following years.

In their early days, Accept had yet to reach the same level of notoriety in the United States that it had enjoyed in Europe, arguably because the group's music was simply too extreme for the wussy American audiences of the day. The release of *Balls to the Wall* in 1983 changed all of that. This version of Teutonic fist-thrusting music showcased a band whose style was toned down enough to dip into AC/DC territory and therefore acceptable for the more timid American musical taste. Predictably, the ship started sinking after this album, as the band vacillated between attempts to return to their heavier past (which never works out for anyone) and to get

another hit (which also never works out). It was at this point that Herr Dirkschneider decided that Accept's *kampf* was kaput, and he embarked on a solo career, resulting in the band's replacing him for another album and tour. Unfortunately, massive indifference on the part of the record-buying and concert-attending public prevailed. The band decided to pack it in. Accept reunited since then for a few albums and tours, but the international runaway-train success of Udo's solo project, the imaginatively named U.D.O., exerted too strong a pull for him to return permanently to the Accept fold. Ultimately, the band gave up on him, and in 2009 they reunited and enlisted vocalist Mark Tornillo to take his place. The group recorded 2010's *Blood of the Nations* with him, and their next album is scheduled for a 2012 release.

Peter Baltes: bass; **Michael Cartellone**: drums (*Predator, The Final Chapter*); **Udo Dirkschneider**: vocals (*Accept* through *Russian Roulette; Staying a Life* through *The Final Chapter*); **Jörg Fischer**: guitars (*Accept* through *Russian Roulette*); **Herman Frank**: guitars (*Balls to the Wall*); **Frank Friedrich**: drums (*Accept*); **Wolf Hoffman**: guitars; **Stefan Kaufmann**: drums (*I'm a Rebel* through *Death Row*); **David Reece**: vocals (*Eat the Heat*); **Jim Stacey**: guitars (*Eat the Heat*); **Gerhard Wahl**: guitar (*Accept*);

Discography: *Accept* (Brain Records, 1979); *I'm a Rebel* (Passport, 1980); *Breaker* (Brain Records, 1981); *Restless and Wild* (Brain Records, 1982); *Balls to the Wall* (Portrait, 1983); *Metal Heart* (Portrait, 1985); *Russian Roulette* (Portrait, 1986); *Eat the Heat* (Epic, 1989); *Staying a Life* (Epic, 1990); *Objection Overruled* (Nuclear Blast, 1992); *Death Row* (RCA, 1994); *Predator* (RCA, 1996); *Blood of the Nations* (Nuclear Blast, 2010)

AC/DC

YEARS ACTIVE: 1973–PRESENT

Two guitar-playing brothers, Malcolm and Angus Young, formed the straightforward crunch-rock quintet AC/DC in Australia in 1973. They joined forces with singer Bon

AC/DC's Angus Young chokes the neck of his signature Gibson SG guitar in 1986.

Scott, who had started off as the band's roadie and whose misdemeanor-ridden background helped reinforce the band's reputation as a gang of drunken, violent ne'er-do-wells. Interestingly, the band members were, for the most part, a bit on the elfin side, which probably made the tough-guy shtick a bit hard to sell. Fortunately, they were able to eradicate any focus on their diminutive stature through the liberal use of alcohol, which they consumed in quantities vast enough to put a frat-house hazing weekend to shame. Angus Young took his overcompensation one step further by exaggerating his height disadvantage and performing in a British schoolboy uniform, complete with shorts, backpack, and tie. In fact, early in their career, the band tried to capitalize on his fashion statement, claiming that he was in fact a bona fide eleven-year-old. The band rose to prominence rather quickly because of the combination of their fist-pumping anthems and adrenaline-torqued live performances. For a time, it seemed like AC/DC

could do no wrong, as they released classic album after classic album, including *Let There Be Rock* and *If You Want Blood You've Got It*, the latter capturing the band in extra frenzied live performances that Angus Young has since conceded that the band has never matched again. All of their albums sold well, both in their native country and abroad. By the time of their 1979 album *Highway to Hell* was released, it was a foregone conclusion that the next logical step for the band was galactic uber-domination. However, in a case of inconvenient timing, Scott dropped dead on February 20, 1980, after a

BELOW: The members of AC/DC accost guitarist Angus Young (lying on the desk) in 1976. Behind Angus Young, left to right: Phil Rudd, Bon Scott, Mark Evans, and Malcolm Young.
RIGHT: AC/DC incites the crowd with on-stage fist thrusting. Left to right: Brian Johnson, Malcolm Young, Angus Young, and Cliff Williams.

ong night of excessive drinking that culminated with the singer dying of alcohol poisoning while in his car. This threw the future of the band into doubt, as the general consensus was that Scott was integral to the band and could never be replaced.

In a stunning, unprecedented turn of events, Scott was replaced. Flat cap enthusiast Brian Johnson was tapped as the new front man, and the band rebounded from almost certain career death by releasing the classic album *Back in Black*. It blew any doubts about the band's survival out of the water by not only the most commercially successful album the band ever made but also one of the rare ones, like Pink Floyd's *Dark Side of the Moon* or the *Saturday Night Fever* soundtrack, that is owned by everyone on earth regardless of personal taste. It would not be an exaggeration to state that the album—which features the one-two punch of the title track and "You Shook Me All Night Long" at its midway point—is a timeless classic from the moment the needle drops on "Hell's Bells" until it gets stuck in the run-off groove after "Rock and Roll Ain't Noise Pollution." This album cemented the band's reputation for all eternity, and the albums they have released since then have sold well. Nevertheless, there is a die-hard Bon Scott fan base that maintains that the band has never been as good with Johnson at the microphone and that AC/DC fell into a stylistic sameness without Scott, as they tried to replicate the formula of *Back in Black* over and over again (as if the earlier albums were a grab bag of stylistic variety). Still, the band has survived multiple trends and lineup changes without missing a beat, and they remain, to this day, one of the most popular bands in the world. They also remain the favorite band of convicted serial murderer and eye-socket fetishist Richard Ramirez.

Mark Evans: bass (*High Voltage, Let There Be Rock*); **Brian Johnson**: vocals (*Back in Black* and later); **Phil Rudd**: drums (*High Voltage* through *Flick of the Switch*; *Ballbreaker* and later); **Bon Scott**: vocals (*High Voltage* through *Highway to Hell*); **Chris Slade**: drums (*The Razor's Edge, AC/DC Live*); **Cliff Williams**: bass

(*Powerage* and later); **Simon Wright**: drums (*Fly on the Wall, Blow Up Your Video*) (see also Dio); **Angus Young**: lead guitar; **Malcolm Young**: rhythm guitar

Discography: *High Voltage* (Atco, 1976); *Dirty Deeds Done Dirt Cheap* (Atco, 1976); *Let There Be Rock* (Atco, 1977); *Powerage* (Atco, 1978); *If You Want Blood You've Got It* (Atco, 1978); *Highway to Hell* (Atco, 1979); *Back in Black* (Atco, 1980); *For Those About to Rock We Salute You* (Atco, 1981); *Flick of the Switch* (Atco, 1983); *Fly on the Wall* (Atco, 1985); *Who Made Who* (Atco, 1986); *Blow Up Your Video* (Atco, 1988); *The Razor's Edge* (Atco, 1990); *Ballbreaker* (Eastwest, 1995); *Stiff Upper Lip* (Eastwest, 2000); *Black Ice* (Columbia, 2008)

ACID KING

Years active: 1993–present

Formed in San Francisco in 1993, Acid King was one of the original stoner doom bands years before the term was coined. In fact, other than the Melvins, nobody else in the area (or, frankly, anywhere) was really doing the downtuned, one-mile-an-hour plod. Acid King had cornered the market, and as if the sheer heft of their material was not enough to set them apart, the band was fronted by a woman whose heavily treated, sporadic vocals are reminiscent of Jefferson Airplane's Grace Slick, stuck at the bottom of a well . . . with a broken leg.

Although Acid King has only a handful of releases to its credit, the band has always been ahead of the curve in terms of sheer pummeling heaviness. By the time of their third release, 1999's *Busse Woods* (a concept album about burnout murderer Ricky Kasso), they had pushed the envelope for slow, lumbering riffs almost to the point of ridiculousness. To top it all off, they even found the time to squeeze in a song from *Jesus Christ Superstar*. It is unclear at this time if future albums will feature somnambulant versions of any other Andrew Lloyd Webber tunes. Depending on where you stand on this issue, sadly, their last album to be released at this time, 2005's *Acid King III*, didn't. But if anybody's going to record the definitive sludge metal version of "Memory" from the soundtrack to *Cats*, it's Acid King.

Brian Hill: bass (*Busse Woods* to *Free*); **Peter Lucas**: bass/vocals (*Zoroaster*); **Joey Osbourne**: drums; **Guy Pinhas**: bass (*Free* and later); **Lori S.**: guitars/vocals; (see also Goatsnake, the Obsessed)

Discography: *Zoroaster* (Sympathy for the Record Industry, 1995); *Busse Woods* (Man's Ruin, 1999); *Free* (Man's Ruin, 2001); *Acid King III* (Small Stone Records, 2005)

AEROSMITH

Years active: 1973–present

Aerosmith escaped from the Boston club circuit in the early 1970s. Although their self-titled first album contained "Dream On," arguably their best-known song, the band didn't really hit the big time until the release of their third album, *Toys in the Attic*—its combination of heavy riffs and Stones-y swagger hit the bull's-eye with an entire generation of dope-smoking burnouts. The band scored hit after hit ("Mama Kin," "Same Old Song and Dance," "Sweet Emotion," "Back in the Saddle," et al.), making it possible for vocalist Steven Tyler and guitarist Joe Perry to afford all the alcohol they could drink and all the cocaine their nostrils could accommodate, which at the time was probably enough to provide the entire population of Colombia with indoor plumbing. Strangely enough, snorting kielbasa-thick lines of cocaine on a nonstop basis began to affect the band in a way that was not entirely positive. Perry soon went out the door, and one album later, guitarist Brad Whitford was right behind him. The band tried to go on without them, but the two albums Aerosmith made with new guitarists Jimmy Crespo and Rick Dufay were poorly received. Not long after that, the band seemed to drop off the radar entirely, leading many to assume that they had broken up, thereby giving them extra free time to pursue their well-documented drug habits.

In a surprising turn of events, however, no one from the band turned up at the bottom of a Dumpster, facedown in a hardened puddle of his own vomit. In the mid-1980s, the original

Steven Tyler serenades the masses at a 1977 Aerosmith concert.

members reconvened, encouraged by the newly burgeoning hair metal movement, which, whether they liked it or not, looked to Aerosmith as a primary influence. With younger groups such as Mötley Crüe starting to gain mainstream popularity, the band decided that it was prime time for a comeback in 1985.

While the album they made upon their return, *Done with Mirrors*, was not the unqualified success they had hoped, it was certainly a respectable showing for a band that had been written off by most critics. Then, in 1986, the rap group Run-DMC covered "Walk This Way," featuring Tyler and Perry in the music video. The single was a huge hit, and it was just the thing Aerosmith needed to launch a full-blown assault on the music scene. Their judgment was apparently right on target, as theirs would prove to be the single biggest comeback in the history of heavy metal, if not all of popular music. The vehicle for their return to the spotlight was 1987's *Permanent Vacation*, which contained such ubiquitous hit songs as "Dude (Looks Like a Lady)" and "Rag Doll." After that, Aerosmith took their place alongside Madonna as a musical entity whose success is guaranteed these days. With the exception of 2004's *Honkin' on Bobo*, every album they have released since their comeback has sold at least a million copies, and in 2001, they performed at the Super Bowl halftime show with 'NSYNC and Britney Spears—thereby adding

High jinks prevail when Steven Tyler and fellow Aerosmith band mate Joe Perry share a stage.

credence to the theory that their revival could be the result only of a pact with the Horned One, inscribed in human flesh and inked with blood of the undead.

Unfortunately, their pact with Satan hit a few speed bumps. In 2006, Tyler underwent throat surgery, forcing them to cancel an upcoming tour. After he recovered, they began recording their new album, but received more bad news when bassist Tom Hamilton was diagnosed with throat cancer. He recovered, but then Perry, Whitford, and Tyler all ended up suffering different medical complaints over the next two years (two leg injuries and a head injury, for those at home keeping score). Then, in 2009, Tyler fell offstage at a show in North Dakota, forcing them to cancel the rest of their tour. He recovered, but then he disclosed that he had become addicted to the painkillers that had been prescribed to him for his injuries, so he entered rehab and slayed the monkey Pfizer had chained to his back. Amusingly, his addiction to drugs garnered far less hostility and recrimination from the fan community than his 2010 decision to sit on the *American Idol* judge's panel. Aerosmith's long-awaited new album is currently rumored to be scheduled for release in 2012. Believe it when you see it.

Jimmy Crespo: guitars (*Night in the Ruts*, *Rock in a Hard Place*); **Rick Dufay**: guitars (*Rock in a Hard Place*); **Tom Hamilton**: bass; **Joey Kramer**: drums; **Joe Perry**: guitars (*Aerosmith* through *Live! Bootleg*; *Done with Mirrors* and later); **Paul Santo**: piano (*Honkin' on Bobo*); **Steven Tyler**: vocals; **Brad Whitford**: guitars (*Aerosmith* through *Night in the Ruts*; *Done with Mirrors* and later)

Discography: *Aerosmith* (Columbia, 1973); *Get Your Wings* (Columbia, 1974); *Toys in the Attic* (Columbia, 1975); *Rocks* (Columbia, 1976); *Draw the Line* (Columbia, 1977); *Live! Bootleg* (Columbia, 1978); *Night in the Ruts* (Columbia, 1979); *Rock in a Hard Place* (Columbia, 1982); *Done with Mirrors* (Geffen, 1985); *Classics Live* (Columbia, 1986); *Classics Live II* (Columbia, 1986); *Permanent Vacation* (Geffen, 1987); *Gems* (Columbia, 1988); *Pump* (Geffen, 1989); *Get a Grip* (Geffen, 1993); *Nine Lives* (Columbia, 1997); *A Little South of Sanity* (Columbia, 1998); *Just Push Play* (Columbia, 2001); *Honkin' on Bobo* (Columbia, 2004); *Rockin' the Joint* (Columbia, 2005)

AIRBOURNE

YEARS ACTIVE: 2001–PRESENT

Australia is home to such legends of no-frills crotch rock as Rose Tattoo, AC/DC, and Warrnambool's Airbourne. The members of that last band are younger than their drunken, rowdy forerunners by as much as four decades, and they were in diapers when those bands went into decline. However, there must be something about growing up around sinks that drain in a counterclockwise motion, because the members of Airbourne seem genetically predisposed to behaving like 24-hour conveyor belts for three-chord anthems about girls, rock, and beer.

Airbourne was founded by singer and guitarist Joel O'Keeffe and his drumming brother Ryan. While their high school chums spent the late 1990s attending raves and listening to the Spice Girls, the brothers O'Keeffe were studiously taking in the sounds of classic rock albums. When they had gotten their fill and sufficient education, the brothers recruited second guitarist David Roads and bassist Justin Street and formed Airbourne, setting about faithfully recreating the sound of the Jimmy Carter years.

The group put out their own EP, *Ready To Rock*, in 2004, and thanks to steady gigging they landed a support slot with Mötley Crüe. Their profile thus raised, Airbourne was signed by Capitol Records in the United States to a five album deal. They recorded their debut album, 2007's *Runnin' Wild*, but were quickly dropped along with several other bands when the label merged with Virgin. Luckily, Roadrunner Records was there to catch Airbourne before it fell through the cracks and *Runnin' Wild* had its worldwide release in 2008. They released the follow-up album, *No Guts. No Glory* in 2010, which was a top 20 album in Australia, Europe, and Scandinavia, and cracked the top 100 of the U.S. *Billboard* chart.

Airbourne frontman Joel O'Keeffe makes pooched-out rock lips for the heatstroke sufferers at some godforsaken festival somewhere.

Joel O'Keeffe: vocals/guitar; **Ryan O'Keeffe**: drums/percussion; **David Roads**: guitar/backup vocals; **Justin Street**: bass/backup vocals

Discography: *Runnin' Wild* (EMI, 2007); *No Guts. No Glory* (Roadrunner)

ALICE IN CHAINS

YEARS ACTIVE: 1987–PRESENT

Alice in Chains emerged from Seattle in the early 1990s, and as such it was always mistakenly lumped in with the grunge movement. While the band's relentlessly bleak music shared elements with grunge, their guitar-heavy sound and high level of musicianship had more in common with the metal bands that preceded them than with the music of their Starbucks-frequenting contemporaries. If Alice in Chains was not

Alice in Chains embodies the spirit of mirth and frivolity for which heavy metal is renowned. Left to right: Sean Kinney, Jerry Cantrell, Layne Staley, and Mike Inez.

recognized as metal, it was more a result of the band's timing than any other factor; at the beginning of the 1990s, metal was synonymous with a bunch of weak pop bands with whom they had next to nothing in common—other than the fact that that they all used sound molecules to displace air. In any event, time has caught up with Alice in Chains, and the influence that they exerted on popular rock music is now obvious. Creed and Nickelback have made entire careers out of copying the band's trademark vocal harmonies, and we can only hope that the god in whose service they

employ said vocal embellishments will bring a wrath against them for such treachery.

Another of Alice in Chains' most notable trademarks had nothing to do with music. Habitual heroin use was not only a theme in much of their work—particularly on 1992's *Dirt*, which contained songs such as "Junkhead" whose lyrics made no effort whatsoever to hide their content—and lead singer Layne Staley was known to have struggled with the brown powder. The band never publicly admitted or denied anything, but their decision not to tour behind two of their most popular releases (1992's *Sap* EP and their self-titled album from 1995) sure smelled fishy. The band did put in one live appear-

ance in 1996, for an episode of MTV's *Unplugged*, but it was their first public performance in three years. With the release of guitarist Jerry Cantrell's solo album *Boggy Depot* (basically an Alice in Chains album sans Staley) two years later, anyone who was paying attention could conclude only that the singer's problems had finally derailed the band. In April 2002, on the eve of the release of Cantrell's second solo album, *Degradation Trip*, Staley was found dead in his Seattle home. The cause of death was an overdose of heroin and cocaine.

The singer's death seemed to indicate the end of Alice in Chains, but in 2006, they joined forces with a new lead singer, William DuVall, who had performed "Rooster" with them at VH1's *Decades Rock Live* concert. They had performed that same night with Phil Anselmo of Pantera and Ann Wilson of Heart, so at the time there was nothing to indicate that DuVall in particular was being groomed to take Staley's place permanently. However, the band announced that he had joined on their official website in 2008, and later that year Blabbermouth.net reported that the band was in the studio, recording their first album of new material in 14 years. The resulting album, *Black Gives Way to Blue*, was released in 2009 and even the most hardcore Layne Staley fan had to concede that the thing was pretty damn good. The band confirmed in 2011 that they were about to start making a new album. This announcement came on the heels of the death of the group's original bassist, Mike Starr. He had succumbed to a prescription drug overdose, despite making what appeared to be a very public return to sobriety and good health one year earlier on VH1's *Celebrity Rehab*.

Jerry Cantrell: guitars/vocals; **William DuVall**: vocals (*Black Gives Way to Blue*); **Mike Inez**: bass (*Jar of Flies* and later); **Sean Kinney**: drums; **Layne Staley**: vocals (*Facelift* through *Alice in Chains*); **Mike Starr**: bass (*Facelift* through *Dirt*)

Discography: *Facelift* (Columbia, 1990); *Dirt* (Columbia, 1992); *Jar of Flies* (Columbia, 1993); *Alice in Chains* (Columbia, 1995); *Unplugged* (Columbia, 1996); *Live* (Sony, 2000); *Black Gives Way to Blue* (Virgin, 2009)

AMORPHIS

YEARS ACTIVE: 1990–PRESENT

Like most heavy metal fans, you probably wonder why it is that Barry Manilow's musical output sucks so fucking bad. The reasons are numerous, and space does not permit us to list them all. However, there is one reason from whence all others come—not one of his songs, not even "Mandy," is based on *The Kalevala*, the 19th-century epic poem of Finland. Amorphis, however, a Finnish band formed in 1990, has used the poem as source material for the lion's share of its songs. The auteur behind "Copacabana" and "I Can't Smile Without You" cannot claim this disctinction. Ergo, suckage.

Amorphis was formed by guitarist Esa Holopainen and drummer Jan Rechberger, who recruited bassist Olli-Pekka Laine and guitarist and lead vocalist Tomi Koivusaari. After

The bouncin' and behavin' hair of Amorphis vocalist Tomi Joutsen.

releasing a well-received demo of death metal laments in 1991, they got signed and released an EP before the year's end. Their first full-length album, *The Karelian Isthmus*, was released in 1992. It was such a successful couple of years that the grim and morbid band members may have even smiled in public once or twice.

Amorphis released the album *Tales From the Thousand Lakes* in 1994. They had already ventured beyond guitar-bass-drums occasionally on previous releases, but they expanded their sound by adding keyboard player Kim Rantala as a full-time member. The lineup extended to six members on 1996's *Elegy*, which included second vocalist and actual tune-carrying singer Pasi Koskinen alongside baritone grunter Koivusaari. The album also saw the band using sitars, folk melodies, and synthesizers. This makes them suspiciously in keeping with John Tesh. For the moment, we'll allow that to slide.

By 2001 the band had lost some blood and the lineup had changed a couple of times, so they said "fuck it" and released *Am Universum*, their most keyboard-centric and un-metal release to date. The thing even had saxophones on it, for the love of all things holy! After some more lineup shuffles the band went all George Lucas on us with a momentous trilogy and released three concept albums based on *The Kalevala*. They began with *Eclipse* in 2006, followed it with *Silent Waters* in 2007 and ended it with *Skyforger* in 2009. In 2010 they released *Magic & Mayhem: Tales from the Early Years*, which featured new versions of material from the band's first three albums, as well as a cover of the Doors' chestnut "Light My Fire," which is one of the most ludicrous things you will ever hear in your entire life. That is a statement made without any qualifications. Check it out on YouTube if you're skeptical. Amorphis's most recent release was the 2011 album *The Beginning of Times*.

Niclas Etelävuori: bass (*Am Universum* and later); **Esa Holopainen**: guitar; **Tomi Joutsen**: vocals (*Eclipse* and later); **Santeri Kallio**: keyboards (*Am Universum* and later); **Pekka Kasari**: drums (*Elegy* through *Am Universum*); **Tomi Koivusaari**: vocals; **Pasi Koskinen**: vocals (*Elegy* through *Far from the Sun*); **Olli-Pekka "Oppu" Laine**: bass (*The Karelian Isthmus* through *Tuonela*); **Kasper Mårtenson**: keyboards (*Tales from the Thousand Lakes*); **Kim Rantala**: keyboards (*Elegy*); **Jan Rechberger**: drums (*The Karelian Isthmus* through *Tales from the Thousand Lakes*; *Far from the Sun* and later)

Discography: *The Karelian Isthmus* (Relapse Records, 1992); *Tales from the Thousand Lakes* (Relapse Records, 1994); *Elegy* (Relapse Records, 1996); *Tuonela* (Relapse Records, 1999); *Am Universum* (Relapse Records, 2001); *Far from the Sun* (Virgin, 2004); *Eclipse* (Nuclear Blast, 2006); *Silent Waters* (Nuclear Blast, 2007); *Skyforger* (Nuclear Blast, 2009); *Magic & Mayhem: Tales from the Early Years* (Nuclear Blast, 2010); *The Beginning of Times* (Nuclear Blast, 2011)

ANGEL

YEARS ACTIVE: 1975–1981; 1987; 1998–PRESENT

Angel was a singer from California who was in the girl group No Secrets. But don't worry, we're not here to talk about that shitty singer.

We're here to talk about the way-awesome Washington, DC metal band from the 1970s of the same name who boldly wore white satin outfits. This band totally ruled but sadly they're not much more than a footnote today, with only keyboard player Gregg Giuffria going on to something resembling mainstream success with House of Lords. Nonetheless, Angel made some excellent music, much of which remains in print today and is worth discovering, particularly their self-titled debut.

Angel was formed by bassist Mickie Jones and guitarist Punky Meadows. The group was rounded out by Giuffria, drummer Barry Brandt, and singer Frank Dimino, owner of one of the finest unibrows in rock. The band was discovered by Gene Simmons of KISS, who helped them get a record deal at his band's label, Casablanca. The band members' signature look was white silk jumpsuits with the occasional cape thrown in, and every live show was an orgy of dry ice and lasers. Needless to say, the critics absolutely fucking despised them and said so whenever the opportunity arose.

With the band's image being as ridiculous as it was, you could say that the ridicule heaped on them was well deserved. Perhaps, but image aside, the music was outstanding. "Tower," which opens their 1975 self-titled debut, revels in swords-and-sorcery imagery and is performed with an abandon that almost rivals the Who. The rest of the album is consistently epic as well, as is the 1976 follow-up, *Helluva Band*. It was followed in 1977 by *On Earth As It Is In Heaven*, which saw the music change from a symphonic sound to something a little less spectacular, probably in a bid for airplay. Founding member Mickie Jones left at this point and was replaced by Felix Robinson, who appeared on 1978's *White Hot*. The album featured "Ain't Gonna Eat Out My Heart Anymore," the band's only single to reach *Billboard*'s top 50.

Despite finally reaching a commercial peak, the band was actually in a state of decline. Their best material was already two albums behind them, and their fifth album, 1979's *Sinful*, was a misguided embarrassment whose pop sound couldn't get it past number 159 on the *Billboard* albums chart. They excreted one more album, 1980's *Live Without A Net*, and after it failed to do anything for them, the band just faded away with no official announcement. Giuffria formed the creatively named band Giuffria, and Dimino sang "Seduce Me Tonight," which appeared on the soundtrack to the very metal film *Flashdance*,

and that was the last that anyone heard about Angel for a while, until they reformed in 1999 and released a new album, *In the Beginning*.

Barry Brandt: drums; **Frank Dimino**: vocals; **Gregg Giuffria**: keyboards; **Randy Gregg**: bass; **Mickie Jones**: bass; **Punky Meadows**: guitar; **Felix Robinson**: bass (*White Hot* through *Sinful*)

Discography: *Angel* (RCA, 1975); *Helluva Band* (PolyGram, 1976); *On Earth As It Is In Heaven* (Mercury, 1977); *White Hot* (PolyGram, 1978); *Sinful* (Mercury, 1979); *In the Beginning* (Coallier Entertainment, 1999)

YEARS ACTIVE: 1981–PRESENT

New York City's Anthrax was one-quarter of the 1980s thrash metal genre's "Big Four" (which also included Megadeth, Metallica, and Slayer), but Anthrax set themselves apart with a streetwise, aggressive, and sometimes comical style that was closely related to hardcore punk. This period in the band's career reached its

RIGHT Foreshadowing its 1991 collaboration with Public Enemy, Anthrax pays homage to rap heavyweights in this 1987 photograph. Left to right: Frank Bello, Dan Spitz, Joey Belladonna, Scott Ian, and Charlie Benante.

You can just imagine the embarrassment that the members of Angel felt when they all showed up the party wearing the same white silk jumpsuits!

pinnacle with 1987's *Among the Living*, which was chock-full of classic tunes (including "I Am the Law," "Caught in a Mosh," and "Imitation of Life"), many of which the band still performs to this day. Unfortunately, the group floundered creatively for the next couple of years, and the albums they produced did not live up to the promise of *Among the Living*.

In 1991 the band appeared on a rerecording of "Bring the Noise" with Public Enemy, and it seemed to give them a renewed sense of purpose. Well, it gave most of them a new sense of purpose: Singer Joey Belladonna belonged squarely to the high-pitched, my-codpiece-is-too-tight school of metal vocalization, and he was promptly given his pink slip. He was replaced by Armored Saint singer John Bush, whose gruffer, lower-range vocals were considered by the remaining band members to be more suitable to their new direction. It was not long afterward that lead guitarist Dan Spitz was informed that his weedly-weedly-wee services were no longer required, and Anthrax's transformation into a hip-hop–influenced metal band was complete. This certainly raised an eyebrow or three at the time, particularly since it appeared that the band was pushing for an "alternative rock" sound; in fact, in the early 1990s, they could not conduct an interview without mentioning that they now felt they should be seriously compared to Jane's Addiction. But today it is clear that Anthrax deserves credit for inspiring groups like Limp Bizkit and Biohazard, whose music incorporates metal and rap in equal measure. Or, depending on your perspective, perhaps they deserve blame. In any event, we can expect this controversy to take its place alongside the single-bullet theory of President Kennedy's assassination as one that will generate heated discourse for generations to come.

Despite inventing a new subgenre of metal, Anthrax had a difficult time of it in the 1990s. After leaving Elektra they signed to two consecutive independent labels, both of which went bankrupt. They then spent much of the 2000s alternating between the lead vocal services of Bush and a returning Belladonna. During that time they released almost no product, save 2003's *We've Come for You All*. Finally, in 2010, the situation apparently resolved itself when Belladonna got his old job back as Anthrax's lead singer, and he appears on 2011's *Worship Music*, the band's first new studio album in eight years.

Joey Belladonna: vocals (*Armed and Dangerous* through *Attack of the Killer B's*, *Worship Music*); **Frank Bello**: bass (*Armed and Dangerous* and later); **Charlie Benante**: drums (see also Stormtroopers of Death); **John Bush**: vocals (*Sound of White Noise* and later) (see also Armored Saint); **Rob Caggiano** (*We've Come For You All* and later); **Scott Ian**: guitars (see also Stormtroopers of Death); **Danny Lilker**: bass (*Fistful of Metal*) (see also Nuclear Assault, Stormtroopers of Death); **Dan Spitz**: guitars (*Fistful of Metal* through *Sound of White Noise*); **Neil Turbin**: vocals (*Fistful of Metal*)

Discography: *Fistful of Metal* (Megaforce, 1984); *Armed and Dangerous* (Megaforce, 1985); *Spreading the Disease* (Megaforce/Island, 1985); *Among the Living* (Megaforce/Island, 1987); *State of Euphoria* (Megaforce/Island, 1988); *Persistence of Time* (Megaforce/Island, 1990); *Attack of the Killer B's* (Island, 1991); *Sound of White Noise* (Elektra, 1993); *Stomp 442* (Elektra, 1995); *Volume 8: The Threat Is Real* (Tommy Boy, 1999); *We've Come for You All* (Nuclear Blast, 2003); *Worship Music* (Megaforce, 2011)

YEARS ACTIVE: 1978–PRESENT

Canada's Anvil, like its German contemporary Accept, exerted a strong influence on the then–newly burgeoning speed metal genre, before the niche had a name. But where Accept preferred an approach of unrefined brutality, Anvil chose a more technical and progressive route; the relationship between the two bands could be compared to that of the Rolling Stones and Yes. As is typical with first-wave innovators, Anvil never got much credit, and certainly did not become particularly famous. However, that changed dramatically with the release of the 2008 documentary *Anvil! The Story of Anvil*. The simultaneously inspiring and cringeworthy film detailed the band's struggle to stay afloat and stay relevant in the face of public indifference, amateur tour promoters, and a nagging sense that the glory that should have been theirs had passed them by. As depressing as the film is at times, the fact remains that Anvil is not only still together, but they're touring and making albums over thirty years after their first release. They released their 14th studio album, *Juggernaut of Justice*, in 2011.

Dave Allison: rhythm guitar (*Hard 'n' Heavy* through *Past and Present Live*); **Ian Dickson**: bass (*Hard 'n' Heavy* through *Worth the Weight*); **Mike Duncan**: bass (*Plugged in Permanent*); **Glenn Gyorffy**: bass (*Absolutely No Alternative* and later); **Ivan Hurd**: guitars (*Plugged in Permanent* and later); **Steve "Lips" Kudlow**: vocals/guitars; **Sebastian Marino**: guitars (*Worth the Weight*) (see also Overkill); **Robb Reiner**: drums

Discography: *Hard 'n' Heavy* (Attic, 1981); *Metal on Metal* (Attic, 1982); *Forged in Fire* (Attic, 1983); *Strength of Steel* (Metal Blade, 1987); *Pound for Pound* (Metal Blade, 1988); *Worth the Weight* (Metal Blade, 1991); *Plugged in Permanent* (Metal Blade, 1996); *Absolutely No Alternative* (Massacre, 1997); *Speed of Sound* (Massacre, 1999); *Plenty of Power* (Massacre, 2001), *Back to Basics* (Attic, 2004); *This is Thirteen* (VH1 Classic Records); *Juggernaut of Justice* (The End, 2011)

ARCH ENEMY

YEARS ACTIVE: 1996–PRESENT

Since time immemorial, the heavy metal community has traditionally been one gigantic sausage fest, one that is as popular with the ladies as your local pharmacy's feminine hygiene aisle is with the fellas. That gender bias has been changing since the glorious aughts, in part because bands like Sweden's Arch Enemy have been out there paving the way. A death metal band, they formed in the 1990s with an all-male lineup, but as of 2000, an enchanting German *fraulein* by the name of Angela Gossow has wielded the microphone, and the sweaty punters in the first row haven't seemed to have any objection.

The group was formed by Michael Amott. It bore a striking resemblance to Carcass, unsurprising since Amott once did a tour of duty with that band long ago. With younger brother Christopher Amott in tow on guitar and the occasionally alarming, penis-wielding Johan Liiva at the microphone, they released their manly first album, *Black Earth*, in 1996, and began losing members almost immediately. On their second album and Century Media debut, 1998's *Stigmata*, they lost two members, and the bleeding continued for 1999's appropriately named *Burning Bridges*. But when Gossow joined in 2000, it provided the band with a more permanent identity and steady success, even if the turnover continued unabated. This change in fortune is likely because most people only notice a band's singer, and this one had tits.

Now known to the headbanging public as the death metal band with the chick singer, Arch Enemy released *Anthems of Rebellion* in 2003 and *Doomsday Machine* in 2005. Their most successful album yet, *Rise of the Tyrant*, followed in 2007 and saw the band hit the road with fellow Swedes Opeth. In 2009, they released *The Root of All Evil*, which featured rerecordings of songs from the band's early years, and in

2011 they released *Khaos Legions*, which actually appeared on the U.S. *Billboard* charts at number 78. Seriously!

Christopher Amott: guitar; **Michael Amott**: guitar; **Martin Bengtsson**: bass (*Stigmata*); **Daniel Erlandsson**: drums; **Sharlee D'Angelo**: bass (*Burning Bridges* and later); **Angela Gossow**: vocals; **Johan Liiva**: vocals (*Black* through *Burning Bridges*); **Per Wiberg**: keyboards (*Anthems of Rebellion*); **Peter Wildoer**: drums (*Stigmata*)

Discography: *Black Earth* (Regain Records, 1996); *Stigmata* (Century Media, 1998); *Burning Bridges* (Century Media, 1999); *Wages of Sin* (Century Media, 2001); *Anthems of Rebellion* (Century Media, 2003); *Doomsday Machine* (Century Media, 2005); *Rise of the Tyrant* (Century Media, 2007); *Khaos Legions* (Century Media, 2011)

Sweden's Arch Enemy. UPPER RIGHT: Singer Angela Gossow tells misogynistic metal fans to talk to the hand.

ARMORED SAINT

YEARS ACTIVE: 1982–1992; 1999–PRESENT

Armored Saint was a rarity among Los Angeles metal bands of the 1980s in that they eschewed the glam metal style that was so popular at the time, preferring instead to play genuine Iron Maiden–influenced Valhalla-metal. One look at the band's album covers, which feature Frank Frazetta–esque images of the armor-clad band astride Harleys in front of medieval castles, and it was a safe bet that there was no

"Unskinny Bop" to be found within the records' grooves. Unfortunately, the band never graduated from the Sunset Strip club circuit, in no small part because of their record label Chrysalis, which marketed metal bands with roughly the same degree of expertise that monkeys solve geometry problems. Furthermore, the band was dealt a final and decisive blow when guitarist David Prichard was diagnosed with leukemia.

Shortly after Prichard's death, the band drafted new guitarist Jeff Duncan to record 1991's *Symbol of Salvation*. Unfortunately, it was not long before vocalist John Bush accepted an offer to join Anthrax. However, much to everyone's

surprise, the band re-formed in 2000 and released the album *Revelation*. Bush remained in Anthrax and bassist Joey Vera not only assumed his pre- and post-Saint gig with Fates Warning, but also took the Anthrax bass slot when Frank Bello briefly left the group in 2004. Both members happily did double duty, and for a while it seemed reasonable to expect Armored Saint to continue, if only in a part-time capacity. However, Bush and Vera would soon have all the time in the world to devote to Armored Saint following the 2005 announcement that Anthrax's classic *Among the Living* lineup was reuniting. Armored Saint followed suit by reforming their year 2000 lineup and recording 2010's *La Raza*.

John Bush: vocals (see also Anthrax); **Jeff Duncan**: guitars (*Symbol of Salvation* and later); **David Prichard**: guitars (*Armored Saint* through *Saints Will Conquer*); **Gonzo Sandoval**: drums; **Phil Sandoval**: guitars; **Joey Vera**: bass (see also Fates Warning)

Discography: *March of the Saint* (Chrysalis, 1984); *Delirious Nomad* (Chrysalis, 1985); *Raising Fear* (Chrysalis, 1987); *Saints Will Conquer* (Metal Blade, 1989); *Symbol of Salvation* (Metal Blade, 1991); *Revelation* (Metal Blade, 2000); *Nod to the Old School* (Metal Blade, 2001); *La Raza* (Metal Blade, 2010)

THE ATOMIC BITCHWAX

YEARS ACTIVE: 1992–PRESENT

The Atomic Bitchwax was the side project of Ed Mundell, whose day job is playing lead guitar for Monster Magnet. Both bands share an obvious affinity to 1970s rock music, but the similarities end there. The Atomic Bitchwax is much more aggressive and seems most at home in the middle of one of its uninhibited free jams. Mundell's primary gig is, by all accounts, held in the viselike clutches of Monster Magnet's founder Dave Wyndorf, so it is easy to see why, with all of his obvious talent, Mundell needed a side project for which he could play whatever he damn well

The members of Armored Saint look like they've come straight out of Camelot. Clockwise from top left: Gonzo Sandoval, Phil Sandoval, David Prichard, Joey Vera, and John Bush.

pleased. As such, the Atomic Bitchwax's albums prominently feature instrumental tracks. The band members had been playing together for almost a decade, but they didn't get around to releasing their self-titled debut until 1999. This gave them plenty of time to develop as a musical unit, which even a cursory listen will reveal was frighteningly cohesive at its height. Mundell left the group after 2002's *Spit Blood*, and drummer Keith Ackerman has since left as well, leaving bassist and vocalist Chris Kosnik the only remaining original member. Mundell was replaced by guitarist and vocalist Finn Ryan, and the drummer's throne is now occupied by one Bob Pantella. Their last release, 2011's *The Local Fuzz*, consists of exactly one (1) song of over 40 minutes in length.

Keith Ackerman: drums (*The Atomic Bitchwax* to *Spit Blood*); **Chris Kosnik**: bass/vocals; **Ed Mundell**: guitars (see also Monster Magnet) (*The Atomic Bitchwax* to *Spit Blood*); **Bob Pantella** (*3* and later); **Finn Ryan** (*3* and later);

Discography: *The Atomic Bitchwax* (MIA, 1999); *The Atomic Bitchwax II* (TeePee, 2000); *Spit Blood* (TeePee, 2002), *3* (Meteor City, 2002); *Boxriff* (Meteor City, 2006); *The Local Fuzz* (TeePee, 2011)

ATOMIC ROOSTER

YEARS ACTIVE: 1969–1975; 1980–1983

Like many bands of the late 1960s and early 1970s, England's Atomic Rooster occupied a stylistic gray area between the sounds of prog rock and heavy metal. The band's music was too keyboard-driven and soulful to be considered straight-up heavy metal, but the song lyrics reeked so strongly of suicidal depression and satanism that the band could never be considered prog rock, the domain of such froufrou bands as Yes and Emerson, Lake & Palmer (although Atomic Rooster did feature ELP drummer Carl Palmer on its first album, interestingly enough). Basically, the problem lay

with ivory-tickling sourpuss Vincent Crane, who played the offending organ and wrote the cranky lyrics. It would have made sense for the band to fire him in order to fit more easily into the defined stylistic dictates of the time. But there was one small problem: Atomic Rooster was Crane's band.

By all accounts, Crane's dark lyrics were completely genuine. He started off playing keyboards with the Crazy World of Arthur Brown, but left to pursue a solo career. However, before he was able to get much of anything off the ground, Crane was hospitalized for a nervous breakdown. Undaunted, he formed Atomic Rooster after his release, and at first the group experienced modest chart ratings with the single "Friday the 13th." But the band was beleaguered with constant lineup changes as members either quit in a huff because of the notoriously difficult Crane or were fired when they failed to live up to his exacting standards. Consequently, the band was prevented from touring, which proved a major, if not fatal, setback. This was, of course, before the time of MTV's *Total Request Live*, and in those simpler, headier days, touring was the only way

to promote a band. Atomic Rooster was prevented from capitalizing on their chart success, and the band suffered from terminal also-ran status for the remainder of their career. Crane kept it going anyway, fronting different lineups until the early 1980s. In a completely bizarre twist, he put the band away for good and joined Dexy's Midnight Runners. Finally, in February 1989, he committed suicide. It is not known how many times he was forced to perform "Come on Eileen" before this occurred.

Steve Bolton: guitar (*Made in England*); **John Cann**: guitar/vocals (*Death Walks Behind You*, *In Hearing of Atomic Rooster*, 1980's *Atomic Rooster*); **Vincent Crane**: organ/vocals; **Chris Farlowe**: vocals (*Made in England* through *Nice 'n' Greasy*); **Pete French**: guitar (*In Hearing of Atomic Rooster*); **Nick Graham**: bass (1970's *Atomic Rooster*); **Paul Hammond**: drums (*Death Walks Behind You*, *In Hearing of Atomic Rooster*); **Carl Palmer**: drums (1970's *Atomic Rooster*); **Rick Parnell**: drums (*Made in England* through *Nice 'n' Greasy*); **Bill Smith**: bass

Discography: *Atomic Rooster* (B&C, 1970); *Death Walks Behind You* (Elektra, 1970); *In Hearing of Atomic Rooster* (Elektra, 1971); *Made in England* (Elektra, 1972); *Nice 'n' Greasy* (Elektra, 1973); *Atomic Rooster* (EMI, 1980); *Headline News* (Towerbell, 1983);

In 1971, Atomic Rooster briefly toyed with a quartet configuration. Left to right: Peter French, Vincent Crane, Paul Hammond, and John Cann.

BAD COMPANY

In 1973, Bad Company was formed in England by former Mott the Hoople guitarist Mick Ralphs, King Crimson bassist Boz Burrell, singer Paul Rodgers and drummer Simon Kirke, both from the recently disbanded Free. They landed a deal on Led Zeppelin's Swan Song vanity label and signed with Zeppelin's hulking colossus of a manager, Peter Grant. With the full weight of the Zeppelin publicity machine behind them, Bad Company was at a decided advantage in the marketplace; a recording of Jim Nabors reading the Warren Commission transcripts would likely have topped the charts under similar circumstances. Fortunately for every living individual who possessed functioning ears at the time, the band did not abuse their advantageous position by force-feeding awful musical tripe down the gaping maws of the record-buying public. Rather, they proved to be highly skilled songsmiths, and as such their eponymously titled debut album, which contained such classics as "Ready for Love" and "Can't Get Enough of Your Love," was a keeper from start to finish.

Their next album, *Straight Shooter*, featured the yuppie sports bar karaoke anthem "Feel Like Makin' Love" and was another enormous hit. The cavalcade of hits continued for the better part of ten years, at which point the band apparently got tired of making money hand over fist and decided to break up. This was, in retrospect, a wise decision, as their last couple of albums saw the band flirting, to disastrous effect, with that

peculiar hybrid of hard rock and disco that thankfully never really caught on. Rodgers eventually turned up in the Firm with Jimmy Page, a band that was notable mainly for having Paul Rodgers and Jimmy Page in it. They released a couple of cringe-inducing albums and then mercifully disbanded before the cacophony of such blasphemous noise deafened the innocent. In 1986, Ralphs and Kirke put the band back together with a new singer and a new bassist, and in 1990 they triumphantly reconquered the *Billboard* charts with four minutes of out-and-out power ballad swill titled "If You Needed Somebody." The song was in no way imitative of Foreigner's "I Want to Know What Love Is"—honest. A few more years followed until, at the tail end of the 1990s, all the original members got back together to exploit the

newly prosperous arena rock nostalgia circuit. They celebrated this joyous turn of events by releasing a retrospective double CD, *The Original Bad Company Anthology*. This release had two newly recorded songs grafted onto the end, whose likely function was to justify a "2 New Songs!" sticker on its packaging in the hopes of distracting the buyer from the $33.99 retail price. They haven't recorded any new material since then, but they've reunited in one form or another numerous times for live appearances. Sadly, Burrell died of a heart attack in 2006, making a full reunion of the original lineup impossible.

Boz Burrell: bass (*Bad Company* through *Fame and Fortune*, *The Original Bad Company Anthology*); **Dave Colwell**: guitar (*Here Comes Trouble* through *Stories Told and Untold*); **Brian Howe**: vocals (*Fame and Fortune*, *The Best of Bad Company Live: What You Hear Is*

The very gifted Paul Rodgers sang for Bad Company. Left to right: Boz Burrell, Paul Rodgers, Simon Kirke, and Mick Ralphs.

What You Get); **Simon Kirke**: drums; **Mick Ralphs**: guitar; **Paul Rodgers**: vocals (*Bad Company* through *Rough Diamonds, The Original Bad Company Anthology, In Concert: Merchants of Cool*); **Rick Wills**: bass (*The Best of Bad Company Live: What You Hear Is What You Get* through *Stories Told and Untold*)

Discography: *Bad Company* (Swan Song, 1974); *Straight Shooter* (Swan Song, 1975); *Run with the Pack* (Swan Song, 1976); *Burnin' Sky* (Swan Song, 1977); *Desolation Angels* (Swan Song, 1979); *Rough Diamonds* (Swan Song, 1982); *Fame and Fortune* (Atlantic, 1986); *Dangerous Age* (Atco, 1988); *Holy Water* (Atco, 1990); *Here Comes Trouble* (Atco, 1992); *The Best of Bad Company Live: What You Hear Is What You Get* (Atlantic, 1993); *Company of Strangers* (EastWest, 1995); *Stories Told and Untold* (EastWest, 1996); *The Original Bad Company Anthology* (Elektra, 1999); *In Concert: Merchants of Cool* (Sanctuary, 2002)\

YEARS ACTIVE: 1987–2006; 2008–PRESENT

Biohazard was formed in Brooklyn, New York, in the late 1980s. The group started off as your garden-variety hardcore/metal crossover band, but by the time they made their move to the Roadrunner record label in 1991, they had transformed into a full-on rap-metal band before rap-metal was an established style. This change in artistic approach is surely the result of the band members' many years of "hanging out in the projects," as stated in the liner notes to the Black Sabbath tribute album *Nativity in Black*, for which Biohazard contributed the first track. A 1994 collaboration with the hardcore rap group Onyx for the *Judgment Night* soundtrack further reinforced this reputation. The band's name became synonymous with the rap-metal movement, and the individual members were recognized as the Johnny Cash, Merle Haggard, David Allan Coe, and Johnny Paycheck of the genre because they were so thoroughly ensconced in the milieu of gritty urban life and correctional facilities. In fact, bassist and vocalist Evan Seinfeld even regularly appeared on HBO's prison series, *Oz*. In 2002, he began dating porn star Tera Patrick, whom he married in 2004, and whom he ejaculated upon in such classic films as *Teradise Island*. Sadly, their union didn't last, and they divorced in 2010, much to the delight of pornography enthusiasts everywhere, who now believed that they, too, could date her. Seinfeld left the group in 2011, and their 2012 offering, *Reborn in Defiance*, was his last album with them.

Leo Curley: guitars (*Uncivilization*); **Rob Echeverria**: guitars (*No Holds Barred: Live in Europe, New World Disorder*) (see also Helmet); **Billy Graziadei**: guitars/vocals; **Bobby Hambel**: guitars (*Biohazard* through *State of the World Address*); **Scott Roberts**: guitar (*Means to an End*); **Keith Rooney**: bass (*Means to an End*); **Danny Schuler**: drums; **Evan Seinfeld**: bass/vocals; **Brian Worland**: bass, vocals (*Means to an End*)

Discography: *Biohazard* (Magnetic Air, 1990); *Urban Discipline* (Roadrunner, 1992); *State of the World Address* (Warner Bros., 1994); *Mata Leao* (Warner Bros., 1996); *New World Disorder* (Polygram, 1999); *Uncivilization* (Sanctuary, 2001); *Means to an End* (Steamhammer, 2005); *Reborn in Defiance* (Nuclear Blast, 2012)

YEARS ACTIVE: 1969–PRESENT

There exists a popular misconception that 1969, the year of the original Woodstock, was universally full of free love, flower power, and generally groovy times. In reality, this couldn't have been less true for a certain group of four working-class kids from the dreary industrial city of Birmingham, England. One of the lads was a singer named Ozzy Osbourne, and he has since recalled that he

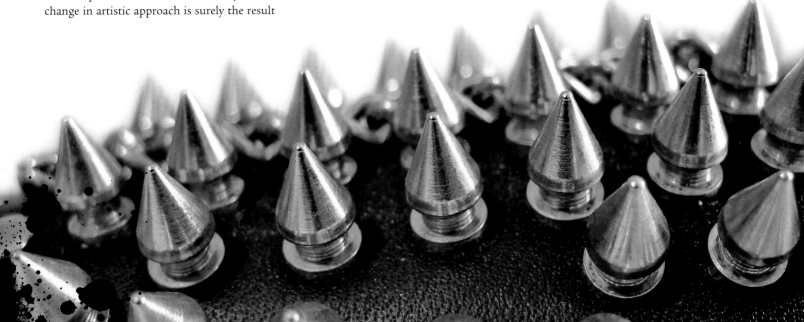

and his bandmates felt that they should make music that reflected the grim reality of their surroundings ("Let's scare people!" was Ozzy's actual quote). At this moment in 1969, Black Sabbath was born. Although their music was essentially blues-based, the tempos were slowed down to a funeral crawl, giving the songs a heft and an epic, theatrical dimension unique for the era. The critics stayed true to their compulsive need to be wrong about everything and lambasted the band whenever they could, characterizing the music as overly amplified stupidity for moronic teens on barbiturates. (They apparently preferred the profoundly meaningful music of the Archies and the 1910 Fruitgum Company.) In all likelihood, the critics were hostile toward Sabbath because the band's lyrics about war, the devil, and death seemed to signal the failure and end of the utopian hippie era.

However, the teenagers of the day clearly identified with Black Sabbath's 1970 self-titled debut, and the band became internationally popular in short order. Later that year, the band released its watershed album, *Paranoid*. If they had never made another album afterward, they would still have their rightful place in his-tory on the merits of this one alone, featuring as it does not only the title track but also such classics as "War Pigs" and the almighty "Iron Man." Happily, Black Sabbath released many more albums. There was *Master of Reality*, possibly Sabbath's heaviest album, which featured the band's love letter to mari-juana, "Sweet Leaf," and both "Children of the Grave" and "Into the Void," songs that can-not be described in terms that eschew either hyperbole or multiple usages of the term "fucking" as a qualifying adjec-tive. The same holds true for the next few releases. They're simply that good, they're still as heavy as the day they were released, and more than forty years later, they're still as heavy as anything else out there.

The band eventually succumbed to the typical late-1970s story of drug abuse and artistic differences, and by 1979, the strain the band was under had revealed itself in the form of two subpar albums. It was at this time that Osbourne left the band (he may actually have been fired, but there has yet to be a definitive statement about what happened). When Osbourne was replaced by former Rainbow vocalist Ronnie James Dio, many of the hard-core faithful decided to jump ship, as they could not accept anything but the band's origi-nal lineup. Much to everyone's surprise, however, the group's maiden release with Dio, *Heaven and Hell*, was their strongest album in years, even garnering enough new interest in the band to justify the reissue of "Paranoid" as a single. It seemed that the band was revitalized by the new blood, but in the middle of the tour to support the album, drummer Bill Ward left for personal and health reasons. Vinny Appice was brought in to replace him, and this lineup recorded *Mob Rules*, which, like its predecessor, was a much stronger album than anyone was expecting. Unfortunately, during the mixing of the band's first live album, *Live Evil*, the two new members developed into a rival faction against the old. In what has to be one of the more idiotic moments of band infighting, each party accused

OPPOSITE: Black Sabbath's Ozzy Osbourne (left) wears groovy fringe, while Tony Iommi sports metallic trimmings. BELOW LEFT: Black Sabbath in an early publicity photograph. LEFT TO RIGHT: Geezer Butler, Tony Iommi, Ozzy Osbourne, and Bill Ward. BELOW RIGHT: Black Sabbath risks its doom-and-gloom reputation by smiling for the camera. LEFT TO RIGHT: Ozzy Osbourne, Tony Iommi, Geezer Butler, and Bill Ward.

BLACK SABBATH
HEAVEN AND HELL

ALL AREA ACCESS

LEFT: It's not quite Stonehenge, but this is a fine example of one of Black Sabbath's modest and unassuming stage props.

the other of sneaking into the studio where the album was being made (perhaps wearing capes and top hats, but surely under cover of darkness) and surreptitiously—nay, diabolically—making themselves louder in the mix. As anyone who has ever had the privilege of mixing an album knows, making anything "louder in the mix" is a protracted nightmare that consumes multiple-digit quantities of hours and would therefore be nearly impossible to do in secret, rendering these accusations somewhat far-fetched. In any case, Dio's crabbiness was compounded when the album credits listed him as simply "Ronnie Dio" minus the "James." Perhaps he was worried that someone might confuse him with Ronnie Ted Dio. In any case, he and Appice walked out the door, and the band was in the can again.

Former Deep Purple vocalist Ian Gillan was brought in, and Black Sabbath released the monstrously heavy and vastly underrated *Born Again*. The supporting tour turned out to be the inspiration for one of the gags in the movie *This Is Spinal Tap*, when dwindling attendance at their live shows forced the band to book smaller halls. As such, they were unable to fit one of their stage props, a life-size model of Stonehenge, into any of the new venues, forcing them to cart it around from city to city and, one presumes, leave it with parking-lot attendants. At the time it probably seemed more depressing than funny, and when the tour was over everyone quit the band. Guitarist Tony Iommi seemed to take it in stride, however, as he now had the opportunity to make a solo album, an idea he had flirted with even before Gillan had been brought into the troubled band. But the record company decided that Iommi's name alone wasn't enough to shift units, and at the company's insistence, the album was credited to "Black Sabbath Featuring Tony Iommi." In the end, it was very likely that this decision by the record company, more than any other factor, reinforced the notion that Black Sabbath was an entity not unlike McDonald's in terms of its rapid turnover of employees. Iommi, now the de facto chief executive officer, kept the band going anyway, and eventually he paired up with powerhouse drummer Cozy Powell and unknown singer Tony Martin. In time, the band started to find its feet again, and by the 1990 release of *Tyr*, Black Sabbath had defied the odds yet again and regained some of their lost credibility.

In 1991, the *Mob Rules* lineup of Iommi, Butler, Appice, and Dio reunited to raised eyebrows the world over. The band made the 1992 release, *Dehumanizer*, and began touring to support it, but the honeymoon was cut short when Dio quit the band again, this time over the possibility of Black Sabbath ending its tour by opening for Ozzy Osbourne. The band was forced to complete their remaining dates with Judas Priest singer Rob Halford, who was briefly rumored to be taking the job full-time. This never happened, and Martin (a talented singer in his own right who certainly deserves better than his reputation as the guy Sabbath got when it couldn't get anyone else) rejoined the band, but by this time there wasn't much left of the band to join. There had been too much instability and too many lineup changes, and Black Sabbath was simply not taken seriously anymore. The band soldiered on and released two more albums, but they did not sell well and the tours were poorly attended.

The band fell silent after the 1995 release of *Forbidden*, and it probably seemed like it was back down the toilet with everything that Iommi had struggled for over the past few years. However, in late 1997, the band's fortunes began improving once more when the original lineup reunited for a series of live dates, recorded and, in 1998, released the album *Reunion*. The album and tour were successful enough to convince everyone involved that there was still significant interest in the band, and a full-scale tour was launched in 1999. Most tantalizingly, Sabbath announced that it would enter the studio with knob-twiddler Rick Rubin. This may have been cause for celebration indeed—Rubin's last involvement with anyone in the Sabbath camp had been in 1991, when he was originally slated to produce Ozzy Osbourne's solo album of that year. According to guitarist Zakk Wylde, Rubin had Ozzy's band writing music "that sounded like we were getting [it] faxed to us straight from Satan every day." Sadly, the project fell through and no new music emerged. In fact, other than Ozzy solo albums, the entire original lineup had gone eerily quiet.

In 2006, the *Mob Rules* lineup of Dio, Iommi, Butler, and Appice surprised the shit out of just about everyone who had been paying attention for the previous 25 years by reuniting to record three new songs for the compilation *Black Sabbath: The Dio Years*. It went so well that they agreed to work together again, this time rechristening themselves Heaven and Hell, a decision that maybe should have been made back in 1980. They went on a wildly successful tour in 2007, and despite their characterization of the reunion as a one-off thing, they announced that they would make a new studio album. Titled *The Devil You Know*, the crushingly heavy album was released in 2009 and sold better than anything any of its members had been involved with in years. It was all systems go, and the band had every intention of not fucking it up this time. They had learned from their mistakes, and now they would enjoy their success.

Unfortunately, it was too good to be true. Dio was diagnosed with stomach cancer at the end of 2009, and he passed away the following year. Naturally, this led to the usual speculation that this cleared the way for a reunion with Ozzy, and after much coyness, false starts, and hemming and hawing, the band announced that the original lineup would, in fact, reunite for an album and tour. Perhaps to bolster their point, they made this announcement on November 11, 2011, or 11/11/11 to *This Is Spinal Tap* enthusiasts. As before, the producer on this album was announced as none other than Rick Rubin, apparently because it had gone so well with him the last time. Despite a fatalistic attitude on the part of fans who'd had the reunion rug yanked out from under them before, the group announced European tour dates for May and June of 2012. If a new album actually, really, truly gets recorded this time, it's expected to come out at the end of that year. Here's hoping.

Vinny Appice: drums (*Mob Rules, Live Evil, Dehumanizer*) (see also Dio); **Bev Bevan**: drums (*Born Again World Tour* to *The Eternal Idol*); **Geezer Butler**: bass (*Black Sabbath* through *Born Again; Dehumanizer, Cross Purposes, Reunion*); **Laurence Cottle**: bass (*Headless Cross*); **Bob Daisley**: bass (*The Eternal Idol*); **Ronnie James Dio**: vocals (*Heaven and Hell* through *Live Evil; Dehumanizer*) (see also Dio, Rainbow); **Ian Gillan**: vocals (*Born Again*) (see also Deep Purple); **Glenn Hughes**: vocals (*Seventh Star*) (see also Deep Purple); **Tony Iommi**: guitars; **Tony Martin**: vocals (*The Eternal Idol* through *Tyr; Cross Purposes*); **Neil Murray**: bass (*Tyr, Forbidden*); **Geoff Nicholls**: keyboards (*Heaven and Hell* and later); **Ozzy Osbourne**: vocals (*Black Sabbath* through *Never Say Die; Reunion*) (see also Ozzy Osbourne); **Cozy Powell**: drums (*Headless Cross, Tyr, Forbidden*) (see also Yngwie Malmsteen, Rainbow); **Bobby Rondinelli**: drums (*Cross Purposes; Live*) (see also Blue Öyster Cult, Rainbow); **Eric Singer**: drums (*Seventh Star, The Eternal Idol*); **Dave Spitz**: bass (*Seventh Star, The Eternal Idol*); **Bill Ward**: drums (*Black Sabbath* through *Heaven and Hell; Born Again, Reunion*)

Discography: *Black Sabbath* (Warner Bros., 1970); *Paranoid* (Warner Bros., 1970); *Master of Reality* (Warner Bros., 1971); *Black Sabbath, Vol. 4* (Warner Bros., 1972); *Sabbath Bloody Sabbath* (Warner Bros., 1973); *Sabotage* (Warner Bros., 1975); *Technical Ecstasy* (Warner Bros., 1976); *Never Say Die!* (Warner Bros., 1978); *Heaven and Hell* (Warner Bros., 1980); *Mob Rules* (Warner Bros., 1981); *Live Evil* (Warner Bros., 1983); *Born Again* (Warner Bros., 1983); *Seventh Star* (Warner Bros., 1986); *The Eternal Idol* (Warner Brothers, 1987); *Headless Cross* (IRS, 1989); *Tyr* (IRS, 1990); *Dehumanizer* (Warner Bros., 1992); *Cross Purposes* (IRS, 1994); *Cross Purposes Live* (IRS, 1995); *Forbidden* (EMI, 1995); *Reunion* (Epic, 1998); *Past Lives* (Sanctuary, 2002)

BLIND GUARDIAN

YEARS ACTIVE: 1984–PRESENT

The original edition of *The Encyclopedia of Heavy Metal* was heavily criticized on numerous fronts. How could it include Jimi Hendrix and omit Ministry? How could it devote such a low word count to Blue Öyster Cult? And how could it be so oddly punctuated?

Good questions all. But the book's most glaring and unforgivable sin was its omission of the German symphonic metal band, Blind Guardian. For this transgression alone, its author should have had his fingers sawed off so that he could never again infect the marketplace with so shitty a volume of prose. Herein lies the author's redemption.

Blind Guardian formed in Krefeld, Germany as a straight-up thrash band. They released their debut album, *Battalions of Fear*, in 1988, and *Follow the Blind* in 1989. Both albums had greater melodic sense than many of those of their contemporaries, but not enough to really set them apart. Next came 1990's *Tales from the Twilight World*, but it was 1992's *Somewhere Far Beyond* that really showed the band taking on elements of the epic, multilayered sound for which they're known today.

In addition to its Tolkien-inspired lyrics and diverse vocals by Hansi Kürsch, guitarists Marcus Siepen and André Olbrich started ripping off Queen's Brian May with abandon. Not that that's a criticism. The lyrics, meanwhile, had more dragons and rainbows than Ronnie James Dio could shake a scepter at, and the double bass of Thomas Stauch sounded like an idling motorcycle. Well played, boys, well played.

In 1994 the group teamed up with former Metallica producer Flemming Rasmussen to create *Imaginations from the Other Side*, released in 1995. It was a sophisticated album, showing that the stylistic advances of *Somewhere Far Beyond* were no fluke. It contained such anthemic highlights as "Mordred's Song" and "The Script for My Requiem." It was followed in 1998 by *Nightfall in Middle-Earth*, an entire con-

cept album based on J.R.R. Tolkien's *The Silmarillion*, which contained such epic tunes as "When Sorrow Sang" and "Noldor (Dead Winter Reigns)," a song so awesome that if you don't like it, you're stupid.

In the new millenium, Blind Guardian did the unthinkable and created an album that was even more complex and overwrought than its predecessors. The album was 2002's *A Night at the Opera*, whose title was both a sign that they were happily paying homage to Queen, as well as an accurate description of the album's contents, which was made up of arias more than mere tunes. Highlights included "Precious Jerusalem," which bears more than a passing resemblance to the *Jesus Christ Superstar* soundtrack, "The Soulforged" and "And Then There Was Silence," a fourteen-minute saga that manages somehow not to be boring. Worth noting that that's a feat many bands can't manage in three minutes. Blind Guardian had already pushed good taste and multichannel overdubbing past its limits, but this song is said to have as many as forty vocal tracks overlaid on it, and one can only assume that ten of them are occupied by the ghost of Freddie Mercury. *A Night at the Opera* was next to impossible to top, but the group did a more than respectable job following it up with 2006's *A Twist in the Myth*. While it may have been slightly less ambitious than its predecessor, it had more than its fair share of absolutely solid material, including "Turn The Page" and "The New Order." Their last album

Blind Guardian guitarists Marcus Siepen (top) and André Olbrich (bottom) bring the harmonized 32nd-note goods.

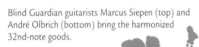

was 2010's *At the Edge of Time*, another consistent effort with such excellent material as the nine-minute orchestral dirge "Sacred Worlds" as well as "Valkyries," which is about valkyries.

With the exception of the studio technology they use, there is nothing really modern about Blind Guardian's music at all. But who gives a shit? It's impossible to deny their complete artistic sincerity, or to propose that they take a half-assed approach to what they do. Blind Guardian keeps the spirit of metal alive and has no use for any modernizing elements in anything that it does. There is really something refreshing about a band that for over twenty years have been absolutely resolute and unapologetic about offering the most fantastical metal available, with a full cast of orcs to populate the lyrics and an army of harmonized guitars to convey the tunes. Blind Guardian is absolutely the real thing, and anyone wishing to hear metal with no pretense should look no further.

Frederik Ehmke: drums, percussion, flute, bagpipes (*A Twist in the Myth* and later); **Hansi Kürsch**: vocals; **André Olbrich**: guitar, vocals; **Marcus Siepen**: rhythm guitar, vocals; **Thomas Stauch**: drums (*Battalions of Fear* through *A Night at the Opera*)

Discography: *Battalions of Fear* (Virgin, 1996); *Follow the Blind* (Virgin, 1989); *Tales from the Twilight World* (Virgin, 1990); *Somewhere Far Beyond* (Virgin, 1992); *Imaginations from the Other Side* (Virgin, 1995); *Nightfall in Middle-Earth* (Virgin, 1998); *A Night at the Opera* (Virgin, 2002); *A Twist in the Myth* (Nuclear Blast, 2006); *At the Edge of Time* (Nuclear Blast, 2010)

BLUE CHEER

Years active: 1966–1972; 1989–1993; 1999–2009

Blue Cheer was one of the most significant bands of the 1960s to have an influence on what became known as heavy metal. The San Francisco power trio—Dickie Petersen, Leigh Stephens, and Paul Whaley—took the acid rock of bands like Cream and pushed it right through the wall, creating the loudest, sludgiest sound that mere mortals had ever heard. The band's career lasted several decades mostly due to Dickie Petersen's ability to keep up with the personnel changes. But it is the band's debut album, *Vincebus Eruptum*, that best distills Blue Cheer's essence and sits on record store shelves to this day. The album's six cuts of lowest-end roar and shrieking-pterodactyl feedback added up to forty minutes of merciless punishment like nothing that had ever come before, with the possible exception of the sound Jimi Hendrix's melting pickups made when he set his guitar on fire. To put it in perspective, in the year when Deep Purple was still doing Neil Diamond covers, Blue Cheer's album-opening studio version of "Summertime Blues" was louder, more chaotic, and more violent than the "definitive" live version that the Who produced two years later. The debut was such a strong statement at the time, in fact, that it rendered subsequent albums impotent-sounding by comparison; it was simply too tough an act to follow. But time has been kind to the band. Blue Cheer's music still holds up today and is as heavy as anything else out there. It has had a pronounced influence on the Aunt Jemima–thick sound of stoner rock bands like Fu Manchu and Nebula, to name but two. Sadly, bassist and founding member Dickie Petersen died in 2009 from prostate cancer that had spread to his liver. Blue Cheer officially disbanded at that point.

Randy Holden: guitar (*New! Improved! Blue Cheer*); **Ralph Burns Kellogg**: keyboards (*Outsideinside* through *The Original Human Being*); **Norman Mayell**: drums (*Blue Cheer, The Original Human Being*); **Dickie Petersen**: vocals/bass; **Tony Rainier**: guitar (*The Beast Is Back: The Megaforce Years*); **Bruce Stephens**: vocals/guitar (*Outsideinside* through *The Original Human Being*); **Leigh Stephens**: guitar (*Vincebus Eruptum*); **Paul Whaley**: drums (*Outsideinside* through *The Original Human Being; The Beast Is Back: The Megaforce Years*); **Gary Lee Yoder**: guitar (*Blue Cheer, The Original Human Being*)

Discography: *Vincebus Eruptum* (Phillips, 1968); *Outsideinside* (Philips, 1968); *New! Improved! Blue Cheer* (Philips, 1969); *Blue Cheer* (Philips, 1969); *The Original Human Being* (Philips, 1970); *Oh! Pleasant Hope* (Philips, 1971); *The Beast Is Back: The Megaforce Years* (Megaforce, 1984); *Blitzkrieg Over Nüremberg* (Magnum, 1989); *Good Times Are So Hard to Find: The History of Blue Cheer* (Mercury, 1990); *Highlights & Low Lives* (Thunderbolt, 1990); *Dining with the Sharks* (Nibelung, 1991); *Highlights & Low Lives* (Thunderbolt, 1996); *Live & Unreleased '68–'74* (Blue Cheer, 1996); *Live at San Jose Civic Center, 1968 & More* (Blue Cheer, 1996)

Blue Cheer was an early purveyor of molten sludge-rock.

GENRES

Although it may seem to the outsider that all heavy metal music is just a longhaired Rob Halford–type guy shrieking into a flame-engulfed microphone while thundering guitar power chords rumble in the background, even the most pedestrian heavy metal fan will happily disabuse the ignorant of this reprehensible stereotype. Here is a basic list of predominant metal subcategories to avoid embarrassment and possible assault from the heavy metal cognoscenti.

Venom

BLACK METAL

The term "black metal" originated from the 1982 Venom album of the same name, although Venom's music has nothing in common with bands associated with this genre. Venom did, however, contribute to the genre's visual aesthetic with their mock-satanic stage presentation. Black metal music is exemplified by bands like Mayhem and Emperor, who favor blindingly fast tempos (known as blast beats), grating guitar sounds, and indecipherable lyrics delivered by a screeching, phlegm-clogged voice. For those who will not tolerate any compromises in their metal, this is the stuff. Detractors describe this genre as silly.

DEATH METAL

Death metal was the stepping stone between thrash metal and black metal. It emerged in the late 1980s, with a striking percentage of bands hailing from Florida, such as Death, Deicide, and Obituary. The music features hyper-speed tempos, extremely down-tuned guitars and Cookie Monster vocals. Despite ridiculous song names like "Stabwound Intercourse" and "Excreted Alive," many of these bands want the public to regard them as serious artists. Good luck with that.

Carcass

GRINDCORE

In the 1990s, grindcore didn't just cross over the line of speed metal's most extreme attributes. It pole-vaulted over it. It was the most extreme sonic onslaught that existed at the time. Early purveyors of this style were Carcass and Napalm Death, the genre's founder. Napalm Death's debut album, *Scum*, possessed every trademark of the style, from indecipherable lyrics, to almost ambient buzzsaw guitars, to drumming so fast it sounds like the drummer is trying to break the sound barrier.

Death

Candlemass

DOOM METAL

Doom metal is a genre based on tempos that are painfully slow, melodies that are absurdly bombastic, and lyrics that are completely morose and hopeless. The movement owes its existence to the 1970 Black Sabbath song that bears the band's name, since it's a veritable sampler platter of all of the genre's attributes. However, unlike its thrash and death metal counterparts, doom metal has yet to find mainstream acceptance, and even its most well known bands, such as Candlemass, have moved only the smallest bit beyond cult status.

Godflesh

INDUSTRIAL METAL

Industrial metal was spearheaded by Godflesh, whose guitarist, Justin Broadrick, had left Napalm Death in the late 1980s. Broadrick took that band's atonal wash of guitars and layered them over slow drum machine tempos. The effect was music that was as unyielding as an industrial-strength laundry mangler. It was not long before this approach, albeit a more accessible one, was co-opted by the likes of Nine Inch Nails to commercially successful effect.

Dio

POWER METAL

Although the movement has its share of American fans, power metal is a European phenomenon. The genre is performed by bands like HammerFall and Jag Panzer, and derives from bands like Dio and Iron Maiden. It emphasizes strong melodies and swords-and-sorcery lyrics, and is sometimes referred to as true metal; some of its most infamous practitioners, the members of Manowar, are in the habit of proudly proclaiming "Death to false metal!" on their website, T-shirts, and albums.

SHRED METAL

Shred was a uniquely 1980s phenomenon. It was basically a bunch of records from the Shrapnel label that featured nonstop guitar solos from beginning to end. The difference between those albums and a Ted Nugent album was that the nonstop soloing was really, really fast. The guitarists who took part in this sixty-fourth-note tom-foolery, such as Jason Becker and David T. Chastain, were inspired by the likes of Eddie Van Halen and Yngwie Malmsteen. The movement really only caught on with other shred guitarists and never went mainstream. It was over by the 1990s.

Yngwie Malmsteen

Def Leppard

NEW WAVE OF BRITISH HEAVY METAL

They were young. They were spunky. And they embraced the energy and do-it-yourself ethos of punk rock, injecting new, aggressive life into a genre that was waning. The New Wave of British Heavy Metal movement started at the end of the 1970s, when bands such as Led Zeppelin and Black Sabbath were a decade old and abject boredom was palpable. With the originators running on fumes, a new generation appeared to reenergize the genre. The best-known bands of the movement are Def Leppard and Iron Maiden, with significant contributions from such bands as Saxon and Tygers of Pan Tang.

PROGRESSIVE METAL

The progressive metal label applies to bands such as Queensrÿche and Fates Warning, who use the elaborate song structures, unusual time signatures, and eyebrow-arching melodies of bands like Yes and King Crimson but to heavier and more aggressive effect. It's sort of redundant to list it as its own genre, since self-indulgent song lengths and masturbatory instrumental showboating exist within the canons of all kinds of metal bands. Metallica certainly has more than its fair share of epic-length threnodies that wind and weave their way through every time signature and key change imaginable. However, the bands generally regarded as progressive metal emphasize their compositional and instrumental prowess with greater finesse and subtlety.

Queensrÿche

Slayer

SPEED METAL/THRASH

Speed metal, a.k.a. thrash, started off as an underground movement, but it became one of the most pervasive styles of the 1980s. When Metallica and Slayer emerged at the beginning of the decade, they were considered unmarketable. Ten years later, they had gone Top 40 and were filling arenas. That original unmarketablity gave it a by-the-fans, for-the-fans characteristic that endeared the bands to their listeners. In the end, it also became the genre's undoing. The original bands' fans went on to form their own bands with the stated intention of being more extreme than their forefathers. This led to death metal and black metal, both of which ate the original genre alive and rendered it obsolete. In retrospect, it is clear that the effect of the speed metal movement on heavy metal as a whole is beyond estimation.

BLUE ÖYSTER CULT

YEARS ACTIVE: 1967–PRESENT

Blue Öyster Cult has been called the thinking man's heavy metal group, likely because of its early associations with rock critics such as Sandy Pearlman and Richard Meltzer. There is also the bit about the band forming at Long Island's Stony Brook University, which is remarkable given that your average heavy metal fan is presumed by the general populace to have an endless reserve of disdain for course work. In any event, this distinction has helped Blue Öyster Cult gain some respect in circles where most other heavy metal bands would not normally find it, and they have had such nonmetallic luminaries contribute to their recorded canon as the Lady Schick–eschewing songstress Patti Smith.

The band went through multiple incarnations until Columbia Records signed them in 1971. Their rise was slow and steady, and after five years of heavy touring they finally got their first Top 40 hit with "(Don't Fear) The Reaper," a song that earned the band enough stoner fans to put the children of butane lighter manufacturers through college. The band had a few more years of chart action ahead of them until the 1980s brought a decade's worth of band member musical chairs, as well as albums that sold progressively less and less well than their predecessors. By the early 1990s, the band seemed to have just sort of gone away, but in 1998 they released a new album, *Heaven Forbid*, on Canada's CMC label, which had for a few years given a home to metal bands that had been dropped by major labels in a rush to sign the next Better Than Ezra. They moved to the Sanctuary label after that, and they released the 2002 album, *A Long Day's Night*. The band is officially still together per their official website, but there are no current plans for any new studio recordings.

Eric Bloom: vocals/guitars; **Albert Bouchard**: drums (*Blue Öyster Cult* through *Fire of Unknown Origin*; *Imaginos*); **Joe Bouchard**: bass (*Blue Öyster Cult* through *Imaginos*); **Rick Downey**: drums (*Extraterrestrial Live* and *The Revolution by Night*); **Allen Lanier**: keyboards (*Blue Öyster Cult* through *The Revolution by Night*; *Imaginos*, *Heaven Forbid*); **Danny Miranda**: bass (*Heaven Forbid*); **Thommy Price**: drums (*Club Ninja*); **Donald "Buck Dharma" Roeser**: vocals/guitars; **Bobby Rondinelli**: drums (*Heaven Forbid*) (see also Black Sabbath, Rainbow); **Tommy Zvoncheck**: keyboards (*Club Ninja*)

Discography: *Blue Öyster Cult* (Columbia, 1972); *Tyranny and Mutation* (Columbia, 1973); *Secret Treaties* (Columbia, 1974); *On Your Feet or on Your Knees* (Columbia, 1974); *Agents of Fortune* (Columbia, 1976); *Spectres* (Columbia, 1977); *Some Enchanted Evening* (Columbia, 1978); *Mirrors* (Columbia, 1979); *Cultösaurus Erectus* (Columbia, 1980); *Fire of Unknown Origin* (Columbia, 1981); *Extraterrestrial Live* (Columbia, 1982); *The Revolution by Night* (Columbia, 1983); *Club Ninja* (Koch, 1986); *Imaginos* (Columbia, 1988); *Heaven Forbid* (CMC, 1998); *Don't Fear the Reaper: The Best of Blue Öyster Cult* (Columbia/Legacy, 2000); *The Curse of the Hidden Mirror* (CMC, 2001); *A Long Day's Night* (Sanctuary, 2002)

BODY COUNT

YEARS ACTIVE: 1987–2006; 2009–PRESENT

Body Count was meant to be a side project for rapper Ice-T, but for a while the band garnered enough outrage and controversy to

In this 1977 photograph, Blue Öyster Cult pounds away at the F chord.

make most people forget that the band was an extracurricular activity. Ice-T already had a few years behind him as a successful rapper when he was invited to play on the first Lollapalooza tour in 1991. He ended his sets by inviting the rest of his recently formed band, Body Count, onstage to play a few songs, and the crowds of suburban teenagers regularly turned into seething mobs in response. Ice-T quite rightly saw a demand for a product, and the following year Body Count released its debut album, an epic jeremiad featuring demonically possessed male sexual organs and the moving account of one individual's urge to test the flame-retardancy of his mother. But the song that got the most attention was "Cop Killer." One day, as the first Tuesday in November neared, then-president George Bush and his running mate, Dan Quayle, decided that the ditty represented a heinous moral outrage, and they called upon the record company to pull the song. Apparently, they had no problems with the trillion depictions of rape and murder to be found on the rest of the album. They also seemed untroubled by similar subject matter on Ice-T's other albums—perhaps because they weren't released during an election year. Things became truly surreal when simian-loathing munitions enthusiast Charlton Heston held a press conference to decry the song, wherein he read aloud its lyrics in a sort of Allen Ginsberg-ish Beat poetry style.

After the "Cop Killer" controversy simmered down, the band soldiered on to record two more albums, which made neither headlines nor hits. Body Count fell off the radar, until the 2006 release of their fourth album, *Murder 4 Hire*. Sadly, in the time between albums, three of the band's original five members had died. Drummer Beatmaster V died of leukemia in 1996, guitarist D-Roc the Executioner succumbed to lymphoma in 2004, and bassist Mooseman died in a 2001 shooting.

Beatmaster V: drums (*Body Count* to *Violent Demise*); **Bendrix**: guitar (*Murder 4 Hire*); **D-Roc**: guitar; **Ernie C**: guitar; **Ice-T**: vocals; **Mooseman**: bass(*Body Count* to *Violent Demise*); **O.T.**: drums (*Murder 4 Hire*); **Vincent Price**: bass (*Murder 4 Hire*)

Discography: *Body Count* (Sire, 1992); *Born Dead* (Capitol, 1994); *Violent Demise: Last Days* (Virgin, 1997); *Murder 4 Hire* (Escapi Music, 2006)

YEARS ACTIVE: 1983–PRESENT

In the year following the 1985 Parents Music Resource Center controversy, and amid the general perception that heavy metal fans were a bunch of mouth-breathing stoner satanists who lived to sacrifice cats to the Father of Lies, Bon Jovi's breakthrough album, *Slippery When Wet*, was responsible for turning heavy metal into a radio-friendly pop format that one could take home to mom and dad. This cleared the way for bands such as Poison and Warrant and, for better or worse, ushered in the era of the power ballad. The 1986 release sold millions of copies on the strength of its hit songs, among them "You Give Love a Bad Name," "Livin' on a Prayer," and "Wanted Dead or Alive." These songs had been cowritten with songwriter Desmond Child (perhaps best known for cowriting "I Was Made for Loving You," KISS' bottomlessly horrible entry in the disco-rock sweepstakes) and then auditioned for local New Jersey audiences; the selections that made the final album reflected

Richie Sambora (left) and Bon Jovi are caught on film during a patriotic moment in 1987.

their popularity at these events. The band pushed things further by taking advantage of the music-video format to showcase lead singer Jon Bon Jovi's dreaminess. They were also notable for being one of the only American metal bands, pop or otherwise, to retain their appeal throughout the 1990s, thanks mostly to their spiffy new haircuts and subtle stylistic changes to their music, which by 1992's *Keep the Faith* had more in common with the arena rock strains of U2 than anything that could remotely be considered metallic. Still, the band deserves credit for handily negotiating the metal-hostile waters of the 1990s, and guitarist Richie Sambora in particular gets a nod for being man enough to successfully maintain a romantic relationship with the habitually augmented Cher. The group was inducted into the Rock and Roll Hall of Fame in 2010.

Jon Bon Jovi: vocals; **David Bryan**: keyboards; **Hugh McDonald**: bass (*These Days* and later); **Richie Sambora**: guitar; **Alec John Such**: bass (*Bon Jovi* through *Keep the Faith*; *One Wild Night: Live 1985–2001*); **Tico Torres**: drums

Discography: *Bon Jovi* (Mercury, 1984); *7800 Fahrenheit* (Mercury, 1985); *Slippery When Wet* (Mercury, 1986); *New Jersey* (Mercury, 1988); *Keep the Faith* (Mercury, 1992); *Cross Road* (Mercury, 1994); *These Days* (Mercury, 1995); *Crush* (Island, 2000); *One Wild Night: Live 1985–2001* (Island, 2001); *Bounce* (Island, 2002); *Have a Nice Day* (Island, 2005); *Lost Highway* (Lost Highway/Island Nashville, 2007); *The Circle* (Island, 2009)

RIGHT: Jersey boy Jon Bon Jovi makes America safe for pop-metal.

BUDGIE

- YEARS ACTIVE: 1967–1998; 2002–2010

Budgie was regulation-issue 1970s heavy rock, most closely related to Black Sabbath and Rush, owing its brontosauran crunch to the former and its front man's high-pitched helium vocals to the latter. To call a band "regulation-issue" might seem an insult, but in this particular band's case, their very simplicity was, in fact, a point of pride with them. The liner notes on the back of their debut album characterize them as "just a rock band, and a freaking good one at that," and you can't really argue with this claim.

Unfortunately, their very simplicity may have played a hand in why they remained little more than a cult band in the rest of the world while in their native Wales they racked up huge business. But Budgie's albums are still in print in the good ol' United States, thanks in part to Metallica's cover of "Crash Course in Brain Surgery" from Budgie's self-titled 1971 debut album.

The Welsh band also distinguished itself from its contemporaries by having incredibly stupid song titles, among them "Nude Disintegrating Parachutist Woman" and "Hot as a Docker's Armpit." Also by virtue of their much-derided folkie passages, the above-mentioned Metallica cover literally excises one such section, presumably because Metallica did not want to be affiliated with any sort of girly sensitivity (at least not until the next year, 1988, when their song "One" was released). Fans of the much vaunted New Wave of British Heavy Metal didn't seem to give a rat's ass, though, and Budgie was a three-time headliner at the Reading Festival. The band has been on hold since bassist and frontman Burke Shelley was hospitalized for an aortic aneurysm in 2010.

Pete Boot: drums (*In for the Kill*); **Tony Bourge**: guitars (*Budgie* through *Impeckable*); **Duncan McKay**: keyboards (*Deliver Us from Evil*); **Ray Phillips**: drums (*Budgie* through *Never Turn Your Back on a Friend*); **Burke Shelley**: bass/vocals; **John Thomas**: guitars (*If Swallowed Do Not Induce Vomiting* and later); **Steve Williams**: drums (*Bandolier* and later)

Discography: *Budgie* (MCA, 1971); *Squawk* (MCA, 1972); *Never Turn Your Back on a Friend* (MCA, 1973); *In for the Kill!* (MCA, 1974); *Bandolier* (A&M, 1975); *If I Were Brittania I'd Waive the Rules* (A&M, 1976); *Impeckable* (A&M, 1978); *Power Supply* (Active, 1980); *Nightflight* (RCA, 1981); *Deliver Us from Evil* (RCA, 1982); *Heavier than Air: Live on the BBC* (Griffin, 1998); *We Came We Saw: Live on the BBC* (Pilot, 1998); *Life in San Antonio* (RCA, 2002);

BUFFALO

YEARS ACTIVE: 1971–1977

Buffalo was an Australian band which was active in the 1970s. The Sydney-based band was ahead of its time in the sheer heft department, and they showcased the same rowdiness evident in many other Australian hard rock bands. Their first album, *Dead Forever...*, was released in 1972, and they followed it up with *Volcanic Rock* in 1973 and the refreshingly frankly titled *Only Want You for Your Body* in 1974. Despite the high quality of the material on all three albums, they gained notice not for their

music but mainly for the decidedly unwholesome scene depicted on the cover of the 1974 offering. It incorporated not only a touch of medieval torture, but also something that might actually be a whiff of granny porn. Buffalo raised eyebrows further with their moronic song titles, such as "I'm a Skirt Lifter, Not a Shirt Raiser," something that's always good to know when you're looking for a new boyfriend on OKCupid.com.

The band dismissed founding guitarist John Baxter in 1975, a move popularly regarded as the cause of their demise. Buffalo released two further albums, 1976's *Mother's Choice* and 1977's *Average Rock 'N' Roller* in his absence, and both were less heavy and more commercial than those

Budgie bassist and vocalist Burke Shelley doesn't let narcolepsy get in the way of his rock star dreams.

which had preceded them. This direction was exactly what people didn't want from them, and Buffalo promptly lost its audience. Despite supporting Rainbow on the band's Australian tour, Buffalo never again regained their mojo. The group broke up in 1977 amidst mounting public indifference, and bassist Peter Wells went on to much greater success with the band Rose Tattoo.

Paul Balbi: drums (*Dead Forever . . .*); **John Baxter**: guitar; **Jimmy Economou**: drums; **Alan Milano**: vocals (*Dead Forever . . .*); **Norm Roue**: guitar (*Mother's Choice*); **Ross Sims**: guitar (*Average Rock 'N' Roller*); **Karl Taylor**: guitar (*Mother's Choice*); **Dave Tice**: vocals; **Chris Turner**: drums, guitar (*Average Rock 'N' Roller*); **Peter Wells**: guitar, bass

Discography: *Dead Forever . . .* (Vertigo, 1972); *Volcanic Rock* (Vertigo, 1973); *Only Want You for Your Body* (Vertigo, 1974); *Mother's Choice* (Vertigo, 1976); *Average Rock 'N' Roller* (Vertigo, 1977)

CACTUS

Years active: 1970–1972; 1973–1982; 2006–present

After the demise of Vanilla Fudge, drummer Carmine Appice and bassist Tim Bogert had a brilliant idea. They would join forces with singer Rod "Ten Pounds of Semen" Stewart and guitar pyrotechnician Jeff Beck and form a supergroup of amazing proportions. Sadly, Beck was tooling around on a motorcycle one fine day when he promptly wiped out and fractured his skull, putting him out of commission for the foreseeable future. Stewart then dropped out to join Ron Wood in the Faces, and Appice and Bogert were in the shits. Luckily, the rhythm section managed to recruit singer Rusty Day from Ted Nugent's Amboy Dukes and guitarist Jim McCarty from Mitch Ryder's Detroit Wheels. The new group was dubbed Cactus, a raw as shit, heavy acid boogie band that blew their proto-metal peers Grand Funk Railroad and Blue Cheer out of the water.

Cactus released their self-titled debut in 1970, which featured such should-have-been-hits as "Bro. Bill" and "Let Me Swim." Despite these musical triumphs, *Cactus* will forever be known as the album that opens with a frenetic reading of Mose Allison's "Parchman Farm." The track will simply melt your face off à la *The Fly II*, and it was easily the best thing the band ever did in the studio. They followed it up the next year with *One Way . . . Or Another*, which was a step forward in terms of studio polish but a step backward in terms of the pure caveman mayhem that defined the debut. Later that year the group released *Restrictions*, which did little to raise the band's commercial profile. Just as the previous album had been redeemed by its title track, *Restrictions* was noteworthy for its sludge-rock take on Howlin' Wolf's "Evil," which, sadly, a lot of people today seem to think is a Monster Magnet song.

Cactus lost both Day and McCarty after *Restrictions* and replaced them with Atomic Rooster singer Peter French, guitarist Werner Fritzschings and keyboard player Duane Hitchings. This lineup was responsible for 1972's *'Ot 'n' Sweaty*, which was half-live and half-studio offering that is best described by the sound "meh." The band broke up afterwards, a wise decision, and the rhythm section went on to their long-delayed supergroup with Jeff Beck. After Cactus, Duane Hitchings led the New Cactus Band, which managed to squeeze out one album, *Son of Cactus*, and then promptly broke up when they realized nobody gave a fuck. Rusty Day formed his own version of Cactus, creatively called "Cactus," which recorded nothing. Day was killed in 1982 by a guitarist, Ron Sanders, to whom he owed money from a past cocaine deal. Sanders also appallingly managed to kill Day's son and a houseguest in the process, then killed himself six weeks later. In 2006, the surviving original members of Cactus reunited

with new singer Jimmy Kunes and released their fifth album, *Cactus V*. Amusingly, when McCarty left the reunited band in 2008, he was replaced for a second time by Werner Fritzschings.

Carmine Appice: drums; **Tim Bogert**: bass; **Rusty Day**: vocals (*Cactus* through *Restrictions*); **Werner Fritzsching**: guitar (*'Ot 'n' Sweaty*); **Duane Hitchings**: keyboards (*Restrictions* through *'Ot 'N' Sweaty*); **Jimmy Kunes**: vocals (*Cactus V*); **Jim McCarty**: guitar (*Cactus* through *Restrictions*; *Cactus V*)

Discography: *Cactus* (Atco, 1970); *One Way . . . Or Another* (Atco, 1971); *Restrictions* (Atco, 1971); *'Ot 'n' Sweaty* (Atco, 1972); *Cactus V* (Escapi Music, 2006)

CANDLEMASS

Years active: 1984–present

In the age of both thrash and hair metal, Candlemass had the thankless task of introducing the slovenly tempos and dark classical melodies of epic doom metal to the general public. Hailing from Sweden, Candlemass started off its mission with the 1986 release *Epicus Doomicus Metallicus*, an album that the band dedicated to the twain wonders of depression and hangovers. *Epicus* contains perhaps their best-known song, "Solitude," and the album remains a milestone in this particular genre. The three albums that followed it, however—*Nightfall*, *Ancient Dreams*, and *Tales of Creation*—ushered in what is widely considered the band's classic era, marked by the arrival of singer Messiah Marcolin, with his operatic vibrato tenor voice and Harlem Globetrotters–worthy afro. Marcolin also dressed like a Trappist monk onstage—said stage having enough candelabras on it to give the impression that the band had won an auction at the Liberace Museum.

After their *Live* album, which featured multiple entreaties by Marcolin for all attendant

Stockholmers to "go doom dancing," the band lost their frocked singer and their music shifted somewhat into a more traditional power metal style. The band lost some of their audience then, and their next album, *Chapter VI*, sold poorly. In truth, the album was every bit as good as its predecessors and deserved to be heard on its own merits, but at the time of its release, there were simply too many people who could not accept the band without Marcolin. Bassist and founding member Leif Edling disbanded the group and started a new one called Abstrakt Algebra. Their first and only album got oodles of bad press, even though its sound was remarkably similar to previous Candlemass albums, except that the vocals were more rock and less opera. Abstrakt Algebra's debut failed to sell well, and shortly after the album's release, Edling hurriedly re-formed Candlemass, mostly with Abstrakt Algebra members. Candlemass' "comeback" album was the incredibly weird *Dactylis Glomerata*, whose unclassifiable sound confounded listeners the world over and sold as badly as the last album. The band underwent another round of lineup changes and in 1999 released *From the 13th Sun*, an album so dark and gloomy it made their previous albums sound like the Archies. In 2002, the "classic" lineup, including Marcolin, reunited and made 2005's *Candlemass*. However, the album sucked and it wasn't long before the befrocked singer parted company with the group again. In 2007 he was replaced by Solitude Aeturnes singer Robert Lowe, and this lineup released *King of the Grey Islands* in 2007 and the very excellent *Death Magic Doom* in 2009.

Mike Amott: guitars (*Dactylis Glomerata*) (see also Carcass); **Mats Björkman**: guitars (*Epicus Doomicus Metallicus* through *Chapter VI*); **Leif Edling**: bass; **Matz Ekström**: drums (*Epicus Doomicus Metallicus*); **Björn Flodkvist**: vocals (*Dactylis Glomerata*, *From the 13th Sun*); **Lars Johansson**: guitars (*Nightfall* through *Chapter VI*); **Johan Längqvist**: vocals (*Epicus Doomicus Metallicus*); **Jan Lindh**: drums (*Nightfall* through *Chapter VI*); **Robert Lowe** (*King of the Grey Islands* and later); **Messiah Marcolin**: vocals (*Nightfall* through *Live*) (see also Memento Mori); **Jejo Perkovic**: drums (*Dactylis Glomerata*, *From the 13th Sun*); **Mats Stahl**: guitars (*From the 13th Sun*); **Tomas Vickström**: vocals (*Chapter VI*); **Carl Westholm**: keyboards (*Dactylis Glomerata*)

Operatic tenor Messiah Marcolin (center) prepares to give his Candlemass band mates a group hug.

Discography: *Epicus Doomicus Metallicus* (Leviathan, 1986); *Nightfall* (Restless, 1987); *Ancient Dreams* (Active, 1988); *Tales of Creation* (Capitol, 1989); *Live* (Metal Blade, 1990); *Chapter VI* (Music for Nations, 1992); *Dactylis Glomerata* (Music for Nations, 1998); *From the 13th Sun* (Music for Nations, 1999); *Doomed for Live—Reunion 2002* (Powerline, 2002); *Candlemass* (Nuclear Blast, 2005); *King of the Grey Islands* (Nuclear Blast, 2007); *Death Magic Doom* (Nuclear Blast, 2009)

YEARS ACTIVE: 1988–PRESENT

Aside from the band's appearance in the 1994 movie *Ace Ventura: Pet Detective*, New York's Cannibal Corpse is perhaps best known as a pioneer in the field of gore metal. This genre is basically death metal (insanely fast tempos, gruff vocals, and so forth) with a pathological fixation on personal injury, typified by delightful song titles such as "Entrails Ripped from a Virgin's Cunt" and "Meat Hook Sodomy," whose lyrics read like the shooting script of a snuff movie. The band's album covers display a similar degree of thematic consistency, depicting human beings in various states of disfigurement, dismemberment, and mutilation. To further cement its nefarious reputation, Cannibal Corpse has also had the distinct privilege of seeing its albums banned by record stores due to the graphic cover artwork. But it couldn't possibly matter less, as the band has enjoyed a fanatical cult following since its inception in 1988. Fans are steadfast because of Cannibal Corpse's refusal to change its sound or subject matter over the years.

Chris Barnes: vocals (*Eaten Back to Life* through *The Bleeding*); **Rob Barrett**: guitars (*The Bleeding, Vile, Kill* and later); **George Fischer**: vocals (*Vile* and later); **Paul Mazurkiewicz**: drums; **Pat O'Brien**: guitars (*Gallery of Suicide* and later); **Jack Owen**: guitars; **Bob Rusay**: guitars (*Eaten Back to Life* through *Hammer Smashed Face*); **Alex Webster**: bass

Discography: *Eaten Back to Life* (Metal Blade, 1990); *Butchered at Birth* (Metal Blade, 1991); *Tomb of the*

Posing in appropriately spooky lighting are forensic pathology enthusiasts Cannibal Corpse.

Mutilated (Metal Blade, 1992); *Hammer Smashed Face* (Metal Blade, 1993); *The Bleeding* (Metal Blade, 1994); *Vile* (Metal Blade, 1996); *Gallery of Suicide* (Metal Blade, 1998); *Bloodthirst* (Metal Blade, 1999); *Live Cannibalism* (Metal Blade, 2000); *Gore Obsessed* (Metal Blade, 2002); *The Wretched Spawn* (Metal Blade, 2004); *Kill* (Metal Blade, 2006); *Evisceration Plague* (Metal Blade, 2009); *Torture* (Metal Blade, 2012)

YEARS ACTIVE: 1985–1995; 2008–PRESENT

Formed in the United Kingdom in 1985, Carcass quickly became one of the most prominent bands in the death metal genre. With Napalm Death guitarist Bill Steer at the helm, the band's sound consisted of chaotic explosions of hyperspeed drumming and guitar riffs, although their arrangements were somewhat more complex than the average death metal band, and a high quality of musicianship could be found by anyone able to look past the blindingly fast tempos. Carcass also distinguished itself on various other fronts, including its song titles ("Crepitating Bowel Erosion," "Excreted Alive," and "Cadaveric Incubator of Endo-Parasites" are all satisfactory examples) and its use of absolutely stomach-churning album artwork. (*Symphonies of Sickness*, from 1989, was adorned by a mixture of surgical photographs and pictures of steaks, which was in retrospect a natural choice for a band made up solely of vegetarians.) Rounding out the picture was the band's lyrics, which consisted almost exclusively of surgical terminology, making it sound as though these Liverpudlians' source material was the thesis paper of a medical student who had just completed an internship in a hospital emergency room.

Unsurprisingly, over time the musicians expanded their musical repertoire. Alas, the band members have made a name for themselves creating music that was so extreme that to tone it down in any sense (for example, to employ melodies from time to time) cried sellout. This is precisely how their

Despite his penchant for singing about disfiguring illnesses, the only disease Carcass guitarist Mike Amott has is boogie fever.

Discography: *Reek of Putrefaction* (Earache, 1988); *Symphonies of Sickness* (Earache, 1989); *Peel Sessions* (Dutch East, 1989); *Necroticism: Descanting the Insalubrious* (Earache, 1991); *Tools of the Trade* (Earache, 1992); *Heartwork* (Earache, 1993); *Swansong* (Earache, 1996); *Wake Up and Smell the Carcass* (Earache, 1996)

CARNIVORE

YEARS ACTIVE: 1982–1987; 2006–2010

Seven-foot-tall Peter Steele, who became famous in the goth metal band Type O Negative, was once a New York City sanitation worker who in his spare time would sing and play bass in a little Brooklyn, New York, combo known as Carnivore. The trio started off in truly Manowar-esque fashion, as live appearances found the band clad in armor, fur, and gas masks, pelting the audience with hunks of raw meat. The soundtrack to the performances included such ditties from their self-titled debut as "Male Supremacy," "Thermonuclear Warrior," and "World Wars III and IV." The band probably would have been written off in short order as a mere novelty act, but they had a secret weapon, and that was Steele's sharp ear for songwriting and melody. To Type O Negative fans, this is old news, but given Carnivore's image and attitude at the time, it was surprising that the band's songs were as well written as they were and, in a few cases, as with "God Is Dead," possessed such a high degree of harmonic sophistication.

For their next album, the band had a new guitarist in Marc Piovanetti, a different image (i.e., they started wearing street clothes), and an expanded sound, which owed a great deal to the hardcore bands of the day, Agnostic Front in particular (in fact, Steele contributed lyrics and drummer Louie Beateaux contributed drum tracks to Agnostic Front's *Cause for Alarm* album). Steele's songwriting had developed by leaps and bounds in the year since *Carnivore*, and musically speaking, the band's 1987 album, *Retaliation* (hands-down the best record ever to start with sixty seconds of vomiting), was New York City hardcore's answer to the Beatles'

Former New York City sanitation worker Peter Steele resumes his bass and vocal duties during a 1995 Carnivore reunion show.

Abbey Road. What had not changed, however, was Steele's ability to raise listener dander with his lyrics. The album contained songs with such ready-to-please titles as "Race War," "U.S.A. for U.S.A.," and "Jesus Hitler." The songs' lyrics fueled speculation that Steele may have been hiding a vintage SS uniform in his closet, but before a thorough investigation could be conducted, Carnivore broke up. Steele resurrected the band with a completely new lineup in 2006, and they played further live appearances throughout Europe and the United States. Sadly, Steele died of heart failure in 2010, bringing the story of Carnivore to a definitive close.

Keith Alexander: guitars (*Carnivore*); **Louie Bateaux**: drums; **Marc Piovanetti**: guitars (*Retaliation*); **Peter Steele**: vocals/bass (see also Type O Negative)

Discography: *Carnivore* (Roadrunner, 1986); *Retaliation* (Roadrunner, 1987)

last two studio albums, *Heartwork* and *Swansong*, were received, and eventually founding member Steer left, effectively pronouncing the group dead, ha ha. The band reunited in 2008 for a tour of the European metal festival circuit, leading longtime fans to party like it's 1993.

Mike Amott: guitars (*Necroticism: Descanting the Insalubrious* through *Heartwork*) (see also Candlemass); **Ken Owen**: drums; **Carlo Regadas**: guitars (*Swansong, Wake Up and Smell the Carcass*); **Bill Steer**: guitars/vocals (see also Napalm Death); **Jeff Walker**: bass/vocals

BAND RIVALRY

Contrary to popular belief, most of the rivalry that crops up in the music industry does not really stem from one band's hatred for another band as much as between the new members and the old members of the same band. There are of course some notable exceptions, such as when Guns N' Roses and Metallica embarked on a tour together in 1992. Many predicted that the two camps would experience some animosity; however, during a tour stop in Montreal, Metallica front man James Hetfield had a run-in with one of the stage pyrotechnics. He was torched like a campfire marshmallow, receiving third-degree burns to half his body. This allowed him to get away from his testy tour mates for a while, and the out-and-out war that many predicted was averted.

Most of the time, these rivalries have been greatly exaggerated—if not downright fabricated—by the heavy metal press, as in the case of Deep Purple and Black Sabbath. Although a spirit of healthy competition surely existed between the two bands, it is a stretch to insinuate that there was any outright hostility. After all, Black Sabbath recorded *Born Again* with Deep Purple singer Ian Gillan, and Deep Purple's Glenn Hughes sang on the *Seventh Star* album. This set of circumstances does not exactly reek of a raging, seething hatred between the two bands. If it's raging, seething hatred you're interested in, look no further than the instances in which someone has been fired from a band and has started his own, particularly because spite was more often than not the primary motivating factor to start anew.

BELOW: Megadeth's Dave Mustaine (left) and Metallica's James Hetfield.

MEGADETH vs. METALLICA

Whether you ask them to or not, most armchair metal historians will be happy to impart to you the fascinating verity that Megadeth's Dave Mustaine was at one time the lead guitar player for Metallica. However, because of his excessive drinking, he was fired from the band right before they recorded their 1983 debut album. While Mustaine has since conceded that his behavior during that period of his life was more than loathsome enough to warrant his dismissal, the way it was handled was so callous that it almost overshadowed the behavior that got him kicked out in the first place. Rather than fire him at home in California, the band instead drove cross-country from San Francisco to New York City, where the sessions were to take place; upon their arrival in the Big Apple, they gave him the boot. They accomplished this task by waking him up, telling him he was fired, and putting him on a Greyhound bus that departed forty-five minutes later. This left Mustaine to stew in his own considerably hateful juices for the better part of what was surely a very long week. Needless to say, when he finally did get home, his old band was not currying much favor with him, and Mustaine would spend the next decade disparaging Metallica.

VAN HALEN vs. DAVID LEE ROTH

BLACK SABBATH vs. OZZY OSBOURNE

Over the course of six hit albums, David Lee Roth was the front man for the band Van Halen, but he was much more than just a lead singer. He had an undeniable stage presence, and at times it seemed that if music didn't work out for him, he could always get a job hosting *Let's Make a Deal*—the end of the video for "Hot for Teacher" certainly seemed to imply that he shared this opinion. However, by the time of *1984*, the band's most successful album to that point, a major rift had grown between the singer and the rest of the band, and he was ultimately fired and replaced by Sammy Hagar. Subsequently, Roth went about the business of building a backing band for himself, and he did so in a way that seemed to indicate a direct challenge to his former band mates. This was most apparent in his choice of guitarist Steve Vai, whose presence seemed like a preemptive strike against accusations that Roth's band could never be as good as Van Halen. In interviews, the singer went to great pains to mention that he found it amusing that Sammy Hagar would have to sing "Jump" every night while Roth himself would never have to perform "I Can't Drive 55" on his own solo tour. It turned out that he was half right. Roth never did perform any of his replacement's material, but Hagar never sang "Jump" on the 5150 tour, either. Rather, when it came time to perform the hit song, the singer would yank some lucky, starry-eyed rube from the audience and give him the microphone, no doubt making his whole year.

When Ozzy Osbourne was fired from Black Sabbath after its 1978 album, *Never Say Die,* conventional wisdom held that it was Osbourne whose career was over. After all, the band had replaced him with Ronnie James Dio, a technically superior singer, and in this configuration, Black Sabbath had crafted *Heaven and Hell*, their strongest album in years. While Black Sabbath appeared to have a new lease on life, Osbourne was considered a fat, washed-up drunk with no future. So it came as quite a surprise when his solo debut, *Blizzard of Ozz*, was released and began to outsell his old band's then-current album. Osbourne soon found himself in a place of public favor superior to that of Black Sabbath, and he used his new platform to publicly trash his old band, singling out Dio for particular abuse. Osbourne went out of his way to call out Dio's height disadvantage at every opportunity. While Osbourne later admitted that he actually admired Dio's undeniable vocal talents, the damage had already been done, and it was permanent. In 1992, a full decade after the rift, a newly reunited Dio-era Black Sabbath received an offer to open for Osbourne at the end of his "farewell" tour, which they accepted—except for Dio, who quit the band on the spot, refusing to open for the man who had done nothing but ridicule him.

CATHEDRAL

YEARS ACTIVE: 1989–PRESENT

Cathedral was formed in England in 1990 by ex–Napalm Death vocalist Lee Dorrian. Perhaps as a reaction to the ultrafast grindcore of Dorrian's previous band, the first Cathedral album, *Forest of Equilibrium*, is a deathly slow, protracted affair that almost seems to stop time. Indeed, the seven-song album is so painfully sluggish that listening to it in a moving car may possibly violate some essential law of physics and cause time to flow backward. Subsequent albums were somewhat perkier (they seemed only to impede time), but the style remained essentially the same mixture of Sabbath worship and pure sludge, with a couple of new elements added, such as heavily pronounced psychedelic influences and peculiar choices made with regard to the vocal delivery.

The band has seen multiple lineup changes throughout their career, but they have gained a loyal cult following over the years and have lasted long enough to see Black Sabbath guitarist Tony Iommi appear as a guest on one of their recordings—surely a high point in Dorrian's life, both professionally and personally. Additionally, Dorrian has achieved something of an elder statesman's status in the doom metal community, and as such he founded his own label, Rise Above, which has released records by bands like Electric Wizard, whose artistic debt to Cathedral is plain to see. Dorrian has since announced that Cathedral's next album will be the last one. It's expected to be released in 2012.

Brian Dixon: drums (*The Carnival Bizarre* and later); **Lee Dorrian**: vocals (see also Napalm Death); **Mark Griffiths**: bass (*Forest of Equilibrium*, *Soul Sacrifice*); **Garry Jennings**: guitars; **Adam Lehan**: guitars (*Forest of Equilibrium* through *Cosmic Requiem*); **Mike Smail**: drums (*Forest of Equilibrium*) (see also Penance); **Leo Smee**: bass (*The Carnival Bizarre* and later); **Mark Wharton**: drums (*Soul Sacrifice* through *Cosmic Requiem*)

Around the release of *Cosmic Requiem* in 1994, Cathedral pauses for a photo shoot. Singer Lee Dorrian is second from right.

Discography: *Forest of Equilibrium* (Combat, 1991); *The Ethereal Mirror* (Earache, 1993); *The Carnival Bizarre* (Earache, 1995); *Supernatural Birth Machine* (Earache, 1996); *Caravan Beyond Redemption* (Earache, 1998); *Endtyme* (Earache, 2001), *The VIIth Coming* (Spitfire, 2002); *The Garden of Unearthly Delights* (Nuclear Blast, 2005); *The Guessing Game* (Nuclear Blast, 2010);

CELTIC FROST

YEARS ACTIVE: 1984–1993; 2001–2008

Celtic Frost was a massively influential band from Switzerland whose impact was most strongly felt in the death metal and black metal bands of the 1990s. They formed in 1984 from the ashes of a previous band, Hellhammer, whose Venom-influenced style was more raw and brutal than anything that had come before. Hellhammer had already gained some notoriety on the strength of its heavily traded demo tape, but guitarist and vocalist Thomas Gabriel Warrior and bassist Martin Ain were at the same time composing material that was much darker and more gothic in nature. A name change was in order to complement their new direction, and Celtic Frost was birthed into existence, bloody and screaming. While the first album under their new mantle, *Morbid Tales*, was widely hailed as a thrash metal masterpiece, the band truly came into its own on its 1985 *To Mega Therion*. The album, which featured the infamous Jesus-in-a-slingshot cover by nutty Swiss artist H. R. Giger, was a mixture of brutal speed metal ("Jewel Throne"), avant-garde electronic experimentation ("Tears in a Prophet's Dream"), and epic symphonic music ("Necromantical Screams"). The band expanded upon this formula in 1987 on *Into the Pandemonium*, the album that is widely regarded as the band's crowning achievement. It features every strength the band had to offer,

Despite the band members' Swiss passports, Celtic Frost sports Americana T-shirts in 1987. Left to right: Reed St. Mark, Martin Ain, Thomas Gabriel Warrior, and tour guitarist Ron Marks.

fully realized. From mercilessly heavy thrash like on "Inner Sanctum" and the metal/hip-hop experimentation of "One in Their Pride" to the crushing doom of "Babylon Fell" and the Middle Eastern–influenced "Caress Into Oblivion," it's all here and fleshed out, and the influence it had on European death and black metal is plainly obvious—when listening to it, one can almost imagine the future members of Emperor taking notes.

Despite the success of this album, however, on the American tour to support it, Celtic Frost fell on hard times, largely due to a clash of personalities among the members and financial difficulties at their label, Noise Records. There is, in fact, one account of the road crew holding the band's equipment hostage in exchange for payment from the record company. In the face of these problems, Celtic Frost broke up, and while conventional wisdom holds that this is the worst thing that can happen to a band, they were actually ahead of the game, given what happened next. A few months after the tour, Warrior decided to re-form the band with two new members and original drummer Steven Priestly for the infamous *Cold Lake* album. Eager fans went

to record stores to pick up the new Frost platter and, to their horror, found that the latest offering was a glam album. The band members who had once worn armor and corpse paint onstage and whose every grunted "Oooh!" had set the bar for all diabolical music to follow were now sporting gargantuan hairdos, dazzling jewelry, and cosmetic products that were not tastefully applied. Perhaps most disturbing was that they were smiling. In a gesture that was possibly a good metaphor for the misguided nature of this affair, one of the new band members was pictured on the

back cover with his fly open, intentionally showing off a tuft of his auburn pubic hair for all the gals to swoon over. Needless to say, fan reaction was of the livid and enraged variety, and it would have come as little surprise to see the entire worldwide heavy metal community descend on Warrior's house, brandishing torches, pitchforks, and lengths of rope. Sensing the degree to which he had misjudged, Warrior tried to exert as much damage control as he could. He fired the new members, rehired original bassist Ain, and dressed in clothes that were not reminiscent of Prince circa *Lovesexy*—but it was already far too late. The stripped-down "comeback" album *Vanity/Nemesis* was a success only in that it stopped the band's disgruntled fans from mailing their own feces to Warrior's alpine chalet. After the failure of that album to do much of anything but clog up record-store shelves, Celtic Frost disbanded yet again, presumably for good.

Warrior went to work on an industrial project called Apollyon Sun and also wrote the book *Are You Morbid?*, which detailed the trials and tribulations of the band with far more humor and good will than one might have expected from the perpetually scowling guitarist. However, as the years passed, fans of the original band couldn't let go of the fantasy that maybe, possibly, somehow, Celtic Frost would reform, and not for that sissy music they had made last time either, but for real, armor-clad, pagan metal with grunted vocals, down-tuned guitars and maybe even a blast-beat or two. Shockingly, this came to pass, and Celtic Frost released *Monotheist* in 2006, almost two full decades after releasing their last good album. The new offering was as dark, grim and negative as anyone could have hoped for, and longtime fans who had written the band off welcomed them back with open arms, as if to say "Welcome back, Thomas Gabriel Warrior! Your room is just the way you left it! We haven't changed a thing!" The guitarist even stated in interviews that things were going well, and that work was to begin soon on a new album. Sadly, Warrior threw cold water on everyone's boners when he announced via the band's official website that the band was breaking up yet again, as a result of "irresolvable, severe erosion." Warrior has since started a new band called Triptykon.

Martin Ain: bass (*Morbid Tales, Emperor's Return; Tragic Serenades* through *Parched with Thirst I Am Dying*); **Oliver Amberg**: guitars (*Cold Lake*); **Curt Bryant**: guitars (*Cold Lake* and later); **Stephen Priestly**: drums (*Morbid Tales, Cold Lake* and later); **Franco Sesa**: drums (*Monotheist*); **Dominic Steiner**: bass (*To Mega Therion*); **Reed St. Mark**: drums

(*To Mega Therion, Into the Pandemonium*); **Thomas Gabriel Warrior**: vocals/guitars; **Erol Unala**: guitar (*Monotheist*)

Discography: *Morbid Tales* (Metal Blade, 1984); *To Mega Therion* (Noise, 1985); *Into the Pandemonium* (Noise, 1987); *Cold Lake* (Noise, 1988); *Vanity/Nemesis* (RCA, 1990); *Monotheist* (Century Media, 2005)

CHEAP TRICK

YEARS ACTIVE: 1973–PRESENT

With such songs as "Surrender" and "I Want You to Want Me" appearing on countless cheesy mixed tapes sent by sixteen-year-old suitors to the objects of their affection, Cheap Trick's aggressive power pop provided the soundtrack to countless parking-lot virginity losses in the late 1970s. In addition to their smart, Beatles-esque songwriting (the Beatles in the sense of *A Hard Day's Night* as opposed to the *White Album*), the Illinois band also had a visual flair: lead singer Robin Zander fulfilled his front man's duty by way of his matinee-idol good looks; incessantly smoking drummer Bun E. Carlos cut a very bizarre figure in his white dress shirt, tie, and ammo belt full of cigarettes; and guitarist Rick Nielsen was utterly inscrutable.

The band was initially slow to catch on in

the United States, but they were megastars right out of the box in Japan, so they wisely chose to record a live album there during a 1978 concert at the world-famous Budokan. This decision resulted in the live single version of "I Want You to Want Me," which finally won the band their first U.S. hit. The single has also provided witty stage banter for every subsequent local band that feels the need to introduce a song in a comical fashion ("This next song . . . is the first song . . . off our new album. . . ."). Cheap Trick entered its most successful era at this time, at one point even recording an album with legendary Beatles producer George Martin. Eventually, however, the band succumbed to the passage of time, and despite a hit single in 1988 with "The Flame" and another in 1994 with the unbelievably irritating "Woke Up with a Monster," they were never able to climb to the same heights they had achieved in the 1970s. But they are still together, are still going strong, and although Carlos no longer tours with the band, Rick Nielsen's son Daxx performs that service for their live appearances.

Jon Brant: bass (*One on One* through *The Doctor*; *Silver*); **Kim Bullard**: keyboards (*Rockford*); **Bun E. Carlos**: drums; **Damon Fox**: keyboards (*Rockford*); **Rick Nielsen**: guitar; **Tom Petersson**: bass (1977's *Cheap Trick* through *All Shook Up*; *Lap of Luxury* through 1997's *Cheap Trick*); **Robin Zander**: vocals

Discography: *Cheap Trick* (Epic/Legacy, 1977); *In Color* (Epic/Legacy, 1977); *Heaven Tonight* (Epic/Legacy, 1978); *Live at Budokan* (Epic, 1979); *Dream Police* (Epic, 1979); *All Shook Up* (Epic, 1980); *One on One* (Epic, 1982); *Next Position Please* (Epic, 1983); *Standing on the Edge* (Epic, 1985); *The Doctor* (Epic, 1986); *Lap of Luxury* (Epic, 1988); *Busted* (Epic, 1990); *Woke Up with a Monster* (Warner Bros., 1994); *Cheap Trick* (Red Ant, 1997); *Special One* (Cheap Trick, 2003); *Rockford* (Cheap Trick, 2006); *The Latest* (Cheap Trick, 2009)

OPPOSITE: While his contemporaries were blowing their money on drugs, Cheap Trick guitarist Rick Nielsen wisely invested in practical purchases.

BELOW: Cheap Trick clean up during their 1978 novelty oversized-sink phase. Left to right: Rick Nielsen, Bun E. Carlos, Robin Zander, and Tom Petersson.

CHILDREN OF BODOM

YEARS ACTIVE: 1993–PRESENT

The Finnish black metal band Children of Bodom formed in 1993. Named after a local lake that had been the site of a 1960 mass murder, the group was founded by guitarist and vocalist Alexi Laiho and drummer Jaska Raatikainen. Predictably, they endured the ongoing lineup instability that's standard operating procedure for bands of this ilk. Their revolving door of rock didn't make a blip on anyone's radar until they recruited keyboard player Janne Warman, who instantly provided a unique sound that made the band stand out from the rest of their Christianity-hating brethren. They soon won a contract with Spinefarm Records, which released their 1997 debut *Something Wild* and 1999's *Hatebreeder* album.

After *Follow The Reaper* in 2000 and *Hate Crew Deathroll* in 2003, the group hilariously released a cover of Britney Spears's "Oops I Did It Again," followed by 2005's *Are You Dead Yet?*, which showcased a simpler sound and was their biggest seller to date. The following year they hit the road with In Flames, Lamb of God, Mastodon, and Slayer as part of the Unholy Alliance tour of Europe and the U.S. In 2007 they were selected to replace the eternally rehab-plagued Velvet Revolver on the Monsters of Rock tour, playing the same stage as Ozzy Osbourne.

The *Blooddrunk* album was released in 2008, and to celebrate the occasion, Children of Bodom decided to do something special—an in-store appearance at a London music store, in which they autographed limited edition versions of the "Blooddrunk" single, of which 666 copies were very cleverly pressed. Speaking of clever, in 2009 they released a covers album, titled *Skeletons in the Closet*, which featured songs by such artists as Creedence Clearwater Revival and Pat Benatar, alongside selections by Sepultura and King Diamond. The group's most recent album was 2011's *Relentless Reckless Forever*.

Alexander Kuoppala: guitar (*Something Wild* through *Hate Crew Deathroll*); **Alexi Laiho**: vocals, guitar; **Roope Latvala**: guitar; **Jaska Raatikainen**: drums; **Henkka Seppälä**: bass, vocals; **Janne Wirman**: keyboards

Discography: *Something Wild* (Spinefarm Records, 1998); *Hatebreeder* (Toy's Factory Records, 1999); *Follow the Reaper* (Nuclear Blast, 2001); *Hate Crew Deathroll* (Century Media, 2003); *Are You Dead Yet?* (Spinefarm Records, 2005); *Blooddrunk* (Spinefarm Records, 2008); *Skeletons in the Closet* (Fontana, 2009); *Relentless Reckless Forever* (Fontana, 2011)

Janne Wirman and Alexi Laiho of Children of Bodom consult their respective war hammers of terror on the concert stage.

CINDERELLA

YEARS ACTIVE: 1983–PRESENT

The *All Music Guide* states that, at the time of Cinderella's debut album, 1986's *Night Songs*, the band was "packaged like a second-rate Bon Jovi imitation." Ha! Nothing could be further from the truth—Cinderella *was* a second-rate Bon Jovi imitation. The Pennsylvania group's first album produced a compelling single, "Nobody's Fool," although the accompanying video seemed to display some hostility toward identical twins, as if it's their fault that the egg split in the womb or something. In any event, the band had little going for them to set them apart from other glam metal bands of the time, their one recognizable attribute being Tom Keifer's vocals, which were reminiscent of nothing so much as AC/DC's Brian Johnson yelping incoherently through a mouthful of shattered glass. Perhaps sensing that a little originality might be in order, the band made a second album, *Long Cold Winter*, which was a much bluesier affair than their debut would have led anyone to expect.

The album sold well enough to give the impression that Cinderella's stylistic gambit had paid off. Accordingly, the band pushed the Rolling Stones and Aerosmith influences to the forefront for 1990's *Heartbreak Station*. Disappointingly, the album didn't sell as well as its predecessors, and the band decided to lie low until it seemed like the world would more readily welcome a new Cinderella offering. For reasons best known to them, they decided that 1994 was the year to do it, despite the fact that during this time playing metal in any form was still a ticketable offense. Predictably, their release that year, *Still Climbing*, was a success on the order of the Gabrielle Carteris afternoon talk show, and the band went on hiatus in 1995. They eventually re-formed, and have been touring the hair metal nostalgia circuit without so much as a new album for their still-unsigned selves to support.

Eric Brittingham: bass; **Fred Coury**: drums; **Tom Keifer**: vocals; **Jeff LaBar**: guitar; **Kevin Valentine**: drums (*Still Climbing*)

Discography: *Night Songs* (Mercury, 1986); *Long Cold Winter* (Mercury, 1988); *Heartbreak Station* (Mercury, 1990); *Still Climbing* (Mercury, 1994); *Looking Back* (Mercury, 1997); *Bad Attitude: 1986–1994* (VSOP, 1998).

Nobody knows why the members of Cinderella lined up in descending height order. Left to right: Eric Brittingham, Tom Keifer, Fred Coury, and Jeff LaBar.

CIRITH UNGOL

Years active: 1972–1992

In the 1980s, Los Angeles produced several metal bands that did not conform to the popular notion that the city churned out nothing but glam and hair metal. One of the best examples has to be Cirith Ungol, a band that, it is generally agreed, was not particularly glamorous. Additionally, little is said with regard to their hair. They played a dark, heavy form of proto-doom and featured the inimitable vocal stylings of Tim Baker, who will surely go down in history as possessing one of the most instantaneously opinion-generating voices in the annals of recorded music (i.e., people either immediately loved his raspy shriek or fled screaming from the room, feeling dirty and violated).

The band's name was taken from J.R.R. Tolkien's *Lord of the Rings* trilogy, and not surprisingly their primary lyrical preoccupations were of the Dungeons & Dragons and winged-steeds-transporting-their-charge-to-Valhalla variety. In 1986, after the release of their third album, *One Foot in Hell*, guitarist Jerry Fogle and bassist Michael Flint left the band, leading to a five-year period of inactivity. In 1991, the band reconvened with replacements for the departed members and recorded *Paradise Lost*, but then founding member Baker left the band, effectively bringing the story to a close.

Tim Baker: vocals; **Jim Barraza**: guitars (*Paradise Lost*); **Michael Flint**: bass (*Frost and Fire* through *One Foot in Hell*); **Jerry Fogle**: guitars (*Frost and Fire* through *One Foot in Hell*); **Robert Garven**: drums; **Vernon Green**: bass (*Paradise Lost*); **Greg Lindstrom**: guitars (*Frost and Fire*)

Discography: *Frost and Fire* (Enigma, 1981); *King of the Dead* (Enigma, 1984); *One Foot in Hell* (Metal Blade, 1986); *Paradise Lost* (Restless, 1991)

ALICE COOPER

Years active: 1964–present

Alice Cooper is widely acknowledged as the father of "shock rock," inspiring the antics of Marilyn Manson and W.A.S.P.'s Blackie Lawless. Cooper's elaborate stage shows featured live snakes, generous to-and-fro spewing of fake blood, and the simulated guillotine execution of the singer, among other things. At the time, there was nothing else like it, and it brought the degree of performance art in rock music to a level that rivaled perhaps only vintage Iggy Pop in its ability to simultaneously repel and fascinate audiences. Other artists, such as G. G. Allin or the Voluptuous Horror of Karen Black, eventually came along and pushed the envelope much further, but they could never have done it without Cooper paving the way.

Born Vincent Furnier, Cooper allegedly got his new appellation during a Ouija board session, when the forces of darkness revealed to him that he was the reincarnation of a seventeenth-century witch by that name. Said forces were not so forthcoming, however, in revealing that it would take him and his band a few years before hitting the big time. The band members had relocated from their native Arizona to find rock-star success in Los Angeles, but their relentlessly negative music, primitive drag outfits, and onstage capital punishment had roughly the same effect on 1968's heavily stoned Whisky A Go-Go patrons as

daylight on Count Dracula. Perhaps sensing the need to subject the entire United States to similar torment, Frank Zappa immediately signed the band to his now-defunct Straight label, for which they released two albums. The releases never caught on, and the dejected band decided to move to the decidedly less groovy climes of Detroit, then home to the MC5, Ted Nugent, and the Stooges. Needless to say, Alice Cooper was far more welcome there than in the City of Angels, and the act had already generated a great deal of buzz for their increasingly theatrical stage show when Warner Bros. finally came knocking, contract and fountain pen in hand.

Collaborating with producer Bob Ezrin, Alice Cooper's band then made the 1971 classic *Love It to Death* album, which contained "I'm Eighteen," their first song ever to get on the charts. This was followed by even more successful albums (including the classic *Billion Dollar Babies*, which is arguably the original band's finest offering) and tours whose stage shows became increasingly extravagant. By 1974, with the *Muscle of Love* album, Cooper decided that it was time for him to strike out on his own. His first album as a solo artist, *Welcome to My Nightmare*, was a Top 10 hit, as was the follow-up album, *Alice Cooper Goes to Hell*. During this time Cooper's struggles with alcohol, which had achieved the wake-up-and-vomit-blood stage during his tenure with the original band, reached George Jones proportions, and he checked himself into rehab. After his recovery, he continued to record and tour throughout the 1980s, but it wasn't until 1989, with the release of *Trash*, that he regained some of his previous fame. Thanks to the song "Poison," the album made it into the Top 20 in the United States. Cooper has since managed to hold on to the modest degree of success that he reclaimed with that album, and he still records and tours to this day. He has also become an avid golfer, and he regularly appeared in an Izod shirt and white visor on VH1's *Fairway to Heaven*, teeing off against members of Hootie and the Blowfish in what had to be the most unwatchable sixty minutes of television since Geraldo Rivera underwent liposuction surgery.

LEFT: One wonders if Alice Cooper had this in mind when he sang "Only Women Bleed."

ABOVE: Vincent Furnier is the caged beast known as Alice Cooper.

Discography: *Pretties for You* (Bizarre, 1969); *Live at the Whiskey, 1969* (Bizarre, 1969); *Easy Action* (Bizarre, 1970); *Love It to Death* (Warner Bros., 1971); *Killer* (Warner Bros., 1971); *School's Out* (Warner Bros., 1972); *Billion Dollar Babies* (Warner Bros., 1973); *Muscle of Love* (Warner Bros., 1974); *Welcome to My Nightmare* (Atlantic, 1975); *Alice Cooper Goes to Hell* (Warner Bros., 1976); *Alice Cooper Show* (Warner Bros., 1977); *From the Inside* (Warner Bros., 1978); *Flush the Fashion* (Warner Bros., 1980); *Special Forces* (Warner Bros., 1981); *Zipper Catches Skin* (Warner Bros., 1982); *DaDa* (Warner Bros., 1982); *Constrictor* (MCA, 1986); *Raise Your Fist and Yell* (MCA, 1987); *Trash* (Epic, 1989); *Prince of Darkness* (MCA, 1989); *Hey Stoopid* (Epic, 1991); *The Last Temptation* (Epic, 1994); *A Fistful of Alice* (Capitol, 1997); *The Life & Crimes of Alice Cooper* (Rhino, 1999); *Brutal Planet* (Spitfire, 2000); *Dragontown* (Spitfire, 2001); *The Eyes of Alice Cooper* (Eagle, 2003); *Dirty Diamonds* (Spitfire, 2005); *Along Came a Spider* (Steamhammer, 2008); *Welcome 2 My Nightmare* (Universal, 2011)

CORROSION OF CONFORMITY

Corrosion of Conformity began in North Carolina in the early 1980s as a metal-influenced hardcore band. Their second release, *Animosity*, is regarded as a classic of hardcore, but by 1989, with the release of *Technocracy*, the band members were at each other's throats, to the degree that their label, Death Records, apparently got sick of putting up with them and dropped C.O.C. like the proverbial bad habit. Under normal circumstances, the story would have ended there, but the band returned in 1991 as an expanded, five-piece metal ensemble, complete with dual-harmony Iron Maiden guitars, an actual singing lead singer, and midtempo songs with discernible melodies. This lineup released one album, *Blind*, before further personnel difficulties gummed up the works. Laughing in the face of career-threatening instability yet again, the band reconvened in 1994 with guitarist Pepper Keenan assuming vocal duties and original bassist Mike Dean returning to the fold. This iteration of Corrosion of Conformity released the southern rock–flavored *Deliverance* album, which sounded like the Marshall Tucker Band as performed by

Pantera. The album was an unqualified success, and it earned them an opening slot on Metallica's world tour. It's also been massively influential, as its mixture of stripped-down heavy metal with southern-rock influences as thick as a wad of chawin' terbacky has been an inspiration to such stoner rock bands as Alabama Thunderpussy and Dixie Witch.

Karl Agell: vocals (*Blind*); **Simon Bob**: vocals (*Technocracy*); **Jimmy Bower**: drums (*Live Volume*) (see also Eyehategod); **Mike Dean**: bass/vocals (*Eye for an Eye* through *Technocracy*; *Deliverance* through *In the Arms of God*); **Eric Eycke**: vocals (*Eye for an Eye*); **Pepper Keenan**: vocals/guitars (*Blind* and later); **Stanton Moore**: drums (*In the Arms of God*); **Reed Mullin**: drums (*America's Volume Dealer*, *Live Volume*); **Phil Swisher**: bass (*Blind*); **Woody Weatherman**: guitars

Discography: *Eye for an Eye* (No Core, 1983); *Animosity* (Combat, 1987); *Technocracy* (1987); *Six Songs With Mike Singing* (1989); *Blind* (Relativity, 1991); *Deliverance* (Sony, 1994); *Wiseblood* (Sony, 1996); *America's Volume Dealer* (Sanctuary, 2000); *Live Volume* (Sanctuary, 2001); *In the Arms of God* (Sanctuary, 2005)

CRADLE OF FILTH

Since 1991, Cradle of Filth has faced an uphill battle, struggling at times just to exist. Through it all, one Daniel Lloyd Davey, better known as Dani Filth, has manned the microphone and steered the ship through a minefield of trials and tribulations. This includes a perpetually unstable lineup that has seen well over twenty people come and go from the band's ranks, and the recording of an entire debut album that was never released. But Dani Filth kept at it, and as a result Cradle of Filth has remained one of the premier black metal bands of the last two decades.

Bolstered by guitarist Paul Ryan, his keyboard-playing brother Benjamin, bassist Jon Pritchard, and a drummer who went by the clearly Satanic name of Darren, Dani Filth founded the group in Suffolk, England. Their debut album, *The Principle of Evil Made Flesh*, was released in 1994,

and the Ryan brothers skedaddled immediately after. Cradle of Filth then released the EP *V Empire or Dark Fairytales in Phallustein* in 1996 to fulfill their contract with Cacophonous Records, then promptly got picked up by Music For Nations. The new label released the full-length *Dusk and Her Embrace* in 1996. The band had lost a lot of blood in a very short period of time, but their consistently strong releases had put them on the map, and when Cradle of Filth returned in 1998 with *Cruelty and the Beast*, the band sounded very much on top of its game.

After 2000's *Midian* and *Bitter Suites to Succubi* in 2001, the group signed to Sony and made 2003's *Damnation and a Day*. With the major label contract came a budget, and the group went full-retard accordingly. They hired a thirty-two-piece choir and forty-piece orchestra for the album, which was based on Milton's "Paradise Lost," an epic poem known to most

Corrosion of Conformity in its brief configuration as a quintet.

OPPOSITE: A member of Cradle of Filth enjoys some quality time in the library.
ABOVE: The two musicians pictured above comprise 10% of the people who have ever played in Cradle of Filth.

fans thanks to the 1978 movie *Animal House*. The new album, whose songs are all enumerated by Roman numerals, runs 77 minutes, has a narrator, and was deemed a sellout by the group's fans. It was also characterized as a pretentious mountain of horseshit by critics, who may have had a point.

The group moved to their next label, Roadrunner, for 2004's *Nymphetamine*. The album sold pretty well for a band whose merchandise included "Jesus Is A Cunt" T-shirts, and amazingly, the title track was nominated for a Grammy. *Thornography* followed in 2006, and 2008's *Godspeed on the Devil's Thunder* cracked the *Billboard* top 50. It was simply no longer possible to call Cradle of Filth an underground band, as their robust sales and successful tours clearly disqualified them from the category. Whatever their status, Cradle of Filth still made music that was as uncompromising as ever, including 2010's *Darkly, Darkly, Venus Aversa*. Their next album is scheduled for release in 2012.

Paul Allender: guitar (*The Principle of Evil Made Flesh* through *Dusk and Her Embrace*; *Midian* and later);

Stuart Anstis: guitar (*Dusk and Her Embrace*); **Nicholas Barker**: drums (*Dusk and Her Embrace*); **Sarah Jezebel Deva: vocals** (*Dusk and Her Embrace* through *Godspeed on the Devil's Thunder*); **Robin Eaglestone**: bass (*The Principle of Evil Made Flesh* through *Cruelty and the Beast*); **Ashley Ellyllon**: keyboards (*Darkly, Darkly, Venus Aversa*); **Adrian Erlandsson**: drums (*Damnation and a Day* through *Thornography*); **Dani Filth**: vocals; **Damien Gregori**: keyboards (*Dusk and Her Embrace*); **Charles Hedger**: guitar (*Thornography*); **James McEllroy**: guitar (*Darkly, Darkly, Venus Aversa*); **Martin Powell**: keyboards (*Damnation and a Day* through *Nymphetamine*); **Dave Pybus**: bass (*Midian* and later); **Gian Pyres**: guitar (*Dusk and Her Embrace* through *Cruelty and the Beast*); **Benjamin Ryan**: keyboards (*The Principle of Evil Made Flesh*); **Paul Ryan**: guitar (*The Principle of Evil Made Flesh*); **Martin Skaroupka**: drums (*Godspeed on the Devil's Thunder*)

Discography: *The Principle of Evil Made Flesh* (Cacophonous, 1994); *Dusk and Her Embrace* (Music for Nations, 1996); *Cruelty and the Beast* (Music for Nations, 1998); *Midian* (Music for Nations, 2000); *Bitter Suites to Succubi* (Snapper, 2001); *Damnation and a Day* (Sony, 2003); *Nymphetamine* (Roadrunner, 2004); *Thornography* (Roadrunner, 2006); *Godspeed on the Devil's Thunder* (Roadrunner, 2008); *Darkly, Darkly, Venus Aversa* (Nuclear Blast, 2010)

CREAM

YEARS ACTIVE: 1966–1968, 2005

The 1960s psychedelic supergroup Cream is about as heavy metal as Jimi Hendrix, which is to say, not very much. However, it's hard to imagine the genre even existing without both entities laying the essential groundwork. Everyone knows the details by now—the group was made up of drummer Ginger Baker, bassist Jack Bruce, and guitarist Eric Clapton, and they only managed to keep the band together for two years before the whole thing collapsed. But in that short time they helped create, among other things, a blueprint for that bastard offspring of rock known as heavy metal. Particularly the kind of metal where musicians solo endlessly and the audience makes a mass exodus for the bathroom.

The group formed in 1966 around Clapton, who was already a superstar after his stints with the Yardbirds, John Mayall's Bluesbreakers, and the appearance of graffiti around London that proclaimed him to be God. Both Baker and Bruce had already played together in numerous bands, long enough to make names for themselves, and also long enough to grow to absolutely hate one another. Hatred aside, neither musician could deny that the other was very, very good at what he did. This left the door open for them to play together once again, this time with Clapton. And we thank them for putting their sheer loathing of one another at the molecular level on hold long enough to help create one of the true godfather bands of metal. Cream's debut album, *Fresh Cream*, featured a six-minute cover of the Willie Dixon classic "Spoonful." This song would pave the way for legions of stoned, shaggy-haired jam-rockers who would populate the airwaves for decades to come. The follow-up, *Disraeli Gears*, was released just months after the debut, and it featured much stronger material, such as "Strange Brew" and "Tales of Brave Ulysses." It also featured "Sunshine of Your Love," their first hit in the U.S.

LEFT: The members of Cream, enjoying some time offstage to take hard drugs. RIGHT: The members of Cream, back at work on stage and taking hard drugs.

and a favorite of fledgling guitarists to this day. Jimi Hendrix himself was so taken with the song, in fact, that he used to cover it at his own concerts.

In 1968, Cream released *Wheels of Fire*, a half-live, half-studio offering that showcased the excellent songwriting of "White Room," and which devoted sides three and four in full to their trademark live jamming. That disc has all of four songs on it, including a sixteen-minute take on "Spoonful" and the drum solo showcase "Toad" that was almost as long. This is where people either gave up on the band as an orgy of rock virtuoso self-indulgence (which it was), or rejoiced that these virtuosi had given up on writing bullshit pop songs and were finally onto something with their nonstop soloing (which they were).

Either way, the group fell apart after just two years together and released one album after the fact, the fittingly named *Goodbye*. A single disc, it was like *Wheels of Fire* in that it was half live and half studio, but apart from "Badge," a collaboration between Clapton and George Harrison, the man whose wife he would later fuck, the studio compositions were the textbook definition of "afterthought." By 1969, all three former members of Cream had pretty much abandoned the high-decibel jamming approach that they had popularized, just as it became a genre in its own right with legions of hungry young musicians as fans and imitators. Over thirty-five years later, the impossible happened and Cream re-formed for a short run of concerts in 2005. Other than that, Clapton has had a very long and successful solo career. Although he never had the radio hits that Clapton had, Bruce went on to have a successful career in his own right. Ginger Baker, whom heroin addiction rendered an all-around hot mess for many years, went on to play with Gary Moore, Hawkwind, and, believe it or not, Public Image Ltd. Go figure.

Ginger Baker: drums; **Jack Bruce**: vocals, bass; **Eric Clapton**: guitar, vocals

Discography: *Fresh Cream* (Reaction, 1966); *Disraeli Gears* (Reaction, 1967); *Wheels of Fire* (Polydor, 1968); *Goodbye* (Polydor, 1969); *Live Cream* (Polydor, 1970); *Live Cream II* (Polydor, 1972); *BBC Sessions* (Polydor, 2003); *Royal Albert Hall London May 2-3-5-6, 2005* (Reprise, 2005)

Danzig singer Glenn Danzig asks who the hell threw that.

DANZIG

YEARS ACTIVE: 1987–PRESENT

Danzig is the project of former Misfits and Samhain front man Glenn Danzig. The band's first album, produced by Rick Rubin for his Def American label, discarded the hardcore punk approach of Danzig's previous bands, opting instead for a straightforward, albeit dark, hard rock sound. This self-titled album, which sounds like Jim Morrison singing for AC/DC, quickly found an audience upon its 1988 release. The lyrics of such songs as "Twist of Cain" and "Mother" were as sinister as anything found in the catalogs of his previous bands, and the group found themselves cast in misanthropic satanist mode—the booklet to their second CD, *Danzig II: Lucifuge*, folded out into an inverted crucifix.

A high point in Danzig's career came in 1994, when the singer contributed a song titled "Thirteen" to American Recordings, the acclaimed album by the original goth himself, Johnny Cash. The song's dark lyrics were consistent with the type of subject matter for which Cash was famous, and they were a natural fit with the atmosphere of the stark, gloomy album. Furthermore, it showed doubters that Glenn Danzig was a more talented lyricist than he was given credit for.

Later, Danzig albums began futzing around with the musical approach that had brought the band success, causing scores of fans to abandon the group for committing the unforgivable crime known as selling out. *Danzig 4*, for example, featured subtle, moody keyboard textures that were a far cry from the violent, mock-satanic material of yore, and was met with a collective shrug by the band's formerly die-hard fan base. That album was followed by *Danzig 5: Blackacidevil* in 1996, which featured a completely new lineup (including Tommy Victor of Prong) and a new sound that flirted with electronica and techno, thereby hammering one more nail into the band's coffin. The band's seventh full-length studio album, *Danzig 777: I Luciferi*, was a return to form of sorts, in that it featured a more guitar-dominated rock sound, although it wasn't the comeback that the front man no doubt hoped for. After 2004's *Circle of Snakes*, Danzig didn't release an album of new, original material until 2010's *Deth Red Sabaoth*. Between those two albums, the singer had released a solo album and a rarities compilation, and since then, the band contributed the original song "Black Hell" to the soundtrack of *The Hangover: Part II*.

Chuck Biscuits: drums (*Danzig* through *Danzig 4*); **Joseph Bishara**: keyboards/programming (*Danzig 5: Blackacidevil*); **Joey Castillo**: drums (*Danzig 5: Blackacidevil, 6:66 Satan's Child*); **Jeff Chambers**: guitars (*6:66 Satan's Child*); **John Christ**: guitars (*Danzig* through *Danzig 4*); **Glenn Danzig**: vocals/keyboards; **Bevan Davies**: drums (*Circle of Snakes*); **Johnny Kelly**: drums (*Deth Red Sabaoth*); **Josh Lazie**: bass (*Danzig 5: Blackacidevil, 6:66 Satan's Child*); **Jerry Montano**: bass (*Circle of Snakes*); **Howie Pyro**: bass (*Danzig 777: I Luciferi*); **Tommy Victor**: guitars (*Blackacidevil* and later); **Eerie Von**: bass (*Danzig* through *Danzig 4*); **Todd Youth**: guitars (*Danzig 777: I Luciferi*);

Discography: *Danzig* (Def American, 1988); *Danzig II: Lucifuge* (Def American, 1990); *Danzig III: How the Gods Kill* (Def American, 1992); *Thrall: Demonsweatlive* (Def American, 1993); *Black Aria* (E-Magine, 1993); *Danzig 4* (Def American, 1994); *Danzig 5: Blackacidevil* (E-Magine, 1996); *6:66 Satan's Child* (E-Magine, 1999); *Live on the Black Hand Side* (Restless, 2001); *Danzig 777: I Luciferi* (Spitfire, 2002); *Circle of Snakes* (Evilive Records, 2004); *Deth Red Sabaoth* (Evilive Records, 2010)

DARK ANGEL

YEARS ACTIVE: 1983–2002; 2002–2005 (NO ALBUMS RECORDED, JUST TOURED AND RECORDED ONE SONG)

Dark Angel was one of the more aggressive bands of the thrash metal heyday of the 1980s. The Los Angeles outfit started off as another Slayer knockoff (not that there's anything wrong with that), but the recruitment of Gene Hoglan, a blindingly fast drummer who possessed unbelievable technical chops, upped the ante considerably. The band followed his lead, and as a result, their second album, *Darkness Descends*, released in 1986, displayed a level of ferocity and originality at which their previous material had not even hinted. Such songs as the title track and "Merciless Death" were furious and terrifying, and they set the bar for the remainder of the band's recorded output.

As their career continued over the decade, they managed to maintain the high esteem in which the heavy metal underground held them. Sadly, by 1991, when they released their final and perhaps best album, *Time Does Not Heal*, the MTV-Mandated Office Where They Run Everything had decided that kids today would be better off in baggy pants and chain wallets and listening to Pearl Jam, and bands like Dark Angel suddenly found themselves without an audience. Consequently, the band broke up, and Hoglan moved on to the drummer's throne of the band Death. In an ironic turn of events, ten years

Dark Angel's guitarists jam out.

after Dark Angel split, they found themselves held in high regard yet again by a new heavy metal underground, based on the fact that they never broke into the mainstream. Can we please get a famous psychologist to figure out that phenomenon?

Don Doty: vocals (*We Have Arrived*, *Darkness Descends*); **Jim Durkin**: guitars (*Darkness Descends* and later); **Brett Eriksen**: guitars (*We Have Arrived*); **Mike Gonzalez**: bass; **Gene Hoglan**: drums (*Darkness Descends* and later) (see also Death, Testament); **Eric Meyer**: guitars (*Darkness Descends* and later); **Ron Rinehart**: vocals (*Leave Scars* and later); **Jack Schwartz**: drums (*We Have Arrived*)

Discography: *We Have Arrived* (Metalstorm, 1985); *Darkness Descends* (Combat, 1986); *Leave Scars* (Combat, 1989); *Live Scars* (Combat, 1990); *Time Does Not Heal* (Combat, 1991)

The Darkness in New York, partying like it's 1973.

YEARS ACTIVE: 2000–2006, 2011–PRESENT

In 1999 or 2000, depending on which side of the debate you fall, British guitarist and singer Justin Hawkins and his guitarist brother Dan recruited drummer Ed Graham and bassist Frankie Poullain to form the Darkness with the sole intention of resurrecting ham-fisted arena rock from the dead. The formula was simple—Justin Hawkins would lift the wardrobe of Steven Tyler and the operatic squeal of Freddie Mercury, and the rest of the band would bash out bombastic anthems that would get you lynched circa Y2K. They trotted out this approach in London's pubs over and over again—lather, rinse, repeat—until their sheer tenacity won over audiences. Atlantic Records could no longer ignore the packed venues even if they tried, and signed the Darkness to a recording contract.

Their first release for the label, 2003's *Permission to Land*, debuted at number two on the U.K. charts, held back from the number one spot by Beyoncé. *Permission to Land*'s popularity was fueled by the single "I Believe in a Thing Called Love," 95% of which was delivered in the castrated falsetto that recalled Tiny Tim of "Tiptoe Through The Tulips" fame. They followed up the album in 2005 with *One Way Ticket to Hell . . . and Back*, which was fittingly enough produced by Queen producer Roy Thomas Baker. Sadly, the album neither topped its predecessor nor charted as well. Justin Hawkins proceeded to do a bang-up job of imitating the frontmen who had inspired him when it came to cocaine and alcohol consumption, and he was forced to enter rehab. Once he completed the program, he left the group, who renamed themselves Stone Gods. But as a phoenix rising from a pile of blow, the Darkness announced in 2011 that they were reuniting with their original lineup and would soon begin work on their third album.

Richie Edwards: bass (*One Way Ticket to Hell . . . and Back*); **Ed Graham**: drums; **Dan Hawkins**: guitar, vocals; **Justin Hawkins**: vocals, guitar; **Frankie Poullain**: bass (*Permission to Land*)

Discography: *Permission to Land* (Atlantic, 2003); *One Way Ticket to Hell . . . And Back* (Atlantic, 2005)

DARKTHRONE

YEARS ACTIVE: 1987–PRESENT

After releasing a more death metal–sounding debut, Norway's Darkthrone adopted the extreme black metal image and sound for which the band became known with their second album, 1991's *A Blaze in the Northern Sky*. Additionally, most of the corpse-painted members adopted pseudonyms to go with their cranky image, taking the names of Viking gods of war, chaos, and so forth.

Darkthrone also gained some unintended notoriety for their not entirely tolerant worldview. Drummer Fenriz was so proud of the band's 1994 album that he wanted the following proviso printed on it: "We would like to state that *Transilvanian Hunger* stands beyond any criticism. If any man should attempt to criticize this LP, he should be thoroughly patronized for his obvious Jewish behavior." Their record label, Peaceville, didn't want to censor its artists outright, so it simply refused to publicize the album. Sensing that an unadvertised album doesn't earn much lutefisk money, the band put their deeply held convictions aside and issued a retraction, wherein they explained that the remark was simply taken out of context; in Norway, they explained, the term "Jewish" is an expression used to describe something that has gone awry. The record label actually fell for this mountain of horseshit and resumed promotion of the album, apparently having no problem with the fact that it featured the slogan "Norwegian Aryan Black Metal" screaming across the back cover in seventy-two-point typeface. After this traumatic turn of events, the deeply wounded band switched from Peaceville to the local Norwegian label Moonfog. The band released six albums for that label, leading one to the conclusion that it never "went Jewish" on them.

Ivar "Zephyrous" Enger: guitars (*Soulside Journey* through *Panzerfaust*, *Goatlord*); **Gylve "Fenriz" Nagell**: drums; **Dag Nilsen**: bass (*Soulside Journey*, *A Blaze in the Northern Sky*); **Ted "Nocturno Culto" Skjellum**: guitars/vocals

Discography: *Soulside Journey* (Peaceville, 1991); *A Blaze in the Northern Sky* (Peaceville, 1991); *Under a Funeral Moon* (Peaceville, 1993); *Transilvanian Hunger* (Peaceville, 1994); *Panzerfaust* (Moonfog, 1995); *Total Death* (Moonfog, 1996); *Goatlord* (Moonfog, 1997); *Ravishing Grimness* (Moonfog, 1999); *Preparing for War* (Peaceville, 2001); *Plaguewielder* (Moonfog, 2002); *Hate Them* (Moonfog, 2003); *Sardonic Wrath* (Moonfog, 2004); *The Cult is Alive* (Peaceville, 2006); *F.O.A.D* (Peaceville, 2007); *Dark Thrones and Black Flags* (Peaceville, 2008); *Circle the Wagons* (Peaceville, 2010)

DARK TRANQUILLITY

YEARS ACTIVE: 1989–PRESENT

Gothenburg, Sweden's Dark Tranquillity formed in 1989 and released their first album in 1993, springing *Skydancer* upon an unsuspecting public. At the time, the band consisted of grunting vocalist Anders Fridén, bassist Martin Hendriksson, drummer Anders Jivarp, and guitarists Mikael Stanne and Niklas Sundin. Don't bother writing that down, as that lineup became a thing of the past as soon as their follow-up EP, *Of Chaos and Eternal Night*, was released in 1995. Fridén left to join fellow Gothenburg band In Flames, leaving

Dark Tranquility plays their inimitable goth-tinged Swede metal.

Stanne to assume lead growling duties. Stanne was replaced on guitar by Fredrik Johansson, and it was this lineup that released the full-length offering, *The Gallery*. It was the first album to earn them the start of a fan base, which they built upon with the subsequent EP *Enter Suicidal Angels* and the full-length *The Mind's I*, both from 1997.

Dark Tranquillity signed to Century Media, which released *Projector* in 1998. The album had more than a hint of goth flavoring and melody to it, which caused some fans to grumble. Had Dark Tranquillity gone soft? Was the group becoming something girls might perhaps listen to while getting mani-pedis and having pillow fights? Well, those fans could file it under tough titty. The band had committed to their musical direction, and even hired keyboard player Martin Brändström to lend the proceedings the distinct spit-shine that they had lacked previously. This was a bridge too far for Johansson, and he left the group. Hendriksson took his place, and his old spot on bass was assumed by Michael Niklasson. This lineup turned in *Haven* in 2000.

The group backpedalled nicely for 2002's *Damage Done*, which saw them lose some of their recently acquired preciousness and return to a heavier style. It was a decision that was reinforced on 2005's similarly heavy *Character* and 2007's *Fiction*. Their most recent album was 2010's *We Are the Void*, and as of the writing of this edition, the band is about to celebrate twenty years since the release of their debut album. The musicians may have swapped instruments several times and the style may not have always been consistent, but nobody can question that Dark Tranquillity has been one of the longest-lasting and most pioneering bands in the melodic death metal field.

Martin Brändström: keyboards (*Haven* and later); **Anders Fridén**: vocals (*Skydancer*) (see also In Flames); **Martin Henriksson**: guitar, bass; **Anders Jivarp**: drums; **Fredrik Johansson**: guitar (*The Gallery* through *Projector*); **Michael Niklasson**: bass (*Haven* through *Fiction*); **Mikael Stanne**: vocals; **Niklas Sundin**: guitar

Discography: *Skydancer* (Toy's Factory Records, 2008); *The Gallery* (Osmose Productions, 1995); *The Mind's I* (Osmose Productions, 2001); *Projector* (Century Media, 1999); *Haven* (Century Media, 2000); *Damage Done* (Century Media, 2002); *Character* (Century Media, 2005); *Fiction* (Century Media, 2007); *We Are the Void* (Century Media, 2010)

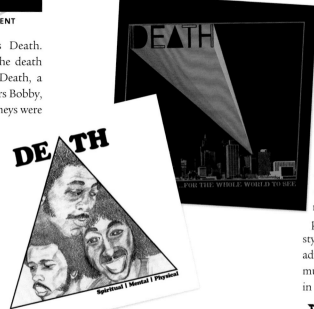

DEATH (DETROIT)

YEARS ACTIVE: 1973–1976, 2009–PRESENT

Before there was Death, there was Death. Specifically, before there was Death, the death metal band from Florida, there was Death, a Detroit band formed in 1973 by brothers Bobby, Dannis, and David Hackney. The Hackneys were black and grew up playing soul and funk, but once they were exposed to Black Sabbath and their fellow Detroit denizens Alice Cooper, they left the Isley Brothers jams behind and dubbed themselves Death, purveyors of a raw and politically charged sound that was too technical to be punk and too lo-fi to be metal.

The group came to the attention of Funkadelic producer Don Davis, who took them into a real studio for the first time and recorded their first handful of singles, including "Keep on Knocking" and "Politicians in My Eyes." The singles were miniature temper tantrums with a political conscience, and it didn't take long for the recordings to reach the desk of Columbia Records bigwig Clive Davis, fresh off of signing Aerosmith and Earth, Wind & Fire. He liked the music and considered giving the group a chance, but with one small proviso— they had to change their name to something, y'know . . . nice. Guitarist David Hackney refused, and Columbia slammed its door in the group's collective face. Bassist and vocalist Bobby and drummer Dannis, enraged at their brother's refusal to throw Columbia Records a bone, had a falling out with unwavering David, and the rift never healed. Another great band was relegated to what-could-have-been status when Death broke up in 1977.

David Hackney died of lung cancer in 2000, and Bobby and Dannis, who had settled down in Vermont, formed a reggae group called Lambsbread. Death had been almost completely forgotten when, in 2009, the independent label Drag City released all of the group's singles on a compilation disc called *For the Whole World to See*. The release finally brought the band some recognition for the recordings that they had produced so many years earlier, and the surviving members played the first Death shows in over thirty years, with Lambsbread guitarist Bobbie Duncan sitting in for the late David Hackney. In 2011, Drag City also released *Spiritual Mental Physical*, a collection of the band's demos and outtakes.

Bobby Hackney: bass, vocals; **Dannis Hackney**: drums; **David Hackney**: guitar

Discography: *For the Whole World to See* (Drag City, 2009); *Spiritual Mental Physical* (Drag City, 2011)

DEATH

YEARS ACTIVE: 1983–2001

At a time when bands like Metallica and Slayer were in the process of slowing their tempos and introducing more subtle elements into their music, Florida's fittingly named Death took brutally aggressive speed metal and morbid lyrics to new depths. In so doing, the band pioneered the death metal style to which groups like Cannibal Corpse and Entombed owe their livelihoods, and today Death is acknowledged as the genre's founder. Actually, it would be more accurate to say that vocalist/guitarist Chuck Schuldiner was death metal's true father. He was there at the band's inception in 1983, and for their first album, *Scream Bloody Gore*, he played every single instrument except for drums. He also guided the band through countless lineup changes and almost as many stylistic ones; despite the fact that death metal is viewed rather simplistically and incorrectly as a genre played by monosyllabic idiots, the band's style became exponentially more technically advanced with every release. Ever the ambitious musician, Schuldiner started a second project in 1996 called Control Denied, which featured

The sun and sand are void in this 1999 photograph of Florida's Death. Left to right: Rick Rozz, Chuck Schuldiner, Terry Butler, and Bill Andrews.

a melodic, straight-ahead metal vocalist over supercomplicated musical compositions. Sadly, in 1999, just as he was in the middle of what seemed to be his most creatively fertile period ever, Schuldiner was diagnosed with brain cancer. He was thirty-four years old when he died on December 13, 2001.

Bill Andrews: drums (*Leprosy*, *Spiritual Healing*); **Terry Butler**: bass (*Leprosy*, *Spiritual Healing*); **Richard Christy**: drums (*Sound of Perseverance*, *Live in L.A.: Death & Raw*) (see also Iced Earth); **Scott Clendenin**: bass (*Sound of Perseverance*, *Live in L.A.: Death & Raw*); **Kelly Conlon**: bass (*Symbolic*); **Steve DiGiorgio**: bass (*Human*, *Individual Thought Patterns*) (see also Iced Earth, Testament); **Shannon Hamm**: guitars (*Sound of Perseverance*, *Live in L.A.: Death & Raw*); **John Hand**: guitars (*Scream Bloody Gore*); **Gene Hoglan**: drums (*Individual Thought Patterns*, *Symbolic*) (see also Dark Angel, Testament); **Bobby Koelble**: guitars (*Symbolic*); **Andy LaRocque**: guitars (*Individual Thought Patterns*) (see also King Diamond); **Paul Masvidal**: guitars (*Human*); **James Murphy**: guitars (*Spiritual Healing*) (see also Obituary, Testament); **Chris Reifert**: drums (*Scream Bloody Gore*); **Sean Reinert**: drums (*Human*); **Rick Rozz**: guitars (*Leprosy*); **Chuck Schuldiner**: guitars/vocals

Discography: *Scream Bloody Gore* (Combat, 1987); *Leprosy* (Combat, 1988); *Spiritual Healing* (Combat, 1990); *Human* (Combat, 1991); *Individual Thought Patterns* (Combat, 1993); *Symbolic* (Roadrunner, 1995); *Sound of Perseverance* (Nuclear Blast, 1998); *Live in L.A.: Death & Raw* (Nuclear Blast, 2001)

DEEP PURPLE

YEARS ACTIVE: 1968–1978; 1984–PRESENT

Deep Purple is one of the most popular bands in the world, and has had one of the greatest influences on the heavy metal genre. While they have the dubious distinction of launching the career of David Coverdale, thereby making Whitesnake, circa 1987, a reality from which humankind is still collectively recovering, they are also noteworthy for appearing in *Guinness World Records* as 1972's loudest band on earth.

Before all that happened, however, Deep Purple was a glorified cover band from England with silly bouffant haircuts whose sole hit, an organ-driven rendering of Joe South's "Hush," was followed by three albums' worth of unfocused quasi-psychedelic yoo-hoo-hooing that made the Strawberry Alarm Clock sound downright crushing by comparison. When their original label, Parlophone, went belly-up in 1970, they followed the lead of virtuoso guitarist Ritchie Blackmore, who wanted to pursue the more aggressive approach of bands like Led Zeppelin and the Jimi Hendrix Experience. Having nothing to lose but their Nehru jackets, they fired their bassist and singer, replaced them with Roger Glover and triple-octave shrieker Ian Gillan, and a rock institution was born. Their first studio album with this lineup, *Deep Purple in Rock*, was a rowdy, borderline-anarchic affair, with recording levels so hot that many listeners must have thought they had blown a speaker. Next came *Fireball*, a worthy enough follow-up, but it was nothing compared to what was around the corner.

In 1972 the band released the legendary *Machine Head*, and life was never the same again. The album contained such classics as "Highway Star," "Space Truckin'," and, of course, "Smoke on the Water," the only song ever to seriously compete with "Stairway to Heaven" in the pantheon of tunes that have been overplayed to gruesome and horrific extremes.

This lineup, known among fans as the "classic" or "Mark II" lineup, also produced *Made in Japan*, which is widely acknowledged as one of the greatest live albums of all time, and that's not an exaggeration; the band members were all well known for their high level of instrumental and improvisational prowess, and this album showcased them at what was,

One year after forming Deep Purple, the members pose for this 1969 photograph in Scotland. Clockwise from top left: Roger Glover, Ian Paice, Jon Lord, Ritchie Blackmore, and Ian Gillan.

at the time, the top of their game. It was also a valuable lesson to anyone who saw the band as primarily Blackmore's. While he certainly deserves the guitar-god accolades that are regularly bestowed upon him, his bandmates were hardly slouches, and the album gave each member the opportunity to showboat for half an album side. Unfortunately, this lineup had only one studio album left in them, the somewhat uneven and disappointing *Who Do We Think We Are?* While the album contained the classic "Woman from Tokyo," it was nowhere near as good as what had come before, and it seemed to crystallize the personal tensions that had been festering between Blackmore and Gillan. Allegedly, the conflict finally came to a head, and the singer ultimately gave his notice. But there was more blood lost as well. The band had been touring for a punishing forty-four weeks of every year, and the schedule had finally taken its toll on Glover. The bassist followed his former Episode Six band mate's example and left as well, hoping to get some much-needed rest and to eventually focus on production work. It appeared likely that the band had reached the end of the road, but management pressure and, very likely, a desire to remain one of the highest-grossing touring acts in the world convinced them to find replacements and go on.

The departed singer and bassist were replaced by the then-unknown Coverdale and Trapeze's singing bass player, Glenn Hughes. While the first album that this version of Deep Purple recorded, *Burn*, was something of a return to form for the band, the honeymoon didn't last long. In short order, Hughes and Coverdale discovered that they loathed each other with the intensity of a thousand suns, making Blackmore's deal-breaking tensions with Gillan seem downright petty. Furthermore, Hughes was beginning to assert more creative control. He had unabashed funk tendencies, which all the other band members enthusiastically latched on to and began exploring—all the other band members, that is, except for Blackmore, who had no love for funk and said so in no uncertain terms. However, for the first time, nobody in Deep Purple cared how he felt, and the guitarist suddenly found himself the odd man out in the band he had helped to form. After the *Stormbringer* album, which he thoughtfully described as both "crap" and "shoeshine music," he left the band, going on to form the swords-and-sandal metal ensemble Rainbow with Ronnie James Dio. This represented a true crisis for the Purple camp, as Blackmore's guitar playing was an

OPPOSITE: Deep Purple rocks this London audience in 1975. Left to right: Jon Lord, Glenn Hughes, David Coverdale, and Tommy Bolin. ABOVE: Deep Purple's Ritchie Blackmore strikes a sleek and feline stage pose.

integral part of the band's sound, and unlike Gillan and Glover, Blackmore was not considered replaceable. He had been with the band from the beginning, and he had been a vital creative force—he wrote the damn "Smoke on the Water" riff, after all.

Despite the reservations of keyboard player Jon Lord and drummer Ian Paice, neither Coverdale nor Hughes wanted to break up the band. They had never been in a band as popular as Deep Purple, and they weren't about to pack it in without a fight. Besides, now that Blackmore was gone, maybe being in the band would be—gasp—an enjoyable experience for those involved. Coverdale recommended James

Gang guitarist Tommy Bolin to his bandmates after hearing him play with fusion drummer Billy Cobham. Bolin had just the right mixture of chops and funk that Deep Purple was looking for, and to the profound shock of many, the band announced that they intended to continue without Blackmore. To the even more profound shock of many, their release with Bolin, *Come Taste the Band*, was the strongest album they had made in a long time, due in no small part to the fact that, for once, the band wasn't going

in several different creative directions. It must have seemed that Deep Purple had achieved the impossible and cheated certain death. However, serious problems began to set in as soon as the band went on tour. Bolin and Hughes had been secretly nursing drug and alcohol problems, which became more severe, as well as more apparent, when the band went on the road. There are stories of bad heroin fixes, onstage nervous breakdowns, and so forth. Although the accounts possess varying degrees

of reliability, no one disputes that in 1976 these problems finally overwhelmed the band. The 1978 release of *When We Rock, We Rock, and When We Roll, We Roll*, an utterly subpar compilation album, represented a once-great band's pathetic last gasp. At least, it seemed that way.

For reasons having absolutely nothing to do with money—honest Abe—the classic Deep Purple lineup re-formed in 1984 for the *Perfect Strangers* album. Although the album was a commercial success, singer Gillan and guitarist Blackmore had not managed to overcome their long-standing, unbridled hatred for each other, and the band was back to where it had found itself a decade earlier. The next few years found Gillan leaving, then returning, thereby causing Blackmore to leave, then return, thereby causing Gillan to leave, etc., etc., ad nauseum. Finally, in 1994, Blackmore was replaced by former Dixie Dregs guitarist Steve Morse, and Deep Purple's situation finally stabilized, surely to the overwhelming relief of everyone involved. This grouping (minus Lord, who packed it in after almost thirty-five years with the band) continues to tour and record today. Lord was replaced by keyboard player Don Airey, who has graced albums by such artists as Ozzy Osbourne, UFO, and Rainbow. Speaking of Rainbow, Blackmore has apparently found happiness in the medieval Gandalf-rock stylings of the modestly named Blackmore's Night, which is surely the favorite band of Renaissance Fair attendees the world over.

Don Airey: keyboards (*Bananas* and later); **Ritchie Blackmore:** guitars (*Shades of Deep Purple* through *Stormbringer*; *Perfect Strangers* through *The Battle Rages On...*) (see also Rainbow); **Tommy Bolin:** guitars (*Come Taste the Band*); **David Coverdale:** vocals (*Burn* through *Come Taste the Band*) (see also Whitesnake);

Rod Evans: vocals (*Shades of Deep Purple* through *Deep Purple*); **Ian Gillan:** vocals (*Deep Purple in Rock* through *Who Do We Think We Are?*; *Perfect Strangers*, *The House of Blue Light*, *The Battle Rages On* and later) (see also Black Sabbath); **Roger Glover:** bass (*Deep Purple in Rock* through *Who Do We Think We Are?*; *Perfect Strangers* and later) (see also Rainbow); **Glenn Hughes:** bass (*Burn* through *Come Taste the Band*) (see also Black Sabbath); **Jon Lord:** keyboards (*Shades of Deep Purple* through *Abandon*) (see also Whitesnake); **Steve Morse:** guitars (*Purpendicular* and later); **Ian Paice:** drums (see also Whitesnake); **Nick Simper:** bass (*Shades of Deep Purple* through *Deep Purple*); **Joe Lynn Turner:** vocals (*Slaves and Masters*) (see also Rainbow, Yngwie Malmsteen)

Discography: *Shades of Deep Purple* (Parlophone, 1968); *The Book of Taliesyn* (Parlophone, 1968*); Deep Purple* (Parlophone, 1969); *Concerto for Group and Orchestra* (Warner Bros., 1969); *Deep Purple in Rock* (Warner Bros., 1970); *Fireball* (Warner Bros., 1971); *Machine Head* (Warner Bros., 1972); *Made in Japan* (Warner Bros., 1972); *Who Do We Think We Are?* (Warner Bros, 1973); *Burn* (Warner Bros., 1974); *Stormbringer* (Warner Bros., 1974); *Come Taste the Band* (Warner Bros., 1975); *Made in Europe* (Warner Bros., 1976); *Deep Purple in Concert* (Harvest, 1980); *Live in London* (Harvest, 1982); *Perfect Strangers* (Mercury, 1984); *The House of Blue Light* (Mercury, 1987); *Nobody's Perfect* (Mercury, 1988); *Scandinavian Nights* (Connoisseur, 1988); *Slaves and Masters* (RCA, 1990); *In the Absence of Pink: Knebworth 85* (Connoisseur, 1991); *The Battle Rages On . . .* (Giant, 1993); *The Gemini Suite* (RPM, 1993); *Come Hell or High Water* (BMG, 1994); *On the Wings of a Russian Foxbat* (Connoisseur, 1995); *Mk III: The Final Concerts* (Connoisseur, 1996); *Purpendicular* (CMC, 1996); *Live at the Olympia, '96* (EMI, 1997); *Abandon* (CMC, 1998); *Total Abandon: Australia '99* (Warner Bros., 1999); *Live at the Royal Albert Hall* (Spitfire, 2000); *Live at the Rotterdam Ahoy* (Thames Thompson, 2001); *The Soundboard Series* (Thames Thompson, 2001); *Bananas* (Sanctuary, 2003); *Rapture of the Deep* (Edeltone, 2005); *Live at Montreux 2006: They All Came Down to Montreux* (Eagle, 2006); *Live at Montreux 2011* (Eagle Rock Ent., 2011)

YEARS ACTIVE: 1977–PRESENT

Def Leppard was the most commercially successful band of the New Wave of British Heavy Metal movement of the early 1980s. The band rose in the heavy metal underground

through relentless touring, but they broke wide open because of their keen ability to recognize the potential marketing power of what was then a new medium, the music video. With MTV still a brand-spanking-new network—and music videos therefore in short supply—the band's video for "Bringin' on the Heartbreak" fell into high rotation simply by virtue of the fact that it existed, and as a result the album on which the song appeared, *High 'n' Dry*, immediately began shifting units. It wasn't until 1983, however, that things went absolutely stratospheric, with the release of *Pyromania*. On the strength of its singles and videos ("Photograph" and "Rock of Ages" are the most noteworthy examples), the album became an absolute monster hit, second in sales that year only to Michael Jackson's *Thriller*. *Pyromania* went on to sell 10 million copies, and the band's tours were hugely successful; they were on their way to rock stardom. But, sadly, disaster was right around the corner.

In 1984, a few weeks into the recording of their next album, drummer Rick Allen was in a car accident that cost him his left arm. While it was tragic enough that Allen could never again successfully navigate a rowboat, this development cast his career as a drummer under the darkest cloud imaginable. However, the Simmons drum company designed a new electronic kit for him, and amazingly, he was soon back in the studio, recording *Hysteria* with his mates. Although Allen's return to drumming is remarkable, the fact that the 1987 reverb-soaked pop-metal mediocrity was actually a bigger hit than its predecessors—thanks to such singles as "Pour Some Sugar on Me" and "Armageddon It"—is even more unbelievable.

A worse tragedy than handstand-threatening dismemberment befell the band in the

87-88 SET LIST
HYSTERIA WORLD TOUR

STAGEFRIGHT
ROCK TILL YOU DROP
WOMEN
TOO LATE
HYSTERIA
STONES SO
GODS OF W
DIE HARD
ROCK DON'T DREAD
ANIMAL
SUGAR
PHOS SOLO
ARMAGEDDON IT
ROCK OF AGES
PHOTOGRAPH
LOVE BITES
TRAVELIN BAND

I THINK THATS RIGHT

new decade, when guitarist Steve Clark died from a fatal mixture of drugs and alcohol. Undaunted as ever, the band replaced him and put out a new album, *Adrenalize*, although by the time of its 1992 release, the public's musical tastes had shifted considerably, and as a result the album's sales were a disappointment. Subsequent releases didn't sell very well, either, and it seemed as though the band's salad days were behind them. They stayed together anyway, and their tenacity paid off when 2008's

Songs From the Sparkle Lounge had a top ten debut on the *Billboard* chart, their first album to do so in years.

Rick Allen: drums; **Vivian Campbell**: guitars (*Adrenalize* and later) (see also Dio); **Steve Clark**: guitars (*On Through the Night* through *Hysteria*); **Phil Collen**: guitars (*Pyromania* and later); **Joe Elliott**: vocals; **Rick Savage**: bass; **Pete Willis**: guitars (*On Through the Night*, *High 'n' Dry*)

Discography: *On Through the Night* (Mercury, 1980); *High 'n' Dry* (Mercury, 1981); *Pyromania* (Mercury,

1983); *Hysteria* (Mercury, 1987); *Adrenalize* (Mercury, 1992); *Retro Active* (Mercury, 1993); *Slang* (Mercury, 1996); *Euphoria* (Mercury, 1999); *X* (Universal, 2002); *Yeah!* (Mercury, 2006); *Songs from The Sparkle Lounge* (Mercury, 2008); *Hysteria/Adrenalize* (Mercury, 2009); *Mirrorball: Live and More* (Mailboat, 2011)

The guitarists of Def Leppard thrust their axes heavenward. Left to right: Rick Savage, Steve Clark, Phil Collen, and Joe Elliott. Thanks to the ingenuity of the people who make Simmons drums, Def Leppard's amazing one-armed drummer Rick Allen has a musical livelihood.

THE DEFTONES

Years active: 1988–present

It's common knowledge that driving under the influence of drugs or alcohol is an inexcusably heinous act that needlessly endangers the lives of many. Drunk drivers are a menace to society, sometimes plowing into gas stations, causing entire banks of fuel pumps to explode, sending flaming shrapnel into the eyes of Flying J customers buying Eddie Rabbitt tapes. Yet the stories of people who have been struck by drunk drivers continue to abound. A case in point is that of guitarist Stephen Carpenter, who luckily survived a run-in with an inebriated motorist. Carpenter won a substantial out-of-court settlement, enough to outfit his entire nu-metal band, the Sacramento-based Deftones, with mountainous quantities of shiny new equipment. The band is often described as a Korn rip-off due to the sound of their debut album, but they have been playing that kind of music for as long as their compatriots. Initially a plain ol' metal band, they were influenced in the early 1990s by groups such as Tool and Rage Against the Machine, and the inspiration the Deftones found was evident on the demo tape that won them a deal on Madonna's Maverick label. The first two albums built the band's fan base slowly and steadily, and by the time of their fourth release, *White Pony*, they had built up enough momentum to see it debut at number three on the *Billboard* charts. They had also built up a considerable amount of artistic credibility, gaining accolades from fans and critics alike for their willingness to incorporate experimental elements into their music, leading some to predict that the Deftones would eventually reach an artistic growth index of Radiohead-esque proportions. Their 2003 self-titled release debuted at number two on the *Billboard* chart and would be the band's commercial high water mark.

In 2008, the band was dealt a crippling blow when bassist Chi Cheng suffered serious injuries in a car accident. When it became clear that Cheng might not recover for a very long time, the band recruited former Quicksand bassist Sergio Vega to sit in, though not as a full member. Although the band had been in the middle of recording a follow-up album at the time of the accident, they eventually chose to shelve those tapes and start over. The new album, *Diamond Eyes*, was released in 2010. Their most recent release was 2011's *Covers,* a vinyl-only release featuring, you guessed it, covers. The material chosen for the album is of a distinctly head-scratching variety, such as "Drive" by the Cars and "No Ordinary Love" by Sade.

Stephen Carpenter: guitars; **Chi Cheng**: bass; **Abe Cunningham**: drums; **Frank Delgado**: keyboards; **Chino Moreno**: vocals; **Sergio Vega**: bass (*Diamond Eyes*)

Discography: *Adrenaline* (Maverick, 1995); *Around the Fur* (Maverick, 1997); *Live Tracks* (Maverick, 1999); *White Pony* (Maverick, 2000); *Deftones* (Maverick, 2003); *Saturday Night Wrist* (Maverick, 2006); *Diamond Eyes* (Reprise, 2010); *Covers* (Warner Brothers, 2011)

DEICIDE

Years active: 1987–present

Deicide is one of the major bands from the Florida death metal scene of the 1990s, which included Death, Morbid Angel, and Obituary, among others. Deicide's particular shtick is that they take their satanist views to a completely over-the-top extreme, such that it would make *700 Club* pledge drive telephones ring off the hook. In interview after interview, the band has gleefully recounted the joys of sacrificing animals, murdering Christians, and other sacrilegious malfeasance. Bassist and vocalist Glen Benton has even taken the liberty of disqualifying himself from burial in a Jewish cemetery by branding an inverted cross into his forehead—how's that for sincerity?

Benton has been quoted as saying that the reason the band still has a substantial fan base behind them after all these years is because of

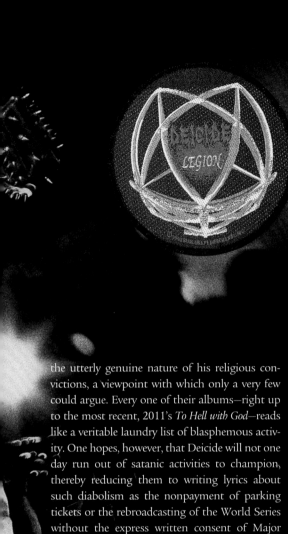

DESTRUCTION

YEARS ACTIVE: 1982–PRESENT

SENTENCE OF DEATH

all hell breaks loose

the utterly genuine nature of his religious convictions, a viewpoint with which only a very few could argue. Every one of their albums—right up to the most recent, 2011's *To Hell with God*—reads like a veritable laundry list of blasphemous activity. One hopes, however, that Deicide will not one day run out of satanic activities to champion, thereby reducing them to writing lyrics about such diabolism as the nonpayment of parking tickets or the rebroadcasting of the World Series without the express written consent of Major League Baseball.

Steve Asheim: drums; **Glen Benton**: bass/vocals; **Brian Hoffman**: guitars; **Eric Hoffman**: guitars; **Jack Owen**: guitar (*To Hell with God*); **Ralph Santolla**: guitar (*Till Death Do Us Part* and later)

Discography: *Deicide* (Roadrunner, 1990); *Legion* (Roadrunner, 1992); *Amon: Feasting the Beast* (Roadrunner, 1993); *Once Upon the Cross* (Roadrunner, 1995); *Serpents of the Light* (Roadrunner, 1997); *When Satan Lives* (Roadrunner, 1998); *Insineratehymn* (Roadrunner, 2000); *In Torment, in Hell* (Roadrunner, 2001); *Scars of the Crucifix* (Earache, 2004); *The Stench of Redemption* (Earache, 2006); *Till Death Do Us Part* (Earache, 2008); *To Hell with God* (Century Media, 2011)

For Deicide's Glen Benton, the term *heavy* metal does not just apply to music.

Destruction was formed in 1983 by drummer Tommy Sandmann, bassist and vocalist Marcel Schirmer, and guitarist Mike Sifringer. Destruction is regularly mentioned in the same breath as Kreator and Sodom when people discuss German thrash metal of the 1980s, and these bands have regularly been credited (or blamed) for helping pioneer what would later become death metal.

Based on their widely-traded demo tape, the German Steamhammer label signed the group and released their debut EP, *Sentence of Death*, in 1984, and 1985's full-length *Infernal Overkill*. Neither release was going to win a Grammy for sound quality, but the band's enthusiasm and aggression came through loud and clear, and they gained enough notice to earn a spot on the WWIII Festival in Montreal, which provided a showcase for other up-and-coming thrash titans like Voivod and Celtic Frost.

The group returned home triumphant and recorded 1986's *Eternal Devastation*, but before they hit the road to support the album, Sandmann left the group. He was replaced by Oliver Kaiser, and the band decided to embrace a little more change by beefing up their sound by adding second guitarist Harry Wilkens to the fold. This lineup produced 1987's *Mad Butcher* EP and the 1988 full-length *Release from Agony*, considered by half of their fans to be the best thing the band ever did. The other half didn't care for the new sophisticated chopsmanship on display and just wanted Destruction to go back to the primitive bludgeoning they used to do.

The band fired Schirmer in 1989, and he was replaced by singer Andre Grieder and bassist Christian Engler. Longtime, loyal fans were pissed, and the 1990 debut of the new lineup, *Cracked Brain*, didn't sell as a result. In fact, neither did anything else they released for the rest of the 1990s. Schirmer, who had responded to getting kicked out of the band by opening a pizzeria, could never quite put the band behind him despite the firing, and he reunited with Sifringer and drummer Sven Vormann.

In 2000, perhaps as a symptom of Y2K fever, this new-old incarnation of Destruction returned with *All Hell Breaks Loose* on the Nuclear Blast label. The label released the band's next two albums, *The Antichrist* and *Metal Discharge*, before Destruction signed to AFM Records. AFM released *Inventor of Evil* in 2005 and *Thrash Anthems* in 2007. *Day of Reckoning* was released in 2011, and the band remains active today. Schirmer sold his pizzeria in 2006.

Wawrzyniec "Vaaver" Dramowicz: drums (*Day of Reckoning*); **Christian Engler**: bass; **Andre Grieder**: vocals (*Cracked Brain*); **Oliver "Olly" Kaiser**: drums (*Release from Agony* through *The Least Successful Human Cannonball*); **Michael "Ano" Piranio**: guitar (*The Least Successful Human Cannonball*); **Marc Reign**: drums (*The Antichrist* through *D.E.V.O.L.U.T.I.O.N.*); **Thomas Rosenmerkel**: vocals (*The Least Successful Human Cannonball*); **Tommy Sandmann**: drums (*Infernal Overkill* through *Eternal Devastation*); **Marcel Schirmer**: bass; **Mike Sifringer**: guitar; **Harry Wilkens**: guitar (*Release from Agony* through *Cracked Brain*)

Discography: *Infernal Overkill* (Steamhammer, 1985); *Eternal Devastation* (Steamhammer, 1986); *Release from Agony* (Steamhammer, 1988); *Live without Sense* (Steamhammer, 1989); *Cracked Brain* (Steamhammer, 1990); *All Hell Breaks Loose* (Nuclear Blast, 2000); *The Antichrist* (Nuclear Blast, 2001); *Metal Discharge* (Nuclear Blast, 2003); *Inventor of Evil* (Candlelight Records, 2005); *Thrash Anthems* (Candlelight, 2007); *D.E.V.O.L.U.T.I.O.N.* (AFM, 2008); *Day of Reckoning* (Nuclear Blast, 2011)

DIAMOND HEAD

YEARS ACTIVE: 1976–1983; 1987–1994; 2000–PRESENT

Formed in 1976, Diamond Head is one of the more famous bands of the New Wave of British Heavy Metal. Diamond Head is also influential as one of the first metal groups to take the do-it-yourself ethos of the punk rock scene and make it their own. Their first singles and first album were completely self-financed affairs, and the band's rise to local-hero status was achieved entirely through grassroots methods. It seemed that the band was going to break out of their cult standing and make it into the major leagues, but it didn't happen. A combination of factors—including managerial incompetence (courtesy of singer Sean Harris's mother), disappointing follow-up albums, and a pressing error that rendered twenty thousand copies of their third album defective—more or less put the kibosh on whatever shot at superstardom the band might once have had. By 1983, Diamond Head was in complete ruin and summarily received the Dr. Kevorkian treatment.

A few years later, a li'l ol' Bay Area combo by the name of Metallica, who had started their illustrious career by covering Diamond Head material, recorded a version of "Helpless" for their 1987 *Garage Days Re-Revisited* EP, igniting new interest in Diamond Head. Metallica drummer Lars Ulrich in particular was a fan of Jehovah's Witness proportions, and he made it his personal mission to champion the splintered group. He and Harris had already collaborated on a greatest-hits compilation, *Behold the Beginning*, in 1986, and it seemed that the time was at hand to attempt a comeback. Mysteriously (or perhaps not so mysteriously, considering all the silliness he had put up with), guitarist Brian Tatler held off on blazing down the comeback trail for another few years, and it wasn't until 1994 that a reunited Diamond Head released a new album, *Death and Progress*. Unfortunately, the band had waited so long to make the album that the interest Metallica had

generated had dwindled considerably, and after a few reunion gigs, Diamond Head broke up again. They reunited in 2000 and five years later released *All Will Be Revealed*. Their most recent album was 2007's *What's in Your Head?*

Andy "Abbz" Abberley: guitar (*What's In Your Head?*); **Mervyn Goldsworthy**: bass (*Canterbury*) (see also Samson); **Sean Harris**: vocals; **Colin Kimberley**: bass (*Lightning to the Nations* through *Borrowed Time*); **Eddie Moohan** (*All Will Be Revealed* and later); **Josh Phillips-Gorse**: keyboards (*Canterbury*); **Duncan Scott**: drums (*Lightning to the Nations* through *Canterbury*); **Brian Tatler**: guitars; **Pete Vuckovic**: drums (*Death and Progress*); **Karl Wilcox**: bass (*Death and Progress*)

Discography: *Lightning to the Nations* (Fan Club, 1979); *Diamond Lights* (Fan Club, 1979); *Four Cuts* (MCA, 1982); *Borrowed Time* (MCA, 1982); *Canterbury* (MCA, 1983); *Behold the Beginning* (Metal Blade, 1986); *Death and Progress* (Blackheart, 1994); *Evil Live* (Castle, 1994); *To Heaven from Hell* (Metal Blade, 1997); *Diamond Nights* (Metal Blade, 2000); *All Will Be Revealed* (Livewire, 2005); *What's In Your Head?* (Livewire/Cargo 2007)

DIO

YEARS ACTIVE: 1982–2010

If Ronnie James Dio was not the best vocalist in all of heavy metal, he was certainly in the top three. That being the case, it would still be difficult to say who the other two singers are. Even Ozzy Osbourne—whom Dio replaced in Black Sabbath and who has had many unkind words for the man—has acknowledged that no Sabbath vocalist who came after Dio could compare. According to many of those who have worked with Dio over the years, he could be a tad on the difficult side—a control freak, just a smidge demanding, an egomaniac. The sheer number of musicians with whom he associated during his long career seems to bear this out. Ultimately, however, it all comes down to his voice and his music, and it is doubtful that anyone without a conflict of interest would seek to impugn either. The music he made with Rainbow, Black

Sabbath, and his own band, Dio, is some of the best, most genre-defining music in all of heavy metal, and he exerted an influence on other bands in the field that is so profound that it defies overstatement. The heavy metal hallmarks that we all take for granted these days, such as Dungeons & Dragons imagery and operatic vocal stylings, were all pioneered by Dio, and his influence is still felt strongly by power metal bands such as Iced Earth, Jag Panzer, and HammerFall. In 2002, the singer, who was at that time 60 years old, toured with Deep Purple and the Scorpions, and by all accounts he regularly blew both bands off the stage. In other words, say what you want about the guy, but note that he was genuinely gifted, and the ends justified the means many times over.

The band Dio was formed in 1982, after the singer quit Black Sabbath in a famously acrimonious split. He took drummer Vinny Appice with him, recruited his old Rainbow bandmate, bassist Jimmy Bain, and hired then-unknown guitarist Vivian Campbell from Sweet Savage. They hit the big time with their very first album, *Holy Diver*, which contained such classic material as the title song and "Rainbow in the Dark." They followed it up with *The Last in Line*, which is considered by many fans to be their best album. "We Rock," "Egypt (The Chains Are On)," and the title track help make a persuasive case for the 1984 offering as the band's crowning achievement. They spent the rest of the decade going from strength to strength, with each new album

selling better than the last, even when, as in the case of *Sacred Heart*, it was possibly not up to snuff. Still, whether or not the albums were any good, the band had achieved such a high level of popularity that it temporarily precluded them from having to release stellar material. If, say, a prop comic, such as Carrot Top, is popular enough, people will laugh at him even if he's not funny. The metaphor certainly applies in the case of this particular album, as well as its follow-up, the live *Intermission* EP, whose justification for release is a mystery that modern detective work has yet to solve. But their final album of the 1980s, *Dream Evil*, was as strong a return to form as anyone could ask for, even if it saw the first of the band's many lineup changes, with Craig Goldy replacing a recently departed Vivian Campbell on guitar. The album is one of the more highly regarded releases in the Dio canon, containing such solid and melodramatic material as "Night People," "Sunset Superman," and "All the Fools Sailed Away."

LEFT: Ronnie James Dio gives the quintessential heavy metal salute.
BELOW: Ronnie James Dio (right) plays tug-of-war with eighteen-year-old wunderkind guitarist Rowan Robertson.

ABOVE: Catching Dio in concert during his 1980s commercial heyday was a treat beyond words.

Augmenting the band's popularity in this era was their stage show, which was more elaborate and extreme than anything else out there at the time. It featured, among other things, laser beams, huge pyrotechnic explosions, and, on the Sacred Heart tour, a smackdown between the sword-wielding singer and a colossal, fire-breathing dragon. Unfortunately, the show had to be downsized when the group's fortunes diminished during the 1990s. It was a difficult decade for most metal bands, who had to take a gigantic step backward from arena-headlining status to playing the small clubs that they surely must have thought they had left behind. During this decade, the band's lineup changed several times (*Lock Up the Wolves* saw Dio as the only remaining original member of the band), and over the course of a few albums with guitarist Tracy G., including *Strange Highways* and *Angry Machines*, the band's sound became darker and more brooding than ever before. Some of the fans simply loathed these albums outright, even though they were, in fact, strong outings; they were simply not what the hardcore faithful wanted to hear, especially at a time when metal bands everywhere seemed to be straying from the fold. But Dio had a comeback of sorts in 2000 with *Magica*, which was the band's first concept album—kind of surprising, considering the lyrical preoccupations of Dio's swords-and-sorcery past. The album also saw the return of original bassist Bain and Dream Evil guitarist Goldy, and it abandoned the doomy style of the Tracy G. releases, instead embracing a more "classic" Dio sound; there were songs on the album that wouldn't have been out of place on *The Last in Line*. The band released two more albums, 2002's *Killing the Dragon* and 2004's *Master of the Moon*, but it was put on hold when the singer went back to work with the *Mob Rules* lineup of Black Sabbath, who were now doing business as Heaven and Hell. That project kept him busy into 2009, but the singer had always intended to return to his band and work on two further installments of the *Magica* saga. Sadly, it would never happen. In November 2009, the singer announced that he had been diagnosed with stomach cancer, and despite aggressive treatments that for a time looked promising, he succumbed to the disease in May 2010.

Discography: *Holy Diver* (Reprise, 1983); *The Last in Line* (Warner Bros., 1984); *Sacred Heart* (Warner Bros., 1985); *Intermission* (Reprise, 1986); *Dream Evil* (Reprise, 1987); *Lock Up the Wolves* (Reprise, 1990); *Strange Highways* (Reprise, 1993); *Angry Machines* (Mayhem, 1996); *Inferno: Last in Live* (Mayhem, 1998); *Magica* (Spitfire, 2000); *The Very Beast of Dio* (Rhino, 2000); *Killing the Dragon* (Spitfire, 2002); *Master of the Moon* (Sanctuary, 2004); *Evil or Divine: Live in New York City* (Spitfire, 2005); *Holy Diver: Live* (Eagle, 2006)

DOKKEN

YEARS ACTIVE: 1978–1989; 1994–PRESENT

Dokken was one of the most popular Los Angeles hair metal bands of the 1980s. Its members distinguished themselves from their contemporaries by combining their surprisingly astute songwriting skills with the virtuoso guitar playing of George Lynch. At the time, fans of heavier, less pop-oriented metal grudgingly admitted that Lynch was a stellar guitarist, while fans of pop who normally shied away from heavy metal found the band accessible because of their radio-friendly melodies. Traditionally, the only heavy metal bands to break out of the Star Trek convention–geek fan ghetto have been those who can appeal to the chicks as well as the dudes, and Dokken had the goods to appeal to both in equal measure.

The band was, unfortunately, inconvenienced by the small matter of Lynch and lead singer Don Dokken despising each other. Their animus was world-famous, and it eventually became more than the band could handle. They broke up in 1988, just before the hair metal explosion would likely have made them one of the most popular bands in the world. Uncowed, their label Elektra decided to

Doug Aldrich: guitars (*Killing the Dragon*); **Vinny Appice**: drums (*Holy Diver* through *Dream Evil*; *Strange Highways* through *Inferno: Last in Live*) (see also Black Sabbath); **Jimmy Bain**: bass/keyboards (*Holy Diver* through *Dream Evil*; *Magica* and later) (see also Rainbow); **Vivian Campbell**: guitars (*Holy Diver* through *Sacred Heart*) (see also Def Leppard); **Teddy Cook**: bass/keyboards (*Lock Up the Wolves*); **Larry Dennison**: bass (*Inferno: Last in Live*); **Ronnie James Dio**: vocals (see also Black Sabbath, Rainbow); **Tracy G.**: guitars (*Strange Highways* through *Inferno: Last in Live*); **Craig Goldy**: guitars (*Intermission, Dream Evil, Magica* and later); **Jens Johansson**: keyboards (*Lock Up the Wolves*) (see also Yngwie Malmsteen); **Jeff Pilson**: bass (*Strange Highways, Angry Machines*); **Rowan Robertson**: guitars (*Lock Up the Wolves*); **Claude Schnell**: keyboards (*The Last in Line* through *Dream Evil*); **Scott Warren**: keyboards (*Angry Machines, Inferno: Last in Live* and later); **Simon Wright**: drums (*Lock Up the Wolves*, *Magica* and later) (see also AC/DC)

George Lynch (left) and Don Dokken have long since given up on making eye contact with each other.

ARENA POLL FOR THE 90S!

YOUR NAME: George Lynch
BEST SOUNDING HALL YOU'VE PLAYED THIS YEAR (OR LAST TOUR): Mason Jar → Nuvo Panton Court
BEST SOLOIST YOU'VE HEARD THIS YEAR:
BEST LIVE BAND YOU'VE SEEN THIS YEAR: Judas Priest
ALBUM OF THE YEAR: → AVIA MUSIC.COM /

YOUR DREAM BAND
--LEAD GUITAR: Allan Holdsworth
--RHYTHM GUITAR: ERIC Johnson
--LEAD VOCALS: Rob Halford
--BACKGROUND VOCALS: Kurt's X
--BASS: Joco Pastorious
--DRUMS: Simon Phillips
--PERCUSSION: Sheil E
--ACOUSTIC PIANO: Chick Corea
--ELECTRONIC KEYBOARDS/ORGAN: Keyboard player in toto
--HARMONICA: Magic Dick
--SOLO SAX/HORN SECTION: De bud
NAME THE BAND: Gay Black Nazis Bikers for chaist

reissue their European debut EP, *Back in the Streets*, in 1989, in a last-ditch effort to cash in on whatever potential Dokken-earmarked dollars were still out there waiting to be spent. Those dollars were certainly not being spent on either Don Dokken's mediocre solo album or the debut by Lynch's band, Lynch Mob. Both ventures were, unsurprisingly, complete and utter commercial failures, and in 1994 the band Dokken re-formed. The happy reunion was short-lived, however, when Dokken and Lynch remembered that they hated each other and Lynch left the band again, this time forever. He was replaced by Reb Beach of Winger and went back to resurrect Lynch Mob. What followed were several years of lineup instability, during which singer Don Dokken and drummer Mick Brown were the only constant members. The situation didn't stabilize until 2004's *Hell to Pay*, which featured the guitar playing services of one Jon Levin, who had previously been the band's lawyer.

Reb Beach: guitar (*Erase the Slate*); **Mick Brown**: drums; **Juan Croucier**: bass (*Breaking the Chains*); **Don Dokken**: vocals; **George Lynch**: guitar (*Breaking the Chains* through *Shadowlife*); **Jon Levin**: guitar (*Hell to Pay* and later); **John Norum**: guitar (*Long Way Home*); **Jeff Pilson**: bass (*Tooth and Nail* through *Erase the Slate*); **Barry Sparks**: bass (*Long Way Home* and later)

Discography: *Breaking the Chains* (Elektra, 1982); *Tooth and Nail* (Elektra, 1984); *Under Lock and Key* (Elektra, 1985); *Back for the Attack* (Elektra, 1987); *Beast from the East* (Elektra, 1988); *Back in the Streets* (Elektra, 1989); *Dysfunctional* (Columbia, 1995); *One Live Night* (CMC, 1996); *Shadowlife* (CMC, 1997); *Erase the Slate* (CMC, 1999); *The Very Best of Dokken* (Rhino, 1999); *Live from the Sun: Best from the West* (CMC, 2000); *Long Way Home* (Sanctuary, 2002); *Hell to Pay* (Sanctuary, 2004); *Lightning Strikes Again* (Rhino, 2007)

DOWN

YEARS ACTIVE: 1991–PRESENT

The music of New Orleans is a jubilant brew of joyful accordion melodies, infectious washboard rhythms, and bittersweet Creole lyrics. When it's played, you can almost smell the étouffée, the red beans and rice, and the tourist vomit stagnating curbside outside of French Quarter titty bars. But did you also know that the city is home to bands whose greatest joy in life is to bludgeon eardrums with slow-motion sludge metal? They should really say so in the tourist pamphlets.

One such ensemble is Down, which was formed by singer Phil Anselmo of Pantera, Corrosion of Conformity guitarist Pepper Keenan, Eyehategod guitarist Jimmy Bower on drums, and Crowbar's Kirk Windstein and Todd Strange. Down was only supposed to be a one-off side project while the various musicians' regular bands were on hiatus. However, their debut album, 1995's *NOLA*, was an accidental masterpiece of ten-ton sludge filtered through the southern rock sound of bands like Molly Hatchet. This approach was typified by such rock-solid songs as "Lifer," "Rehab," and the magnificent single "Stone the Crow." The

Despite their southern pedigree, Phil Anselmo and Pepper Keenan of Down will not be performing "Gimme Three Steps" at tonight's performance.

band only did a brief tour, and then everyone went back to their regular projects. But the cat was out of the bag—Down had caught on, and not as a side project, but as a standalone band in its own right.

Down didn't release a follow-up until 2002, long after bassist Todd Strange had left the crew. He was replaced by Pantera bassist Rex Brown, and the new lineup recorded and released 2002's *Down II: A Bustle in Your Hedgerow*. The album wasn't as well received by critics as Down's debut, but fans bought it in larger numbers, and Down was well-received when they played the second stage at that year's Ozzfest. Down went back on hiatus for five years, releasing *Down III: Over the Under* in 2007. The band toured, but had to do so without the services of Rex Brown, who was suffering from acute pancreatitis. Their last offering was the live recording *Diary of a Mad Band*, which was released in 2010.

Phil Anselmo: vocals; **Jimmy Bower**: drums; **Rex Brown**: bass (*Down II* and later); **Pepper Keenan**: guitar; **Kirk Windstein**: guitar

Discography: *NOLA* (Elektra, 1995); *Down II: A Bustle in Your Hedgerow* (Elektra, 2002); *Down III: Over the Under* (Roadrunner Records, 2007); *Diary of a Mad Band: Europe in the Year of VI* (Down Records, 2010)

Dirty Rotten Imbeciles (henceforth referred to as D.R.I.) began its life as a blindingly fast Texas hardcore band whose first album, 1982's *Dirty Rotten LP*, featured more than twenty songs and clocked in at less than half an hour. It was raw, brutal stuff, and the album remains a hardcore classic, mainly because of songs such as "I Don't Need Society" and how ridiculously fast the tracks are. The only competition the band received in that department was the last thirty seconds of Slayer's "Raining Blood," which didn't arrive until four years later.

After the band moved to San Francisco in 1984, the next full-length album, *Dealing with It*, saw them introduce heavy metal elements into their sound, typified by the inclusion of (gasp) guitar solos and other embellishments, causing the album to explode to a sprawling thirty-three minutes in length. By the time of their fourth release, *Crossover*, the band was combining metal and hardcore influences in equal measure, which was certainly in the spirit of the times; by 1987, hardcore and thrash metal were nearly indistinguishable from each other. The band's sound

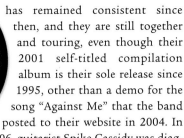

has remained consistent since then, and they are still together and touring, even though their 2001 self-titled compilation album is their sole release since 1995, other than a demo for the song "Against Me" that the band posted to their website in 2004. In 2006, guitarist Spike Cassidy was diagnosed with colon cancer, and although he was free and clear of it in 2008 after a chemotherapy course, it returned in 2011, forcing him to have a total colectomy in January 2012.

Eric Brecht: drums (*Dirty Rotten LP, Violent Pacification*); **Kurt Brecht**: vocals; **Spike Cassidy**: guitars; **Felix Griffin**: drums (*Dealing with It* through *Thrash Zone*); **Dennis Johnson**: bass (*Dirty Rotten LP*); **John Menor**: bass (*Thrash Zone* through *Live*); **Mikey Offender**: bass (*Dealing with It*); **Josh Pappe**: bass (*Violent Pacification, Crossover, Four of a Kind*); **Chumly Porter**: bass (*Full Speed Ahead*); **Rob Rampy**: drums (*Definition* and later)

Discography: *Dirty Rotten LP* (Radical, 1982); *Violent Pacification* (Radical, 1984); *Dealing with It* (Metal Blade, 1985); *Crossover* (Metal Blade, 1987); *Four of a Kind* (Metal Blade, 1988); *Thrash Zone* (Metal Blade, 1989); *Definition* (Rotten, 1992); *Live* (Rotten, 1995); *Full Speed Ahead* (Rotten, 1995); *Dirty Rotten Imbeciles* (Cleopatra, 2001)

Dream Theater has been in business since 1985, ever since bassist John Myung, guitarist John Petrucci, and drummer Mike Portnoy met at the Berklee College of Music in Boston. They joined forces with keyboard player Kevin Moore and singer Charlie Dominici and signed to Mechanic Records, which put out the band's debut, *When Dream and Day Unite*, in 1989. The promotion given to the album is best described as shit-tastic, and the group severed its ties with the label, also parting ways with Dominici while they were at it. The band replaced him with James LaBrie and signed to Atco for

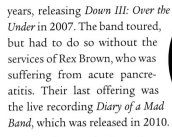

Bassist John Myung can finally execute that 64th-note run in the Locrian mode, now that Dream Theater has been included in *The Encyclopedia of Heavy Metal*.

their second album, *Images and Words*. Released in 1992, the album proved a very different experience for the band, whose video for "Pull Me Under" went into heavy rotation on MTV. The follow-up album, *Awake*, came next.

After the 1996 tour, the band's label underwent a change of personnel, and the person who had served as their main liaison was fired.

The band suddenly had to deal with new people who didn't particularly like their music and saw their progressive sound as a flaw to be corrected, not their main selling point. To fix this "issue," the label hired hack writer and producer Desmond Child to "polish" the band's sound. Child had been responsible for such crimes against humanity as "I Was Made for Loving You" by KISS and "She Bangs" by Ricky Martin, perfected by William Hung of *American Idol* fame. The resulting album, 1997's *Falling into Infinity*, was the group's most overtly radio-friendly effort, which their long-time fans were none too happy about. Portnoy agreed with his fans and reacted so negatively to the entire experience that he considered disbanding the group rather than subject it to any further record company wisdom.

The band got back on track with the concept album *Scenes from a Memory*, which they would perform in its entirety on tour. Then the group suffered a ridiculous turn of fate when their album *Live Scenes from New York*, whose cover depicted the Big Apple consumed by flames, was released on September 11, 2001, complete with the World Trade Center right there on the cover. Awkward! Undeterred, in 2002 they released *Six Degrees of Inner Turbulence*, the double disc they had always wanted to make and whose second disc consisted of exactly one song, the forty-two-minute title track. It was followed in 2003 by *Train of Thought*, the most overtly metal album in their catalog, and *Octavarium* in 2005. They went back to the live album trough in 2006 for *Score*, which featured the backing of a full orchestra.

Dream Theater moved to the far more sympathetic Roadrunner label for their next album,

2007's *Systematic Chaos*. It reached the *Billboard* top 20 in part thanks to the record company actually promoting it. In 2010, the unthinkable happened and drummer and founding member Mike Portnoy left the band, leaving many people to wonder if they could even go on without him and remain credible. The group replaced him with Mike Mangini, doing so just weeks after Portnoy's departure. Somehow, even with all that upheaval going on in the late months of 2010, the group managed to record *A Dramatic Turn of Events*, which was released in 2011.

Charlie Dominici: vocals (*When Dream and Day Unite*); **James LaBrie**: vocals (*Images and Words* and later); **Mike Mangini**: drums (*A Dramatic Turn of Events*); **Kevin Moore**: keyboards (*When Day and Dream Unite* through *Awake*); **John Myung**: bass; **John Petrucci**: guitar; **Mike Portnoy**: drums; **Jordan Rudess**: keyboards (*Metropolis Pt. 2: Scenes from a Memory* and later); **Derek Sherinian**: keyboards (*A Change of Seasons* through *Falling into Infinity*)

Discography: *When Dream and Day Unite* (Mechanic, 1989); *Images and Words* (Atco, 1992); *Live at the Marquee* (Warner Music, 1993); *Awake* (East West, 1994); *A Change of Seasons* (East West, 1995); *Falling Into Infinity* (East West, 1997); *Once in a Livetime* (Elektra, 1998); *Scenes from a Memory* (Elektra, 1999); *Live Scenes from New York* (Elektra, 2001); *Six Degrees of Inner Turbulence* (Elektra, 2002); *Train of Thought* (Elektra, 2003); *Live at Budokan* (Atlantic, 2004); *Octavarium* (Atlantic, 2005); *Score* (Rhino, 2006); *Systematic Chaos* (Roadrunner, 2007); *Black Clouds and Silver Linings* (Roadrunner, 2009); *A Dramatic Turn of Events* (Roadrunner, 2011)

DUST

YEARS ACTIVE: 1969–1972

New York City's Dust is one of the most criminally underrated heavy metal bands of the early 1970s. Why they never achieved a high level of celebrity is a complete, baffling mystery, as they certainly seemed to have everything going for them. They possessed top-notch musicianship and classic songwriting skills that were easily as good as, if not better than, anything else that was out at the time. But the band never went anywhere, for reasons that are anybody's guess. Their self-titled debut album was released in 1971 but failed to chart, despite such strong material as "Chasin' Ladies" and "Love Me Hard." Undeterred, the band returned to the studio in 1972 for *Hard Attack*, an album was that even stronger and heavier than its predecessor. But it, too, failed to catch on, even with such excellent material as "Pull Away/So Many Times," "Walk in the Soft Rain," "Learning to Die," and the pummeling "Suicide."

While Dust did not receive even a fraction of the recognition that it deserved, the story does have a happy ending—actually, three happy endings. Bassist Kenny Aaronson went on to become a high-in-demand session musician, and singer and guitarist Richie Wise coproduced the first two KISS albums. The sweetest outcome, however, was reserved for drummer Marc Bell, who went on to join another local New York City band. The only caveat was that he would have to change his surname to the one adopted by all the members of the group. Bell agreed, and he finally won his stardom as Marky Ramone.

Kenny Aaronson: bass; **Marc Bell**: drums; **Richie Wise**: vocals/guitar

Discography: *Dust* (Kama Sutra, 1971); *Hard Attack* (Kama Sutra, 1972)

ELECTRIC WIZARD

YEARS ACTIVE: 1993–PRESENT

Formed in 1993, England's Electric Wizard is one of the more extreme specimens of stoner doom. Almost all of the group's "songs" are more accurately described as long, slow plods, which employ vocal and guitar effects in Butthole Surfers quantities and at least flirt with the ten-minute mark if not simply crawl right past it. Needless to say, this music is not about whistleable melodies or verse-chorus-verse-chorus tunesmithery—it's about pounding the listener into a narcotic haze. This

music is also not about the precision execution of virtuoso licks with which heavy metal is normally associated. Anyone who's seen one of Electric Wizard's incredibly loose (okay, sloppy) live shows can attest to this fact.

The band members are first and foremost about creating an atmosphere, and it's not a stretch to say that they are similar to the Syd Barrett–era Pink Floyd, whose live performances were considered "happenings," designed to expand the listener's consciousness. Of course, ingesting LSD certainly helped, and Electric Wizard is consistent in this respect as well, since the band enthusiastically champions the speed-gorging technique of marijuana ingestion, and their music produces a baggy-eyed, too-stoned effect in the listener (no matter if said listener has been doing push-ups and drinking milk all day). Regrettably, on the band's 2002 U.S. tour the whole show collapsed, and Greening and Bagshaw left to form Ramesses. Any rational person would have expected this to be the end of the story, but Osborn simply replaced his departed comrades and got on with it. The new lineup released the next Electric Wizard album in 2004, not coincidentally titled *We Live*.

Rob Al-Issa: bass (*We Live* and *Witchcult Today*); **Tim Bagshaw**: bass (*Electric Wizard* to *Let Us Pray*); **Liz Buckingham**: guitar (*We Live* and later); **Tas Danazoglou**: bass (*Black Masses*); **Justin Greaves**: drums (*We Live*); **Mark Greening**: drums (*Electric Wizard* to *Let Us Pray*); **Jus Oborn**: vocals; **Shaun Rutter**: guitar (*Witchcult Today*)

Discography: *Electric Wizard* (Rise Above, 1994); *Come My Fanatics...* (Music Cartel, 1996); *Chrono.Naut* (Man's Ruin, 1997); *Supercoven* (Bad Acid, 1998); *Dopethrone* (Music Cartel, 2000); *Let Us Prey* (Music Cartel, 2002); *We Live* (Music Cartel, 2004); *Witchcult Today* (Candlelight, 2007); *Black Masses* (Rise Above, 2011)

EMPEROR

YEARS ACTIVE: 1991–2001

Emperor was an archetypal Norwegian black metal band, and despite the members'

involvement in various criminal activities, they actually managed to gain recognition based on the merits of their music. While they were just as satanic as any other black metal band in the 1990s, they expressed it in a variety of thoughtful and interesting ways. Musically speaking, they took the usual jet-engine sound of black metal and expanded upon it, including elements of classical and Norwegian folk music. Lyrically speaking, they added Viking and pre-Christian pagan imagery to the usual "We don't like Jesus very much" subject matter.

Emperor has had its share of personnel difficulties, some of which were simply the result of artistic differences. Original bassist Mortiis, for example, left the band to pursue a solo career, and he can now be found adorning album covers dressed as some kind of carrot-nosed winged demonic elf, to amusing effect. The majority of the problems, however, were the result of illegal pursuits. Drummer Faust was imprisoned for murder, guitarist Samoth was convicted of a church arson, and bassist Tchort was brought up on assault charges. Remarkably, the band bounced back from these "professional" obstacles and resumed their recording career, reestablishing Emperor on the basis of the musical adventurousness for which they are known today. In 2001, they broke up to focus on other bands and solo projects.

Alver: bass (*Reverence, Anthems to the Welkin at Dusk*); **Faust**: drums (*Emperor, In the Nightside Eclipse*); **Ihsahn**: vocals/bass; **Mortiis**: bass (*Emperor, As the Shadows Rise*); **Samoth**: guitars; **Tchort**: bass (*In the Nightside Eclipse*); **Trym**: drums (*Reverence* and later)

Discography: *In the Nightside Eclipse* (Candlelight, 1994); *Anthems to the Welkin at Dusk* (Candlelight, 1997); *Thorns vs. Emperor* (Moonfog, 1999); *IX Equilibrium* (Candlelight, 1999); *Emperial Live Ceremony* (Candlelight, 2000); *Prometheus: The Discipline of Fire and Demise* (Candlelight, 2001)

HEAVY METAL

Like any other cultural movement, heavy metal has visual cues that identify its members to one another. There are variations, of course—the Morbid Angel fan is recognizable only because he wears the band's T-shirt, while an Immortal fan is found in corpse paint and possibly wields a sword. Unlike in hardcore or punk rock, the heavy metal dress code is not strictly adhered to, and all that matters to the metalhead is rocking out to the music and throwing the horns. Still, there are a few recurring themes in the heavy metal fan's appearance.

COLOR SCHEMES

Although black is the de rigueur color of heavy metal clothes, there was a time in the 1980s when the more colorful one's outfit was, the better. One need only look at Poison in its prime to spy every shade of yellow and pink in zebra-stripe patterns. But once the 1990s hit, loud colors were out, and the only acceptable colors to wear were black, black, and, on casual Fridays, black. The scene has never recovered.

FABRICS

For most metal fans, fabric isn't an issue, since jeans and a Manowar T-shirt constitute the evergreen choice. Denim in particular is in every fan's wardrobe. One doesn't see it so much today, but in the 1980s, every teenage burnout owned a jean jacket that stunk to high heaven of Marlboro reds and pot, and it had an Iron Maiden back patch for good measure. Those willing to make an investment in the heavy metal lifestyle eventually sprung for a leather jacket and ripped the arms off the denim jacket, rendering it a vest.

Also popular with metal fans was spandex, a favorite of the movement's women. Spandex's form-fitting qualities resulted in the attention of sexually excitable males, either to the delight or horror of the wearer. Spandex was also at the center of one of the darker moments in heavy metal history, when men started wearing it, presumably to showcase their crotch bulges. Luckily, this period proved to be short-lived, since nobody wants to see that shit.

FOOTWEAR

The headbanger shoe of choice is usually the sneaker, thanks to the advent of the mosh pit. The pit had been a fixture at punk rock shows for a decade, and the behavior expected of its participants was well known—stay in an orderly, clockwise formation and when someone falls down, help them up. When pits were transplanted to metal shows in the early 1990s, the rubes knew none of this, and viewed the pit as a license to transform into a pack of violent mouth-breathers who punched people in the back, started fights and responded to a fallen mosher with a ten-man pile-on. This made sneakers useful, as anyone in a mosh pit was in effect at football practice without protective gear. Prior to this, boots were popular with metal audiences, particularly cowboy boots made of fake snakeskin or rumpled imitation leather. The ladies seemed fond of the latter in white.

"FASHION"

MAKEUP

Makeup has been the subject of three distinct approaches within the heavy metal community. First, there were artists like King Diamond, KISS, and countless black metal bands, who refused to appear onstage without full geisha makeup. The second approach involved effeminate makeup worn by 1980s glam metal bands, such as Poison, who had tarted themselves up like cheap whores. The third approach was no makeup whatsoever. In the 1980s this was a proactive choice and a reaction against the glam bands who had made makeup par for the course. Bands that refused to wear makeup were afforded a degree of respect for forgoing the lipstick, as though this decision constituted "integrity." Seriously, that was all you had to do!

HAIR

While it was certainly no problem to be both a well-shorn metal fan, it is more desirable to sport generous, Christlike tresses. As such, the list of heavy metal musicians with long hair is stacked much higher than the list of those without it. Just ask Robert Plant, who still refuses to get a haircut despite being over 90. Long hair also came in handy during the glam metal era, when fans and band members alike would tease and plaster their hair with half the contents of an Aqua Net can, resulting in a towering follicular edifice that made the simple act of walking through a doorway a backbreaking chore. The final variation on heavy metal hair was the short-in-front, long-in-back style known as the mullet, a popular source of ridicule to this day.

HOMOEROTIC CLOTHING

The heavy metal community has always been rabidly homophobic. This is why in all of human history, there has been no greater act of collective self-delusion than that practiced by Judas Priest fans, who overlooked lead singer Rob Halford's very obvious homosexuality for decades. In retrospect, they had little choice, as they had been copying his blatantly homoerotic style of dress for just as long, decking themselves out in head-to-toe leather, studded belts and bracelets, spiked collars, and all manner of marital aid–related accoutrements. These were later supplemented with tattoos and piercings, many of which are on parts of the body that cannot be discussed in a family publication such as this.

T-SHIRTS

The single most important article of heavy metal fashion has always been the T-shirt. It is worn by every metal fan regardless of preferred subgenre, and serves the purpose of advertising the band affiliation of the wearer. The public display sends a signal to others, partially in the hopes of finding friends with common interests and partially as a public service to the band emblazoned on one's chest, which very likely could use the advertising.

ENTOMBED

Years active: 1987–present

The crabby Swedes known collectively as Entombed started out in the late 1980s as your average death metal band, with a recording contract with Earache to boot. Their first album, *Left Hand Path*, was immediately seized upon as a death metal milestone, and countless bands began copying its sound outright. Amazingly, Entombed was able to follow up on the genre-defining album with an even better one, *Clandestine*, which brought the band to an international audience and won critical acclaim, a commodity that very

The men of Entombed are Sweden's death metal deities.

few death metal bands, Swedish or otherwise, ever see much of. They seemed poised to be crowned the Kings of Swedish Death Metal when, in 1993, they released the *Hollowman* EP and the *Wolverine Blues* album back to back, and all hell broke loose. It featured slower tempos, traditional song structures, and, most upsettingly, articulate vocals. The die-hard death metal fans who had made Entombed famous were now crying sellout. Clearly not sensitive to such criticisms, the band continued to develop their new sound, to the point where they were known for playing a unique if unsolicited mixture of death metal and Stooges-style punk rock. However, by the time of 1998's *Same Difference*, the death metal influence was almost completely gone, as was a considerable portion of their once-loyal audience. In response, the band suddenly did a complete 180-degree turn, and their later releases, such as *Uprising* and *Morning Star*, found the band clinging to their death metal past like a squealing puppy to its owner's

leg. In late 2002, they collaborated with—no joke—the Swedish Royal Ballet Ensemble, on a project called Unreal Estate, which certainly pleased their hardcore death metal fans to no end. Their last album, *Serpent Saints: The Ten Amendments*, was released in 2007.

Nicke Andersson: drums (*Left Hand Path* through *To Ride, Shoot Straight, and Speak the Truth*; vocals on *Clandestine*); **Uffe Cederlund**: guitars; **Johnny Dordevic**: vocals (*Stranger Aeons*); **Alex Hellid**: guitars; **L. G. Petrov**: vocals (*Left Hand Path*, *Hollowman* and later); **Lars Rosenberg**: bass (*Clandestine* through *Out of Hand*); **Orvar Säfström**: vocals (*Crawl*); **Jörgen Sandström**: bass (*To Ride, Shoot Straight, and Speak the Truth*); **Peter Stjärnvind**: drums (*Same Difference* and later)

Discography: *Left Hand Path* (Earache, 1990); *Crawl* (Earache, 1991); *Clandestine* (Earache, 1991); *Stranger Aeons* (Earache, 1992); *Hollowman* (Earache, 1993); *Wolverine Blues* (Earache, 1993); *Out of Hand* (Earache, 1994); *Entombed* (Earache, 1997); *To Ride, Shoot Straight, and Speak the Truth* (Music for Nations, 1997); *Wreckage* (Music for Nations, 1998); *Same Difference* (Roadrunner, 1998); *Monkey Puss: Live in London* (Earache, 1999); *Black Juju* (Man's Ruin, 1999); *Uprising* (Sanctuary, 2000); *Morning Star* (Koch, 2002); *Inferno* (Candlelight, 2003); *Serpent Saints: The Ten Amendments* (Threeman, 2007)

EXCITER

YEARS ACTIVE: 1978–PRESENT

Exciter, like fellow Canadian group Anvil, was among the first of the speed metal bands to achieve prominence in the early 1980s. In fact, the band's first album, *Heavy Metal Maniac*, released in 1983, is considered by some to be one of the first speed metal albums ever. The band seemed to be on its way up, particularly when, in 1985, they toured with Megadeth and Motörhead to support their best-selling album *Long Live the Loud*. But this proved to be the zenith of their career. By 1987, with the release of *Unveiling the Wicked*, their music had grown steadily less aggressive and more melodic and consequently it was much less accepted by their fans, who infinitely preferred the thrashy tendencies of their beloved Exciter of yore. The band was then dropped by their label, but they refused to be counted out, and they released another album independently. Stylistically speaking, it was more of what got them into trouble in the first place: slower tempos, greater emphasis on melody, and so on. As a result, it was met with a degree of consumer enthusiasm equal to that which would befall a rack of barbecued ribs to a wearer of white gloves. The band went through a major lineup shift at that point, and released *New Testament* in 2004. While the album was simply a selection of older Exciter songs, rerecorded, it was preferable for their remaining fans to the band simply breaking up, which seemed like a real possibility not long before. The band released *Thrash Speed Burn* in 2008 and *Death Machine* in 2010, which were real albums of new material and everything!

Dan Beehler: drums/vocals (*Heavy Metal Maniac* through *Better Live Than Dead*); **Jacques Bélanger**: vocals (*The Dark Command* and later); **Marc Char-** ron: bass (*The Dark Command* and later); **Rick Charron**: drums (*The Dark Command* and later); **Robert "Clammy" Cohen:** bass (*Thrash Speed Burn* and later); **Allan James Johnson**: bass (*Heavy Metal Maniac* through *Exciter*); **David Ledden**: bass (*Kill After Kill*); **Jeff MacDonald**: bass (*Better Live Than Dead*); **Rob Malnati**: vocals (*Exciter*); **Brian McPhee**: guitars (*Exciter, Unveiling the Wicked*); **John Ricci**: guitars (*Heavy Metal Maniac* through *Long Live the Loud*; *Kill After Kill* and later); **Kenny Winter** (*Thrash Speed Burn*)

Discography: *Heavy Metal Maniac* (Enigma, 1983); *Violence and Force* (Music for Nations, 1984); *Long Live the Loud* (Music for Nations, 1985); *Feel the Knife* (Music for Nations, 1985); *Exciter* (Maze/Kraze, 1986); *Unveiling the Wicked* (Music for Nations, 1987); *O.T.T.* (Maze/Kraze, 1989); *Kill After Kill* (Spy, 1993); *Better Live Than Dead* (Bleeding, 1993); *The Dark Command* (Osmose, 1998); *Blood of Tyrants* (Osmose, 1999); *New Testament* (Osmose, 2004); *Thrash, Speed, Burn* (Massacre, 2008); *Death Machine* (Massacre, 2010)

EXODUS

YEARS ACTIVE: 1980–1992; 1997–2002; 2004–PRESENT

San Francisco has been dubbed "the Birthplace of Thrash," and Exodus is a major reason why. Although the band was at one time on the same level as Metallica in terms of both initial popularity and influence on the speed metal genre, Exodus rarely receives the credit it deserves. Like Metallica,

Taking a five-minute break from global devastation, the members of Exodus pose for the paparazzi. Left to right: Gary Holt, Rob McKillop, Rick Hunolt, Steve Souza, and Tom Hunting.

the band's initial style owed a lot to the New Wave of British Heavy Metal bands and a whole lot more to Motörhead. Their initial underground audience was the result of the widespread practice of tape trading, which was very often the sole reason many bands ever got a following in those days—it was not exactly common practice for radio stations to play crappy-sounding demos by unknown speed metal bands. By the time their first album, *Bonded by Blood*, was released in 1985, they had a die-hard following, thanks in no small part to the grassroots methods their fan base used to spread the word.

Exodus suffered a series of setbacks that ultimately kept them at a second-tier level,

where they did not deserve to languish. Before they had even recorded their first album, they endured a major blow when lead guitarist and founding member Kirk Hammett left the band to join Metallica, a decision he is no doubt happy about today. Lead singer (and yet another founding member) Paul Baloff was next to go. After the addition of new vocalist Steve Souza for 1987's *Pleasures of the Flesh*, the band's lineup stabilized, affording them the opportunity to rebound in 1989 with *Fabulous Disaster*. But after the tour, drummer Tom Hunting was diagnosed with an irregular heartbeat, which sidelined him from any future touring. Subsequent albums did not do much to capitalize on the success of *Fabulous Disaster*, and by the time of their final studio album in 1992, the unfortunately named *Force of Habit*, the writing was on the wall, and the band broke up. However, in the decidedly less metal-hostile environment of 1997, the band reunited with original singer Baloff for a few shows, which were recorded and released on the live album *Another Lesson in Violence*. While a full-fledged reunion seemed unlikely, the band continued to get together sporadically and perform. Sadly, a seemingly insurmountable setback was dealt to the band when Baloff suffered a massive stroke on January 31, 2002. He died three days later, and it seemed certain that the book had been closed forever on this band. However, the group was determined to press on, and with Souza back in the fold they released *Tempo of the Damned* in 2004.

The band lost guitarist Rick Hunolt, drummer Tom Hunting and, yet again, Souza after *Tempo of the Damned*, so guitarist Gary Holt, who was now the only original member left, simply replaced everybody except for bassist Jack Gibson, who had appeared on the last two Exodus albums and was still showing up for rehearsal. This lineup produced *Shovel Headed Kill Machine*. *The Atrocity Exhibition . . . Exhibit A* followed in 2007 and saw Hunolt return to the fold. In 2008 the group released *Let There Be Blood*, a rerecording of the band's 1985 debut,

Exodus' wailing guitarists are Rick Hunolt (foreground) and Gary Holt.

Bonded by Blood, which featured the drumming services of the twice-departed Tom Hunting. The band's most recent album was *Exhibit B: The Human Condition*, released in 2010.

Lee Altus: guitar (*Shovel Headed Kill Machine* and later); **Paul Baloff**: vocals (*Bonded by Blood, Another Lesson in Violence*); **Paul Bostaph**: drums (*Shovel Headed Kill Machine*); **Mike Butler**: bass (*Force of Habit*); **Rob Dukes**: vocals (*Shovel Headed Kill Machine* and later); **Jack Gibson**: bass (*Another Lesson in Violence* and later); **Gary Holt**: guitars; **Rick Hunolt**: guitars; **Tom Hunting**: drums (*Bonded by Blood* through *Fabulous Disaster, Another Lesson in Violence* and later); **Rob McKillop**: bass (*Bonded by Blood* through *Impact Is Imminent*); **Steve Souza**: vocals (*Pleasures of the Flesh* through *Force of Habit, Tempo of the Damned*); **John Tempesta**: drums (*Impact Is Imminent* through *Force of Habit*) (see also Testament, White Zombie)

Discography: *Bonded by Blood* (Combat, 1985); *Pleasures of the Flesh* (Combat, 1987); *Fabulous Disaster* (Combat, 1989); *Impact Is Imminent* (Capitol, 1990); *Good Friendly Violent Fun* (Combat, 1991); *The Best of Exodus: Lessons in Violence* (Combat, 1992); *Force of Habit* (Capitol, 1992); *Another Lesson in Violence* (Century Media, 1997); *Tempo of the Damned* (Nuclear Blast, 2004); *Shovel Headed Kill Machine* (Nuclear Blast, 2005); *The Atrocity Exhibition . . . Exhibit A* (Nuclear Blast, 2007); *Let There Be Blood* (Zaentz Records, 2008); *Exhibit B: The Human Condition* (Nuclear Blast, 2010)

YEARS ACTIVE: 1985–1996; 2007–PRESENT

While Boston's Extreme is best known for its ballads, closer inspection of the band's albums reveals a high level of musicianship, particularly on the part of lead guitarist Nuno Bettencourt, whose accomplished playing exhibits the undeniable influence of Queen's Brian May. Unfortunately, the band became a household name because of their second album, *Extreme II: Pornograffitti*. It was released in 1990, the Year of the Power Ballad, and like so many of their contemporaries, the band members were responsible for power ballad proliferation. They reached their highest point of commercial

EXTREME

Only the Dark One knows what Gary Cherone was searching for when he lined up his Extreme band mates in this frisk-ready manner. Left to right: Pat Badger, Paul Geary, Gary Cherone, and Nuno Bettencourt.

success with the Everly Brothers–esque single "More Than Words," and their reputation as deeply sensitive fancy boys was cast in quick-drying cement when they followed it up with "Hole Hearted," which was slightly less wussyish only because it included the actual strumming of acoustic guitar chords with a pick.

If 1990 was the Year of the Power Ballad, 1992 was the Year of All Bands Who Made Power Ballads Being Lined Up and Shot, and Extreme was no exception. The group's follow-up album, *III Sides to Every Story*, was released that year and shifted only a fraction of its predecessor's units. The band took one more futile stab in 1995 and released *Waiting for the Punchline*, an album that was met with massive indifference and made its dismally selling predecessor seem like *Thriller* by comparison. Extreme broke up at this point, and Bettencourt went on to make solo albums that

were aimed at an audience yet to be identified. Lead singer Gary Cherone went on to front Van Halen for the single worst-selling album of the band's career, presumably because Van Halen fans cannot accept a singer who doesn't own a tequila still at his own private retreat in Mexico. Bettencourt currently tours with Rihanna, and in 2010, the members of Extreme threatened to start writing a new album, but so far, nothing.

Pat Badger: bass; **Nuno Bettencourt**: guitar; **Gary Cherone**: vocals (see also Van Halen); **Kevin Figuerido**: drums (*Saudades de Rock*); **Paul Geary**: drums; **Mike Mangini**: drums (*Extreme* to *Waiting for the Punchline*)

Discography: *Extreme* (A&M, 1989); *Extreme II: Pornograffitti* (A&M, 1990); *III Sides to Every Story* (A&M, 1992); *Waiting for the Punchline* (A&M, 1995); *Saudades de Rock* (Universal, 2008)

EYEHATEGOD

Years active: 1988–present

New Orleans. NOLA. The Crescent City. Home of Dr. John, Tippitina's, and the springtime bartering of strung beads in exchange for public displays of female mammary glands. The Big Easy is also the birthplace of the sludge-core movement. For those not in the know, sludge-core is the preferred nomenclature for a style of music composed mainly of tempos slowed to a crawl, guitars tuned down to the key of Q, and vocals suitable for a Septic Death album. For reasons that are anybody's guess, this style of music was invented in a fun-time party town, and the band that seems to receive the most credit for its inception is Eyehategod. One possible reason why the band gets credit is that they have broken up as many times as most people change their underwear, only to find the members going on to play in other prominent sludge-core groups in the same city. Guitarist Brian Patton plays in Soilent Green, and guitarist Jimmy Bower can be found slamming the skins for not one but two such bands, Crowbar and the very successful Down, a collaboration with his fellow Crowbar members, Corrosion of Conformity guitarist Pepper Keenan, and Pantera vocalist Phil Anselmo. However, the band has gotten back together just as frequently, and in 2000 they released a new studio album, *Confederacy of Ruined Lives*, and a compilation album *Southern Discomfort*. Then, in 2001, they released a live album, *Ten Years of Abuse (and Still Broke)*.

Jimmy Bower: guitars (see also Corrosion of Conformity); **Steve Dale**: bass (*In the Name of Suffering*); **Joe LaCaze**: drums; **Vince LeBlanc**: bass (*Dopesick*); **Daniel Nick**: bass (*Confederacy of Ruined Lives*); **Brian Patton**: guitars; **Mark Schultz**: bass (*Take As Needed for Pain*); **Michael Williams**: vocals

Discography: *In the Name of Suffering* (Century Media, 1992); *Take As Needed for Pain* (Century Media, 1993); *Dopesick* (Century Media, 1996); *Southern Discomfort* (Century Media, 2000); *Confederacy of Ruined Lives* (Century Media, 2000); *Ten Years of Abuse (and Still Broke)* (Century Media, 2001)

FAITH NO MORE

YEARS ACTIVE: 1981–1998

San Francisco's Faith No More was an anomaly in that the band achieved commercial success without a misrepresentative pop single to make them more accessible to mainstream audiences. Under normal circumstances, they really should have been a cult band, since their fusion of styles, including metal, hip-hop, and funk, was not yet a mainstream practice (the eternal underground status of Fishbone bears this out). However, the band had gone through several vocalists (no less a luminary than Courtney Love had passed through their ranks early on) and spent two albums fine-tuning their sound, so in 1989 when they released their third album, *The Real Thing*, all the kinks were worked out; in a stroke of sheer good luck, the timing was exactly right. The record-buying public responded cash-positively to their single and video for "Epic," a song that distilled the band's essence perfectly in just a couple of minutes, making the album a huge commercial success. It was a tough act to follow, however, and their next studio album, *Angel Dust*, didn't do as

It appears as if Faith No More's singer, Mike Patton, greedily eats some trail mix while his band mates look away in disgust. Left to right: Roddy Bottum, Mike Patton, Billy Gould, and Jim Martin.

well as everyone had expected. The album was simply too weird, and it lacked any material with the same mainstream appeal as "Epic." The band began to fragment at this point, with guitarist Jim Martin being the first casualty. The band made two more studio albums, but the individual members were turning to outside projects. Vocalist Mike Patton began working with the incredibly bizarre band Mr. Bungle, and drummer Mike Bordin started touring and recording with Ozzy Osbourne. In 1998, the band split up, and the members went to work on their individual endeavors full-time. Patton worked with Mr. Bungle as well as Fantômas, and Bordin was hired to surreptitiously replace the drum tracks on the albums in Osbourne's back catalog.

Mike Bordin: drums; **Roddy Bottum**: keyboards; **Billy Gould**: bass; **Jon Hudson**: guitars (*Album of the Year*); **Jim Martin**: guitars (*We Care a Lot* through *Angel Dust*); **Chuck Mosely**: vocals (*We Care a Lot, Introduce Yourself*); **Mike Patton**: vocals (*The Real Thing* and later); **Trey Spruance**: guitars (*King for a Day, Fool for a Lifetime*)

Discography: *We Care a Lot* (Mordam, 1985); *Introduce Yourself* (Slash/Rhino, 1987); *The Real Thing* (Slash, 1989); *Live at Brixton Academy* (Polygram, 1991); *Angel Dust* (Slash, 1992); *King for a Day, Fool for a Lifetime* (Slash/Reprise, 1995); *Album of the Year* (Slash/Reprise, 1997);

FASTER PUSSYCAT

YEARS ACTIVE: 1981–1998

Taking its name from a movie by hardcore schlockophile filmmaker Russ Meyer, Faster Pussycat was one of the bands that personified the trashy Hollywood glam explosion of the late 1980s. Although they were always described as heavy metal, they could probably be more accurately categorized as a highly amplified rock'n'roll band; like many of their Sunset Strip contemporaries, Faster Pussycat sounded more like Aerosmith than Judas Priest. Lead singer Taime Downe was even in the practice of tying *shmattes* to his microphone stand, à la Steven Tyler, whom Downe has claimed as a primary influence.

Faster Pussycat hit the big time on their second album, *Wake Me When It's Over*, released in 1989. The album featured the popular single "House of Pain," which at the time was classified as a power ballad. In reality, the song probably sat more comfortably alongside a song like the Rolling Stones' "Wild Horses" (which raises the question of whether the alt.country bands weren't really just glam bands with haircuts and Fender Telecasters). The band members have since gone on record as stating that they believed "House of Pain" did more to damage their career than anything else, as it was unrepresentative of the rest of their material. This created a situation where people who liked the song and therefore bought the album were displeased with its contents, while people who probably would have enjoyed the band's harder-edge material were put off by the drippy treacle of the single. In any event, the whole point was moot in two years' time anyway, when grunge broke and every band suspected of being affiliated with the dreaded "metal" tag was dropped from their labels and shipped off to forced labor camps for their horrific crimes against humanity.

Brett Bradshaw: drums; **Taime Downe**: vocals; **Brent Muscat**: guitar (*Faster Pussycat* to *Whipped!*); **Danny Nordhal**: bass (*The Power and the Glory Hole*); **Xristian Simon**: guitar (*The Power and the Glory Hole*); **Eric Stacy**: bass (*Faster Pussycat* to *Whipped!*); **Greg Steele**: guitar (*Faster Pussycat* to *Whipped!*); **Chad Stewart**: drums (*The Power the Glory Hole*)

Discography: *Faster Pussycat* (Elektra, 1987); *Wake Me When It's Over* (Elektra, 1989); *Whipped!* (Elektra, 1992); *The Power and the Glory Hole* (Full Effect, 2008)

FASTWAY

YEARS ACTIVE: 1983–1990; 2007–PRESENT

A veritable who's who of musicians who left their previous bands on lousy terms, England's Fastway was formed by legendary guitarist

With its popularity in decline, Faster Pussycat's ability to attract groupies reached its lowest ebb yet. Left to right: Eric Stacy, Brent Muscat, Greg Steele, Brett Bradshaw, and Taime Downe.

Fast" Eddie Clarke after his famously atrocious split from Motörhead in 1982. He joined forces with freshly fired U.F.O. bassist Pete Way and with drummer Jerry Shirley, who was best known for his work in Humble Pie. With this pedigree, the band, it was generally assumed, would be a monster. Unfortunately, it was fatally crippled before it ever even got off the ground. In a decision that probably seemed like a good idea on paper, Clarke came to the conclusion that there was no way in hell he could possibly match the sheer sonic might of his last gig. He decided instead that his latest band should make music that was more polished and commercial, officially rendering Fastway's ass grass. Motörhead fans were not then, nor are they now, nor will they ever be, fans of the slick stuff, particularly not when it's being made by a former member. As such, Fastway's debut album was moderately well received in the United States, but back home in Motörhead country, it was another story. Things did not improve. Perhaps thinking that the band needed to be even slicker and more poplike, Clarke added a keyboard player to the band's ranks. This did not have the desired effect, and in 1990 Fastway said bye-bye. The group remained inactive until Clarke put together a new lineup, who released the album *Eat Dog Eat* in 2011.

Shane Carroll: keyboards/guitar (*Waiting for the Roar, Trick or Treat*); **Charlie McCraken**: bass (*All Fired Up, Trick or Treat*); **"Fast" Eddie Clarke**: guitar (*Fastway, Waiting for the Roar, On Target, Bad Bad Girls*) (see also Motörhead); **Alan Connor**: drums (*Waiting for the Roar, Trick or Treat*); **Lea Hart**: vocals (*On Target, Bad Bad Girls*); **Toby Jepson**: vocals (*Eat Dog Eat*); **Paul Reid**: bass (*Waiting for the Roar, Trick or Treat*); **Jerry Shirley**: drums (*Fastway*); **Pete Way**: bass (*Fastway*) (see also U.F.O.).

Discography: *Fastway* (Columbia, 1983); *All Fired Up* (Columbia, 1984); *Waiting for the Roar* (Columbia, 1986); *The World Waits for You* (CBS, 1986); *Trick or Treat* (Columbia, 1987); *On Target* (Enigma, 1988); *Bad Bad Girls* (Enigma, 1990); *Eat Dog Eat* (SPV, 2011)

FATES WARNING

YEARS ACTIVE: 1982–PRESENT

Although not as well known as Dream Theater and certainly not as popular as Queensrÿche, Fates Warning still holds its own as a band whose progressive tendencies have influenced many others (for example, Dream Theater and Queensrÿche). Following the lead of progressive heavy rock groups of the 1970s such as Rush, Fates Warning's music has been consistently sophisticated and challenging, with the possible exception of their solid but slightly more straightforward debut album. While it was the band's second release, *The Spectre Within*, that introduced the public to their more progressive tendencies, the 1986 follow-up, *Awaken the Guardian*, was the most intricate offering of their career. The album's style was hardcore progressive metal like nothing before, featuring hairpin time changes and Mahavishnu-intricate arrangements that would likely have caused a casual musician's head to explode, *Scanners*-style. Later albums found the band refining their technique, if pulling back somewhat on the aggressively radio-unfriendly approach of their past albums. This is not to say, however, that the band had in any sense wussed out when it came to doling out the complicated stuff. Their 1997 album, *A Pleasant Shade of Gray*, consisted wholly of one single forty-minute song, broken up into what could only be described as movements. It was considered by some fans to be a comeback, since for most of the 1990s the band had been writing material that, while still unusual, was not as uncompromisingly

Fates Warning brings the math-metal goods to dedicated fans. Left to right: Jim Matheos, Ray Alder, Joe DiBiase, and Frank Aresti.

impenetrable as their 1980s work (i.e., they were writing songs with verses and choruses as opposed to seemingly arbitrarily chosen nine-minute riffs). On their 2000 album, *Disconnected*, the band struck a balance between their progressive leanings and their more conventional urges. The band's last album was 2004's *FWX*, and the band's next release is due sometime in 2012. It doesn't have a name yet, but if the past is any indication, it will most likely offer a challenging and interesting listening experience.

Ray Alder: vocals (*No Exit* and later); **John Arch**: vocals (*Night on Bröcken* through *Awaken the Guardian*); **Victor Arduini**: guitars (*Night on Bröcken*, The *Spectre Within*); **Frank Aresti**: guitars (*Awaken the Guardian* through *Inside Out*); **Joe DiBiase**: bass (*Inside Out* and later); **Jason Keaser**: keyboards (*Still Life*); **Jim Matheos**: guitars; **Kevin Moore**: keyboards (*A Pleasant Shade of Gray*); **Joey Vera**: bass (*A Pleasant Shade of Gray* and later) (see also Armored Saint); **Bernie Versailles**: guitars (*Still Life*); **Steve Zimmerman**: drums (*Night on Bröcken* through *No Exit*); Mark **"Thunderchild" Zonder**: drums (*Perfect Symmetry* and later) (see also Warlord)

Discography: *Night on Bröcken* (Metal Blade, 1984); *The Spectre Within* (Metal Blade, 1985); *Awaken the Guardian* (Metal Blade, 1986); *No Exit* (Metal Blade, 1988); *Perfect Symmetry* (Metal Blade, 1989); *Parallels* (Metal Blade, 1991); *Inside Out* (Metal Blade, 1994); *A Pleasant Shade of Gray* (Metal Blade, 1997); *Still Life* (live double album) (Metal Blade, 1998); *Disconnected* (Metal Blade, 2000); *FWX* (Metal Blade, 2004);

FEAR FACTORY

YEARS ACTIVE: 1989–PRESENT

If you've ever wondered what it would sound like if Sepultura played covers of Einstürzende Neubauten tunes—and who hasn't?—then Fear Factory is for you. The Los Angeles–based band was arguably the first to fuse death metal and industrial styles, proving themselves to be several years ahead of their time in the process. Their debut album in 1992, *Soul of a New Machine*, blended the two styles seamlessly several years before this became common. Indeed, it was not until the band's fifth album, *Obsolete*, released in 1998, that it seemed like the rest of the alternative metal scene had finally caught up with them. It is worth noting, however, that this occurred a full five years after the band had already smashed yet another stylistic barrier by releasing the EP *Fear Is the Mindkiller*, which featured songs from their debut album as remixed by members of Front Line Assembly. While this kind of thing would become commonplace, it is important to remember that this was simply not done in the early 1990s.

On the set of Fear Factory's "Launch.com" video shoot in 2001, guitarist Dino Cazares hopes that the director gets it right on the first take.

The band did another album of remixes in 1997, and at this point the individual members started taking part in a number of side projects. Guitarist Dino Cazares (who also played in Nailbomb) and drummer Raymond Herrera took part in Brujeria, a band that was started largely as a joke; Brujeria's press kit stated that the members all had substantial criminal records and were part of a murderous Colombian drug-running cartel. Amazingly, people actually believed this and it was stated as fact in magazines and among fans who were surely deeply humiliated upon learning the less-sensational truth. Vocalist Burton C. Bell joined Black Sabbath bassist Geezer Butler's solo project, g/z/r, surely helping to play a hand in securing Fear Factory a slot on the 1999 Ozzfest tour. However, by the time Fear Factory released its 2001 album, *Digimortal*, Bell had decided that he had had his fill, and he packed his bags. The rest of the members followed suit shortly thereafter, and the band was considered dead and buried. However, after some time had passed, it emerged that the source of most of the problems that had caused the band's demise was a rift between Cazares and the rest of the group, particularly that no-good varmint Bell. The singer and Herrera put a new lineup of the band together that was conspicuously free of their old guitar player, and released 2004's *Archetype*. *Transgression* came just one year later. Fans who thought this meant that the band was now on an accelerated release schedule were no doubt disappointed by the five-year lag between *Transgression* and 2010's *Mechanize*, but the new album heralded the return of Cazares, so there you go. The band has announced that their next album will be released in 2012.

Burton C. Bell: vocals (*Soul of a New Machine* to *Archetype*, *Transgression* and later); **Dino Cazares**: guitars; **Raymond Herrera**: drums(*Soul of a New Machine* to *Transgression*); **Gene Hoglan**: drums (*Mechanize*); **Byron Stroud**: bass (*Archetype* and later); **Christian Olde Wolbers**: bass (*Soul of a New Machine* to *Transgression*)

Discography: *Soul of a New Machine* (Roadrunner, 1992); *Fear Is the Mind Killer* (Roadrunner, 1993); *Demanufacture* (Roadrunner, 1995); *Remanufacture* (remixes) (Roadrunner, 1997); *Obsolete* (Roadrunner, 1998); *Digimortal* (Roadrunner, 2001); *Concrete* (Roadrunner, 2002); *Archetype* (Liquid 8, 2004); *Live on Sunset Strip* (Calvin Records, 2005); *Transgression* (Roadrunner, 2005); *Mechanize* (Candlelight, 2010)

YEARS ACTIVE: 1982–PRESENT

Just as William Shatner can never go out in public without some dork asking him why he didn't pursue peaceful negotiations with the Romulans, Arizona thrash metal band Flotsam & Jetsam will likely forever be known as the group that Jason Newsted left so that he could join Metallica. In truth, the most significant strike the band had against them came in the form of their timing. They had been together for a few years already before they finally got a deal with Metal Blade Records, but by the time their debut album, *Doomsday for the Deceiver*, was released in 1986, the marketplace was hopelessly overcrowded with thrash bands—most of whom, Flotsam & Jetsam included, just sounded too much like Metallica to be noticed by that point.

Regardless of the fact that the band was, to a large extent, Newsted's baby (he wrote all of the lyrics as well as a significant portion of the music), the remaining members chose to soldier on after his departure in 1986. But despite the combination of high-quality recorded material and nonstop touring to back it up, the band simply failed to catch on. Maybe the aforementioned glut in the thrash metal marketplace held them back, or maybe it was simply the fact that they had to conduct their entire career in the extremely long, dark shadow that Metallica cast. Whatever the case, the band never graduated from also-ran status. However, absent a couple of hiatuses and mysterious absences, the

Flotsam and Jetsam rocks the Metropole Ruhr Festival in 2010.

band never broke up, and as recently as 2010 they had a new studio album called *The Cold*, whose cover looked like it had been stolen from Mortiis' drafting table.

Ed Carlson: guitars; **Michael Gilbert**: guitars (*Doomsday for the Deceiver* through *High*); **Troy Gregory**: bass (*No Place for Disgrace, When the Storm Comes Down*) (see also Prong); **Eric "A.K." Knutson**: vocals; **Craig Nielsen**: drums (*Unnatural Selection, My God* and later); **Jason Newsted**: bass (*Doomsday for the Deceiver*) (see also Metallica); **Mark T. Simpson**: guitars (*Unnatural Selection, My God* and later); **Kelly David Smith**: drums (*Doomsday for the Deceiver* through *High*); **Jason Ward**: bass (*Cuatro* and later)

Discography: *Doomsday for the Deceiver* (Metal Blade, 1986); *No Place for Disgrace* (Elektra, 1988); *When the Storm Comes Down* (MCA, 1990); *Cuatro* (MCA, 1992); *Drift* (MCA, 1995); *High* (Metal Blade, 1997); *Unnatural Selection* (Metal Blade, 1999); *My God* (Metal Blade, 2001); *Dreams of Death* (Crash Music, 2005); *The Cold* (Driven Music, 2010)

Years active: 1968–1973; 2004–2010

To this day, Flower Travellin' Band remains virtually unknown outside of its native Japan, despite creating some of the best and most original heavy rock of the 1970s. Originally formed as the Flowers as the 1960s drew to a close, the group was created by Yuya Uchida, a Japanese entertainer who was friendly with John Lennon and Frank Zappa. He dreamed of bringing the primordial sludge of such bands as Cream and Blue Cheer to the Land of the Rising Sun, and saw the Flowers as the ideal vehicle. The group released one album, *Challenge!* in 1969, but it garnered only limited notice. This was not because of the music, but because the band had made the bold choice to appear fully naked on the cover.

Uchida stepped out of the picture after the failure of *Challenge!*, but guitarist Hideki Ishima, bassist Jun Kowzuki, and drummer Joji Wada decided to carry on. They recruited afro-sporting singer Joe Yamanaka, changed their name to the Flower Travellin' Band and released *Anywhere* in 1970, which featured the band in the nude yet again on the cover, but this time astride motorcycles. Good visual, probably not so comfortable. The album consisted entirely of covers, such as "Black Sabbath" and "21st Century Schizoid Man," but the group decided that for the next album they would finally write their own tunes.

That album was 1971's *Satori*, which was split into five segments, simply titled "Satori, Pt. 1," "Satori, Pt. 2," and so on. However, the lack of creativity plaguing the song titles existed nowhere else on the album. As heavy as Black Sabbath and exotic as a Turkish opium den, the group created a sound with undeniable roots in heavy rock but sounded like little else out there. The album's peak comes in the form of "Satori, Pt. 3," a creepy, wordless meditation on a serpentine, Eastern-tinged riff that would be revisited on subsequent albums.

The Flower Travellin' Band would never again make an album as watertight as *Satori*, but the follow-ups certainly had their fair share of great material. *Made in Japan* features "Kamikaze," in which singer Joe Yamanaka predates the falsetto shrieks of Rob Halford by two years and those of King Diamond by a full decade. Sadly, the album did nothing for them in terms of making them more popular, and the half-live, half-studio follow-up, 1973's *Make Up*, fared poorly as well despite a 25-minute version of "Hiroshima" that gave Deep Purple at its most jamming a run for its money.

Flower Travellin' Band closed up shop after *Make Up*, but in 2007 they reunited and released the album *We Are Here* in 2008. It was their first album of new material in 35 years. Sadly, Yamanaka was diagnosed with cancer in 2010 and he died the following year.

FLOWER TRAVELLIN' BAND

SATORI

¥2,000

Remi Aso: vocals (*Challenge!*); **Hiroshi Chiba**: vocals (*Challenge!*); **Hideki Ishima**: guitar (*Anywhere* and later); **Takeshi Hasimoto**: bass (*Challenge!*); **Katsuhiko Kobayashi**: guitar (*Challenge!*); **Jun Kowzuki**: bass (*Anywhere; Satori* and later); **Nobuhiko Shinohara**: keyboards (*We Are Here*); **Joji Wada**: guitar; **Joe Yamanaka**: vocals (*Anywhere* and later)

Discography: *Challenge!* (Phoenix Records, 1969); *Anywhere* (Universal, 1970); *Satori* (Phoenix Records, 1971); *Made in Japan* (Phoenix Records, 1972); *Make Up* (Phoenix Records, 1973); *We Are Here* (Pony Canyon Records, 2008)

LITA FORD

Years active: 1976–1995; 2008–present

A significant portion of the human race only remembers Lita Ford from her 1988 "Kiss Me Deadly" video. The video featured her crawling around on the floor of some Los Angeles parking lot, perhaps in search of a lost contact lens, and clad in revealing outerwear that recalled a dominatrix who had recently purchased a Bedazzler. This is truly unfortunate, and not just because the video ends without resolving the issue of whether or not Ford would have to go back to LensCrafters in the morning. Ford was then and is now a serious, accomplished guitarist, and she can hold her own against any musician, be it man, woman, transgender, castrato, or eunuch.

She started her professional career at age sixteen, and that alone should indicate that she knows her way up and down a fretboard. She was then with the teenage girl group known as the Runaways, sharing the stage with none other than Joan Jett. When the band broke up, Ford resisted immediately embarking on a solo career, instead disappearing from the public eye for a few years. During this time, she took voice lessons and developed as a musician. Although her first couple of albums as an adult went nowhere, her third, 1988's *Lita*, was released at exactly the right moment. The album was a slick, polished pop-metal affair, featuring both "Kiss Me Deadly" and a duet with Ozzy Osbourne, "Close My Eyes Forever." While those attributes were probably enough to move product, it was her video for "Kiss Me Deadly" that inspired unwholesome thoughts in adolescent boys the world over, turning the album into a smash hit. Ford celebrated this milestone in her career by marrying W.A.S.P. guitarist Chris Holmes. Unfortunately, neither commercial success nor her marriage lasted for very long. Poor

sales of *Stiletto* and *Dangerous Curves* led to her major label departure in the early 1990s. After a four-year absence, *Black* was released, but the thing just didn't sell. It would be 14 years before the next Lita Ford album, *Wicked Wonderland*, was released, and there is currently a new album on the release schedule for 2012.

Discography: *Out for Blood* (Mercury, 1983); *Dancin' on the Edge* (Mercury, 1984); *Lita* (Dreamland, 1988); *Stiletto* (RCA, 1990); *Dangerous Curves* (RCA, 1991); *Black* (ZYX, 1995); *Greatest Hits Live!* (Dead Line, 2000); *Kiss Me Deadly* (BMG, 2001); *Wicked Wonderland* (JLRG, 2010)

While rubbing her inner thighs with a guitar, Lita Ford wonders why she is not viewed as a serious musician.

FREE

Free will forever be associated with the 1970 radio hit "All Right Now," a two-chord party anthem with lyrics about nothing. The band had written it as an afterthought so that they'd have at least one uptempo song in their set. But afterthought or not, it topped U.S. and U.K. singles charts upon its release. "All Right Now" remains the group's best-known song which is, weirdly, totally not representative of anything else in their catalog. At their best, Free trafficked in a plodding, heavy, bluesy thud that predated Led Zeppelin and belied the fact that when the group was founded the band members were all teenagers.

The group was founded in 1968 by guitarist Paul Kossoff and singer Paul Rodgers, whose Otis Redding growl was already setting him apart as one of the best voices in rock. The band was rounded out by drummer Simon Kirke and Bluesbreakers bassist Andy Fraser, who was then all of sixteen years old. They issued their debut, *Tons of Sobs*, that same year, and the slow, heavy grind of such tunes as "I'm a Mover" and "Moonshine" was by turns sludgy enough and morose enough that it should have been the product of musicians three times their age.

The self-titled follow-up was solid, consistent, and like the debut, nobody bought it. A pattern of disappointing sales had been set on their first two albums, and it would plague them for their entire existence. *Fire and Water* from 1970, which featured "All Right Now," would be the only exception, but listeners would have to wade through such sullen material as the title track and "Heavy Load" before they could get to the single upbeat tune closing out the album. The follow-up, *Highway*, was supposed to strike while the iron of their sole hit was hot, but it took a stylistic turn for the mellower and didn't sell well, despite inspired material like "The Stealer" and "Ride on a Pony." Demoralized and disappointed, the group broke up, and the album *Free Live!* was released posthumously.

The band re-formed in 1972 and made *Free at Last*. It didn't sell well, but it actually wasn't supposed to. Kossoff had been emotionally wrecked by the demise of Free and turned to heroin to fill the void. The drug quickly took hold of him, and Free re-formed in the naïve hope that somehow, with the band active again, the guitarist would be inspired to kick the black tar and return to his old self. Sadly and predictably, it didn't work out. Fraser left for good but the devastated band returned to the stu-

LEFT: Paul Kossoff of Free, who would not live to see his 26th birthday.

dio to record *Heartbreaker*. Although Kossoff's name appears on the album credits, he was in such poor health that he only played on half of it. The album was mostly realized by Kirke and Rodgers, but despite the skeleton crew involved, the album turned out to be one of

Fu Manchu tears it up onstage during one of its never-ending tours. Left to right: Bob Balch, Scott Hill, and Brad Davis.

FU MANCHU

YEARS ACTIVE: 1987–PRESENT

their best, and a worthy note to go out on. Kirke and Rodgers went on to form Bad Company, and Kossoff recorded a solo album, *Back Street Crawler*. The drugs had an unrelenting hold on him at this point, and his health quickly deteriorated. Kossoff died of a heart attack in 1976 at the age of twenty-five.

John "Rabbit" Bundrick: vocals, keyboards (*Heartbreaker*); **Andy Fraser**: bass (*Tons of Sobs* through *Free at Last*); **Simon Kirke**: drums; **Paul Kossoff**: guitars; **Paul Rodgers**: vocals; **Tetsu Yamauchi**: bass (*Heartbreaker*)

Discography: *Tons of Sobs* (Island, 1968); *Free* (Island, 1969); *Fire and Water* (A&M, 1970); *Highway* (Island, 1971); *Heartbreaker* (Island, 1973); *Free & Easy Rough & Ready* (Island, 1976)

If Kyuss was the Black Sabbath of stoner rock, then Fu Manchu is certainly its Ted Nugent. Far more straightforward and rock'n'roll–oriented than their compatriots in psychedelic fuzz, Fu Manchu has for the most part focused on an aggressive, song-oriented sound. They are also notable for their influence on stoner rock's visual aesthetic, as the band's album artwork was among the first to feature muscle cars, gaseous astronomical entities, and that goofy *Battlestar Galactica* typeface. While it could be argued that the band is merely trafficking in an oversimplified imitation of 1970s pop culture, this has had exactly no effect whatsoever on the profound influence they have exerted over other stoner rock bands, many of whom have made their careers out of the verbatim regurgitation of these attributes.

Naturally, Fu Manchu has not been without its share of turmoil, as almost every band member, except for founding guitarist and vocalist Scott Hill, has left the group at one time or another (in fact, the stoner rock trio Nebula consists entirely of former Fu Manchu members). But as the band's continued tours and album releases prove, this hasn't really hurt them. Fu Manchu has put in some high-profile appearances as an opening act, supporting mainstream metal bands like White Zombie and Marilyn Manson, and they have continued to release new material at a consistent pace. Their most recent album was 2009's *Signs of Infinite Power*.

Mark Abshire: bass (*No One Rides for Free*) (see also Nebula); **Bob Balch**: guitars (*The Action Is Go* and later); **Brant Bjork**: drums (*The Action Is Go* and later) (see also Kyuss); **Brad Davis**: bass (*Daredevil* and later); **Scott Hill**: vocals/guitars (*Start the Machine* and later); **Eddie Glass**: guitars (*No One Rides for Free* through *In Search Of . . .*) (see also Nebula); **Scott Reeder**: drums (*Start the Machine* and later); **Ruben Romano**: drums (*No One Rides for Free* through *In Search Of . . .*) (see also Nebula)

Discography: *No One Rides for Free* (Bong Load, 1994); *Daredevil* (Bong Load, 1995); *In Search Of . . .* (Mammoth, 1996); *The Action Is Go* (Mammoth, 1997); *Return to Earth '91–'93* (Elastic, 1998); *Godzilla's Eatin' Dust* (Man's Ruin, 1999); *King of the Road* (Mammoth, 2000); *California Crossing* (Mammoth, 2001); *Go For It! Live* (Steamhammer, 2003); *Start the Machine* (DRT, 2004); *We Must Obey* (Century Media, 2007); *Signs of Infinite Power* (Century Media, 2009)

GIRLSCHOOL

Years active: 1978–present

The Runaways may have been the first all-female band to make inroads with the exclusively male heavy metal audience, but South London's Girlschool rocked harder and heavier. The group started in 1975 around singer and guitarist Kim McAuliffe and bassist Enid Williams under the name Painted Lady. After multiple lineup shuffles, one of which saw Kathy Valentine of the Go-Go's join their ranks, they drafted drummer Denise Dufort and guitarist Kelly Johnson in 1978. Girlschool was born, and at the perfect time. The New Wave of British Heavy Metal was gaining steam, and it created the ideal environment in which to release their debut single, "Take It All Away." The single gained them the attention of Motörhead's manager, Doug Smith, and Motörhead's label, Bronze, both of whom took Girlschool onto their rosters. Their debut, *Demolition*, was released in 1980 and made the U.K. top 30. The follow-up, *Hit & Run*, came one year later and sold even better, this time making the U.K. top 10. They even had time to record the *St. Valentine's Day Massacre* EP, a

MAGAZINES

The advent of the Internet has made it possible for any fool with a computer and a modem to create his or her own e-zine, most of which possess a visual sense and content quality that are beneath criticism. Worse yet, this medium cannot be read on the toilet. As such, there is still plenty of demand for good old-fashioned print publications. These magazines rely on advertisers and need to be purchased in retail outlets, thereby raising the standard as well as the breadth of information they must convey—a magazine that is limited to covering industrial metal will reach only a limited audience, and consequently it will die a quick death in the marketplace. It logically follows that even underground magazines like *Terrorizer* and *Unrestrained!* will have surprisingly high production values and feature a cornucopia of information on a variety of different metal genres. However, a few magazines have managed to stand out, so here's a short list of those that have satisfied the curiosity and the bathroom needs of metalheads.

BRAVE WORDS AND BLOODY KNUCKLES

A relatively new publication, this one focuses mainly on underground and extreme metal and devotes an unusually large amount of print space to independent bands, many of whom are reviewed in the "Unearthing the Unsigned" section. Each issue also contains a CD, *Knuckle Tracks*, which any band with $400 can appear on, thereby creating compilations that could, hypothetically, kick off with a track by Pantera, followed by one from Sons of Otis, then one by Slayer, then one by Borgo Pass, and so forth, affording unknown bands a level of visibility they would otherwise be unable to achieve.

KERRANG!

This is the United Kingdom's best-known metal magazine. It's been in business for many years, and rather than focus on one specific genre or category of metal, the magazine is jam-packed with news, articles, and information about bands from every conceivable level of notoriety. It would not be unusual to see King's X, Neurosis, and Rammstein, for example, sharing a single news column. The magazine is, hands-down, one of the most voluminous ever devoted to the subject of heavy metal, and one issue can thoroughly entertain you for the entire month before the next one arrives in your mailbox.

METAL EDGE

Metal Edge is a bit more on the "vanilla" side than some people might like, but it's an informative and entertaining read nonetheless. The magazine mainly covers mainstream metal acts du jour, such as Slipknot and Marilyn Manson, but it still devotes relatively generous amounts of ink to underground and unsigned bands. As a bonus, it features a classified ad section that, apart from the usual "gtr sks drms, OH, influs: Bizkit, Korn" fare, also possesses romantic entreaties from mullet-adorned men who are looking for a good time with the Lita Ford or Doro Pesch of their dreams.

METAL MANIACS

Metal Maniacs is one of the most successful American heavy metal magazines to focus primarily on the underground scene. A current issue devoted much of its print space to Darkthrone, Cathedral, and Armored Saint, with bands like Dio and Cannibal Corpse comprising the bulk of its mainstream coverage. Suited for readers who want in-depth access to musicians via question-and-answer interviews and tour diaries, this magazine will not disappoint.

collaboration with Motörhead that included a Motörhead cover of Girlschool's "Emergency" and a Girlschool cover of Motörhead's "Bomber."

Unfortunately, the good times were short-lived. Williams gave up her bass duties in 1982, and 1983's more pop-sounding *Play Dirty* became their first album to miss the U.K. top 50 entirely. Johnson was next to quit the band, and Bronze dropped them, although they were on such shaky financial ground that it was probably for the best. Mercury Records picked them up, but it was a curse in disguise. The label pushed them in an even more commercial direction, in the hope that they could compete with the latest incarnation of Heart. This effort produced 1985's *Running Wild*, an album whose commercial chances were hobbled from the outset by the label's decision to release it only in the United States. For once, the label, the music press and the band itself were all in agreement, and they all characterized the album as rubbish, which is British for dogshit.

Mercury dropped them, but Motörhead was there yet again to pick them up from the pavement onto which they had fallen. The lads of Motörhead helped the maidens in distress get a contract with their own label, GWR Records, making them labelmates for the second time. Girlschool's 1986 album, *Nightmare at Maple Cross*, marked a return to a harder sound and it received some good reviews as a result. Unfortunately, Girlschool never again recaptured their original mojo, perhaps in part because the New Wave of British Heavy Metal movement with which they had been so heavily identified was over.

The group broke up after 1988's *Take a Bite*. McAuliffe, Williams, and Dufort reunited in 1991 as Strange Girls, and there was a proper Girlschool reunion in 1992, complete with a new self-titled album. Kelly Johnson returned to the fold the following year, and remained in the band for seven years, a tenure longer than her original stint with the group. Girlschool have remained in session (ha ha) ever since,

LEFT: Girlschool take in the local color in New York City in 1982. ABOVE: Girlschool in New York City in 1984.

although the band's level of activity has waxed and waned. Johnson died of spinal cancer in 2007 at the age of 49, and the following year the group released *Legacy*, which was both a tribute to their fallen bandmate and a celebration of the fact that one of the original hard-rocking girl groups still existed after thirty years of trial and tribulation.

Jackie Bodimead: vocals, keyboards (*Running Wild*); **Cris Bonacci**: guitar (*Nightmare at Maple Cross* through *Girlschool*); **Jackie Carrera**: bass (*Girlschool*); **Denise Dufort**: drums; **Jackie Chambers**: guitar (*21st Anniversary: Not That Innocent* and later); **Kelly Johnson**: guitar, vocals (*Demolition* through *Play Dirty*; *21st Anniversary: Not That Innocent*; *Legacy*); **Tracey Lamb**: bass (*Take a Bite*; *21st Anniversary: Not That Innocent*); **Kim McAuliffe**: guitar, vocals; **Ghislaine 'Gil' Weston**: bass (*Running Wild* through *Nightmare at Maple Cross*); **Enid Williams**: bass, vocals (*Demolition*)

Discography: *Demolition* (Bronze, 1980); *Hit & Run* (Bronze, 1981); *Screaming Blue Murder* (Bronze, 1982); *Running Wild* (Mercury, 1985); *Nightmare at Maple Cross* (GWR, 1986); *Take a Bite* (GWR, 1988); *21st Anniversary: Not That Innocent* (Communique, 2002); *Legacy* (Wacken, 2008); *Hit and Run Revisited* (Wacken, 2011)

YEARS ACTIVE: 1996–2002; 2004–PRESENT

Although Goatsnake's entire recorded output could be heard in the amount of time it takes to watch a movie, what material the band did release before their 2002 breakup is some of the higher-quality music to come out of the stoner doom movement of the late 1990s. The

band was a supergroup of sorts, consisting of the Obsessed's former rhythm section (bassist Guy Pinhas and drummer Greg Rogers), former Engine Kid guitarist Greg Anderson, and singer Pete Stahl, who had been a member of Wool and, prior to that, 1980s hardcore legend Scream (not to be confused with the Scream, a commercial metal band led by Mötley Crüe's John Corabi). The members of the band had played professionally for several years, so by the time they released their first album as *Goatsnake, I*, in 1999, it was so tight and focused that you might have thought it was their fifth.

Goatsnake also distinguished itself from the pack by virtue of its high degree of musicianship, particularly on the part of Stahl, whose smooth, soulful vocals contrasted perfectly with the extreme, plodding, bottom-heavy guitar sound. Unfortunately, Goatsnake lasted only long enough to release two albums and one EP, and when the band broke up, it was with little fanfare or explanation. Bassist Pinhas went on to San Francisco's Acid King, Stahl joined Earthlings?, and Anderson had his hands full with his record label, Southern Lord, as well as with various massively downtuned, doom- and drone-centric side projects—Sunn O))), Teeth of Lions Rule the Divine—whose sole raison d'être seemed to be to create frequencies so extremely subsonic that they would cause anyone in their vicinity to soil their undergarments. Anderson and Stahl reunited to record the *Trampled Under Hoof* EP in 2004.

Greg Anderson: guitars; **G. Stuart Dahlquist**: bass (*Dog Days, Flower of Disease*); **Guy Pinhas**: bass (*I*) (see also Acid King, the Obsessed); **Greg Rogers**: drums (see also the Obsessed); **Pete Stahl**: vocals/guitars

Discography: *I* (Man's Ruin, 1999); *Dog Days* (Southern Lord, 2000); *Flower of Disease* (Man's Ruin, 2000); *Trampled Under Hoof* (Southern Lord, 2004)

GODFLESH

Years active: 1988–2002; 2009

Godflesh was yet another in a long line of British bands that was formed in the late 1980s by Napalm Death escapees and sounded nothing like that group whatsoever. Guitarist Justin Broadrick, who had also played drums for Head of David, took the down-tuned guitars of grindcore and slowed them to seemingly interminable tempos that were so stunted it seemed as though he was trying to simultaneously undo and atone for the ultrafast gait of his previous ensemble. Whether by necessity, accident, or intent, Broadrick and cofounding member and bassist Ben Green used a drum machine, as opposed to a real, live human percussionist, and the resulting sound was impenetrably mechanical, rigid, and cold, intensifying the already hostile style of the band. The band added tape loops and various other electronic embellishments to the mix, and voilà! Industrial grind-core was born.

Godflesh continued to experiment with its sound throughout its existence, releasing albums that were either emphatically embraced or unconditionally despised by fans and critics. For example, *Love and Hate in Dub*—an album consisting entirely of dub remixes of songs from the band's 1996 album, *Songs of Love and Hate*—was aptly named, as it garnered both forms of extreme emotion in equal measure. In 2001, the same year that Godflesh released the compilation *In All Languages*, Green left the band. Although Broadrick replaced Green, after the release of *Hymns* the band broke up in early 2002. They reunited in 2009 for some live appearances, and although they have mentioned the possibility of recording a new studio album, nothing definite has been announced yet. Whatever happens, the band will remain widely acknowledged and highly respected for their influence on the fusion of metal and industrial musical styles.

Justin Broadrick: guitars/vocals (see also Napalm Death); **Ben Green**: bass; **Robert Hampson**: guitars (*Pure*); **Brian Mantia**: drums (*Songs of Love and Hate*);

Justin Broadrick, of Godflesh, reenacts his favorite scene from *Carrie*.

Paul Neville: guitars (*Streetcleaner, Slavestate*); **Ted Parsons**: drums (see also Prong)

Discography: *Streetcleaner* (Earache, 1989); *Pure* (Earache, 1992); *Selfless* (Earache, 1994); *Us and Them* (Earache, 1999); *Hymns* (Koch, 2001); *In All Languages* (Earache, 2001)

GRAND FUNK RAILROAD

Years active: 1988–2002; 2009

For as long as music has been a commercially available commodity, there has been a divide between the people who buy it and the people who review it. Just like contemporaries Black Sabbath and Led Zeppelin, Grand Funk Railroad experienced this rift firsthand. The band also had become one of the most popular groups of the early 1970s, almost overnight, while critics of the day met them with a degree of hatred normally reserved for convicted pedophiles. Thanks to the miracle of revisionist history, however, these bands now regularly receive their due, very often in the same publications that lambasted them during the "me decade."

Grand Funk Railroad came from blue-collar Flint, Michigan (the band's name is based on the town's Grand Trunk Railroad). Flint's glamour and wealth of opportunity are vividly depicted in Michael Moore's excellent documentary *Roger and Me*. The band's straightforward rock hit their disaffected-working-class target audience

This is where most rock critics wanted to see Grand Funk Railroad end up. Clockwise from top left: Mel Schacher, Mark Farner, Craig Frost, and Don Brewer.

with bull's-eye precision. In four years' time, an unprecedented eight of their albums went platinum, including *Closer to Home*, considered by many to be the band's finest. In 1972 they expanded their roster with the addition of keyboard player Craig Frost, at the same time shortening their name to simply Grand Funk. This change coincided with the release of the band's highest-selling and best-known single, "We're an American Band."

After such amazing commercial success, there was, of course, nowhere to go but down. The band's audience began to lose interest in Grand Funk as the power-trio (or in this case, power-quartet) era passed and musical tastes shifted. At the same time, the creatively exhausted and tour-weary band began to churn out uninspired albums whose only high points were cover versions of other people's songs, such as "The Loco-Motion." The band members stuck it out for one more album, the Frank Zappa–produced *Good Singin', Good Playin'*, and then went their separate ways, with the exception of two indifferently received reunion albums released in the early 1980s.

However, once the Reagan decade came to a close, there was renewed interest in the much-maligned music of the 1970s, and Grand Funk benefited greatly from the resurgence. Interest in the band remains strong to this day, and curious record buyers, many of whom grew up well after *Rolling Stone* told them not to like the band, can find Grand Funk's output very well documented on *Thirty Years of Funk: 1969–1999*, an extremely satisfying, though sadly out of print, three-disc set.

Dennis Bellinger: bass (*Grand Funk Lives, What's Funk?*); **Don Brewer**: drums; **Mark Farner**: guitar/vocals; **Craig Frost**: keyboards; **Mel Schacher**: bass (*On Time* through *Good Singin', Good Playin'; Bosnia*)

Discography: *On Time* (Capitol, 1969); *Grand Funk* (Capitol, 1970); *Live Album* (Capitol, 1970); *Closer to Home* (Capitol, 1970); *E Pluribus Funk* (Capitol, 1971); *Survival* (Capitol, 1971); *Phoenix* (Capitol, 1972); *We're an American Band* (Collector's, 1973); *Shinin' On* (Capitol, 1974); *All the Girls in the World Beware!!* (Capitol, 1974); *Caught in the Act* (Capitol, 1975); *Born to Die* (Capitol, 1976); *Good Singin', Good Playin'* (EMI, 1976); *Grand Funk Lives* (Full Moon, 1981); *What's Funk?* (Full Moon, 1983); *Bosnia* (Capitol, 1997); *Thirty Years of Funk: 1969–1999* (Capitol, 1999); *Live: The 1971 Tour* (Capitol, 2002)

GRANICUS

YEARS ACTIVE: 1973; 2010

Although Granicus originally released only one album, unknown except to the most hardcore of 1970s heavy metal collector geeks (and let's not forget the band members' parents), the group warrants inclusion in this volume, if only because that lone album absolutely rules and deserves to be documented in a book, dag nabbit. They hailed from Cleveland but moved to New York City in the hopes of securing a record deal without having to slog through years of deeply demoralizing Ohio nightclubbery. As it turned out, the band got signed after their first show. But the good news ended right there, and Granicus took its place alongside Dust, Bloodrock, and who knows how many other talented and highly deserving American bands of the era that never got their piece of the pie.

The band members (who took their name from a river in Turkey where the army of Alexander the Great defeated the Persians) based their utilitarian hard rock sound on the dual guitars of Wayne Anderson and Vietnam vet Al Pinell, as well as the completely out-of-hand vocals of Woody Leffel, who sang like an unholy hybrid of Deep Purple's Ian Gillan and Rush's Geddy Lee. Granicus' musical stylings are well represented on its self-titled debut/swan song, although the band members were reportedly very unhappy with what they perceived to be a substandard final mix. This disappointment was compounded by several other factors, among them RCA's inability to properly promote the album, personal differences among the band members, and a seemingly terminal lack of money. It all eventually conspired to make the Granicus story a short one, and the band broke up in 1973, the same year in which they had, it seemed, struck gold. Fortunately, they made enough of an impression in the short time that they were around to keep the band's name alive (or at least on life support), and in 1998 their sole album was reissued on the Free Records label. The reissue must have made enough noise to convince the Granicus boys to give it another go, and in 2010, they released a second album, *Thieves, Liars and Traitors*, on their own label. Buy two copies.

Wayne Anderson: guitar; **Joe Battaglia**: drums; **Dale Bedford**: bass; **Woody Leffel**: vocals; **Al Pinell**: guitar

Discography: *Granicus* (RCA, 1973); *Thieves, Liars and Traitors* (CDBY, 2010)

GRAVE DIGGER

YEARS ACTIVE: 1980–1986; 1993–PRESENT

Grave Digger has the neat-o distinction of being one of the first bands to be signed to Noise Records, which would later be called home by such ammunition-belt sporters as Voivod and Celtic Frost. However, while its labelmates were riding the initial waves of thrash metal in the early 1980s, Germany's Grave Digger stayed true to its traditional metal sound, and the three studio albums that the band released for the label would all be described as power metal had they been released today. Of course, had they been released today, they would never have possessed the wretched production values with which they were saddled, but that's of no consequence. Noise Records' releases in the 1980s were not known for their sterling production values—one spin of Voivod's *Rrrooooaaarrr!* will demonstrate this with stunning clarity. At any rate, for no apparent reason, in 1986 the band suddenly decided that they must immediately and forthwith shorten their name to simply Digger. Then they broke up. Seven years later, they got back together, and today they can be found playing alongside the power metal progenitors who were their contemporaries, such as Helloween and the extremely goofy Running Wild, who at one point boasted not just one, but two members of Grave Digger. Their most recent album was 2010's *The Clans Will Rise Again*, but who gives a shit about that when there's the band's 2003 album, *Rheingold*, which is based on the works of Richard Wagner?

Stefan Arnold: drums (*Tunes of War* and later); **Jens Becker**: bass (*Knights of the Cross* and later) (see also Running Wild); **Chris Boltendahl**: vocals; **C. F. Brank**: bass (*War Games*); **Albert Eckardt**: drums (*Heavy Metal Breakdown* through *War Games*); **Tomi Gottlich**: bass (*Symphony of Death* through *Tunes of War*); **Thilo Hermann**: guitar (*Ballads of a Hangman*); **H. P. Katzenburg**: keyboards (*Excalibur* and later); **Willi Lackmann**: bass (*Heavy Metal Breakdown, Witch Hunter*); **Uwe Lulis**: guitars (*Symphony of Death* through *Excalibur*); **Peter Masson**: guitars (*Heavy Metal Breakdown* through *War Games*); **Jörg Michael**: drums (*The Reaper*) (see also Running Wild); **Alex Ritt**: guitar (*The Clans Will Rise Again*); **Manni Schmidt**: guitars (*The Grave Digger*); **Frank Ullrich**: drums (*Heart of Darkness*)

Discography: *Heavy Metal Breakdown* (Noise, 1984); *Witch Hunter* (Noise, 1985); *War Games* (Noise, 1986); *Symphony of Death* (GUN, 1993); *The Reaper* (GUN, 1993); *Best of the Eighties* (compilation) (Noise, 1994); *Heart of Darkness* (GUN, 1995); *Tunes of War* (GUN, 1996); *The Dark of the Sun* (GUN, 1997); *Knights of the Cross* (GUN, 1998); *Excalibur* (GUN, 1999); *The Grave Digger* (Nuclear Blast, 2001); *Rheingold* (Nuclear Blast, 2003); *The Last Supper* (Nuclear Blast, 2005); *Liberty or Death* (Locomotive, 2007); *Ballads of a Hangman* (Napalm, 2009); *The Clans Will Rise Again* (Napalm, 2010)

GRIM REAPER

YEARS ACTIVE: 1979–1988; 2006–PRESENT

Grim Reaper was yet another of the New Wave of British Heavy Metal bands, although it failed to attract as much attention as many of its counterparts. This is quite possibly because Metallica never got around to covering any of the band's songs. Anyway, Grim Reaper released two by-the-numbers Euro-metal albums for the dinky Ebony Records label, which mysteriously managed to attract the attention of RCA Records. RCA had the privilege of releasing what turned out to be the band's last studio album, *Rock You to Hell*, which is perhaps not surprising, given that label's less-than-stellar track record when it came to promoting metal bands.
The band broke up in 1987,

Grim Reaper, in 1987, beckons you to Hell. Left to right: Lee Harris, Nick Bowcott, Steve Grimmett, and Dave Wanklin.

but they managed to achieve, as a bonus, an additional ten seconds of fame when their "See You in Hell" video appeared on MTV's vehicle for those animated arbiters of musical taste, Beavis & Butt-Head.

Nick Bowcott: guitars; **Steve Grimmett**: vocals; **Lee Harris**: drums (*Rock You to Hell*); **Mark Simon**: drums (*See You in Hell, Fear No Evil*); **Dave Wanklin**: bass

Discography: *See You in Hell* (Ebony, 1984); *Fear No Evil* (Ebony, 1985); *Rock You to Hell* (RCA, 1987);

YEARS ACTIVE: 1985–PRESENT

In the summer of 1988 after much chart-topping success, it seemed like just about everybody on earth was singing the praises of Guns N' Roses, regardless of their musical tastes. The group's debut album, *Appetite for Destruction*, seemed to sell on the basis of the band members' offstage antics (in particular, lead singer Axl Rose's) as much as on the strength of its seemingly bottomless wellspring of hits ("Sweet Child O' Mine," "Mr. Brownstone," "Welcome to the Jungle," "Paradise City," and so on). The band also owed a great deal of their success to the fact that they simply represented an image and an attitude that was diametrically opposed to the time period in which they existed; with few exceptions, popular music in 1988 was very slick, very glossy, and very overproduced. Guns N' Roses' raw rock'n'roll style provided exactly the steaming puddle of vomit that the spotless white rug of popular music required. And just to satisfy the public's lust for scandal, some of the band members had well-publicized drug problems.

The band members found themselves embroiled in controversy right from day one. The original cover of *Appetite for Destruction* depicted a freshly raped woman with her panties at her ankles. In the face of heavy criticism and threats of censorship, the cover, designed by artist Robert Williams, was quickly withdrawn and replaced, but the damage was done, and it set the tone for the rest of the band's career. In 1989, *G N' R Lies* was released, an EP featuring four slices of sensitive acoustic balladry, including the hit single "Patience." The song that got all the attention, though, was "One in a Million," and not because of the James Taylor–esque tenderness of the acoustic guitars. No, it was most likely due to Rose's incendiary lyrics, which referred to members of the African-American community with a term beginning with the letter "N" that is not their preferred nomenclature, at least not coming from a white guy. The song featured other, equally impolite statements regarding immigrants, as well as individuals who engage in sexual practices with members of their own gender. When asked by the press to justify his statements, Rose was only too happy to expound on his prejudicial views pertaining to these particular demographics. As a result, the song brought the band a degree of controversy and negative publicity that was beyond the reach of even David Geffen's substantial coffers.

By the time the band began recording *Use Your Illusion I* and *Use Your Illusion II*, there had been some blood lost, and it would not be for the last time. Drummer Steven Adler

During the *Appetite for Destruction* heyday, the members of Guns N' Roses look fairly content and smug backstage. Left to right: Slash, Duff McKagan, Axl Rose, Izzy Stradlin, and Steven Adler.

was the first to go. He was fired because of alleged drug problems, which one assumes must have been pretty extreme for anyone in the band to even notice. He was replaced by former Cult drummer Matt Sorum, and the two albums were recorded without further personnel-related incident. However, before the new albums were released, guitarist and primary songwriter Izzy Stradlin left the group, reportedly to pursue a solo career, although it was rumored that he and Rose were regularly butting heads over the band's artistic direction. He was replaced by Gilby Clarke, and finally, the albums saw the light of day in the fall of 1991. The original release date had actually been slated for 1990, but delay after delay kept the albums from getting out the door. By the time they were finally released, public demand was at a stage rivaling that of a prison riot. As expected, the albums sold like crazy, but this might not have been the case had their release been postponed any further; close behind on the calendar was Nirvana's *Nevermind*.

Perhaps feeling the pressure to follow up four very successful albums, Guns N' Roses began to eat itself alive. By 1994, an imminent breakup was heavily rumored, with Rose and guitarist Slash apparently in a state of perpetual conflict. Quite clearly fed up with Rose's histrionics and the band's seemingly endless state of hiatus, the guitarist went on to form Slash's Snakepit, intended as a side project whose main function was to keep his fingers limber while his main gig figured out what the hell its direction was supposed to be. However, it was announced in 1996 that Slash was officially no longer a member of Guns N' Roses, and Slash's Snakepit turned into an official full-time job. One would have expected Guns N' Roses to dissolve at this point, as Slash was not only an integral part of it and a highly accomplished guitarist but also one of its most recognizable visual trademarks, he of the top hat and the perpetual cigarette dangling from his lips. It is not an exaggeration to say that, in many people's minds, Guns N' Roses without Slash was like the Rolling Stones without Keith Richards—sacrilege.

The band did not officially break up at this point, but it entered a state of limbo made conspicuous mostly by the group's absence. During this time, Rose almost completely retreated from the public eye, becoming more or less the Howard Hughes of Sunset Strip hair metal. Producing no music whatsoever, Rose perpetuated his celebrity by turning into a raving nutcase whose band mates changed from hour to hour. He was rumored to have consorted with a veritable whirligig of musicians too numerous to mention in a book not rivaling the length of a James Michener novel. Yet, in 1999, with Rose now the only remaining original member of the band, Guns N' Roses contributed a song to the soundtrack of the Arnold Schwarzenegger movie *End of Days*. This was followed by two concerts the following year, which were supposedly warm-ups for a full-scale tour to support a new album called *Chinese Democracy*. However, what actually followed was a sprinkling of sightings, most notably a New Year's Eve 2001 concert and a five-minute performance at the 2002 MTV Video Music Awards. By the end of 2002, Rose had settled down with Tommy Stinson of the Replacements, Robin Finck of Nine Inch Nails, and the unclassifiable guitarist Buckethead (who, with the possible exception of Bronski Beat's Jimmy Somerville, is absolutely the last person one would ever expect to see sharing an album credit with Rose). However, Guns N' Roses canceled their tour late that year and never released the new album.

What followed was a six-year comedy of errors in which band members quit, concerts were cancelled, rumors were spread, songs leaked onto the internet, and Rose seemed

When this photo was taken in 1993, who could have guessed that Guns N' Roses singer Axl Rose (left) and guitarist Slash would part ways within a year.

increasingly like someone who had long since ceased to be relevant. His sole interesting attribute was that he was a full-on hot mess who was likely to die penniless and insane, and would never release the goddamn album. However, naysayers were shocked when *Chinese Democracy*, the first new Guns N' Roses product in 15 years, appeared on new release schedules with a street date of November 23, 2008. With that kind of gestation time, there was no possible way the album could live up to what were now sky-high expectations, and as a matter of fact, it didn't. The album sold one million copies, which would have been great for almost anyone else, but constituted an "Oh, the humanity" moment for Rose and especially for Geffen Records, which the *New York Times* estimated had sunk $13 million just into its production.

But was the thing any good? The consensus on this seemed to be an emphatic "meh." Alexis Petridis of *The Guardian* summed up what a lot of fans were probably thinking when he wrote "Bloody hell, is that *the* best you could come up with? It's not like you haven't had time to think about it."

It's impossible to say what's next for Guns N' Roses. Although it's hard to look at *Chinese Democracy* as anything but a gigantic fuckup of comical proportions, the band remains a very popular concert attraction, and by every account, when they launch into "Welcome to the Jungle" or "Paradise City," all is forgiven, and it's like the last 20 years never took place. Naturally, if Rose spends another 15 years on the next album, every bit of good will that the band has earned back will permanently disappear. However, it's a fact that the band has made some timeless music that is beloved to this day, and whatever the future holds, that will never go away.

Steven Adler: drums (*Appetite for Destruction*, *G N' R Lies*); **Buckethead**: guitar (*Chinese Democracy*); **Gilby Clarke**: guitar (*The Spaghetti Incident?*);**Frank Ferrer**: drums (*Chinese Democracy*); **Richard Fortus**: guitar (*Chinese Democracy*); **Duff "Rose" McKagan**: bass; **Chris Pitman**: keyboards (*Chinese Democracy*); **Dizzy Reed**: keyboards (*Use Your Illusion I* and later); **Axl Rose**: vocals; **Slash**: guitar; **Matt Sorum**: drums (*Use Your Illusion I* through *The Spaghetti Incident?*); **Izzy Stradlin**: guitar (*Appetite for Destruction* through *Use Your Illusion II*); **Ron "Bumblefoot" Thal**: guitar (*Chinese Democracy*)

Discography: *Appetite for Destruction* (Geffen, 1987); *G N' R Lies* (Geffen, 1989); *Use Your Illusion I* (Geffen, 1991); *Use Your Illusion II* (Geffen, 1991); *The Spaghetti Incident?* (Geffen, 1993); *Live Era: '87–'93* (Geffen, 1999); *Chinese Democracy* (Geffen, 2008)

YEARS ACTIVE: 1984–PRESENT

GWAR would not be nearly as well known as it is today had its members relied solely on their music to bring them attention. They owe their success to an elaborately conceived stage show, which takes the theatrics of KISS and dumbs them down. Realizing the futility of trying to fashion larger explosions or make the flaming stage rise higher into the stratosphere, they opted instead for cartoonishly violent papier-mâché theatrics that recall late-1960s Japanese Godzilla movies (for the uninitiated, these are the ones that featured a guy in a rubber suit stepping on miniature tanks). GWAR's show also features copious amounts of violent dismemberments and executions, each of which provides the opportunity for the first fifteen or so rows of the audience to be hosed down with fake blood, as though Gallagher had grown weary of smashing watermelons and instead began using decapitated human heads. Needless to say, it's probably the best live show you'll ever see, discounting of course the possibility that you will take three hits of acid and catch the Osmond Brothers in Branson, Missouri.

The band members all claim to be warriors from an extraterrestrial world whose earthly mission to conquer mankind began upon their landing in Antarctica. As such, they have names that would do Arthur C. Clarke proud, such as Jizmak Da Gusha and Flattus Maximus. There are also loincloth-garbed cavemen ambling, simian-like, up and down the sides of the stage, occasionally coming to the band's aid to do their bidding and assist in a mock execution. Because of the fantastic scale of such a show and the elaborate artistry it involved, it should come as no surprise that, prior to their Antarctic reincarnation, the band members were all art students at a college in Virginia. What is surprising, however, is that GWAR was not conceived as an elaborate joke to enable the procrastination of a term paper on abstract expressionism. Rather, the band was an experiment in marketing strategies for which several

Danyell "Slymenstra Hymen" Stampe directs a slavering minion to his fate.

students hoped to gain course credit. Needless to say, the band is just about the best-marketed underground metal group in existence, so you could say that the strategy paid off, whether or not they got course credit.

It might be argued by some that GWAR has in effect won the battle but lost the war, to the extent that a person could probably attend ten consecutive concerts and still have no idea what any of the songs are called. This may sound like an indictment of their music (which is, admittedly, pretty standard, straightforward metal), but the truth is that, like KISS, who came before them, GWAR's live shows are really the main attraction, and also like KISS, the band members are usually the first to admit this. As if to demonstrate the forgettable nature of their generic music, the band was nominated for a Grammy in 1993. They did not win the highly coveted golden statuette, but we can all close our eyes and collectively imagine a tearful

Beefcake the Mighty thanking his parents, his producer, and God in his acceptance speech, while Celine Dion, Brooks & Dunn, and everyone else in the first twenty rows are hosed down with fake blood.

Mike "Beefcake the Mighty" Bishop: bass (*Hell-O* through *This Toilet Earth*); **Dave "Oderous Urungus" Brockie**: vocals; **Mike "Balsac the Jaws of Death" Derks**: guitars (*Scumdogs of the Universe* and later); **Steve Douglas**: guitars (*Hell-O*); **Todd "Beefcake the Mighty" Evans**: bass (*War Party*); **Peter "Flattus Maximus" Lee**: guitars (*The Road Behind* and later); **Rob Mosby**: drums (*Hell-O*); **Casey Orr**: bass (*RagNaRok* and later); **Brad "Jizmak Da Gusha" Roberts**: drums (*Scumdogs of the Universe* and later); **Dewey Rowell**: guitars (*Hell-O* through *America Must Be Destroyed*); **Cory "Flattus Maximus" Smoot**: guitar (*War Party*); **Danyell "Slymenstra Hymen" Stampe**: backing vocals (*Scumdogs of the Universe* and later); **Chuck "Sexecutioner" Varga**: backing vocals

Discography: *Hell-O* (Metal Blade, 1988); *Scumdogs of the Universe* (Metal Blade, 1990); *America Must Be Destroyed* (Metal Blade, 1991); *The Road Behind* (Metal Blade, 1992); *This Toilet Earth* (Metal Blade, 1994); *RagNaRok* (Metal Blade, 1995); *Carnival of Chaos* (Metal Blade, 1997); *We Kill Everything* (Metal Blade, 1999); *Violence Has Arrived* (Metal Blade, 2001); *War Party* (DRT, 2004); *Live from Mt. Fuji* (DRT, 2005); *Beyond Hell* (DRT, 2006); *Lust in Space* (Metal Blade, 2009); *Bloody Pit of Horror* (Metal Blade, 2010)

LEFT: GWAR poses for a family photo in 1992. LEFT TO RIGHT: Sleazy P. Martini (manager), Dave "Oderous Urungus" Brockie, Mike "Beefcake the Mighty" Bishop, Mike "Balsac the Jaws of Death" Derks, Brad "Jizmak Da Gusha" Roberts, Peter "Flattus Maximus" Lee, Chuck "Sexecutioner" Varga, and Danyell "Slymenstra Hymen" Stampe.
ABOVE: GWAR, the hottest band in Antarctica, performs in 1990.

HALLOWS EVE

YEARS ACTIVE: 1984–1989, 2004–PRESENT

The reason why forms of music other than metal ultimately suck is because they will never ever produce an artist whose stage name is inspired by one of the characters in the *He-Man and the Masters of the Universe* cartoon. As amusing as it might be to see one of the members of R.E.M. refer to himself as Man-at-Arms or even Orko, it just won't happen. So we must collectively turn to our good friends the metal bands to perform this important public service. Atlanta's Hallow's Eve is one such band to which we all owe a debt of gratitude, as it featured a guitarist who was known simply as Skullator. Other than this, there isn't really very much that set the band apart from their mid-1980s thrash contemporaries. They produced classic, high-velocity speed metal with somewhat predictable death-and-torment lyrics and promptly broke up after three albums, following the departure of lead singer Stacy Anderson. However, by the power of Grayskull, they reunited in 2004 and have made two new albums since then.

Chris Abbamonte: guitars (*History of Terror* and later); **Stacy Andersen**: vocals; **Ronny Appoldt**: drums (*Tales of Terror*); **Doyle Bright**: guitars (*History of Terror* and later); **Rob Clayton**: drums (*Monument*); **Tym Helton**: drums (*Death and Insanity*); **Pat "Scooch" Pascucci**: drums (*History of Terror* and later); **Skullator**: guitars (*Tales of Terror*); **Tommy Stewart**: bass; **David Stuart**: guitars

Discography: *Tales of Terror* (Metal Blade, 1985); *Death and Insanity* (Metal Blade, 1986); *Monument* (Metal Blade, 1988); *History of Terror* (Metal Blade, 2006); *The Neverending Sleep* (Hallows Eve, 2008)

HAMMERFALL

YEARS ACTIVE: 1993–PRESENT

"Big in Europe"—it's a phrase that garners quite the surfeit of chuckling in America. However, once the laughter has subsided, most American metal bands eventually must make their way across the pond if they expect to have any kind of a career. Metal is much more widely accepted in Europe than it is in the United States, and as if to prove this theorem (as well as that the U.S. possesses a culture completely at odds with the rest of the world), the debut album by Sweden's HammerFall, *Glory to the Brave*, landed in the German Top 100 upon its release in 1997. So even though the band may be little more than an underground phenomenon in the culturally advanced Home of Backyard Wrestling, HammerFall started off immediately popular on the Continent and has remained so to this day. The moral of the story is that metal may not be as hip in the good ol' U.S. of A. as it is in Europe, but that's an American handicap.

HammerFall is a classic example of the European power metal that emerged in the late 1990s. For those interested in this sub-genre, this style of metal got off the ground thanks mostly to Ritchie Blackmore's post–Deep Purple band, Rainbow, with its heavy classical music influences and mystical lyrics about ladies of the lake, stargazing, and the liberation of Rapunzel-esque characters from tower-bound incarceration. The style was expanded upon in previous decades by bands like Iron Maiden and Germany's Helloween, and HammerFall's epic approach obviously owes quite a bit to these bands, Helloween in particular. Today, HammerFall is considered a leading proponent of the genre and is widely credited with influencing the dozens of other power metal bands that

have seemingly materialized out of thin air in the new millennium.

Joacim Cans: vocals; **Oscar Dronjak**: guitars/backing vocals; **Stefan Elmgren**: guitars (*Legacy of Kings* through *Masterpieces*); **Anders Johansson**: drums (*Renegade* and later); **Fredrik Larsson**: bass/backing vocals (*Glory to the Brave*, *Steel Meets Steel* and later); **Glenn Ljungstrom**: guitars (*Glory to the Brave*); **Pontus Norgren**: guitar (*No Sacrifice, No Victory* and later); **Patrik Räfling**: drums (*Glory to the Brave* through *I Want Out*); **Magnus Rosén**: bass (*Glory to the Brave* through *Threshold*); **Jesper Strömblad**: drums (*Glory to the Brave*) (see also In Flames)

Discography: *Glory to the Brave* (Nuclear Blast, 1997); *Legacy of Kings* (Nuclear Blast, 1998); *I Want Out* (Nuclear Blast, 1999); *Renegade* (Nuclear Blast, 2000); *Crimson Thunder* (Nuclear Blast, 2002); *Chapter V: Unbent, Unbowed, Unbroken* (Nuclear Blast, 2005); *Threshold* (Nuclear Blast, 2006); *No Sacrifice, No Victory* (Nuclear Blast, 2009); *Infected* (Nuclear Blast, 2011)

HANOI ROCKS

YEARS ACTIVE: 1979–1985; 2001–2009

Hanoi Rocks was one of the first high-profile glam metal bands, and there are many fans who maintain to this day that it was the best of the bunch. Taking the hardcore sleaze of groups like the New York Dolls and running it through earsplitting amplification, this Finnish band was second only to Aerosmith in terms of the impact it had on the genre. The music notwithstanding, the Mick Jagger–like stage frolics of heavily lipsticked and hairsprayed lead singer Michael Monroe was hugely influential on just about every glam metal band to follow.

The band did not have as long a run as they deserved, releasing only a few albums over the course of four years. They certainly seemed to be on the way up, and one can only guess what they might have accomplished had they

OPPOSITE: Fashion template Hanoi Rocks poses with befringed hepcat Michael Monroe front and center.

Hanoi Rocks epitomized glam metal in the 1980s. Left to right: Sam Yaffa, Michael Monroe, and Andy McCoy.

Geffen, 1982); *Oriental Beat* (Uzi Suicide, 1982); *Back to the Mystery City* (David Geffen, 1983); *Two Steps from the Move* (Epic, 1984); *Rock 'n' Roll Divorce* (Bootlick, 1985); *All Those Wasted Years* (David Geffen, 1985); *True Live Rarities* (Vodka Records, 1985); *Dead by Christmas* (Raw Power, 1986); *Tracks from a Broken Dream* (Caroline, 1990); *Lean on Me* (Castle, 1996); *Hanoi Rocks* (Castle, 1996); *Decadent Dangerous Delicious: The Best of Hanoi Rocks* (Essential, 2000); *Twelve Shots on the Rocks* (Liquor and Poker Music, 2002); *Another Hostile Takeover* (Major Leidén, 2005); *Street Poetry* (Wolfgang, 2007)

HATEBREED

YEARS ACTIVE: 1994–PRESENT

The year was 1993. The former governor of Arkansas, Bill Clinton, had just been sworn in as president of the United States. The Maastricht Treaty had taken effect, thereby establishing the European Union. And Lorena Bobbitt had cut her husband's penis off, making John Wayne Bobbitt a household name. Amidst these excitements, Connecticut's Hatebreed was founded. Their raison d'étre was thus: They would imbue metal with a hardcore sensibility via songs that were short blasts of harsh vocals, crushing guitars, and primal, caveman 'tude. The band's first release was a split 7" single with the band Neglect, made in 1995, followed by *Under the Knife*, their own EP, in 1996. Hatebreed then secured a deal with Victory Records, who released their debut, *Satisfaction Is the Death of Desire*, in 1997. The band toured with such luminaries as Entombed, Napalm Death, and Slayer. Perhaps referring to the five-year wait between albums, the group's second album, *Perseverance*, was released in 2002. It was followed one year later with *The Rise of Brutality*. After 2006's *Supremacy* the group was struck by tragedy when former guitarist Lou Richards, who had left the group in 2002, committed suicide. Seven years later in 2009 Hatebreed released two albums, one

stayed together. In 1983, they signed an international deal with CBS Records and even scored a minor hit with a cover of Creedence Clearwater Revival's "Up Around the Bend," but it all came to a screeching halt in late December of that year, when drummer Nicholas "Razzle" Dingley made the fateful decision to ride shotgun on a liquor-store run with Mötley Crüe singer Vince Neil. Like his passenger, Neil was drunk, and when he plowed into another automobile, the drummer was killed instantly. Hanoi Rocks hired a replacement and tried to continue, but it proved too difficult to go on without their friend; Monroe in particular is said to have been devastated by the loss. At the beginning of 1985, just a little over a year after the accident, the singer decided that he just didn't have the heart to go on, and he quit the band. The remaining members followed suit that May. However, the breakup may have had unintentional good side effects. By breaking up before the glam metal explosion, the band managed to avoid all the bad press that dogged those who followed in their footsteps, and in their absence Hanoi Rocks achieved something akin to legendary status, a fact that is more than well demonstrated by the spate of compilation and live albums that have been released on a regular basis since the band's 1985 breakup. Monroe and guitarist Andy McCoy reunited in 2001 for what they referred to as a "rebirth," not a reunion, of Hanoi Rocks. The reborn band hit the live circuit and made three new studio albums before breaking up again in 2009. Today the band remains well respected, and they duly receive their share of credit for the genre that they helped to create.

Conny Bloom: guitars (*Another Hostile Takeover* and later); **Gyp Casino**: drums (*True Live Rarities*); **Terry Chimes**: drums (*True Live Rarities*); **Andy Christell**: bass (*Another Hostile Takeover* and later); **Nicholas "Razzle" Dingley**: drums (*Bangkok Shocks, Saigon Shakes, Hanoi Rocks* through *Two Steps from the Move*); **Costello Hautamäki**: guitars (*Twelve Shots on the Rocks*); **Lacu**: drums (*Twelve Shots on the Rocks* and later); **Andy McCoy**: guitar; **Michael Monroe**: vocals; **Nasty Suicide**: guitar; **Timpa**: bass (*Twelve Shots on the Rocks*); **Sam Yaffa**: bass

Discography: *Bangkok Shocks, Saigon Shakes, Hanoi Rocks* (David Geffen, 1981); *Self Destruction Blues* (David

Hatebreed bassist Chris Beattie makes the "Who farted?" face onstage.

all covers called *For The Lions*, and a self-titled album of original material.

Chris Beattie: bass; **Matt Byrne**: drums (*Perseverance* and later); **Jamey Jasta**: vocals; **Wayne Lozinak**: guitar (*For the Lions* and later); **Sean Martin**: guitar (*Perseverance* through *Supremacy*); **Matt McIntosh**: guitar (*Satisfaction Is the Death of Desire*); **Frank Novinec**: guitar (*Supremacy* and later); **Jamie Pushbutton**: drums (*Satisfaction Is the Death of Desire*); **Lou "Boulder" Richards**: guitar (*Satisfaction Is the Death of Desire* through *Perseverance*);

Discography: *Satisfaction is the Death of Desire* (Victory Records, 1997); *Perseverance* (Universal, 2002); *The Rise of Brutality* (Universal, 2003); *Supremacy* (Roadrunner, 2006); *For the Lions* (Koch, 2009); *Hatebreed* (Koch, 2009)

HEART

YEARS ACTIVE: 1973–PRESENT

When Heart released their debut album, *Dreamboat Annie*, in 1975, there were precious few women in hard rock, much less heavy metal. In fact, if you were in possession of both a guitar and a vagina and you expected to make music released by a record company, your only hope was to be named Carole King or Melissa Manchester. Furthermore, you had better be able to sing the shit out of "Have You Never Been Mellow." A daunting state of affairs, to be sure, but one that Heart overcame. Sisters Ann and Nancy Wilson joined Heart after the band had already been around for a while. The group was originally formed in 1963 in Vancouver by brothers Mike and Roger Fisher, and it was an all-male, penises-only proposition for several years, thank you very much. Ann, a singer, was the first to join, and upon doing so she began a relationship with Mike Fisher that included such activities as sexual intercourse. Nancy, a guitarist, joined in 1974 and began shacking up with Roger. Perhaps feeling that things were getting a little too incestuous to remain healthy, Mike Fisher quit the group and became its sound engineer. The new coed lineup signed to the Canadian label Mushroom, which released *Dreamboat Annie*. After strong sales in the Great White North, the album was issued in the United States and quickly went platinum, spurred on by such strong singles as "Crazy on You" and "Magic Man," still staples of classic rock radio today. Mushroom decided that it would be appropriate to celebrate the sales success of *Dreamboat Annie* by taking out a full-page ad in *Rolling Stone* depicting the Wilson sisters, bare-shouldered, with the caption "It was only

Heart in the middle of a very glamorous early tour.

our first time." Unhappy with being portrayed as bimbos, or possible residents of the Isle of Lesbos, and realizing that they had a big success on their hands, the band signed to Portrait. Portrait was a label affiliated with CBS Records, which released *Little Queen* in 1977. The album features one of the group's best-known songs, "Barracuda," and easily moved a million copies. Unfortunately, the move to Portrait was not 100% kosher on the part of the band. They had broken their existing contract with Mushroom, prompting a protracted legal battle between the band and the label. In the ensuing chaos, Mushroom released *Magazine*, an incomplete album that Heart had been working on. A Seattle court ruled that the album had to be taken off the market, but that Heart still owed Mushroom another record. So they rerecorded *Magazine* and rereleased it in 1978, and despite its extremely disorganized origins, it went platinum. The album itself sounds somewhat phoned-in, unsurprising considering that it was recorded to satisfy a court order. The next record, 1978's *Dog and Butterfly*, was a much more solid effort and more of a "real" follow-up to *Little Queen*. Unfortunately, Heart entered a turbulent state after these glory days. The Wilson sisters ended their relationships with the Fisher brothers, and what followed was a period of lineup changes and declining album sales. By 1983, the group simply wasn't selling like they used to, and after leaving their label they were largely forgotten. But in 1984, the public saw a preview of things to come when Ann Wilson and Loverboy singer Mike Reno sang "Almost Paradise" for the soundtrack to the movie *Footloose*. The song was absolutely horrible, but its power ballad sound would be a prominent component of the band's next offering. Heart signed to Capitol Records and released a self-titled album in 1985, which spawned such hits as "What About Love?" and "These Dreams," both of which ate shit out of diapers and

Heart in concert, prior to becoming a band that yuppies aero-bicized to.

would never be considered heavy metal in a million years. The album hit number one and moved five million copies, dwarfing the sales of their 1970s heyday. So who cares if it was a crime against humanity? The group rehashed their sound in this vein throughout the rest of the decade and into the 1990s, until they eventually experienced the same downturn in their sales that had occurred a decade earlier. Still, the band has never really gone away. They have remained together in one form or another to this day, and the band gained some unexpected cool points when Ann Wilson sang on three songs on Alice in Chains' *Sap* EP. The Seattle grungesters returned the favor when their bassist, Mike Inez, joined the band on their 2002 tour. Their music still turns up on movie soundtracks, such as *The Virgin Suicides*, and Nancy Wilson composed the soundtrack to the films *Jerry Maguire*, *Almost Famous*, and *Vanilla Sky*. The fact that her husband, Cameron Crowe, directed those movies, had nothing to do with it, honest.

Mark Andes: bass (*Passionworks*); **Craig Bartock**: guitar (*Red Velvet Car*); **Denny Carmassi**: drums (*Passionworks*); **Gilby Clarke**: vocals, guitar (*Jupiters Darling*); **Schuyler Deale**: bass (*Desire Walks On*); **Michael DeRosier**: drums (*Little Queen* through *Passionworks*); **Roger Fisher**: guitar (*Dreamboat Annie* through *Bebe le Strange*); **Steve Fossen**: bass; **Mike Inez**: bass (*Jupiters Darling*); **Rick Keefer**: synthesizer (*Dog and Butterfly*); **Howard Leese**: guitar; **Ric Markmann**: bass (*Red Velvet Car*); **Ben Mink**: guitar (*Red Velvet Car*); **John Purdell**: keyboards (*Desire Walks On*); **Darian Sahanaja**: keyboards (*Jupiters Darling*); **Ben Smith**: drums (*Jupiters Darling* and later); **Ann Wilson**: vocals; **Nancy Wilson**: guitar, vocals

Discography: *Dreamboat Annie* (Mushroom, 1976); *Little Queen* (Portrait, 1977); *Magazine* (Mushroom, 1978); *Dog and Butterfly* (Portrait, 1978); *Bebe le Strange* (Epic, 1980); *Private Audition* (Epic, 1982); *Passionworks* (Epic, 1983); *Heart* (Capitol, 1985); *Bad Animals* (Capitol, 1987); *Brigade* (Capitol, 1990); *Rock the House Live!* (Capitol, 1991); *Desire Walks On* (Capitol, 1993); *Jupiters Darling* (Sovereign, 2004); *Red Velvet Car* (Legacy, 2010)

Here are the members of Helloween looking as spooky as they can be. Left to right: Uli Kusch, Roland Grapow, Andi Deris, Michael Weikath, and Markus Grosskopf.

HELLOWEEN

YEARS ACTIVE: 1984–PRESENT

Germany's Helloween was one of the most influential European metal bands of the 1980s. Helloween melded a traditional metal approach with thrash, expanding on the work of bands like Iron Maiden and Judas Priest, and in the process helped to invent what is known today as power metal. The band took a few years to nail down their formula; founding guitarist Kai Hansen handled vocal duties at first, but after two releases he relinquished the microphone, feeling that he was at best a mediocre singer and that his limitations were holding back the band. The job was handed off to one Michael Kiske, who was still a teenager at the time of his maiden release with the band, the *Judas* EP, released in 1987. This set the stage for what is widely regarded as the band's crowning achievement, *Keeper of the Seven Keys, Part I*. The album broke them wide open in Europe, and they even managed to attract some attention in fickle old America. The following year saw the release of the creatively titled *Keeper of the Seven Keys, Part II*, but the album

was nowhere near as good or as well received as its predecessor. Not long after *Part II*'s release, Hansen left the band, claiming that he had done his best work with them and had taken the band as far as it could go. Apparently, his bandmates did not agree with the second half of that sentence and replaced him, unwilling to give up so quickly on the rising popularity that they were enjoying at the time.

Helloween appeared to be on the verge of superstardom when major label EMI offered the band a deal, but unfortunately, this led to a legal dispute with Noise Records that sidelined them for two years. Perhaps it should have been a longer holdup, as an album that they eventually released in 1991, *Pink Bubbles Go Ape*, was universally considered not fit for human enjoyment. The next studio album, 1994's *Chameleon*, was just as unpopular, and it was followed by the delivery of pink slips to Kiske and drummer and founding member Ingo Schwichtenberg. For the 1994 release *Master of the Rings*, the band set about furiously backpedaling in the stylistic direction of their earlier, more popular musical approach, and they seemed to regain some of the ground they had lost with their last two studio albums.

Tragedy struck the band in 1995 when the recently downsized Schwichtenberg committed suicide. He had suffered from manic depression for his entire life, and his unstable behavior was in fact one of the reasons for his dismissal in the first place. Apparently, in the middle of a particularly acute depressive episode, the drummer jumped in front of an oncoming train. The band dedicated their 1996 album *Time of the Oath* to Schwichtenberg. It turned out to be their strongest release in quite some time, and it went a long way toward reestablishing Helloween's popularity in Europe. In 2005, the band revisited the *Keeper of the Seven Keys* saga when they released *Keeper of the Seven Keys: The Legacy*. Today, they continue to pack 'em in in Europe as well as Japan, where they are superstars of the Monkees variety.

Andi Deris: vocals (*Master of the Rings* and later);

Sascha Gerstner: guitars (*Rabbit Don't Come Easy* and later); **Roland Grapow**: guitars (*Pink Bubbles Go Ape* through *The Dark Ride*); **Markus Grosskopf**: bass; **Kai Hansen**: guitars/vocals (*Helloween* through *Keeper of the Seven Keys, Part II*); **Michael Kiske**: vocals (*Keeper of the Seven Keys, Part I* through *Chameleon*); **Uli Kusch**: drums (*Master of the Rings* through *The Dark Ride*); **Dani Löble**: drums (*Keeper of the Seven Keys* and later); **Ingo Schwichtenberg**: drums (*Helloween* through *Chameleon*); **Michael Weikath**: guitars

Discography: *Helloween* (Noise, 1985); *Walls of Jericho* (Noise, 1986); *Judas* (Combat, 1987); *Keeper of the Seven Keys, Part I* (RCA, 1987); *Keeper of the Seven Keys, Part II* (RCA, 1988); *I Want Out: Live* (RCA, 1989); *Live in the U.K.* (Noise, 1989); *Pink Bubbles Go Ape* (EMI, 1991); *The Best, the Rest, the Rare* (Noise, 1991); *Chameleon* (EMI, 1994); *Master of the Rings* (EMI, 1994); *Time of the Oath* (Castle, 1996); *High Live* (Castle, 1996); *Better than Raw* (Velvel, 1998); *Metal Jukebox* (Never, 1999); *The Dark Ride* (Sanctuary, 2000); *Treasure Chest* (Metal-Is, 2002); *Rabbit Don't Come Easy* (Nuclear Blast, 2003); *Keeper of the Seven Keys: The Legacy* (Steamhammer, 2005); *Gambling with the Devil* (Steamhammer, 2007); *7 Sinners* (Steamhammer, 2010)

YEARS ACTIVE: 1989–1998; 2004–PRESENT

Three years after the band formed, New York City's Helmet cut a strange figure when it broke into the rock mainstream in 1992. Looking more like members of a professional rugby team than a metal band, the neatly coiffed, polo shirt-sporting quartet created a harsh, clipped sound that bleached all the niceties out of metal, imbuing it with a dissonance normally associated with Sonic Youth or Jesus Lizard. The band was formed by an accomplished jazz guitarist named Page Hamilton, who had fallen under the spell of Manhattan's noise rock scene of the late 1980s. They quite appropriately signed to the Amphetamine Reptile label and in 1990 released their debut album, *Born Annoying*, an exercise in absolutely grating sheer noise torture, not for the faint of heart. Helmet seemed to have found its little niche in the world, and then grunge hit.

In a frenzy to cash in on the fad, labels began signing any and every flannel-clad ensemble they could find, and word soon got out that Helmet was just the Pearl Jam soundalike they were looking for. This must have come as something of a surprise to the band, who sounded a great deal more like a free-jazz version of Prong than anything on Pearl Jam's *Ten* album. In fact, one wonders if anyone from the various labels had heard Helmet's music in the first place. Refusing to let the facts get in the way, the companies launched a bidding war, culminating in Interscope Records finally winning the privilege of releasing the band's next effort, *Meantime*. No numbers were ever released publicly, but the album was reportedly brought in at a cost that is best characterized as "astronomical" and, more to the point, impossible for any band but the most commercially successful to recoup. Fortunately, their videos were popular, which translated into strong sales. The band surely must have been relieved when it actually appeared possible for them to sell enough records to keep Interscope's stockholders happy. They spent the next couple of years on the A-list, appearing on the soundtracks for both *Judgment Night* and *The Crow*.

Naturally, expectations were high for their follow-up album, *Betty*, which certainly looked promising at first. The album was heavier than *Meantime* but at the same time possessed greater musical sophistication, as Hamilton had become more comfortable flexing his jazz chops. Bad! Bad! Bad! For the transgression of broadening their sound, the band paid the ultimate price. Nobody bought the album, and accountants at Atlantic (which had taken over the band's contract from Interscope) must have started thinking "write-off" at this point, as if it was the band's fault that the A&R idiots at the label had thrown away millions of dollars stupidly believing that they had signed the next Nirvana. By the time of the band's final release in 1997, it was readily apparent that Hamilton had been sufficiently demoralized by the whole sordid experience, and Helmet broke up in 1999. Hamilton moved from New York to Los Angeles and busied himself with session work, most notably playing guitar for David Bowie. He joined forces with drummer John Tempesta of Testament and White Zombie for what was intended to be a brand new project, but ultimately the new project was dubbed Helmet. With Hamilton now the only original member, Helmet released *Size Matters* in 2004, and the band has remained together ever since.

Dan Beeman: guitar (*Seeing Eye Dog*); **Frank Bello**: bass (*Size Matters*); **Henry Bogdan**: bass (*Born Annoying* through *Aftertaste*); **Rob Echeverria**: guitars (*Betty*) (see also Biohazard); **Page Hamilton**: guitars/vocals; **Mike Jost**: drums (*Monochrome*); **Peter Mengede**: guitars (*Strap It On*, *Meantime*); **John Stanier**: drums (*Born Annoying* through *Aftertaste*); **Kyle Stevenson**: drums (*Seeing Eye Dog*); **John Tempesta**: drums (*Size Matters*); **Chris Traynor**: guitars (*Aftertaste* and later)

Discography: *Born Annoying* (Amphetamine Reptile, 1990); *Strap It On* (Amphetamine Reptile, 1991); *Meantime* (Interscope, 1992); *Betty* (Atlantic, 1994); *Aftertaste* (Atlantic, 1997); *Size Matters* (Interscope, 2004); *Monochrome* (Warcon, 2006); *Seeing Eye Dog* (Work Song, 2010)

JIMI HENDRIX

YEARS ACTIVE: 1963–1970

While the inclusion of Jimi Hendrix in an alphabetical listing of heavy metal artists may seem like a bit of a stretch at first, it really isn't when you consider the groundbreaking effect that he had in introducing elements that are now commonplace in the genre. For one thing, he changed the way people thought about the guitar, one of heavy metal's most potent tools. Before he exploded onto the scene, the instrument was commonly viewed as occupying a supporting role, its primary function being to back up a song's vocal melody. Hendrix put it front and center, combining his jaw-dropping technique with a battery of feedback and distortion, attributes that most of the day's recording artists normally tried to eradicate. In the process, he gave the instrument its own personality, on a par with that of any human

Jimi Hendrix lounges about in heavily psychedelic environs.

being (to oversimplify, it was the stringed-instrument equivalent of transforming a casual shower-singer into one of those Buddhist monks who can sing octaves simultaneously). Since then, artists such as Ritchie Blackmore, Ted Nugent, Eddie Van Halen, and countless others have had the opportunity to create music that is unabashedly guitar-centric, and they owe it to Jimi Hendrix. Furthermore, Hendrix is responsible for the practice of basing songs around the almighty guitar riff, as opposed to the vocal melodies of old. "Purple Haze," the song that served as most people's introduction to the guitarist, is as well known for its dissonant, tritone-based guitar intro as Black Sabbath's "Iron Man" is for its opening chord pattern. Ditto Led Zeppelin's "Black Dog," Deep Purple's "Smoke on the Water," and so forth. This type of songwriting and arrangement is taken for granted these days, but it was practically unheard-of in its time. To put it in its appropriate context, the debut album of the Jimi Hendrix Experience, *Are You Experienced?* came out in 1967. One year prior to that, the Beatles' *Revolver*, regarded by many to be the greatest rock'n'roll album of all time, was released. Chances are that *Revolver* is in your collection somewhere, so pull it out and look at the songs on the back. Got it? Okay. Name one riff on the album that is as well known as the one in "Purple Haze." What are you going to pick—"Taxman"?

Jimi Hendrix's band—or, more appropriately, the Jimi Hendrix Experience—was also notable in that it brought to the world's attention the concept of the power trio (actually, some might argue that Cream came first, but those who would belabor this point are mostly irritating collector-geek types who would never be caught dead with this book). Since the rhythm section consisted of a grand total of exactly two guys, they had to work overtime to fill out the empty spaces that Hendrix left when he played lead, which was a considerable portion of the time. Consequently, Experience bassist Noel Redding and drummer Mitch Mitchell developed fearsome chops in order to pull off this daunting task, becoming rock heroes in their own right. Redding's thunderous bass was

in a state of constant forward momentum, at once anchoring and complementing the busy jazz chops of Mitchell, whose playing had little in common with most rock drummers of the day, sounding more like a pissed-off Buddy Rich than anything else. Almost every heavy metal power trio that came after them in the 1970s—and there were a lot—followed this exact template.

Given the virtuoso playing of everyone in the band, it probably would have been enough to simply set up some microphones and press the "record" button, but that would have cheated Hendrix out of another area in which he proved to be an innovator. He had already begun tinkering pretty heavily with studio technology on his first album (listen to "Third Stone from the Sun") and more so on *Axis: Bold As Love*, but he went completely nuts on the sprawling double album *Electric Ladyland*. In much the same way that he had given the guitar enough character to make it a personality in its own right, he manipulated technology to such a degree that it was almost as though he had made the studio itself an honorary band member. By using every means at his disposal, from backward recording to aggressive back-and-forth panning between stereo speakers, Hendrix created sounds that no one before him had ever even imagined. This had short-term negative consequences, however. So unprecedented were some of the sounds on the album that its initial pressing was temporarily halted when plant engineers thought they

were mistakes. While *Electric Ladyland* can get somewhat bogged down in knob-twiddling, particularly around side three's midway point, it remains a landmark album in the history of heavy metal. After all, the middle section of Led Zeppelin's "Whole Lotta Love" owes its entire existence to Hendrix's experimentation in the recording studio.

The last album to be released in Hendrix's lifetime was the live *Band of Gypsys*, which had initially been thrown together in order to appease Capitol Records. In the early 1960s, it was not uncommon for a record company's A&R representatives to hang around recording sessions, offering "Amazing Deals!" to the session musicians, who naively signed, assuming they had gotten just the break they were looking for. Ultimately, the true purpose of offering these contracts was to preemptively gain exclusive rights to artists on the off-chance that these musicians became famous. Hendrix had signed just such a contract with Capitol Records early in his career, before he had the business savvy to understand the ramifications of the vicelike hold the record company would later assert. In 1969, with Hendrix an international superstar, Capitol wanted to cash in. Bassist Redding had already left the band in the middle of sessions for *Electric Ladyland*, and the Experience was effectively on ice, so the guitarist opted to record with a drummer from his club days, Buddy Miles, and an old army buddy, bassist Billy Cox. They recorded a few live shows at the Fillmore East, hoping to produce a quickie live album to toss into the gaping maw of the record company, thereby fulfilling the contractual requirements and making the label go away. Although they surely didn't realize it at the time, the album that resulted from these slapdash, just-get-me-out-of-my-contract concerts was a heavy funk masterpiece that at times predicted later generations of noise rockers like Sonic Youth,

OPPOSITE: This photograph of the Jimi Hendrix Experience, taken in 1967, catches Hendrix (left) and bassist Noel Redding in a rather subdued moment.

particularly on the twelve-minute screeching feedback showstopper "Machine Gun."

With Capitol off his back, Hendrix probably felt that he could now breathe easy and go back to the recording studio to work on songs for his next album. What nobody knew was that he now had only a few months left to live. His enthusiasm for drugs was the stuff of legend, even in the late 1960s when supposedly everyone was high; for example, there was one account of a concert where the revolutionary virtuoso was so stoned that Redding had to tune his guitar for him. Hendrix was indeed the Evelyn Wood of drug consumption, gleefully shoveling all manner of mind-altering substances into every orifice in his body, so his death by drug overdose was not much of a surprise. What is not known is the degree to which he had gone "downhill" before then, as some sources seem to indicate he had. This seems highly unlikely; right up until his death, he was always in the studio, jamming and recording, but he had not released any of this work. Hendrix was known as an exacting perfectionist, and it would have been unlike him to release any material that did not meet his high standards. In all likelihood, his lack of post–*Electric Ladyland* album releases is indicative not of an artist who had "lost it" but rather of one who had been through the wringer for the past few years and who was just trying to slow down. When he died, his unreleased material fell into much less caring hands, and those particular bloodsucking opportunistic vultures decided to—kachiiiing!—cash in on his death. For twenty-five extremely painful years, fans endured inferior material that Hendrix never approved for release, much of which was made worse through the miracle of overdubbing (the most infamous example being the addition of

Jimi Hendrix sets his guitar on fire at the 1967 Monterey Pop Festival. But what did he do for an encore?

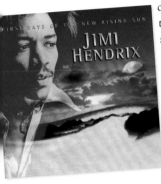

drummer Bruce Gary of the Knack on the classic song "Angel"). Most likely it was this wealth of subpar material, which Hendrix never green-lighted, that contributed to the fallacy that he was all washed up by the time he died.

Fortunately, in 1995, the Hendrix family won the rights to his work and has been turning out quality material ever since. These releases include the original albums remastered by their original engineer, Eddie Kramer, as well as the material Hendrix was working on at the time of his death. This material was mixed by Kramer and sequenced according to the guitarist's own handwritten notes, which were also the source of the 1997 album title *First Rays of the New Rising Sun*. The Hendrix family also released several live performances that serve as a shocking reminder of just how good a guitar player Hendrix actually was; with so much talk about his influence, sometimes he gets overlooked as just a great guitar player. Naturally, these releases, the live ones in particular, are also sad reminders of how much he obviously still had to offer. It's anybody's guess what he would have accomplished had he lived, but we'll all just have to be satisfied that he completely changed the scale and scope of rock music and invented what have become heavy metal cornerstones today. Not too bad for four years' work, huh?

Discography: *Are You Experienced?* (MCA, 1967); *Axis: Bold As Love* (MCA, 1967); *Electric Ladyland* (MCA, 1968); *Smash Hits* (Reprise, 1969); *Band of Gypsys* (Capitol, 1970); *Blues* (MCA, 1994); *First Rays of the New Rising Sun* (MCA, 1997); *South Saturn Delta* (MCA, 1997); *BBC Sessions* (MCA, 1998); *Experience Hendrix: The Best of Jimi Hendrix* (MCA, 1998); *Live at the Fillmore East* (MCA, 1999); *Live at Woodstock* (MCA, 1999); *Merry Christmas and Happy New Year* (MCA, 1999); *The Jimi Hendrix Experience* (MCA, 2000); *Voodoo Child: The Jimi Hendrix Collection* (MCA, 2001); *Valleys of Neptune* (Legacy, 2010)

HOLOCAUST

YEARS ACTIVE: 1977–PRESENT

Scotland's Holocaust was lumped in with the New Wave of British Heavy Metal movement on the basis of its 1981 debut album, *The Nightcomers*. The album is considered a classic today, but at the time of its release it didn't sell particularly well. The disappointment that this caused made the band's situation considerably strained, and by the time they began recording their 1984 album, *No Man's Land*, vocalist John Mortimer was the sole remaining member. In a show of truly awe-inspiring testicular mass, the vocalist went ahead and recorded the whole album by himself, handling every single instrument except for drums, which came courtesy of Steve Cowen. Sadly, the album sold poorly, and at this point the "band" ceased to exist. Or so it appeared.

In 1987, "The Small Hours," a song off their second album, was recorded by a certain Bay Area thrash band (that is, Metallica), whose personal mission seemed to be the resurrection of every forgotten New Wave of British Heavy Metal group in the world. Encouraged by the newfound attention, Mortimer and Cowen put the band back together as a trio, recruiting bassist Graham Hall. The band has stayed together since then, in one form or another, and unlike many of its contemporaries, the band's members did not use a reunion as an excuse to launch a series of demoralizing nostalgia tours. Rather, they refused to rest on their laurels, and they have consistently released albums that have been progressive and musically challenging.

Nicky Arkless: drums (*The Nightcomers* through *Live*); **Robin Begg**: bass (*The Nightcomers* through *Live*); **Graham Cowen**: bass (*The Courage to Be*); **Steve Cowen**: drums (*No Man's Land* and later); **Ed Dudley**: guitars (*The Nightcomers* through *Live*); **Graham**

Hall: bass (*The Sound of Souls*); **Gary Lettice**: vocals (*The Nightcomers* through *Live*); **Iain McKenzie**: guitars (*The Courage to Be*); **John Mortimer**: guitars/vocals; **David Rosie**: bass (*Hypnosis of Birds* through *Covenant*)

Discography: *The Nightcomers* (Phoenix, 1981); *Heavy Metal Mania* (Phoenix, 1981); *Comin' Through* (Phoenix, 1982); *Live (Hot Curry and Wine)* (Phoenix, 1983); *No Man's Land* (Phoenix, 1984); *The Sound of Souls* (Chrome, 1989); *Hypnosis of Birds* (Taurus Moon, 1992); *Spirits Fly* (Neat, 1996); *Covenant* (Neat, 1997); *The Courage to Be* (Neat, 2000); *Primal* (Edgy, 2003)

HUMBLE PIE

YEARS ACTIVE: 1968–1975; 1980–1983; 1988–2003

One of the first bands to be associated with the term "heavy metal" was England's Humble Pie. It was not a compliment. The term was used in a review of their 1969 debut album, *As Safe as Yesterday Is*, written by Mike Saunders. The write-up ran in *Rolling Stone* and dubbed the group a "heavy metal-leaden shit-rock band." He also used the term in *Rolling Stone* #70 to describe the sound of their self-titled third album as "more of the same 27th-rate heavy metal crap" that was "worse than the first two put together, though I know that sounds incredible." So if anyone asks you who the first heavy metal band was, and you want to say Humble Pie, you now have the words of at least one highly-respected rock scribe to bolster your case. You're welcome. Humble Pie formed when Small Faces singer and guitarist Steve Marriott joined forces with guitarist Peter Frampton, Spooky Tooth bassist Greg Ridley, and 17-year-old drummer Jerry Shirley. The new band spent a good chunk of 1969 holed up in Marriott's house, practicing, practicing, and practicing. The strategy paid off when they issued their debut single, "Natural Born Boogie," which was a top ten hit in their native U.K. They followed it up with *As Safe as Yesterday Is* and the follow-up, *Town and Country*, but the label that issued them, Immediate, went

Group singer Bobby Tench. They produced the *On To Victory* LP and followed it up in 1981 with *Go for the Throat*, but apparently God hated Steve Marriott and sidelined him with both a hand injury and an ulcer. Humble Pie broke up yet again, and while Shirley went on to happier times as a member of Fastway, Marriott became something of a recluse and never really got his mojo back. He died in a house fire in 1991 at the age of 44. Ten years later, Ridley, Shirley, and Tench reunited under the cobweb-strewn Humble Pie banner, enlisting the services of guitarist Dave Colwell to stand in for their departed colleague. This lineup produced the 2002 album *Back on Track*, but Ridley's death in 2003 put a definitive end to any further activities under the Humble Pie name.

Dave Clempson: guitar (*Smokin'* and later); **Peter Frampton**: vocals (*As Safe as Yesterday Is* through *Performance: Rockin' the Fillmore*); **Anthony Jones**: guitar (*On to Victory*); **Bobby Keyes**: saxophone (*Rock On*); **Alexis Korner**: vocals (*Rock On*); **Steve Marriott**: vocals; **Greg Ridley**: bass; **Jerry Shirley**: drums; **Bobby Tench**: guitar (*On to Victory*)

Discography: *As Safe as Yesterday Is* (Immediate, 1969); *Town and Country* (Immediate, 1969); *Humble Pie* (A&M, 1970); *Rock On* (A&M, 1971); *Performance: Rockin' the Fillmore* (A&M, 1971); *Smokin'* (A&M, 1972); *Eat It* (A&M, 1973); *Thunderbox* (A&M, 1974); *Street Rats* (A&M, 1975); *On to Victory* (Atco, 1980); *Go for the Throat* (Atco, 1981); *Back on Track* (Sanctuary, 2002)

bankrupt, shuttering its doors right after the group's inaugural U.S. tour. After moving to their new label A&M, the group issued a self-titled album in 1970 and *Rock On* in 1971. As the band forged ahead, Frampton's musical tastes were beginning to make him feel like the odd man out. Humble Pie's music was becoming heavier, sludgier, and more plodding, a direction typified by the balls-out riffing on *Rock On*'s "Stone Cold Fever." Frampton left the group after their very popular 1971 live album, *Performance: Rockin' the Fillmore*. The album featured a crushing, devastating take on the Ray Charles chestnut "I Don't Need No Doctor," and one presumes that this type of thing was exactly what prompted Frampton to leave the band and pursue a solo career. He probably also left so that he could have time to nurse his little girl eardrums whilst drinking chocolate milk and wearing footie pajamas. The band replaced him with Dave Clempson and recorded 1972's *Smokin'*. It was

their most commercially successful album yet and the only one to reach the U.S. top ten album charts. It features some of their best-known songs, including "Hot 'n' Nasty" and the oft-covered "30 Days in the Hole," which name-checks every strain of marijuana known to man. The 1973 part-studio/part-live *Eat It* was almost as successful, although the live portion of it is most accurately described as "utter dogshit." The albums made less and less of an impact after that, due in part to the very strong possibility that the band just wasn't feeling it so much anymore. Of 1974's *Thunderbox*'s twelve songs, fully six were covers, and 1975's *Street Rats* was thrown together by the record company, using material the band members had intended for another project entirely. The surviving musicians have since disowned it, and Humble Pie broke up soon after its release. A reconstituted Humble Pie emerged in 1980 around Marriott, Shirley, bassist Anthony Jones, and former Jeff Beck

ICED EARTH

YEARS ACTIVE: 1985–PRESENT

Iced Earth is the Great White Hope of American power metal. This genre is mostly acknowledged as a European phenomenon, as the demand for metal is significantly greater than it is in the United States. Nevertheless, the band has a faithful following both in and out of America, particularly in Greece. None of this would have happened without the commendable efforts and perseverance of founding guitarist Jon Schaffer, who has stuck it out through personnel changes so frequent that they border on the ludicrous. The band even managed to build their audience on the club circuit of Florida, the erstwhile Home of Death Metal and treacherous ground indeed for bands of the Iron Maiden ilk.

While the band was undergoing lineup changes right up to the time of this writing, their situation had stabilized to some degree on their third album, *Burnt Offerings*. The 1995 album saw the debut of singer Matthew Barlow. With this grouping, the band was able to capitalize on the buzz their music generated, and their next release, 1996's *The Dark Saga*, was their best to date, featuring cover art by none other than comic artist Todd MacFarlane, of Spawn fame. The band now had considerable notoriety on the underground metal circuit, and their 1998 album, *Something Wicked This Way Comes*, was their best seller yet. To celebrate the occasion, they embarked on a world tour of epic proportions, taking the opportunity to record a live album in Greece, their home away from home. The band produced *Horror Show*, in 2001, as well as the *Dark Genesis* box set and *Tribute to the Gods* cover album.

Barlow remained until 2003, when he left the band to become a police officer in Georgetown, Delaware. The band then gained the vocal services of Tim "Ripper" Owens, who had just been elbowed out of Judas Priest to make room for a returning Rob Halford. Barlow returned in 2007 but left again, and their current singer at the time of this writing is Stu Block of Into Eternity. This lineup released *Dystopia* in 2011, and has tour dates scheduled for 2012 in China.

Dave Abell: bass (*Iced Earth* through *Days of Purgatory*); **Gene Adam**: vocals (*Iced Earth*); **Matthew Barlow**: vocals (*Burnt Offerings* and later); **Rodney Beasley**: drums (*Burnt Offerings*); **Stu Block**: vocals (*Dystopia*); **Richard Christy**: drums (*The Horror Show*) (see also Death); **Steve DiGiorgio**: bass (*The Horror Show*) (see also Death, Testament); **John Greely**: vocals (*Night of the Stormrider*); **James MacDonough**: bass (*Something Wicked This Way Comes, Alive in Athens, The Glorious Burden*); **Mike McGill**: drums (*Iced Earth*); **Tim "Ripper" Owens**: vocals (*The Glorious Burden* through *Framing Armageddon: Something Wicked Part 1*); **Mark Prator**: drums (*The Dark Saga*); **Rick Risberg**: keyboards (*Alive in Athens*); **Ralph Santolla**: guitar (*The Glorious Burden*); **Jon Schaffer**: guitars; **Richey Secchiari**: drums (*Night of the Stormrider*); **Troy Seele**: guitar (*The Crucible of Man* and later); **Randy Shawver**: lead guitar (*Iced Earth* through *Days of Purgatory*); **Brent Smedley**: drums (*Days of Purgatory, Alive in Athens, Framing Armageddon* and later); **Larry Tarnowski**: guitars (*Alive in Athens* through *Tribute to the Gods*); **Freddie Vidales**: bass (*The Crucible of Man* and later)

Discography: *Iced Earth* (Century Media, 1991); *Night of the Stormrider* (Century Media, 1992); *Burnt Offerings* (Century Media, 1995); *The Dark Saga* (Century Media, 1996); *Days of Purgatory* (Century Media, 1997); *Something Wicked This Way Comes* (Century Media, 1998); *Alive in Athens* (Century Media, 1999); *Horror Show* (Century Media, 2001); *Dark Genesis* (Century Media, 2002); *Tribute to the Gods* (Century Media, 2002); *The Glorious Burden* (SPV, 2004); *Framing Armageddon: Something Wicked Part 1* (SPV, 2007); *The Crucible of Man: Something Wicked Part 2* (SPV, 2008); *Dystopia* (Century Media, 2011)

IMMORTAL

YEARS ACTIVE: 1990–PRESENT

Anyone wishing to take an introductory course in Norwegian black metal is hereby advised to journey to their local vendor of recorded music and purchase one of the first four albums by Immortal. This band caught some flak for slowing the tempos a tad on their fifth album, 1999's *At the Heart of Winter*, so you might want to steer clear of that one if you want only the meat and potatoes of the black metal movement. However, every previous album featured all the attributes for which the genre is

known the world over, such as blast beats (the sound of the drummer playing at absolute top speed by performing what amounts to a closed roll, split evenly between the snare drum on the left hand and the ride cymbal, or hi-hat, on the right), corpse paint (otherwise known as KISS makeup), and raspy vocals that are at times reminiscent of Popeye the spinach aficionado. The band's lyrics are consistent with the norms of the genre, being almost entirely inspired by paganism, and the members have never revealed their real names, referring to themselves by their pseudonyms only.

Immortal was founded in 1990 by guitarist Demonaz Doom Occulta and bassist and vocalist Abbath Doom Occulta (no relation), who had previously played in the death metal band Old Funeral with none other than convicted murderer and noted anti-Semite Varg Vikernes, of Burzum fame. Abbath and Demonaz took the forbidding forests and testicle-shriveling cold weather of Norway as their inspiration, ultimately creating a fictional world called Blashyrkh, which provided the basis for all of the demonic entities and Viking raids of their lyrics. The band recruited drummer Armagedda, completing their lineup, but his tenure was short-lived—he quit after their first album. This left Abbath to perform triple duty on the next two albums—bass, vocals, and drums. After a few candidates had come and gone, Abbath was finally relieved of the drummer's throne by Horgh, who made his first appearance on the 1997 album *Blizzard Beasts*. With that little problem out of the way, the band was now free to focus on the fact that guitarist Demonaz had contracted acute tendonitis and could no longer play, forcing him to leave the group. This put all the songwriting responsibilities squarely on Abbath's shoulders, who took the opportunity to fashion a somewhat slower, more sophisticated musical style for their next album. Now playing every instrument except for drums, Abbath produced

Abbath Doom Occulta of Immortal is especially cranky before he's had his morning coffee.

At the Heart of Winter, whose more epic, polished sound brought new fans and acclaim to Immortal. It also had the effect of producing the usual legion of idiots who always come out of the woodwork to say that a band sucks when they release an album with production values. Bassist Iscariah joined the fold afterward, relieving Abbath of his three-tiered *kransekake* of responsibility and allowing the poor guy to just vocalize and play the damn guitar. The band split up in 2003, but they didn't know how to quit each other, and they reunited and released *All Shall Fail* in 2009.

Abbath Doom Occulta: bass/drums/guitars/vocals; **Apollyon**: bass (*All Shall Fail*); **Armagedda**: drums (*Diabolical Fullmoon Mysticism*); **Demonaz Doom Occulta**: guitars (*Diabolical Fullmoon Mysticism* through *Blizzard Beasts*); **Horgh**: drums (*Blizzard Beasts* and later); **Iscariah**: bass (*Damned in Black* and later)

Discography: *Diabolical Fullmoon Mysticism* (JL America, 1992); *Pure Holocaust* (Osmose, 1993); *Battles in the North* (Osmose, 1995); *Blizzard Beasts* (Osmose, 1997); *At the Heart of Winter* (Osmose, 1999); *Pure Tranquility* (Osmose, 1999); *Damned in Black* (Osmose, 2000); *Sons of Northern Darkness* (Nuclear Blast, 2002); *All Shall Fail* (Nuclear Blast, 2009)

IN FLAMES

YEARS ACTIVE: 1990–PRESENT

In Flames was formed in Gothenburg, Sweden by guitarist Jesper Strömblad in 1990. Wrong Again Records issued their debut album, *Lunar Strain*, in 1993, and it was based on the combination of aggressive death metal with Iron Maiden's melodic approach. The group didn't have a regular vocalist at this point, so Mikael Stanne of Dark Tranquility loaned his services. Another session vocalist, Henke Forss, appeared on their 1994 EP *Subterranean*. Even though the lineup was in constant disarray, it didn't stop the Nuclear Blast label from

signing them. The group wisely decided to get their shit together and get some full-time musicians. They enlisted drummer Björn Gelotte and vocalist Anders Fridén, another Dark Tranquility alumnus. The new In Flames lineup released *The Jester Race* in 1996, and in 1997 the group recorded *Whoracle*, which they promoted through some far-ranging touring that took them as far as Japan. The group continued a relentless pace of albums and touring, but on 2002's *Reroute to Remain*, they changed their style, losing the growling vocals and adding in some toe-tapping choruses. This laid the foundation for 2004's *Soundtrack to Your Escape*, which was their best-selling album by far. Their profile now heightened through capitalism, they found themselves sharing the stage with such titans as Motörhead and Judas Priest, and playing the main stage at Ozzfest. In 2009, the group's unbroken string of releases and tours came to a grinding halt when they cancelled their U.K. tour. Strömblad, it seemed, was struggling with the bottle, and the group was giving him some much-needed time to dry out in rehab. He ultimately left the band in 2010, which could very well have been the kiss of death—normally, when the founding member packs his bags, the rest of the group usually follows suit. Happily, they stayed together by replacing Strömblad and releasing *Sounds of a Playground Fading* in 2011 like nothing had happened. Ouch.

Anders Fridén: vocals (*The Jester Race* and later) (see also Dream Theater); **Björn Gelotte**: drums (*The Jester Race* and later); **Peter Iwers**: bass (*Colony* and later); **Johann Larsson**: bass; **Glenn Ljungström**: guitar (*Lunar Strain* through *Whoracle*); **Carl Näslund**: guitar (*Lunar Strain*); **Örjan Örnkloo**: keyboards (*Soundtrack to Your Escape*); **Mikael Stanne**: vocals (*Lunar Strain*); **Jesper Strömblad**: guitar, drums; **Daniel Svensson** (*Colony* and later)

Discography: *Lunar Strain* (Wrong Again, 1994); *The Jester Race* (Nuclear Blast, 1996); *Whoracle* (Nuclear Blast, 1997); *Colony* (Nuclear Blast, 1999); *Clayman* (Nuclear Blast, 2000); *The Tokyo Showdown* (Nuclear Blast, 2001); *Reroute to Remain* (Nuclear Blast, 2002); *Soundtrack to Your Escape* (Nuclear Blast, 2004); *Come Clarity* (Nuclear Blast, 2008); *Sounds of a Playground Fading* (Century, 2011)

Anders Fridén of In Flames plays on despite being doubled over with gas pains.

Iron Butterfly poses outside its garden of Eden. Left to right: Erik Brann, Ron Bushy, Lee Dorman, and Doug Ingle.

YEARS ACTIVE: 1966–PRESENT

San Diego's Iron Butterfly was a leading proponent of acid rock, which was rapidly mutating into heavy metal in its late-1960s heyday. The band was brought to the masses through high-profile supporting slots on tours with Jefferson Airplane and the Doors, as well as through their hit single "In-A-Gadda-Da-Vida," unquestionably their best-known song. The original track clocked in at an unprecedented seventeen minutes, two and a half of which are the kick-drum solo. The rest of the song features showboating turns from guitarist Erik Brann and organ player Doug Ingle, whose basso profundo vocal delivery has been the source of equal amounts of ridicule and tribute in the intervening years. Perhaps more bands today should follow this formula, since the song sold 4 million copies and spent an entire year in the Top 10.

When it came to airplay, the band's record company excised all the solos and other superfluities, chopping the song down to a trim three minutes. This decision conformed to the rules of AM radio, the standard-bearer and all-around Big Kahuna at the time. However, FM radio, still an underground phenomenon, was not bound by the same constraints as its mainstream counterpart; there, the album version of the song, all seventeen minutes of it, played to great success. This cleared the way for other artists without traditional single-length material to get airplay, and one genre to benefit from this was the often highly roundabout musical form known as heavy metal. It was now possible for five- or six-minute songs, such as "Whole Lotta Love" and "Iron Man," to receive heavy rotation and mass adulation. Unfortunately, inadvertently creating Album-Oriented Rock wasn't enough to keep the band in the spotlight for long. Their next album, *Ball*, released in 1969, sold only a fraction of its predecessor's total units, and rather than endure a long, slow decline, Iron Butterfly broke up in 1971. That is, until 1975 when, for some reason, guitarist Erik Brann and drummer Ron Bushy put the band back together and released two albums that were poorly reviewed by critics and largely ignored by record buyers. Iron Butterfly split yet again after releasing 1976's *Sun and Steel* on the self-fulfillingly monikered Edsel label. The band has since gotten back together from time to time to cash in on whatever nostalgia value they can scrape up. Sadly, Erik Brann, the guitarist who appeared on "In-A-Gadda-Da-Vida," died of heart failure in 2003. Bassist Philip Taylor Kramer, meanwhile, disappeared in 1995 under very bizarre circumstances. In the 1970s, after leaving Iron Butterfly, Kramer had become an aerospace engineer. He was in the midst of developing a data compression technique for CD-ROMs when he drove to the airport to meet a potential investor for his project. When he got there, he called the police, and according to the 2007 book *Mysterious Deaths and Disappearances*, he told them "I'm going to kill myself. And I want everyone to know O. J. Simpson is innocent. *They* did it." That was on February 12, 1995, and he was never heard from again. Ultimately, his minivan was found in 1999, with his remains inside, at the bottom of a canyon in Malibu. Perhaps he had died and decomposed listening to an unedited version of "In-A-Gadda-Da-Vida" with an extra long drum solo?

Erik Brann: guitar (*In-A-Gadda-Da-Vida* and later); **Ron Bushy**: drums; **Darryl DeLoach**: vocals (*Heavy*); **Lee Dorman**: bass (*In-A-Gadda-Da-Vida* through *Metamorphosis*); **Doug Ingle**: vocals/organ (*Heavy* through *Metamorphosis*); **Jerry Penrod**: bass (*Heavy*); **Danny Weis**: guitar (*Heavy*)

Discography: *Heavy* (Rhino, 1968); *In-A-Gadda-Da-Vida* (Atco, 1968); *Ball* (Collectors', 1969); *Iron Butterfly Live* (Rhino, 1970); *Metamorphosis* (Rhino, 1970); *Scorching Beauty* (Repertoire, 1975); *Sun and Steel* (Edsel, 1976); *Light and Heavy: The Best of Iron Butterfly* (Rhino, 1993)

Without a doubt, Iron Maiden was one of the best heavy metal bands of the 1980s. Left to right: Dave Murray, Bruce Dickinson, Steve Harris, and Adrian Smith.

IRON MAIDEN

YEARS ACTIVE: 1975–PRESENT

Chances are that if you were born between 1965 and 1975, give or take a few years, there was at least one kid in your high school who bore certain intriguing visual trademarks. His hair was long and greasy, and his eyes were bloodshot from recreational marijuana inhalation. The number one article, however, was the ever-present denim vest, whose back displayed an image that seemed to say everything you needed to know about its owner. The image featured a partially decomposed ghoul sporting long hair, empty eye sockets, and a diabolical smile. This figure might have been depicted with a bloody axe in hand, his victim clawing at him from beneath. Or perhaps he was occupying a padded cell and wearing a straitjacket, his newly shaven head revealing a skull that was hinged for easy access to the brain. Or maybe he was manipulating none other than the devil himself with marionette strings. Whatever the activity might have been, the one constant factor was the logo above the image, two words written in a blocky, angular typeface: IRON MAIDEN. At this point, your reaction was either to find out more or to get up to sit at a different desk, preferably the one next to the girl in the Laura Ashley skirt.

Iron Maiden (or "Fuckin' Maiden," as it was often called) was without question the most influential band from the New Wave of British Heavy Metal movement. They have championed the cause of true, honest-to-Satan, back-patch metal for more than thirty years, rarely straying from their formula but also never sounding stagnant, a rare accomplishment indeed. More than thirty years after their self-titled debut album was released, not only does it still hold up, it sounds like the album that a lot of the other metal bands—who shall remain nameless—are still ripping off. All the criteria that are used to judge the degree to which a band is "truly" metal can be found on any of Iron Maiden's albums, from the twin-harmony guitars and the banshee shriek of the vocals to Steve Harris' foot-on-the-monitor flurry of bass notes and the belligerent yet progressive drumming. These are all trademarks of any true metal band worth its salt, and they all started with Iron Maiden. The man who deserves the lion's share of the credit for this is Harris, who appears on every album (a feat that no other member, except for guitarist Dave Murray, has accomplished) and who writes the majority of the band's material.

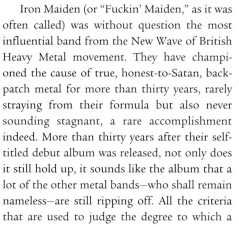

Iron Maiden slays 'em in 1988 on the *Seventh Son of a Seventh Son* tour.

ARENA POLL FOR THE 90S!

YOUR NAME: STEVE HARRIS YOUR BAND: IRON MAIDEN

BEST SOUNDING HALL YOU'VE PLAYED THIS YEAR (OR LAST TOUR): BERCY (PARIS)

BEST SOLOIST YOU'VE HEARD THIS YEAR: JOE SATRIANI

BEST LIVE BAND YOU'VE SEEN THIS YEAR: GOLDEN EARRING

ALBUM OF THE YEAR: ANDY CURRAN

BEST PERSONAL PERFORMANCE OF THE YEAR (include date and venue): LAST TOUR LISBON, PORTUGAL

BEST TRACK ON YOUR LATEST ALBUM: PUBLIC ENEMA Nº 1.

GEAR OF THE YEAR (Your favorite new piece of equipment): ZOOM UNIT

UNDISCOVERED GUITAR HERO: MYKE GRAY

YOUR DREAM BAND (OPTIONAL)

--LEAD GUITAR: TREVOR RABIN

--RHYTHM GUITAR:

--LEAD VOCALS: GEOFF TATE

--BACKGROUND VOCALS: JOHN SLOMAN

--BASS: CHRIS SQUIRE

--DRUMS: NICKO MCBRAIN

--PERCUSSION:

--ACOUSTIC PIANO:

--ELECTRONIC KEYBOARDS/ORGAN: KEITH EMERSON

--HARMONICA:

--SOLO SAX/HORN SECTION:

NAME THE BAND: NATIONAL FLAG

While band mascot Eddie looks on approvingly, superstar Iron Maiden bassist and principal songwriter Steve Harris spits out a million-note-per-second flurry.

The band originally started out with singer Paul Di'Anno, whose gruff, lower-octave vocals often come as something of a shock to newer fans who are accustomed to the sound of his replacement, Bruce Dickinson. The original, Paul Di'Anno–fronted lineup recorded the band's self-titled debut and the follow-up, *Killers*. The debut won the band a hit single in the form of "Running Free," but it's hardly the only good song from that period. On the contrary, what is amazing is not only how fully realized the band's sound was at the time but also the quality of the material on the first two albums. Together, they contain such classics as "Prowler," "Remember Tomorrow," "Phantom of the Opera," "Wrathchild," "Murders in the Rue Morgue," the unexpectedly delicate "Prodigal Son," and the pre-speed metal of "Purgatory," and that's just a Whitman's Sampler. With such strong material and their dues fully paid on the British club circuit, the band was hugely successful with these albums, especially considering that, to most people outside the United Kingdom, they were new. Unfortunately, Di'Anno parted ways with Iron Maiden after

Maiden Japan, allegedly because of serious problems with alcohol. In spite of the anxieties inherent in replacing someone as essential to the band's sound as a singer, Dickinson was brought in from the group Samson to take over the microphone. His voice—dubbed "the air raid siren" by some—was well suited to the material the band was writing for the next album, *Number of the Beast*, which contained such classic material as "Run to the Hills," the concert favorite "Hallowed Be Thy Name,"

IRON MAIDEN

and the title track, among others. All worries were laid to rest when the album was released. It was Iron Maiden's biggest hit ever, and it certified the band members as international superstars. Subsequent albums, such as *Piece of Mind* and *Powerslave*, found the band solidifying their approach and still turning out high-quality material.

Around 1990, after what could only be described as Iron Maiden's classic era, some cracks were starting to show. The first personnel change in several years came when guitarist Adrian Smith quit the band. He was replaced with little fanfare by Janick Gers, but it was impossible to keep the next change quiet; Dickinson, the voice of the band for a decade, announced that he too would be leaving, to focus on his solo career. He was replaced by ex-Wolfsbane singer Blaze Bayley, who should be commended for having the confidence it surely took to accept a gig replacing one of the most imitated singers in all of heavy metal. He recorded just two albums with Iron Maiden, neither of which sold particularly well, probably because of a mixture of metal's extreme lack of hipness at the time and the perception on the part of many fans that Dickinson was just not replaceable—not by Bayley, not by anyone. Apparently, the Maiden camp felt the same way, and both Dickinson and Smith returned to the fold. Although Bayley had

been given the old heave-ho to make room for the returning vocalist, Smith's replacement, Gers, stayed on, making the band a three-guitar ensemble, the implications of which are truly gargantuan and awe-inspiring. The six-piece band recorded *Brave New World* in 2000, and it was the first Maiden album since Dickinson's departure to sell respectably and to be received well by both fans and critics. Subsequent releases have been of a consistently high quality, a remarkable achievement for a band that's hung around as long as this one. Even more remarkable is the fact that Iron Maiden is more commercially successful now than at any other time in their history—their last album, 2010's *The Final Frontier*, was their highest-charting album ever in the United States, debuting at number 4 on the *Billboard* charts. Hopefully, the Iron Maiden story will keep going, and tomorrow's fifteen-year-olds will be able to confuse and confound their classmates with their scary back patches.

Blaze Bayley: vocals (*The X-Factor*, *Virtual XI*); **Clive Burr**: drums (*Iron Maiden* through *Number of the Beast*); **Paul Di'Anno**: vocals (*Iron Maiden* through *Maiden Japan*); **Bruce Dickinson**: vocals (*Number of the Beast* through *A Real Dead One*; *Brave New World* and later) (see also Samson); **Janick Gers**: guitars (*No Prayer for the Dying* and later); **Steve Harris**: bass; **Nicko McBrain**: drums (*Piece of Mind* and later); **Dave Murray**: guitars; **Adrian Smith**: guitars (*Killers*

through *Seventh Son of a Seventh Son*; *Brave New World* and later); **Dennis Stratton**: guitars (*Iron Maiden*)

Discography: *Iron Maiden* (EMI, 1980); *Killers* (EMI, 1981); *Maiden Japan* (EMI, 1981); *Number of the Beast* (EMI, 1982); *Piece of Mind* (EMI, 1983); *Powerslave* (EMI, 1984); *Live After Death* (EMI, 1985); *Somewhere in Time* (EMI, 1986); *Seventh Son of a Seventh Son* (EMI, 1988); *No Prayer for the Dying* (EMI, 1990); *Fear of the Dark* (EMI, 1992); *A Real Live One* (EMI, 1993); *A Real Dead One* (EMI, 1993); *Live at Donnington '92* (Virgin/ EMI, 1994); *The X-Factor* (CMC, 1995); *Virtual XI* (CMC, 1998); *Brave New World* (Sony, 2000); *Rock in Rio* (Sony, 2002); *Dance of Death* (EMI, 2003); *A Matter of Life and Death* (EMI, 2006); *The Final Frontier* (EMI, 2010)

IRON MAN

Years active: 1988–present

Formed in 1988 as a Black Sabbath tribute band, Iron Man was one of the groups that made up the Maryland underground doom scene of the early 1990s, which included Unorthodox, Wretched, and the Obsessed, among others. Most of the bands from this movement were signed to the Hellhound label, which went belly-up in 1995, promptly taking its entire roster of bands down with it, many of whom never recorded again. Iron Man, however, managed to keep it together, and the band released *Generation Void* through the Brainticket label in 1999. The album featured a completely new lineup, except for Alfred Morris III, whose guitar sound was almost identical to that of Sabbath's Tony Iommi, and *The Passage* singer Dan Michalak. As for the rest of the band members, they had a more modern metal sound (well, "modern" as in post-1973, anyway), especially singer Michalak, whose Sabbath influence seemed to be drawn more from Ronnie James Dio or Tony Martin than from Ozzy Osbourne. This lineup didn't continue for long after the album was released, however, and Morris put a whole new band together for a 2000 tour. This group disintegrated the minute they stepped out of the van at the tour's end. However, the band had the metaphorical defibrillator applied to its chest in 2004, and they released the *Submission* EP in 2007, their first new product in eight years. They have since released a new album and another EP and continue to perform today.

Larry Brown: bass (*Black Night*, *The Passage*); **Screaming Mad Dee**: vocals (*I Have Returned*); **Ginger**: bass (*Generation Void*); **Gary Isom**: drums (*The Passage*) (see also *Spirit Caravan*); **Ronnie Kalimon**: drums (*Black Night*) (see also Unorthodox); **Rob Levey**: vocals (*Black Night*); **Dan Michalak**: vocals (*The Passage* and later); **Alfred Morris III**: guitars; **Louis Strachan**: bass (*I Have Returned*); **Vic Tomaso**: drums (*Generation Void*); **Mot Waldmann**: drums (*I Have Returned*)

Discography: *Black Night* (Hellhound, 1993); *The Passage* (Hellhound, 1994); *Generation Void* (Brainticket, 1999); *I Have Returned* (Shadow Kingdom, 2009)

Years active: 1997–2010

Isis, also known as ISIS, plays music that is a mixed stylistic bag. Their sound can be characterized as metal, in the sense that it's aggressive and there are a lot of heavy guitars, but that's only part of the picture. They employ elements used by bands like Swans and Godflesh, namely a ten-ton droning plod that comes in handy when you want the guests you're entertaining to go home. The music also has a plaintive vibe not seen in a lot of metal, and the arrangements rely on frequent and

Aaron Turner of Isis keeps his head down while Cliff Meyer stays in the background.

extreme dynamic shifts that don't turn up on a lot of Great Kat albums either. But just when you think you've got them figured out, the guitars lurch into a downtuned roar, and the vocals go full Cookie Monster. So even though Isis has plenty of metal bona fides, nobody will ever mistake them for Lizzy Borden. The band is the brainchild of vocalist Aaron Turner, the owner of Hydra Head Records, who made Agoraphobic Nosebleed and Xasthur the household names that they are today. He joined up with bassist Jeff Caxide and drummer Aaron Harris in 1997 and brought keyboard player and sample generator Chris Mereschuk onboard to record the EP *The Mosquito Control* in 1998. Mereschuk didn't stay onboard for long, but the band replaced him with Jay Randall and gained guitarist Mike Gallagher. Isis experienced ongoing lineup instability until 2000, which was the year in which they released *Celestial*. Despite its vintage, many fans still consider this one of

their best and most defining works. The period in which the album was made proved so fertile that a lot of the songs recorded didn't get used. The remaining material was released as the EP *SGNL>05* in 2001, which came complete with a version of the song "Celestial," remixed by Godflesh's Justin Broadrick. The next year they released the album *Oceanic*, which became their commercial breakthrough despite how goddamn long the songs were. They followed it up with 2004's *Panopticon*. Both albums received widespread critical acclaim. After 2007's *In the Absence of Truth*, Isis toured with Tool, whose guitarist Adam Jones was so impressed with them that he performed on two songs from the band's 2009 effort, *Wavering Radiant*. However, after touring to support the album, the band surprised their many fans by announcing on their blog that they were hanging up their jerseys. Calling it quits. Packing it in. Nobody in the band had become a huffer or fucked anyone's girlfriend, they simply felt that they had realized their artistic goals and wanted to go out on a high note. How thoughtful.

Jeff Caxide: bass; **Michael Gallagher**: guitar; **Aaron Harris**: drums; **Bryant Clifford Meyer**: guitar; **Aaron Turner**: vocals

Discography: *Celestial* (Escape Artist, 2000); *Oceanic* (Ipecac, 2002); *Panopticon* (Ipecac, 2004); *In the Absence of Truth* (Ipecac, 2006); *Wavering Radiant* (Ipecac, 2009)

JAG PANZER

YEARS ACTIVE: 1981–1988; 1994–2011

Colorado's Jag Panzer is an Aerosmith for the American power metal scene in that the band's comeback put them in a much better position than they ever enjoyed during their earlier, 1980s incarnation. Jag Panzer started out as a Judas Priest–influenced, traditional metal band in 1981, and they gained a high degree of notoriety based on

their first full-length album, *Ample Destruction*, which is still widely regarded as a power metal classic. Unfortunately, the band was never able to build upon that success, as lineup changes slowed things down considerably. Lead singer Harry "Tyrant" Conklin left Jag Panzer and eventually formed his own new band, Titan Force, whose music was remembered for as long as several minutes by those lucky enough to have experienced it. Jag Panzer tried to soldier on as best they could, with guitarist Mark Briody and bassist John Tetley finding new members and recording a follow-up album, *Chain of Command*. Their label never released it, though, for reasons that are unclear. By the mid-1990s, Jag Panzer was completely forgotten, apparently unable to weather the swirling miasma of bad luck that seemed to dog them

without mercy at every turn. However, in an unexpected move, the *Ample Destruction* lineup of Briody, Conklin, and Tetley reconvened with a new drummer, Rikard Stjenquist, and a new guitarist, Joey Tafolla, and released *The Fourth Judgement* in 1997. Even more surprising, the album sold well, at least by American power metal standards. Having finally caught a much-anticipated break, Jag Panzer followed up the album almost every year afterward. One of these releases, 2000's *Thane to the Throne*, was a power metal adaptation of Shakespeare's Macbeth—honest. All of the band's albums were well received since its return, right up to 2011's *The Scourge of the Light*. Perhaps hoping to go out on a high note, the band announced their breakup later that year.

Mark Briody: guitars; **Chris Broderick**: guitars (*Age of Mastery* and later); **Daniel J. Conca**: vocals (*Dissident Alliance*); **Harry "Tyrant" Conklin**: vocals (*Jag Panzer*, *Ample Destruction*, *The Fourth Judgement* and later); **Rick Hilyard**: drums (*Jag Panzer*, *Ample Destruction*); **Chris Kostka**: guitars (*Dissident Alliance*); **Christian Lasegue**: guitar (*Chain of Command*); **Bob Parduba**: vocals (*Chain of Command*); **Rikard Stjernquist**: drums (*The Fourth Judgement* and later); **Joey Tafolla**: guitars (*Ample Destruction*, *The Fourth Judgement*); **John Tetley**: bass

Discography: *Jag Panzer* (Azra, 1983); *Ample Destruction* (Metal Blade, 1984); *Dissident Alliance* (Pavement, 1995); *The Fourth Judgement* (Century Media, 1997); *Age of Mastery* (Century Media, 1998); *Thane to the Throne* (Century Media, 2000); *Mechanized Warfare* (Century Media, 2001); *Chain of Command* (Century Media, 2004); *Casting the Stones* (Century Media, 2004); *The Scourge of the Light* (Steamhammer, 2011)

JANE'S ADDICTION

YEARS ACTIVE: 1985–1991, 2001–PRESENT

Among those not in the know, Nirvana regularly receives credit for "inventing" alternative rock. If you're cool enough to have bought this book, however, then you know that this is a falsehood that the surviving band members would surely

deny in the most vehement manner possible. In fact, Kurt Cobain would likely claw his way out of his dirt-swathed casket, Lucio Fulci–style, to appear on VH1 and set the record straight himself. Alternative rock, like heavy metal, was never "invented"; it was the result of a gradual evolution, a slow, steady, but unstoppable change. One band that let a lot of people know that this particular change was right around the corner was Jane's Addiction. The album that served as their introduction to the general public was 1988's *Nothing's Shocking*. Its off-putting naked-mannequins-on-fire cover art and often uncomfortable subject matter made it a hard sell at first, but against all odds and all conventional wisdom, it finally started to catch on in 1989, a full year after its release. The album doesn't carry quite the same weight today as it did then, mostly because of the fact that the changes in the musical landscape that it foretold have since come and gone. Nevertheless, it was a truly unique album at the time, showing the band using the familiar old tool of Zeppelin-esque riff rock to stake out new territory. Avoiding the ultimately harmless sexual suggestiveness of then-current glam bands, Jane's Addiction preferred lyrics that carried a very real sense of sexual menace ("Sex is violent! Sex is violent! Sex is violent!") and depicted drug abuse in a way that recalled the Velvet Underground, unflinchingly real one moment and almost poignant the next. Anyone who had ever known (or, worse, been) a heroin addict knew all too well the phrase "I'm gonna kick tomorrow" that featured prominently in the song "Jane Says."

The band released their follow-up, *Ritual de lo Habitual*, in 1990 and immediately started pissing people off. The cover depicted three dolls, two female and one male, naked and involved in group sex. This inspired the usual puritanical reactionary response from conservative groups, whose ire prompted the release of a more "family-oriented" cover: a completely white slate with the First Amendment printed on it. Furthermore, the album's big hit single, "Been Caught Stealing," was seized upon by like-minded arbiters of American morality as glorifying the mortal sin of shoplifting. Their own teenage offspring must have no doubt found this amusing, considering that shoplifting has been one of the favorite pastimes of suburban adolescents for several decades now. All controversy aside, the album was both a commercial and a creative success, a sprawling and ambitious work that hinted at a great artistic future for the band. But Jane's Addiction started to unravel because of personal differences between the band members, which, according to some accounts, actually resulted in preshow fisticuffs. Singer and founding member Perry Farrell was also beginning to feel that the band's increasing popularity was actually working against them, making them into a commercial entity that was too large and unwieldy to remain within their control. He decided to send the band off in grand style, mounting the Lollapalooza festival tour in 1991. The tour featured bands as diverse as the Butthole Surfers, the Rollins Band, Ice-T, Nine Inch Nails, and Siouxsie and the Banshees. Farrell went on to form Porno for Pyros, and guitarist Dave Navarro did a brief stint with the Red Hot Chili Peppers. Jane's Addiction did a brief but successful reunion tour in 1997, and reunited again in 2001 to make the album *Strays* with producer Bob Ezrin. After performing at 2003's Lollapalooza, they broke up yet again, then reunited in 2008, this time with original bassist Eric Avery, who had declined to participate in every reunion before. However, he didn't stay on past 2010, and in 2011 they recorded *The Great Escape Artist* with TV on the Radio bassist Dave Sitek.

Eric Avery: bass (*Jane's Addiction* to *Ritual de lo Habitual*); **Chris Chaney**: bass (*Strays*); **Perry Farrell**: vocals; **Dave Navarro**: guitar; **Stephen Perkins**: drums; **David Andrew Sitek**: bass, keyboards (*The Great Escape Artist*)

Discography: *Jane's Addiction* (Triple X, 1987); *Nothing's Shocking* (Warner Bros., 1988); *Ritual de lo Habitual* (Warner Bros., 1990); *Live and Rare* (Warner Bros., 1991); *Strays* (Capitol, 2003); *The Great Escape Artist* (Capitol, 2011)

JOAN JETT

YEARS ACTIVE: 1975–PRESENT

Joan Jett was the most significant role model available to female hard rockers in the 1980s. Born Joan Larkin in Philadelphia, she relocated with her family to Los Angeles when she was twelve years old. A scant three years later, a newly rechristened Joan Jett was sharing the stage with none other than Lita Ford in the Runaways, a teenage girl group put together by record producer Kim Fowley. The band was popular in Los Angeles and deeply beloved in Japan, but they never achieved much commercial success anywhere else. They broke up in 1980 and Jett, at the ripe old age of twenty, moved to New York City to pursue her solo career. But the Big Apple was not kind to her, and it quickly became apparent that there were no labels interested in signing her. Never one to be particularly concerned about where she was or wasn't wanted, an undaunted Jett released her first album independently. Fans who were accustomed to the hard bubblegum sound of the Runaways were surprised to hear her solo record, a straightforward hard rock outing that at times recalled AC/DC. Fortunately, the surprise they manifested was of the good variety. The album sold well enough to net her a contract with Boardwalk Records, which did her the courtesy of reissuing the formerly eponymous album under the title *Bad Reputation*.

Jett's second album was the monster hit that removed her from the shadow of the Runaways for the rest of her natural life. *I Love Rock 'n' Roll* was released in 1981, and the single of the same name (a cover of an Arrows song) became an omnipresent, unavoidable hit that year, reaching the Top 10. Apparently seeing no reason to screw around with a good thing, Jett released other cover songs to great success, including "Crimson and Clover" by Tommy James and the Shondells and "Do You Wanna Touch Me" by Gary Glitter, a man who has

no doubt learned how to fix computers on his own in recent years. But none of them reached the level of popularity of "I Love Rock 'n' Roll." Jett has not revisited the Top 10 since then, but she has managed to keep her career choices and reputation respectable as the years have passed, with the sole exception of her appearance as Michael J. Fox's sister in the very stupid 1987 movie *Light of Day*. More recently, she has had to suffer the indignity of seeing Britney Spears cover Jett's version of "I Love Rock 'n' Roll" in the 2002 movie *Crossroads*, a chilling fate that would surely cause any artist to question his/her belief in a benevolent god. She also made the questionable decision to perform "I Love Rock 'n' Roll" with Trans-Siberian Orchestra at Madison Square Garden in 2005, and she has only herself to blame for that one. However, on the plus side, Jett began receiving accolades in the mid-1990s from female artists such as Babes in Toyland, Bikini Kill, Hole, and L7, all of whom have claimed Jett and the Runaways as hugely influential. Indeed, it is difficult to imagine where our snarlingly confrontational female artists would be today without having had Joan Jett to kick down the door for them.

Discography: *Bad Reputation* (Blackheart, 1981); *I Love Rock 'n' Roll* (Blackheart, 1981); *Album* (Blackheart, 1983); *Glorious Results of a Misspent Youth* (Blackheart, 1984); *Good Music* (Epic, 1986); *Up Your Alley* (Epic, 1988); *The Hit List* (Epic, 1990); *Notorious* (Epic, 1991); *Pure and Simple* (Warner Bros., 1994); *Sinner* (Blackheart, 2006)

JUDAS PRIEST

YEARS ACTIVE: 1969–PRESENT

Judas Priest is one of the most influential heavy metal bands of all time, period. They inspired not only the New Wave of British Heavy Metal (Iron Maiden, itself the most influential band of that movement, owes its entire sound to the twin

Mess with Joan Jett at your own peril.

guitars and screaming vocals of vintage Priest) but also thrash metal. As an unintended bonus, Judas Priest also has the unique distinction of helping to shape heavy metal fashion, thanks to the virtual founder of the classic heavy metal vocal style, lead singer Rob Halford. He publicly announced his homosexuality in 1997, revealing that he got his leather-and-chains look from the gay bar scene. Amusingly enough, it caught on with the notoriously homophobic males of the metal scene, who were perhaps not aware that they were dressed in a manner similar to that of one of the Village People.

Formed in 1970 by guitarist K. K. Downing and bassist Ian Hill, the band underwent various personnel and label changes before reaching anything even remotely resembling a stable situation. Although their second album, *Sad Wings of Destiny*, is considered by many aficionados to be an indispensable classic—Megadeth's Dave Mustaine claims it was a primary influence on him—the band didn't reach a wide audience until they signed with Columbia Records. Their debut for the label, 1977's *Sin After Sin*, represented a major step forward in terms of their popularity, which became even greater the

following year with the release of *Stained Class*. Both albums contained material that was heavier and more aggressive than anything else on the market, and Priest quickly found favor with the future members of thrash bands (Slayer actually covered the *Sin After Sin* track "Dissident Aggressor" in 1988, and its version was almost identical to Priest's). In 1978, when *Hell Bent for Leather* was

OPPOSITE: Unlikely candidates, the members of Judas Priest, in 1979, prepare for roller boogie in New York City's Central Park. Left to right: Glenn Tipton, Dave Holland, Ian Hill, Rob Halford, and K.K. Downing.

RIGHT: The foggy effects of dry ice combined with onstage motorcycle riding—much like the scene here—would lead Rob Halford to break his nose in a 1990 Judas Priest performance.

released, it was becoming apparent that Judas Priest was having a profound effect on the new breed of groups just coming out of the gate. The metal "uniform" now consisted of leather, chains, spikes, and so forth, and all of the bands had deeply morbid lyrical preoccupations, both of which were Priest mainstays. The New Wave of British Heavy Metal was officially under way, and the Birmingham quintet was responsible.

When they weren't busy starting cultural upheavals, the band occupied themselves by breaking into the British Top 10, as they did with their 1980 album, *British Steel*. The release had such hits to its credit as "Breaking the Law" and "Living After Midnight," and at this time the band began making significant inroads in America, with the help of new network MTV and the new format of the music video. Despite the fact that the videos, particularly the one for "Breaking the Law," were moronic beyond belief, they extended the band's commercial reach to places it had never gone before. As a result, when two years had passed and the *Screaming for Vengeance* album was released, the pump was fully primed. The 1982 album captured arguably the band's finest hour. It contained "You've Got Another Thing Comin'," a hit single for Judas Priest, and it was ultimately an artistic success. The album was their heaviest and most brutal, reaching its apex with the title track, whose opening salvo is among the most fearsome eight seconds of music in 1980s metal history.

The album was followed up in fine style with *Defenders of the Faith*, but the band made its first major misstep in 1986 on the glossy, keyboard-driven *Turbo* album. The record seemed especially flaccid when compared to thrash bands like Metallica and Slayer, who regularly cited Priest as a primary influence but who were now drawing the spotlight away from Priest. The band backpedaled nicely with the less anemic sounding *Ram It Down*. However, it was 1990's *Painkiller*, with insanely technical former Racer X drummer Scott Travis, that saw Judas Priest in their most hyperactive and aggressive mode since *Screaming for Vengeance*; they were clearly trying to make up the ground that they had lost and also win respect among the hardcore metal fans whose interest was beginning to wane.

Unfortunately, by that point lead singer Rob Halford had decided that he wanted to move on, and he left Judas Priest to form his own group, which went by the very silly name of Fight. His departure dealt the band a life-threatening blow, as Halford's voice was as strong a trademark as their twin lead guitars. Quite understandably, the band reacted by going into hiding, and except for the 1993 *Metal Works '73–'93* compilation, it would be seven years before they were heard from again.

By 1997, Halford had disbanded Fight and signed with Nothing Records, the label owned by Nine Inch Nails' Trent Reznor and home to Marilyn Manson. Halford's project for the label, *Two*, was in truth somewhat derivative of Reznor's band and didn't sell very well, despite a shocking turn of events occurring on the eve of the album's release, when Halford came out of the proverbial closet. His revelation surprised possibly as many as six people in the entire world (five of whom were infants). Meanwhile, as this completely super-fluous event was tak-ing place in one part of the world, Judas Priest had regrouped with a new singer, Tim "Ripper" Owens, who had, in all seri-ousness, sung for a Judas Priest cover band. The newly re-formed band released their first new offer-ing in seven years, at almost the

exact same time as their old band-mate released his. Unfortunately, Priest's album, called *Jugulator*, was an unfocused and pedes-trian effort despite the much-ballyhooed claim that it signi-fied a return to the band's roots. Apparently they believed that revisiting their heyday meant releas-ing albums whose song titles were 30 percent "Dead"- or "Death"-centric, 20 percent concerned with head trauma, and, if you count the title track, another 20 percent focused on blood, the most popular red liquid in all of heavy metal.

Just when it seemed that things couldn't get any nuttier, an extremely bizarre situation developed where there were, in effect, two differ-ent Judas Priests releasing albums at the same time. Halford had disbanded Two because of a complete lack of public interest and started a full-on, no-bullshit metal band that was creatively named Halford. Their debut album was released in 2000, and the band's live set constituted—surprise!—a whole lot of Judas Priest material. The following year, Halford released a live double CD, *Live Insurrection*, which was interesting considering Judas Priest had released one of its own, *'98 Live Meltdown*. Since the Halford CD was very heavy on the Priest material, there were essentially two live Judas Priest double CDs out at the same time and competing with each other. As if 2001 wasn't creepy enough, that year also saw the deeply moving story of Owens' journey to the Priest microphone brought

to the silver screen—well, not quite. Originally, the story of Judas Priest and its new singer was supposed to be made with the band's involvement. However, pos-sibly sensing that the film was going to be a big pile of cow chips, the band pulled out of the project. It eventually became the unwatchable movie *Rock Star*, featuring Marky Mark as an aver-age Joe who gets to join his favorite band, Steel Dragon. The movie, with acting, writing, and direction at levels slightly lower than those found in the 1995 film *Showgirls*, features a scene involving the original, gay lead singer quitting the band to join an Irish dance company. This was probably meant as a slight against Halford, but the film-makers would have been well served to know that people need to see a movie to be able to laugh at its jokes.

Since 1991, Judas Priest had been plagued by the same question, relentlessly asked of them by fans and media outlets alike: "Is Rob Halford coming back to Judas Priest?" Eventually, in 2003, they made the announcement that fans had been waiting over a decade to hear—the singer would, in fact, take his rightful place at the Judas Priest microphone stand, and when they released their 2005 reunion album, *Angel of Retribution*, the clouds parted, the seas rose, and the firmament sang joyously. People bought the album, too, perhaps not knowing that its closing track, "Lochness" was a 13-minute orgy of ridicu-lousness about the titular Scottish beast that has eluded cryptozoologists for centuries. Then the band went completely off the reservation for

OPPOSITE: Judas Priest slays 'em live in concert. Left to right: K.K. Downing, Rob Halford, Glenn Tipton, and Ian Hill.

through *Ram It Down*); **Alan Moore**: drums (*Sad Wings of Destiny*); **Tim "Ripper" Owens**: vocals (*Jugulator* through *Live In London*); **Simon Phillips**: drums (*Sin After Sin*); **Glenn Tipton**: guitars; **Scott Travis**: drums (*Painkiller* and later)

Discography: *Rocka Rolla* (Gull, 1974); *Sad Wings of Destiny* (Gull, 1976); *Sin After Sin* (Columbia, 1977); *Stained Class* (Columbia, 1978); *Hell Bent for Leather* (Columbia, 1978); *Unleashed in the East* (Live in Japan) (Columbia, 1979); *British Steel* (Columbia/Legacy, 1980); *Point of Entry* (Columbia/Legacy, 1981); *Screaming for Vengeance* (Columbia/Legacy, 1982); *Defenders of the Faith* (Columbia/Legacy, 1984); *Turbo* (Columbia, 1986); *Priest . . . Live!* (Sony, 1987); *Ram It Down* (Columbia, 1988); *Painkiller* (Columbia, 1990); *Jugulator* (CMC, 1997); *'98 Live Meltdown* (SPV, 1998); *Demolition* (Atlantic, 2001); *Angel of Retribution* (Epic, 2005); *Nostradamus* (Epic, 2008)

2008's *Nostradamus*, a two-disc concept album about the 16th-century French seer and alchemist. Containing keyboards, choirs and the occasional lyric sung in Latin, the album was easily the goofiest thing the band had ever recorded, which is saying a lot. Still, they deserve credit for the sheer balls it took to see through a project that cooler heads no doubt tried to talk them out of many times. Two years later, the band announced that their upcoming tour, the appropriately titled Epitaph World Tour, would be their last. However, founding guitarist K. K. Downing would never finish it. In April 2011 he made the somewhat surprising decision to retire from the band, effective immediately. The band replaced him with Richie Faulkner, a relative unknown who had been plucked from the band of Lauren Harris, daughter of Iron Maiden bassist Steve Harris. He made his live debut with the band in May 2011 on *American Idol*, and Downing can now go to his deathbed knowing he quit the group in time to avoid so horrific a fate.

Les Binks: drums (*Stained Class* through *Unleashed in the East*); **K.K. Downing**: guitars; **Rob Halford**: vocals (*Rocka Rolla* through *Painkiller*, *Angel of Retribution* and later); **Ian Hill**: bass; **John Hinch**: drums (*Rocka Rolla*); **Dave Holland**: drums (*British Steel*

One of the newer metal subcategories to emerge in the new millenium was that of doom-death (or, depending on your preferences, death-doom—but there is, apparently, some kind of difference). The style incorporates the slovenly tempos and epic song structures of doom and marries them with the growling vocals of death metal, and one of its leading proponents is Sweden's Katatonia. The band was formed in 1992, and its releases from that period are emblematic of the style. But as the 1990s gave way to the noughties, the band started changing their sound, incorporating cleaner, nay, human-sounding vocals and the occasional jaunty tempo here and there. Their style progressed into somewhat more accessible, melodic territory, although it would still be something of a stretch to characterize any of this music as commercial in any sense. In 2001 Katatonia released the album *Last Fair Deal Gone Down*, which is the title of a song by 1930s blues

guitarist Robert Johnson, and their most recent album was 2009's *Night Is the New Day*.

Mikael Åkerfeldt: vocals (*Brave Murder Day*); **Guillaume "Israphel Wing" Le Huche**: bass (*Dance of December Souls*, *For Funerals to Come*); **Daniel Liljekvist**: drums (*Last Fair Deal Gone Down* and later); **Fredrik Norrman**: guitars (*Brave Murder Day* and later); **Mattias Norrman**: bass (*Last Fair Deal Gone Down* and later); **Anders "Blakkheim" Nyström**: guitars; **Mikael Oretoft**: bass (*Saw You Drown*, *Discouraged Ones*); **Jonas "Lord Seth" Renkse**: vocals/drums

Discography: *Jhva Elohim Meth: The Revival* (Vic, 1992); *Dance of December Souls* (No Fashion, 1993); *For Funerals to Come* (Avantgarde, 1995); *Brave Murder Day* (Century Media, 1997); *Sounds of Decay* (Avantgarde, 1997); *Saw You Drown* (Avantgarde, 1998); *Discouraged Ones* (Century Media, 1998); *Tonight's Decision* (Peaceville, 1999); *Last Fair Deal Gone Down* (Peaceville/Snapper, 2001); *Viva Emptiness* (Peaceville, 2003); *The Great Cold Distance* (Peaceville, 2006); *Night Is the New Day* (Peaceville, 2009)

Killswitch Engage was formed by bassist Mike D'Antonio, drummer Adam Dutkiewicz, vocalist Jesse Leach, and guitarist Joel Stroetzel. The group secured a deal with Ferret Records, which released their self-titled 2000 debut. It didn't take long before Roadrunner caught wind of Killswitch Engage, and the label released *Alive or Just Breathing* in 2002. The band underwent a major lineup shift at this point, when Leach left the group and Dutkiewicz left the drummer's throne to become the band's second guitarist. Dutkiewicz was replaced by Justin Foley. A new vocalist was recruited by the name of Howard Jones. Sorry, but no, it was a different Howard Jones than the "No One Is to Blame" guy, although that would have been awesome. Jones debuted on the song "When Darkness Falls" from the soundtrack to the incredibly shitty horror movie *Freddy vs. Jason*. The new lineup debuted in full-length form on 2004's *The End of Heartache*, which almost

Killswitch Engage gets sweaty in the U.K. in December 2002.

made the *Billboard* top 20 and even earned the band a Grammy nomination. It was Killswitch Engage's best seller to date, and in 2007 it was certified gold with 500,000 copies sold in the U.S. of A. In 2006, the band released *As Daylight Dies*, which was also certified gold in 2007. In 2009 the band released their second self-titled album, and this one debuted at number seven on the *Billboard* 200, putting them within striking distance of Katy Perry territory. In 2010, Jones was sidelined with back pain, so they toured with replacement vocalist Philip Labonte, and had original vocalist Jesse Leach join in on a few

tunes. Killswitch Engage announced that they expected to return to the studio in early 2012 to start making a new album, but just a couple of days into the new year they announced that Jones had left the group. The singer revealed that he had left because he had been diagnosed with type 2 diabetes, and the prospect of becoming metalcore's answer to Bret Michaels and managing the disease on the road was just not appealing to him. The band has stated their intention to go on with a new singer, whoever that unnamed, mysterious, hypothetical person may be.

Mike D'Antonio: bass; **Adam Dutkiewicz**: drums; **Justin Foley**: drums (*The End of Heartache* and later); **Howard Jones**: vocals (*The End of Heartache* and later) **Jesse Leach**: vocals; **Joel Stroetzel**: guitars

Discography: *Killswitch Engage* (Ferret, 2000); *Alive or Just Breathing* (Roadrunner, 2002); *The End of Heartache* (Roadrunner, 2004); *As Daylight Dies* (Roadrunner, 2006); *Killswitch Engage* (Roadrunner, 2009)

RECORD LABELS

The major labels may have been involved in a signing frenzy in the late 1980s, snatching up every metal band they could find, but metal would never have reached its level of commercial prestige had there not been a group of independent imprints willing to take a chance and invest what little money they had into an unproven band solely because they liked the music. Once the majors lost interest and decided that it would make brilliant long-term sense to sign alternative pop bands like Dishwalla, the indies were there yet again to catch the bands when they fell. Here are some of the more significant non-corporate labels that specialize in heavy metal.

CENTURY MEDIA RECORDS

Century Media is one of the biggest independent metal labels out there. In fact, if you're a fan of newer metal bands, particularly power metal bands like Iced Earth or Jag Panzer, chances are that any CD you pick up will bear the Century Media imprint. But the company is not strictly a power metal label by any means, and its roster has boasted bands as diverse as Eyehategod and Voivod.

EARACHE RECORDS

It would not be a stretch to say that Earache Records pretty much put grindcore on the map. While the label has at times deviated from its formula and released albums by bands like Cathedral and Sleep, Earache is mainly known for its grindcore releases, many from pioneering bands, from the sublime (Napalm Death, Carcass, Morbid Angel) to the ridiculous (Anal Cunt).

MEGAFORCE RECORDS

Megaforce is easily the most important and influential underground metal label in the genre's history. Earache may have put grindcore on the map, but it wouldn't have been able to do that had Megaforce not brought underground metal to the mainstream in the first place. Megaforce released landmark albums by bands such as Anthrax, King's X, Testament, and Manowar, but the label is most famous for releasing Metallica's 1983 debut, *Kill 'Em All*, the album that opened the floodgates for everything that came afterward.

METAL BLADE RECORDS

While Metal Blade Records cannot take credit for bringing Metallica to the masses, the label's impact on the underground metal movement was certainly highly significant, and it still releases quality material today. Metal Blade started off giving a home to Fates Warning, D.R.I., Slayer, and Celtic Frost, but also branched out into releasing material from classic artists like Deep Purple and Alice Cooper. The company even had the Goo Goo Dolls on its roster awhile back for some reason. Recently, it gave a home to King's X, which was fresh off a soured deal with Atlantic.

NOISE RECORDS

Noise Records is very similar to Metal Blade and signed many early thrash bands which went on to great things. However, Noise's artists are a little darker, as evidenced by its roster's inclusion of Kreator, Celtic Frost, and Voivod, all bands that had a huge effect on extreme music in following years. Now aligned with Sanctuary Records, the label continues to bring metal bands to fans worldwide.

PEACEVILLE RECORDS

Peaceville picked up where the first wave of independent metal labels left off, signing bands who proved to be as influential in the 1990s as the Megaforce and Metal Blade bands were in the 1980s. Peaceville's bands include some of metal's most notorious, such as My Dying Bride, Paradise Lost, and Darkthrone.

ROADRUNNER RECORDS

Originally called Roadracer, Roadrunner Records was at one time home to Carnivore, among others. With the name change also seemed to come a newfound shrewdness, and the label began to sign bands that became massively successful, such as Sepultura and Fear Factory. It also issued albums by established artists like Motörhead and Mercyful Fate, and even had a few head scratchers on its roster, such as the alt.country group Blue Mountain. As if that were not weird enough, the label at one time issued *The Legend of Jim Croce*—no kidding—and one can only imagine what a tour featuring the "Time in a Bottle" singer and Type O Negative would have been like.

KING DIAMOND

YEARS ACTIVE: 1974–PRESENT

There is perhaps no singer in all of heavy metal who garners such extreme reactions, both negative and positive, as King Diamond (no relation to Neil). The former Mercyful Fate vocalist possesses an expansive singing voice that ranges over multiple octaves, and he seems to really, really want you to know that he's going to use all of them. This has caused him to win a devoted legion of fans who marvel at his impressive technique as well as a legion of disparagers whose hatred for him is so intense that, if it could be correctly harnessed, could light our cities. The caped singer also insists on using a microphone stand that consists of two human bones grafted together to form an inverted cross, and until recently he always appeared in Gene Simmons–inspired stage makeup—that is, of course, until the real Gene Simmons sued him. Diamond was forced to change his makeup design, and he chose a charming wraparound motif that recalls a bleeding zebra.

Diamond and Mercyful Fate had musical differences that ultimately caused the band to break up after two promising and well-received albums. The singer took it in stride, however, forming his own band and taking with him two former Mercyful Fate band mates, guitarist Michael Denner and bassist Timi Hansen. To the surprise of absolutely no one, the new band sounded a whole lot like Diamond's old band, the major difference being King Diamond's greater emphasis on the vocals. The first three albums—1986's *Fatal Portrait*, 1987's *Abigail*, and 1988's *Them*—are widely held to be the group's strongest releases.

In the 1990s, Diamond got a little sidetracked by extracurricular entanglements. Aside from his legal

Oops! King Diamond in 1989 after spilling some Easter egg dye on his face.

discomfiture with the KISS camp, he took some flak for his outspoken views on the joys of satanism, the almost exclusive subject of his lyrics. Sensationalist newsman Geraldo Rivera, on a break from getting chairs thrown at his face by white supremacists, based an episode of his television talk show on satanism in rock music. Diamond, an avowed and outspoken devotee of the Dark One, was accused of that old chestnut, "backward masking." Apparently, Rivera and his panel of "experts" completely overlooked the richly satanic content to be heard when Diamond's records are played forward. Also, if the guy makes records that, when played in their intended direction, glorify satanism, then wouldn't it stand to reason that playing them backward would cause the listener to embrace Christianity?

After Diamond's career stoppages were dispensed with (including a substantial settlement paid to KISS in the aforementioned Battle of the Stage Makeup), Mercyful Fate reconvened with their singer in the mid-1990s and began making new albums. At the same time that he was reuniting with his old band mates, Diamond was still releasing his own albums, and at one point, both King Diamond and Mercyful Fate went on tour together, with one band opening for the other. King Diamond released a sequel to one of their best-received albums, *Abigail*, in 2002. The album, *Abigail II: The Revenge*, was met enthusiastically by the King Diamond faithful, who, one assumes, had been waiting fifteen years for that moment to arrive. In 2010, the singer had a major health scare when he was hospitalized for multiple heart attacks, necessitating triple-bypass surgery. The procedure was successful, but he understandably put all of his upcoming musical projects on hold while recovering. A little over a year later, in December 2011, he took to the stage for the first time since his surgery to appear at Metallica's 30th anniversary concert in San Francisco. Here's hoping the singer and his tibia-and-femur microphone stand make a full recovery.

Darrin Anthony: drums (*The Spider's Lullabye*); **Pete Blakk**: guitars (*Them* through *The Eye*); **Mikkey Dee**: drums (*Fatal Portrait* through *Conspiracy*) (see also

Motörhead); **Michael Denner**: guitars (*Fatal Portrait*, *Abigail*) (see also Mercyful Fate); **King Diamond**: vocals (see also Mercyful Fate); **Glen Drover**: guitars (*House of God*); **Chris Estes**: bass (*The Spider's Lullabye* through *Voodoo*); **Timi Hansen**: bass (*Fatal Portrait*, *Abigail*) (see also Mercyful Fate); **David Harbour**: bass (*House of God*); **John Luke Hebert**: drums (*The Graveyard* through *House of God*); **Andy LaRocque**: guitars (see also Death); **Hal Patino**: bass (*Them* through *The Eye*; *Abigail II: The Revenge* and later); **Snowy Shaw**: drums (*The Eye*) (see also Memento Mori, Mercyful Fate); **Herb Simonsen**: guitars (*The Spider's Lullabye* through *Voodoo*); **Matt Thompson**: drums (*Abigail II: The Revenge* and later); **Mike Wead**: guitars (*Abigail II: The Revenge* and later) (see also Memento Mori, Mercyful Fate); **Livia Zita**: vocals (*The Puppet Master* and later)

Discography: *Fatal Portrait* (Roadrunner, 1986); *Abigail* (Roadrunner, 1987); *Them* (Roadrunner, 1988); *The Dark Sides* (Roadrunner, 1988); *Conspiracy* (Roadrunner, 1989); *The Eye* (Roadrunner, 1990); *In Concert 1987: Abigail* (Roadrunner, 1991); *A Dangerous Meeting* (Roadrunner, 1992); *The Spider's Lullabye* (Metal Blade, 1995); *The Graveyard* (Metal Blade, 1996); *Voodoo* (Metal Blade, 1998); *House of God* (Metal Blade, 2000); *Black Rose: 20 Years Ago—A Night of Rehearsals* (Metal Blade, 2001); *Abigail II: The Revenge* (Metal Blade, 2002); *The Puppet Master* (Massacre, 2003); *Deadly Lullabyes* (Massacre, 2004); *Give Me Your Soul . . . Please* (Massacre, 2007)

KING'S X

Years active: 1980–present

King's X is without question one of the most unjustly underrated bands in heavy metal, or any other genre, for that matter. Their combination of high-quality songwriting, intoxicating vocal harmonies, and instrumental prowess—Ty Tabor has got to be one of the best Hendrix-influenced guitarists ever (listen to the *Faith Hope Love* track "Moanjam" if you are skeptical)—should have guaranteed them a shot at superstardom, but it just wasn't in the cards. There are different theories: mismanagement, unrealistic label expectations. There is even the deeply disturbing possibility that conservative, white, suburban metal audiences of the late 1980s were unable

When Doug Pinnick (left) and Ty Tabor of King's X perform live, they're more than likely to put any other band playing that night to shame.

to accept a band with a—gasp!—black member. Whatever the reason, it's a goddamn shame King's X never received more credit. This Texas band nevertheless managed to carve out a considerable niche for itself. The band's sound is so unique and immediately identifiable that almost no one attempts to duplicate it. On top of that, their fan base is about as die-hard as anyone could ask for, and the band is deeply respected in the heavy metal musicians' community. Case in point: they count among their admirers no less an authority than Deep Purple/Rainbow guitarist Ritchie Blackmore, who has praised them effusively. Blackmore has been particularly forthcoming in his admiration of their live shows, which prompted him to concede that he "wouldn't want to follow them." Considering that Blackmore appears on Deep Purple's *Made in Japan*, widely considered one of the greatest live albums of all time, this is high praise indeed.

In 1988, King's X released its debut album, *Out of the Silent Planet*, to universal confusion, and it died a quiet commercial death. However, the group's next album, *Gretchen Goes to Nebraska*, released the following year, developed a strong buzz as other, more prominent bands—such as Living Colour—cited them in the music press as one of the best new bands around. This, coupled with MTV putting their "Over My Head" music video on semiheavy rotation, got the band's name out there and helped to set the stage for a major breakthrough with their next album, *Faith Hope Love*. This is an ambitious near-masterpiece that won the band more converts, as well as an opening slot on AC/DC's world tour. Sadly, management problems began to slow the upward climb that the band had been experiencing. The buzzkill was fully manifested on their self-titled fourth album, which seemed a bit uninspired compared with the band's previous work, perhaps because they had their hands full cleaning up the mess that their old management had left them.

The next album, however, put King's X right back at center stage where the band belonged.

In 1994, *Dogman*, helmed by Pearl Jam producer Brendan O'Brien (a huge fan of King's X), was possibly the band's finest hour, both in terms of the songwriting and the sound of the recording. The band had always been heavy, but O'Brien's mixing-board expertise resulted in an aggressive, muscular sound that was a shock to fans and resulted in the band's greatest commercial success to date. Naturally, their label, Atlantic, wanted a smash hit to follow it up, and 1996's *Ear Candy* failed to meet those expectations, most likely because the label did nothing to advertise or promote it. The band and the label parted company afterward—whether King's X was dropped or left the label is not known. They were not homeless for long, however. In mainstream circles they may have been little more than a cult phenomenon, but in the metal underground they were well-respected superstars, and their contract was picked up in short order by Metal Blade Records. The label was clearly happy to have King's X on its roster and exerted no pressure on the band members to do anything but make the records they wanted to make. Their first release for the label, 1998's *Tape Head*, coincided with solo releases from Tabor and bassist/vocalist Doug Pinnick, who made his under the name Poundhound and also collaborated with former Trouble guitarist Bruce Franklin on a project called Supershine. After four albums for Metal Blade, King's X signed to InsideOut Music and released 2005's *Ogre Tones*, their best album in years. Three years later they released the very well-received *XV*, their first album to chart since the Atlantic days.

Jerry Gaskill: drums/backing vocals; **Doug Pinnick**: bass/vocals; **Ty Tabor**: guitars/vocals

Discography: *Out of the Silent Planet* (Megaforce, 1988); *Gretchen Goes to Nebraska* (Megaforce, 1989); *Faith Hope Love* (Megaforce, 1990); *King's X* (Atlantic, 1992); *Dogman* (Atlantic, 1994); *Ear Candy* (Atlantic, 1996); *Best of King's X* (Atlantic, 1997); *Tape Head* (Metal Blade, 1998); *Please Come Home . . . Mr. Bulbous* (Metal Blade, 2000); *Manic Moonlight* (Metal Blade, 2001); *Black Like Sunday* (Metal Blade, 2003); *Live All Over the Place* (Metal Blade, 2004); *Ogre Tones* (InsideOut, 2005); *Live & Live Some More* (Molken, 1994); *XV* (InsideOut, 2008)

KISS

YEARS ACTIVE: 1973–present

KISS was one of the most popular bands of the 1970s, and as the many reunion tours have indicated with stunning clarity, its appeal has not diminished in the intervening years. Almost everyone who plays in a heavy metal band can count the group as an influence, whether they realize it or not. Even black metal bands, who probably consider KISS to be about as metal as John Tesh, owe their corpse-painted appearance to these nice Jewish boys from Queens.

While these Knights In Satan's Service certainly had their share of solid material to earn them their place on the FM radio stations of the 1970s, they were, by their own admission, a triumph of style over substance. The band was first and foremost about spectacle, an attribute probably best personified by bassist and singer Gene Simmons, who took KISS' image to its furthest extreme. While the rest of the band was content to wear makeup that recalled either a domesticated house pet or an entity of ambiguous celestial origin, Simmons sported demonic kabuki face paint, a bat cape with a six-foot wingspan, eight-inch platform boots, and an extremely long tongue. He also had a propensity for spitting blood and breathing fire, no doubt to the joy of the blue-haired audience who got to experience firsthand the band's debut/final performance on the *Mike Douglas Show*.

In actuality, the band never wrote a single song that captured even an iota of the terror and mystery that their appearance inspired. Their brand of heavy metal was really a mixture of hard rock and glam that at times recalled the New York Dolls and that ultimately predicted 1980s arena rock. But it hardly matters. The message was the medium in this case, and it worked like a charm, as it has worked for no band before or since. When KISS was first playing showcases to court a recording contract, Casablanca Records president Neil Bogart agreed to sign the band on the sole condition that they get rid of the makeup. The band members wisely refused, and the rest is history, since it's probably safe to say that KISS without greasepaint would never have achieved the level of notoriety that they did. The songs were far from groundbreaking, and with the possible exception of lead guitarist Ace Frehley, the individual musicians did not exactly possess jaw-dropping instrumental prowess. Ultimately, however, this worked in their favor. Out of necessity, they were limited to crafting straight-forward material, and the resultant simplicity of the songs allowed them to be easily accessible to the arena rock denizens of the day.

KISS had three albums to their credit before their commercial breakthrough. Although these albums—*KISS*, *Hotter Than Hell*, and *Dressed to Kill*—are all considered classics today, at the time the band was struggling to get the records to sell, bankrupting their label in the process. They had, however, toured incessantly to build their fan base, and it was the recording of one of these tours that produced the *Alive!* double album. The album and its hit single, "Rock & Roll All Nite," made the band superstars. Conventional wisdom holds that the album captured the energy of a KISS concert in a way

Before Gene Simmons existed, there was Chaim Witz, a nice Jewish boy.
OPPOSITE: Another nice Jewish boy, Stanley Eisen, later became known as Paul Stanley.

that no studio recording ever could. Based on the momentum that *Alive!* had generated, the group's follow-up album, 1976's *Destroyer*, went platinum, and its single "Beth," sung by drummer Peter Criss, was their first to make it to the Top 10.

Seizing upon this success, the band—actually, Simmons and guitarist/singer Paul Stanley–initiated the KISS merchandising machine, and suddenly scores of products with the band's name were everywhere. This may not seem like a big deal today, but at the time it was highly unusual for a band to market itself this aggressively as a commodity. Most groups wanted you to view them as serious artists but secretly hoped you never found out that they liked making money as well. KISS didn't care what you thought of them as long as you bought the lunch box, or the board game, or the comic books, which had the band members' blood mixed into its ink in a brilliantly conceived publicity stunt. They just never seemed to run out of ways to hawk their wares, and a lot of this is attributable to the band's uncanny ability to take the ordinary and dress it up as something new. For example, you did not join a fan club but rather you could, for a

mere five dollars, join the KISS Army, an organization whose military applications are still unclear at this point. There were also pinball machines, masks, home makeup kits . . . it just went on and on. There is, however, such a phenomenon as too much of a good thing, and it eventually became evident that the KISS merchandising operation was starting to seriously overplay its hand.

Regardless of the fact that after *Love Gun* the band was simply not creating music of the same caliber as before, they were still as popular as ever and still trying to tap every possible source of income. That the band was now shilling themselves to their detriment became evident in 1978 when they made the TV movie *KISS Meets the Phantom of the Park*, which was so bad that it all but filled living rooms accommodating television sets with a rancid, fishlike odor. While nobody was expecting Kurosawacaliber work, it was of so poor a quality that it fell beneath even the ankle-high standards of a medium that delivers moving images to your house for free.

The next misstep occurred later that same year, when all four band members released separate solo albums simultaneously, all dedicated to one another and all consistently ranging in quality from crappy to insulting. Finally, the band released *Dynasty* in 1979, with session drummer Anton Fig sitting in for Criss. This album featured KISS' contribution to disco, "I Was Made for Loving You," and at this point many fans decided to jump ship. Things did not improve from there. Criss left the band for good after 1980's *Unmasked*, and was replaced by Eric Carr, who had the privilege of starting his tenure with the band on what many peo-

The classic KISS lineup plays in all of its glorious makeup, circa 1992. Left to right: Gene Simmons, Peter Criss, Paul Stanley, and Ace Frehley.

After KISS' first lineup change, Eric Carr became the man behind the drums. Clockwise from top left: Gene Simmons, Paul Stanley, Eric Carr, and Ace Frehley.

ple, band members included, consider their worst album, *Music from the Elder*. Frehley was the next one out the door, citing a loathing for the album so intense that he actually destroyed his own copy. But he was kind enough to allow his former band mates to use his likeness on the cover of their next album, *Creatures of the Night*.

KISS replaced Frehley with Vinnie Vincent, but the group was without question experiencing a commercial downturn. Sensing the need to shake things up, they made the highly questionable decision to persevere, sans makeup, in 1983. While they certainly are to be commended for the courage it took to continue without their most well-known visual trademark, the ensuing period produced music so dismal that it might have been more advisable for them to protect their identities at all costs. Their work at this time was exemplified by *Lick It Up* and *Animalize*, among other albums. This point in world history was also the heyday of glam metal. Never ones to turn their noses up at a possibly lucrative trend (see "I Was Made for Loving You" above), the band decided to throw their hats into the ring and make their own contributions to this much-maligned genre. They have since disavowed most of the music as well as the professional deci-

Here are the members of KISS in 1987—four years after taking off their makeup, and nine years before they wisely put it back on. Clockwise from top left: Eric Carr, Gene Simmons, Paul Stanley, and Bruce Kulick.

sions they made during this period, which is indicative of the wisdom and insight that often accompany hindsight. Still, it is worth noting that the albums and tours that they produced in the post-makeup 1980s were very successful, and the band even managed to score their second Top 10 hit with the power ballad "Forever," their first such chart success since "Beth" more than a decade earlier.

The band was struck by tragedy when Carr died of cancer in 1991. He was replaced by Eric Singer, and the band turned in two more studio albums with him. However, their 1980s second coming was in the process of petering out, as grunge broke and heavy metal, particularly KISS' oversized arena variety, began to lose its audience. Either out of intuitive acumen or sheer desperation, the band reunited in 1996 with its original members, put the makeup back on, and went on a hugely profitable tour. They mounted another one in 2000, promising that it would be their last. But there was trouble in paradise when Criss left the group yet again, this time on the eve of the Japanese leg of the tour. Apparently, he was unhappy with his salary, even though it was surely the biggest payday the drummer had received in decades, if not ever. KISS replaced him with former drummer Singer, who, ironically, had been kicked out to make room for Criss to return. Nuttier still was the negative fan reaction that ensued when Singer took to the stage wearing Criss' feline makeup. (Simmons and Stanley own the rights to the makeup designs of both Criss and Frehley, so no one could do anything about it.) The tour continued, everyone made money, and KISS was allegedly laid to rest after a run of almost thirty years. In a gesture symbolic of the transient nature of all things on God's green earth, the group even produced what seemed to be their final piece of merchandising: the KISS Kasket.

In 2003, the supposedly retired group appeared on *That 70's Show* and *Dick Clark's American Bandstand 50th Anniversary Show*. The following year, they recorded with the Melbourne Symphony Orchestra. Later that year, the band gave up all pretense of aging gracefully and announced that they were going back out on tour, this time with Aerosmith. Frehley officially quit the group at that point, and the band inserted guitarist Tommy Thayer into the now vacant Space Ace makeup and costume. KISS hasn't slowed down since. They released a new album in 2009, *Sonic Boom*, but more importantly they introduced new merchandising opportunities, such as the KISS Kruise, launched in October 2011 and featuring onboard activities that the band's official website refers to as "krazy." The seafaring adventure brings discriminating vacationers from Miami to the Bahamas for the low, low price of just $895 for an interior cabin. Act now!

Eric Carr: drums (*Music from the Elder* through *Hot in the Shade*); **Peter Criss**: drums (*KISS* through *Alive II*, *Psycho Circus*); **Anton Fig**: drums (*Dynasty*); **Ace Frehley**: lead guitar (*KISS* through *Music from the Elder*, *Psycho Circus*); **Bruce Kulick**: lead guitar (*Asylum* through *Carnival of Souls: The Final Sessions*); **Gene Simmons**: bass/vocals; **Eric Singer**: drums (*Revenge* through *Carnival of Souls: The Final Sessions* and later); **Paul Stanley**: rhythm guitar/vocals; **Mark St. John**: lead guitar (*Animalize*); **Tommy Thayer**: guitar, vocals (*Sonic Boom*); **Vinnie Vincent**: lead guitar (*Creatures of the Night*, *Lick It Up*)

Discography: *KISS* (Casablanca, 1974); *Hotter Than Hell* (Casablanca, 1974); *Dressed to Kill* (Casablanca, 1975); *Alive!* (Casablanca, 1975); *Destroyer* (Casablanca, 1976); *Rock and Roll Over* (Casablanca, 1976); *Love Gun* (Casablanca, 1977); *Alive II* (Casablanca, 1977); *Peter Criss* (Casablanca, 1978); *Ace Frehley* (Casablanca, 1978); *Gene Simmons* (Casablanca, 1978); *Paul Stanley* (Casablanca, 1978); *Dynasty* (Casablanca, 1979); *Unmasked* (Casablanca, 1980); *Music from the Elder* (Casablanca, 1981); *Creatures of the Night* (Casablanca, 1982); *Lick It Up* (Mercury, 1983); *Animalize* (Mercury, 1984); *Asylum* (Mercury, 1985); *Crazy Nights* (Mercury, 1987); *Hot in the Shade* (Mercury, 1989); *Revenge* (Mercury, 1992); *Alive III* (Mercury, 1993); *MTV Unplugged* (Mercury, 1996); *Carnival of Souls: The Final Sessions* (Mercury, 1996); *Psycho Circus* (Mercury, 1998); *KISS Symphony: Alive IV* (Sanctuary, 2003); *Alive! The Millennium Concert* (Mercury, 2006); *Sonic Boom* (Kiss Records, 2009)

KORN

YEARS ACTIVE: 1993–PRESENT

While today there are countless thousands of down-tuned-guitar bands who owe a rhythmic debt to hip-hop and a vocal debt to the fine art of yelling really loud, the still-new rapcore style seemed pretty out there when Korn first showcased it on the band's massively influential 1994 debut. The band started off under the name LAPD when they formed in Bakersfield, California (home of Buck Owens and Merle Haggard), rechristening themselves Korn upon making the acquaintance of vocalist Jonathan Davis. Then a struggling student mortician, a vocation he was perhaps drawn to for its easy access to photographic subjects suitable for death metal album covers, Davis was relieved of any further contact with wound filler when Korn signed to Epic Records. The band subsequently found themselves on all manner of high-profile tours, including a slot opening for none other than Ozzy Osbourne. The exposure helped push their debut to eventual gold status and increased the demand for a follow-up.

In 1996, *Life Is Peachy* was released to satisfy that call, and the album was a smash hit. Its out-of-the-box platinum sales helped propel the band to headlining status at Lollapalooza, which surely caused festival founder Perry Farrell to get a Paxil prescription filled, pronto. However, the band had to drop off the tour when guitarist J. "Munky" Shaffer contracted viral meningitis—a condition that has been known to inhibit one's ability to project rage to an audience of one thousand body-surfing teenagers wearing very large pants, among

If joining the KISS Army is not for you, there's plenty room at the Korn Kamp. Left to right: Brian Welch, Reginald "Fieldy Snuts" Arvizu, and Jonathan Davis.

other symptoms. Any ground that they might have lost was quickly regained when the band made national headlines the following year. A Michigan high school student was suspended for wearing one of the band's shirts, on the grounds that Korn's music was, according to the school's assistant principal, "indecent, vulgar, and obscene." She forgot to mention "prosecutorial." The band served the school district with a cease-and-desist order, thereby making the Zeeland, Michigan, institution a paragon of free speech for all of the United States to use as a model. Things remained uncharacteristically placid in the Korn camp until 2005, when founding guitarist Brian "Head" Welch left the band and became a born-again Christian after struggling with methamphetamine addiction. The band finished their untitled 2007 album without him, then took a year off to pursue other projects. Korn's most recent album was 2011's The Path of Totality.

Reginald "Fieldy Snuts" Arvizu: bass; Jonathan Davis: vocals; Ray Luzier: drums (Korn III and later); J. "Munky" Shaffer: guitars; David Silveria: drums (Korn through See You on the Other Side); Brian "Head" Welch: guitars (Korn through Take a Look in the Mirror)

Discography: Korn (Immortal/Epic, 1994); Life Is Peachy (Immortal/Epic, 1996); Follow the Leader (Immortal/Epic, 1998); Issues (Immortal/Epic, 1999); Untouchables (Epic, 2002); Take a Look in the Mirror (Epic, 2003); See You on the Other Side (EMI, 2005); Untitled (EMI, 2007); Korn III: Remember Who You Are (Roadrunner, 2010); The Path of Totality (Roadrunner, 2011)

YEARS ACTIVE: 1982–PRESENT

The German band Kreator has spent the better part of twenty years as one of Europe's leading proponents of thrash metal. Their heyday may have been in the late 1980s, and they are undoubtedly nowhere near as financially successful now as they were in the good ol' days, but they have outlived most of their contemporaries and are still delivering the high-velocity goods. In 1984, Kreator was founded by guitarist and vocalist Mille Petrozza, and soon after the band's formation, they gained a reputation as one of the more brutal thrash outfits of the era. As it turned out, their style was actually a precursor to death metal, which certainly explains why their music sounded so chaotic and violent at the time. This was particularly evident on their 1988 offering, Terrible Certainty, which from its lead-off track, "Blind Faith," showed that the band was absolutely, unequivocally not playing around.

In the early 1990s, the band hit a wall, as did most of their contemporaries. Alternative music was all the rage, and the thrash scene was widely considered to be all played out. This left a lot of bands, Kreator included, fighting an uphill battle to remain relevant. Renewal, for example, saw the band experimenting with industrial music to unimpressive effect. It's not a bad album; it's just that one gets the feeling while listening to it that the experimentation is not the result of artistic curiosity but instead a semidesperate gambit from a band in mortal fear of being forgotten. Despite the fact that the band would clearly never be as popular as they had been in the previous decade, they stuck it out, and in the new millennium, they were rewarded for their tenacity. Their 2001 album Violent Revolution apparently represented enough of a step in the right direction to renew fan interest in them. While a 100 percent throwback to Kreator's glory days is not likely to be in the cards, the band seems to have regained a sizable portion of their following—one that had, to all outward appearances, stopped tuning in.

Joe Cangelosi: drums (Cause for Conflict); Rob Fioretti: bass (Endless Pain through Renewal); Christian Geisler: bass (Cause for Conflict and later); Frank Gosdzik: guitars (Coma of Souls through Cause for Conflict); Mille Petrozza: vocals/guitars; Jürgen "Ventor" Reil: drums (Endless Pain through Renewal; Scenarios of Violence and later); Jörg "Tritze" Trzebiatowski: guitars (Terrible Certainty through Extreme Aggression); Tommy Vetterli: guitars (Outcast, Endorama); Sami Yli-Sirniö: guitars (Violent Revolution and later)

Discography: Endless Pain (Noise, 1985); Pleasure to Kill (Noise, 1986); Flag of Hate (Noise, 1987); Terrible Certainty (Noise, 1988); Out of the Dark . . . Into the Light (Noise, 1989); Extreme Aggression (Epic, 1989); Coma of Souls (Epic, 1990); Renewal (Futurist, 1992); Cause for Conflict (Noise, 1995); Scenarios of Violence (FAD, 1996); Outcast (FAD, 1997); Endorama (Pavement, 1999); Voices of Transgression (Pavement, 2000); Violent Revolution (Steamhammer/SP, 2001); Past Life Trauma (1985–1992) (FAD, 2001); Live Kreation (Steamhammer, 2002); Enemy of God (Steamhammer, 2005); Hordes of Chaos (Steamhammer, 2009)

YEARS ACTIVE: 1974–PRESENT

Switzerland's Krokus started out in the mid-1970s as a borderline prog rock band. This musical direction proved incapable of paying the band members enough to keep them from working at the Ricola factory, and so, in the early 1980s, they switched to AC/DC-influenced hard rock. They scored their biggest hits with covers of other people's material, chief among these Sweet's "Ballroom Blitz" and Alice Cooper's "School's Out," but they dropped off the radar quite a long time ago even though they have not disbanded and are still releasing albums, albeit sporadically. The Swiss misters were plagued by constant turnover in their ranks—they changed band members more often than Italy changes its ruling party. They also enjoyed playing musical chairs with existing members, as in the sad case

In 1986, the Swiss members of Krokus thrust their guitars at you. Left to right: Fernando Von Arb, Marc Storace, Freddy Steady, Mark Kohler, and Chris Von Rohr.

of guitarist Tommy Kiefer, whose position in the band was usurped by Mark Kohler, a former Krokus roadie. Then there is the downright heartbreaking case of Chris Von Rohr, who had started out as the band's lead singer and, thus, primary recipient of groupie favors. He was demoted to playing bass when they made their stylistic switch to cock-rock fist-pumpery, surely signaling a second, more humiliating devaluation to a position as the band's primary Jergens lotion abuser. However, in 2008, they abandoned the personnel-swapping chicanery and announced that their classic lineup of Kohler, Storace, Von Rohr, guitarist Fernando Von Arb, and drummer Freddy Steady would reunite for a new album and world tour. The result of this union, *Hoodoo*, was released in 2010.

Tony Castell: guitars (*Stampede*, *Rock the Block*); **Dani Crivelli**: drums (*Change of Address* through *Heart Attack*); **Dominique Favez**: guitar (*Rock the Block*); **Peter Haas**: drums (*Stampede*, *Round 13*); **Tommy Keiser**: bass (*Change of Address*); **Tommy Kiefer**: guitars (*To You All* through *Hardware*); **Jeff Klaven**: drums (*The Blitz*, *Change of Address*); **Mark Kohler**: guitars (*One Vice at a Time* through *Change of Address*; *To Rock or Not to Be*, *Hoodoo*); **Chris Lauper**: guitars (*Round 13*); **Many Maurer**: bass (*Stampede* and later); **Jürg Naegeli**: bass (*To You All*, *Pay It in Metal*); **Steve Pace**: drums (*Headhunter*); **Carl Sentance**: vocals (*Round 13*); **Freddy Steady**: drums (*To You All* through *One Vice at a Time*; *To Rock or Not to Be*); **Marc Storace**: vocals (*Metal Rendezvous* through *Heart Attack*; *The Dirty Dozen*, *Round 13* and later);

Peter Tanner: vocals (*Stampede*); **Fernando Von Arb**: guitars; **Chris Von Rohr**: bass/vocals (*To You All* through *Headhunter*, *Alive and Screamin'* (*Live 1986*), *Heart Attack*, *Hoodoo*)

Discography: *Krokus* (Mercury, 1976); *To You All* (Schnoutz, 1977); *Painkiller* (Mercury, 1978); *Pay It in Metal* (Philips, 1978); *Metal Rendez-vous* (Arista, 1980); *Hardware* (Ariola, 1981); *One Vice at a Time* (Arista, 1982); *Headhunter* (Arista, 1983); *The Blitz* (Arista, 1984); *Change of Address* (Arista, 1985); *Alive and Screamin' (Live 1986)* (Arista, 1986); *Heart Attack* (MCA, 1987); *Stampede* (Justin, 1991); *The Dirty Dozen* (BMG Ariola, 1993); *To Rock or Not to Be* (Phonag, 1995); *Round 13* (Angel Air, 2000); *Rock the Block* (WEA, 2003); *Hoodoo* (AFM, 2010)

KYUSS

Whether they like it or not—and given some recent statements in the press, the latter is likely to be the case—no band had a greater influence or impact on the stoner rock movement than Kyuss. More than two decades after the release of their breakthrough album, *Blues for the Red Sun*, countless bands have come and gone who imitated them, using the record as primary source material. At the time of its release, it sounded like nothing that had ever come before, with the sole exception of *Vincebus Eruptum* by Blue Cheer. Kyuss' absurdly bottom-heavy sound was the product of extreme down-tuning and of guitarist Josh Homme's use of a bass cabinet, enabling him to convey his lowest notes with devastating, intestine-melting clarity. At the time of its release, *Blues for the Red Sun* was classified somewhat inaccurately as metal, which actually played in the band's favor. The majority of metal releases at that moment in history followed the model of Metallica's . . . *And Justice for All*, all of them possessing a trebly, highly processed sound characterized by clicky drums and paper-thin guitars. *Blues for the Red Sun* went as far in the other direction as possible, pushing the bass right up into the foreground, à la *Master of Reality* by Black Sabbath. The sounds of the drums, vocals, and guitars were all completely organic, the only effects seeming to come from Homme's wa-wa pedal.

When it was stacked up against everything else that fell under the "heavy metal" rubric, *Blues for the Red Sun* stood out like a cold sore, and as a result it suffered the same fate that befalls most innovators. Kyuss was greeted with clueless indifference by about 75 percent of the record-buying public, sheer hatred by 15 percent, and outright sycophantic worship

With the sun setting on its career, Kyuss poses for a photograph one year before the band went kaput. Left to right: Josh Homme, Alfredo Hernandez, John Garcia, and Scott Reeder.

by the remaining 10 percent. However, everyone in that last bracket apparently went on to form their own, emulative bands, calling their style of music desert rock, a reference to Kyuss' home in California's Palm Desert. Interestingly enough, most of the Kyuss-clone bands hailed from Scandinavia, Sweden in particular. These dozens of bands were almost uniformly unable to capture the essence of the music that they were copying with such utter attention to detail. Many of them had drafted vocalists who sounded almost exactly like Kyuss singer John Garcia, and they went so far as to purchase the same equipment as their heroes, all to no avail.

Kyuss may have had a massive impact years after its demise, but while it was active, members were struggling to get by. They had started out on the independent label Dali, which was bought out—Kyuss contract in tow—by the faceless corporate oligarchy known as Elektra Records. Their first album for the label, 1994's *Welcome to Sky Valley*, was received with the same demographic split as its predecessor. Matters were not helped when the band made the decision to index the CD into three parts (four if you count the hidden track, the deeply poignant "Lick My Doo"), each containing three or four songs and recalling the format of an eight-track tape. This had the effect of discouraging both attention-deficient listeners and A&R executives from skipping from track to track in a vain search for "the single." The strategy won the band no new markets, and they failed to make friends at their record company. But for the people who were already on board, *Welcome to Sky Valley* was a godsend. Its liner notes bore an instruction to "listen without distraction," which translates roughly to "sit down, shut up, and listen to the damn record from end to end." The fully realized rock album was an uncommon commodity at the time, and it was a rarity to find one that functioned in the traditional sense, as a whole, in the way that *Led Zeppelin IV* did, for example. *Welcome to Sky Valley* enveloped the listener in an organic atmosphere for fifty minutes, becoming more than a listening experience in the process—it was a place to visit.

This is not to say that the album was without strong individual songs—the powerful instrumental "Asteroid," the ferocious roar of "100°," the exotic acoustic beauty of "Space Cadet," and the psychedelic wash of "Whitewater" are among the band's best material.

Kyuss had undergone lineup changes on each album, and after the tour for *Welcome to Sky Valley* drummer Brant Bjork became the latest casualty. The band went into the studio with his replacement, Alfredo Hernandez, but the album with which they emerged, *. . . And the Circus Leaves Town*, was a little unfocused, especially compared with its two masterful, groundbreaking predecessors. Though the 1995 release was certainly not without its share of strong material, it conveyed a weariness that couldn't be overlooked. Behind the scenes, the band's label had been exerting pressure on them to produce more accessible material, apparently free of the knowledge that this is the worst possible strategy for coaxing good work out of a band. There had also allegedly been some internal clashes among the personnel, particularly between Garcia and Homme. Finding themselves besieged from both within and without, the band broke up in 1995. The Man's Ruin label released a ten-inch single of Kyuss' cover of Black Sabbath's "Into the Void" in 1996, and after that, one of the most promising bands of the 1990s was finished after just a few short years. Garcia went on to front a number of bands, including Slo Burn and Hermano, finally settling down with Unida, which released a well-received straight rock album on the now-defunct Man's Ruin label. Homme went on to form Queens of the Stone Age with his former Kyuss buddies Hernandez and original bassist Nick Oliveri. However, the "When is Kyuss going to re-form?" question never went away, and in 2011 Garcia, Bjork and Oliveri recruited Belgian guitarist Bruno Fevery and began touring under the name "Kyuss Lives!" Missing from the lineup, of course, was guitarist Josh Homme, without whom Garcia said that there is no Kyuss, hence the modified name. Still, fans were more than happy to

see the band reunited, if only in abbreviated form, and the tours did gangbuster business, so there's no telling what the future might bring.

Brant Bjork: drums (*Wretch* through *Welcome to Sky Valley*) (see also Fu Manchu); **John Garcia**: vocals; **Alfredo Hernandez**: drums (*. . . And the Circus Leaves Town*) (see also Queens of the Stone Age); **Josh Homme**: guitars (see also Queens of the Stone Age); **Nick Oliveri**: bass (*Wretch, Blues for the Red Sun*) (see also Queens of the Stone Age); **Scott Reeder**: bass (*Welcome to Sky Valley*, *. . . And the Circus Leaves Town*) (see also the Obsessed)

Discography: *Wretch* (Dali, 1991); *Blues for the Red Sun* (Dali, 1992); *Welcome to Sky Valley* (Elektra, 1994); *. . . And the Circus Leaves Town* (Elektra, 1995); *Into the Void* (Man's Ruin, 1996); *Muchas Gracias: The Best of Kyuss* (Elektra, 2000)

Years active: 1985–2011

L7 was an all-female Los Angeles band that originally got its start on the Epitaph label in 1988. That company's punk credentials were as well known then as they are now, and it was perhaps a better home for L7's style and orientation than the one where they eventually ended up. The band's sound—a mixture of equal parts grunge (in the Jack Endino sense), metal (in the AC/DC sense), and punk (in the garage-rock sense)—landed them in 1991 on the Sub Pop label, which was then representing such bands as Nirvana and Mudhoney, who at the time were just barely scraping by. The label appeared to be slowly but steadily growing, making it a natural choice for an upwardly climbing band like L7. But later that year, it was a very different situation. Seattle became a word on the lips of every man, woman, and child, whether they knew why or not, and suddenly every major label snatched up any band they could get their grubby little mitts on who had even the most tangential relationship to the city.

By virtue of being signed to a label that made its home in the northwestern mecca, L7, a punk band from Los Angeles, was now magically a grunge band, in the Pearl Jam sense. As such, they got wooed by Slash, a division of Reprise, which put Nirvana producer Butch Vig behind the controls for their 1992 album, *Bricks Are Heavy*. They had a minor MTV hit in the form of "Pretend We're Dead," and the band also saw "Shitlist," another song from the album, included on the soundtrack to Oliver Stone's idiotically pretentious movie *Natural Born Killers*, which, if memory serves, was about fifteen hours long. However, their follow-up, *Hungry for Stink*, didn't do much to increase the band's following, and after their third album for Slash, the band parted company with the

label. They released two more albums for independent labels, but by 2001 they had stopped touring and a notice went up on their website saying that they were on "indefinite hiatus," which is shorthand for "we were raped by the music business so we're taking our ball and going home." Guitarist and vocalist Donita Sparks currently plays with former L7 drummer Demetra Plakas in Donita Sparks and the Stellar Moments, bassist Jennifer Finch plays in a band called The Shocker (look it up on UrbanDictionary.com) and guitarist Suzi Gardner appears to have left the music business entirely. After all, in 2000 she became the first woman to have her breasts cast in plaster by recovering groupie Cynthia Plaster Caster, so what else was there to achieve?

Jennifer Finch: bass/vocals (*L7* through *Hungry for Stink*); **Suzi Gardner**: guitars/vocals; **Gail Greenwood**: bass (*The Beauty Process: Triple Platinum* through *Slap-Happy*); **Roy Koutsky**: drums (*L7*); **Demetra Plakas**: drums (*Smell the Magic* and later); **Donita Sparks**: guitars/vocals

Discography: *L7* (Epitaph, 1990); *Smell the Magic* (Sub Pop, 1991); *Bricks Are Heavy* (Slash, 1992); *Hungry for Stink* (Slash/Reprise, 1994); *The Beauty Process: Triple Platinum* (Slash/Reprise, 1997); *Live: Omaha to Osaka* (Man's Ruin, 1998); *Slap-Happy* (Bongload, 1999); *Best of L7: The Slash Years* (Slash, 2000)

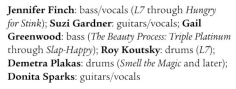

L.A. GUNS

YEARS ACTIVE: 1983–PRESENT

As human beings, we are all embattled by our own personal demons: depression, alcoholism, substance abuse, etc. These are all painful conditions, but there is an especially cruel circle of hell populated by especially cursed denizens of the earth. These selfsame individuals toss and turn in their beds on a nightly basis, digging their chewed and ragged fingernails into their 380-thread-count sheets, so excruciating is their distress. The source of this agonizing torment, you ask? They suffer from a question that has gone unanswered in popular literature, leaving them to ponder endlessly a soul-burning question, whose answer is perhaps more desired than proof of the existence of God or an afterlife: Where did Guns N' Roses get their name? The "Roses" portion was contributed by gibbering lead singer Axl Rose, a factoid that is widely known and, consequently, will not bring the relief that is so heavily sought. Now, this book will seek to emancipate its readership from their collective suffering: the "Guns" portion was contributed by guitarist Tracii Guns.

Guns founded the legendary Los Angeles

L7 strikes a glamorous pose.

Imported from England, Philip Lewis was L.A. Guns' haunting vocalist.
RIGHT: In 1988, L.A. Guns hoped that you would like them more than Guns N' Roses. Clockwise from top left: Mick Cripps, Tracii Guns, Steve Riley, Philip Lewis, and Kelly Nickels.

band with Rose but parted ways with it in 1987, for reasons that are unclear. He must surely have been cursing his luck the following year, when he saw his old band achieve megastardom. (However, a persuasive argument could be made that he was extremely fortunate not to be handcuffed to a band that recorded no new material for fifteen years.) Undaunted, the guitarist went on to form his own band with W.A.S.P. drummer Steve Riley, and L.A. Guns was born. The band was very similar to Guns N' Roses in that it was a twin-guitar quintet that took the raunchy blues-based riff rock of groups like Aerosmith as their primary inspi-

ration. Their 1988 debut was overshadowed by the huge success of *Appetite for Destruction*, but their 1989 follow-up, *Cocked & Loaded*, benefited from the glam metal explosion for which Guns' former band had been a catalyst. Any and all Los Angeles glam bands seemed to have a spotlight shining on them at that point, L.A. Guns included. They took advantage of the opportunity by releasing "The Ballad of Jayne," which, like every other power ballad released in 1989, was a huge hit and stimulated sales of

their album to eventual gold status. Their next album, released in 1991, *Hollywood Vampires*, did almost as well. But as heavy metal gave way to grunge, the band saw the writing on the wall and went into hiding as they waited for the public to abandon the silly new fad and come home to heavy metal. Realizing that this was not going to happen anytime in the foreseeable future, the band members ended their four-year hiatus and released *Vicious Circle* in 1995. The album was poorly received and sold only to their most hardcore followers, creating a black hole into whose unforgiving pull most of the band's lineup was siphoned. The next few years saw a succession of other poorly selling albums and corresponding turns of the revolving-door lineup until finally, in 2001, original vocalist Philip Lewis and original guitarist Mick Cripps returned to L.A. Guns to record *Man in the Moon*. The album was produced by none other than ex–Guns N' Roses guitarist Gilby Clarke, who surely had a consistent topic of discussion for the entire length of the album's sessions.

In 2002, the band was dealt a crippling blow when founding guitarist Guns quit. Unthinkable! Even more unthinkable was that they just replaced him and kept right on going. Guns himself started a new band, The Tracii Guns Band, but apparently didn't much cotton to his old one using the L.A. Guns name, particularly since he owned 50% of the rights to it. And so, the Tracii Guns-fronted version of the band and the Philip Lewis–fronted version of the band did what any mature, thinking, adult musicians would do—they had two competing versions of the same band going at the same time. Amazingly, this situation has persisted to the present day. It seems that both entities have a legal right to use the "L.A. Guns" name since, like Tracii Guns, drummer Steve Riley also has a 50% claim to the name. So, the next time you're on the Sunset Strip and you see L.A. Guns perform, don't get sad when their set is over. Just go across the street and see them somewhere else!

Stacey Blades: guitar (*Tales from the Strip*); **Mick Cripps**: guitar (*L.A. Guns* through *Hollywood Vampires, Live! A Night on the Strip, Man in the Moon*); **Johnny Crypt**: bass (*American Hardcore* through *Shrinking Violet*); **Tracii Guns**: guitar; **Adam Hamilton**: bass (*Tales from the Strip*); **Philip Lewis**: vocals (*L.A. Guns* through *Hollywood Vampires; Live! A Night on the Strip* and later); **Kelly Nickels**: bass (*L.A. Guns* through *Hollywood Vampires; Live! A Night on the Strip*); **Jizzy Pearl**: vocals (*Shrinking Violet*); **Steve Riley**: drums (*L.A. Guns* through *Hollywood Vampires; Live! A Night on the Strip* and later) (see also W.A.S.P.); **Ralph Saenz**: vocals (*Wasted*); **Chris Van Dahl**: vocals (*American Hardcore*)

Discography: *L.A. Guns* (Polydor, 1988); *Cocked and Loaded* (Polydor, 1989); *Hollywood Vampires* (Polydor, 1991); *Vicious Circle* (Polydor, 1995); *American Hardcore* (CMC, 1996); *Wasted* (Standback, 1998); *Shrinking Violet* (Perris, 1999); *Greatest Hits and Black Beauties* (Cleopatra, 1999); *Live! A Night on the Strip* (Cleopatra, 2000); *Cocked and Re-Loaded* (Cleopatra, 2000); *Man in the Moon* (Spitfire, 2001); *Waking the Dead* (Spitfire, 2002); *The Ultimate L.A. Guns* (Cleopatra, 2002); *Tales from the Strip* (Shrapnel, 2005)

LACUNA COIL

YEARS ACTIVE: 1998–PRESENT

Italy is much more than just the birthplace of Leonardo da Vinci, Federico Fellini, and Chef Boyardee. It is also home to the goth metal wunderkinds known as Lacuna Coil. They emerged in 1998 with a self-titled EP and caught the attention of the metal community thanks to their female vocalist, Cristina Scabbia. She served as counterpoint to Andrea Ferro, the band's male vocalist, and even though no offense is meant to him, it was her vocals that caught metal fans' ears and made the group one to watch. Lacuna Coil, which means "empty spiral" in Italian, released two full-length albums and another EP through Century Media from 1999 through 2001, all of which sold respectably enough. It was their 2002 release, *Comalies*, that gave them their real breakthrough to wider audiences. The band went on high-profile tours with Danzig and Opeth and even saw some radio play with the single "Heaven's a Lie," and by the time they performed at Ozzfest in 2004, *Comalies* had become the best-selling release in Century Media history. The band released *Karmacode* in 2006, and its success could be directly attributed to the headway the band had made thanks to *Comalies*. There had been precious few Italian goth metal bands on the U.S. charts, but the new album debuted at number twenty-eight on *Billboard*. The group returned to the Ozzfest stage in 2006, becoming the first female-fronted band to co-headline the festival in the process. *Shallow Life* followed in 2009, and was followed by *Dark Adrenaline* in 2012.

Mamma mia! Cristina Scabbia performs with Italy's Lacuna Coil.

Marco Biazzi: guitar (*Unleashed Memories* and later); **Andrea Ferro**: vocals; **Cristiano Mozzati**: drums (*Unleashed Memories* and later); **Cristiano Migliore**: guitar; **Cristina Scabbia**: vocals; **Marco Coti Zelati**: bass

Discography: *In a Reverie* (Century, 1999); *Unleashed Memories* (Century, 2001); *Comalies* (Century, 2002); *Karmacode* (Century, 2006); *Shallow Life* (Century, 2009); *Dark Adrenaline* (Century, 2012)

ABOVE AND RIGHT: Lamb of God is the finest purveyor of beard metal in all of Christendom.

LAMB OF GOD

YEARS ACTIVE: 1994–PRESENT

Richmond, Virginia's Lamb of God is often referred to as a leader of the "New Wave of American Heavy Metal." Like their fellow southern brethren Pantera, most of Lamb of God's early releases channel thrash metal, death metal, and sludge metal, all with growling vocals to top it off. However, the group was never one to just ape other people, and it ultimately charted its own course. They're now an influential band in their own right. Lamb of God released their debut album, *New American Gospel*, in 2000 and immediately gained notice for it. They sold themselves as a pure death metal band, and the album brought the thundering double-bass and 32nd-note rhythm guitar goods in spades. However, it never did so at the expense of coherent melody. The album was so successful and inspired so much

time on the road that Lamb of God took three years to record a follow-up. However, when *As the Palaces Burn* finally emerged in 2003, the consensus among the metal community was that it had been worth the wait. Unlike the leisurely rollout of its predecessor, *Ashes of the Wake* turned up just a year later in 2004. Featuring guest appearances by Testament's Alex Skolnick and Megadeth's Chris Poland, its chart performance convinced Epic Records to reissue the band's debut, a self-titled 1998 release from when the band was still called Burn the Priest. After 2006's *Sacrament* and 2009's *Wrath*, Epic kept up its bout of reissue fever and released the three-disc retrospective box set *Hourglass: The Anthology* in 2010. The retrospective was followed in 2012 by *Resolution*.

Chris Adler: drums; **Willie Adler**: guitar (*New American Gospel* and later); **Randy Blythe**: vocals; **John Campbell**: bass; **Mark Morton**: guitar; **Abe Spear**: guitar

Discography: *Burn the Priest* (Legion, 1998); *New American Gospel* (Prosthetic, 2000); *As the Palace Burns* (Epic, 2003); *Ashes of the Wake* (Epic, 2004); *Sacrament* (Epic, 2006); *Wrath* (Epic, 2009); *Resolution* (Epic, 2012)

LARD

YEARS ACTIVE: 1988–2000

Perhaps one of the more unlikely pairs of artists to join forces in recent memory is that of former Dead Kennedys singer Jello Biafra and Ministry's Al Jourgensen, although a strong argument could be made for pairing Biafra with Tipper Gore or Jourgensen with Steven Spielberg. Speculation aside, Biafra and Jourgensen did come together in 1989 to form the band Lard, one of Jourgensen's roughly eleventy-fifty billion side projects. The band fuses industrial styles with hardcore, although Jourgensen's industrial tendencies definitely seem to dominate the proceedings, which should not come as much of a surprise. Consequently, the music is very close to Ministry circa *The Mind Is a Terrible Thing to Taste*. Lyrically, however, it's Biafra's show, and his subjects are the usual political and social targets that he has always favored, albeit to more comic effect than he displayed in the Dead Kennedys.

Sadly, the band was touched by tragedy in 1993 when drummer Jeff Ward, formerly of Revolting Cocks, committed suicide after a long struggle with heroin addiction. Lard was not heard from for another four years, when they returned with 1997's *Pure Chewing Satisfaction*, an album that was very similar in style to 1990's *The Last Temptation of Reid*, the last album the band made before Ward's death. The new album featured Swans alumnus William Rieflin on drums and Mike Scaccia, a member of both Ministry and Revolting Cocks, playing guitar. In 2000, they released the EP *70's Rock Must Die*, apparently not aware of the exponentially more egregious musical forms that have transpired in the intervening decades since Ambrosia and James Taylor were hot, and which would make both Biafra and Jourgensen run to their nearest purveyor of recorded music to purchase Kansas' *Leftoverture* album and the complete Styx catalog.

Paul Barker: bass; **Jello Biafra**: vocals; **Al Jourgensen**: guitars; **William Rieflin**: drums (*Pure Chewing Satisfaction*); **Mike Scaccia**: guitar (*Pure Chewing Satisfaction*); **Jeff Ward**: drums (*The Power of Lard, The Last Temptation of Reid*)

Discography: *The Power of Lard* (Alternative Tentacles, 1988); *The Last Temptation of Reid* (Virus, 1990); *Pure Chewing Satisfaction* (Alternative Tentacles, 1997)

LAS CRUCES

YEARS ACTIVE: 1994–PRESENT

Texas' Las Cruces has been around since 1994. Their output has been sporadic at best, thanks to constant lineup changes as well as other inconveniences thrust upon them by former band members, the nature of which is at once too complicated and too childish to expound upon here. However, they have still managed to make a name for themselves in underground doom metal circles, where they are widely acknowledged as one of the genre's leading proponents. The band's music used to be based around the muscular vocals of Mark Zammaron (who in real life looks exactly like a professional wrestler, fulfilling the listener's mental image of him when he sings) and the slow and steady chug of the songs' epic, guitar-dominated structures. However, he's out of the picture now. All the same, the band recovered from the loss of more than half of their personnel as well as their record label, re-forming with new members. Somehow, they've managed to keep their house in order, and in 2010 they released *Dusk*, their first new product in nine years.

Art Cansino: bass (*Ringmaster, Lowest End*); **Paul DeLeon**: drums (*Lowest End*); **Dana Hawkins**: guitars (*Lowest End*); **Michael Hosman**: drums (*S.O.L.*); **Mark Lopez**: guitars (*S.O.L., Ringmaster*); **Ben Regio Montano**: drums (*Ringmaster*); **Mando Tovar**: guitars (*Lowest End*); **George Trevino**: guitars (*Ringmaster*); **Mark Zamarron**: vocals/bass

Discography: *S.O.L.* (Brainticket, 1996); *Ringmaster* (Brainticket, 1998); *Lowest End* (self-released, 2001); *Dusk* (Brainticket, 2010)

YEARS ACTIVE: 1968–1980

This book would probably refer to Led Zeppelin as the ultimate heavy metal band, were it not for the fact that the three surviving members have consistently taken great pains to distance themselves from that particular tag. While the band should certainly be proud of the merciless crunch they forged with material such as "Communication Breakdown," "The Immigrant Song," "Black Dog," and, of course, "Whole Lotta Love," it is understandable that they might be a little squeamish about the scores of truly dismal bands who cite them as a primary influence and for whom no sane individual would want to shoulder responsibility. Besides, the tag is also just too limiting to do justice to the band's vast diversity. Although they certainly excelled in the heavy metal arena, anyone who is more than a casual fan knows that Led Zeppelin was far from being limited to pentatonic riffs, thunderous drum fills, and screaming vocals. The band's affinity for classic blues material is prominent on all of their albums (sometimes to a degree that has actually gotten them in legal trouble, as in the case of "Whole Lotta Love," whose lyrics were lifted verbatim from Willie Dixon's "You Need Love," resulting in the band having to pay a substantial out-of-court settlement for years and years of back royalties), and they have never shied away from riskier, more exotic material. When they made the decision to pursue a style, they wouldn't just dip in a toe; they would immerse themselves to the fullest extent possible. Their catalog features countless experiments with folk music, world music ("Kashmir" has made it impossible for any heavy rock band to use Middle Eastern textures without drawing Zeppelin comparisons), funk,

OPPOSITE: Led Zeppelin in an early publicity photo, circa 1968. Left to right: Jimmy Page, John Bonham, John Paul Jones, and Robert Plant.

Jimmy Page (left) enjoys some refreshments backstage, in a happier, more innocent time before he discovered drugs, while Robert Plant (far right) eyes the fruit basket.
OPPOSITE: Led Zeppelin's Robert Plant (left) and Jimmy Page live onstage in the 1970s.

reggae, and synthesizer pop, and that's just a brief overview. Had drummer John Bonham lived and the band continued, there's no telling where they might have taken us next.

The Led Zeppelin saga started in 1967, when professional session guitarist Jimmy Page landed a slot playing bass for the Yardbirds, erstwhile home to guitar heroes Eric Clapton and Jeff Beck. Page came into the band just in time to see it fracture and deteriorate, and by the time the smoke had cleared, he was the only man left standing. The good news was that he now owned the exclusive rights to the Yardbirds name. The bad news was that the band for which he was now solely responsible was contractually bound to fulfill a rapidly approaching series of tour dates. He immediately set about finding a new band, and his first acquisition was bassist John Paul Jones, a colleague from his session work. Jones, already an experienced and gifted

musician, had scored the string arrangements for Donovan's "Hurdy Gurdy Man," among his many other accomplishments. The band was rounded out by singer Robert Plant and Bonham, both of whom, in contrast to the two

seasoned professionals, were as green as they come. Both were the ripe old age of twenty and had only regional club experience under their belts. Regardless, when the quartet played together at their first rehearsal, everyone in the room, according to Jones, was smiling from ear to ear within the first few seconds. The band fulfilled the old Yardbirds' tour dates under the name the New Yardbirds, which they promptly scrapped at tour's end, rechristening themselves Led Zeppelin. Popular mythology alleges that the band got this new name when Who drummer Keith Moon joked that Page's new band would go over like the world's largest lead balloon, nay, a dirigible, whose mass was composed entirely of that dense and unyielding matter. Page must have either agreed with Moon or else simply took the slight in stride, because the name stuck. The one change was the alteration of the word "lead" to "led." This may have been a very astute move indeed, as it prevented generations of stoner burnouts from mispronouncing the homophonous band name so as to suggest an airship that was the brand preferred by blimp pilots the world over.

The band immediately set to work recording their first album. Amazingly, the seminal work, which contains such classics as "Dazed and Confused" and "Good Times Bad Times," was recorded in a mere thirty hours. Today it is not uncommon for drummers to consume the same amount of studio time tweaking their snare drum sound. Released in January 1969, the album was a hit with the young ones, but the press was infamously and openly hostile toward the band, in a manner that employed many superlative terms used in a pejorative sense. *Rolling Stone* magazine was particularly unkind to them, referring to their albums as joyless, empty exercises in sheer volume whose only possible appeal was to listeners too

stoned on horse tranquilizers to turn them off. The magazine even went so far as to compare the band's concerts to Nazi Party rallies, leading one to conclude that its staff had been in attendance at Nuremberg.

Apparently realizing that they were not going to get anywhere through critical acclaim, the band got out there and played, to earthshaking effect. By all accounts, Zeppelin was a ferocious live creature with no equal, and one that you certainly would never want to follow—or precede, for that matter. Aware that they were building a rabid fan base as their maiden tour continued, the band decided quite rightly that some new product should be released as soon as possible. During the course of the tour, they squeezed in whatever studio time they could get their hands on and recorded when and where it was possible to do so. These sessions yielded what would become known as *Led Zeppelin II*, which was released in October 1969, a scant nine months after the debut. Unlike its predecessor, which took some time to establish itself in the marketplace, the new album was a hit immediately upon its release. The band got back on the road for another long and punishing tour, during which they developed a reputation among the groupie community for engaging in sexual activity that bordered on the psychotic. A well-publicized but unconfirmed piece of Zeppelin lore held that one of the band members had inserted a live mudshark into a groupie's nether regions. Whether this is true will likely forever remain a mystery, but what is less hotly debated is that the band was clearly going completely nuts from a full year of nonstop touring with any downtime used to record an album.

When the exhausted musicians finally got off the road, the peace, quiet,

Reinforcing Frau Eva Von Zeppelin's objections to the sullying of her family's good name, Led Zeppelin's Jimmy Page (left) and Robert Plant have a raucous time.

and privacy they enjoyed were sorely needed. Besides simply relaxing at home, however, Page and Plant also felt the need to creatively ramp down from the crushing volume of the tour. They decided to use the time between albums to retire to a remote cottage in the woods, where they collaborated on acoustic material that fully embraced the folk music of groups like Pentangle and Fairport Convention, for whom both the singer and the guitarist had always had a soft spot. The resultant album, *Led Zeppelin III*, saw the band's sound deepen and reach levels of light and shade that the previous albums had only hinted at, particularly on its almost entirely acoustic side two. The experimentation left some fans scratching their heads, but it set a precedent for the diversification of the band's sound and paved the way for their next album, one that saw the band's combination of acoustic folk and heavy metal achieve crystallization. The album was untitled and did not bear the band's name, a rejoinder to accusations in the press that the mindless hordes who bought Led Zeppelin records had been sucked into a massive hype machine and were buying the records simply because of the name and not because they liked the music. Now commonly referred to as *Led Zeppelin IV* (or *Zoso* or, in an extremely distant third place, *The Runes Album*), the release was an out-and-out masterpiece, containing some of the band's most beloved material, including "Rock and Roll," "When the Levee Breaks," and of course its centerpiece, "Stairway to Heaven," which started as a folk song and gradually built to a state of complete hard rock Armageddon. The song, as we all know, went on to become the most requested song in the history of radio, but that's just a footnote. "Stairway to Heaven" made it impossible for the band to be perceived any longer in the traditional sense. Led Zeppelin was now a cultural phenomenon that was larger than the individual band members or even their collective identity, and there could be no turning back. With one song, they were officially launched into superstardom.

The band's fortunes seemed to grow at geometric rates for the next couple of years. They could do no wrong during this period, which saw the *Houses of the Holy* and *Physical Graffiti* albums released to a frenzied public, like chum to a school of rabid piranhas. The tour for *Houses of the Holy* was an unprecedented success, breaking attendance records previously set by none other than the Beatles. Naturally, expectations were high for the *Physical Graffiti* tour. Given the massive out-of-the-box sales of the album, the band had every reason to expect financial success on a scale similar to or greater than that of the previous tour. Instead, a series of setbacks occurred that ultimately kept them off the road for the better part of four years. In 1975, Plant and his wife were involved in a major car accident while on vacation in Greece, and he sustained injuries so serious that there was some question as to whether he would actually pull through. The singer did, eventually, recuperate to the point where the band could begin to entertain possibilities for how they would deal with their short-term future. With Plant still very much on the mend, touring was out of the question, so the decision was made to return to the studio and put out another album. Plant recorded all of his vocals from a wheelchair and spent the rest of his time recovering. The album that eventually emerged from these sessions, *Presence*, was a dark and claustrophobic affair, which reflected the high degree of uncertainty under which the band was operating at the time. *Presence* debuted in England and America at number one, but it simply didn't stick with audiences in the same way their previous albums had. It quickly fell out of the spotlight and has since become their only album to appear in Kmart bargain bins. Plant, however, was healed enough that he felt able to resume his front man duties, albeit in a somewhat more subdued fashion that was not likely to include any triple cartwheels. The band came to America to tour, but a couple of months into it, Plant received devastating news: his six-year-old son, Karac, had died of a stomach infection. The singer returned home immediately, and the tour was canceled.

Plant spent the next two years out of the spotlight, grieving with his family. During this time, the band released a movie culled from live footage from the *Houses of the Holy* tour titled *The Song Remains the Same*. It did well at midnight screenings, but for the most part the general consensus was that it was just a stopgap measure, released mainly to make sure people remembered that Led Zeppelin still existed. It was, in fact, important to reinforce this because for a time it seemed as though the singer really might not return, forcing Zeppelin to disband. Happily, though, in the middle of 1978, two years after his son's death, Plant reemerged, and the band began work on their next album. Actually, it would be more accurate to say that

OPPOSITE: If your guitarist dressed like the Gorton's Fisherman you'd laugh, too. Left to right: John Paul Jones, John Bonham, Robert Plant, and Jimmy Page.

Plant and Jones began work on their next album because they were the only ones showing up for the sessions. Page had apparently been nursing a heroin addiction for some time, and it had worsened during the band's long period of inactivity. Bonham, on the other hand, had become a full-blown alcoholic. Always a heavy drinker in the past, the drummer was now in the habit of getting stinking, falling-down drunk on a daily basis. Needless to say, the men's addictions rendered them too unreliable. As such, the new album, *In Through the Out Door*, bore the stamps of Jones' and Plant's work in as dominating a fashion as Page had exerted over *Presence*. It was rich with keyboard textures and flirted with samba on "Fool in the Rain," country on "Hot Dog," and barrelhouse piano on "South Bound Saurez." It was unquestionably Led Zeppelin's most commercial and least heavy album, and even though it made the now-customary debut at number one, it left some fans grumbling. It simply did not offer much in the way of the guitar-oriented crunch that fans expected, and some of the material, such as "All My Love," was simply more precious than fans of "Immigrant Song" could tolerate. Of course today, "All My Love," like the album, is acknowledged as a classic on a par with any of Zeppelin's other work, but at the time they caught a fair amount of flak for it. No matter, though; they hit the road soon enough, where they won their fans' hearts all over again, just as they had the first time around and every time after that.

They spent the spring and summer of 1980 touring Europe and then began rehearsals at Page's house for the American leg of the tour, which was scheduled later that year. It never occurred. On September 24, the band rehearsed, and when it was over, Bonham followed it up with his daily drinking binge, which invariably culminated with the drummer passing out. The band's handlers had dealt with an unconscious Bonham many times before and were well versed in the routine, so he was taken to bed and laid on his side, in a manner that had become commonplace. The drummer must have shifted during the night, however, and

the next day he was found lifeless in the bed where he had been left, having choked to death on his own vomit. Unsubstantiated speculation immediately followed about how the band would continue, with famous drummers like Carl Palmer having their names bandied about in fits of wild conjecture. However, it all came to an end in December of that year, when the band formally announced that they were disbanding. In the end, they simply didn't have the heart to go on without their friend. Although everyone in the band was utterly devastated, Plant took Bonham's death particularly hard. Prior to Zeppelin, when the two of them were still teenagers, he had played with the drummer in Band of Joy, and he had been the one who had recommended Bonham to Page when the guitarist was initially trying to fill Zeppelin's ranks.

Since the band's demise, the surviving members have pursued solo careers to varying degrees of success. None of them have had a major hit, most likely because of the simple fact that their careers will forever exist in the shadow of their former band. Jones, never one to particularly enjoy the spotlight anyway, arguably made the easiest transition back into civilian life, returning to the behind-the-scenes persona of his session days. One could in fact argue that his career has come full circle, as he recently produced an album by Texas' own Butthole Surfers, a band who, a decade earlier, had made an album titled *Hairway to Steven*. Plant had a moderately successful solo career in the mid-1980s, and Page was involved in projects with singers Paul Rodgers and David Coverdale. The whole time, however, rumors of a Led Zeppelin reunion persisted among the band's fans, who by and large just couldn't let it go. The rumors flared up most strongly in 1985, when the surviving members played a short set at Live Aid, and in 1988, when they got together yet again to perform at Atlantic Records' 40th Anniversary Concert. Finally, in 1994, Page and Plant, who had had some unkind words for each other in the press over the years, put aside their differences and rerecorded some underrated Zeppelin chestnuts with acoustic instruments and a full Egyptian orchestra. The album, *No Quarter*, sold

well, although nowhere near as well as one would have expected given the band's hysterical following. Further complicating matters was the decision to exclude Jones from the get-together, which was never explained and was viewed by many as an unfair slight. The bassist, while clearly not thrilled by the decision, took it in stride, continuing his tour with Diamanda Galas, the terrifying singer from another dimension for whom he had produced an album, *The Sporting Life*, on which he also played and collaborated. Page and Plant went on to record their long-awaited studio album of new material. The 1997 release, *Walking into Clarksdale*, was seen as a huge disappointment among fans, and the two parted company soon after.

In 2003, *How the West Was Won* was released, a three-disc set documenting 1972 live shows performed in California. It was a powerful document, and easily the best live offering Led Zeppelin ever officially released. At the same time, they also released the *Led Zeppelin* DVD, a six-hour leviathan of live performance footage spanning their entire history. Both products did a lot to remind people of why they loved this band so much in the first place. It even made some of them forget that Page had last been seen performing with the artist formerly known as P. Diddy. Finally, in 2007, they violated two of their major taboos. The first was when they released their entire catalog digitally, thereby violating the sanctity and the running order of the classic Led Zeppelin album forever. Then, they did what they had sworn a million times that they would never do—they reunited, and performed their first full set as a band in 27 years. With John Bonham's son Jason sitting in on drums, Jones, Page, and Plant ended years of feuding and turned in a triumphant 16-song set, which immediately led to conjecture that there would be a full-scale reunion. However, in January 2009, the band confirmed that any such plans had been abandoned. It was over. That was it. End of story. Jimmy Page's manager, Peter Mensch, even poured salt in the wound by telling MusicRadar "Led Zeppelin are over! . . . It's done. I can't be any clearer than that." Still, the band had done themselves a solid by going out on so high a note, and it seems to have freed them from the fan expectations yoke. John Paul Jones has been playing in Them Crooked Vultures with Josh Homme of Queens of the Stone Age and Dave Grohl of the Foo Fighters. Robert Plant has been dabbling in Americana and making great music with Alison Krauss, of all fucking people. And Jimmy Page is currently the subject of a push on the part of the conservative member of the British Parliament, Louise Mensch, to be knighted. The fact that she's married to Page's manager has nothing to do with it.

John Bonham: drums; **John Paul Jones**: bass/keyboards; **Jimmy Page**: guitars; **Robert Plant**: vocals

Discography: *Led Zeppelin I* (Atlantic, 1969); *Led Zeppelin II* (Atlantic, 1969); *Led Zeppelin III* (Atlantic, 1970); *Led Zeppelin IV* (Atlantic, 1971); *Houses of the Holy* (Atlantic, 1973); *Physical Graffiti* (Swan Song, 1975); *Presence* (Swan Song, 1976); *The Song Remains the Same* (Swan Song, 1976); *In Through the Out Door* (Swan Song, 1979); *Coda* (Swan Song, 1982); *Led Zeppelin Box Set* (Swan Song, 1990); *Led Zeppelin Box Set 2* (Swan Song, 1993); *BBC Sessions* (Atlantic, 1997); *Early Days: The Best of Led Zeppelin, Vol. 1* (Atlantic, 1999); *Latter Days: The Best of Led Zeppelin, Vol. 2* (Atlantic, 2000); *How the West Was Won* (Atlantic, 2003)

LEGS DIAMOND

YEARS ACTIVE: 1975–PRESENT

Legs Diamond coulda been a contender, but sadly it was not to be, and the 1970s Los Angeles band remains a cult favorite to this day. Their music was always first-rate, and deserves to be explored by rock fans just as much as the music of their contemporaneous also-rans, like Dust and Granicus. The group was founded in San Francisco's Bay Area by bassist Michael Diamond and drummer Jeff Poole, but they didn't meet the rest of their band lineup until they moved to Los Angeles. There they met keyboard player and guitarist Mike Prince, guitarist Roger Romeo, and singer Rick Sanford. After signing to Mercury Records, they released two back-to-back albums in 1977, a self-titled debut and its follow-up, *A Diamond Is a Hard Rock*. They toured relentlessly with arena-filling acts like KISS and Ted Nugent, but their upbeat, hard-rocking party anthems simply didn't go over, for reasons that are still hard to divine.

Songs like "Stage Fright" and "A Diamond Is a Hard Rock" not only held their own compared to the output of the bands they shared stages with, but also foreshadowed the music of the next decade. "Come With Me" in particular sounds like the lost single that Mötley Crüe never recorded. After their third album, *Fire Power*, charted as dismally as their first two, Legs Diamond understandably called it quits. Happily for grateful fans, they reunited in 1984 and released *Out on Bail*. They followed it with *Land of the Gun* in 1986 and *Town Bad Girl* in 1990. All three albums sold as badly as their seventies albums, leading to another breakup. Undeterred, like a zombie that hasn't been shot in the head, Legs Diamond rose and reunited once more. After 2001's *The Wish*, they released *Diamonds Are Forever* in 2006. Rumors are currently swirling about that the band is back together and working on another album. Who knows, maybe this one will sell?

Michael Diamond: bass; **John Levesque**: vocals (*Diamonds Are Forever*); **Jeff Poole**: drums; **Michael Prince**: keyboards; **Roger Romeo**: guitar; **Rick Sanford**: vocals (*A Diamond Is a Hard Rock* through *The Wish*)

Discography: *A Diamond Is a Hard Rock* (Mercury, 1977); *Firepower* (Cream, 1979); *Out on Bail* (Music

RADIO

It may be hard to believe, but heavy metal Heavy metal reached its initial audience through radio airplay. At the end of the 1960s, AM radio was what everyone listened to, and FM radio was considered a no-man's-land. Heavy metal—or "acid rock," as it was known in the day—was not considered commercially viable by the top brass. Where were the three-minute pop songs? The epic tracks of heavy metal were unplayable on AM radio stations with conventional advertising concerns, so it fell to FM stations, which had no such restrictions, to play the music.

Iron Butterfly's seventeen-minute-long "In-A-Gadda-Da-Vida" could only be played only on the underground stations that were the preferred choice of acid casualties with no use for Perry Como. This demographic loved the expansive vistas available to them on FM radio, and bands like Black Sabbath were quick to find a home and a following there. Freed of the constraints of the two-minute ditty, these bands created epic tracks with impunity. Led Zeppelin, in fact, didn't even bother to release single any more. Fans loved the new music and the subculture that it was creating, and they turned FM radio into a legitimate commercial force.

Over time, AM radio was relegated to a distant second-tier status, and without angry, bellowing conservative talk-show hosts, nobody would even listen to it any more. The album-oriented rock format created by heavy metal and FM radio became the most popular in America, eventually reaching a ludicrous point where stations would feature "perfect album side" blocks, which basically consisted of disc jockeys playing all of side two of Dark Side of the Moon while they snorted coke in the bathroom.

Sadly, FM radio has since overtaken AM radio as the primary venue for three-minute, advertiser-friendly ditties. But for a brief moment, it was possible to rest your dial in a fabled place, where you could clean your bong and listen to all of "Cygnus X-1: Book II" uninterrupted and in its entirety.

For Nations, 1984); *Land of the Gun* (Target, 1985); *Town Bad Girl* (Metal Blade, 1990); *The Wish* (Music for Nations, 1993); *Diamonds Are Forever* (AOR Heaven, 2006)

LIVING COLOUR

YEARS ACTIVE: 1984–1995; 2000–PRESENT

New York City's Living Colour was a heavy rock band in the 1980s whose members were all black. As such, they were mischaracterized in every imaginable way and compared to bands with whom they had nothing in common, save pigment. Had they been white, nobody would have compared them to Fishbone. Nobody would have referred to their music as funk metal. So here follows the truth about this extremely talented and woefully overlooked band. First of all, they were musically light years ahead of any commercial rock band operating at the time.

Next, guitarist Vernon Reid (an accomplished experimental jazz guitarist who had played with Defunkt, Bill Frisell, and Ronald Shannon Jackson) could play circles around anybody. Finally, if they had anything in common with any existing bands, it was with Rush or Yes in terms of complexity and *Larks' Tongues in Aspic*–era King Crimson in terms of how dark, heavy, and improvisationally frightening they were capable of being. However, the band was described in the press as a "Black Zeppelin," thereby proving that people can be equally as stupid, ignorant, and reactionary when it comes to music as they are about race.

Living Colour plugged away in obscurity until they were discovered by Mick Jagger, who was quite rightly impressed with the band's simultaneously complex yet accessible music. He got them a deal at Epic Records, which issued their debut, *Vivid*, in 1988. The video for "Cult of Personality" was all over MTV by year's end and helped propel the album to platinum sta-

tus, as well as providing footage of singer Corey Glover's manhood bulging from a Body Glove that will surely plague him to his deathbed.

For a while there, the honeymoon was pretty sweet. *Vivid* went platinum, "Cult of Personality" won a Grammy, and perhaps most gratifying, the band had the privilege of opening for the Rolling Stones on its Steel Wheelchairs tour. Living Colour's follow-up, *Time's Up*, was diverse and ambitious and featured more sophisticated material than its predecessor, but it failed to live up to the sales expectations that the previous album's success had created. The band's subsequent release, an EP of covers called *Biscuits*, was received about as well and was followed by bassist Muzz Skillings' decision to leave the group because of "artistic differences." He was replaced by Doug Wimbish for the

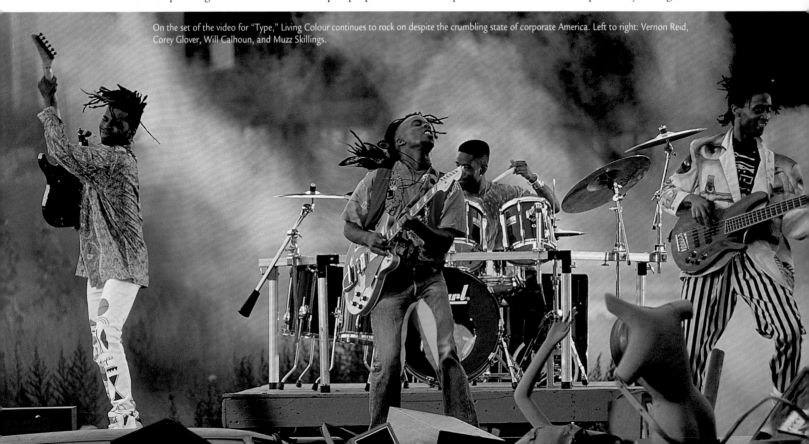

On the set of the video for "Type," Living Colour continues to rock on despite the crumbling state of corporate America. Left to right: Vernon Reid, Corey Glover, Will Calhoun, and Muzz Skillings.

1993 release *Stain*, Living Colour's heaviest and most musically advanced album. There had always been speculation among the band's faithful that behind their commercial exterior there was a much darker, heavier, and more progressive band aching to get out. *Stain* proved that hunch correct, and though the band's most loyal fans were pleased by the direction the album had taken, it alienated many of those who had come on board in 1988. Finally, after sessions for a fourth full-length album were thwarted by the band members' pulling in different artistic directions, they

broke up in 1995. The greatest-hits compilation *Pride* followed shortly thereafter, that same year. They went their separate ways and worked on their own projects for a few years, until 2001, when Living Colour reunited and went on tour, their first in six years. In 2002, the band signed to Sanctuary Records, and released a new studio album, *Collideøscope*, in 2003. They released their last album, *The Chair in the Door*, in 2009, and it featured a cover of John Cage's "4'33" that's faithful to the original.

Will Calhoun: drums; **Corey Glover**: vocals; **Vernon Reid**: guitar; **Muzz Skillings**: bass (*Vivid* through *Biscuits*); **Doug Wimbish**: bass (*Stain* and later)

Discography: *Vivid* (Epic, 1988); *Time's Up* (Epic, 1990); *Biscuits* (Epic, 1991); *Stain* (Epic, 1993); *Pride* (Epic, 1995); *Collideøscope* (Sanctuary, 2003); *The Chair in the Doorway* (Megaforce, 2009)

YEARS ACTIVE: 1981–PRESENT

The band Loudness, like their fellow Axis-power colleagues the Scorpions, had been successful in their homeland Japan and had already peaked creatively before they ever became known in America. Guitarist Akira Takasaki and drummer Munetaka Higuchi

BELOW: Loudness—pictured here in 1986—provided inspiration for the legions of Japanese metal bands that are so popular throughout the world today. Left to right: Masayoshi Yamashita, Minoru Niihara, Akira Takasaki, and Munetaka Higuchi.

Guitarist Akira Takasaki has scores of fans all over the world.

formed the band in the late 1970s after leaving Lazy, a more mainstream rock group that they felt was becoming too commercial for their tastes. Their new band was a hit with Japanese audiences almost immediately, partially because, aside from Bow Wow, fans had very few metal bands of their own to follow, particularly ones that sang in their native tongue, as Loudness originally did.

In the first few years that they were together, their pure metal sound and Takasaki's Randy Rhoads–inspired guitar histrionics provided a template that the majority of Japanese metal bands in the early 1980s followed almost exactly. Later, they began to gain some attention in the West, based on their first live album, *Live-Loud-Alive: Loudness in Tokyo*, and *Disillusion*, their fourth studio release. The band even issued an English-language version of *Disillusion* in the hopes of expanding their following outside Japan. They got what they wanted, and Atlantic Records signed them. In 1985, they released *Thunder in the East*, which

abandoned much of the traditional metal sound that had won them their initial following in favor of a more commercial metal sound. Considering that their core members had left their original band because they felt it was becoming too middle-of-the-road, this seems like a bizarre choice, but Loudness followed the advice of their producers. They crafted more mainstream material in an effort to achieve international superstardom, and the record sold well enough as a result. Ultimately, however, they didn't have staying power in America. Their next couple of albums, which followed the formula of *Thunder in the East* to the letter, simply didn't sell in the market for which they were geared. Still, the band retained a sizable portion of their original Japanese fan base, which was happy to have them back when they returned from their vain quest to conquer the United States. The original lineup reunited, and in 2001, they released a new album, *Spiritual Canoe*. The band has kept up a relentless release schedule, even when original drummer Munetaka Higuchi died of liver cancer in 2008. Their most recent studio album was 2011's *Eve to Dawn*.

Munetaka Higuchi: drums (*The Birthday Eve* through *Loudness*; *Spiritual Canoe* and later); **Hirotsugu Homma**: drums (*Heavy Metal Hippies* through *Engine*); **Minoru Niihara**: vocals (*Jealousy* through *Heavy Metal Hippies*; *Spiritual Canoe* and later); **Taiji Sawada**: bass (*Loudness*); **Naoto Shibata**: bass (*Heavy Metal Hippies* through *Engine*); **Masayuki "Ampan" Suzuki**: drums (*Eve to Dawn*); **Akira Takasaki**: guitars; **Mike Vescera**: vocals (*Soldier of Fortune*, *On the Prowl*); **Masaki Yamada**: vocals (*Loudness* through *Engine*); **Masayoshi Yamashita**: bass (*The Birthday Eve* through *On the Prowl*; *Spiritual Canoe* and later)

Discography: *The Birthday Eve* (Columbia, 1981); *Devil Soldier* (Columbia, 1982); *Law of Devils Land* (Columbia Japan, 1983); *Live-Loud-Alive: Loudness in Tokyo* (Columbia Japan, 1983); *Disillusion* (Music for Nations, 1984); *Thunder in the East* (Atlantic, 1985); *Lightning Strikes* (Atco, 1986); *8186 Live* (Warner Japan, 1986); *Hurricane Eyes* (Atco, 1987); *Jealousy* (Warner Japan, 1988); *Soldier of Fortune* (Atco, 1989); *On the Prowl* (Atlantic, 1991); *Loud & Rare* (Warner Japan, 1991); *Loudness* (Warner Japan, 1992); *Once and for All* (Warner Japan, 1992); *Heavy Metal Hippies* (Warner

Japan, 1994); *Ghetto Machine* (Rooms, 1997); *Dragon* (Rooms, 1998); *Engine* (Rooms, 1999); *Spiritual Canoe* (Rooms, 2001); *The Soldier's Just Come Back* (Nippon Columbia, 2001); *Pandemonium* (Columbia, 2001); *Re-Masterpieces: The Best of Loudness* (Columbia, 2002); *Biosphere* (Tokuma, 2002); *Live 2002* (Tokuma, 2003); *Terror* (Tokuma, 2004); *Racing* (Drakkar, 2005); *Breaking the Taboo* (Tokuma, 2006); *Metal Mad* (Tokuma, 2008); *The Everlasting* (Tokuma, 2009); *Live Loudest at the Budokan '91* (Warner Music Japan, 2009); *King of Pain* (Tokuma, 2010); *Eve to Dawn* (Tokuma, 2011)

YNGWIE MALMSTEEN

YEARS ACTIVE: 1978–PRESENT

Sweden's Yngwie Malmsteen was one of the most technically accomplished heavy metal guitarists of the 1980s and an inspiration to aspiring metal musicians everywhere. Upon his arrival on the scene, he immediately set the bar higher than ever before, and if you were a heavy metal guitarist at the time who was unable to duplicate his sixty-fourth-note arpeggios, your band demoted you to playing bass. Guitar heroes of the previous decade, such as Jimmy Page and Ace Frehley, had played in a raunchy, blues-based style that only occasionally threw in the odd classical flourish here and there. Malmsteen, however, appeared to take very little inspiration from that decade, with the sole exception of Ritchie Blackmore's classically influenced work in Deep Purple and Rainbow. On second thought, it's best in Malmsteen's case to just disregard the 1970s entirely. The influence of classical composers, including Bach, Mozart, and Vivaldi, has always been the defining characteristic of his work, and those guys had already spent a full two centuries decomposing.

Malmsteen's career began at age eighteen, when he joined Steeler, a band whose mainstream metal sound bored him stiff almost overnight, thereby guaranteeing that his tenure would be short-lived. He quit after a single album but was quickly snatched up by Alcatrazz, a more classical-sounding metal band, which even featured former Rainbow singer Graham Bonnett. One would have guessed at this point that the scallop-fretted Swede had met his ideal match in this band and would make his home there. Nope. He quickly moved on, probably realizing that he just wasn't much of a team player, and he finally decided to form his own group, which he called Rising Force. The new band's 1984 debut was a mostly instrumental affair, based without exception around Malmsteen's lead guitar playing. Needless to say, it was a big hit with gear-head subscribers to *Guitar Player* magazine, most of whom eschewed a personal life in order to remain confined to their bedrooms with only their new hero's lead guitar tablature and a metronome.

Malmsteen's talents aside, the guitarist gained considerable press during his 1980s heyday for his allegedly difficult personality—the word "ego" was thrown around quite a bit, as if other heavy metal lead guitarists at the time were paragons of modesty and temperament. In truth, if he had been born a century earlier, he probably would have fit right in, as his stormy and tempestuous personality seemed to be a tribute, conscious or not, to the nineteenth-century violinist Nicola Paganini, of whom he has always claimed to be an admirer. The violinist was a massively talented musician whose skill with the instrument was so considerable that many people believed he had made a deal with the Father of Lies in order to get it (in fact, there are accounts from concertgoers of the day who claimed to have seen Satan himself manipulating Paganini's hands as he executed one of his lightning-fast runs, thereby proving that the phenomenon of the silly Internet rumor existed for many years prior to the advent of Hotmail).

He was also, by all accounts, a crabby jerk, and many who have worked with Malmsteen have characterized him as a bit on the difficult side, too. Indeed, the number of people with whom he has worked reads like a laundry list of . . . well, people who have worked with other notoriously "difficult" heavy metal personalities, namely Ronnie James Dio and Ritchie Blackmore. However, in the new millennium, when people like Courtney Love behave insufferably and still become famous musicians despite the fact that no musical skills are actually in evidence, it is refreshing to look back to the salad days of the 1980s, when celebrities behaved insufferably but actually had the goods to back it up. Today Malmsteen is still recording and touring, although his godlike stature of the 1980s is a thing of the past. However, he weathered the 1990s better than almost any other "shredder" and he still provides inspiration for guitarists everywhere who want to push themselves and excel at their chosen instrument.

Yngwie Malmsteen, in 1987, wears his many implements of godly wrath.

Discography: *Rising Force* (Polydor, 1984); *Marching Out* (Polydor, 1985); *Trilogy* (Polygram, 1986); *Odyssey* (Polygram, 1988); *Live in Leningrad: Trial by Fire* (Polygram, 1989); *Eclipse* (Polygram, 1990); *The Yngwie Malmsteen Collection* (Polygram, 1991); *Fire and Ice* (Elektra, 1992); *The Collection* (Polygram, 1992); *The Seventh Sign* (CMC, 1994); *Magnum Opus* (CMC, 1995); *Inspiration* (CMC, 1996); *Facing the Animal* (Mercury, 1997); *Yngwie Malmsteen Live!!* (Canyon Intl., 1998); *Alchemy* (Pony Canyon, 1999); *War to End All Wars* (Spitfire, 2000); *Best of Yngwie Malmsteen: 1990–1999* (Spitfire, 2000); *Double Live* (Spitfire, 2000); *Live at Budokan* (Polygram, 2001); *Concerto Suite LIVE with the New Japan Philharmonic* (Pony Canyon, 2002); *Attack!!* (Pony Canyon, 2002); *The Genesis* (Pony Canyon, 2002); *G3: Rockin' in the Free World* (Epic, 2004); *Unleash the Fury* (Universal, 2005); *Perpetual Flame* (Rising Force, 2008); *Angels of Love* (Rising Force, 2009); *High Impact* (Rising Force, 2009); *Relentless* (Rising Force, 2010)

The members of Manilla Road flaunt their metal-plated guitar and sleek locks for the camera.

MANILLA ROAD

Years active: 1977–1990; 2001–present

Like the band Kansas, Manilla Road is from Kansas. The similarities end there, but it's a neat point anyway. Manilla Road has trafficked almost exclusively in epic sword-metal; their fantastical lyrics usually cover the same sort of territory with which fans of Dio, Manowar, and Warlock should have more than a nodding acquaintance. As is often the case with this genre of metal, the band's American fan base has been a virtually nonexistent commodity, but at the same time they enjoy the strong following that they have always had in Europe. Manilla Road's aggressive, chugging sound is based around down-tuned guitars (very downtuned by the standards of the early 1980s) and the distinctive vocals of Mark Shelton, whose nasal delivery has the Geddy Lee effect

of engendering either immediate adoration or blood-frothing, psychopathic hatred. The band has stayed together in one form or another right up to the present day, although it should be noted that this appearance of stability is due mainly to the fact that Shelton, now the only original member, keeps the band alive one way or another. In 2001, he hired new members for the band and released the first Manilla Road album in almost a decade.

Mark Anderson: bass (*Atlantis Rising*); **Aaron Brown**: bass/keyboards/vocals (*The Circus Maximus*); **Cory Christner**: drums (*Voyager* and later); **Andrew Coss**: drums/vocals (*The Circus Maximus*); **Rick Fisher**: drums (*Metal*, *Crystal Logic*); **Randy Foxe**: drums/keyboards/backing vocals (*Open the Gates* through *The Courts of Chaos*); **Scott Parks**: bass (*Invasion* through *The Courts of Chaos*); **Bryan Patrick**: drums/backing vocals (*Atlantis Rising*); **Harvey Patrick**: bass (*Voyager*); **Mark Shelton**: vocals

Discography: *Invasion* (Black Dragon, 1981); *Metal* (Black Dragon, 1982); *Crystal Logic* (Black Dragon, 1983); *Open the Gates* (Black Dragon, 1985); *The Deluge* (Black Dragon, 1986); *Live Roadkill* (Black Dragon, 1987); *Mystification* (Black Dragon, 1987); *Out of the Abyss* (Black Dragon, 1988); *The Courts of Chaos* (Black Dragon, 1990); *The Circus Maximus* (Black Dragon, 1992); *Atlantis Rising* (Iron Glory, 2001); *Spiral Castle* (Iron Glory, 2002); *Mark of the Beast* (Monster, 2002); *Gates of Fire* (Battle Cry, 2005); *Voyager* (My Graveyard Productions, 2008); *After Midnight Live* (MRI, 2010); *Playground of the Damned* (Shadow Kingdom, 2011)

MANOWAR

Years active: 1980–present

Heavy metal is a form of music whose artists regularly fall into the "love 'em or hate 'em" category, and there is perhaps no band that embodies this rift more than Manowar. Their fans really and truly love them in a manner that is as absolute and unconditional as the love one has for one's own children. Their detractors, on the other hand, hate them with a blood-boiling, seething rage. The band was formed in 1979 around singer Eric Adams and bassist and main songwriter Joey DeMaio, a former bass tech for Black Sabbath. They were joined by drummer Donnie Hamzik and the legendary guitarist Ross "the Boss" Funicello, whose relationship to original Mouseketeer Annette Funicello is still shrouded in mystery.

Other bands play; Manowar kills. Left to right: Scott Columbus, Eric Adams, Ross "The Boss" Funicello, and Joey DeMaio.

Capitol Records picked up Manowar in 1981, and to commemorate the happy occasion, the band members signed the contract in their own blood, setting the tone for the way they would present themselves for their entire career. The soaring, majestic, yet aggressive sound of their 1982 Capitol debut, *Battle Hymns*, was like no other, particularly in the use of extended time-outs, in which DeMaio performed an unaccompanied bass guitar arrangement of "The William Tell Overture" and the corpulent, drunken actor Orson Welles provided a spoken narration on the song "Dark Avenger." The album's uncompromisingly he-manly music and lyrics were matched only by its visual

imagery, featuring apparently steroid-enhanced band members wearing loincloths and animal pelts and wielding broadswords, suggesting that they had seen *The Beastmaster* one too many times. Claiming that "Other bands play; Manowar KILLS!" and using "Death to false metal!" as their battle cry, the band took everything to such an extreme level that it was difficult to tell if it was all just an elaborate joke (which would be wonderful) or if they were being 100 percent serious (which would be even more wonderful).

For the band's next album, *Into Glory Ride*, drummer Scott Columbus, who sadly passed away in 2011, replaced a departing Hamzik.

Mano-lore holds that Columbus was so feral and untamed a drummer that normal kits would regularly go to rack and ruin beneath his pummeling attack, with broken splinters flying to and fro until the kit was finally smashed down to its particle atoms. Naturally, this necessitated the construction of a stainless steel kit, custom-built to withstand the flams, ruffs, and ratamacues that his hands, his Twin Hammers of Thor, inflicted. Subsequent albums, particularly those released in the mid-1980s, saw the band pushing their music and image to even further extremes, culminating in their 1984 tour for *Sign of the*

nder communism, residents of the Iron Curtain had to make do with whatever music they could get their hands on. Music was heavily censored and Western albums were almost impossible to come by through legitimate, legal means. As a result, a black market thrived for many years. This was how the forbidden sounds of metal got into the hands of the region's citizens, who only wanted to chill out with some Stolichnaya and groove to a few Manowar tunes. Some metal heads stuck behind the iron curtain went one step further and took matters into their own hands by forming their own groups.

HUNGARY's Karthago is one of the oldest active bands to have played while communism reigned. Formed in 1979, the band was most popular during the 1980s, when they specialized in traditional European metal. They are also noteworthy for the cover of their self-titled debut album, which features elephants shooting laser beams from their eyes and is better than anything Pink Floyd paid Hipgnosis half a mil for. Despite a few hiatuses, the band is still together and still rocking Budapest on a regular basis.

THE CZECH REPUBLIC has had a lot to offer the thrash and black metal genres. Arakain released their first album, *Thrash the Trash*, in 1990 and has since made sixteen albums, while Debustrol has been in business since 1986. Their most recent album, 2009's *Rwanda*, has a cover featuring a hand gripping a bloody machete that looks like it might have been drawn by Mike Diana, or John Wayne Gacy. Törr is a thrash band from Prague which formed in 1987, but whose sound has incorporated elements of black metal. Master's Hammer and Root have both been making black metal since 1987. Silent Stream of Godless Elegy formed in 1995 and call themselves a doom metal band with influences of Moravian folklore. Also—vagina alert!—there's a chick in the band.

POLAND has been a haven for extreme metal for decades. Poland's Decapitated, which is not to be confused with Decapitated from the Philippines, are a death metal band which formed in 1996, when the members ranged in age from 12 to 16, making them a Polish death-metal Jonas Brothers. Meanwhile Behemoth, who should not be confused with Behemoth from Brazil, Greece, Singapore, Spain, or the two different ones from Sweden, formed in 1991 as a black metal band but has shifted its style to death metal. In 2007 they made the All-Polish Committee for Defense Against Sects list of bands that promote Satanism and murder.

Vader is the best-known Polish death metal band, and are considered the country's first. Hate, from Warsaw, formed in 1990 as a death metal band but changed to black metal later. Their last album was 2010's *Erebos*. Mgla is a black metal duo from Krakow formed in 2000, with "M" on vocals, guitar and bass. Vesania has been bringing the symphonic black metal and death metal goods since 1997. Poland's more traditional metal bands include KAT, which formed in 1979 and whose name means "executioner.". TSA formed at the same time. Their name stands for "Tajne Stowarzyszenie Abstynentów" or "Teetotalers Secret Association," and their sound has been compared to that of the New Wave of British Heavy Metal bands.

While Poland, Hungary, and the Czech Republic are all fine and good, it wouldn't have been much of an Iron Curtain without **RUSSIA** to secretly monitor them. Russian metal bands have played in every subgenre there is, from the most extreme black metal to hair metal. Aria formed in 1985 and plays traditional metal, à la Iron Maiden, while Cherniy Obelisk formed in 1986 and wavered between hard rock and speed metal. Old Wainds formed in 1995 and plays black metal. But it's essential to note that the most internationally successful Russian metal band by far was Gorky Park. A glam band, they enjoyed a brief moment of mainstream international popularity in the late 1980s, when the members of Bon Jovi got them a deal with their label, Mercury Records. The fruits of that deal were released as their self-titled debut in

Poland's Czeslaw Niemen (1939-2004), one of the few heavy progressive rockers to emerge from the Iron Curtain in the late 1960s. Respect.

1989, which was followed by an appearance alongside Ozzy Osbourne, Scorpions, and Bon Jovi among others at the Moscow Music Peace Festival.

A much less popular but no less present Russian metal band is Korrozia Metalla, founded in 1982 by Sergey "Spider" Troitsky. According to legend, their first show took place in a basement and was busted four songs in by the KGB. Originally fronted by the Schizophrenic, who left and was replaced by the Pussycat, their first album was called *The Order of Satan*, and as a testament to the power of the black market at that time, it sold thousands of copies without ever being officially released by a label. The band was also notorious for its live shows, which featured partially clothed dancers gyrating away alongside the giant robots and spiders that infested the stage. All good fun, but unfortunately the band took a nationalist turn in the 1990s and began singing songs about white power and Nazism. According to *The Wall Street Journal* things got even weirder when Troitsky made the unsavory decision to run for Mayor of Moscow in 1993.

GORKY PARK

ПАРК ГОРЬКОГО

and the Who as the loudest band in the world, according to Guinness World Records.

After the 1988 release of *Kings of Metal*, which featured a one-hundred-piece choir and a full orchestra, Funicello, feeling they had toned down their music a tad, left the band and moved on to what one assumes were manlier pastures. The band replaced him, but it was four more years before they released their next album, *The Triumph of Steel*. As if to prove that the band had not wussed out in the intervening years, the first track on the album was a twenty-eight-minute retelling of Homer's *Iliad*. On tour for this album, the band broke their own Guinness record in Hanover, Germany, where they played at a deafening 129.5 decibels, roughly the same volume as a jet engine. Afterward, they released four consecutive albums with the word "Hell" in their titles, two of which were double-CD live albums, released back to back. If this is a sign of stagnation, their perpetually rabid fans certainly don't seem to care, and neither do their detractors, who still hate the band with a fanatical intensity. Perhaps, to settle the matter once and for all, both camps should, in tribute to the band, declare full-scale war on each other, featuring hand-to-hand combat à la *Braveheart*—this would surely do Manowar proud.

Eric Adams: vocals; **Scott Columbus**: drums (*Into Glory Ride* through *Kings of Metal*; *Louder Than Hell* through *Hell on Stage*; *Gods of War*); **Joey DeMaio**: bass; **Kenny Earl "Rhino" Edwards**: drums (*The Triumph of Steel*); **Ross "the Boss" Funicello**: guitars (*Battle Hymns* through *Kings of Metal*); **Donnie Hamzik**: drums (*Battle Hymns*; *Battle Hymns MMXI*); **Karl Logan**: guitars (*Louder Than Hell* and later); **David Shankle**: guitars (*The Triumph of Steel*)

Discography: *Battle Hymns* (Capitol, 1982); *Into Glory Ride* (Megaforce, 1983); *Hail to England* (Music for Nations, 1984); *Sign of the Hammer* (10, 1984); *Fighting the World* (Atlantic, 1987); *Kings of Metal* (Atlantic, 1988); *The Triumph of Steel* (Atlantic, 1992); *Hell of Steel: The Best of Manowar* (Atlantic, 1994); *Louder Than Hell* (Geffen, 1996); *Hell on Wheels* (BMG, 1998); *Hell on Stage* (Metal Blade, 1999); *Kingdom of Steel: The Best of Manowar* (MCA, 1999); *Warriors of the World* (Metal Blade, 2002); *Gods of War* (Magic Circle, 2007); *Battle Hymns MMXI* (Magic Circle, 2010)

BELOW: The metal gods from Manowar charm their legions with the fine art of appropriate foot placement. Left to right: Joey DeMaio, Eric Adams, and Ross "The Boss" Funicello.

MARILYN MANSON

YEARS ACTIVE: 1989–PRESENT

Since the 1970s, when Alice Cooper became a household name equivalent to soap scum or vermin, every decade has had its own heavy metal personality for uptight parents to blame for the fact that their fat, pimply teenagers detest them. In the 1980s, Ozzy Osbourne fit the bill, with all those wacky rumors about him biting the heads off live bats and his records subliminally commanding impressionable teenagers to off themselves. In the late 1990s, the position was supplanted by Marilyn Manson, a showman of unparalleled talents, who milked the sex-drugs-and-Satan-worship angle for everything it was worth. One would have thought that the championing of these pastimes had gone out with the previous decade along with acid-washed jeans and shoulder pads, but one would have been wrong. Apparently, landing on the "pro" side of the aforementioned has lost none of its ability to upset Pat Robertson and his ilk, whose condemnations of Manson have helped propel sales of his albums to multiplatinum status several times over. You'd think they would have learned by now, but apparently those who bristled at Manson's shock tactics have yet to understand that proclaiming him the messenger of Satan is roughly equivalent to driving a teenager to a record store and putting $20 in his/her hand.

Born Brian Warner, Manson grew up in Ohio, leaving at the age of eighteen for Florida, home to guitarist Scott Mitchell Putesky. The two became fast friends and decided to form a band, prompting them to adopt stage names. Following Manson's lead, Putesky took the persona of Daisy Berkowitz, and everyone who joined the band thereafter chose monikers that were similarly one-half sexy female celebrity and one-half serial killer. After the group, known then as Marilyn Manson and the Spooky Kids, had built a reputation around the Florida club circuit, Trent Reznor of Nine Inch Nails offered them a contract on his Nothing label in 1993.

One year later, their debut, *Portrait of an American Family*, was released, and they went on the road, opening for their label's CEO. Their stock rose immensely as a result, and their follow-up, the *Smells Like Children* EP, was released in 1995 to a rapidly growing fan base. It featured a cover of the Eurythmics' "Sweet Dreams (Are Made of This)," and like all those that feature transvestite singers cavorting with oversize swine in an abandoned insane asylum, the video for the song was an MTV smash.

The next album, *Antichrist Superstar*, capitalized on the buzz that was building for the intriguing new band, and it

debuted in the *Billboard* Top 10. Manson now had his biggest audience ever, with a group of detractors to match. Every sold-out concert was picketed by one conservative religious group or another, causing his fame to grow exponentially. Clearly enjoying the notoriety, Manson made the most of the public outrage by appearing on magazine covers and on television as much as humanly possible. He even brought actress and onetime girlfriend Rose McGowan into the picture when the two appeared at an MTV awards ceremony with McGowan's naked hindquarters on full display. It was the Posterior That Launched a Thousand Shutters, and photos of Manson arm in arm with the body attached to McGowan's ass ran in every magazine on earth, with the possible exception of *Martha Stewart Living* and the Aryan Nations newsletter.

In 1998, *Mechanical Animals* was released to enthusiasm that was somewhat dampened compared with the excitement that surrounded his previous albums. The cover featured a gender-

neutral Manson, bulgeless and sporting gray B-cups, going *Aladdin Sane*–era David Bowie one better. The album was released concurrently with his autobiography, *The Long Hard Road Out of Hell*, a document reflecting the keen insight and wisdom that Manson had earned in his vast thirty years. That same year, he went on tour with Hole, an arrangement that, to nobody's surprise, deteriorated quickly. Right off the bat it was clear that Manson and Hole front woman Courtney Love loathed each other, and their relationship degenerated into the type of whiny feuding

Marilyn Manson appears to be surveying the audience for innocent underage Christian souls to consume.

normally associated with teenage siblings as they aired their grievances to their thousands of concert attendees and to MTV audiences numbering in the millions. In any event, the media, as well as all fans of schadenfreude, had a field day covering this public relations disaster, and the attendant press kept Manson's name in the spotlight. The band has since released three more albums, with another due in 2012. In 2008, the singer engaged in an entrepreneurial endeavor by launching his own beverage, an absinthe named Mansinthe. A panel of tasters on Epicurious.com described the flavor as "mediocre" and compared the aroma to "sewage water."

Daisy Berkowitz: guitars (*Portrait of an American Family, Smells Like Children*); **Ginger Fish**: drums (*Smells Like Children* through *The Golden Age of the Grotesque*; *The High End of Low*); **Madonna Wayne Gacy**: keyboards; **Gidget Gein**: bass (*Portrait of an American Family*); **John 5**: guitars (*Mechanical Animals*; *The Golden Age of the Grotesque*); **Sara Lee Lucas**: drums (*Portrait of an American Family*); **Marilyn Manson**: vocals; **Twiggy Ramirez**: bass (*Smells Like Children* through *Holy Wood*; *The High End of Low*); **Tim Sköld**: bass (*The Golden Age of the Grotesque* and later); **Chris Vrenna**: keyboards (*The High End of Low*); **Zim Zum**: guitars (*Antichrist Superstar*)

Discography: *Portrait of an American Family* (Nothing/Interscope, 1994); *Smells Like Children* (Nothing/Interscope, 1995); *Antichrist Superstar* (Nothing/Interscope, 1996); *Mechanical Animals* (Nothing/Interscope, 1998); *The Last Tour on Earth* (Nothing/Interscope, 1999); *Holy Wood (In the Valley of the Shadow of Death)* (Nothing/Interscope, 2000); *The Golden Age of Grotesque* (Nothing/Interscope, 2003); *Eat Me, Drink Me* (Interscope, 2007); *The High End of Low* (Interscope, 2009).

YEARS ACTIVE: 2000–PRESENT

The music of Mastodon is hard to define, and calling them a metal band only tells a small portion of the story. Yes, the guitars are heavy.

Yes, the drummer does lots of bashing. Yes, there are guitar solos up the yin yang. And yes, they wind up on most lists of "New Wave of American Heavy Metal" bands. At the same time, there's something too cerebral about them for them to qualify as a pure metal band, particularly when they do things like make a whole concept album based on the work of Herman Melville.

Based in Atlanta, Mastodon consists of drummer Brann Dailor, guitarist and vocalist Brent Hinds, guitarist Bill Kelliher, and bassist and vocalist Troy Sanders. Their music is equal parts Neurosis and Iron Maiden, influences that were detectable from the get-go on Mastodon's 2001 debut EP, *Lifesblood*. After 2002's full-length album, *Remission*, the band released 2004's *Leviathan*, and metal fans promptly lost their shit. Based on the novel *Moby Dick*, it was named album of the year by *Kerrang!* magazine, earning the band metal cred that it's never lost. *Leviathan* was followed in 2006 by *Call of the Mastodon*, a reissue of the band's early demos which served to fulfill the band's contract with Relapse. Mastodon's major label debut, *Blood Mountain*, was released in the fall of 2006 by Reprise, which had been itching to sign them since *Leviathan* blew the doors off of their A&R division's conference room. The album's arrangements were strong representations of prog metal, and the guitars bore a more than passing resemblance to the approach of *Jailbreak*-era Thin Lizzy. Even though it had clean production and clear vocals, the band survived their transition to the majors without earning the cries of "sellout!" that often accompany this kind of career move. There was, however, the spectacle of them performing "Colony of Birchmen" on *Late Night with Conan O'Brien* to remind people that this wasn't your father's Mastodon any more. While not sellouts, they knew a good PR move when it came a-knockin'. On 2009's *Crack the Skye*, Mastodon dug even deeper into prog territory, offering a mere seven songs, two of which stretched well past the ten-minute mark. The title of the album alluded to

Skye, the late sister of drummer Brann Dailor, who committed suicide as a teenager. The subject matter of the album, however, has nothing to do with that unfortunate event. Rather, it has something to do with a quadriplegic man who astrally projects backwards in time to tsarist Russia. This suggests that the members of Mastodon were either very interested in metaphysical matters, or simply taking a lot of very hard drugs.

Next up, the band recorded an instrumental EP, *Jonah Hex: Revenge Gets Ugly*, which was used in the soundtrack to the appallingly bad film *Jonah Hex*. Most recently, they released 2011's *The Hunter*, a return to the riff-heavy approach

and shorter songs found on *Leviathan*, which suggests that they may have had enough of the Jethro Tull shit and wanted to get back to basics. As of January 2012, the band was back in the studio, recording their next album.

Brann Dailor: drums, vocals; **Brent Hinds**: bass; **Bill Kelliher**: guitar; **Troy Sanders**: bass

Discography: *Remission* (Relapse, 2002); *Leviathan* (Relapse, 2004); *Blood* (Reprise, 2006); *Crack the Skye* (Reprise, 2009); *The Hunter* (Reprise, 2011)

Mastodon frontman Brent Hinds wants to know if anyone in the crowd can recommend a good chiropractor.

MAYHEM

YEARS ACTIVE: 1984–PRESENT

Perhaps no band's music is as overshadowed by their extracurricular activities as is that of Norway's Mayhem. While they would probably warrant inclusion here simply for the impact they had as one of the first Norwegian black metal bands, their musical accomplishments are likely to remain eclipsed by the crimes that were committed both by and against the band members. Originally formed in 1984 by guitarist Oystein "Euronymous" Aarseth, the band first

achieved prominence in the underground metal circles of their homeland, based on their 1987 debut album, *Deathcrush*, and their scarce live appearances. In the next couple of years, however, their style shifted from the death metal they had started with to a much more aggressive, violent form of metal that, once refined, would come to be known as black metal. Today their 1993 release, *De Mysteriis Dom Sathanas*, is widely regarded as one of the most influential black metal albums of all

time, but it was a full decade after their initial formation before Mayhem was stable enough to capitalize on the recognition they received.

The band was struck by what most rational people would consider tragedy in 1991, when singer Per Yngve Ohlin, who performed under the self-fulfilling pseudonym of "Dead," committed suicide by slashing his wrists to ribbons and then firing a shotgun at his head, causing it to explode—he was found with his brain literally sitting in his lap. In a somewhat unorthodox quest to find closure, his bandmates used the many available shards of his skull to make necklaces. A rumor also circulated that Aarseth ate pieces of the singer's brain, although this is surely a crock, as it positively reeks of a desperate cry for a reputation of blackest diabolism, which, by all accounts, the guitarist sought to court whenever possible. Bassist Varg Vikernes, on the other hand, saw no reason to rely on rumor and innuendo and, in a show of personal initiative, went about setting churches on fire by his own bad self. His next kooky publicity stunt involved murdering Aarseth in 1993. Vikernes stabbed his former bandmate twenty-three times, for reasons that have been theorized as ranging from personal jealousy to financial disagreement (Vikernes recorded for an independent label that Aarseth ran, rather incompetently, so the latter explanation seems most likely). Whatever the reason was, Vikernes went to prison, and he has become one of those White Power guys who tries to pretend that their impulsive and badly planned criminal actions were in fact an expression of their proud Aryan warrior heritage and their incarcerations politically motivated by "Them." In interviews, he has justified stabbing his underwear-clad bandmate in the head and setting churches on fire as: (1) a tribute to the Viking gods, which will certainly win him a seat next to Odin when he goes to Valhalla, and (2) a blow to the Jewish conspiracy's ultimate weapon against the master race, Christianity.

You can read his idiotic and almost exclusively contradictory statements on the matter in the excellent book *Lords of Chaos*. And if you're interested in what Vikernes is doing musically,

he has a one-man synthesizer project called Burzum, which he worked on when he wasn't getting abused in the prison shower. He was released on parole in 2009.

Oystein "Euronymous" Aarseth: guitars (*Deathcrush* through *De Mysteriis Dom Sathanas*); **Attila Csihar**: vocals (*De Mysteriis Dom Sathanas*; *Ordo Ad Chao*); **Rune "Blasphemer" Ericksen**: guitars (*Wolf's Lair Abyss* and later); **Sven Erik "Maniac" Kristiansen**: vocals (*Deathcrush*; *Wolf's Lair Abyss* and later); **Kjetil Manheim**: drums (*Deathcrush*); **Per Yngve "Dead" Ohlin**: vocals (*Live in Leipzig*); **Jorn "Necrobutcher" Stubberud**: bass; **Varg "Count Grishnackh" Vikernes**: bass (*De Mysteriis Dom Sathanas*); **Jan Axel "Hellhammer" von Blomberg**: drums (*Live in Leipzig* and later)

Discography: *Deathcrush* (Deathlike Silences, 1987); *Live in Leipzig* (Obscure, 1992); *De Mysteriis Dom Sathanas* (Voices of Wonder, 1993); *Wolf's Lair Abyss* (Misanthropy, 1998); *Mediolanum Capta Est* (Avantgarde, 1999); *A Grand Declaration of War* (Necropolis, 2000); *Live in Marseille* (Season of Mist, 2001); *U.S. Legions* (Season of Mist, 2001); *Chimera* (Season of Mist, 2004); *Ordo Ad Chao* (Season of Mist, 2007)

THE MC5

Years active: 1964–1972

Detroit's MC5 is widely regarded as one of the forerunners of punk rock, but the group's raw, distorted style certainly helped define heavy metal as well. They are usually mentioned by rock historians in the same breath as the Stooges, and the comparison, musically speaking, is an apt one. However, where Iggy Pop in his Stooges heyday was primarily known for covering his chest in peanut butter, the MC5 took a hard-line, far-left-wing political stance that later influenced bands that mixed their politics and their music in equal measure, such as Rage Against the Machine. The MC5 were strongly influenced by John Sinclair, a former high school teacher who did a Timothy Leary and dropped out of academic society to become a leading figure in Detroit's hippie culture, founding an organization called Trans-Love Energies. Its many different ventures included the infamous White Panther Party, as well as other radical hippie movements whose many

functions included an assault on the status quo of society, using any means necessary, including the tactics of "rock'n'roll, dope, and fucking in the streets," as quoted from their November 1968 statement. Sinclair heard about the MC5's transcendent, high-energy performances and took the band under his wing, eventually acting as their manager. In short order, they became the musical arm of the White Panthers, in much the same way that the Velvet Underground had functioned in Andy Warhol's Exploding Plastic Inevitable. The MC5 had always been politically active, but under Sinclair's guidance they produced live sets that gave off energy so volatile that it seemed to concertgoers that the revolution was right around the corner. Even fellow Detroit-area musician Ted Nugent, himself as far to the right of the MC5 as it is possible to be, has conceded that the band was one of his favorites of the era simply on the strength of their powerful live shows.

Thanks to Sinclair's considerable pull, the band won a spot at the 1968 Yippies' Festival of Life in Chicago, which ran concurrently with the infamous full-scale riot known as the Democratic National Convention. In attendance at the festival was an Elektra Records A&R executive, who was so impressed with the band's performance that he signed them immediately. Wisely realizing that the energy of a live performance is rarely if ever, captured in the recording studio, the band was recorded live at Detroit's Grande Ballroom on Halloween, in 1968. The resulting album, *Kick Out the Jams*, was as anarchic and orgiastic as the band's concerts, and the high-energy set actually landed in the Top 40. However, it also gained the band some unintended controversy, the effects of which dogged them until they broke up. The album's title track was preceded by some presong banter that famously concluded with singer Rob Tyner exhorting the audience to "kick out the jams, motherfuckers!" While today the average Eminem album contains scores of similarly colorful phrases, it was a huge scandal back then and prompted retailers to refuse to carry the album. Chief among those boycotting was a large chain called Hudson's, the 1969 equivalent of Wal-Mart. The band responded

Leftist radicals, the MC5 preach revolution to the young and impressionable. Left to right: Fred "Sonic" Smith, Rob Tyner, Wayne Kramer, and Dennis Thompson.

by running advertisements for the album in the underground press that bore the rejoinder "Fuck Hudson's!" Elektra, however, caved and released a cleaned-up version of the album that replaced the offending article with the words "brothers and sisters," thereby turning the original into a highly sought-after collectors' item. Elektra could not have cared less about the eventual resale value of the record and—already having its hands full with the drunken jackass behavior of the Stooges and the Doors—dropped the band. The MC5 signed to Atlantic Records, but Sinclair had gotten busted for marijuana possession and landed in prison. Without their hippie Svengali, the band lost the political rhetoric of their previous album, along with their chaotic,

feedback-and-distortion-driven sound. The 1970 album with which they emerged from the studio, *Back in the U.S.A.*, saw the band completely castrated, sonically speaking, and the clean-sounding, upbeat material could almost have been described as bubblegum. The next album, *High Time*, recaptured some of the MC5's sound and politics but failed to chart, prompting Atlantic to drop them. They broke up the following year, thanks to the twin wonders of drugs and bankruptcy. Tyner died in 1991, guitarist Fred "Sonic" Smith died in 1994, and bassist Michael Davis died in February 2012, leaving only guitarist Wayne Kramer and drummer Dennis Thompson from the original lineup. However, they have never really gone away. Almost every

band in existence today whose sound possesses any kind of raw, aggressive rock'n'roll quality considers the MC5 a primary influence. It is also remarkable that a band that broke up more than thirty years ago and had minimal commercial impact in its day not only still has all its albums in print but is an ongoing source of compilations and bootlegged live performances.

Michael Davis: bass; **Wayne Kramer**: guitar; **Fred "Sonic" Smith**: guitar; **Dennis Thompson**: drums; **Rob Tyner**: vocals

Discography: *Kick Out the Jams* (Elektra, 1969); *Back in the U.S.A.* (Atlantic, 1970); *High Time* (Atlantic, 1971); *Babes in Arms* (ROIR, 1983); *Greatest Hits Live* (Cleopatra, 1999); *The Big Bang: The Best of the MC5* (Rhino, 2000)

Megadeth trots out its umpteenth lineup for the metal masses. Left to right: Marty Friedman, Dave Mustaine, and Dave Ellefson.

MEGADETH

YEARS ACTIVE: 1983–2002; 2003–PRESENT

Guitarist and vocalist Dave Mustaine formed Megadeth in 1983 after being fired from Metallica for his drunken shenanigans, raising the question of how much one must drink to get fired from "Alcoholica" for excessive snifter consumption. Though Megadeth has suffered countless lineup changes (an early incarnation briefly included Slayer guitarist Kerry King), the core of the group has always been Mustaine and bassist Dave Ellefson, who have appeared on every album through 2001's *The World Needs a Hero*. At the band's inception, their approach was more instrumentally focused and technical than Metallica's comparably more melodic style, an artistic direction made possible by Mustaine's initial choice of high-caliber musicians, including guitarist Chris Poland and jazz drummer Gar Samuelson, who brought his considerable technique into the band, thereby upping the ante for everyone else. Megadeth quickly gained a following in thrash's heyday, and when the band signed to Combat Records, their 1985 debut, *Killing Is My Business . . . and Business Is Good!*, sold well enough in underground metal circles to eventually attract major-label interest from Capitol Records. Their debut for the label, which asked the musical question *Peace Sells*

"My name is Dave M., and I'm the front man for Megadeth."

new drummer Nick Menza and guitarist Marty Friedman, a Shrapnel Records alumnus who is beloved by gear-head *Guitar Player* magazine subscribers the world over. In subsequent albums, the band released somewhat more mainstream material, which, although perhaps alienating some of their original core followers, caused them to be embraced by a wider audience than ever before; in the early 1990s, every album they made debuted in the Top 10. The whole time, Mustaine had varying degrees of success dealing with his addictions—there was the small matter of the one time he overdosed and was pronounced dead for a couple of minutes. In all, he has gone to drug rehab a staggering, record-smashing fifteen times, surely qualifying him for a plaque of some kind or perhaps a quantity of frequent freebaser miles that could earn him free coffee at Starbucks. In 2002, Mustaine was injured and diagnosed with radial neuropathy, preventing him from playing the guitar for the foreseeable future. Megadeth disbanded that spring, while Mustaine went about the business of undergoing physical therapy and teaching himself how to play guitar all over again, with no guarantee of success.

A year later, the guitarist emerged, able to play again and ready to record. Originally intending to make a solo album, he started work on the next Megadeth album, mostly because he still owed one to his European label, EMI. He was able to convince original guitarist Chris Poland to play on the record, but for the first time, Ellefson was not involved. The two had fallen out bitterly since Megadeth originally disbanded, and though Mustaine

. . . But Who's Buying?, was released in 1986, at almost exactly the same time that Mustaine's former band released their landmark album, *Master of Puppets.* Megadeth's *Peace Sells . . . But Who's Buying?* went platinum and the band became a major concert attraction, but Mustaine was beginning to succumb to his various chemical dependencies.

The entire band had substance-abuse problems of one form or another, but their main drug of choice was heroin, which caused Mustaine's work to suffer and his behavior to become so erratic as to qualify for evil-twin status. For reasons that are unclear, he fired Poland and Samuelson before sessions commenced for their third album, *So Far, So Good . . . So What!* The album eventually went platinum, but Mustaine's drug and alcohol problems were worse than ever. Penelope Spheeris, who directed *Decline of Western Civilization Part II: The Metal Years*, was assigned to direct Mustaine in a video for Megadeth's cover of Alice Cooper's "No More Mr. Nice Guy." Spheeris recalled that the guitarist was so visibly impaired by chemical refreshment that it was a Herculean task of many hours to get him to simply stand still, play guitar, and lip-synch the song. In 1990, Mustaine was arrested for drunk driving and entered rehab.

A newly sober Mustaine emerged, and the reunited band recorded *Rust in Peace*, the first Megadeth album whose title did not feature punctuation marks of any kind, a common side effect of drug rehabilitation. The album was their most popular yet as well as their most progressive, in part because of the contributions of had tried to reach out to him, they simply couldn't come to terms. Using session bassist Jimmie Lee Sloas, Megadeth recorded 2004's very commercially successful *The System Has Failed*, and the band released two further albums after that which also sold well. However, in 2010, on the eve of a tour to commemorate the 20th anniversary of the *Rust in Peace* album, Ellefson returned to the band, and appeared on their 2011 album, *Th1rte3n*. In 2012, Mustaine endorsed the bestiality-obsessed Rick Santorum for President of the United States.

Chuck Behler: drums (*So Far, So Good . . . So What!*); **Chris Broderick**: guitar (*Endgame*); **Vinnie Colaiuta**: drums (*The System Has Failed*); **Jimmy DeGrasso**: drums (*Risk* and later) (see also Suicidal Tendencies, Y&T); **Glen Drover**: guitar (*United Abominations*); **Shawn Drover**: drums (*United Abominations* and later); **Dave Ellefson**: bass (*Killing Is My Business . . . and Business Is Good!* through *The World Needs A Hero*; *Th1rt3en*); **Marty Friedman**: guitars (*Rust in Peace* through *Risk*); **James LoMenzo**: bass (*United Abominations* and later); **Nick Menza**: drums (*Rust in Peace* through *Cryptic Writings*); **Dave Mustaine**: vocals/guitars (see also Metallica); **Al Pitrelli**: guitars (*The World Needs a Hero, Rude Awakening*) (see also Savatage); **Chris Poland**: guitars (*Killing Is My Business . . . and Business Is Good!, Peace Sells . . . But Who's Buying?*); **Gar Samuelson**: drums (*Killing Is My Business . . . and Business Is Good!, Peace Sells . . . But Who's Buying?*); **Jimmie Lee Sloas**: bass (*The System Has Failed*); **Jeff Young**: guitars (*So Far, So Good . . . So What!*)

Discography: *Killing Is My Business . . . and Business Is Good!* (Combat, 1985); *Peace Sells . . . But Who's Buying?* (Capitol, 1986); *So Far, So Good . . . So What!* (Capitol, 1988); *Rust in Peace* (Capitol, 1990); *Countdown to Extinction* (Capitol, 1992); *Youthanasia* (Capitol, 1994); *Hidden Treasures* (Capitol, 1995); *Cryptic Writings* (Capitol, 1997); *Risk* (Capitol, 1999); *Capitol Punishment: The Megadeth Years* (Capitol, 2000); *The World Needs a Hero* (Sanctuary, 2001); *Rude Awakening* (Sanctuary, 2002); *The System Has Failed* (Sanctuary, 2004); *United Abominations* (Roadrunner, 2007); *Endgame* (Roadrunner, 2009); *Th1rt3n* (Roadrunner, 2011)

THE MELVINS

YEARS ACTIVE: 1983–PRESENT

The Melvins emerged from the primordial ooze in 1986 with two releases, *10 Songs* and *Gluey Porch Treatments*. The band's primary accomplishment was the creation of, arguably, the first ever post-punk sludge album, *Gluey Porch Treatments*, which featured Buzz "King Buzzo" Osborne on guitar and vocals, Matt Lukin on bass, and, on drums, Dale Crover, whose last gig had been with an Iron Maiden cover band. At the time of its release, the album probably sold about ten copies, as it was neck-deep in Sabbath worship, a musical characteristic that simply was not in great supply at the time. In fact, Black Sabbath itself released an album the next year, *The Eternal Idol*, which was not as good a Sabbath release as *Gluey Porch Treatments*.

Originally formed in Aberdeen, Washington, home of Nirvana's Kurt Cobain and Krist Novoselic, the Melvins got their name from a fellow employee at Osborne's grocery store day job who was by all accounts a detestable, loathsome little man, wholly deserving of an extreme-noise-torture band using him as their namesake. The deep grinding slop of their sound had a profound effect on the then-burgeoning Seattle scene, particularly on bands like Nirvana and Mudhoney, both of which applied the extreme guitar filth of the Melvins to their pop songwriting, creating a sound that became known the world over as grunge. Perhaps sensing that they might one day have to take the blame for a lot of bands they would never want associated with them, the Melvins moved to San Francisco. Lukin stayed in Seattle and joined Mudhoney, and the Melvins began a long and proud tradition of losing bassists. In California, the band gained bassist Lori "Lorax" Black, who—this is a neat little tidbit—is the daughter of Shirley Temple.

The band spent the next few years releasing a series of albums that were as alienating and idiosyncratic as they were heavy and sludgy, sort of like the Butthole Surfers as performed by Eyehategod. The songs, already a structural labyrinth on *Gluey Porch Treatments*, became borderline impenetrable on these albums, particularly on *Bullhead* and the *Eggnog* EP, both of which feature tracks that never even pay lip service to traditional song structure. This is in no small part because of the inestimable talents of Crover, who, it seems, has never played a conventional drumbeat in his life, with the exception of the band's cover of "Candy-O" by the Cars. His style propels the music forward and functions as a discernible rhythm, but it never goes in a straight line. It would be more accurate to describe it as a series of lumbering twists and turns whose net effect is similar to that of watching a building collapse in slow motion. The song lyrics are no help, either. They are at times completely indecipherable, and it would be worth investigating whether they may in fact be in a nonexistent, purely phonetic language of Osborne's own invention. The band is really and truly out there, and the degree to which they have risked alienating audiences in order to make the music they want to make shows true testicular fortitude.

The band was briefly signed to Atlantic Records in the 1990s, an ill-advised move that was most likely the result of their Seattle affiliation, although they have as much in common with Pearl Jam as they do with Slim Whitman. They continued to make exactly the same music they had made on the independent labels, and it fell largely on deaf ears. While the Melvins were releasing albums for Atlantic, they were also releasing albums for smaller, independent labels that, unthinkably, were even less accessible than the mystifying major-label offerings. The most notable indie-label offering was their 1992 Boner Records album originally released as *Lysol* (which had to be retitled simply *Melvins* after the purveyors of the fart-masking aerosol spray sued the band for sullying their good name). The album consisted of a single thirty-

The members of the Melvins, in 1993, embark on a vision quest atop scenic Mount Tamalpais, where they plan to write their next commercially successful album. Left to right: Kevin Rutmanis, Dale Crover, and Buzz "King Buzzo" Osborne.

minute song, the first third of which was nothing but feedback and, eventually, a kick drum. After three albums for Atlantic, the Melvins were dropped in 1996 for—get this—poor sales. The band responded by releasing a deluge of material in the remaining 1990s and at the beginning of the new millennium, the majority of them on Ipecac Records, the label run by former Faith No More singer Mike Patton. Osborne also teamed up with Patton and Slayer drummer Dave Lombardo in Fantômas,

another extremely radio-unfriendly outfit. Back on the Melvins front, the band released 2001's *Colossus of Destiny*, a live album consisting of two tracks, one of which is nearly an hour long and the other clocking in at five seconds. The longer one is a version of "Eye Flys" from *Gluey Porch Treatments*, preceded by about 56 minutes or so of synthesizer and sample fuckery that was described on TheMelvins.net by an attendee as ". . . so loud most people were holding their ears. My friends were lying on the floor in

agony . . ." In 2010, the band released *The Bride Screamed Murder*, which was the first album in the Melvins' 25-plus-year history to chart. It peaked on the *Billboard* Top 200 at number 200. Who says perseverance doesn't pay off?

Lori "Lorax" Black: bass (*Ozma* through *Eggnog*); **Dale Crover**: drums; **Mark Deutrom**: bass (*Houdini* through *Alive at the Fucker Club*); **Adam Jones**: guitar (*Pigs of the Roman Empire*); **Matt Lukin**: bass (*10 Songs, Gluey Porch Treatments*); **Buzz "King Buzzo" Osborne**: guitars/vocals; **Joe Preston**: bass (*Melvins*);

Kevin Rutmanis: bass (*The Maggot* through *Pigs of the Roman Empire*); **Jared Warren**: bass (*(A) Senile Animal* and later); **Coady Willis**: drums (*(A) Senile Animal* and later)

Discography: *10 Songs* (C/Z, 1986); *Gluey Porch Treatments* (Alchemy, 1986); *Ozma* (Boner, 1989); *Bullhead* (Boner, 1991); *Eggnog* (Boner, 1991); *Dale Crover* (Boner, 1992); *Joe Preston* (Boner, 1992); *King Buzzo* (Boner, 1992); *Melvins* (Boner, 1992); *Houdini* (Atlantic, 1993); *Your Choice Live Series* (Your Choice, 1994); *Prick* (Amphetamine Reptile, 1994); *Stoner Witch* (Atlantic, 1994); *Stag* (Atlantic, 1996); *Honky* (Amphetamine Reptile, 1997); *Singles 1–12* (Amphetamine Reptile, 1997); *Alive at the Fucker Club* (Amphetamine Reptile, 1998); *The Maggot* (Ipecac, 1999); *The Bootlicker* (Ipecac, 1999); *The Crybaby* (Ipecac, 2000); *Electroretard* (Man's Ruin, 2001); *The Colossus of Destiny* (Ipecac, 2001); *Hostile Ambient Takeover* (Ipecac, 2002); *Pigs of the Roman Empire* (Ipecac, 2004); *(A) Senile Animal* (Ipecac, 2006); *Nude with Boots* (Ipecac, 2008); *The Bride Screamed Murder* (Ipecac, 2009)

MEMENTO MORI

YEARS ACTIVE: 1992–1997

Singer Messiah Marcolin formed Memento Mori after his departure from Swedish doom-mongers Candlemass in 1992. Those who expected the new band to follow in the dark and plodding footsteps of his former group were somewhat surprised to find a much more technical, progressive and, at times, experimental outfit than its forerunner. That's not to say that it was a 180-degree departure from Candlemassian epic bombast—the music still retained a sizeable chunk of the gloom and doom. And besides, any band with Marcolin at the microphone will always sound like Candlemass to some extent, even when they're covering the Scorpions' "Animal Magnetism," as they did on their final album, *Songs for the Apocalypse, Vol. 4*.

The one album that Memento Mori did record without Marcolin, *La Danse Macabre*, did go so far as to discard the doom influences almost entirely and embrace a more complex, technical direction that the previous albums had only flirted with. Tad Morose singer Kristian Andren took over for Marcolin, the keyboards were promoted to a more front-and-center role, and Mercyful Fate guitarist Mike Wead's classical lead guitar work became much more prominent. The result was a Memento Mori that sounded almost like a completely different band. Fan opinion was sharply divided, but not for long, as the issue was rendered moot when the band decided to back-pedal furiously to their previous sound. *Songs for the Apocalypse, Vol. 4* marked both the return of Marcolin and the complete and utter abandonment of the previous album's symphonic keyboards and classical flourishes.

Marcolin left the band again to pursue a Candlemass reunion, and the other members became involved in projects of their own, most notably drummer Snowy Shaw, whose pet project *Dream Evil* entered Sweden's Top 100. Nevertheless, Memento Mori represents a worthwhile tangent for those who want to do a little exploring and check out one of the less well-known, but certainly high-quality, doom metal bands.

Kristian Andrén: vocals (*La Danse Macabre*); **Nikkey Argento**: bass, guitar; **Tom Björn**: drums (*Songs for the Apocalypse, Vol. 4*); **Messiah Marcolin**: vocals (*Rhymes of Lunacy* through *Life, Death, and Other Morbid Tales*; *Songs for the Apocalypse, Vol. 4*); **Marty Marteen**: bass (*Rhymes of Lunacy* and later); **Miguel Robaina**: keyboards (*Life, Death, and Other Morbid Tales* and later); **Snowy Shaw**: drums (*Rhymes of Lunacy* through *Life, Death, and Other Morbid Tales*); **Billy St. John**: drums (*La Danse Macabre*); **Mike Wead**: guitar

Discography: *Rhymes of Lunacy* (Black Mark, 1993); *Life, Death, and Other Morbid Tales* (Black Mark, 1994); *La Danse Macabre* (Black Mark, 1996); *Songs for the Apocalypse, Vol. 4* (Black Mark, 1997)

THE MENTORS

YEARS ACTIVE: 1977–PRESENT

Probably one of the most ingenious bands ever to walk the earth, the Mentors were the forerunners of a decidedly low-tech brand of shock rock that eschewed the elaborate stage theatrics and publicity-courting techniques of the genre's more mainstream acts. Except for one brief, shining moment in the mid-1980s, the band was relegated to the deepest, darkest underground, and the full extent of their stage "theatrics" was embodied by the band members' donning of black executioner's hoods. Originally formed in Seattle, the band members relocated with their roadies to a one-bedroom apartment in Hollywood, reveling in the truly scummy, gutter-level environs that only Bones Alley could provide. They gained a cult following through their live performances, which were really drunken rambles through primitive two-minute punk/metal songs, each of which was preceded by five or ten minutes' worth of what was essentially stand-up comedy, courtesy of drummer and vocalist Eldon "El Duce" Hoke, the band's unofficial leader. On the strength of these infamous "performances," the Mentors won their first recording contract, and a few years later they wound up on Death Records, which released their 1985 album, *You Axed for It*. Indeed, who among us cannot remember where they were when they first heard such unforgettable classics as "Golden Showers" or "My Erection Is Over," both of which rival Journey's "Open Arms" in the hearts and minds of the generation that was ensnared in its loving embrace?

The album would probably have remained completely unknown anywhere but in the most subterranean of metal circles were it not for a Tennessee senator's bored wife, Tipper Gore. She and a few other friends who were also the wives of prominent politicians decided that

The Mentors give a disapproving thumbs down to those who would encroach upon their First Amendment rights. Left to right: Eldon "El Duce" Hoke, Steve "Dr. Heathen Scum" Broy, and Eric "Sickie Wifebeater" Carlson.

rock music was a form of auditory pornography that would hold sway over the nation's adolescents, causing them to become hypnotized by myriad insidious evils, such as magazine-assisted self-abuse, devil worship, bestiality, unsupervised gunplay, mass consumption of angel dust, running with scissors, horseplay conducted at poolside without benefit of an on-duty lifeguard, voter fraud, smoking in bed, and other behavior generally considered inconsistent with upstanding citizenship. As such, they wanted a rating system for albums similar to that used by the motion picture industry. Records would have their objectionable content indicated by letters, such as "O" for occult lyr-

ics, "V" for violent lyrics, and so forth. Along with the Prince and Twisted Sister songs that got Tipper's panties in a bunch, the ladies who lunch cited the lyrics of the Mentors, whose oeuvre would likely have required the use of a labeling system consisting of the entire alphabet supplemented by a subset of bulleted lists, footnotes, and an appendix. The band's moment in the spotlight included a truly surreal and disorienting moment in American political history when then-senator Al Gore read their lyrics aloud in a congressional hearing, delivering the couplet, "Bend up and smell my anal vapor/Your face will be my toilet paper" in his usual robotic speech pattern.

It's anybody's guess how anyone involved in these hearings ever heard of the band in the first place, as it received no radio airplay whatsoever, its independent distribution gave the band a very low degree of visibility, and the album covers presented compelling arguments for the abolition of the display rack. Perhaps in an attempt to shed some light on this mystery, the Mentors have since stated that the reason the Gores took such an interest in the band was because bassist Steve "Dr. Heathen Scum" Broy had taken the former Second Lady "around the world, sexually speaking," as her husband "had fallen victim to the syndrome of 'turning gay when [he] hit middle age.'" Apparently believing their encounter to have been one of two ships passing in the night, Broy claims to have refused to return her many desperate phone calls despite the fact that "her chunky slutty look gave me a major hard-on." While this is obviously a crock, it's as acceptable an explanation as any for how the Mentors entered mass public consciousness, as they were impeccably designed to repel any and all mainstream attention.

One year after the hearings, the band released *Up the Dose*, which contained more classic material in the form of "Heterosexuals Have the Right to Rock," "Service Me or Be Smacked," and their ode to domestic violence, "Rock 'em Sock 'em." After its release, they were contacted by Al Jourgensen of Ministry, a fan of the band, who offered them a slot on the Revolting Cocks' tour, bringing the Mentors to a larger audience than they had probably ever even considered within the realm of possibility. After this tour, Hoke was kicked off the drummer's throne and replaced, as his nonstop drinking made him unable to keep up with the rest of the band's high degree of musicianship. Perhaps taking inspiration from Don Henley, the band kept him on as lead singer, which was probably a better gig for him anyway, as it allowed him to pursue as much drunken rambling as he wished without having to worry about those nagging timekeeping duties. The newfound freedom also afforded him the opportunity to perform live sex acts onstage, an impossibility when attempting to execute a press roll.

Now an even sexier and more glamorous front man than David Lee Roth, Hoke exploited his celebrity to the fullest by claiming in the press that Hole singer Courtney Love had offered him $10,000 to kill her husband, Nirvana singer Kurt Cobain. Hoke also appeared on the *Jerry Springer Show* in 1997 on an episode whose subject was shock rock that featured members of the band GWAR. At one point in the show, a member of the audience claimed that she didn't find Hoke's pro-rape comments amusing, as she had been a victim of a gang rape. He responded that she looked familiar, possibly because he had been a participant. Sadly (or

perhaps not so sadly for certain talk-show audience members), Hoke's alcoholism was decisively and permanently cured in 1997, when he was killed after drunkenly wandering onto some railroad tracks and being struck by an oncoming train. It is, however, inspiring to report that the Mentors were not felled by this tragedy. Clark "Moosedick" Johnson inherited the drummer's throne, and a new singer, "El Rapo," was enlisted to help the band record its first new offering in 14 years, 2005's *Over The Top*, which featured "Suck for Rent" as its lead-off track. Hoke would have wanted it that way.

Steve "Dr. Heathen Scum" Broy: bass; **Eric "Sickie Wifebeater" Carlson**: vocals/guitar; **Marc "Mad Dog" DeLeon**: drums (*Ducefixion*); **El Rapo**: vocals (*Over the Top*); **Eldon "El Duce" Hoke**: vocals/drums; **Clark "Moosedick" Savage**: drums (*Over the Top*); **Sickie J**: guitar (*Over the Top*)

Discography: *Get Up and Die* (Mystic, 1982); *Live at the Whiskey/Cathey de Grande* (Mystic, 1983); *You Axed for It* (Death, 1985); *Up the Dose* (Death, 1986); *Sex Drugs & Rock'n'Roll* (Ever Rat, 1989); *Rock Bible* (Mentors, 1990); *To the Max* (Mentors, 1991); *Over the Top* (Mentors, 2005); *Ducefixion* (Mentors, 2009)

YEARS ACTIVE: 1981–1985, 1992–1999

Denmark's Mercyful Fate was one of the most influential metal bands of the 1980s. Their dark, complex sound and the theatrical nature of their live appearances paved the way for death metal, black metal, and pretty much every other dark, uncommercial metal you could name. Their trademark elephant-stampede guitar riffs, courtesy of Hank Shermann and Michael Denner, were offset by the over-the-top vocals of King Diamond, who brought the heavy metal vocal style to its highest plateau of absurdity. He was able to deliver the lowest-register bowel-churning growls, and at the same time he could hit notes so high that it seemed they would cause glass to shatter. As such, he pioneered the Cookie Monster vocal

delivery of death metal and also produced the most preposterous, shrillest shrieks around, beyond even the abilities of Judas Priest's Rob Halford. He truly sounded like no other singer in any genre, and nobody else has ever been able to compete with him, nor should they try. The singer won most of the headlines, thanks largely to his vocal histrionics, but he also earned a great deal of printer's ink on the basis of his carefully cultivated stage persona, which included KISS-inspired makeup and the occasional cape and top hat, depending on whether it was good cape-and-top-hat weather.

Diamond and Shermann formed the band in 1981 in Copenhagen. The singer had previously been a member of Black Rose, a Deep Purple–inspired band for whom his puppy-agitating vocals were absolutely not appropriate in any regard. Shermann had been a member of the Brats, a punk band that had actually made a respectable dent in their native country. Shermann brought in his band mate Denner to play guitar; he in turn brought in bassist Timi Hansen, who had played with him in Denner's post-Brats band, Danger Zone. The new group, Mercyful Fate, released their own EP in 1982, which, although self-titled, has come to be known to fans as the *Nuns Have No Fun* EP. It is rumored that the real title is *A Corpse Without Soul*. The rest of us can only sit back and hope that this conflict will be resolved in a peaceful fashion. The next release was the band's first proper album, 1983's *Melissa*. It was instantly seized upon by the underground metal community as a classic—there had simply never been anything like it. At the time, it was some of the darkest, most inhuman music imaginable, as well as some of the most original. It also gained more than a little notoriety for its controversial occult lyrics. Between his voice

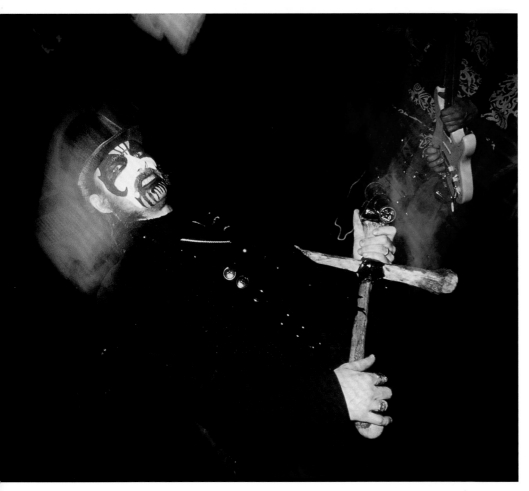

Mercyful Fate front man King Diamond with his favorite microphone, complete with its stand made of human bones.

the singer was pursuing his very successful solo career, the rest of the band members were involved in their own projects. Apparently putting aside their creative differences, Denner and Shermann reunited for a new band, Zoser Mez, which sounded an awful lot like Mercyful Fate. Apparently King Diamond thought so, too; even though Roadrunner had released yet another vault-clearing cash-in attempt that year with *Return of the Vampire: The Rare and Unreleased* compilation, Mercyful Fate reunited in 1992 with all of its original members to bring acts of extreme satanism back to the masses. The only no-show was drummer Kim Ruzz, who was replaced by King Diamond drummer Snowy Shaw. Stylistically speaking, the 1993 reunion album, *In the Shadows*, featured music that was almost identical to that which the band had created nine years earlier, and it sold as well as anyone could have hoped for. Since then, both Mercyful Fate and King Diamond have existed at the same time, alternating album releases and at one point even going on tour together, leading one to speculate whether Diamond had two separate tour riders, each stipulating different quantities of cold cuts, bottled water, and Christian babies to be kept for him in the backstage area.

and his stage persona, one would have thought that King Diamond had all his bases covered, but he raised more than a few eyebrows when he employed his multiple-octave range to convey his openly satanic views. Fan reaction aside, the rest of the band didn't share his enthusiasm for the glorification of the mischievous sprite of the underworld, and the rift sparked tension amid their ranks almost immediately. Making matters worse was a creative tug-of-war between the two guitarists, with one side pushing for Mercyful Fate to stick with their dark, heavy sound and the other wanting to pursue a more mainstream direction. After they released their second full-length album, the 1984 landmark proto–black metal masterpiece *Don't Break the Oath*, the friction among the band members

reached critical mass, causing Mercyful Fate to break up in 1985 at what was the highest point in their career. It was truly a shame, as all three of their original releases were extremely well received in the underground metal community, and even a cursory listen to them shows that this band obviously had a lot left to offer. In any event, the band was considered over and done with, and Mercyful Fate received the customary posthumous compilation treatment with 1987's *In the Beginning*.

In the wake of Mercyful Fate's demise, King Diamond took bandmates Denner and Hansen with him and started his own eponymous group, which sounded almost exactly like Mercyful Fate, only with more of the King's trademark dry-heaving and yodeling. While

Sharlee D'Angelo: bass (*Time* and later); **Michael Denner**: guitars (*Mercyful Fate* through *Into the Unknown*) (see also King Diamond); **King Diamond**: vocals (see also King Diamond); **Timi Hansen**: bass (*Mercyful Fate* through *In the Shadows*) (see also King Diamond); **Bjarne T. Holm**: drums (*Into the Unknown* and later); **Kim Ruzz**: drums (*Mercyful Fate* through *Don't Break the Oath*); **Snowy Shaw**: drums (*In the Shadows*, *Time*) (see also King Diamond, Memento Mori); **Hank Shermann**: guitars; **Mike Wead**: guitars (*Dead Again*, 9) (see also King Diamond, Memento Mori)

Discography: *Mercyful Fate* (Rave-On, 1982); *Melissa* (Megaforce, 1983); *Don't Break the Oath* (Roadrunner, 1984); *In the Beginning* (Roadrunner, 1987); *Return of the Vampire* (Roadrunner, 1992); *In the Shadows* (Metal Blade, 1993); *Time* (Metal Blade, 1994); *Bell Witch* (Scarface, 1994); *Into the Unknown* (Priority, 1996); *Dead Again* (Metal Blade, 1998); *9* (Metal Blade, 1999)

METAL CHURCH

YEARS ACTIVE: 1980–1994; 1999–2009

Metal Church started in 1983 in a typically modest fashion, playing cover material in Seattle-area bars. After tiring of performing "Takin' Care of Business" and "Sweet Home Alabama" on a thrice-nightly basis, the group eventually graduated to writing their own material, hoping that it would help them to escape the bar circuit. Taking their name from the designation given to guitarist Kurdt Vanderhoof's house—the site of countless hours of metal worship by him and his friends—the band put out a self-titled, self-financed, and self-released debut in 1984, just as the thrash revolution was getting under way. The album's melodic traditional metal stood in stark contrast to the Anthraxes and Celtic Frosts of the day, but it was every bit as heavy as its thrash counterparts while tenaciously sticking to its pre–power metal sound. Thanks mostly to a grassroots following that had been trading the band's demos, the debut sold well enough for an independent release to attract Elektra Records, which reissued Metal Church's debut album in 1985. Like their other major-label counterparts, Elektra was in the process of attempting to capitalize on the rapidly growing thrash movement, and the company devoured whatever metal bands it could get its claws into. As such, it signed the band and in the process made Metal Church the first in a long line of Seattle bands to be signed to major labels because of a perceived marketing connection that was questionable at best.

After their follow-up, 1987's *The Dark*, singer David Wayne left the band and was replaced by former Heretic vocalist Mike Howe for the 1989 release *Blessing in Disguise*. The album lived up to its title by displaying a band at its creative peak, with a completely fleshed out sound at which the two previous albums had only hinted. Guitarist and primary songwriter Vanderhoof left the band after the album's release, however, refusing to do

During the busy holiday season, Metal Church took a minute to stop in at a Seattle-area Sears portrait studio. Clockwise from far left: Duke Erickson, Craig Wells, Kirk Arrington, John Marshall, and Mike Howe.

any further touring. He was replaced by John Marshall, whose previous claim to fame was acting as a guitar tech for Metallica. But it seemed that Vanderhoof was sick only of touring with Metal Church, as he formed a side project called

Hall Aflame, which inexplicably won an opening slot for ZZ Top after the integrity-wracked Black Crowes vacated the post in protest of the tour's corporate sponsorship. While his new band was doing well, his old band had lost a considerable amount of its focus after Vanderhoof's departure, turning out two somewhat directionless albums. The second of these, *Hanging in the Balance*, sold poorly in the face of the alternative rock revolution, and Metal Church broke up shortly thereafter.

They did reunite in 1999, with almost the entire original lineup of drummer Kirk Arrington, bassist Duke Erickson, singer Wayne, and even tour-disparaging guitarist Vanderhoof. The one member to sit out the reunion was guitarist Craig Wells, whose slot was filled by Marshall. The band released an album, *Masterpeace*, for Nuclear Blast and toured to support it, but they went back on ice soon after. It had been a few years since the original breakup, after all, and in that time a couple of the members had settled down and become family men—the tumult and craziness of touring life simply held no appeal for them anymore. Wayne went on to form his own solo project, with the ingeniously chosen name of Wayne. In what one hopes was simply an unfortunate lapse in judgment, the title of the first Wayne album was *Metal Church*, a decision that likely has cost him whatever relationship he might once have had with his former bandmates. Wayne died in 2005 from injuries he had sustained in a car accident, and the band's last album was 2008's *This Present Wasteland*. They broke up in 2009.

Kirk Arrington: drums (*Metal Church* through *The Weight of the World*); **Duke Erickson**: bass (*Metal Church* through *Masterpeace*); **Mike Howe**: vocals (*Blessing in Disguise* through *Hanging in the Balance*); **John Marshall**: guitars (*Blessing in Disguise* and later); **Ronny Munroe**: vocals (*The Weight of the World* and later); **Jeff Plate**: drums (*A Light in the Dark* and later); **Jay Reynolds**: guitar (*The Weight of the World*); **Steve Unger**: bass (*The Weight of the World* and later); **Kurdt Vanderhoof**: guitars (*Metal Church, The Dark,*

Masterpeace, A Light in the Dark and later); **David Wayne**: vocals (*Metal Church, The Dark, Masterpeace*); **Craig Wells**: guitars (*Metal Church* through *Hanging in the Balance*); **Rick van Zandt**: guitar (*This Present Wasteland*)

Discography: *Metal Church* (Elektra, 1985); *The Dark* (Elektra, 1987); *Blessing in Disguise* (Elektra, 1989); *The Human Factor* (Epic, 1991); *Hanging in the Balance* (Blackheart, 1993); *Masterpeace* (Nuclear Blast, 1999); *Live* (Nuclear Blast, 2000); *The Weight of the World* (Steamhammer/SPV, 2004); *A Light in the Dark* (SPV, 2006); *This Present Wasteland* (Steamhammer/SPV, 2008)

YEARS ACTIVE: 1981–PRESENT

Metallica is a lot of things, such that trying to qualify its impact in one glib sentence (or even a series of paragraphs) is an exercise doomed to failure. It holds the distinction of being the most influential heavy metal band of the 1980s, and that alone should be more than enough to say about it, but the band is a lot more besides. It is also one of the best, one of the most original, one of the most musically accomplished, one of the most creatively resourceful, one of the most imitated—you really could go on heaping accolades upon Metallica forever and still not come even close to capturing the band's full essence.

That Metallica started from modest means only adds to the underdog charm that has always worked in the band members' favor. Theirs is both a literal and figurative rags-to-riches story, sort of an ignored-to-innovators story, if you will. Originally based in Los Angeles, singer and guitarist James Hetfield met Danish drummer and New Wave of British Heavy Metal fanatic Lars Ulrich in 1980 through an advertisement for potential bandmates in the *Recycler*, a local magazine. Actually, the reality is that they both ran ads at the same time, and nobody else answered either one, leaving the two to shrug and call each other. Their initial meeting didn't yield much, with Hetfield going on record saying that he found Ulrich's drumming to be lacking,

although his choice of words was a smidgen more colorful. Ulrich's technical ability notwithstanding, however, he more than made up for it in sheer determination, and he was then, as he is now, a promotion machine of superhuman proportions. He somehow managed to finagle a slot for his band, which did not even exist yet, on Metal Blade Records' *Metal Massacre* compilation. The band was hastily assembled and turned out a recording of "Hit the Lights," which seemed to bear out Hetfield's assessment of Ulrich's drumming capabilities. The recording, credited to "Mettalica," was performed by Ulrich on drums; Hetfield on vocals, rhythm guitar, and bass; and Lloyd Grant, a friend of the band's, on lead guitar. The collective performance on this particular track stank like a garbage bag full of medical waste that had been left out in the sun for three days, but it did its job of putting Metallica on the map as far as the heavy metal underground was concerned. Eventually, the band acquired a full roster of musicians with the joining of bassist Ron McGovney and lead guitarist Dave Mustaine. This first true configuration of Metallica recorded the *No Life 'til Leather* demo, which contained songs that eventually ended up on its debut album and that, as in the case of "Seek and Destroy," remain in the band's live set to this day. The much-ballyhooed heavy metal tape-trading community simultaneously and collectively shit themselves over the demo, and made it in all probability the most widely circulated demo tape in the history of recorded sound.

As Metallica's demo continued to circulate, the band was generating considerable word-of-mouth publicity. However, as luck would have it, all was not well in Metallicaland. Hetfield and Ulrich were dissatisfied with bassist McGovney and decided that they should seek a replacement. Metal Blade's Brian Slagel advised them to check out a band called Trauma, whose bassist he thought they should approach. The bassist in question was one Cliff Burton, whose high-energy Steve-Harris-with-a-wa-wa-pedal lead-bass style won the pair over immediately. Burton was asked to join Metallica, and he accepted the offer on the sole condition that the band relocate to his hometown of San Francisco. Because the band members regarded Los Angeles as the focus of all evil in the universe, the condition was happily agreed to and the foursome headed north, leaving the smog-shrouded desert oasis behind them. Metallica spent the next year playing locally, and almost immediately it was clear that San Francisco audiences were far more receptive to the band's music than those they had left behind, which surely must have relieved the members of any second thoughts to return to L.A. The band had little trouble cultivating an intense level of fanaticism and audience loyalty, which reached its peak when other bands on bills with them were greeted by the sight of entire audiences with their backs turned to them, giving them the finger, and refusing to face the stage until their heroes began playing.

The growing buzz eventually worked its way east to a New York City–based record-store owner named Jon Zazula, who took it upon himself to secure a deal for Metallica, realizing that it was going to be only a matter of time before they exploded. The labels he approached didn't share either his insight or his enthusiasm, so ultimately he formed his own label, Megaforce, with Metallica being the first signing. The band trekked across the country to New York to record their debut for the label, but it was at this time that Mustaine's legendary drinking problems began to get seriously out of hand, and his bandmates realized that they would have to replace him, quite astutely reasoning that being trapped with a violent drunk in a recording studio, on a tour bus, or in any other high-pressure situation would spell certain death for the band. The perpetually inebriated guitarist was excused from further service, and he was replaced by Exodus' Kirk Hammett in time to record their debut album, Kill 'Em All. The album was released in 1983, and although the band surely couldn't have realized it at the time, it was the auspicious beginning of both a highly successful career and a style that would influence other bands on a massive scale. While the album has moments that don't hold up particularly well today, it

served as a blueprint for what would follow and contains all of the band's trademarks, from sudden, drastic tempo changes to Hetfield's signature chugging guitar rhythms.

Metallica released Ride the Lightning one year later, and the progress that they had made in twelve months' time was staggering. The album contained such classic material as "For Whom the Bell Tolls," "Fade to Black," and "Creeping Death," a favorite at concerts in that it affords attendees the opportunity to chant "Die! Die! Die! Die!" for several minutes, depending on how long the band wants to milk it. The album was a huge success and set the stage for the 1986 release Master of Puppets, arguably Metallica's masterpiece. Master of Puppets was an epic excursion into places both light and dark, furious and delicate, and it silenced once and for all anyone attempting to advance the argument that the band was just about speed. The best known songs off the album, such as the title track and "The Thing That Should Not Be," provided the required crunch of previous albums, but they were creatively imagined and possessed attributes far more sophisticated than anyone expected. This is perhaps best embodied by the instrumental track "Orion," which takes the listener from progressive metal chug to almost Pink Floydian psychedelia and back again, all over the course of an eight-minute voyage that seems significantly shorter. The band had already spawned a host of imitators based on its first two releases, but this album left them all hopelessly outpaced and permanently made Metallica the premier thrash metal band, the bearers of a standard by which all other such bands would be judged.

They were now enjoying their greatest peak, commercially and creatively, and they began promoting the new album by opening for Ozzy Osbourne, very likely showing him up in the process. The good times were short-lived, however. In late September of that year, the band's tour bus crashed in Sweden during an overnight drive to Copenhagen. The bus hit a patch of black ice and flipped onto its side, tossing a sleeping Burton out of the window in the process. He was

RIDE THE LIGHTNING

MASTER OF PUPPETS

Metallica (left: Cliff Burton; right: James Hetfield) forging a completely new sound in 1984.

crushed beneath the bus' weight, and Burton—who had redefined the role of bass playing in the heavy metal context and who had so impressed his bandmates that they had relocated hundreds of miles in order to play with him—was dead at the age of twenty-four.

The band chose to continue, eventually taking on Flotsam & Jetsam bassist Jason Newsted to finish up the remaining tour dates. During the tour the new boy was mercilessly hazed by his bandmates, who had chosen to resume touring despite the fact that they were very obviously in the thick of their grief over Burton's death. Newsted survived his initiation and made his first recorded appearance with the band on an EP of covers, *Garage Days Re-Revisited*. Those who were impressed by his playing on the EP were in for a nasty shock, however, when the band released

their follow-up studio album, . . . *And Justice for All*, in 1988. The album contained no audible bass guitar anywhere in its sixty-five minutes, for reasons that have never been given by the band. Although it was hailed as a creative tour de force thanks to its extreme progressive song structures and virtuoso musicianship, it was a major step backward in terms of sound quality. The album is tinny, dry, and utterly lacking in power, with Ulrich's drums undermined by an irritating, clicky sound that saps all the life and presence out of the songs. Hammett's lead guitar fares no better, and Hetfield's usual battery of rhythm guitars sounds anemic and toothless, despite the fact that on several tracks he had overdubbed as many as fifteen rhythm guitars. Still, the band was more popular than ever, and the album hit the Top 10 without the benefit of so much as a minute of radio airplay. The only promotion that the album received was a video for the song "One," which mostly consisted of scenes that alternated between clips from the movie *Johnny Got His Gun* (the song was based on the Dalton Trumbo novel of the same name, from which the film was adapted) and Ulrich making lots of goofy faces to show what an intense and authoritative drummer he is. This was the band's first music video, and the decision to make it ruffled some feathers in the fan community, as the band had gone on record as stating that they never would. As it turned out, it was not the last time that their fans were asked to accept something that seemed to undermine Metallica's uncompromising image.

After a year in the recording studio with Mötley Crüe producer Bob Rock (Judas!), the band emerged with their 1991 self-titled album, known to some as *The Black Album* for its resemblance to Spinal Tap's fictional *Smell the Glove* album. It was,

hands down, the most commercial thing they had ever released, trading in the thrash and progressive tendencies of their previous work for a polished sound and four-minute songs that were as spit-shined and radio-ready as anyone could ask for. While Rock's production was blamed for the inexcusable crime of paring down the band's songwriting, he certainly succeeded in rectifying everything that was wrong with the sound of . . . *And Justice for All*. The new album, which even went so far as to acknowledge the presence of Newsted's bass, was the thickest and heaviest of anything in Metallica's catalog. While many grumbled that the band had sold out (an accusation that has been

hurled at them on an hourly basis since *Master of Puppets*), the album nonetheless debuted at number one, eventually going on to sell more than 22 million copies, putting it in *Eagles' Greatest Hits* territory in terms of units shifted. Touring to support the album went on for two years, and by the time all the smoke had cleared, Metallica was the best heavy metal band in the world and certainly the first to have critical acceptance to match its commercial success.

Metallica finally came off the road and reentered the studio in 1995 to begin work on their next album. By the time they emerged in 1996 with *Load*, five years had passed since their last studio album and the musical terrain had shifted considerably. It was no longer a simple matter of alternative rock becoming popular; guitar-oriented rock music itself, alternative or otherwise, was at its lowest ebb since its inception, and concern over whether the public wanted a new Metallica album must have been on the band's collective mind as the June release date approached. When the album finally came out, its greeting was mixed. *Load* sold multiple millions of copies in a matter of months, but the band members had committed the unforgivable crime of cutting their hair, which seemed to upset their fans to an alarming degree. It was in all likelihood a textbook case of people listening with their eyes, since the album was stylistically not all that different from its predecessor. Regardless, the cries of "sellout" were louder than ever. Metallica was subjected to further damnation for its decision to headline that summer's Lollapalooza tour, causing some to label the band "Alternica" and proving the final straw for a number of fans. A considerable portion of Metallica's core jumped ship at this point, or at least they claimed to—after all, somebody bought three million copies of *Load*.

Apparently trying to make up for the five years between albums, Metallica released what was, for them, a flurry of product. A year after *Load*, they released *ReLoad*, which contained all the songs left from the previous album's sessions. This was followed in 1998 by *Garage Inc.*, a two-CD set of covers, with one full disc of newly recorded material and the other containing older material that had been out of print for years, including the *Garage Days* EP. The following year, they released *S&M*, a live recording of their performance with the San Francisco Symphony.

When they weren't touring or releasing albums, the band members spent their time bringing legal action against entities. The litigious rumpus began in 1999 when the band sued Victoria's Secret for releasing a lip pencil bearing the brand name Metallica, which, trademark infringement notwithstanding, surely caused fans to erroneously patronize the women's haberdashery with the intention of purchasing a product that was, unlike other lip pencils, endorsed by the ill-tempered foursome. More famous, however, was the band's very public feud with Napster. The Internet service allowed its users to download music files from one another's computers, basically amounting to the dissemination of the band's music without compensation. Metallica became aware of the service when an unfinished version of its

OPPOSITE: Metallica's dynamic guitarists James Hetfield (left) and Kirk Hammett.
ABOVE: James Hetfield pays homage to Glenn Danzig's post-Misfits band, Samhain.
RIGHT: Metallica pose for a City of San Francisco Tourism Board brochure.

song for the *Mission Impossible II* soundtrack, "I Disappear," turned up on the site for anyone to download free of charge. Although it is perfectly understandable that the band members, who make their living off the sales of their music, wanted to protect their interests, the dispute lasted for more than a year, during which time Metallica lost a considerable amount of their hard-won credibility. This was, after all, the band who had built their fan base through tape trading, which was nothing more than an early-1980s analog method of disseminating the band's music for free. The suit was eventually dropped when Napster agreed to become a pay service, but Ulrich's appearance before a judicial committee had considerably undermined the band's "regular Joe" image. Finally, in January 2001, Newsted announced that he would be leaving the band in a press statement that was vague enough to fuel all manner of wild speculation.

The band reconvened without Newsted that same year to begin work on their next studio album, and as they did so, they were joined by filmmakers Joe Berlinger and Bruce Sinofsky, who intended to make a movie about the recording of their next album. They got much more than that. The recording almost stopped before it started when Hetfield entered rehab, citing alcoholism and "other addictions." When he emerged, he was limited to working just a few hours a day, which was barely enough time to do anything. Complicating matters was the band's decision to record in a completely untried, improvisatory fashion, without any real game-plan as to what they were going to come out with. They hadn't even replaced Newsted—bass duties on the album were handled by producer Bob Rock. The process of recording the album was incredibly contentious, and at times it wasn't clear if the band would actually survive the process. However, survive they did, and the record they emerged with was *St. Anger*. The nicest thing that can be said about the 2003 album is that it accurately depicts the turmoil that the band was going through at the time. This is a diplomatic way of saying that it's an unfocused, incoherent,

overlong mess that one doesn't listen to so much as suffer through. It still sold millions of copies, but this is no Metallica fan's favorite album by any stretch.

Then there was the matter of Berlinger and Sinofsky, who had captured the spectacle on film. The results were released as the 2004 documentary *Some Kind of Monster*, and it showed the band fighting, recording, and attending group therapy sessions with a "performance enhancing coach." Finally, the film showed the band auditioning new bassists, including members of Marilyn Manson, Kyuss, and Jane's Addiction. Ultimately, they chose Robert Trujillo, formerly of Suicidal Tendencies and Ozzy Osbourne's band. But while *St. Anger* was a terrible album and possibly the worst thing the band had produced up to that point, the film was a hypnotizing schadenfreude train-wreck, and when one watches it, one wonders why the group ever signed off on it.

In 2006, Metallica announced that they would not work with longtime producer Bob Rock on their next album. Instead, they chose Rick Rubin, who had been the man behind albums that had elevated careers, including those of Slayer and Johnny Cash. The fan community was hopeful. Perhaps he could assist them in coming up with something that would get the horrible taste of *St. Anger* out of their mouths? As it turned out, he did exactly that. The new album, *Death Magnetic*, appeared in 2008, and it was the album that many fans had been waiting over twenty years for. It was a triumphant return to the classic Metallica sound, but it wasn't a throwback or an apology either. It went a long way towards rehabilitating the group with its fans, even those who had written Metallica off two decades before.

The honeymoon was short-lived. In 2011, Metallica announced that their next album

Metallica gave an awesome performance in 1994 despite Jason Newsted's haircut. Clockwise from top: Lars Ulrich, Kirk Hammett, James Hetfield, and Jason Newsted.

would be a collaboration with Lou Reed, of all fucking people. He had performed with them at the Rock and Roll Hall of Fame 25th Anniversary Concert in 2009, and both parties had been so taken with one another that they decided they simply must work together again. Two years later, the fruits of that collaboration arrived in the form of *Lulu*, a double CD consisting of ten pieces that can't really be called songs. Reed had written lyrics based on the works of Frank Wedekind, a 19th-century German playwright, and they were recited over instrumental tracks that the band had recorded. The end result sounds like a mashup of an amateur metal band rehearsing in a basement and a 70-year-old man barking idiocies into a microphone simultaneously, with neither party realizing that the other is there too. The lyrics include such gems as "I beg you to degrade, is there waste that I could eat?" as well as the occasional vocal from Hetfield, who at one point sings "I am the table!" The album was quite rightly ripped to shreds by critics, such as Julian Marszalek of TheQuietus.com, who wrote that the time spent listening to *Lulu* could be better spent "wanking into a sock," and veteran journalist Don Kaye, who called it "a catastrophic failure on almost every level" on Blabbermouth.net. The fans were no more merciful. In fact, the best thing about *Lulu* was chuckling at their comments beneath the online reviews, such as one beneath Kaye's which referred to it as a "pile of DuDu."

Ah, well. In October 2011, the band announced that they were due to start recording their next album, and that Rick Rubin would again twiddle the knobs. Whether this can make fans forget about *Lulu* remains to be seen, but if time has proven anything, it's that Metallica's loyal following is always willing to hear what the band does next, even when they've strayed far off the reservation.

Cliff Burton: bass (*Kill 'Em All* through *Master of Puppets*); **Kirk Hammett**: guitars (see also Exodus); **James Hetfield**: guitars/vocals; **Jason Newsted**: bass (*Garage Days Re-Revisited* through *S&M*) (see also Flotsam & Jetsam); **Robert Trujillo**: bass (*Death Magnetic* and later); **Lars Ulrich**: drums

Discography: *Kill 'Em All* (Megaforce, 1983); *Ride the Lightning* (Megaforce, 1984); *Master of Puppets* (Elektra, 1986); *Garage Days Re-Revisited* (Elektra, 1987); . . . *And Justice for All* (Elektra, 1988); *Metallica* (Elektra, 1991); *Live Shit: Binge and Purge* (Elektra, 1993); *Load* (Elektra, 1996); *ReLoad* (Elektra, 1997); *Garage Inc.* (Elektra, 1998); *S&M* (Elektra, 1999); *St. Anger* (Elektra, 2003); *Death Magnetic* (Warner Bros., 2008); *Lulu* (Warner Bros., 2011)

MONSTER MAGNET

YEARS ACTIVE: 1989–PRESENT

Monster Magnet is as influential a band in the stoner rock movement as either Fu Manchu or Kyuss. In 1990, the band members released their first EP, and its feedback-laden, psychedelic metal sound was condemned by some as nothing more than a cynical attempt to recycle the bloated stadium rock of the early 1970s. In many respects, they were right. However, there were also a lot of people at this time who were rapidly outgrowing the music, sensibility, and aesthetics of the 1980s, and tastes were beginning to shift. The heavy guitar rock of the "me decade" had been marginalized for long enough to be viewed as a breath of fresh air upon its return. The good people at Caroline Records felt the same way, and they signed the band in 1991. Monster Magnet emerged that year with *Spine of God*, whose back cover proclaimed, "It's a Satanic drug thing . . . you wouldn't understand." The band's own tongue-in-cheek attitude proved as prominent a characteristic of their music as the psychedelic wash of vintage guitars and crunch of vintage Orange amplifiers. One listen to the lyrics of "Nod Scene" bears this out, as it details comical situations involving, but not limited to, cranial mishaps incurred while doing whipits. Monster Magnet had not only rehabilitated heavy rock for a new decade but also informed it with an ironic attitude that suited the time in which *Spine of God* was released.

Perhaps believing that it had found a band capable of producing a second *Badmotorfinger*, A&M Records, the home of Soundgarden,

signed Monster Magnet the following year. They produced two excellent albums of somewhat more straightforward rock for the label, *Superjudge* in 1993 and *Dopes to Infinity* in 1995. However, despite a considerable push from the label and heavy touring with popular bands such as Corrosion of Conformity, Monster Magnet barely made a dent in the marketplace, save for *Dopes to Infinity*'s single "Negasonic Teenage Warhead," which received a decent amount of airtime on MTV and helped the album sell slightly better than its predecessor. They finally got their breakthrough with their 1998 album, *Powertrip*, thanks to the single "Space Lord," which received radio airplay practically every ten minutes. The album reached gold sales status, vindicating Dave Wyndorf and company, who had endured almost a full decade of indifference and disrespect but nevertheless had stuck to their guns the whole time in order to make the music they wanted to make. Their new high profile got them on two years' worth of tours, both as headliners and as the opening act for bands such as Metallica and Aerosmith. In 2001, they released *God Says No*, which must have been a commercially successful album since everyone in the stoner rock movement that Monster

Monster Magnet radiates joy. Left to right: Jon Kleiman, Joe Calandra, Ed Mundell, and Dave Wyndorf.

In between committing extreme acts of Satanism, Morbid Angel's Steve Tucker stopped in for a visit to the cloisters.

Magnet had helped to create began crying "sellout" upon its release, thereby carrying on the fans' proud tradition of eating their own. After 2004's *Monolithic Baby!*, the band was set to release a new album and go on tour, but Wyndorf overdosed on prescription drugs in February 2006, according to the band's management. He recovered, and the group finally released their next album, *4-Way Diablo*, in 2007. Their most recent album was 2010's *Mastermind*.

Jim Bagliano: bass (*Monolithic Baby!*); **Phil Caivano**: guitars (*God Says No* and later); **Joe Calandra**: bass; **Jon Kleiman**: drums; **John McBain**: guitars (*Monster Magnet* through *Spine of God*); **Ed Mundell**: lead guitar (*Superjudge* through *God Says No*) (see also the Atomic Bitchwax); **Michael Wildwood**: drums (*Monolithic Baby!*); **Dave Wyndorf**: vocals/guitars

Discography: *Monster Magnet* (Glitterhouse, 1990); *Tab 25* (Glitterhouse, 1991); *Spine of God* (Caroline, 1991); *Superjudge* (A&M, 1993); *Dopes to Infinity* (A&M, 1995); *Powertrip* (A&M, 1998); *God Says No* (A&M, 2001); *Monolithic Baby!* (SPV, 2004); *4-Way Diablo* (SPV, 2007); *Mastermind* (Napalm, 2010)

MORBID ANGEL

YEARS ACTIVE: 1984–PRESENT

What the hell is the deal with Florida and death metal bands anyway? Death, Deicide, Obituary—these groups and numerous others have all hailed for reasons that are anyone's guess from the state that is home to Burt Reynolds, the pregnant chad, Disneyworld, and retirees. Deicide's own Glen Benton once opined that the Sunshine State produced heavily satanic bands because "it's so hot down here, all you can think about is hell." This is a compelling argument, to be sure, but it comes from a guy who burned an inverted crucifix into his forehead, leaving one with the strong impression that the sinner-roasting magma at the earth's core is on his mind most of the time anyway, even when he goes to the grocery store to buy toilet paper and cat food. Whatever the reason, most of the major bands

of the subgenre have hailed from this state, and Morbid Angel is no exception. Like the band's contemporaries, they grabbed the baton that had been passed to them by bands like Slayer and Venom and ran with it, taking thrash to such an extreme degree that it came to be known as death metal.

Founded by guitarist Trey Azagthoth in 1984, Morbid Angel hung around for a few years before finally getting a record deal, and they spent the time refining their approach. In retrospect, this probably worked out well for them, as they have no back catalog of crappy albums that find them trying to figure out what their style is, a trap that has befallen many an extreme metal band, from Slayer to Mayhem. When Morbid Angel finally got signed to Earache, their approach was well in hand, and their 1989

debut, *Altars of Madness*, exuded a confidence that made their sound all the more menacing. Morbid Angel has since released a flurry of albums for the label, and although the band has been dogged by constant lineup changes throughout its career, the members have never changed their style and have never capitulated to whatever might have been trendy at a given time.

Trey Azagthoth: guitars/keyboards; **Richard Burnelle**: guitars (*Altars of Madness, Blessed Are the Sick*); **Thor Anders "Destructhor" Myhren**: guitar (*Illud Divinum Insanus*); **Erik Rutan**: guitars (*Abominations of Desolation* through *Entangled in Chaos: Live*; *Gateways to Annihilation*); **Pete Sandoval**: drums (*Altars of Madness* through *Heretic*); **Steve Tucker**: vocals/bass (*Formulas Fatal to the Flesh* through *Heretic*); **David Vincent**: vocals/bass (*Altars of Madness* through *Entangled in Chaos: Live*); **Tim Yeung**: drums (*Illud Divinum Insanus*)

Discography: *Altars of Madness* (Earache, 1989); *Blessed Are the Sick* (Earache, 1991); *Abominations of Desolation* (Earache, 1991); *Covenant* (Giant, 1994); *Domination* (Giant, 1995); *Entangled in Chaos: Live* (Earache, 1996); *Formulas Fatal to the Flesh* (Earache, 1998); *Gateways to Annihilation* (Earache, 2000); *Heretic* (Earache, 2003); *Illud Divinum Insanus* (Season of Mist, 2011)

MÖTLEY CRÜE

YEARS ACTIVE: 1981–PRESENT

Mötley Crüe is without question the premier hair metal band of the 1980s, influencing every single one that followed in that decade, from Poison to Warrant to who knows how many others that never graduated from Los Angeles' Sunset Strip. Bassist Nikki Sixx and drummer Tommy Lee formed the band in 1981, drafting singer Vince Neil from Rock Candy, a Cheap Trick cover band, and Mick Mars, who ran an ad proclaiming that there was a "loud, rude guitarist available" in his unctuous person. In addition to providing six-string histrionics, Mars also gave the band their misspelled moniker, although they went through several different misspellings before

settling on the one we have all come to know and love. The band hit Los Angeles' club circuit and became a hit with local audiences, thanks in part to their transvestite-linebacker makeup, Judas Priest–inspired S&M costumes, and use of every form of pyrotechnical device that would fit in the dinky clubs they played. One of the audiences that they succeeded in wowing included Allan Coffman, who was so impressed with the band that he offered to finance the recording of an album for them. The resulting debut, *Too Fast for Love*, was released in 1981, and it was an aggressive, trashy affair that at times flirted with the naked antagonism and belligerence of punk. It sold an amazing twenty thousand copies, prompting Elektra Records to pick them up posthaste. The band's first release for Elektra, 1983's *Shout at the Devil*, was an immediate hit, in no small part due to the video for "Looks That Kill," which featured flying laser-generated pentagrams and a caged Amazonian warrior babe submitting to the collective will of the diabolical Crüe. They

tame her, you see, through the sheer force of rock.

Having successfully capitalized on adolescent male anxieties, Mötley Crüe saw *Shout at the Devil* go platinum, establishing them as a major force on Los Angeles' metal scene. However, not long after

OPPOSITE: After *Shout at the Devil* went platinum in 1984, Mötley Crüe was on fire. Clockwise from left: Nikki Sixx, Mick Mars, Vince Neil, and Tommy Lee.

BELOW: At one of its numerous stadium shows, Mötley Crüe encourages its audience to do the wave. Left to right: Tommy Lee, Mick Mars, Vince Neil, and Nikki Sixx.

the album's release, Neil, driving while intoxicated, plowed into another car. The accident killed his passenger, drummer Nicholas "Razzle" Dingley of Hanoi Rocks, and permanently injured the passengers in the car he hit. Ironically, the singer walked away without a scratch. He was found guilty of drunk driving and vehicular manslaughter, but he avoided serving more than thirty days in prison by performing community service and paying a substantial cash settlement to his surviving victims. The reasoning behind the judgment was that if Neil were incarcerated for any serious stretch of time, he would be unable to earn a living and therefore unable to pay damages. Fair enough, but the public perception was that he bought his way out of jail, and literally got away with murder. Mötley Crüe's fans didn't seem to mind, though, and the band's 1985 album, *Theatre of Pain*, which was released just after Neil's sentencing, met with sales figures that can only be quantified using terms such as megaton. The band even managed to score their first Top 40 hit with their cover of "Smokin' in the Boys' Room" by Brownsville Station. The video for this song, which featured that creepy cone-headed actor from *The Hills Have Eyes*, went into heavy rotation on MTV, but it was soon left in the dust upon the premiere of the video for the Crüe's

power ballad "Home Sweet Home." The song became the most requested clip in the station's history up to that time, occupying the top spot for four consecutive months.

In 1987, Mötley Crüe released *Girls, Girls, Girls* to similar fan enthusiasm and strong sales. The band members, on the other hand, were in very, very bad shape. Neil had cleaned up after his car accident, but his bandmates were in the grips of major substance-abuse problems, Sixx in particular, whose drug of choice was heroin. Actually, by this point

SA

WA
107.

Write dow
songs you he
11pm and mi
home from th
Then mail this
box 107.3 Boa
as soon as po
50 received will get a
Mötley Crüe's *D*

UNTAME

"choice" was no longer a factor, as the bassist was, by his own admission, a full-fledged addict. At one point, the drug had even briefly claimed his life. Following an overdose, his heart had stopped, and he was technically dead for a moment. He was successfully resuscitated by emergency workers, but he recalls the whole out-of-body shebang, complete with the white light, hovering above his own dead body, and so forth. But Sixx was not one to be cowed by

OPPOSITE: In 1986, Mötley Crüe wanted you to know that on the Sunset Strip, it was all right for sleazy guys to wear as much makeup as sleazy women. Clockwise from top left: Mick Mars, Nikki Sixx; Vince Neil, and Tommy Lee.
BELOW: Mötley Crüe shows off the registered nurses that the band keeps on call in case Nikki Sixx dies again. Left to right: Nikki Sixx, Vince Neil, Tommy Lee, and Mick Mars.

a little thing like his own death, so against medical advice, he checked himself out of the hospital the next day.

Sixx went home and proceeded to cook himself up a fix that was his personal record holder for the Most Heroin I Have Ever Injected. Immediately upon injecting it into his arm, he passed out, not reviving until the following day. The first sight to greet him that sunny morning was the hypodermic needle still dangling from his arm. He had bled from the needle site into the palm of his hand, where a miniature tide pool of blood had dried. Sixx recounts that it was not until this point that he realized the extent of his addiction, and that the only certain course for him to stop was either treatment

or death. With Neil having already set a precedent by entering rehab after his car accident, the other members of the group, Sixx included, decided that they would follow his lead and clean up.

A newly cleaned-up Mötley Crüe emerged and in 1989 released *Dr. Feelgood*. There was some trepidation, as some in the band worried that a Crüe sans dangling syringes and wrecked cars could no longer be considered bad-ass. Whatever fears they may have manifested were allayed when the album went to number one. It was fueled by strong singles, two of which, the title track and "Kickstart My Heart," used the band's struggles with drugs as their subject matter. This was followed up in 1991 with

Decade of Decadence, the band's first compilation album. After the album's release and subsequent chart success, the band was in an advantageous position in the marketplace, and they renegotiated their contract with Elektra to the tune of $25 million. Naturally, it was at this point that everything went to hell.

By 1992, the band was tearing itself apart, with tensions running especially high between Neil and Lee. At this point, Neil either quit or was fired from the band, depending on who you ask (the singer maintains that he was fired while Sixx claims that he quit). The band hired singer John Corabi, previously of The Scream (not to be confused with the D.C. hardcore band Scream), and Neil went solo. Unfortunately for all parties involved, it was 1994 before anyone got any goods manufactured, and in that year any metal product was doomed in the marketplace. However, no metal was more doomed than that associated with womanizing or any other such frivolity. The band seemed to believe that their new singer was what was holding them back as opposed to massive shifts in the public's musical taste, and in 1997, the band reunited with Neil for the *Generation Swine* album. It didn't sell very well either, perhaps forcing the band to consider that their lack of multiplatinum sales was attributable to issues beyond whoever happened to be at the microphone at any given moment.

At the same time, a home video surfaced on the Internet that Lee and his silicone-enhanced wife Pamela Anderson had made while locked in beautiful, loving coitus during their honeymoon. The videotape was the focus of many uninteresting party conversations and unfunny penis-length jokes, but it didn't unclog much of the Mötley Crüe product that was out there. It did go on to become the biggest-selling pornographic videotape of all time up to that point, so Lee must have been happy to be a winner again. However, the glory with which his gargantuan rhinoceros penis was regaled was short-lived. Possibly mistaking her face for a snare drum, Lee pounded on Anderson, prompting his arrest for spousal abuse. The drummer remained incarcerated for the better part of a year, returning to the band after his release. While jail time might have taught Lee a thing or two about the laws against wife beating, his relationship with Neil was as bad as it had ever been, and this time Lee went out the door, forming his own band, Methods of Mayhem, in 1999.

Lee was replaced by Randy Castillo, who had previously occupied the throne for Ozzy Osbourne, and Crüe recorded a new album with him in 2000, *New Tattoo*. However, Castillo fell ill and couldn't tour, forcing the band to find a replacement. As it turned out, it was a girl, girl, girl. None other than Hole drummer Samantha Maloney, herself a huge fan of the band since time immemorial, took over for Castillo and the tour was able to take place. Ironically, the tour was with none other than Megadeth, featuring Dave Mustaine, who throughout the 1980s had singled out Mötley Crüe as the band who best represented everything that was "gay" about Los Angeles metal. As if that were not enough, the irony was doubly rich as Mustaine, like Sixx, had a few years earlier overdosed on drugs to the point of being momentarily pronounced dead. One can just imagine the laughter and good times in which the pair surely engaged on the tour bus, recounting the sight of emergency workers stabbing their lifeless torsos with adrenaline syringes. One can also imagine nobody wanting to sit next to them on said bus, lest they be subjected to two separate versions of the "I almost died!" story on a nightly basis. The Crüe's next album of original material was 2008's *Saints of Los Angeles*. Sixx told *Rolling Stone* magazine in late 2011 that the band was starting to consider packing it in. "At some point—whether it's within a year or a few years—we're probably gonna have that conversation about maybe it's time, maybe it's time to go out on top."

Randy Castillo: drums (*New Tattoo*); **John Corabi**: vocals (*Mötley Crüe*); **Tommy Lee**: drums (*Too Fast for Love* through *Live: Entertainment or Death*; *Saints of Los Angeles*); **Mick Mars**: guitar; **Vince Neil**: vocals (*Too Fast for Love* through *Dr. Feelgood*; *Generation Swine* and later); **Nikki Sixx**: bass

Discography: *Too Fast for Love* (Elektra, 1981); *Shout at the Devil* (Elektra, 1983); *Theater of Pain* (Elektra, 1985); *Girls, Girls, Girls* (Elektra, 1987); *Dr. Feelgood* (Elektra, 1989); *Mötley Crüe* (Elektra, 1994); *Generation Swine* (Elektra, 1997); *Live: Entertainment or Death* (Beyond, 1999); *New Tattoo* (Mötley/Beyond, 2000); *Saints of Los Angeles* (Mötley/Eleven Seven, 2008)

MOTÖRHEAD

YEARS ACTIVE: 1975–PRESENT

When asked to sum up Motörhead's musical approach, stalwart bassist and vocalist Lemmy Kilmister once stated that his wish was for

Motörhead's Lemmy Kilmister (left) and "Fast" Eddie Clarke destroy the earth, town by town.

them to be the band that, were they to move in next door to you, "your lawn would die." While their effect on the landscaping efforts of the United Kingdom has yet to yield significant results, the band's considerable influence on heavy metal is beyond question. A year before the punk movement was even officially under way, Motörhead was already crossing metal with the fast, furious, as-yet-unnamed style, thereby inventing thrash metal in the process.

In 1976, a full fifty-two weeks before the Sex Pistols released their debut and the death of Elvis Presley, Motörhead was portending the apocalypse with its first recorded supersonic onslaught, which resembled nothing so much as the soundtrack for a nuclear strike. Unfortunately, this recording was not released to the public until the next decade, an indication of the type of inconveniences that the band encountered throughout their long career.

However, Kilmister has proven to be dedicated and resilient enough to keep rising every time he's been knocked down, and his band has kept on destroying otherwise well-maintained frontages, in one form or another, for more than thirty-five years. Somehow, despite its long tenure, Motörhead has managed to avoid being perceived as an over-the-hill nostalgia act, even though as of this writing Kilmister is now more than 65 years old. If anything,

age has actually worked in the wart-stricken bassist's favor, as his now graying hair and faded tattoos seem to place him comfortably in the category that he has cultivated from day one, that of outlaw biker trash. One could say that his appearance and public persona is something like that of a British David Allen Coe.

Kilmister, who is, amusingly, the son of a church vicar, had played in a variety of bands and even worked as a roadie for Jimi Hendrix before joining the progressive rock group Hawkwind. His term with the space-rock outfit lasted four years, and upon his departure, he took with him the title of the last song he had written for them, using it as the name for his new band. Almost immediately, Motörhead encountered every type of turmoil imaginable. Dave Edmunds, a prominent producer, was originally put in charge of the band's debut album for the United Artists label but was fired after violently clashing with the bassist over the album's artistic direction. Kilmister already knew what he wanted the band to sound like and could not be persuaded otherwise. The label felt differently, however, and rejected the completed album, shelving it until further notice. Additional salt was poured into the metaphorical wound at roughly the same time, when drummer Lucas Fox quit the band. This was actually a blessing

On stage during a Motörhead show in 1988, Lemmy Kilmister is caught looking like he's experiencing an acid flashback from his Hawkwind days.

in disguise, however, as he was replaced by the legendary Phil "Philthy Animal" Taylor, the only member of the band ever to compete with Kilmister in terms of celebrity. Along with original guitarist Larry Wallis, another guitarist "Fast" Eddie Clarke was recruited to round out the band, but the four-piece version of Motörhead lasted exactly one rehearsal, after which Wallis walked out the door.

The remaining trio of Kilmister, Taylor, and Clarke are now generally regarded as Motörhead's "classic" lineup, and after much toil, they recorded, and even released, their self-titled debut. After getting their product out, the musicians finally hit their stride, releasing a string of albums that are all considered classics, such as *Overkill*, *Bomber*, and the infamous *Ace of Spades*, which charted in the British Top 10. The single by the same name didn't do too shabby, either, peaking at number fifteen. With the band now a safe bet to sell a few records, the opportunistic parasites at United Artists decided to grace the public with the album they had shelved four years earlier, dubbing it *On Parole*, perhaps implying that theirs was not so much a record label as a forced labor camp.

But the salad days were soon to end, as Clarke and Kilmister started developing considerable animus for each other during the Iron Fist tour in 1982. The guitarist quit that year and was replaced by Brian Robertson of Thin Lizzy, who didn't last long either, sticking around for *Another Perfect Day* and then walking out in 1983. It was at this point that the band's lineup became an unstable nightmare, with members changing place left and right, leaving only Kilmister standing in place and waiting for the smoke to clear. During this whole time, Motörhead managed to squeeze out exactly one single, "Killed by Death," but after its release in 1984 the band members became embroiled in a lawsuit with their label, Bronze, that precluded them from releasing any of the new recordings they had made, including a collaboration between Kilmister and breast-brandishing pseudosinger Samantha Fox.

While two years' worth of inaction and legal hassles would have surely spelled certain career death for almost any other band, Motörhead carried on somehow, and when the lawsuit with Bronze was finally resolved in 1986, they had lost none of the die-hard following that they had in 1991, when Taylor rejoined the band for their *1916* album. However, the reunion didn't last beyond the recording, and former King Diamond drummer Mikkey Dee took over and remains with the band. In 1995, Motörhead found a stable home in Canada's CMC label, for which the band released five albums, their longest-lasting label affiliation since their 1984 split with Bronze. They moved to the Steamhammer label in 2002 and released four albums with them, and their most recent album, 2010's *The Wörld Is Yours*, was released through Future PLC. When Motörhead wasn't recording or touring, Kilmister turned up in British television commercials for insurance firms and in movies such as *Hellraiser 3* and the pornographic blockbuster *John Wayne Bobbit Uncut*. Ladies, no! Lemmy does not get naked in the film, so calm down.

Phil Campbell: guitars (*No Remorse* and later); **"Fast" Eddie Clarke**: guitars (*Motörhead* through *Iron Fist*) (see also Fastway); **Mikkey Dee**: drums (*March or Die* and later) (see also King Diamond); **Lucas Fox**: drums (*On Parole*); **Pete Gill**: drums (*No Remorse, Orgasmatron*) (see also Saxon); **Lemmy Kilmister**: bass/vocals; **Brian Robertson**: guitars (*Another Perfect Day*) (see also Thin Lizzy); **Phil "Philthy Animal" Taylor**: drums (*Motörhead* through *Ace of Spades*; *No Sleep 'Til Hammersmith* through *Another Perfect Day*; *1916*); **Larry Wallis**:

guitars (*On Parole*); **Wurzel**: guitars (*No Remorse* through *Bastards*)

Discography: *Motörhead* (Bronze, 1977); *Overkill* (Bronze, 1979); *Bomber* (Bronze, 1979); *Ace of Spades* (Bronze, 1980); *On Parole* (EMI, 1980); *No Sleep 'Til Hammersmith* (Bronze, 1981); *Iron Fist* (Bronze, 1982); *Another Perfect Day* (Bronze, 1983); *No Remorse* (Roadrunner, 1984); *Orgasmatron* (GWR, 1986); *Rock'n'Roll* (GWR, 1987); *No Sleep at All* (Roadrunner, 1990); *Lock Up Your Daughters* (Trojan, 1990); *1916* (Sony, 1991); *March or Die* (Sony, 1992); *Bastards* (ZYX, 1993); *All the Aces: The Best of Motörhead* (Roadrunner, 1993); *The Best of Motörhead, Vol. 2* (Roadrunner, 1995); *Sacrifice* (CMC, 1995); *Overnight Sensation* (CMC, 1996); *Stone Dead Forever* (Receiver, 1997); *Snake Bite Love* (CMC, 1998); *Everything Louder Than Everyone Else* (CMC, 1999); *We Are Motörhead* (CMC, 2000); *Hammered* (Steamhammer, 2002); *Inferno* (Steamhammer, 2004); *Kiss of Death* (Steamhammer, 2006); *Motörizer* (Steamhammer, 2008); *The Wörld is Yours* (Future PLC, 2010)

MOUNTAIN

Years active: 1969–1972; 1973–1974; 1981–1985; 1996–present

Very few of the bands who played at Woodstock in 1969 could credibly be called heavy, much less heavy metal. One exception was Mountain, whose appearance at the seminal hippie rock concert was their fourth live performance ever. The band was the brainchild of former Cream producer Felix Pappalardi and guitarist Leslie West, who had released an album under his own name titled *Mountain* in 1968. The title is rumored to be an allusion to West's physical form, which at the time was, uh . . . well . . . very fat. Pappalardi had seen West in a local Long Island band called the Vagrants and was completely blown away by his exquisite guitar

playing, so he got them signed to Atlantic Records and produced their first joint effort. From a commercial standpoint, nothing came of it. West left the Vagrants to make his solo album, *Mountain*, which Pappalardi again produced. Pappalardi also played bass on it, and though it was marketed as a solo album, it was really total heavy blues power trio awesomeness. The album still retains the power to tear listeners a new asshole with its sludgy psychedelic goods.

The pair eventually realized that they formed the nucleus of one hell of a band, and they took the name of West's solo album for themselves. After Woodstock, they enlisted drummer Corky Laing, and Mountain's classic lineup was now in place. This lineup recorded its proper debut, *Climbing!*, which was released in 1970. Its first track and debut single is "Mississippi Queen," whose eight introductory cowbell smacks are instantly recognizable, as is its very heavy and very exciting main riff. The single charted at number twenty-one, but it's led a life since then that has far outweighed whatever commercial impact it had at the time, a major reason why the album keeps selling to this day.

Fans who bought the album looking for more southern-fried metallic chug were rewarded with "Silver Paper," the heavy "Sittin' on a Rainbow," the heavier still "For Yasgur's Farm," and the very, very heavy "Never in My Life." What also came across on the album was an enthusiasm that the band sadly never recaptured and that is usually found only on debut albums. While the tunes were momentous, Mountain had another very important weapon in their arsenal—they could really play. They pulled out all the stops when they played live, and every concert was a jam fan's dream. The band displayed the pure pummeling capability of Cream at their peak with the skillful interplay of the Allman Brothers.

After barnstorming live shows to promote their debut album, the band returned in 1971 with *Nantucket Sleighride*, an album that was not quite the equal of its predecessor, but only by the smallest measure. The standout track was the title cut, which became an improvisational showcase when performed live. Recordings exist wherein the song stretches out to as much as 30 or 40 minutes, and whether or not this is a good thing probably depends on the listener's patience, enthusiasm for very long guitar solos, and the number of bong hits in play.

Flowers of Evil came next at the end of 1971, but it was already clear that Mountain had overextended itself by this point. There had been just ten months between albums and there had been almost nonstop touring during that time as well, so the album unsurprisingly came off like the contractual obligation of a bunch of very tired people.

After a 1972 live album, *Mountain Live: The Road Goes Ever On*, the group packed it in. West and Laing joined former Cream bassist Jack Bruce for the trio West, Bruce & Laing. Pappalardi went back to studio production. Mountain reunited in 1973, but Laing didn't participate, so the new lineup featured drummer Allan Schwartzberg and keyboard and guitar player Bob Mann. This lineup performed on the 1974 live album *Twin Peaks*. Laing returned to the fold for their next studio album, *Avalanche*, and the group broke up again soon afterwards.

In 1983, any possibility of the original lineup reuniting came to a definitive end when Pappalardi's wife, Gail Collins, shot and killed him. The circumstances behind the killing were never clear, and to this day Collins, who designed some of the band's album covers and collaborated on their music, maintains that the shooting was an accident. West and Laing recruited bassist Mark Clarke for the 1985 album *Go For Your Life*, and after parting ways for over a decade, this lineup returned to record *Man's World* in 1996.

Since then, Mountain has made two further releases, 2002's *Mystic Fire* and 2007's *Masters of War*, which was made up entirely of Bob Dylan covers. Both albums featured different lineups, although both albums retained the core duo of West and Laing.

In 2011, West had his right foot amputated after complications from diabetes became life-threatening. It is not known how his health situation will impact his career going forward or if we'll hear any new music from him afterwards. Here's hoping he rebounds. It would be a shame not to hear him play again, since he's one of hard rock's all-time finest guitar players.

Mark Clarke: bass (*Man's World*); **Chuck Hearne**: bass (*Mystic Fire*); **Rev Jones**: bass (*Masters of War*); **Steve Knight**: keyboards (*Climbing!* through *Avalanche*); **Brian John Mitchell**: keyboards (*Masters of War*); **Corky Laing**: drums; **Felix Pappalardi**: bass (*Climbing!* through *Avalanche*); **David Perry**: guitar (*Avalanche*); **Leslie West**: guitar; **Todd Wolfe**: slide guitar (*Mystic Fire* and later)

Discography: *Climbing!* (Windfall, 1970); *Nantucket Sleighride* (Sony, 1971); *Flowers of Evil* (Sony, 1971); *Mountain Live: The Road Goes Ever On* (Island, 1972); *Avalanche* (Columbia, 1974); *TwinPeaks* (Columbia, 1974) *Go For Your Life* (Axe Killer, 1985); *Man's World* (Viceroy, 1996); *Mystic Fire* (Lightyear, 2002); *Masters of War* (Big Rack, 2007)

Mr. Bungle vocalist Mike Patton eliminates all peripheral distractions that would detract from his vocal performance.

MR. BUNGLE

YEARS ACTIVE: 1985–2004

Mr. Bungle has spent its entire career crafting wildly chaotic, idiosyncratic music that does not even pay lip service to any conventional concept of genre or classification. Founded in Eureka, California, in 1985, when all of the members were still in high school, the band took their name from the title of an educational film whose focal point was the cultivation of grooming habits appropriate for those in their formative years, with special attention paid to techniques used in combing one's hair and methods for maintaining the crease in one's pant legs. Catchy moniker in tow, they released several demos with names like *The Raging Wrath of the Easter Bunny* that were guaranteed to have major-label A&R representatives in a feeding frenzy, elbowing one another in the teeth to get to the highly coveted band first and award them a contract worth a multimillion-dollar amount so astronomical as to defy quantification. Strangely, this never occurred. Whatever the reason, Mr. Bungle went completely unnoticed, and so the band spent their time making music that developed progressively into a weirder and weirder mishmash of metal and experimental jazz, crossed with occasional ska and disco influences for good measure. The resulting sound was a wash of styles that was uniquely theirs and was absolutely impossible to describe, much less imitate.

Their fortunes improved when singer Mike Patton won the lead vocalist slot in Faith No More on the basis of his performance on one of the Mr. Bungle demos. Rather than leave the band, Patton decided to keep both gigs going, and he used his newfound clout to secure a deal for his high school buddies. Mr. Bungle, which had never created so much as a note of commercial music and whose ability to alienate listeners was equaled only by the Residents, was now a major-label band. Their self-titled debut was released on Warner Bros. in 1991, and perhaps as a nod to the Residents, the band members disguised themselves with masks, refusing to reveal their true identities. They won over crowds on their first tour with their visual presentation, migraine-inducing music, and unlikely choice of cover songs, such as the theme to *Welcome Back Kotter*. The band members have all been involved in various side projects, such as Fantômas, Mike Patton's collaboration with Melvins guitarist Buzz Osborne and former Slayer drummer Dave Lombardo. In 2004, Patton confirmed to *Rolling Stone* magazine that Mr. Bungle had broken up.

Trevor Dunn: bass; **Danny Heifetz**: drums; **Theobald Lengyel**: alto saxophone; **Clinton McKinnon**: tenor saxophone/clarinet; **Mike Patton**: vocals (see Faith No More); **Trey Spruance**: guitar

Discography: *Mr. Bungle* (Warner Bros., 1991); *Disco Volante* (Warner Bros., 1995); *California* (Warner Bros., 1999)

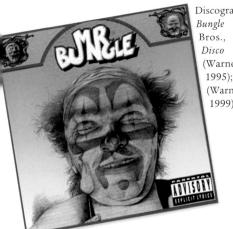

In 1994, as the last night of Hanukkah approaches, My Dying Bride poses for a group portrait. Left to right: Ade Jackson, Andy Craighan, Rick Miah, Aaron Stainthorpe, Martin Powell, and Hamish Glencross.

MY DYING BRIDE

YEARS ACTIVE: 1990–PRESENT

Those who find the music of Candlemass too modest and unassuming are advised to check out My Dying Bride, whose style is based around epic, symphonic compositions that flirt with, if not exceed, the ten-minute mark and create a mood as oppressively negative as anything in the early Swans catalog. At the start of their career, My Dying Bride ranked right alongside Anathema and Paradise Lost as forerunners in the doom-death field, based on their 1991 debut EP, *Symphonaire Infernus*

et Spera Empyrium, and the 1992 full-length *As the Flower Withers*. These releases were as gloomy as they were aggressive, and they employed the growling vocals of death metal as a counterpoint to the epic nature of the songs, which brought them back down to earth. The band's style began to shift in 1993, around the time of the release of the EP *The Thrash of Naked Limbs*. They expanded their roster by adding violin player Martin Powell and began incorporating cleanly sung vocals, immediately separating them from the rest of the pack. The fruits of their new approach were released to the public in 1994 on their landmark album *Turn Loose the Swans*, and it was at this point that people dropped the doom-death tag with which the band had originally been stuck and began referring to them as goth metal. Since then, a lot of doom-death bands have followed My Dying Bride's lead and added strings and melodic vocals to their music, but My Dying Bride did it first and were awarded forerunner status as a result.

The band now had carte blanche to do any damn thing they pleased, and they took full advantage of their new standing, first in 1995 with the release of *Trinity*, a compilation of their EPs, and then in 1996 with the release of *The Angel and the Dark River/Live at the Dynamo '95*. The 1996 album consisted of six songs clocking in at almost an hour and was combined with a live EP, which coalesced to make their previous recordings sound like *Now That's What I Call Music* collections by comparison. They continued to expand upon their popularity in underground metal circles, eventually winning opening slots on tours with such bands as Iron Maiden and Dio. After a few more albums, tours, and lineup changes, they released *The Light at the End of the World* in 1999, which was, surprisingly, almost a complete throwback to their original sound. In 2001, My Dying Bride released the *Meisterwerk 1* and *Meisterwerk 2* compilation albums, and a studio album, *The Dreadful Hours*. The following year marked the release of *The Voice of the Wretched*, another live set. My Dying Bride remains one of the most significant and highly regarded bands of this particular subgenre.

Lena Abé: bass (*For Lies I Sire*); **Yasmin Ahmid**: keyboards (*The Dreadful Hours*); **Johan Baum**: cello (*Evinta*); **John Bennett**: drums (*A Line of Deathless Kings*); **Andy Craighan**: guitars; **Hamish Glencross**: guitars (*The Dreadful Hours* and later); **Adrian Jackson**: bass; **Bill Law**: drums (*34.788% . . . Complete*); **Rick Miah**: drums (*Symphonaire Infernus et Spera Empyrium* through *Like Gods of the Sun*); **Dan Mullins**: drums (*For Lies I Sire*); **Alice Pembroke**: viola (*Evinta*); **Martin Powell**: vocals/violin (*Turn Loose the Swans* through *Like Gods of the Sun*); **Calvin Robertshaw**: guitars (*Symphonaire Infernus et Spera Empyrium* through *The Light at the End of the World*); **Lucie Roche**: vocals (*Evinta*); **Aaron Stainthorpe**: vocals; **Sarah Stanton**: keyboards (*Songs of Darkness, Words of Light* through *A Line of Deathless Kings*); **Shaun Steels**: drums (*The Light at the End of the World* through *Songs of Darkness, Words of Light*); **Katie Stone**: keyboards (*For Lies I Sire*)

Discography: *Symphonaire Infernus et Spera Empyrium* (Peaceville, 1991); *As the Flower Withers* (Peaceville, 1992); *The Thrash of Naked Limbs* (Peaceville, 1993); *Turn Loose the Swans* (Peaceville, 1994); *I Am the Bloody Earth* (Peaceville, 1994); *Trinity* (Peaceville, 1995); *The Angel and the Dark River/Live at the Dynamo '95* (Peaceville, 1996); *Like Gods of the Sun* (Peaceville, 1997); *34.788% . . . Complete* (Peaceville, 1998); *The Light at the End of the World* (Peaceville, 1999); *The Dreadful Hours* (Peaceville, 2001); *The Voice of the Wretched* (Peaceville, 2002); *Songs of Darkness, Words of Light* (Peaceville, 2004); *A Line of Deathless Kings* (Peaceville, 2006); *An Ode to Woe* (Peaceville, 2008); *For Lies I Sire* (Peaceville, 2009); *Evinta* (Peaceville, 2011)

NAPALM DEATH

YEARS ACTIVE: 1981–PRESENT

In the late 1980s, the thrash metal genre split in two directions, with some bands choosing a more mainstream approach and others trying to push the envelope as far as they could. The most extreme purveyors of the latter approach were the bands playing in a new style known as grind-core, which distinguished itself with song tempos that were almost too fast to register, track lengths that sometimes clocked in at only a few seconds, and indecipherable vocals delivered in the ridiculous Cookie Monster growl that somehow caught on and turned into a legitimate style. Napalm Death founded this movement on its 1987 debut, *Scum*, which contained almost thirty songs, some of them barely clearing the one-minute mark and all of them utterly dispensing with conventional notions of melody, songwriting, or any other aesthetic niceties that most people associate with music. The lyrics showcased the band's social consciousness, but unless one

followed very closely with a lyric sheet, making them out was impossible thanks to the warp-speed tempos. The album was also noteworthy for having two almost completely different lineups on each of its sides, drummer Mick Harris being the sole member to grace both. The band's second album, *From Enslavement to Obliteration*, was released in 1988 and pushed the formula even further. It featured fifty-four songs, almost double the amount of its predecessor and many of them lasting only a few seconds. Perhaps feeling that the album format was turning them into a self-indulgent progressive rock band, they appeared on a split single with the Electro Hippies, with each side lasting exactly one second. It is difficult to imagine that it could have been possible to expand upon the formula, and the band lost yet more members afterward. The first round of downsizing had seen *Scum* guitarist Justin Broadrick go on to form Godflesh, and exiting vocalist Lee Dorrian and guitarist Bill Steer would, like Broadrick, each go on to form their own influential bands—Dorrian formed Cathedral, and Steer formed the herbivorous musical collective known as Carcass.

In 1990, after a new lineup was established, the band recorded *Harmony Corruption*. The album was a more commercial offering, at least by Napalm Death standards. Perhaps tired of making music that could be measured only in nanoseconds, for the new album, the band increased song lengths, which now sometimes exceeded as many as two minutes, and tempos fell back to a lazy, Neil Young–esque two hundred beats per minute. The sellout didn't last long, however, and Napalm Death returned a year later with the *Mass Appeal Madness* EP, a complete return to the supersonic blast beats of the band's earlier sound. Sadly, the lineup changes that had been de rigueur for the band claimed Harris the following year. When he left to found Scorn, Napalm Death chose to perse-

vere despite the fact that the band now featured no original members. They returned in 1992 with *Utopia Banished*, but the real surprise came in 1994 with *Fear, Emptiness, Despair*, which somehow landed in the U.S. Top 10. Since then, they have not had anything even remotely resembling that type of chart success, but they have stayed together and in 2012, they released their latest album, *Utilitarian*.

Justin Broadrick: guitars (*Scum*) (see also Godflesh); **Nik Bullen**: bass/vocals (*Scum*); **Lee Dorrian**: vocals (*Scum, From Enslavement to Obliteration*) (see also Cathedral); **Shane Embury**: bass (*From Enslavement to Obliteration* and later); **Mark "Barney" Greenway**: vocals (*Harmony Corruption* and later); **Mick Harris**: drums (*Scum* through *Mass Appeal Madness*); **Mitch Harris**: guitars (*From Enslavement to Obliteration* and later); **Danny Herrera**: drums (*Utopia Banished* and later); **Jesse Pintado**: guitars (*Harmony Corruption* and later); **Bill Steer**: guitars (*Scum, From Enslavement to Obliteration*) (see also Carcass); **Jim Whitely**: bass (*Scum*)

Discography: *Scum* (Earache, 1987); *From Enslavement to Obliteration* (Combat, 1988); *Harmony Corruption* (Earache, 1990); *Mass Appeal Madness* (Earache, 1991); *Utopia Banished* (Earache, 1992); *Fear, Emptiness, Despair* (Earache, 1994); *Greed Killing* (Earache, 1995); *Diatribes* (Earache, 1996); *Inside the Torn Apart* (Earache, 1997); *Words from the Exit Wound* (Earache, 1998); *Leaders Not Followers* (Dreamcatcher, 1999); *Enemy of the Music Business* (Dreamcatcher, 2001); *Order of the Leech* (Spitfire, 2002); *Leaders Not Followers: Part 2* (Century Media, 2004); *The Code is Red . . . Long Live the Code* (Century Media, 2005); *Smear Campaign* (Century Media, 2006); *Time Waits for No Slave* (Century Media, 2009); *Utilitarian* (Century Media, 2012)

LOS NATAS

YEARS ACTIVE: 1992–PRESENT

Los Natas is a stoner rock band hailing from Buenos Aires. There are a few other Argentine stoner rock bands, such as Dragonauta, but the movement is still deeply underground in South America, and as such Los Natas has its strongest following outside the members' native land, in the United States in particular. The band has virtually cloned the Kyuss sound, but the musicians have done a better job than most imitators of mining the spirit of their heroes, whereas their contemporaries have been content just to copy them. As such, Los Natas' albums contain quite a bit of material that evokes a mood similar to that found on *Welcome to Sky Valley*, particularly in its mellower moments. Los Natas' catalog is a strong one, and all of the group's albums have their shining moments, but the best offering is also, strangely, the worst-sounding one, their 1996 debut, *Delmar*. The album sounds like it was recorded at a cost that likely could not buy a week's worth of groceries. The drums in particular are the most tragic casualty of the budgetary constraints. They don't even sound like drums, really. Perhaps in tribute to Captain Beefheart's *Trout Mask Replica*, it sounds as though drummer Walter Broide is executing his fills on a series of milk cartons and landing them on cymbals muted with corrugated cardboard. Regardless, the band members' enthusiasm for making their first album is palpable and comes through loud and clear, even when the instruments don't. Subsequent albums, particularly the 1999 Dale Crover-helmed *Cuidad de Brahman*, were well recorded even if the excitement level isn't 100 percent of what it was on the debut. In 2002, the band released its third studio album, *Corsario Negro*, which also marked the first time the members billed themselves as Los Natas, in order not to be confused with the rap artist named Natas. In more recent years, the band's sound has gotten much less derivative and more experimental. They can be heard using South

American folk instruments, and they engage in long, feedback-and-effects-pedal jams that occasionally get into Grateful Dead territory.

Walter Broide: drums; **Sergio Chotsourian**: guitars/vocals; **Miguel Fernandez**: bass

Discography: *Delmar* (Man's Ruin, 1996); *Unreleased Dopes* (Vinyl Magic 3, 1999); *Cuidad de Brahman* (Man's Ruin, 1999); *Corsario Negro* (Smallstone, 2002); *Toba Trance, Vol. 1* (Elektro, 2005); *Toba Trance, Vol. 2* (Elektro, 2005); *El Hombre Montaña* (Small Stone, 2006); *Nuevo Orden de la Libertad* (Small Stone, 2009)

NAZARETH

YEARS ACTIVE: 1968–PRESENT

Scotland's Nazareth is normally referred to as a 1970s hard rock band, mostly because the band experienced their greatest commercial triumphs during the Me Decade. This assertion is totally bogus, as the band has been employed on an ongoing basis for forty years, having just released their last album, *Big Dogz*, in 2011, a full thirty-six years since their biggest radio hit, "Love Hurts." The band may be associated with a bygone era, but they're by no means a relic of the "have a nice day" decade.

The band was formed in 1968 by bassist Pete Agnew, guitarist Manny Charlton, singer Dan McCafferty and drummer Darrell Sweet. Sensing that their hometown Dunfermline might not offer them many opportunities, they moved to London in 1970. One year later they released their self-titled debut, which got good press and favorable fan reaction for its bevy of no-bullshit hard rock stompers. As is frequently the way, the band fucked up in 1972 with their second release *Exercises*, a mostly acoustic album that their small fan base welcomed as warmly as one would a leprosy diagnosis.

Sensing the degree to which they had erred, Nazareth did some masterful stylistic backpedalling. The result was 1973's meat & potatoes hard rock outing *Razamanaz*. Featuring the singles "Bad Bad Boy," "Broken Down Angel,"

and the hard-charging title track, the album brought the hard rock goods that the fans wanted, and Nazareth was forgiven for the egregious sin of its previous album.

Nazareth released two albums in 1974, *Loud 'n' Proud* and *Rampant*, both of which traveled the same stylistic road as *Razamanaz*. But it was their 1975 album, *Hair of the Dog*, that was their true breakthrough. *Hair of the Dog* was the band's best album yet, and truth be told, they still haven't topped it. There are simply no bad songs on *Hair of the Dog*, and it offers a dizzying array of stomping hard rock ("Beggar's Day"), leaden plodders ("Miss Misery"), and even evocative mood pieces ("Please Don't Judas Me").

The title track was famously covered by Guns n' Roses on the 1993 album *The Spaghetti Incident?*, and it could have made a good single for Nazareth if only the phrase "son of a bitch" wasn't repeated *ad nauseam* throughout its four minutes and nine seconds. Nazareth released their cover of the Everly Brothers' "Love Hurts" as the single instead, and it became their biggest hit. It was the band's first foray into ballad territory, and some more punterly fans were displeased to see them trafficking in a song that could be accused of being a bit on the trite side. But who cares, because *Love Hurts* was by far the band's biggest hit, and it helped the album sell over one million copies in the United States alone. So there you go.

Nazareth kept up a steady stream of releases and tours, and remained a popular act throughout the 1970s. Until 1979 when things began to go south. The band changed its lineup numerous times and saw their ability to chart shrink away. There were no specific missteps; Nazareth simply hadn't found a way to keep pace and stay fashionable as the 1980s wore on.

By the middle of the '80s they had disappeared, but they returned in 1991 with *No Jive*. After two more albums, the band was struck by tragedy when drummer Darrell Sweet died of a heart attack in 1999 while the band was touring the U.S. Nazareth certainly would have been forgiven for packing it in at that point, but the band returned in 2008 with *The Newz*, and they released *Big Dogz* in 2011.

Dan McCafferty of Nazareth performs ear-shattering, skull-pounding METAL, just as Satan intended it.

Lee Agnew: drums (*The Newz*); **Pete Agnew**: bass (*Nazareth*); **Manny Charlton**: guitar (*Nazareth* through *Snakes 'N' Ladders*); **Zal Cleminson**: guitars (*No Mean City* through *Malice in Wonderland*); **Ronnie Leahy**: keyboards (*Boogaloo*); **Dan McCafferty**: vocals (*Nazareth*); **Jimmy Murrison**: guitar (*Boogaloo* and later); **Billy Rankin**: guitar (*2XS* through *Sound Elixir*); **Darrell Sweet**: drums (*Nazareth* through *Boogaloo*)

Discography: *Nazareth* (A&M, 1971); *Exercises* (Mooncrest, 1972); *Razamanaz* (Mooncrest, 1973); *Loud 'n' Proud* (A&M, 1973); *Rampant* (Mooncrest, 1974); *Hair of the Dog* (Mooncrest, 1975); *Close Enough for Rock 'n' Roll* (Mountain Records, 1976); *Play 'n' The Game* (Sahara, 1976); *Expect No Mercy* (Mountain Records, 1977); *No Mean City* (Mountain Records,

1979); *Malice in Wonderland* (Mountain Records, 1980); *The Fool Circle* (NEMS, 1980); *Snaz* (A&M, 1981); *2XS* (A&M, 1982); *Sound Elixir* (A&M, 1983); *The Catch* (Vertigo, 1984); *Cinema* (Vertigo, 1986); *Snakes 'n' Ladders* (Vertigo, 1989); *No Jive* (Griffin, 1991); *Move Me* (Eagle Records, 1994); *Boogaloo* (Steamhammer, 1998); *At the Beeb* (Snapper, 1998); *Homecoming* (Eagle, 2002); *Alive & Kicking* (Direct, 2003); *The Newz* (Edel Records, 2008); *Big Dogz* (Edel Records, 2011)

YEARS ACTIVE: 1997–2010

Stoner rock, like any other metal genre, can be sliced into as many finely diced multiple-hyphen subcategories as there are types of marijuana. One of the defining questions is whether a given band is more influenced by Black Sabbath or by the Stooges, that is, more metal or more punk. Los Angeles' Nebula fell definitively into the latter category. This is not to say that the band was without metal attributes or that the influence of Ozzy and company wasn't plain to see; it's just that Nebula cruised along where other bands plodded, and its songs were short and economical where other bands were too stoned to remember to just repeat that riff twice, not sixteen times. They even covered the Stooges' "I Need Somebody" on their album *Charged*. Formed in 1997 after guitarist and vocalist Eddie Glass and drummer Ruben Romano left Fu Manchu, they briefly counted ex-Kyuss bassist Scott Reeder among their ranks. After Reeder moved on,

former Fu Manchu bassist Mark Abshire replaced him. The power trio was now composed entirely of former Fu Manchu members, which is probably significant in some respect. While the band found itself filed in the same record-store sections as "the Fu," in reality Nebula was a little more psychedelic, owing a good deal to the 13th Floor Elevators and Syd Barrett–era Pink Floyd. These influences turned up frequently enough to keep things interesting but not enough to undermine the band's hard rock sound, which was really what they were all about at the end of the day. Where they truly distinguished themselves, however, is in the live setting. Nebula was, by all accounts, a hypercharged live unit, and they never came off the road for very long. The group broke up in 2010.

Mark Abshire: bass (see also Fu Manchu); **Eddie Glass**: guitars/vocals (see also Fu Manchu); **Ruben Romano**: drums (see also Fu Manchu)

Discography: *Let It Burn* (Relapse, 1998); *Sun Creature* (Man's Ruin, 1999); *To the Center* (Sub Pop, 1999); *Charged* (Sub Pop, 2001); *Dos Eps* (Meteor City, 2002); *Apollo* (Liquid and Poker, 2006)

YEARS ACTIVE: 1985–PRESENT

Neurosis is a rare example of a band that has managed to carve out a niche for itself despite its lack of mainstream appeal and its refusal to embrace familiar formats. The Oakland, California, group started in 1985 as a straight

Nebula counters accusations that it is a stoner rock band. Left to right: Mark Abshire, Ruben Romano, and Eddie Glass.

hardcore band, which is plainly evident on their 1987 debut, *Pain of Mind*. It was four years before they released any further material, and in that time, their sound shifted considerably. Neurosis released two albums within a year, *The Word as Law* in 1991 and *Souls at Zero* in 1992, both of which incorporated elements that eventually defined the band's signature style. The albums retained the metallic guitars of Neurosis' past, but now the sound was complemented by industrial-music influences and tribal drumming. These characteristics must surely have come as something of a shock to those who had known Neurosis only in their hardcore incarnation of old.

In a live setting, the band's performances recall the considerable fury of their hardcore past, but now they supplement it by projecting

Neurosis' Scott Kelly delights fans while on tour to support *Through Silver in Blood* in 1996.

deeply unpleasant film-strips behind them for the audience's enlightenment. Neurosis built themselves up, slowly but surely, via the tried-and-true methods of touring, touring, and touring. Eventually, they won a slot on Ozzfest, thanks to the relative success of their 1996 album, *Through Silver in Blood*. This marked not only the band's largest audiences to date but also the first time they had ever played during daylight hours. Their next full-length album, the 1999 Steve Albini–produced *Times of Grace*, broadened Neurosis' sound with the addition of traditional acoustic instruments, such as bagpipes, brass, woodwinds, and violins, among others. Since then, the band has released three more successful studio albums plus three live recordings and has also been involved in a variety of side projects, such as Tribes of Neurot, the dark, brooding solo acoustic recordings of guitarist and vocalist Steve Von Till, and Neurosis & Jarboe, a collaboration with Swans' former singer.

Dave Edwardson: bass; **Scott Kelly**: guitars/vocals; **Noah Landis**: keyboards/samples (*Through Silver in Blood* and later); **Simon McIlroy**: keyboards (*Souls at Zero, Enemy of the Sun*); **Jason Roeder**: drums; **Steve Von Till**: guitars/vocals

Discography: *Pain of Mind* (Alternative Tentacles, 1987); *The Word as Law* (Lookout, 1991); *Souls at Zero* (Virus, 1992); *Enemy of the Sun* (Alternative Tentacles, 1994); *Through Silver in Blood* (Relapse, 1996); *Locust Star* (Relapse, 1997); *Times of Grace* (Relapse, 1999); *Sovereign* (Relapse, 2000); *A Sun That*

Never Sets (Relapse, 2001); *Live in Lyon* (Neurot, 2002); *Live in Stockholm* (Neurot, 2003); *Live at Roadburn* (Neurot, 2003)

NIGHTWISH

YEARS ACTIVE: 1996–PRESENT

Many metal bands have vocalists who are described as "operatic." This is a thoughtful thing to say. While there are indeed many metal singers with wide vocal ranges and the ability to carry a tune, very few have had actual operatic training, and fewer still would make the callback list after auditioning for "The Barber of Seville." One exception to this rule is Tarja Turunen, the former lead singer of Finland's Nightwish. She received vocal training at the Sibelius Institute and Karlsruhe University of Music, and has a three-octave range that at its high end can shatter glass.

OPPOSITE: Fuck operatic vocals, Nightwish's Tarja Turunen (left) is an actual opera singer!
ABOVE: Nightwish with their new singer, Anette Olzon, hangs out in the snowy climes of a soundstage.

Keyboard player Tuomas Holopainen formed the band in 1997. He had originally teamed up with Turunen for an acoustic music project, but eventually decided, "fuck that shit." Turunen's voice was simply too powerful to back up with anything but the he-manliest of metal musicians, and the pair found them in the form of drummer Jukka Nevalainen, bassist Sami Vänskä, and guitarist Emppu Vuorinen. This lineup released *Angels Fall First* on the Spinefarm label, and though the album has its moments, it's clearly evidence of a group still in search of a coherent direction. It also features the well-below-average vocals of Holopainen, stinking up the joint on a couple of tracks. Fortunately he was smart enough not to do that again on subsequent albums, something for which we can all be grateful.

Oceanborn, from 1998, saw Nightwish embrace with a vengeance the direction that they would follow for the next several years. Boasting such balls-out material as "Stargazers" and "The Pharaoh Sails to Orion," the album is a near-perfect, shimmering example of epic, operatic, symphonic metal, with an expansive sound that seems like the product of dozens of musicians, not just five. The album's highlight is a vocal version of the Rainbow instrumental "Snowman," titled "Walking in the Air," which became a concert favorite for several years. All told, the album brought Nightwish mainstream success, and they've never looked back. The band went from strength to strength on 2000's *Wishmaster*, which was a smash hit in their native country and their first album to get a U.S. release. Unfortunately, fans of their more bombastic approach were disappointed when 2002's *Century Child* saw them moving in a more commercial direction. This move was repeated on 2004's *Once*, which was also a much poppier outing than the first couple of albums, but the songwriting was better and the tracks featured the London Philharmonic Orchestra, so all was forgiven by originally skeptical fans.

In 2005, the unthinkable happened and Turunen was fired from the band after a Helsinki concert. She got the news when Holopainen first handed her a note after the show to that effect, and then posted it on the band's website for everyone on earth to see. Classy. The note accused her of having a shitty attitude ever since marrying Argentine businessman Marcelo Cabuli. Turunen responded that she had no idea anyone even had a problem with her until she read the note. Turunen went on from there to start her own solo career, but since her voice was the band's single most identifiable characteristic, fans were doubtful that the band had a future without her.

Turunen was replaced by Swedish singer Anette Olzon, who is not an opera singer by any stretch. Rather, she has a much more commercial pop voice that at times recalls the vocal on "Knowing Me Knowing You" by ABBA. If anyone had a problem with that, it wasn't reflected in the band's sales. Her debut with the group, 2007's *Dark Passion Play*, sold better than any of its predecessors, and it was supported by a world tour that went on for two full years. The band released the album *Imaginaerum* in 2011.

Marco Hietala: bass (*Century Child*); **Tuomas Holopainen**: keyboards; **Jukka Nevalainen**: drums; **Anette Olzon**: vocals (*Dark Passion Play* and later); **Tarja Turunen**: vocals (*Angels Fall First* through *Once*); **Sami Vänskä**: bass (*Oceanborn* through *Wishmaster*); **Emppu Vuorinen**: guitars

Discography: *Angels Fall First* (Spinefarm, 1997); *Oceanborn* (Spinefarm, 1998); *Wishmaster* (Spinefarm, 2000); *Century Child* (Spinefarm, 2002); *Once* (Spinefarm, 2004); *Dark Passion Play* (Spinefarm, 2007); *Imaginaerum* (Nuclear Blast, 2011)

NINE INCH NAILS

YEARS ACTIVE: 1988–PRESENT

While it would be difficult to say who "invented" industrial music and even more difficult to say who was the first to successfully fuse it with heavy metal, the first band to merge the styles and translate the combination into mainstream commercial success was unquestionably Nine Inch Nails ("NIN" to its friends). The band is really the one-man project of Trent Reznor, who sings, writes all the music, and plays all the instruments, except at live performances, where he employs a full backing band made up of actual humans. Originally influenced by such industrial artists as Einstürzende Neubauten and Ministry, Reznor recorded his first demo in 1988 and sent it to various labels, manifesting what he felt were appropriately low expectations. He was offered deals by no fewer than ten major labels, eventually signing to TVT, which released the debut, *Pretty Hate Machine*, in 1989. A band was hastily assembled for an upcoming tour with Skinny Puppy, after which Reznor decided to never again tour with industrial bands. He chose instead to open for alternative rock groups, hoping to bring the industrial sound

Nine Inch Nails main man Trent Reznor terrorizes an already frightened public.

to an audience for whom it was brand-new. This proved to be a prescient strategy, as NIN began catching on with alternative rock fans and in mainstream dance clubs, where industrial music had never been heard before. Nine Inch Nails truly broke wide open in 1991, when MTV aired the video for "Head Like a Hole" and the band appeared on the first Lollapalooza tour. Reznor was officially on the map now, and *Pretty Hate Machine* reached platinum status, the first industrial album to do so.

Since the 1989 debut had been such a great commercial success, TVT decided that the best course of action was to pressure Reznor into crafting another commercial behemoth, proving that no good deed goes unpunished. The label constantly interfered with his work, causing him to go on creative strike while he tried to get out of his contract with the company. While the legal battle raged on, Reznor busied himself with side efforts, most notably participating in the 1000 Homo DJs project, led by Ministry's Al Jourgensen. The

album was noteworthy mostly because of its cover of "Supernaut" by Black Sabbath, on which Reznor made a vocal contribution, much to TVT's chagrin. The label ordered that the legally dubious guest appearance be removed, and at first, it appeared that Jourgensen had acquiesced. However, as it turned out, he had only altered the offending vocal track ever so slightly and simply lied to TVT about removing it.

Once the TVT debacle was finally sorted out, it was 1992, and Reznor had signed to Interscope. The label helped him set up his own company, Nothing Records, which operated out of his hometown of Cleveland and allowed him to release Nine Inch Nails material without outside interference. His first Nothing release was *Broken*, a compilation of all the material he had been recording on his own while all the TVT foolishness was being hashed out. The album debuted in the Top 10, vindicating Reznor and, one hopes, causing rage-induced steam geysers to shoot out of the ears of the TVT suits who had tried to push him around. To add insult to injury, the hit single off the album, "Wish," won a Grammy. He was even given the opportunity to release *Fixed*, a companion piece to *Broken* that was composed entirely of remixed versions of that album's songs. Reznor was now a major star, and where but Los Angeles should a star reside? He relocated to Beverly Hills to work on his next album, retiring to the spacious digs of the house where representatives of the Manson Family had murdered Sharon Tate.

Reznor emerged in 1994 with *The Downward Spiral*, which debuted at number two and went platinum several times over, thanks in part to the single "Closer," which contains the charming couplet "I want to fuck you like an animal" (raising the question of what kind of animal—a giraffe, an osprey?). The album was followed one year later by the now-customary companion remix album, this one called *Further Down the Spiral*. It was also at this time that he began expanding his résumé to include the composition of film soundtracks, creating the score to Oliver Stone's 1994 self-congratulatory exercise in heavy-handedness, *Natural Born Killers*. Reznor repeated this three

years later, when he scored David Lynch's *Lost Highway*. All the while, he was holed up in New Orleans, where he had relocated after leaving Los Angeles. This time, he had converted a funeral home into a recording studio, ostensibly for use on his next album.

However, between composing movie soundtracks and signing Marilyn Manson to his label, Reznor wasn't really spending much time getting a new album together, quite possibly because he simply wasn't sure how to follow up the massive success of his previous album. By the time of the *Lost Highway* soundtrack, the industrial metal sound had already crept into the mainstream, with bands like Filter making a significant impact on the charts and allegedly causing Guns N' Roses front man Axl Rose to go crazy and fire his entire band while he tried to recast it in Nine Inch Nails' image. In fact, he even drafted Nine Inch Nails guitarist Robin Finck. Finally, five years after the last NIN album of new material, *The Fragile* was released in 1999. It debuted at number one and was followed the next year by a remix album, then a live album two years later. But 2002 proved to be a banner year for Nine Inch Nails fans for another reason: the 1987 movie *Light of Day*, starring Michael J. Fox and Joan Jett and featuring Reznor as a keyboard player in the bar band the Problems, was finally released on DVD. Sadly, Reznor does not appear on the commentary track, and we will all have to pray for a collector's edition to someday grace video-store shelves.

Fully six years would pass between Nine Inch Nails studio albums. A lot had happened during that time, very little of it good. Despite seeing commercial success for *The Fragile* and selling out everywhere the band played, Reznor had struggled with drugs and alcohol during the recording of the album and he had suffered a heroin overdose in London in 2001, according to the *Sydney Morning Herald*. However, the hiatus hadn't hurt his popularity, and the 2005 album *With Teeth* debuted at number one on the *Billboard* charts.

Another album, *Year Zero*, followed in 2007, and it signaled the end of Nine Inch Nails' contract with Interscope Records. The Null Corporation, a label founded by Reznor, released 2008's *Ghosts I-IV*, an instrumental album that drew comparisons to the work of Brian Eno. Just a few months later, the band released *The Slip*, a more traditional Nine Inch Nails album, in the respect that unlike *Ghosts I-IV*, it had both lyrics and song titles. In 2009, Reznor announced on the band's official website that they wouldn't tour "for the foreseeable future," although he clarified that the group was still going to be actively creating and releasing new music. Outside of Nine Inch Nails, Reznor co-wrote the soundtrack for the 2010 film *The Social Network* with British musician Atticus Ross, and the pair won the Oscar for Best Original Score. The duo also co-wrote the soundtrack to the 2011 film *The Girl with the Dragon Tattoo*.

Discography: *Pretty Hate Machine* (TVT, 1989); *Broken* (Nothing/ Interscope, 1992); *Fixed* (Nothing/ Interscope, 1992); *The Downward Spiral* (Nothing/ Interscope, 1994); *Further Down the Spiral* (Nothing/ Interscope, 1995); *The Fragile* (Nothing/Interscope, 1999); *Things Falling Apart* (Interscope, 2000); *And All That Could Have Been* (Nothing, 2002); *With Teeth* (Nothing, 2005); *Year Zero* (Interscope, 2007); *Ghosts I-IV* (Null Corporation, 2008); *The Slip* (Null Corporation, 2008)

With a battery of Marshall stacks, Nuclear Assault is prepared to take the world by storm on its *Handle With Care* tour. Left to right: Danny Lilker, Glenn Evans, John Connelly, and Anthony Bramante.

NUCLEAR ASSAULT

YEARS ACTIVE: 1984–1995; 2002–PRESENT

Here's a neat little factoid supporting the argument that Danny Lilker is out of his goddamn mind: he was the original bassist for Anthrax, and he quit after the band's 1984 debut so that he could form a heavy band instead. He created Nuclear Assault with guitarist and extremely grating vocalist John Connelly, who had himself been a member of Anthrax for roughly ten minutes. The pair joined forces with lead guitarist Anthony Bramante and drummer extraordinaire Glenn Evans, resulting in a hardcore/metal hybrid that was equal parts social commentary, criticism-proof musicianship, brutalizing heaviness, and blinding speed. They truly had all their bases covered, and they quickly distinguished themselves among the New York City thrash metal community. Although their sound was simply too extreme and aggressive for them to ever approach any kind of broad commercial appeal, Nuclear Assault was a popular live attraction both at home and abroad, opening for the era's more prominent acts, such as Exodus, Savatage, and Testament, among others. Unfortunately, the band lasted for only a few years, and after the 1991 release of *Out of Order*, Lilker left the band to form Brutal Truth, a death metal group whose sound was so extreme that it made Nuclear Assault sound like James Taylor performing "How Sweet It Is." Nuclear Assault released one more album, 1993's *Something Wicked*, but by then much of their enthusiasm, as well as much of their fan base, had disappeared, and they broke up soon after. *Assault and Battery*, a best-of compilation, was released in 1997. They reunited in 2002 and released *Third World Genocide*, their first studio album since *Something Wicked*, in 2005.

Anthony Bramante: guitars (*Game Over* through *Out of Order*; *Third World Genocide*); **John Connelly**: guitars/vocals; **Dave DiPietro**: guitars (*Something Wicked*); **Glenn Evans**: drums; **Danny Lilker**: bass (*Game Over* through *Out of Order*; *Third World Genocide*) (see also Anthrax, Stormtroopers of Death); **Scott Metaxas**: bass (*Something Wicked*)

Discography: *Game Over* (Combat, 1986); *The Plague* (Combat, 1987); *Survive* (IRS, 1988); *Handle with Care* (In-Effect, 1989); *Out of Order* (IRS, 1991); *Live at Hammersmith Odeon* (Combat, 1992); *Something Wicked* (IRS, 1993); *Assault and Battery* (Receiver, 1997); *Third World Genocide* (Screaming Ferret, 2005)

TED NUGENT

YEARS ACTIVE: 1958–PRESENT

Legendary guitarist Ted Nugent is as adept at playing his instrument as he is at raining all over the Love Generation's parade. Since the advent of *Laugh-In*, the guitarist has publicly and defiantly championed the profoundly un-politically correct triumvirate of Meat, Guns, and Serial Womanizing. He has also been completely alcohol- and drug-free for his entire life, which, it goes without saying, is an anomaly in the world of rock music. This is not to say, however, that he doesn't know the value of a good time—all work and no play makes the Nuge a dull Motor City madman, after all. In his adolescence, while most of his contemporaries alleviated stress by building model airplanes and watching *My Mother the Car*, Ted played with the rainbow assortment of deadly firearms available in his military household. He was raised under the iron fist of his authoritarian father, who, besides showing him how to reduce a bowling pin to smoking shards, taught him the meaning of discipline, which Nugent in turn applied to his study of his other favorite pastime, playing guitar. So while his peers were busy dropping acid and sleeping until two o'clock in the afternoon, Nugent was doggedly practicing his scales, modes, and Hendrix solos. Needless to say, his diligence paid off.

Nugent grew up outside Detroit, and his band, the Amboy Dukes, were contemporaries of the MC5 and the Stooges—Motor City bands who were also too incendiary for their own good. The Amboy Dukes enjoyed some chart success in 1968 with the song "Journey to the Center of the Mind," which the guitarist claims he didn't know was about drugs. They wouldn't achieve that level of success again, but Nugent stuck with the band despite the nonstop personnel changes. In the end, the turnover proved irrelevant. He was such a ferocious guitar player and raging showman that the spotlight always followed him, so by the time he made it official and changed the band's name to Ted Nugent and the Amboy Dukes, it had been a foregone conclusion for some time that he was the star of the show. By the mid-1970s, he had dumped the Amboy Dukes name for good and began casting about for musicians to back him. The results of this search were released to the public in 1975 on his self-titled debut album, featuring such classics as "Stranglehold" and "Stormtroopin'," which were basically showcases for his lead guitar work. There was turmoil within his band almost immediately, as second guitarist and lead vocalist Derek St. Holmes began clashing with Nugent over the band's power structure—somehow, St. Holmes had managed to overlook the fact that Nugent was the undisputed leader of the band that bore his name. The second guitarist quit before sessions for the second album, but he returned in time to tour and to appear on the third album, 1977's *Cat Scratch Fever*, which, like the single of the same name, was a massive hit and the band's commercial breakthrough. Nugent hit the road to support the album, and he rapidly became the number one concert attraction in America. It certainly made sense: Nugent was always meant for the stage rather than the confines of the recording studio; the live setting allowed him to play the Terrible Ted angle to the hilt, as he emerged at the beginning of shows swinging onstage from a rope, Tarzan-style, clad in only a loincloth.

Nugent's star dimmed considerably in the 1980s, in part because of an inevitable shift in public tastes but also, perhaps, because he was perceived by many as simply repeating himself. Many artists, like Motörhead and AC/DC, have managed to sustain fertile careers over the course of several decades without changing their music one iota, but for some reason this phenomenon didn't extend to Nugent. He continued to tour and release albums regardless, but he was unable to replicate the success he had experienced during the 1970s, and, to make matters worse, he was completely bank-

OPPOSITE: Ted Nugent proves that doing drugs is not a necessary precursor to playing interminably long and self-indulgent guitar solos.

RIGHT: Ted Nugent performs dressed as his favorite member of the Village People.

rupt. While he was earning millions of dollars as the nation's top concert draw, his management was using the miracle of creative accounting to facilitate the spending of said millions on themselves. It wasn't until he joined forces with former members of Styx and Night Ranger for the band Damn Yankees that he reached the top of the mountain again, thanks to their 1990 Top 10 single, "High Enough," a power ballad that surely made hardcore fans of Nugent's hyperamplified guitar playing break out in hives. Chart success notwithstanding, however, the honeymoon was short-lived, as the guitarist proved himself to be as much of a team player as ever, clashing with his bandmates and contributing to a hostile atmosphere that led to the band's breakup after just one more album. He returned to touring and recording, but he also

began lending his celebrity to a variety of right-wing causes, chief among these being his personal favorite, those wacky firearms. He owns a bow-hunting school for the young ones, with a promotional videotape that features truly moving footage of a grinning Nugent showing a very small child how to put down Bambi. He also makes instructional videotapes for the munitions enthusiast, owns a hunting accessories store, sits on the board of directors of the National Rifle Association, and sells his own brand of beef jerky. He also likes to squeeze off a few rounds from time to time with impeachment-happy Georgia Republican Bob Barr. In 2001, he published his autobiography, *God, Guns, and Rock & Roll*, a title that will be extremely helpful to those who, because of the guitarist's soft-spoken modesty, are not aware that his enthusiasms extend to the spiritual realm.

Discography: *Ted Nugent* (Epic, 1975); *Free-for-All* (Epic, 1976); *Cat Scratch Fever* (Epic, 1977); *Double Live Gonzo* (Epic, 1978); *Weekend Warriors* (Epic, 1978); *State of Shock* (Epic, 1979); *Scream Dream* (Epic, 1980); *Great Gonzos! The Best of Ted Nugent* (Epic, 1981); *Intensities in 10 Cities* (Epic, 1981); *Nugent* (Atlantic, 1982); *Penetrator*

(Atlantic, 1984); *Little Miss Dangerous* (Atlantic, 1986); *If You Can't Lick 'em . . . Lick 'em* (Atlantic, 1988); *Spirit of the Wild* (Atlantic, 1995); *Live at Hammersmith '79* (Sony, 1997); *Full Bluntal Nugity* (Spitfire, 2001); *The Ultimate Ted Nugent* (Epic/Legacy, 2002); *Craveman* (Spitfire, 2002); *Love Grenade* (Eagle, 2007)

OBITUARY

Years active: 1988–1997; 2003–present

Obituary was among the first of the many Florida death metal bands, emerging at roughly the same time as its peers Death, Deicide, Morbid Angel, and so forth. Obituary's debut, *Slowly We Rot*, was released in 1989 and heralded death metal as a bona fide style, with the genre's trademarks in all their disemboweled glory. The album featured a towering wall of muddy guitars and painfully sluggish tempos that set Obituary apart from their speed-freak counterparts, as their shifts in tempo ranged from "slow" to "slower" to "stop." But the most recognizable trait of the band was the growled vocals of John Tardy, whose lyrical subject matter centered on the type of obsessively graphic violence that became all the rage of the next generation of death metal bands, such as Cannibal Corpse. Of course, Tardy's lyrics were impossible to decipher, so he could just as well have written lyrics about the joys of baking cookies as the many varieties of decapitation. The band's output remained consistent throughout the 1990s, which kept their fans happy and kept them touring and selling records, but in 1997 vocalist Tardy quit the band, allegedly tired of the relentless grind of touring. After he quit, the rest of the band soon followed suit and packed their bags. Roadrunner released *Anthology*, an anthology, in 2001, and prior to that, in 1998 they released an album called *Dead*, which was, in fact, live, to the pleasure and merriment of many. The band reunited in 2003 and released *Frozen in Time* in 2005, then released two further albums. At the time of this writing, they are diligently plugging away in the studio on a third.

James Murphy: guitars (*Cause of Death*) (see also Death, Testament); **Trevor Peres**: guitars; **Ralph Santolla**: guitar (*Xecutioner's Return* and later) (see also Deicide); **Donald Tardy**: drums; **John Tardy**: vocals; **Daniel Tucker**: bass (*Slowly We Rot*); **Frank Watkins**: bass (*Cause of Death* and later); **Allen West**: guitars (*Slowly We Rot*, *The End Complete* through *Frozen in Time*)

Discography: *Slowly We Rot* (Roadrunner, 1989); *Cause of Death* (Roadrunner, 1990); *The End Complete* (Roadrunner, 1992); *World Demise* (Roadrunner, 1994); *Back from the Dead* (Roadrunner, 1997); *Dead* (Roadrunner, 1998); *Anthology*

(Roadrunner, 2001); *Frozen in Time* (Roadrunner, 2005); *Xecutioner's Return* (Candlelight, 2007); *Darkest Day* (Candlelight, 2009)

THE OBSESSED

YEARS ACTIVE: 1976–1995

The Obsessed was one of several D.C.-area doom metal bands signed to the Hellhound label in the 1990s. The doom metal genre first got off the ground in the mid-1980s, and met a level of enthusiasm normally reserved for herpes outbreaks. As a result, the band, which was

formed early in the decade, broke up after just a couple of years, much to the dismay of the six people who made up its fan base. Singer and guitarist Scott "Wino" Weinrich moved to Los Angeles to front Saint Vitus, a similarly Black Sabbath–fixated band on the SST label that gained a bit more notoriety than its East Coast cousin. But after a few years, Weinrich came home and resurrected his old band. The rhythm section was brand-new, making him the sole original member, and the new incarnation of the Obsessed was signed to Hellhound in 1990. Their two albums for the label, the self-titled debut and the 1991 release *Lunar Womb*, were exercises in raw, slow doom that seemed like collections of *Master of Reality* outtakes. The band signed with Columbia in 1994, serendipitously leaving Hellhound right when the fledgling doom label went bankrupt. Unfortunately, their new lease on life managed to last for only one album, *The Church Within*. While it was a respectable enough release, it wasn't quite as raw as the two that came before, causing a bit of grumbling among the band's fans, now a full thirty people. Beyond any perceived slickness or defanging, however, was the greater problem of the label simply not knowing what to do with the album, and it disappeared not long after its release. The band broke up shortly thereafter, with the rhythm section of Guy Pinhas and Greg Rogers going on to form Goatsnake, and Weinrich founding the more successful Spirit Caravan. Those looking for a compilation that spans the Obsessed's history can thank the Southern Lord label for releasing such an album, *Incarnate*, in 1999.

Ed Gulli: drums (*The Obsessed*); **Mark Laue**: bass (*The Obsessed, Lunar Womb*); **Guy Pinhas**: bass (*The Church Within*) (see also Acid King, Goatsnake); **Scott Reeder**: bass (*Lunar Womb*) (see also Kyuss); **Greg Rogers**: drums (*Lunar Womb, The Church Within*) (see also Goatsnake); **Scott "Wino" Weinrich**: vocals/guitars (see also Saint Vitus, Spirit Caravan)

Discography: *The Obsessed* (Hellhound, 1990); *Lunar Womb* (Hellhound, 1991); *The Church Within* (Columbia, 1994); *Incarnate* (Southern Lord, 1999)

LEFT: The Obsessed's Scott "Wino" Weinrich embraces his beloved.
OPPOSITE: John Tardy rocks the mike at an Obituary show.

OPETH

YEARS ACTIVE: 1990–PRESENT

Although it usually gets lumped in with the death metal movement, Stockholm's Opeth is too progressive and eclectic for any single classification to do it justice. Artistically speaking, the band simply can't sit still. This is not to say that they don't deliver the death metal goods—their output, particularly on their first two albums, is certainly as brutal as anything else on the Century Media imprint. However, at the same time, they employ too many subtle elements, mood shifts, and dynamic changes to fit too comfortably alongside a band like, say, Pungent Stench. Opeth's songs often stretch past the ten-minute mark, as they constantly try to encompass every possible style and direction in each composition. Their albums have become

Opeth front man Mikael Akerfeldt sings bathed in a heavenly glow.

more progressive with each release, particularly 2001's *Blackwater Park*. That was probably the idea—the band unveiled its prog roots with the title of the album, which is the name of an obscure proto-metal band from the 1970s. The band then released two albums back-to-back, 2002's crushingly heavy *Deliverance* and 2003's *Damnation*, which sounds not unlike an early Genesis album. Since then, the band has released three further studio albums, the latest of which was 2011's *Heritage*.

Mikael Akerfeldt: guitars/vocals; **Martin Axenrot**: drums (*Watershed*); **Johan De Farfalla**: bass (*Orchid*, *Morningrise*); **Peter Lindgren**: guitars; **Martin Lopez**: drums (*My Arms, Your Hearse* and later); **Martin Mendez**: bass (*My Arms, Your Hearse* and later); **Anders Nordin**: drums (*Orchid*, *Morningrise*); **Per Wiberg**: keyboards (*Ghost Reveries* and later)

Discography: *Orchid* (Century Media, 1995); *Morningrise* (Century Media, 1996); *My Arms, Your Hearse* (Century Media, 1998); *Still Life* (Peaceville, 1999); *Blackwater Park* (Koch, 2001); *Deliverance* (Koch, 2002); *Damnation* (Koch, 2003); *Ghost Reveries* (Roadrunner, 2005); *Watershed* (Roadrunner, 2008); *Heritage* (Roadrunner, 2011)

OZZY OSBOURNE

YEARS ACTIVE: 1968–PRESENT

Ozzy Osbourne truly needs no introduction. His name is synonymous with images of decapitated bats flapping at his feet as he commands the unconditional loyalty and blind adoration of his teenaged minions, whom he hypnotizes into doing his satanic bidding and so forth. In the real world, however, the Ozzman is a family man who has always adhered to his Christian upbringing, and his infamous antics are either urban legends or the results of his well-publicized struggles with drugs and alcohol. This has never stopped his detractors from denouncing him as the cause of all evil in the universe, particularly during the conservative 1980s, when, coincidentally or not, the singer experienced some of his greatest commercial success.

Of course, before all the hoopla, Osbourne was simply the lead singer for Black Sabbath, one of the most influential metal bands of all time, so he already had a distinct advantage when he went solo after his famously acrimonious split with the group. Sabbath had been managed by Don Arden, whose daughter, Sharon, wanted to start her own management company and took John Michael "Ozzy" Osbourne under her wing. While everyone else believed that the singer was nothing but a fat, washed-up drunk whose days were numbered, Sharon saw him as a solo artist of great potential, a perception based solely on the undeniable charisma and showmanship that was on full display during his Sabbath tenure. She fought uphill to convince a record company to sign her new client and future husband, finally finding a label that grudgingly agreed to add him to its roster, although it had no plans to give him anything but the most threadbare recording budget and promotional push. Hoping to improve the singer's standing with the label, Sharon suggested that she and Osbourne go to the company's offices and release live doves during a promotions meeting, signifying Osbourne's desire to have a friendly and peaceful relationship with his new business partners. A drunken Osbourne stumbled into the meeting, set the doves free, and plopped himself down on the lap of one of the executives. One of the doves landed on Osbourne's lap, and he promptly snatched it and bit its head off, much to the chagrin of the attendant executives. Without knowing it, the singer had just launched a thousand tangentially related urban legends and irrevocably created his persona. He was now officially the "Prince of Fuckin' Darkness."

Osbourne's debut album, *Blizzard of Ozz*, was released in 1980 and contained such songs as "Crazy Train" and "Mr. Crowley," classics that remain in the singer's live set to this day. Apart from strong songwriting, the album also featured the blazing guitar work of Randy Rhoads, whose mixture of heavy metal and classical styles influenced a whole generation of guitarists. Ultimately, the album sold far beyond the expectations of the label, and the executives were forced to accept the dove decapitator as a legitimate commercial prospect. In order to capitalize on the singer's newfound buzz, they decided to squeeze another album out of him as soon as possible. The result, *Diary of a Madman*, was released in 1981 and sold even more than the debut, fueled by such hits as "Flying High Again" and, perhaps more significantly, by the singer's infamous reputation, which had been enhanced when a fan at a concert threw what Osbourne believed was a rubber bat onstage and he summarily snatched it up, stuck it in his mouth, and decapitated it. As it turned out, the bat was real, and the concert had to be stopped while the singer was rushed to the hospital for a rabies vaccination. Another "oopsy-daisy" occurred on the same tour when guitarist Randy Rhoads was in a small plane with members of the band's crew. The pilot decided it would be a great idea to fly close to the band's tour bus. The genius flew the plane right into a house, killing everyone on board. Osbourne, who had grown very close to the guitarist, was devastated by the loss, and although he replaced Rhoads and soldiered on, he never really recovered from the shock.

Although Osbourne had never shied away from controlled substances before, he began consuming them at an alarming rate reminiscent of Tony Montana in the last fifteen minutes of *Scarface*. His behavior crossed the line from Life of the Party to Dangerously Unstable Psychotic. Mötley Crüe drummer Tommy Lee has since recalled an incident when, on tour supporting Osbourne, he personally observed the singer snorting a line of live ants. The blackout-drunk singer further rendered Lee dumbstruck by defecating on his hotel room floor and smearing the fresh, steaming feces on its walls. Somehow, in the face of his borderline-psychotic substance-abuse problems, Osbourne still continued to sell albums and play to capacity crowds. Even the odd frivolous lawsuit didn't slow him down. In 1986 he was sued by the family of a teenager who had killed himself, allegedly while listening to the *Blizzard of Ozz* track "Suicide Solution." Although Osbourne's song was actually an anti-alcohol jeremiad (written about AC/DC singer Bon Scott's death from alcohol poisoning), lawyers for the plaintiffs claimed that the song contained—you guessed it—backward masking, subliminally commanding the teenager to kill himself, as if he was a perfectly well-adjusted, Brylcreemed individual with no personal problems of any kind who was suddenly overcome by the urge to kill himself after hearing thirty seconds of the song and its patent glorification of suicide. The case was eventually dropped, but it helped the singer maintain his reputation as an agent of Satan who actively endeavored to bring about the death of joy on earth.

Weakened by years of drug and alcohol abuse, Ozzy Osbourne buckles under the tremendous weight of a balsa wood cross.

In the 1990s, Osbourne continued to release successful albums and tour, despite the fact that he had claimed his 1992 No More Tours tour would be his last. Apparently, what he meant to say was that it would be his last tour until the next one, and he hit the road again in 1995 to support *Ozzmosis*, one of his best-selling albums to date. The tour proved to be just as commercially successful as its predecessors, and in 1996 he created Ozzfest, a festival that featured several of the day's popular metal acts, including Marilyn Manson and Pantera, all leading up to a reunion of the original lineup of Black Sabbath. To this day, Ozzfest continues to be a major concert attraction, and it has since expanded to feature a second stage, where lesser-known, up-and-coming bands have the opportunity to strut their stuff before a raging sea of teenagers. Inspired by their popularity at Ozzfest, the four original members of Black Sabbath reunited again in 1998 to record the live *Reunion* album and to tour into the following year.

At the beginning of 2002, Osbourne added a

facet to his public persona that took many by surprise, that of clueless, bumbling father, on the MTV reality series *The Osbournes*. The network sent a camera crew to his family's house at the end of 2001 to film a host of footage of the singer, Sharon, and their children Kelly and Jack. His eldest daughter, Amy, declined

OPPOSITE: Osbourne cites alcoholic blackouts as the cause for several of his questionable decisions, those fashion-related and otherwise.

ABOVE: Ozzy Osbourne is the Prince of Fuckin' Darkness.

involvement, a decision leading one to assume that she is an extremely well-adjusted individual. The program turned out to be one of the biggest successes in the network's history, as its entire viewership tuned in with nearly religious regularity to watch the family argue and their pets vomit while the proud patriarch stuttered incessantly and wandered confused about their palatial Los Angeles estate. That same year, the singer found himself invited to the White House to meet former President George W. Bush, and later

he performed "Paranoid" with Tony Iommi in front of Queen Elizabeth. Here's hoping he simply didn't know where he was. In 2005, he released a 4-disc retrospective box set, *Prince of Darkness*, which included hits, demos, rarities and duets with other artists, including a cover of Steppenwolf's "Born To Be Wild" performed with Miss Piggy. In 2010, scientists from Knome, a human genome mapping company, mapped the singer's genetic code to find out how the fuck he's still alive after being on a nonstop bender for over 40 years.

Discography: *Blizzard of Ozz* (Jet, 1980); *Diary of a Madman* (Jet, 1981); *Speak of the Devil* (Jet, 1982); *Bark at the Moon* (Epic, 1983); *The Ultimate Sin* (Epic, 1986); *Tribute* (Epic, 1987); *No Rest for the Wicked* (Epic, 1989); *Just Say Ozzy* (Epic, 1990); *No More Tears* (Epic, 1991); *Live & Loud* (Epic, 1993); *Ozzmosis* (Epic, 1995); *The Ozzman Cometh: Greatest Hits* (Sony, 1997); *Down to Earth* (Sony, 2001); *Live at Budokan* (Sony, 2002); *Black Rain* (Epic, 2007); *Scream* (Epic, 2010).

YEARS ACTIVE: 1980–PRESENT

New York City's Overkill (not to be confused with the Los Angeles–based SST band of the same name) have been crafting straightforward thrash metal for the better part of thirty years, and their style has remained consistent, even when their lineup hasn't. Originally formed by vocalist Bobby "Blitz" Ellsworth and guitarist Bobby Gustafson, the band released their self-titled debut in 1984, which delivered the high-velocity, chugging-freight-train goods and was right up there with anything that any of their contemporaries were churning out. Overkill found what was arguably their true voice in the years between 1987 and 1989, particularly on the 1988 album *Under the Influence*, which featured such industrial-strength material as the epic "Drunken Wisdom." After releasing *The Years of Decay*, Gustafson left the band in 1989 and was replaced by two guitarists for Overkill's 1991 album, *Horrorscope*. The album earned the band better reviews than they had ever received, even if it did tone down the all-out thrash assault a notch or three. Since then there have been numerous lineup changes, with Ellsworth and bassist D. D. Verni the only remaining original members. However, neither they nor their fans seem to care, and Overkill continues to release albums and tour.

Rob Cannevino: guitars (*Horrorscope* through *Wrecking Your Neck*); **Joe Comeau**: guitars (*The Killing Kind* and later); **Bobby "Blitz" Ellsworth**: vocals; **Sid Falck**: drums (*Under the Influence* through *Horrorscope*); **Merritt Gant**: guitars (*Horrorscope* through *Wrecking Your Neck*); **Bobby Gustafson**: guitars (*Overkill* through *The Years of Decay*); **Dave Linsk**: guitars (*Bloodletting* and later); **Ron Lipnicki**: drums (*Immortalis* and later); **Tim Mallare**: drums (*I Hear Black* and later); **Sebastian Marino**: guitars (*The Killing Kind* and later) (see also Anvil); **Rat Skates**: drums (*Overkill* through *Taking Over*); **Derek Tailer**: guitars (*Killbox 13* and later); **D. D. Verni**: bass

Discography: *Overkill* (Azra, 1984); *Feel the Fire* (Megaforce, 1985); *Taking Over* (Megaforce, 1987); *Under the Influence* (Megaforce, 1988); *The Years of Decay* (Megaforce, 1989); *Horrorscope* (Megaforce, 1991); *I Hear Black* (Atlantic, 1993); *W.F.O.* (Atlantic, 1994); *Wrecking Your Neck* (CMC, 1995); *The Killing Kind* (CMC, 1996); *From the Underground and Below* (CMC, 1997); *Necroshine* (CMC, 1999); *Coverkill* (CMC, 1999); *Bloodletting* (Metal-Is, 2000); *Wrecking Everything: Live* (Spitfire, 2002); *Killbox 13* (Spitfire, 2003); *ReliXIV* (Spitfire, 2005); *Immortalis* (Bodog, 2007); *Ironbound* (Nuclear Blast, 2010); *The Electric Age* (Nuclear Blast, 2012)

The members of Overkill seem deeply irked in this 1990 photo. Left to right: Bobby Gustafson, Bobby "Blitz" Ellsworth, D.D. Verni, and Sid Falck.

PANTERA

Years active: 1981–2004

Pantera unapologetically flew the metal banner during the 1990s, a decade when other bands were attempting to prolong their survival by distancing themselves from the genre as much as they could. Although they were one of the most visible metal bands of that decade, Pantera's roots actually go back to the 1980s. They released four albums then, all of them in a more or less traditional hard rock mold that, at times, flirted with glam in a manner reminiscent of early Mötley Crüe. The only indicators of what was to follow came in the form of "Diamond" Darrell Abbott's impressive guitar playing, the powerful drumming of his brother, Vince "Vinnie Paul" Abbott, and the vocals of Phil Anselmo, who replaced original vocalist Terrence Lee on the 1988 *Power Metal* album, the band's fourth. Pantera was not yet the juggernaut of brutality that we know and love today, but by the time of this album the band members were certainly on their way. It won them a deal with Atlantic Records, and by the time of their 1990 debut for the label, the thrash-influenced *Cowboys from Hell*, it was clear that this was no longer the li'l ol' band from Texas that had been making albums throughout the 1980s. Because of this, both the band and fans treat the album as Pantera's unofficial debut, and there are in fact many people who are not even aware that the band has any prior recordings to their credit.

In 1992, Pantera released what many consider to be their finest offering, *Vulgar Display of Power*. The album featured such classics as "Mouth for War" and "Walk," a song that probably started more mosh pits in the 1990s than any other. It also saw the musicians come into their own and define their style, which abandoned thrash's speed-and-technique fetish

Pantera's "Diamond" Darrell Abbott gazes heavenward in search of inspiration for his next run of thirty-second notes.

ONE OF MY GREATEST MOMENTS AS A GUITAR PLAYER WAS WINNING 1ST PLACE IN A GUITAR CONTEST. I WAS 16 YRS OLD AND THE PRIZE WAS A DEAN "ML"! I RAN THROUGH VARIOUS RIFFS FROM VAN HALEN'S ERUPTION TO RANDY'S MOTHER EARTH ALL MIX'D TOGETHER ALONG WITH SOME OF MY OWN SHIT.. THAT GUITAR I WON IS STILL MY MAIN AXE! YOU KNOW, THE BLUE ONE WITH THE LIGHTNING BOLTS!!

Dimebag Darrell

in favor of a simpler, heavier sound. More significant, however, the album set a new standard for what the word "metal" came to mean in the 1990s, even though the band probably did not yet realize it. Metallica was no longer the underdog hero of heavy metal's marginalized—the group had been arena headliners for a few years already. Glam was over. The thrash movement was in its final, gurgling death throes. The alternative rock revolution was in full swing, hammering the final nails into the coffin of all that metal had been in the 1980s. It was during this fulcrum point in metal history that *Vulgar Display of Power* was released, and it not only upped the ante for how heavy mainstream metal could be but also offered a glimpse into the genre's future. One need only listen to the debut recordings of bands like Korn and Slipknot to understand the effect that Pantera had in 1992. If anyone had any doubts that the band's impact was major, those doubts were silenced in 1994 when Pantera released their follow-up, *Far Beyond Driven*. The album debuted at number one, surely the harshest and least radio-friendly album to do so up to that time. It was just one continuous stretch of bludgeoning punishment from back to front, and it saw the band completely abandon any pretense of finesse or subtlety. It was also their most commercially successful album. Go figure.

In 1996 Pantera released *The Great Southern Trendkill*, which saw them diversify their approach somewhat, with Anselmo turning in much more reflective and self-loathing lyrics than were his usual stock in trade, and for good reason. Since not long after the success of *Far Beyond Driven*, Anselmo had been privately struggling with drug problems, which reached their apex in July 1996, when the vocalist succumbed to a heroin overdose and was actually pronounced dead for four full minutes. Amazingly, not only did he not run to the light, he quit heroin cold turkey afterward,

Defenders of the metal faith, the members of Pantera refuse to compromise their style—or smile for the camera. Left to right: Vince "Vinnie Paul" Abbott, "Diamond" Darrell Abbott, Rex Brown, and Phil Anselmo.

withdrawal and everything, while still on tour. In fact, the band didn't miss a single date. This was the story for the next two years as the band toured relentlessly from the moment the singer was declared dead through the middle of 1998. In reality, this was in part because they had little choice. Their popularity had dwindled somewhat, the result of the twin inevitable factors of the passage of time and the shift in audience tastes, and touring was the only proven method of retaining their existing fans and attracting new ones.

By the time they released their next studio album, *Reinventing the Steel*, it was the year 2000 and a full four years had passed since their previous release (except for a 1997 live album). *Reinventing the Steel* was a complete return to basics and by far the heaviest thing the band had ever recorded. Whether this was an attempt to recapture their former commercial glory or an abandonment of any and all mainstream aspirations is any-

body's guess. Whatever the motivation, the band hit the road again, this time with Slayer. While both bands had long since put their glory days behind them, the tour was a massive success and went a long way toward proving that not only does metal always have some kind of die-hard following, but fans appreciate the bands that stick to their guns and make the music that they need to make. The tour to support the album ended in Yokohama, Japan, in August 2001, and though they didn't know it at the time, it was the last time the members of Pantera would ever share a stage.

After returning to the United States, the band was set to take a year-long break and recharge. Instead Rex Brown played on the second Down album with Anselmo, who also made *Use Once and Destroy* with Superjoint Ritual, another side project, that same year. The Abbott brothers interpreted this as a sign that Anselmo had abandoned Pantera, and in 2003 they broke up the band. The brothers and Anselmo then formed two warring camps who fought openly in the metal press, with the singer telling *Metal Hammer* magazine that the guitarist "deserves to be beaten severely." This comment, tongue-in-cheek or not, would come back to haunt him in December 2004.

The Abbott brothers had formed a new band, Damageplan, and they had a successful album out, *New Found Power*, that they were touring to support. On December 8, 2004, as they were starting their set at a Columbus, Ohio nightclub, a 25-year-old ex-Marine named Nathan Gale climbed onstage, produced a 9mm Beretta and fired five rounds into Darrell Abbott, killing him instantly. He also murdered the band's head of security, a club employee, and an audience member. The band's drum technician and tour manager were also shot, but survived. Gale

was shot and killed by police, so there was no way to know what his motive was, but he had been diagnosed with paranoid schizophrenia, and his mother told a local Columbus television station that he had been a Pantera fan to an obsessive degree, and he believed that they had stolen lyrics from him. Friends corroborated this account and also said that Gale believed the band had tried to steal his identity.

The musician was buried the following week with his guitar, which he had gotten from Eddie Van Halen. The outpouring of grief from the fan community was immense, both because of the affection that fans had for the music but also because of the senselessness of the murder. One also has to wonder about the effect that it had on Anselmo, who had made unfortunate comments prior to the guitarist's murder that he surely regretted, and who was barred from attending the funeral by the Abbott family. As for Vinnie Paul, he eventually joined Hellyeah, which features Damageplan bassist Bob Zilla, and Brown was a member of Down until 2011.

Darrell "Dimebag" Abbott: guitars; **Vince "Vinnie Paul" Abbott**: drums; **Phil Anselmo**: vocals (*Power Metal* and later); **Rex Brown**: bass; **Terrence Lee**: vocals (*Metal Magic* through *I Am the Night*)

Discography: *Metal Magic* (Metal Magic, 1983); *Projects in the Jungle* (Metal Magic, 1984); *I Am the Night* (Metal Magic, 1985); *Power Metal* (Metal Magic, 1988); *Cowboys from Hell* (Atlantic, 1990); *Vulgar Display of Power* (EastWest, 1992); *Far Beyond Driven* (EastWest, 1994); *The Great Southern Trendkill* (EastWest, 1996); *Official Live: 101 Proof* (EastWest, 1997); *Reinventing the Steel* (EastWest, 2000)

PARADISE LOST

YEARS ACTIVE: 1988–PRESENT

Paradise Lost is one-third of what is commonly called the Peaceville Three, referring to bands of the doom-death genre who recorded for that label, Anathema and My Dying Bride being the other two. Hailing from Halifax, England, Paradise Lost had their commercial breakthrough with their second release, 1991's *Gothic*, which also won them their reputation as progenitors of the genre. Like My Dying Bride, they were among the first to integrate symphonic and orchestral elements into their music right alongside the growled vocals and stunted tempos. Their more recent work minimizes their connection to metal and has at times become almost straight goth—the band members nowadays refer to their music simply as dark rock. Still, the influence they had on other bands in their original genre has been profound enough for them to retain a sizable portion of their fan base. In 2001, Paradise Lost released *Believe in Nothing*, which surprised fans by downplaying their recent sojourns into dark wave and electronica and returning to a more guitar-oriented sound. That same year they toured with Sisters of Mercy, further obscuring the line between the metal and goth genres that they have been straddling all these years. As of 2002's *Symbol of Life*, the band has begun to re-incorporate more metallic influences into their music. They were even allowed to release their 2007 album, *In Requiem*, on Century Media, an unabashedly metal label.

Aaron Aedy: guitars; **Matthew Archer**: drums (*Lost Paradise* through Icon); **Stephen Edmondson**: bass; **Peter Damin**: drums (*Faith Divides Us—Death Unites Us*); **Nick Holmes**: vocals; **Gregor Mackintosh**: guitars; **Lee Morris**: drums (*Draconian Times* and later); **Jeff Singer**: drums (*Paradise Lost* through *In Requiem*)

Discography: *Lost Paradise* (Peaceville, 1990); *Gothic* (Peaceville, 1991); *Shades of God* (Metal Blade, 1992); *Icon* (Metal Blade, 1993); *Draconian Times* (Music for Nations, 1995); *One Second* (Music for Nations, 1997); *Reflections: The Best of Paradise Lost* (Mayhem, 1998); *Host* (EMI, 1999); *Believe in Nothing* (EMI, 2001); *Symbol of Life* (Koch, 2002); *Paradise Lost* (Bartelsmann, 2005); *In Requiem* (Century Media, 2007); *Faith Divides Us—Death Unites Us* (Century Media, 2009)

PENANCE

YEARS ACTIVE: 1990–2004

Originally named Dream Death, the Pittsburgh doom metal band Penance got their first break when Cathedral front man Lee Dorrian heard their demo tape and asked drummer Mike Smail to play on Cathedral's infamous debut, *Forest of Equilibrium*. The singer returned the favor later by signing the group, now called Penance, to his Rise Above label, for which they recorded their 1992 debut, *The Road Less Traveled*. The album generated enough buzz to attract the attention of the Century Media label, which released Penance's 1994 album, *Parallel Corners*. Unfortunately, the band was plagued by persistent changes in their lineup that prevented them from being able to support the album with a tour, and eventually Penance was dropped from Century Media.

With Smail and guitarist Terry Weston now the only remaining original members, the band got back to business in 1997 after the recruitment of bassist Ron Leard and front man Brian "Butch" Balich, with whom they recorded 1999's *Proving Ground*, a sophisticated and accomplished album that compromised none of the band's trademark heaviness. In 2000, the band brought in ex-November's Doom bassist Mary Bielich to replace the departed Leard, and added ex-Wickerman guitarist Matt Tuite. This new, expanded, five-piece incarnation of Penance released *Alpha and Omega* in December 2001; the album's dark, oppressive melancholy and crushing heaviness was the perfect soundtrack for the Christmas season. The band's last album was 2003's *Spiritualnatural*, and they broke up in 2004.

Brian "Butch" Balich: vocals (*Proving Ground* and later); **Mary Bielich**: bass (*Alpha and Omega*); **Richard Freund**: bass (*The Road Less Traveled*); **Brian Lawrence**: vocals/guitars (*The Road Less Traveled*); **Ron Leard**: bass (*Proving Ground*); **Frank Miller**: bass (*Parallel Corners*); **Mike Smail**: drums (see also Cathedral); **Lee Smith**: vocals (*Parallel Corners*); **Matt Tuite**: guitars (*Alpha and Omega*); **Terry Weston**: guitars

Discography: *The Road Less Traveled* (Rise Above, 1992); *Parallel Corners* (Century Media, 1994); *Proving Ground* (self-released, 1999); *Alpha and Omega* (Martyr Music, 2001); *Spiritualnatural* (Martyr Music, 2003)

PENTAGRAM

YEARS ACTIVE: 1971–1976; 1980–PRESENT

Pentagram is one of the most influential bands of the doom metal movement, although few people realize it. The band members have played together in one form or another since 1971 but didn't release their first album until 1985, which is a good example of the type of problems checkering their history since day one. The sole remaining original member is vocalist Bobby Liebling, who helped found the band and has seen it through more than forty years of turmoil and instability, a remarkable feat considering that there has been plenty of both. Originally formed in Virginia by Liebling and guitarist Geof O'Keefe, the band experienced its first round of musical chairs right off the bat as various members came and went, a situation that was exacerbated when bassist Vince McAllister switched to guitar, compelling O'Keefe to switch from guitar to drums. This lineup, the most stable in Pentagram's career, was rounded out by bassist Greg Mayne and stayed together for a miraculous six years. With the lineup established, the band decided to play with their newfound stability by changing their name with alarming frequency, sporting such monikers as Stone Bunny, Virgin Death, and Macabre. The group inevitably changed their name back to Pentagram and released a series of self-financed singles under that tag. Major labels began to court them on the basis of their singles' Blue Cheer-meets-Black Sabbath sound, but nothing materialized, and by 1976 they appeared to have reached the end of the line.

Pentagram was resurrected a few years later when Liebling met drummer Joe Hasselvander, who was playing in a band called Death Row with guitarist Victor Griffin. Upon the addition of bassist Martin Swaney, the band took up the Pentagram mantle anew and slugged it out in D.C.-area clubs for a few years. Finally, in 1985, the cruel forces that had conspired to hold the band back for so long were banished to the land of wind and ghosts, and the group released their debut album at long last, fourteen years after they first formed. The self-titled album, later renamed *Relentless*, was followed up by *Day of Reckoning* in 1987. By this time, the doom metal movement was just beginning, and it was populated by other D.C.-area bands, such as the Obsessed and Unorthodox, who were among the first generation to be influenced by Pentagram. Unfortunately, the pioneering band was unable to capitalize on the movement they had helped to spearhead, and it was a full seven years before they released their next album, *Be Forewarned*. Its 1994 release date was perhaps the worst possible time for any metal band to release anything, regardless of how influential they happened to be or how high the quality of the product was. It really is a shame, because in the case of *Be Forewarned*, the quality is very high indeed. It is hands down the band's best album ever, from the songwriting to the performances. If there is anything to criticize on the album, it would have to be Liebling's questionable decision to abandon his own trademark singing style for one that is identical to Ozzy Osbourne's. This was compensated for, however, by Griffin's unbelievably heavy guitar playing, which was put front and center where it belonged. Ultimately, though, it made no difference. The album went largely unheard, and the doom metal movement it was meant to capitalize on never managed to escape the underground.

The band seemed to have broken up for good when, in 1999, Liebling and Hasselvander released *Review Your Choices* under the Pentagram name, much to the shock of the many people who had written off the band. The duo were the only ones to appear on the album, with Liebling on vocals and Hasselvander on drums as well as every other instrument, which he quite capably handled. The release was also an enormous shock to naysayers in that it was much stronger than anyone would have expected, had they even been expecting it in the first place. It was followed up two years later by *Sub-Basement*, which was distributed in the United States by the Southern Lord label, owned by Greg Anderson of Goatsnake, a Pentagram fan for many years. By this time, the band had finally managed to cultivate a following of respectable proportions within the stoner rock and doom metal communities. This justified the release of their earliest material, beginning with *First Daze Here*, the first-ever authorized compilation of the band's official 1970s output, and *Turn to Stone*, which covered the band's three albums for Peaceville from the 1980s.

Despite the fact that the band was enjoying its highest profile ever, Hasselvander moved on, and Liebling recruited an entirely new crew for the next studio album, 2004's *Show 'Em How*. The band then went quiet, and one could be forgiven for assuming that Liebling had finally said "fuck this shit" and moved on to something that was less of an uphill climb. However, fans were stunned in 2011 to find out that not only was there a new album, *Last Rites*, but it would be released on Metal Blade, the most legit label the band had been involved with yet. Furthermore, it also heralded the return of Griffin to six-string duty. This was a pretty big deal. Griffin had his own band, Place of Skulls, which he had spent the past decade establishing, and his return lent the proceedings a level of credibility that would not have existed otherwise. That same year, Liebling was the subject of a documentary film, *Last Days Here*.

Kelly Carmichael: guitar (*Show 'Em How*); **Victor Griffin**: guitars (Pentagram through *Be Forewarned*; *Last Rites*) (see also Place of Skulls); **Joe Hasselvander**: drums/guitars/bass (*Be Forewarned* through *Sub-Basement*) (see also Raven); **Adam Heinzmann**: bass (*Show 'Em How*); **Bobby Liebling**: vocals; **Greg Mayne**: bass (*Human Hurricane, First Daze Here*); **Vince McAllister**: guitars (*Human Hurricane, First Daze Here*); **Geof O'Keefe**: drums (*Human Hurricane, First Daze Here*); **Stuart Rose**: drums (*Pentagram, Day of Reckoning*); **Mike Smail**: drums (*Show 'Em How*);

Martin Swaney: bass (*Pentagram* through *Be Forewarned*); **Tom Tomaselli**: drums (*Last Rites*); **Greg Turley**: bass (*Last Rites*)

Discography: *Pentagram* (Peaceville, 1985); *Day of Reckoning* (Peaceville, 1987); *Be Forewarned* (Peaceville, 1994); *Review Your Choices* (Black Widow, 1999); *Sub-Basement* (Southern Lord, 2001); *A Keg Full of Dynamite* (Black Widow, 2003); *Show 'Em How* (Black Widow, 2004); *Last Rites* (Metal Blade, 2011)

PLACE OF SKULLS

YEARS ACTIVE: 2000–PRESENT

Knoxville, Tennessee's Place of Skulls was formed in 2000 by guitarist Victor Griffin. After leaving the legendary cult doom band Pentagram, he did various stints here and there, at one time playing with Cathedral on its European tour supporting Black Sabbath. Eventually, he teamed up with Lee Abney, the bassist from his pre-Pentagram band, Death Row, and drummer Tim Tomaselli to form Place of Skulls. Based on a biblical reference, the name refers to the hill of Golgotha, where Jesus Christ was crucified. Much to the shock and horror of the tongue-pierced Marilyn Manson fans of America, Griffin had converted to Christianity since the demise of Pentagram, and although the band's sound is 100 percent old-school Sabbath-worship doom metal, the lyrics reflect his commitment to that faith. However, even the most devoted unbaptized, baby-consuming disciple of Lucifer can find things to enjoy on the band's 2002 debut, *Nailed*—from Griffin's stellar guitar work to the heavy-as-hell cover of the Animals' "Don't Let Me Be Misunderstood." Regrettably, after the band toured to promote the album, Abney left Place of Skulls. He was replaced first by Trouble bassist Ron Holzner, and then by Greg Turley, and the band also added former Spirit Caravan singer and guitarist Scott "Wino" Weinrich. This lineup recorded 2003's *With Vision*, and where *Nailed* consisted entirely of songs written by Griffin (or Bennie Benjamin and Sol Marcus), the 2003 album was a collaborative effort. The band carried on, releasing *The Black Is Never Far* in 2006, but the lineup shuffles would not relent, and Griffin finally put the band on hiatus. However, in 2010, Abney returned to the band, as did Tomaselli, who had left a few years earlier. As unlikely as it seemed, Place of Skulls was now back to its original personnel. This lineup released the band's most recent album, *As a Dog Returns*.

Lee Abney: bass; **Dennis Cornelius**: bass (*The Black Is Never Far*); **Mike Dearing**: drums (*As a Dog Returns*); **Victor Griffin**: guitars/vocals (see also Pentagram); **Tim Tomaselli**: drums; **Greg Turley**: bass (*With Vision*); **Scott Weinrich**: guitar (*With Vision*) (see also The Obsessed)

Discography: *Nailed* (Southern Lord, 2002); *With Vision* (Southern Lord, 2003); *The Black is Never Far* (Exile on Mainstream, 2006); *As A Dog Returns* (Giddy Up!, 2010)

YEARS ACTIVE: 1983–PRESENT

One would be hard-pressed to find a band that better epitomized the Los Angeles hair metal scene of the 1980s than Poison. The band was criticized, and justifiably so, as a triumph of image over music, but for the time they were at the top of the heap it really didn't make any difference what people said about them because they were far too busy selling records and packing arenas to notice. Originally hailing from Pennsylvania, the band relocated to Los Angeles in 1984 with the stated intention of becoming rich and famous. Upon their arrival, they met guitarist C. C. DeVille, who went on to become the band's mascot of obnoxious excess. In short order, they found themselves signed to Enigma, and their 1986 debut, *Look What the Cat Dragged In*, was an out-of-the-box success, selling two million copies and spawning the Top 10 hits "I Want Action" and "Talk Dirty to Me," the latter of which is the band's best-known song. They were all over the radio and MTV, and had—with just one album—achieved the type of commercial recognition that it normally takes bands three or four albums to attain. Their follow-up, 1988's *Open Up and Say . . . Ahh!*—which featured such hits as "Nothin' But a Good Time" and the mother of all power ballads (for that year, anyway), "Every Rose Has Its Thorn"—permanently carved their commercial status in granite.

Poison's third release, *Flesh and Blood*, was released in 1990 to the now-customary audience feeding frenzy, but by this time they were experiencing major problems within their ranks, typified by a live appearance on MTV where DeVille, clearly under the influence of some type of behavior-modifying substance, refused to play the same song as the rest of the band, breaking into a disastrous rendition of "Talk Dirty to Me" that lasted all of about twenty seconds. Despite the group's best efforts to save face and act like the aborted set was in fact an intentional homage to the truest spirit of rock'n'roll, it was clear that something was awry within the Poison camp—a suspicion confirmed the moment the band got backstage and began pounding the lights out of the guitar-playing narcotics aficionado. DeVille was fired shortly thereafter; the official reason given was his addiction to drugs and alcohol, which the guitarist has since confirmed was true. DeVille was replaced by Richie Kotzen, who performed on the 1993 *Native Tongue* album. By this time, however, Poison was in the opening stages of the nauseatingly

Poison epitomized glam metal's fixation on superficial good looks. Left to right: Rikki Rockett, C.C. DeVille, Bobby Dall, and Bret Michaels.

slow but sure wane of their popularity, and the album sold only a fraction of its predecessors' totals. Kotzen was summarily given the boot and replaced by Blues Saraceno, who recorded *Crack a Smile* with the band in 1996. But for four years that album would not even get the chance to become a commercial failure, as the label shelved it, opting for the less commer-

cially risky release of a greatest-hits compilation instead. Saraceno quite understandably moved on after this, which opened the door for DeVille to return once the band's considerable differences with him and his personal problems were sorted out. The restored Poison hit the road for a reunion tour in 1999, which was more successful than anybody expected and made a

compelling case for the longevity and popularity of the band's party anthems and power ballads. They released *Crack a Smile* as *Crack a Smile . . . and More* in 2000, and in 2002 they released *Hollyweird*, their first studio album with DeVille in twelve years.

In 2007, Michaels became the star of the VH1 reality show *Rock of Love with Bret Michaels*,

By 1993, Poison had left the lipstick behind. Left to right: Richie Kotzen, Bret Michaels, Rikki Rockett, and Bobby Dall.

a dating show similar to *Flavor of Love*, only with skanks competing for the singer's affections as opposed to ho's. The show ended when the frontman picked pink-haired Jess over his "soul-mate" Heather, despite the fact that she had tattooed his name on the back of her neck. Shockingly, the union didn't yield fruit, and a second season became necessary. This time, he passed on surgically butchered Daisy in favor of Ambre (pronounced Amber), and again, sadly, the bandanna'd one was unable to form a lasting union. So in its third season, the locale was moved from a mansion to a tour bus, for the creatively named *Rock of Love Bus with Bret Michaels*. In 2009, he required medical attention when he performed "Nothin' But a Good Time" at the 63rd Tony Awards, and upon turning to exit the stage, he was smashed in the head by a lowering set piece. The video footage is available for relentless repeat viewings on YouTube.

Bobby Dall: bass; **C. C. DeVille**: guitar (*Look What the Cat Dragged In* through *Swallow This Live*; *Hollyweird* and later); **Richie Kotzen**: guitar (*Native Tongue*); **Bret Michaels**: vocals; **Rikki Rockett**: drums; **Blues Saraceno**: guitar (*Crack a Smile . . . and More*)

Discography: *Look What the Cat Dragged In* (EMI-Capitol, 1986); *Open Up and Say . . . Ahh!* (Capitol, 1988); *Flesh and Blood* (Capitol, 1990); *Swallow This Live* (Capitol, 1991); *Native Tongue* (Capitol, 1993); *Crack a Smile . . . and More* (Capitol, 2000); *Power to the People* (Cyanide Music, 2000); *Hollyweird* (Cyanide Music, 2002); *Poison'd!* (EMI, 2007)

Years active: 1983–1987; 1990–1993; 2007–present

The members of San Francisco's Possessed were death metal pioneers. Inspired by *Show No Mercy*–era Slayer, Possessed's raw, brutal approach proved massively influential to the

On the brink of their 1987 breakup, Possessed performed at New York's legendary club CBGB.

legions of gore- and satanism-obsessed bands that followed in their footsteps. But they almost didn't even escape from the garage, as their vocalist Barry Fisk committed suicide in 1983, before they had so much as their first demo tape in hand. They persevered, however, and after an appearance on the *Metal Massacre VI* compilation, they won a deal with Combat Records. Their 1985 debut for the label, *Seven Churches*, was many people's introduction to death metal, and today there are some who maintain that it was, in fact, the first death metal album ever made. We can surely expect this point to be perpetually and inconclusively argued until the next Ice Age. In an interesting footnote, after the band's breakup in 1987, guitarist Larry LaLonde traded in his pitchfork and suction-cup devil horns and went on to play in Primus.

Jeff Becerra: vocals/bass; **Larry LaLonde**: guitars; **Mike Sus**: drums; **Mike Torrao**: guitars

Discography: *Seven Churches* (Combat, 1985); *Beyond the Gates* (Combat, 1986); *Agony in Paradise* (Agonia, 2004)

Years active: 1986–1997; 2000–present

Starting out in the New York City hardcore scene, Prong was a basic thrash metal band with hardcore overtones. But even in their earliest stages, anyone listening carefully enough could spot subtle indications of a behind-the-scenes artistic sensibility that was utterly tweaked. By the time they were signed to Epic for the 1990

Prong does not like you. Left to right: Tommy Victor, John Bechdel, Paul Raven, and Ted Parsons.

start midtempo riffing and the marksmanlike precision of Ted Parsons' drumming. One can almost imagine the members of Helmet dropping their vegan Tofu Pups in amazement. The album was a modest hit, but bassist and vocalist Mike Kirkland handed in his notice afterward, for reasons that are unclear. He was replaced by Flotsam & Jetsam bassist Troy Gregory for 1991's *Prove You Wrong*, a decent enough album but one that paled in comparison to its predecessors. Each Prong album had been radically different from the one before, but this one seemed to find the band in a bit of rut, repeating the *Beg to Differ* formula to less convincing effect. Allegedly, the relationship between Gregory and his band mates never really took off either, and the bassist soon found himself relegated to the Prong history books. As if trying to compensate for the lost creative opportunity, Victor and Parsons enlisted former Killing Joke bassist Paul Raven and keyboard player John Bechdel for *Cleansing*, the 1994 album that was creatively light years ahead of anything the band had done. It was one of the first metal albums to embrace the sound of industrial music, which in retrospect was always a perfect match for Prong's robotically accurate sound. The album was also the band's most melodic, and it possessed some of the strongest grooves in their catalog, which is saying a lot. Basically it was a winner from start to finish, but unfortunately it was as criminally overlooked as Prong itself. After the 1996 release of the somewhat tired-sounding *Rude Awakening* album, the band broke up, with Victor going on to play with Danzig and Parsons joining Godflesh, where Raven also had a stint not long afterward. Victor re-formed the band in 2000 with a completely new lineup, which released *Scorpio Rising* in 2003. The album didn't exactly set the world on fire, so Victor returned to Danzig and did a stint with Ministry as well. However, Prong released *Power of the Damager* in 2007, and it was described by critics as a welcome return to form.

John Bechdel: keyboards (*Cleansing* through *Rude Awakening*); **Troy Gregory**: bass/vocals (*Prove You Wrong*) (see also Flotsam & Jetsam); **Mike Kirkland**: bass/vocals (*Primitive Origins* through *Beg to Differ*); **Dan Laudo** (*Scorpio Rising*); **Ted Parsons**: drums (*Primitive Origins* through *Rude Awakening*) (see also Godflesh); **Monte Pittman**: bass (*Scorpio Rising* and later); **Paul Raven**: bass (*Whose Fist Is This Anyway?* through *Rude Awakening*); **Aaron Rossi**: drums (*Power of the Damager*); (see also Ministry); **Tommy Victor**: guitars/vocals (see also Danzig)

Discography: *Primitive Origins* (Spigot, 1987); *Force Fed* (In-Effect, 1987); *Beg to Differ* (Epic, 1990); *Prove You Wrong* (Epic, 1991); *Whose Fist Is This Anyway?* (Epic, 1992); *Cleansing* (Epic, 1994); *Rude Awakening* (Epic, 1996); *Scorpio Rising* (Locomotive, 2003); *Power of the Damager* (13th Planet, 2007).

release *Beg to Differ*, they had come into their own, and what would have been described as idiosyncratic elements on their first two releases became their most recognizable traits. *Beg to Differ* reflected Prong's jettisoning of its thrash elements almost entirely, with the focus instead on guitarist Tommy Victor's staccato, stop-and-

DRUGS

While heavy metal is its own distinct musical style, complete with its own aesthetic that separates it from other forms of music, there's one thing it has in common with punk rock, avant-garde jazz, hip-hop, classical music, and show tunes, as well as every other form of music: drugs. From its fans to its practitioners to its critics, heavy metal's past, present, and future are as inexorably linked with drug use as Manuel Noriega is. There are of course exceptions, such as Ted Nugent and KISS' Gene Simmons, but for the most part, any company that these two may have are only sober thanks to the Betty Ford Center. In many of those cases, it's a miracle that they lived long enough to make it to rehab.

Although there is not a particular drug of choice associated with heavy metal, there is a recurring theme of collective overindulgence. Heavy metal musicians who take drugs or drink alcohol have been infamous in this regard—look at AC/DC's Bon Scott and Def Leppard's Steve Clark, both of whom died of alcohol poisoning, literally drinking themselves to death. Poison guitarist C. C. DeVille recalls the Mt. Kilimanjaro–worthy drifts of cocaine that he regularly consumed in his late-1980s heyday, but he seems like an absolute amateur when you consider the amount of heroin Mötley Crüe bassist Nikki Sixx took around the time of the 1987 *Girls, Girls, Girls* album. Even Nugent and Simmons, who have never taken drugs in their lives, overindulged when it came to their sexual conquests—the KISS bassist claims to have slept with more than two thousand women and to have the photographs to prove it. So while some substances, such as cocaine and marijuana, have been more popular in the metal community than, say, LSD or ecstasy, they are usually consumed in massive quantities that recall the Nathan's hot dog–eating competition and its nau-

limited to heavy metal musicians, of course, and there are plenty of people who are simply fans who consume drugs on Keith Richards' level. A visit to the parking lot of any venue hosting a heavy metal concert will reveal fans of all ages who are up to their eyeballs in beer and marijuana.

While overindulgence certainly fits the heavy metal lifestyle and ethos, one cannot say that it is the music that causes drug abuse, any more than ballet causes eating disorders, poetry causes alcoholism, or rockabilly causes barroom brawls. Nevertheless,

hol are consumed within the heavy metal community is certainly cause for investigation, and the argument that heavy metal's inherently extremist aesthetic fosters overindulgence is not without its persuasive qualities. But to blame a genre of music for drug abuse is to ignore the fact that drugs were a popular source of recreational activity for centuries prior to the release of the first Budgie album and will most likely remain popular for centuries after the last heavy metal musician breathes his or her dying breath.

QUEEN

YEARS ACTIVE: 1971–1991; 2004–PRESENT

The heavy metal credentials of Queen are beyond question. The theatrical, over-the-top showmanship of lead singer Freddie Mercury has been as much of an inspiration to front men everywhere as his incredible vocal technique, which was unparalleled even when the singer was literally on his deathbed. One would also be hard-pressed to find a single living rock guitarist who would not concede that Brian May possesses a style as instantly recognizable as it is inimitable and among the best and most original in the entire history of recorded sound. But the band members were never content to rest on their laurels or remain confined to a single style. Even the most cursory listen to a single Queen album side will reveal a band working in an infinite array of styles, many of which most heavy metal bands would as soon attempt as soak themselves from head to toe in gasoline and then light a match. Queen gave it a shot in literally every genre you can think of, including glam, barbershop quartet, nightclub torch balladry, blues, country, vaudeville, piano dirges, disco, funk, rockabilly, and so on, and they were able to pull it off every time, to 100 percent convincing effect. Whatever the genre, it was as if they had been playing in that style for their entire musical career. Case in point: the 1980 hit "Another One Bites the Dust" had charted well as a rock single, but due to its thoroughly convincing disco sound, disc jockeys at R&B radio stations began playing the song of their own volition, leading their

Queen performs the crushing heavy metal anthem, "Bohemian Rhapsody." Left to right: John Deacon, Freddie Mercury, and Brian May.

audiences to the completely understandable conclusion that Queen was in fact a black funk band, like Chic. If you imagine that your first and only exposure to the group was via this particular song, you will see that it is entirely possible to make this assumption.

When the four members of Queen first met and began playing together in Britain, they were in college, and they made the decision to finish that up. They spent two years working toward their undergraduate degrees first and rehearsing second, with only the odd gig thrown in here and there. That was about it until 1973, when all diplomas were dispersed to their appropriate parties, after which time the band members entered the studio, emerging with their self-titled debut.

It was for the most part a standard-issue hard rock album, with occasional piano flourishes and grandiose tendencies that were somewhat muted and gave only the slightest indication of the epic ridiculousness that became the band's trademark. Queen featured strong material, such as "Keep Yourself Alive" and "Great King Rat," but it went largely unnoticed. Undaunted, the band returned to the studio with producer Roy Thomas Baker for the 1974 *Queen II* release, which was rife with concept-album overtones and improved upon its predecessor's relatively reined-in sound by elaborating on the dynamics and theatrics that the debut had held in check. Its single, "Seven Seas of Rhye," broke into the U.K. Top 10, and in an attempt to

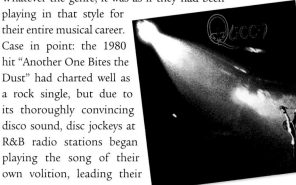

OPPOSITE: Here's hoping that in this early photograph of Queen, the members are still wearing pants. Clockwise from top left: Roger Taylor, John Deacon, Brian May, and Freddie Mercury.

THE ENCYCLOPEDIA OF HEAVY METAL 251

capitalize on the momentum they had gained, they immediately returned to the studio to churn out another album, *Sheer Heart Attack*, before 1974 even ended. This is all the more remarkable considering that it was recorded while May was laid up with hepatitis. The guitarist regained his health and the band returned to the studio to record 1975's aptly named *A Night at the Opera*. After its release, things would never be quite the same again for Queen.

The liner notes for *A Night at the Opera* listed "tantrums" as one of Mercury's many contributions to the album. It's amazing he had the time for them, as his hands were full to capacity with the performance of the album's thousand or so vocal overdubs. This included, for example, a three-minute portion of "The Prophet's Song," which was in its entirety an unaccompanied vocal solo. Furthermore, Queen had always proudly stated on their album sleeves that "nobody played synthesizer," a proclamation of their devotion to pure rock. The downside of having this sort of integrity, however, was that every instrument that appeared on the album had to somehow be sought out, acquired, and recorded. This presented something of a logistical challenge, as the album featured a vast selection of exotic, un-rock instruments, including the harp—not the harmonica kind, but the kind that's eight feet tall and is employed in the performance of music whose function is to evoke in the listener mental images of unicorns and cherubim. This particular instrument's entire contribution was confined to a mere two seconds of the album's duration, but for those two seconds to be committed to vinyl, a harp had to be located, rented, shipped to the recording studio, unpacked, set up in a booth, and hooked up to a microphone, a job that in itself represents a multiple-hour nightmare for any engineer not familiar with the recording of acoustic instruments normally used in symphony orchestras. Upon the successful completion of these tasks, the harp music then had to be recorded, subjected to multiple playbacks, and finally approved by both the band and the producer, all while the clock ticked away and marked the rapid passage

of extremely expensive studio time. Finally, the instrument had to be repackaged, picked up by movers who could be trusted to handle fragile items, and returned to the original site of its rental. And the harp was not the only instrument whose blink-and-you-missed-it appearance on the album entailed an inordinate consumption of time and money.

When the hellish, grueling torment of the recording process was finally over, *A Night at the Opera* had won the dubious distinction of being the most expensive album ever made. Happily, it was a smash hit on both sides of the Atlantic, surely a coup for Queen, who had hoped to break big in the United States since their formation. The album featured strong material, including the single "You're My Best Friend," but everything paled in comparison to "Bohemian Rhapsody," the highlight of the album and the song that marked the band's true arrival. Although later releases like "We Are the Champions," are also intimately identifiable with the band's persona, none better encapsulates the vast territory and musical extremes with which the band was associated during their long career than "Bohemian Rhapsody." The song began

Queen in concert, live and ready to explode. Left to right: Freddie Mercury and Brian May.

as a piano-based ballad, developing into a crushingly heavy guitar anthem by way of an operatic call-and-response section that took three weeks to record and that contained so many vocal overdubs that sections of the recording tape had been rendered transparent.

When they weren't in the recording studio destroying reels of quarter-inch tape, the band members liked to blow off a little steam by engaging in behavior that pushed their reputations as decadent, hedonistic rock stars into the upper atmosphere. Their considerable substance consumption was overshadowed by their sexual triumphs, which are recalled as among the most infamous in the annals of groupie abuse, rivaling only those of Led Zeppelin. They also rivaled Zeppelin in terms of how much the press hated them. Yes, believe it or not, Queen, a popular 1970s rock band, was mercilessly derided in the press as the embodiment of all the worst traits of overbloated dinosaur rock. The band members no doubt wiped their tears of emotional distress with phone book–size royalty statements reflecting their massive earnings. These earnings were of especially gargantuan proportions after *News of the World* was released, as it was consumed in mass quantities based on its opening one-two punch of the back-to-back singles "We Will Rock You" and "We Are the Champions." The following year's *Jazz* was just as successful, in part because of a publicity stunt that was staged to promote the album's first single, "Bicycle Race." The stunt in question was—you guessed it—a bicycle race, with the angle that all of the contestants were naked women.

Queen started off the 1980s well enough. *The Game* featured some of the band's most famous singles, including "Crazy Little Thing Called Love," and eventually hit number one in the United States, their first and only album to do so. However, despite the awesome film

soundtrack to *Flash Gordon* and Mercury's 1981 duet with David Bowie, "Under Pressure," the band's popularity began to wane, disappearing entirely and permanently in the United States. They made up for some of the lost ground in 1985, thanks to a highly impressive performance at Live Aid that served as a shocking confirmation of both how good Queen actually was and how terrible Led Zeppelin's performance had been that day. Subsequently, Queen saw themselves recapture a considerable portion of their sales clout in Europe and wisely chose to expand their touring to include Africa, Asia, and South America, markets that most European and American bands overlooked despite the fact that they were all populated by vast numbers of people who bought records and concert tickets. They were still unable to break sales records in the United States, but one supposes that they just had to be satisfied with playing to fanatical sellout crowds everywhere but Antarctica and the good ol' U.S. of A., home of Alf and the Flowbee.

As the 1980s drew to a close, the band drastically cut back on touring. Despite possessing a level of showmanship that almost any rock singer would have killed for, Mercury had never been a particularly devoted fan of touring, and the band's scaled-back tour itinerary was at first attributed to his distaste for the grind of the road. However, as time passed and the singer was seen in public less and less often, people began to suspect that there was more at work than a simple aversion to bus rides. Finally, in 1991, Mercury laid all the rumors to rest by issuing a press statement declaring that, as many people had already guessed, he was dying from complications related

to AIDS. On November 24, two days after issuing the statement, he died. Although it was pretty obvious that he enjoyed the company of men, Mercury had always stopped short of declaring his sexual preferences to the public. Surprisingly, the master showman was in reality a deeply private person who cherished what little solitude he could find and was fiercely protective of whatever scant pieces of himself he was not obligated to share with the public. After his death, many gay-rights organizations expressed disappointment with his lifelong refusal to come out, as he could have been part of the general effort to destigmatize homosexuality in society's mainstream by serving as a positive role model. In any event, after Mercury's death, the music of Queen enjoyed a renaissance of sorts, due in part to the vulture-like mass consumption of product that occurs whenever a celebrity drops dead, as well as to a serendipitously timed sequence in the movie *Wayne's World* that rendered "Bohemian Rhapsody" ever-present for the remainder of 1992, guaranteeing that no one on earth would ever want to hear it again for the rest of their lives.

Queen's surviving band members kept a low profile after Mercury's death. Their music, however, never really went away. Suggestions that they replace Mercury never did either. Even Elton John, a close friend of the band and of the late singer in particular, had suggested that they should get back out there after recording with them for a greatest hits package. "You guys should go out and play again," the Rocket Man told them. "It must be like having a Ferrari in the garage waiting for a driver." Finally, in 2004, May and Taylor took his advice and announced that they were getting

back together, and had enlisted a new singer to take Mercury's place. They had chosen Paul Rodgers, the former Bad Company and Free singer. He would front the band under the moniker "Queen + Paul Rodgers," and they would take the show public in 2005. Bassist John Deacon would be absent from the proceedings, a decision that most people respected.

The union, though dignified and well-intentioned, simply didn't work. Rodgers is a stellar talent, so it wasn't a matter of him not being up to the job. However, Mercury's take on the classic material was simply too unique, and the pairing of Rodgers and Queen never quite gelled. There were exceptions, of course—Rodgers acquitted himself well of later material, like "The Show Must Go On." But when it came to the band's earlier, classic material, like "Bohemian Rhapsody" or "We Are the Champions," it just didn't work. The songs were too well-known and too beloved in their original form, and they would always sound somehow off with someone else singing them.

The musicians enjoyed working together regardless, and audiences were happy to have them back, but the studio album that the new group released in 2008, *The Cosmos Rocks*, received a lukewarm reception, and when Rodgers left in 2009 to reunite with Bad Company, no flags were flown at half-mast to mourn the sad occasion. In February 2012, Queen announced that *American Idol* runner-up Adam Lambert would front the band for dates later that year in both Moscow and the U.K.

John Deacon: bass; **Brian May**: guitar/vocals; **Freddie Mercury**: vocals/keyboards; **Roger Taylor**: drums/vocals

Discography: *Queen* (EMI, 1973); *Queen II* (Elektra, 1974); *Sheer Heart Attack* (Elektra, 1974); *A Night at the Opera* (Elektra, 1975); *A Day at the Races* (Elektra, 1976); *News of the World* (Elektra, 1977); *Jazz* (Elektra, 1978); *Live Killers* (Elektra, 1979); *The Game* (Elektra, 1980); *Flash Gordon* (Elektra, 1981); *Hot Space* (Elektra, 1982); *The Works* (Capitol, 1984); *A Kind of Magic* (Capitol, 1986); *Live Magic* (EMI, 1986); *The Miracle* (Capitol, 1989); *Live at the Beeb* (Hollywood, 1989); *Innuendo* (Hollywood, 1991); *Live at Wembley '86* (Hollywood, 1992); *Made in Heaven* (Atlantic, 1995); *Queen on Fire—Live at the Bowl* (Atlantic, 2004); *Queen Rock Montreal* (Atlantic, 2007)

QUEENS OF THE STONE AGE

YEARS ACTIVE: 1996–PRESENT

After the demise of the massively influential stoner rock band Kyuss in 1995, fans waited with bated breath for guitarist Josh Homme's next move, saving up their lunch money for the *Kyuss Redux* album that his new band was certain to produce. When it was revealed that Homme's new band, Queens of the Stone Age, was rounded out by bassist Nick Oliveri and drummer Alfredo Hernandez, both former Kyuss members, it seemed that their enthusiasm and patience had been thoroughly justified. Then the group's self-titled debut was released in 1998, resulting in immense confusion the world over. The album was a quirky, progressive affair that went in many different directions, none of which bore even the slightest resemblance to the stoner rock band that had been an exalted divinity to its fans. However, thanks to the slavish loyalty that Kyuss had engendered in its adherents, the fans were willing, for the most part, to give the somewhat upsetting album a few more spins than most albums receive when their contents are not immediately appreciated by the listener.

In 2003, Queens of the Stone Age was nominated for the Best Hard Rock Performance Grammy, for "No One Knows." Left to right: Brendon McNichol, Nick Oliveri, Gene Trautmann, and Josh Homme.

But just when people thought they had Queens of the Stone Age pegged and expected more of the same music on the band's sophomore offering, *Rated R*, the album turned out to bear almost no resemblance to its predecessor, to say nothing of Kyuss. Instead, the album flirted with pop and had an atmosphere of high-energy gusto that one finds only on albums designed to piss people off. The pop angle was pushed even further on their 2002 album *Songs for the Deaf*, which featured the extraordinary drumming of the Foo Fighters' Dave Grohl and Homme's canniest songwriting to date, particularly on the album's first single, the almost Beatles-esque "No One Knows."
In 2005 the band released *Lullabies to Paralyze*, this time without the services of Oliveri, who had been relieved of his bass duties the previous year and replaced by Troy Van Leeuwen. It debuted at number 5 on the *Billboard* chart, far outpacing any position they had reached before, and making it impossible to classify them as an underground band any longer. Their last album was 2007's *Era Vulgaris* which, like its predecessor, was well-received and sold well. However, rather than work on the follow-up, Homme took a detour in 2009 to join Them Crooked Vultures, a group featuring the Foo Fighters' Dave Grohl and some dude named John Paul Jones, plonking away at a bass. Grohl said that they were already intending to work on a second album, leaving the fate of Queens of the Stone Age up in the air for now.

Joey Castillo: drums/piano (*Lullabies to Paralyze* and later); **Dave Catching**: guitars/keyboards (*Rated R*); **Alfredo Hernandez**: drums (*Queens of the Stone Age*) (see also Kyuss); **Josh Homme**: guitars/vocals (see also Kyuss); **Nick Lucero**: drums (*Rated R*); **Brendon McNichol**: guitar/lap steel/keyboards (*Songs for the Deaf*); **Nick Oliveri**: bass (see also Kyuss); **Gene Trautmann**: drums (*Rated R*); **Troy Van Leeuwen**: guitar/bass/keyboards (*Lullabies to Paralyze* and later)

Discography: *Queens of the Stone Age* (Loosegroove, 1998); *Rated R* (Interscope, 2000); *Songs for the Deaf* (Interscope, 2002); *Lullabies to Paralyze* (Interscope, 2005); *Era Vulgaris* (Interscope, 2007)

QUEENSRŸCHE

YEARS ACTIVE: 1981–PRESENT

Seattle's Queensrÿche was formed in 1981 by a group of high school buddies who, upon coming together, fastidiously rehearsed their Iron Maiden–esque songs for a full two years without recording so much as a note. When they finally made their four-song demo tape, it caught the attention of record-store owners Kim and Diana Harris, who ended up managing the band and who made it their personal mission to get them a record deal. Their work culminated in a contract with EMI, which reissued the band's self-released *Queen of the Reich* EP, supplementing it with extra tracks and renaming it Queensrÿche. The band hit the road soon after and released two well-received albums, *The Warning* in 1984 and *Rage for Order* in 1986, the latter peaking only seven slots shy of the American Top 40. All the while, the band was expanding upon their somewhat standard Euro-metal sound, gradually incorporating more and more progressive elements.

In 1988 they reached their true breakthrough, both as a progressive metal band and as a commercial force, with *Operation: Mindcrime*, a concept album whose progressive elements were supplemented by symphonic arrangements played by a live orchestra. The album stayed on the charts for a full year, eventually going platinum. In 1990, the band followed it up with the even more successful *Empire*, which went double platinum on the strength of the video and single "Silent Lucidity," a song that bore more than a passing resemblance to Pink Floyd's "Comfortably Numb." The group managed to maintain its fan base with the 1994 studio album *Promised Land*, and they remained close to their fans' hearts throughout the rest of the decade, with the exception of their 1997 release, *Hear in the Now Frontier*, for which they abandoned their trademark progressive tendencies in favor of a more straightforward sound.

ABOVE: Queensrÿche sports hairdos in 1987 that would be seen years later on the likes of non-metalheads such as Patrick Swayze. Left to right: Michael Wilton, Eddie Jackson, Geoff Tate, Chris DeGarmo, and Scott Rockenfield.

OPPOSITE: After Queensrÿche landed a record deal with EMI, Geoff Tate (left) and Chris DeGarmo hit the road along with the rest of the band to support *The Warning*.

They got back on track in 1999 with the *Q2K* album, and in 2000 they went on tour in support of Rob Halford and a reunited Iron Maiden, surely the wet dream of metalheads worldwide.

In 2006 the group recorded *Operation: Mindcrime II*, and when they toured to support it they played both the original album and the sequel in their entireties, one assumes in chronological order. In 2009 they released *American Soldier*, a concept album about war. In 2010 they were in fact playing for American soldiers in Iraq when the base was bombed. Nobody was hurt, but it certainly gave the band all the cred they needed when it came to playing songs in front of military personnel. Their most recent album was 2011's *Dedicated to Chaos*.

Chris DeGarmo: guitars (*Queensrÿche* through *Hear in the Now Frontier*; *Tribe*); **Kelly Gray**: guitars (*Q2K*); **Eddie Jackson**: bass; **Scott Rockenfield**: drums; **Mike Stone**: guitar (*Tribe* through *Take Cover*); **Geoff Tate**: vocals; **Michael Wilton**: guitars

Discography: *Queensrÿche* (EMI, 1983); *The Warning* (EMI, 1984); *Rage for Order* (EMI, 1986); *Operation: Mindcrime* (EMI, 1988); *Empire* (EMI, 1990); *Operation: LIVEcrime* (EMI America, 1991); *Promised Land* (EMI, 1994); *Hear in the Now Frontier* (EMI, 1997); *Q2K* (Atlantic, 1999); *Live Evolution* (Sanctuary, 2001); *Tribe* (Sanctuary, 2003); *The Art of Live* (Sanctuary, 2004); *Operation: Mindcrime II* (Rhino, 2006); *Mindcrime at the Moore* (Rhino, 2007); *Take Cover* (Rhino, 2007); *American Soldier* (Atco/Rhino, 2009); *Dedicated to Chaos* (Loud & Proud, 2011)

QUIET RIOT

Years active: 1973–1989; 1993–2003; 2004–2008; 2010–present

Quiet Riot is often—and inaccurately—credited with being the first metal band whose debut album reached number one. *Metal Health*, the album in question, was actually the band's third. Their two prior albums, 1977's *Quiet Riot* and 1978's *Quiet Riot II*, featured none other than legendary guitarist Randy Rhoads, who left the band to play for Ozzy Osbourne. The

drummer and bassist walked as well, leaving Kevin DuBrow by himself. After DuBrow recruited a completely new lineup, the band pressed on and eventually signed to Pasha Records, for whom they released *Metal Health* in 1983. Spurred by the video and single for "Cum On Feel the Noize," a cover of a song by the British glam band Slade, the album rocketed to the number one slot, and the band members, who had previously been slugging it out in dinky little clubs, were suddenly arena-metal megastars. The group immediately rushed back into the studio, where they cranked out their next album, *Condition Critical*, which was

a virtual clone of *Metal Health*. The band even went so far as to feature as its first single another Slade cover, "Mama Weer All Crazee Now." The only respect in which it was not an exact copy of the previous album was that of its sales. Fans were keenly aware that the album was simply a cynical verbatim regurgitation of *Metal Health* with different cover art and a new title, and they stayed away in droves.

Exacerbating matters was DuBrow's behavior. Spurred by

At the height of its popularity, Quiet Riot entrances its many fans. Left to right: Rudy Sarzo, Kevin DuBrow, and Carlos Cavaso.

With a brand-new lineup, in 1983 Kevin DuBrow led Quiet Riot to number one with *Metal Health*. Left to right: Frankie Banali, Kevin DuBrow, Carlos Cavaso, and Rudy Sarzo.

the disappointing sales of the album and a fondness for cocaine, the singer turned into an obnoxious loudmouth who enjoyed speaking disparagingly about every person or entity on which he was able to fixate long enough to craft a witty barb at their expense. His targets included other metal bands and Quiet Riot's own label, creating a situation that his bandmates realized would cost them dearly. By 1986, with the release of *QR III*, the band, who had been at the top of the mountain only three years prior, couldn't even give away copies of the album. Their disappointment manifested itself in an intense hatred focused on the singer, whom they rightly characterized as responsible for the band's downward slide. It was ironic considering that DuBrow had rescued the band and guided it to its most successful period through the very same egotistic persistence that had cost them their popularity, their connections, and whatever other bridges the singer seemed gleefully hell-bent on reducing to smoking ruins. The crestfallen band members decided once and for all that they had had enough of DuBrow, and in Hawaii, after the final date on the disastrous tour to support *QR III*, the rest of the band and their road crew sneaked out of the hotel early to fly home sans the singer, who woke up several hours later to find himself completely abandoned.

Upon their return home, the remaining band members drafted singer Paul Shortino for their sixth album, *QR*, only to find themselves being sued by DuBrow, who still owned the rights to the Quiet Riot name. This proved the final straw, and Quiet Riot broke up shortly thereafter. They reunited in 1993 minus *Metal Health* bassist Rudy Sarzo, who, after fulfilling his commitments on the *Condition Critical* tour, had quit the band, running out the door so fast that he left a Wile E. Coyote cloud of dust behind him. Sarzo came back into the fold in 1997 to perform with Quiet Riot at a party held by Marilyn Manson, and one hopes the band was aware that their presence at the party was pretty much a joke at their expense. Since Sarzo's return, the band busied themselves with club tours, and in 2001, they released *Guilty Pleasures*, the first album by the *Metal Health* lineup in seventeen years. However, they weren't able to keep it together, and the band broke up again in 2003.

DuBrow and drummer Frankie Banali put together a new lineup in 2004 and released the album *Rehab* in 2006. The unfortunately titled album would be DuBrow's last. In November 2007, the singer died of a cocaine overdose, and in January 2008, Banali posted a statement to his official website to the effect that it would be unseemly to even consider continuing with Quiet Riot in the wake of DuBrow's passing. "I reject any and all suggestions to have Quiet Riot continue as a live performing entity," the statement read. "My friendship, love and respect for Kevin DuBrow as well as my personal love and affection for Kevin's mother and his family makes it inconceivable for me to ever entertain any ovation to reform or to continue Quiet Riot." In 2010, Banali took to the band's official website to announce the return of Quiet Riot.

Frankie Banali: drums (*Metal Health* and later) (see also W.A.S.P.); **Carlos Cavaso**: guitars (*Metal Health* and later); **Neil Citron**: guitar (*Rehab*); **Kevin DuBrow**: vocals (*Quiet Riot* through *QR III*; *Terrified* and later); **Drew Forsuth**: drums (*Quiet Riot*, *Quiet Riot II*); **Tony Franklin**: bass (*Rehab*); **Kelli Garni**: bass (*Quiet Riot*, *Quiet Riot II*); **Kenny Hillary**: bass (*QR* through *Terrified*); **Sean McNabb**: bass (*QR*); **Randy Rhoads**: guitars (*Quiet Riot*, *Quiet Riot II*) (see also Ozzy Osbourne); **Rudy Sarzo**: bass (*Metal Health*, *Condition Critical*, *Alive and Well* and later); **Paul Shortino**: vocals (*QR*); **Chuck Wright**: bass (*QR III*, *Down to the Bone*)

Discography: *Quiet Riot* (Columbia, 1977); *Quiet Riot II* (Columbia, 1978); *Metal Health* (Pasha, 1983); *Condition Critical* (Pasha, 1984); *QR III* (Pasha, 1986); *QR* (Pasha, 1988); *The Randy Rhoads Years* (Pasha, 1993); *Terrified* (Moonstone, 1993); *Down to the Bone* (Kamikaze, 1995); *Alive and Well* (Cleopatra, 1999); *Guilty Pleasures* (Bodyguard, 2001); *Rehab* (Chavis, 2006)

RAGE AGAINST THE MACHINE

YEARS ACTIVE: 1991–2000; 2007–PRESENT

When Rage Against the Machine's 1992 debut was unleashed upon an unsuspecting public, the group's incendiary rap-metal sound came as an aggressively confrontational shock to most rock fans. The Los Angeles band dealt exclusively with left-wing political subjects such as imperialism, oppression, poverty, and corporate oligarchism, the last of which did not go unnoticed when the band members signed their deal with Epic Records, whose parent company was itself the evil corporate oligarchy known as Sony Music. Nevertheless, the members of Rage Against the Machine would consistently put their money where their mouths were, happily supporting a variety of organizations such as Rock for Choice and Refuse and Resist. Whether their political bent was appreciated by their fans is a subject deserving of closer inspection, but there can be no doubt that the band instilled in at least some of their listeners the intellectual curiosity to find out more about the subjects of their songs.

After a four-year hiatus, during which the band's breakup was heavily rumored, they returned in 1996 with *Evil Empire*, which debuted at number one. They performed at a 1999 benefit concert for death-row inmate

Mumia Abu-Jamal, who has become something of a left-wing media hero due to his possible status as a wrongly incarcerated victim of a racist justice system. He is in jail because he was convicted of murder, but the main point is that the concert ruled. Later that year, the band released *The Battle of Los Angeles*, which, like the album before it, debuted at number one, eventually selling two million copies. In 2000 the band performed across the street from the Democratic National Convention, and

Rage Against the Machine railed against political apathy. Left to right: Zack de la Rocha, Brad Wilk, and Tom Morello.

munication issues within the group. The rest of the band chose to continue under a different name, Audioslave, with Soundgarden's Chris Cornell as lead vocalist, but when Audioslave broke up in 2007, the group reunited with de la Rocha to play at that year's Coachella festival. This led to a full tour, which naturally led to speculation that they would also make a new album. So far, guitarist Tom Morello has denied it. The band has, however, continued to tour, and has continued to issue qualified, passive-aggressive semi-denials that they will ever record again.

Tim Commerford: bass; **Zack de la Rocha**: vocals; **Tom Morello**: guitars; **Brad Wilk**: drums

Discography: *Rage Against the Machine* (Epic, 1992); *Evil Empire* (Epic, 1996); *Live & Rare* (Epic, 1998); *The Battle of Los Angeles* (Epic, 1999); *Renegades* (Epic, 2000); *Live at the Grand Olympic Auditorium* (Epic, 2003)

RAINBOW

YEARS ACTIVE: 1975–1984; 1994–1997

After leaving Deep Purple in 1975, guitarist Ritchie Blackmore decided to form his own band, in which he would be the focus of attention and have the last word on any and all creative decisions. Unfortunately, his first singer was Ronnie James Dio, whose inability to share the spotlight made Ted Nugent look like a shrinking violet by comparison. Blackmore formed his band in a fashion that was quite

the following month bassist Tim Commerford climbed on top of a twenty-foot sculpture on the side of the stage at the MTV Video Music Awards while a clearly confused Limp Bizkit front man Fred Durst tried to accept one of the many statuettes honoring the artistically worthless that are regularly doled out during this travesty. The next month, vocalist Zach de la Rocha quit the band, citing com-

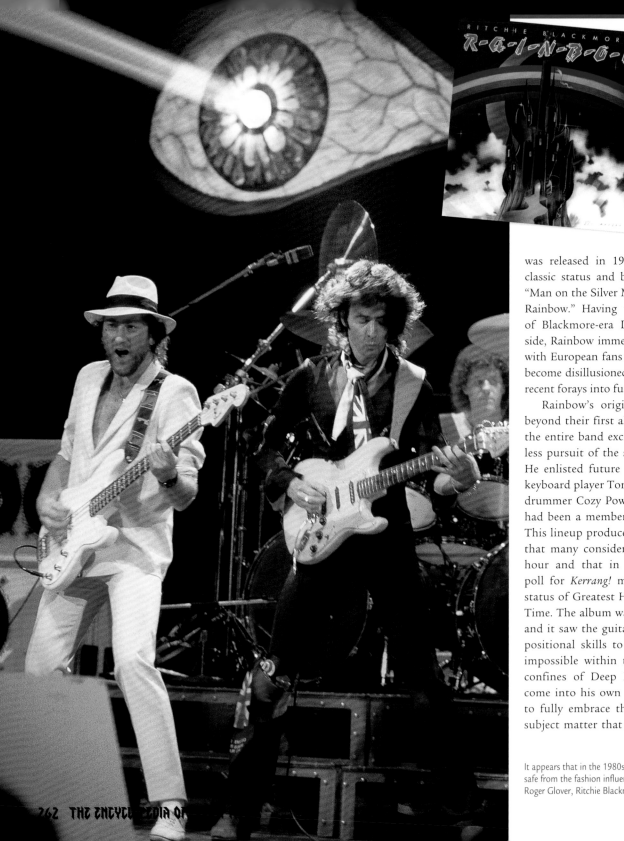

simple—he took over the band Elf, which had opened for Deep Purple and had been produced by Purple bassist Roger Glover, and fired their guitarist. In two easy steps, Rainbow was birthed into existence. The band's debut, *Ritchie Blackmore's Rainbow*, was released in 1975, assuming immediate classic status and boasting such material as "Man on the Silver Mountain" and "Catch the Rainbow." Having the advantage of legions of Blackmore-era Deep Purple fans on its side, Rainbow immediately caught on, mostly with European fans who, like Blackmore, had become disillusioned with his previous band's recent forays into funk.

Rainbow's original lineup did not last beyond their first album, as Blackmore fired the entire band except for Dio in his relentless pursuit of the sound that was his ideal. He enlisted future Dio bassist Jimmy Bain, keyboard player Tony Carey, and powerhouse drummer Cozy Powell, who until that point had been a member of the Jeff Beck Group. This lineup produced *Rising*, the 1976 album that many consider to be the band's finest hour and that in 1981 topped a reader's poll for *Kerrang!* magazine, granting it the status of Greatest Heavy Metal Album of All Time. The album was a success on all fronts, and it saw the guitarist developing his compositional skills to a degree that had been impossible within the relatively democratic confines of Deep Purple. It also saw Dio come into his own as a lyricist, as he began to fully embrace the Dungeons & Dragons subject matter that became the primary pre-

It appears that in the 1980s, no one—not even Rainbow—was safe from the fashion influences of *Miami Vice*. Left to right: Roger Glover, Ritchie Blackmore, and Chuck Burgi.

occupation of most of his lyrics. But the happy marriage proved short-lived. The next album, 1978's *Long Live Rock'n'Roll*, marked the total breakdown of the singer's relationship with the guitarist, who was in the process of considering a complete stylistic change from mystical epics to the straightforward rock sound of the album's title track, which had been a successful single. In typical fashion, the issue of whether Dio quit or was fired is murky at best, so suffice it to say that in 1979 he was no longer a part of the band, and he went on to join Black Sabbath.

As history has proven, replacing Ronnie James Dio is not as simple a task as it appears. Blackmore tried his best, though, and in addition to casting about for a new singer, he sent the rest of the band the way of the Elf lineup, firing them all with the exception of Powell. Blackmore eventually rounded out the band with keyboard player Don Airey and former Deep Purple bassist Roger Glover, an interesting choice considering that it had been Blackmore who had lobbied for the bassist's ouster from Purple in the first place. The quest for a singer came to an end with the recruitment of Graham Bonnet, whose short hair and aviator sunglasses provided a sharp, striking contrast to the band's visual image of the previous four years. More shocking, however, was Rainbow's new musical direction, which was revealed to horrified listeners on the 1979 album *Down to Earth*. The band had turned to crafting straightforward rock radio hits, typified by the singles "All Night Long" and the atrocious "Since

You've Been Gone," which resembled nothing so much as a sped-up version of Boston's "More Than a Feeling." This was quite shocking, especially coming from the band who gave us "Kill the King." Not so surprisingly, this was the band's worst-selling effort in history. Bonnet was shown the door, and, to add insult to injury, rock-solid uber-drummer Cozy Powell left the band, leaving Blackmore to find new replacements yet again.

American-born singer Joe Lynn Turner replaced Bonnet, and the band's first album in this incarnation, 1981's *Difficult to Cure*, helped them make up some of the ground they had lost with their previous offering. But even though it seemed as if the band was experiencing an upswing, its years had already come and gone. The next album, released the following year, *Straight Between the Eyes*, should have expanded upon the success of *Difficult to Cure*, but it simply didn't sell. The 1983 release *Bent Out of Shape* suffered a similar fate, and after a 1984 tour, Blackmore read the writing on the wall and disbanded Rainbow, going on to take part in a very successful reunion of the Mark II Deep Purple lineup. The Rainbow story seemed to be really and truly over at this point, an impression that was reinforced by the 1986 release of a live compilation album, pessimistically titled *Finyl Vinyl*. However, in 1995, after Blackmore's second and final split from Purple, he drafted a group of unknown musicians and released a new Rainbow album, *Stranger in Us All*. He has since formed Blackmore's Night, a medieval folk music ensemble consisting of himself and singer Candice Night.

Don Airey: keyboards (*Down to Earth, Difficult to Cure*) (see also Whitesnake); **Jimmy Bain**: bass (*Rising*) (see also Dio); **Ritchie Blackmore**: guitars (see also Deep Purple); **Graham Bonnet**: vocals (*Down to Earth*); **Chuck Burgi**: drums (*Bent Out of Shape*); **Tony Carey**: keyboards (*Rising*); **Bob Daisley**: bass (*Long Live Rock'n'Roll*) (see also Uriah Heep); **Ronnie James Dio**: vocals (*Ritchie Blackmore's Rainbow* through *Long Live Rock 'n' Roll*) (see also Black Sabbath, Dio); **Gary Driscoll**: drums (*Ritchie Blackmore's Rainbow*); **Roger Glover**: bass (*Down to Earth* through *Bent Out of Shape*) (see also Deep Purple); **Craig Gruber**: bass (*Ritchie Blackmore's Rainbow*); **Paul Morris**: keyboards (*Stranger in Us All*); **Cozy Powell**: drums (*Rising* through *Down to Earth*) (see also Black Sabbath, Yngwie Malmsteen); **John O'Reilly**: drums (*Stranger in Us All*); **Bobby Rondinelli**: drums (*Difficult to Cure, Straight Between the Eyes*) (see also Black Sabbath, Blue Öyster Cult); **David Rosenthal**: keyboards (*Straight Between the Eyes, Bent Out of Shape*); **Greg Smith**: bass (*Stranger in Us All*); **Mickey Lee Soule**: keyboards (*Stranger in Us All*); **David Stone**: keyboards (*Long Live Rock'n'Roll*); **Joe Lynn Turner**: vocals (*Difficult to Cure* through *Bent Out of Shape*) (see also Deep Purple, Yngwie Malmsteen); **Doogie White**: vocals (*Stranger in Us All*)

Discography: *Ritchie Blackmore's Rainbow* (Polydor, 1975); *Rising* (Polydor, 1976); *On Stage* (Polydor, 1977); *Long Live Rock'n'Roll* (Polydor, 1978); *Down to Earth* (Polydor, 1979); *Difficult to Cure* (Polydor, 1981); *Straight Between the Eyes* (Polydor, 1982); *Bent Out of Shape* (Polydor, 1983); *Finyl Vinyl* (Polydor, 1986); *Stranger in Us All* (BMG, 1995); *Live in Europe* (Mausoleum, 1996); *The Very Best of Rainbow* (Polydor, 1997); *Live in Munich 1977* (Eagle, 2006)

Rainbow does its Rapunzel-metal shtick live in 1976. Left to right: Tony Carey, Ronnie James Dio, Jimmy Bain, and Ritchie Blackmore.

While the issue of rivalries between bands has been somewhat overhyped by the media through the years, one phenomenon requiring no outside help whatsoever is that of conflicts taking place among members of the same band. Sometimes there is just one member who, in a need to assert control over the project, goes through band members the way most households go through toilet paper (Ritchie Blackmore, Ronnie James Dio, Ted Nugent, Yngwie Malmsteen, and Axl Rose are notable examples). Then there is the opposite situation, where one member will be the odd one out, such as drummer Dave Lombardo of Slayer or singer Kevin DuBrow of Quiet Riot. The most common experience, however, aside from when the whole band simply goes nuts and eats one another alive, is when one member clashes with another, leaving the rest of the band to simply duck and hope the projectiles miss their heads. It is perhaps not a coincidence that, in the majority of these situations, the members involved in the clashes are the singer and the guitar player.

EDDIE VAN HALEN *vs.* SAMMY HAGAR

GEORGE LYNCH *vs.* DON DOKKEN

When Van Halen fired original front man David Lee Roth in 1985, most people thought that the band had made a ruinous mistake that was made worse by the major miscalculation of replacing him with some guy named Sammy Hagar, whom most of the band's teenage fans had never heard of. As it turned out, Van Halen was more popular than ever with Hagar, and the band went on to produce some of their best-loved material with him. So it came as something of a surprise when, in 1986, the band announced that they had fired Hagar, apparently over a flap between the singer and the guitarist that had to do with a song they were to contribute to a movie soundtrack. Both parties had their own side of the story, but it was Eddie Van Halen who came up with the most memorable sound bite. He accused Hagar of being stricken by the same condition that had befallen Roth, that of "L.S.D.," or "Lead Singer's Disease."

In the mid-1980s, Dokken was one of the commercial metal bands to beat. The group had to their credit a deadly combination of deft songwriting and the impressive lead guitar skills of George Lynch. Unfortunately, Lynch and singer Don Dokken had a deeply adversarial relationship. The singer wanted the band to continue churning out hits as it had been, while Lynch wanted the band to become more musically adventurous, which is guitar player's code for "I want the band to back me while I play solos forever." Neither side would budge, and eventually the band broke up, with the singer going on to form his own solo project and the guitarist going on to form Lynch Mob, the guitar-dominated ensemble he had always wanted. However, apparently the band Dokken was greater than the sum of its parts, for neither member could individually capture the glory that had been theirs as a unit. Eventually the band reunited, but the same tensions cropped up again almost immediately, and Lynch left Dokken for good.

OZZY OSBOURNE *vs.* BOB DAISLEY AND LEE KERSLAKE

RITCHIE BLACKMORE *vs.* IAN GILLAN

(OR "THE OZZMAN ERASETH")

Bassist Bob Daisley and drummer Lee Kerslake were the rhythm section on Ozzy Osbourne's first two solo albums, 1980's *Blizzard of Ozz* and 1981's *Diary of a Madman*. For many years after those albums were released, the duo maintained that they had a substantial settlement coming to them because they did not receive the performance royalties that they claimed were owed to them. Rather than get into a long, protracted legal battle, particularly one that they might lose, Osbourne and his manager/wife, Sharon, reissued the two albums in 2002, but with a small, unadvertised difference. Customers who bought the reissues were surprised, and not pleasantly, when they got home and found that the original bass and drum tracks had been rerecorded by bassist Robert Trujillo and drummer Mike Bordin, both of whom were regular members of Osbourne's touring band. Therefore, the issue of performance royalties was rendered moot, but many people, fans included, found the decision mildly creepy at best and downright sacrilegious at worst. Caveat emptor!

Before forming Rainbow and having the undisputed authority t[o] hire and fire band members with impunity, guitarist Ritchie Black[more] more was part of Deep Purple, and he clashed with singer Ian Gilla[n] on a regular basis. Although the pair managed to set aside their di[f]ferences for long enough to craft some of the band's best and mo[st] classic material, Gillan eventually couldn't take it and left in 197[3]. Deep Purple carried on for a few years, and then Blackmore left [to] form Rainbow. When that band ended, it appeared that there wa[s] a cash cow waiting to be milked—the classic Mark II lineup of Dee[p] Purple was reunited in 1984, and they found massive public acce[p]tance that suggested a fruitful career for the remainder of their na[t]ural lives. Apparently, however, a decade apart had done nothing [to] dull the animosity between Blackmore and Gillan, and for the ne[xt] several years, the band put up with a ridiculous situation where [where] Gillan would return to the fold, thereby causing the departure [of] Blackmore, who would then return, causing Gillan to leave, and s[o] on. It all came to an end in 1994, when Blackmore was permanentl[y] replaced by Dixie Dregs guitarist Steve Morse, an arrangement tha[t] has been in place ever since.

THE CASE OF THE TAPE-TAMPERING GUITARIST

While it had taken eight studio albums for Ozzy Osbourne's relationship with Black Sabbath to deteriorate, his replacement, singer Ronnie James Dio, seemed to be well on his way out the door after just two. Guitarist Tony Iommi and bassist Geezer Butler had formed one camp in the band, and the singer was developing his own with drummer Vinnie Appice. Over time, the situation between the two factions became obviously and irreparably frayed, and things came to a head in 1982, during mixing for *Live Evil*, the band's first authorized live album. Dio had problems with the amount of time it was taking to mix the

album, as well as the seemingly interminable length of "Heaven and Hell," which was so long that it was broken up over two album sides. The big problem, however, was that the singer believed that Iommi and Butler were sneaking into the studio on the sly and mixing their parts loude[r] than they had been when he was present. Interest[ingly, Iommi and Butler believed that Dio and Appice were doing the same thing. While both theories are most likely a pile of poop, they must have seemed per[fectly plausible to the parties involved, and at the end of the day, Dio and Appice left Black Sabbath in what has to be one of the dumbest moments in the history of recorded sound.

RAMMSTEIN

YEARS ACTIVE: 1994–PRESENT

The list of foreign-language bands that have made a name for themselves in the United States is a slim volume. The last such band to find a warm welcome on American shores was Menudo, a commercial juggernaut whose practice of replacing its members once they reached manhood virtually guaranteed the band's immortality. However, times changed, tastes changed, and the business strategy that allowed an adult Ricky Martin to exist side by side with his still-adolescent former group was not invulnerable to the phenomenon of diminished interest. Menudo was sent to the mythical land of Avalon, and a new foreign-language sensation was required. Thank God, this arrived in the form of Germany's Rammstein. The group took its name from a U.S. Air Force base in Germany that was the site of an air show gone horribly wrong, killing pilots and spectators alike. The literal translation of the word is "stone-battering ram," and it certainly provides an adequate description of Rammstein's sound. The band's clipped, stuttering guitar riffs and mechanical techno beats are heightened by the harsh, angular mother tongue in which the singer delivers the lyrics. As a bonus for the concertgoer, these lyrics are delivered from the stage while former Olympic swimmer and lead singer Till Lindemann is on fire. As a result of this type of theatrical tomfoolery, they quickly built a strong following in Europe, particularly in their own Deutschland, where they regularly play to thousands of people and their albums debut at the top of the charts. Even in other countries, where they are merely a cult phenomenon at best, the band members continue to regularly win over new converts on the basis of their flaming histrionics.

Till Lindemann gives the audience at a Rammstein show a lesson in proper stop-drop-and-roll techniques.

Richard Kruspe: rhythm guitar; **Paul Landers**: lead guitar; **Till Lindemann**: vocals; **Flake Lorenz**: keyboards; **Oliver Riedel**: bass; **Christoph Schneider**: drums

Discography: *Herzeleid* (Ils, 1995); *Sehnsucht* (Motor Music, 1997); *Live Aus Berlin* (Slash, 1999); *Mutter* (Universal, 2001); *Reise, Reise* (Motor, 2004); *Rosenrot* (Universal, 2005); *Liebe ist für alle da* (Universal, 2009)

ABOVE: Ratt on tour to support their wildly successful debut, *Out of the Cellar*. Left to right: Robbin Crosby, Juan Croucier, and Stephen Pearcy.

RATT

YEARS ACTIVE: 1976–1992; 1996–2010

Ratt was one of countless Los Angeles hair metal bands of the 1980s. They might not have amounted to much of anything were it not for their ability to craft a lethally effective pop hook, an attribute that received a hefty boost thanks to the impressive lead guitar playing of Warren DeMartini, truly one of the most underrated musicians in the genre. Originally known as Mickey Ratt, the band was signed to Atlantic in 1983. Later dubbed simply Ratt, the band released their debut, *Out of the Cellar*, in 1984, and it immediately became a major hit thanks to the single "Round and Round," the video of which featured the famous comedian Milton Berle in multiple roles. The album went triple platinum, and while none of their later releases accomplished this feat, they remained popular throughout the 1980s, and all of their albums charted well and sold at least 1 million copies.

In 1990, however, the honeymoon ended when the band was touring to support the *Detonator* album. It is unclear whether it was time, fatigue, close quarters, or any other factor, but the bottom line is that the band members all began to bristle at one another's presence, and they couldn't get off the bus fast enough at the tour's merciful end. Lead singer Stephen Pearcy formed his own band, Arcade, and the rest of the group rightly assessed that any albums they released during this time would go unpurchased now that glam metal had come to its inauspicious end. But they also realized that the downturn in the genre's fortunes couldn't last forever, so they simply put Ratt on the back burner as opposed to breaking up outright. In 1997, the band reconvened, returning to the public eye with their *Collage* album, following it up in 1999

Ratt at the height of its career, in 1984.
Left to right: Juan Croucier, Robbin
Crosby, Stephen Pearcy, Warren
DeMartini, and Bobby Blotzer.

with a self-titled release. However, Pearcy left the band for good soon after, and fans wondered what had become of guitarist Robbin Crosby, who had not taken part in the band's return and had not made any public appearances in several years. In 2001, Crosby made a public statement disclosing that he had contracted the AIDS virus, and it claimed his life in 2002, although later reports surfaced that said that the cause of death may actually have been a heroin overdose. The rest of the band chose to continue, with former Love/Hate singer Jizzy Pearl replacing Pearcy and former Mötley Crüe vocalist John Corabi replacing Crosby on guitar. This incarnation of the band never recorded any new material, and for years, multiple band members were involved in legal disputes over who was a legitimate member, who owned the rights to the Ratt name, and who had been fucked out of what contract by whose lawyer. Whatever the case may have been, an entertainment entity doing business as Ratt and featuring Pearcy, DeMartini, bassist Robbie Crane and drummer Bobby Blotzer released its first new album in 11 years, 2010's *Infestation*. The album featured former Quiet Riot guitarist Carlos Cavazo and debuted at number 30 on the *Billboard* charts, surely surprising the shit out of many people. However, just months after the triumphant return of the band to the top 40, Ratt went back on indefinite hiatus, when the members went back to hating each other again. The band is currently rumored to be working on new material, although which musicians are actually involved remains a mystery.

Bobby Blotzer: drums; **Carlos Cavazo**: guitar (*Infestation*); **Robbie Crane**: bass (*Collage* and later); **Robbin Crosby**: guitar (*Out of the Cellar* through *Detonator*); **Juan Croucier**: bass (*Out of the Cellar* through *Detonator*); **Warren DeMartini**: guitar; **Stephen Pearcy**: vocals

Discography: *Out of the Cellar* (Atlantic, 1984); *Invasion of Your Privacy* (Atlantic, 1985); *Dancin' Undercover* (Atlantic, 1986); *Reach for the Sky* (Atlantic, 1988); *Detonator* (Atlantic, 1990); *Ratt and Roll 81–91* (Atlantic, 1991); *Collage* (D-Rock, 1997); *Ratt* (Portrait, 1999); *Infestation* (Roadrunner, 2010)

RIGHT: The intramural rockers of Raven horse around in 1985. Left to right: John Gallagher, Rob "Wacko" Hunter, and Mark Gallagher.

RAVEN

YEARS ACTIVE: 1974–PRESENT

Raven was one of the Great White Hopes of the New Wave of British Heavy Metal. However, as with so many of its contemporaries, a combination of unfortunate factors ultimately conspired to keep Raven from reaching their full potential. Brothers Mark Gallagher, a guitarist, and John Gallagher, a bassist and vocalist, formed the band in the late 1970s. After recruiting drummer Rob "Wacko" Hunter, Raven signed with Neat Records (home of the crucifix-inverting Venom) and released *Rock Until You Drop*. The 1981 album was an exercise in a very early version of thrash metal, a genre in

which bands like Motörhead and Venom were already making inroads. However, this album saw the style executed with a considerably greater degree of competence. The Raven lads were highly skilled musicians, and they took the still-primitive thrash genre to places where it had not yet gone. The band referred to the style as athletic rock, a genre name that thankfully did not catch on, although in retrospect it's not like "thrash" is a name borne of creative genius either.

Raven won over many fans with *Rock Until You Drop*, and they continued their streak throughout their stay with Neat Records. In 1985, they signed to Atlantic, and Raven's sound promptly went down the toilet. Their Atlantic debut, *Stay Hard*, was anything but hard. Rather, the band abandoned the aggressive, nay, "athletic," style that had won them their loyal fan base in favor of a more poplike sound that provided listeners with a sensation slightly less pleasant than a pelvic exam. Their fans abandoned them in droves, and matters were not helped when the pop sound continued for three more albums, all of which sold poorly. The band finally got the picture and released *Nothing Exceeds Like Excess* in 1988, an album that returned to their glorious sound of old. The band even signed to Combat Records for this auspicious occasion, which sweetened the deal. But it was too little too late, and Raven has never regained the following it had inadvertently alienated. Raven has not broken up, and continues to release albums on independent metal labels.

John Gallagher: vocals/bass; **Mark Gallagher**: guitars; **Joe Hasselvander**: drums (*Nothing Exceeds Like Excess* and later) (see also Pentagram); **Rob "Wacko" Hunter**: drums (*Rock Until You Drop* through *Life's a Bitch*)

Discography: *Rock Until You Drop* (Neat, 1981); *Wiped Out* (Neat, 1982); *All for One* (Neat, 1983); *Live at the Inferno* (Neat, 1984); *Stay Hard* (Atlantic, 1985); *Mad* (Atlantic, 1986); *The Pack Is Back* (Atlantic, 1986); *Life's a Bitch* (Atlantic, 1987); *Nothing Exceeds Like Excess* (Combat, 1988); *Architect of Fear* (Steamhammer, 1991); *Heads Up* (Steamhammer, 1993); *Glow* (X-Zero, 1994); *Destroy All Monsters* (X-Zero, 1995); *Everything Louder* (EMI, 1997); *Stark Raven Mad: The Best of Raven* (Mayhem, 1998); *One for All* (Metal Blade, 2000); *Walk Through Fire* (SPV, 2009)

If Patrice Guers of Rhapsody of Fire squints hard enough, he might see the last winged unicorn.

RHAPSODY OF FIRE

YEARS ACTIVE: 1993–PRESENT

There are two kinds of people in the world—people who think that heavy metal is too silly to listen to, and people who only want to hear songs about unicorns. It is for the latter group that Rhapsody of Fire exists. Originally called Rhapsody until 2005, this Italian band is the brainchild of keyboard player Alex Staropoli. He and his band of merry men have been bringing the high-pitched melodramatic goods since "Friends" started airing which, for all you kids out there, is a long time ago.

The band formed in 1993 when Staropoli joined forces with guitarist Luca Turilli and drummer Daniele Carbonera. After a brief period working under the moniker Thundercross,

the group changed their name to Rhapsody and recruited singer Fabio Lione. This lineup released *Legendary Tales* in 1997, an album so steeped in classical music, medieval folklore, and beast-slaying that it made Dio sound like Wilco. The album was part one in the "Emerald Sword Saga," a series of five albums that the band made between 1997 and 2002. The protagonist on these narrative albums is the Ice Warrior, who seeks the fabled Emerald Sword so that he might exact vengeance against the Dark Lord Akron. If any of that is confusing, don't worry. It's all helpfully spelled out in the CD booklet should you decide to go old school and eschew the download.

The second part of the saga was 1998's *Symphony of Enchanted Lands*. This wasn't just the album where the Ice Warrior joins forces with Tharos the dragon to search for the three Keys of Wisdom. Fuck, no. It was also

Fabio Lione demonstrates his golden-throated technique with Rhapsody of Fire.

the debut of bassist Alessandro Lotta on a Rhapsody album, and was promoted via the band's first tour. The *Dawn of Victory* album followed in 2000 and featured the band's most well-known song, "The Last Winged Unicorn." *Rain of a Thousand Flames* arrived in 2001 and *Power of the Dragonflame* followed in 2002, and with that the Emerald Sword Saga came to an end. Wagner and his *Ring* series had nothing on these guys.

Now with their five-album saga behind them, Rhapsody had the opportunity to make a bold break with their past and forge a new direction. Instead, they released *Symphony of Enchanted Lands II: The Dark Secret* in 2004, which is both a sequel to their second album and part one of their second saga, the "Dark Secret Saga." It features Christopher Lee, who provided both narration and a Tolkienesque flair to the proceedings.

In July 2006, the band was forced to change their name from Rhapsody to Rhapsody of Fire, citing trademark issues. Three months later they released *Triumph or Agony*, with highlights including the sixteen-minute "The Mystic Prophecy of the Demonknight." This epic output was followed by a four-year hiatus during which the band members went their separate ways and worked on various outside projects. When they returned in 2010, they had a new album, *The Frozen Tears of Angels*, followed just a month later by *The Cold Embrace of Fear: A Dark Romantic Symphony*.

From Chaos to Eternity came the following year, but in August 2011 the group announced that founding guitarist Luca Turilli was leaving the band. He would mount his winged steed and ride on crimson flames to glory. Either that or he would just start a solo career. He was replaced by Roberto De Micheli, and the band is now free to go on with whatever nine-part epic odyssey they choose to forge next in the fires of their rehearsal space.

Daniele Carbonera: drums (*Symphony of Enchanted Lands*); **Patrice Guers**: bass (*Triumph or Agony* and later); **Tom Hess**: guitar (*From Chaos to Eternity*); **Alex Holzwarth**: drums (*Dawn of Victory*; *Triumph or Agony* and later); **Dominique Leurquin**: guitar (*The Frozen Tears of Angels*); **Fabio Lione**: vocals; **Alessandro Lotta**: bass (*Symphony of Enchanted Lands* through *Dawn of Victory*); **Alex Staropoli**: keyboards; **Luca Turilli**: guitar

Discography: *Legendary Tales* (SPV, 1997); *Symphony of Enchanted Lands* (Limb Music, 1998); *Dawn of Victory* (Limb Music, 1998); *Rain of a Thousand Flames* (Limb Music, 2001); *Power of the Dragonflame* (Limb Music, 2002); *Symphony of Enchanted Lands II: The Dark Secret* (SPV, 2004); *Triumph or Agony* (SPV, 2006); *Live in Canada 2005: The Dark Secret* (Magic Circle, 2006); *The Frozen Tears of Angels* (Nuclear Blast, 2010); *From Chaos to Eternity* (Nuclear Blast, 2011)

RIOT

YEARS ACTIVE: 1975–2011

Although New York City's Riot never managed to grow beyond cult status, the group's commitment to pure metal has not gone unappreciated by lifelong fans, even when the band experienced major changes to its lineup, location, or label. Formed in 1976 by guitarist and main songwriter Mark Reale, Riot released its Capitol Records debut, *Rock City*, in 1977. The 1979 album *Narita* marked trouble within their ranks, as guitarist L. A. Kouvaris was replaced by Rick Ventura. Then the band switched to the Elektra label and lost more blood in the process, as original bassist Jimmy Iommi (no relation to Tony Iommi) and drummer Peter Bitelli moved on and were replaced by Kip Leming and Sandy Slavin, respectively. While it may have seemed like the lineup that was in place was simply an arbitrary result of the band's ongoing instability, this incarnation of Riot experienced the band's greatest success and is considered by many fans to be its classic lineup. They toured with AC/DC and Molly Hatchet during this period, and in 1981 they released the album that many consider their best, *Fire Down Under*. The success was soon dampened, however, when lead singer Guy Speranza turned in his notice, and things were never the same again. Riot replaced him and released two more albums, but at this point the band members were basically just going through the motions, hoping to recapture the glory that they had so briefly had in their possession. In 1983, Reale disbanded Riot and moved to Texas. However, three years later he re-formed the band with completely

What the members of Riot lack in physical beauty, they make up for with fringe. Left to right: Tony Moore, Mark Reale, Don Van Stavern, and Bobby Jarzombek.

new members, and Riot did well from that point on, particularly in Japan, where they were immensely popular. The band's last release was 2011's *Immortal Soul*. Tragically, just months after its release, Reale died of complications from Crohn's Disease.

Peter Bitelli: drums (*Rock City*, *Narita*); **Mike DiMeo**: vocals/keyboards (*Nightbreaker* and later); **Mike Flyntz**: guitars (*Riot Live: In Japan* and later); **Rhett Forrester**: vocals (*Restless Breed*, *Born in America*); **Frank Gilchrist**: drums (*Army of One*); **Jimmy Iommi**: bass (*Rock City*, *Narita*); **Bobby Jarzombek**: drums (*Thundersteel* and later); **L. A. Kouvaris**: guitars (*Rock City*); **Kip Leming**: bass (*Fire Down Under* through *Born in America*); **John Macaluso**: drums (*Brethren of the Long House*); **Tony Moore**: vocals (*Thundersteel* through *Riot Live: In Japan*); **Pete Perez**: bass (*Riot Live: In Japan* and later);

Mark Reale: guitars; **Sandy Slavin**: drums (*Fire Down Under* through *Born in America*); **Guy Speranza**: vocals (*Rock City* through *Fire Down Under*); **Don Van Stavern**: bass (*Thundersteel*, *The Privilege of Power*, *Immortal Soul*); **Rick Ventura**: guitars (*Narita* through *Born in America*)

Discography: *Rock City* (Capitol, 1977); *Narita* (Capitol, 1979); *Riot Live* (Elektra, 1980); *Fire Down Under* (Elektra, 1981); *Restless Breed* (Elektra, 1982); *Born in America* (Quality, 1983); *Thundersteel* (CBS, 1988); *Riot Live: In Japan* (Sony, 1989); *The Privilege of Power* (CBS, 1990); *Nightbreaker* (Sony, 1993); *Brethren of the Long House* (Sony, 1995); *Inishmore* (Metal Blade, 1998); *Shine On* (Metal Blade, 1998); *Sons of Society* (Metal Blade, 1999); *Through the Storm* (Metal Blade, 2002); *Army of One* (Metal Heaven, 2006); *Immortal Soul* (SPV/Steamhammer, 2011)

YEARS ACTIVE: 1976–1986; 1998–PRESENT

After the demise of the very wonderful Australian band Buffalo, guitarist Peter Wells formed his new band, Rose Tattoo, in 1976 with other musicians who had been similarly orphaned by their previous outfits. A raucous, rowdy outfit whose hard rock swagger predated the glam metal movement, Rose Tattoo incorporated a ferocity that recalled early AC/DC, and that the glam bands of the subsequent decade never possessed. The band members built a strong following based on their live performances, and

By showing off their tattoos, the members of Rose Tattoo hope to win guest appearances on the HBO series *Oz*. In this publicity photo, clockwise from far left: Peter Wells, Robin Riley, Dallas "Digger" Royal, Geordie Leech, and "Angry" Anderson Troat.

it was not long before they were signed and recording their debut album. Upon its release, the band began a three-year cycle of nonstop touring, pausing in 1981 to record their second album, *Assault and Battery*, only to pack their suitcases yet again and hit the road anew. This tour won Rose Tattoo the dubious distinction of being the loudest band ever to play at the Marquee Club in London, a record previously held by Led Zeppelin. After releasing their second album for 1981, *Rock'n'Roll Outlaw*, the band released another album the following year and embarked on yet another grueling tour cycle, this time opening for Aerosmith and ZZ Top. When it was over, three members, including founding guitarist Wells, had had enough and quit the band, unwilling to board another tour bus even at gunpoint. Remarkably, the remaining lineup

chose to continue and without missing a beat hired new members, cut another album, and launched a new tour, almost as if nothing had happened. By 1986, however, vocalist "Angry" Anderson Troat was the only remaining original member, and when he left to start a solo career, it effectively broke up the band, seemingly once and for all. However, seven years later, Rose Tattoo reunited to accept an invitation from Guns N' Roses to open for the fivesome's Australian tour. Apparently, Axl and company had all been longtime fans of the band. Rose Tattoo split after the tour ended, but they re-formed yet again in 1998 and have toured and recorded since then in various incarnations. Wells and bassist Ian Rilen, also a founding member, both died in 2006 from cancer. Founding member Mick Cocks followed suit in 2009.

Mick Cocks: guitar (1978's *Rose Tattoo* through *25 to Life*); **Paul DeMarco**: drums (*25 to Life* and later); **Scott Johnston**: drums; **Greg Jordan**: guitar (*Beats from a Single Drum*, 1990's *Rose Tattoo*); **Steve King**: bass (*25 to Life* and later); **Geordie Leach**: bass (1978's *Rose Tattoo* through *Southern Stars*); **John Meyer**: guitar (1990's *Rose Tattoo*); **Ian Rilen**: bass (*Never Too Old*, *Nice Boys Don't Play Rock and Roll*); **Robin Riley**: guitar (*Beats from a Single Drum* through *Never Too Old*); **Dallas "Digger" Royal**: drums (1978's *Rose Tattoo* through *Southern Stars*); **"Angry" Anderson Troat**: vocals; **Peter Wells**: guitar (*Rose Tattoo* through *Best of Rose Tattoo*)

Discography: *Rose Tattoo* (Mirage, 1978); *Assault and Battery* (Mirage, 1981); *Rock'n'Roll Outlaw* (Carrere, 1981); *Scarred for Life* (Carrere, 1982); *Southern Stars* (Albert, 1984); *Beats from a Single Drum* (Mushroom, 1986); *Rose Tattoo* (Repertoire, 1990); *The Best of Rose Tattoo* (Dojo, 1995); *Never Too Old* (Repertoire, 1996); *25 to Life* (Steamhammer/SP, 2000); *Pain* (Steamhammer/SP, 2002); *Bloodbrothers* (Armageddon, 2007)

AUSTRALIA

The Unspoken Hymns

ustralia, depending on how you want to look at it, is either the world's smallest continent or its sixth largest country. What's not disputed, however, are the contributions that it's made to heavy metal. Its most famous heavy metal export is, of course, the mighty AC/DC, though lesser-known bands like Buffalo and Rose Tattoo, along with a few others, have made important contributions as well.

Although Norway's black metal bands have gotten the most media attention, that doesn't mean that the genre hasn't thrived in other parts of the world. Australia made its own contribution when Deströyer 666 was founded by guitarist K. K. Warslut in 1994. He played every instrument but drums

on the debut EP, *Violence Is the Prince of This World*, but got a full band soon after. Sadly for his native land, Warslut left Australia and relocated to the metal-friendly Netherlands in 2001.

Adelaide's Mournful Congregation is a band that traffics in the highly unpopular genre known as funeral doom. Which, yes, seems slightly redundant. For those not in the know, playing funeral doom involves tuning guitars down to a key so low that note values are hard to discern, and using tempos so slow as to be almost nonexistent. Mournful Congregation originally formed in 1993 and released their debut album, *Tears from a Grieving Heart*, in 1999. A full decade later, they finally performed live

for the first time! In 2011 they released *The Unspoken Hymns*, their first album to see a U.S. release.

AFRICA

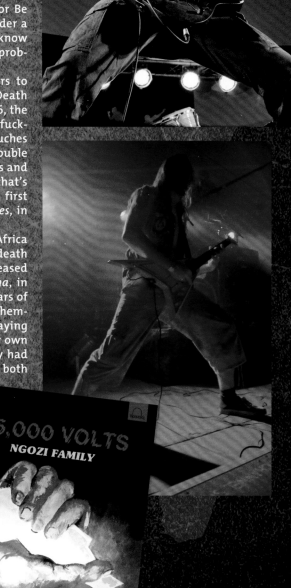

When most people think about heavy metal from a geographical standpoint, they think of snow, battle axes, and at least one of the former Axis powers. They do not think of zebras, Nubians, or Bushmen. In other words, they don't think of Africa. That's certainly the case as far as brick-and-mortar retail music stores go. A brief perusal of the African music section will turn up very little in the way of guitar crunch, castrati vocals, or lyrics about burning down churches. But maybe that's just to make more room for Putamayo samplers.

Popular misconceptions aside, the African continent has, in fact, produced some noteworthy metal, both in the past and present. Zambia spawned one of the earliest known examples of this claim with the output of the Ngozi Family. Led by Paul Ngozi, the band was active in the 1970s and dubbed its genre, "Zamrock." What this boiled down to was raw, dirty, lo-fi guitar riffs that split the difference between the Stooges and some highly stoned Black Sabbath rehearsal circa 1971. The rhythms didn't plod like much traditional metal does, and could get pretty damn intricate at times.

Finding a copy of this band's music in any conventional retail outlet in the United States is almost certainly out of the question, and their best-known album, *45,000 Volts*, is accessible mainly through illegal piracy on Ted Stevens' intertubes. However, some good souls have been kind enough to load samples to YouTube, and they're worth investigating if you like to have your preconceived notions smashed.

Today, there's Botswana's Wrust. Led by vocalist and guitarist Stux Daemon, their sound is pretty fucking brutal, with lots of double bass, stuttering machine-gun guitar riffs, and growling. They cite Morbid Angel, Carcass, and Napalm Death as influences, and they opened for Sepultura on the Brazilian band's first South African jaunt in 2003. Their video for "Kill or Be Killed" features them performing under a freeway underpass, and if you didn't know where this band was from you would probably think they were in Los Angeles.

Scarab hails from Egypt and refers to itself on its website as "Egypt's Death Metal Band." Formed in Cairo in 2006, the band's sound is pure death metal, no fucking around whatsoever, no exotic touches of any kind. Just blindingly fast double bass, harmonized Iron Maiden guitars and Cookie Monster vocals in a language that's anyone's guess. They released their first full-length album, *Blinding the Masses*, in 2010.

Mind Assault hails from South Africa and refers to itself as a melodic death metal band. Formed in 2004, they released their debut full-length album, *Stigma*, in 2008. This event came after a few years of heroic efforts to build a name for themselves, such as making demos, playing local festivals, and transporting their own audiences to gigs on buses that they had chartered. The group's lyrics are in both English and Afrikaans, making them quite possibly the first extreme metal band to deliver their lyrics in the native language of South Africa. They've played several festival dates with SacriFist, who have been in the South African melodic death metal business since 1992.

45,000 VOLTS
NGOZI FAMILY

Toward the end of their career, the Runaways manifest as a four-piece incarnation. Left to right: Lita Ford, Joan Jett, Sandy West, and Vicki Blue.

OPPOSITE: Barely old enough to drive a car—much less drink alcohol—the Runaways led the charge for all-female bands for years to come. Clockwise from top left: Sandy West, Jackie Fox, Joan Jett, Cherie Currie, and Lita Ford.

THE RUNAWAYS

YEARS ACTIVE: 1975–1979

The Runaways spawned the solo careers of both Lita Ford and Joan Jett, which in and of itself is more than enough to warrant the band's inclusion here. However, the group did a lot more than that, and although they received slightly less respect than the Monkees during the brief time that they were together, there can be no doubt today that the Runaways were major trailblazers whose impact is still felt. They became the first all-female hard rock band to have a serious impact on popular culture, and while woman-fronted rock bands are still as heavily stigmatized as ever, the Runaways kicked the door down and the bands who followed in their wake, from Hole to L7 to Veruca Salt, regularly cite them as a major influence even though none of these groups sound anything like the Runaways. Los Angeles promoter Kim Fowley (a man) formed the band and guided them through various incarnations, from a power trio featuring bassist Micki Steele (a woman, who went on to play in the Bangles, and whose contribution to the Runaways can be heard on the Joan Jett–less *Born to Be Bad* album, which was recorded when the band had been together for all of five days) to the final five-piece classic model.

Fowley was well known for his expertise in the fields of hype and gimmickry, and as a result, the Runaways' 1976 debut album was lambasted in the press as an opportunistic exploitation of minors in language suggesting that Fowley was profiting from white slavery or snuff films. There was, of course,

The Runaways favored spandex for live performances in 1977. Left to right: Vicki Blue, Joan Jett, and Lita Ford.

fall apart in the face of management problems, interpersonal tensions, artistic differences, power struggles, and so forth. In 1979, the Runaways disbanded. Afterward, Ford and Jett went on to become the solo artists we know and love today, and bassist Vicki Blue became a filmmaker. She made the very enlightening 2004 documentary *Edgeplay: A Film About the Runaways*. In 2010, *The Runaways*, a biographical account of the band based on Currie's book *Neon Angel*, was released, and it starred Dakota Fanning—Dakota Fanning!—as Cherie Currie. Joan Jett is portrayed by Kristen Stewart of the *Twilight* movies, which are about closet-case emo vampires.

Vicki Blue: bass (*Waitin' for the Night, And Now . . . the Runaways*); **Cherie Currie**: vocals; **Lita Ford**: guitar; **Jackie Fox**: bass (*The Runaways, Queens of Noise*); **Joan Jett**: guitar; **Laurie McCallister**: bass; **Micki Steele**: bass (*Born to Be Bad*); **Sandy West**: drums

Discography: *The Runaways* (Touchwood, 1976); *Waitin' for the Night* (Mercury, 1977); *Live in Japan* (Mercury, 1977); *Queens of Noise* (Touchwood, 1977); *Mama Weer All Crazee Now* (Rhino, 1978); *And Now . . . the Runaways* (Cherry Red, 1978); *Born to Be Bad* (Marilyn, 1993)

RUNNING WILD

YEARS ACTIVE: 1976–2009; 2011–PRESENT

When it comes to German power metal bands who dress like pirates, there can be little disagreement that Running Wild is hands down the finest example. Anyone who would attempt to dispute this truism doubtless has their own German power metal band in which the members dress like pirates, and is seeking, truculently, to defame their betters in the hopes of advancing their own career.

The musicians started their career in a fashion similar to their fellow countrymen and labelmates Grave Digger; both bands were signed to the nascent Noise Records and both used mildly satanic imagery. Based on their first two releases, *Gates to Purgatory* and *Branded*

ample evidence to support the argument that Fowley was simply manipulating the band members to line his pockets. Everyone in the group was, after all, still in the throes of adolescence, and there were in fact band members, who shall remain nameless, who could barely play their instruments. So it is completely understandable that it appeared to the outside observer that Fowley had pushed lead singer Cherie Currie onstage in lingerie and backed her up with a band whose musical credentials were dubious at best. But beneath the surface, the real explanation for this extreme criticism of the Runaways was a very simple, sexist one—they were a female hard rock band. It was easier for people to characterize the band as being the product of a nefarious male's manipulation of five fragile, impressionable young innocents as opposed to something the members were involved in of their own free will. There was also the issue

of the band members being "easy on the eyes," as they say, thereby violating a central tenet of 1970s rock culture: the music was supposed to be played by men for adoring, slavering young nubiles. The Runaways turned that dynamic around, much to the chagrin of many males. In other words, they made the sexually frustrated male rock press lash out, an act that betrayed their own male shame.

Radio stations wouldn't play the Runaways' music, and their stateside sales suffered mightily as a result. However, when the band toured Japan, it was a completely different story. "Cherry Bomb," the band's best-known single, had been a number one hit in the Land of the Rising Sun, and the Runaways were selling out arenas there. Unfortunately, they never replicated even a fraction of that success at home, and although they probably could have made decent careers by simply touring Asia and Europe, the band began to and Exiled, Running Wild gets a three or four on a scale of one to ten on the Lucif-o-meter. Furthering their metal chops, the band members opened for Mötley Crüe in 1986, and their careers seemed poised for a breakthrough. However, on the 1987 album *Under Jolly Roger*, their third release, they completely abandoned the notion of presenting themselves under the banner of any sort of commonly recognized metal aesthetic or any reasonable facsimile thereof. It was at this time that they began dressing like Long John Silver, for no reason that was ever given and with no party in the band's ranks ever taking responsibility for the decision. In any event, this actually ended up being exactly what brought the band to a larger audience, against all logic and reason. In over thirty years, Running Wild has never changed its style and only broke up once, only to hurriedly re-form two years later. The fact that the band members dress like pirates bars the need to conclude this entry on a humorous note.

Jens Becker: bass (*Under Jolly Roger* through *Blazon Stone*) (see also Grave Digger); **Stephan Boriss**: bass (*Gates to Purgatory*, *Branded and Exiled*); **Ian Finlay**: drums (*Port Royal* through *Bad to the Bone*); **Wolfgang "Hasche" Hagemann**: drums (*Gates to Purgatory*, *Branded and Exiled*); **Thilo Hermann**: guitars (*The Privateer* through *Victory*); **Rolf Kasparek**: vocals/guitars; **Matthias Liebetruth**: drums; **Jörg Michael**: drums (*Wild Animal* through *The Rivalry*) (see also Grave Digger); **Axel Morgan**: guitars (*Wild Animal* through *Pile of Skulls*); **Majk Moti**: guitars (*Branded and Exiled* through *Bad to the Bone*); **Peter Pichl**: bass (*The Brotherhood*); **Angelo Sasso**: drums (*Victory* and later); **Stefan Schwarzmann**: drums (*Under Jolly Roger* through *Pile of Skulls*); **Thomas Smuszynski**: bass (*Lead or Gold* through *Victory*); **Gerald Warnecke**: guitars (*Gates to Purgatory*)

Discography: *Gates to Purgatory* (Noise, 1984); *Branded and Exiled* (Noise, 1985); *Under Jolly Roger* (Noise, 1987); *Ready for Boarding* (Noise, 1988); *Port Royal* (Noise, 1988); *Death or Glory* (Noise, 1989); *Bad to the Bone* (Noise, 1989); *Wild Animal* (Noise, 1990); *Blazon Stone* (Noise, 1991); *Lead or Gold* (Noise, 1992); *Pile of Skulls* (Noise, 1992); *The Privateer* (Noise, 1994); *Black Hand Inn* (Noise, 1994); *Masquerade* (Noise, 1995); *The Rivalry* (GUN, 1998); *Victory* (GUN, 2000); *The Brotherhood* (GUN, 2002); *Rogues en Vogue* (GUN, 2005)

RUSH

YEARS ACTIVE: 1968–PRESENT

Metal qualifications notwithstanding, Rush has charted musical territory as fearlessly progressive as anything in the Yes or King Crimson catalogs. All three of Rush's members are world-class musicians who have been an inspiration to aspiring guitarists, bassists, drummers, keyboard players, glockenspiel players, crotales players, and Taurus pedal players the world over. While all that should be more than enough to distinguish them from their peers, the band members have also consistently displayed uncanny melodic sensibility and sharp songwriting skills, giving even their most dauntingly odd-metered and key-shifting compositions a basic appeal that has allowed for their popularity, even in Peoria. The sole fly in the ointment is the singing of bassist and keyboard player Geddy Lee, whose shrill, piercing voice has alienated as many people as it has won over. As they have consistently done for decades, Rush continues to pack in fans on its sold-out arena tours, and their albums still sell with the regularity of cigarettes, milk, toilet paper, and other staples. At the same time, the group continues to win the respect of both the musicians' community and the metal community. If they could do all of this while simultaneously juggling chainsaws, they would truly have all their bases covered.

The band began in 1968 in the suburbs of Toronto as a modest power trio. Lee and guitarist Alex Lifeson crafted Cream-inspired acid rock with drummer John Rutsey, and this lineup recorded Rush's self-titled debut. Although it was hopelessly overshadowed by their later albums, the debut was a straightforward hard rock classic in its own right, epitomized by songs like "Finding My Way" and, in particular, the very heavy showstopper "Working Man." However, a rift was already growing in the band even at this early stage. Lifeson and Lee were pushing hard in a more progressive direction, while Rutsey favored a more basic rock approach. With neither side budging, it was not long before the two camps parted company.

Neil Peart, or "the Professor" to his legion of admirers, replaced Rutsey and entered the Rush fray. Throughout Peart's career, he has been praised as a drummer's drummer, and it's easy to see why—the guy has chops to burn. Even the lay listener who has no knowledge or understanding of the complexities of playing an instrument can appreciate Peart's skills, to say nothing of the swarms of amateur drummers who cite him as a major influence. The drummer also brought to the band his lyric writing, a task that neither Lee nor Lifeson was particularly fond of, as the eighth-grade poetry contest–esque lyrics of the band's debut will bear out. Peart's writing, on the other hand, was brainy and highbrow and full of wordplay, focusing mainly on science fiction topics—his effect on the group cannot be overstated. His drumming and his lyrics are trademarks as identifiable with the band as Lee's unique voice. This is not to say that Peart's bandmates could even remotely be considered slouches; both the guitarist and the bassist are widely recognized as among the best in their particular fields, and they too have inspired countless musicians. It's simply that Peart's entrance made it possible for the band to realize their considerable collective potential. Rush began releasing monolithically progressive albums, such as *Fly by Night* and *Caress of Steel*, both of which included epic-length compositions that served as showcases for their instrumental prowess. Clearly, this was no longer the band that had released "In the Mood."

In 1976, Rush released *2112*, the group's most progressive effort yet. The album kicked off with the title track, which took up all of side one, a decision that many would have considered commercial suicide. Based on the work of Ayn Rand, the lyrics concerned a totalitarian society of the future that crushed the spirit and individuality of one of its inhabitants. It would have been a pretentious disaster in the hands of any other band; however, against all conventional wisdom, it struck a chord with listeners, and with this album the band graduated to the major leagues. Rush had put its progressive inclinations directly in the spotlight, which resulted in the band's greatest success. This unlikely turn of events provided a valuable lesson for up-and-coming musicians: crafting radio-friendly three-minute consumable units was not necessarily the one and only path to commercial success, and this lesson was not lost on bands like Dream Theater, Metallica, and Queensrÿche, to name but a very few.

Rush stuck to this approach for the remainder of the 1970s, during which time the band crafted such superlative progressive rock epics as "Xanadu," "Cygnus X-1," and "La Villa Strangiato." These multiple-movement compositions were all balanced out by shorter, more accessible, but no less challenging songs, such as "Closer to the Heart," "A Farewell to Kings," and "The Trees." However, as the years passed and the 1970s gave way to the 1980s, the band began to favor more prominent keyboard textures and began crafting shorter songs that eschewed the twenty-minute lengths of old, instead clocking in at a lean and economical nine minutes. Nevertheless, the material

remained as idiosyncratic and challenging as ever. Their 1980 album, *Permanent Waves*, had its share of lengthy material but also contained "The Spirit of Radio," their first major radio hit. Rush hit the proverbial jackpot in 1981 with *Moving Pictures*. The album contained what is surely the band's most famous single, "Tom Sawyer," with an opening beat that inspired twelve-year-olds everywhere to beg their parents for drum lessons. *Moving Pictures* also contained well-known songs like "Red Barchetta" and "Limelight" but continued to offer the band's technical chops, as showcased on the instrumental "YYZ." If anything, the band had proven that they could survive the always difficult transition from one decade to the next, not by copying the sounds of the new decade but rather by reimagining themselves in a leaner, tighter form.

Their next few albums followed the *Moving Pictures* formula, but as the 1980s reached its halfway point, some fans of Rush's earlier, heavier material began to feel as though the band was straying too far into synthesizer pop. Despite this criticism, the albums kept selling like crazy, even *Roll the Bones* in 1991, when many of the band's longtime faithful permanently abandoned them. It is interesting to note, however, that during Rush's slick pop years of the mid-1980s and early 1990s, while new wave was giving way to glam metal which in turn gave way to grunge, Rush managed to remain above the fray the whole time. The band had established themselves to the point where it didn't matter what the other trends were. In 1993 they released *Counterparts* and won back a considerable portion of the fan base they had lost when they released material that was a tad too polite for some. The album was not a full-fledged return to the band's past, but it was the first heavy, guitar-driven album Rush had made in more than a decade. They followed it up three years later, to similar effect, with *Test for Echo*. By this time, they had experienced

Rush feels that it's important to have more guitar necks on stage than band members. Left to right: Alex Lifeson, Neil Peart, and Geddy Lee.

a cultural renaissance of sorts, as then-current bands began to openly declare their extremely unhip love of the band, with King's X and Living Colour's Vernon Reid among those citing Rush as profoundly influential.

In the middle of this newfound acceptance, Peart was struck with unimaginable tragedy—twice, no less. Shortly after Rush concluded its *Test for Echo* tour in 1997, Peart's daughter was killed in a car accident. One year later, he lost his wife to cancer. The band quite understandably put everything on indefinite hold, and fans wondered if that was the end of Rush. This suspicion was exacerbated when Lee released a solo album, *My Favorite Headache*, in 2000.

The following year, however, the rumor mill began to circulate and the news was good—Rush was back in the studio, working on another album. In 2002, after a five-year hiatus, the band released its seventeenth studio album, *Vapor Trails*, to veritable mass hysteria. The album featured absolutely no keyboards whatsoever and was quite possibly the band's heaviest offering ever, to say nothing of its return to progressive structures and extreme chopsmanship, qualities for which the band was known and loved.

The band embarked on their 30th anniversary tour in 2004, and in 2007 they released *Snakes and Arrows*, their 18th studio album. In 2008 they made their first appearance on U.S. television in 30 years when they appeared on *The Colbert Report*, where they performed "Tom Sawyer." They were also asked by the host if they had ever written a song so long that by the end of it, they had influenced themselves. In 2011, the band surprised their fans when they announced that they were leaving their long-time major label Atlantic Records for the very

In this 1977 photograph, Rush's Alex Lifeson and Geddy Lee flawlessly execute a thirty-second note run in 11/8 time that modulates to the fourth degree of the scale during an eighteen-minute song with science fiction-based lyrics that feature clever wordplay ... in their bathrobes.

metal Roadrunner Records, home to Opeth, Killswitch Engage, and Megadeth. In retrospect, however, it should not have come as a surprise. Unlike many of their contemporaries, who just kind of hang around for decades churning out assembly-line crap, the members of Rush continue to push themselves to new places.

Geddy Lee: bass/vocals/keyboards; **Alex Lifeson**: guitars; **Neil Peart**: drums (*Fly by Night* and later); **John Rutsey**: drums (*Rush*)

Discography: *Rush* (Mercury, 1974); *Fly by Night* (Mercury, 1975); *Caress of Steel* (Mercury, 1975); *2112* (Mercury, 1976); *All the World's a Stage* (Mercury, 1976); *A Farewell to Kings* (Mercury, 1977); *Hemispheres* (Mercury, 1978); *Permanent Waves* (Mercury, 1980); *Moving Pictures* (Mercury, 1981); *Exit . . . Stage Left* (Mercury, 1981); *Signals* (Mercury, 1982); *Grace Under Pressure* (Mercury, 1984); *Power Windows* (Mercury, 1985); *Hold Your Fire* (Mercury, 1987); *A Show of Hands* (Mercury, 1989); *Presto* (Mercury, 1989); *Roll the Bones* (Atlantic, 1991); *Counterparts* (Atlantic, 1993); *Test for Echo* (Atlantic, 1996); *Different Stages* (Atlantic/Anthem, 1998); *Vapor Trails* (Atlantic, 2002); *Snakes & Arrows* (Atlantic, 2007).

SACRED REICH

YEARS ACTIVE: 1985–2000; 2007

Arizona's Sacred Reich was truly a victim of lousy timing. The band members seemed to have everything going for them—musicianship, intelligence, and a sense of humor, a scarce commodity in the thrash metal genre. However, their first album was not released until 1987, by which time the marketplace was flooded with every Metallica wannabe on the planet, making it difficult, if not hopeless, for any straightforward thrash band to gain recognition no matter how good they were (see Flotsam & Jetsam). Still, Sacred Reich certainly made a dent, gaining underground recognition for its thrash novelty song "Surf Nicaragua" and earning a loyal cult following that stuck with it through the years. The band broke up and re-formed many times during the 1990s, but they broke up in 2000 and re-formed to play some reunion shows in 2007.

Despite obvious talent, Sacred Reich suffered from bad timing.

Wiley Arnett: lead guitar; **Greg Hall**: drums (*Ignorance* through *A Question, Still Ignorant*); **Dave McClain**: drums (*Independent, Heal*); **Jason Rainey**: rhythm guitar; **Phil Rind**: bass/vocals

Discography: *Ignorance* (Metal Blade, 1987); *Surf Nicaragua* (Metal Blade, 1988); *Alive at the Dynamo* (Metal Blade, 1989); *The American Way* (Metal Blade, 1990); *Independent* (Metal Blade, 1992); *Heal* (Metal Blade, 1996); *Still Ignorant* (Metal Blade, 1997)

YEARS ACTIVE: 1988–2000

Miami's Saigon Kick formed in 1988, at the height of metal's commercial dominance. The original members were guitarist Jason Bieler, bassist Tom Defile, singer Matt Kramer, and drummer Phil Varone. Two years later, they had a record deal, courtesy of Atlantic Records affiliate Third Stone, and a self-titled debut that sold modestly. In 1991, they released *The Lizard*, which featured the hit single "Love Is on the Way." Its acoustic texture and vocal harmonies in no way constituted an effort to

Florida's very smoldering and nattily attired Saigon Kick.

replicate on the success of "More Than Words" by Extreme, really. No. Really.

Things began to go south during the recording of Saigon Kick's 1993 effort, *Water*. Kramer decided that he didn't like the band's direction, and he left the group, leaving Bieler to take one for the team and handle lead vocals. A nice gesture, but the album didn't sell, and the band was dropped by their label in 1994. Saigon Kick had officially joined the long list of bands who were signed by major labels looking for the next Guns n' Roses, and then dropped just as quickly when it didn't pan out.

Saigon Kick still had a following in Asia, which was a factor in the group's decision to stay together. They issued their fourth album, *Devil in the Details*, in 1995, mainly so they would have something to promote when they toured outside of the U.S.

The band attempted a reconciliation with Kramer in 1997. The reunited lineup recorded one song, "Dizzy's Vine," and played two shows, but then Bieler left. *Bastards* was released in 1999 in Asia only, and it would be the last album released under the Saigon Kick name.

Currently, the most well-known member of the band is most likely Varone. Apart from appearing on the VH1 reality show *Sex Rehab with Dr. Drew*, he entered into a partnership with California Exotic Novelties in 2011 to have a Phil Varone replica dildo manufactured. Nice work if you can get it.

Jason Bieler: guitar; **Tom Defile**: bass (*Saigon Kick* through *The Lizard*); **Pete Dembrowski**: guitar (*Devil in the Details* and later); **Matt Kramer**: vocals (*Saigon Kick* through *The Lizard*); **Chris McLernon**: bass (*Water* and later); **Ricky Sanders**: guitar (*Bastards*); **Phil Varone**: drums

Discography: *Saigon Kick* (Third Stone, 1990); *The Lizard* (Third Stone, 1992); *Water* (Atlantic, 1993); *Devil in the Details* (CMC International, 1995); *Bastards* (Pony Canyon Records, 1999)

SAINT VITUS

YEARS ACTIVE: 1978–1996; 2003–PRESENT

When it comes to doom bands whose influence on the movement has been criminally underacknowledged, Saint Vitus is almost without rival. Unlike Pentagram, which got its start in the early 1970s and therefore counted Black Sabbath and Blue Cheer among its contemporaries, Saint Vitus emerged a full decade later, counting among its contemporaries such nonpurveyors of monolithic doom as the Go-Go's and Fun Boy Three. Saint Vitus emerged from the Los Angeles hardcore scene, no less, where their stunted plodding and longhaired biker image could not have been any less welcome. Named after the Black Sabbath song "Saint Vitus' Dance" and, to a lesser degree, a medieval saint, the band was formed in 1979 and was signed to the SST label by Black Flag guitarist Greg Ginn. The label's roster included such bands as Hüsker Dü and the Minutemen, whose styles were far different from Saint Vitus. In short,

Saint Vitus was the odd man out, to say the very least, and the sales—or lack thereof—of its 1984 self-titled debut reflected this sorry fact.

In 1986, original vocalist Scott Reagers left Saint Vitus and was replaced by former Obsessed front man Scott "Wino" Weinrich. With Weinrich in place, the band produced *Born Too Late*, which fans generally consider to be Saint Vitus' finest work. Perhaps as a vain attempt to fit in with their labelmates, they followed the album up in 1987 with the *Thirsty and Miserable* EP, whose title track was a cover of a Black Flag song. The album did not expand their audience numbers, and attendees at concerts by more successful SST bands were never particularly happy to see Saint Vitus as the opening act. When they performed, the band members were regularly subjected to either outright hostility or, on a good night, plain old indifference, and after 1988's *Mournful Cries*, they parted ways with SST, signing to the more doom-friendly Hellhound label the following year. The band released *V* that year and *Live* in 1990, but despite the best efforts of both themselves and their label, Saint Vitus was absolutely, terminally, pathologically incapable of finding an audience. Weinrich quit the band at this point to move back to Washington, D.C. and re-form the Obsessed, and when Saint Vitus' next move was the release of *Heavier Than Thou*, a best-of compilation, it seemed as though they had, quite understandably, closed up shop once and for all. However, the band reemerged in 1992 with a new singer, Christian Lindersson, and a new album, *C.O.D.*, produced by Don Dokken. The album was saddled with production values so hopelessly wretched that it was rendered nearly unlistenable, making the band's previous albums, which were not exactly of high quality, seem downright overproduced by comparison. In 1995, Saint Vitus reunited with original vocalist Scott Reagers and issued one more album for Hellhound, *Die Healing*. They broke up soon after, having gained no more notoriety or respect than they'd had when they started.

The *Born Too Late* lineup reunited in 2003 and toured Europe in 2009, but drummer Armando Acosta left the band before all the

Saint Vitus guitarist Dave Chandler shows off his charming smile.

dates were completed. He died on Thanksgiving Day, 2010, from undisclosed causes. The band's first album in 17 years, *Lillie: F-65*, is scheduled for a 2012 release.

Armando Acosta: drums; Mark Adams: bass; Dave Chandler: guitars; Christian Lindersson: vocals (*C.O.D.*) (see also Terra Firma); Scott Reagers: vocals (*Saint Vitus* through *The Walking Dead*, *Die Healing*); Scott "Wino" Weinrich: vocals (*Born Too Late* through *Live*, *Die Healing*) (see also the Obsessed, Spirit Caravan)

Discography: *Saint Vitus* (SST, 1984); *Hallow's Victim* (SST, 1985); *Born Too Late* (SST, 1986); *Mournful Cries* (SST, 1988); *V* (Hellhound, 1989); *Live* (Hellhound, 1990); *Heavier Than Thou* (SST, 1991); *C.O.D.* (Hellhound, 1992); *Die Healing* (Hellhound, 1995)

YEARS ACTIVE: 1977–2002

The history of Samson, a band that was part of the New Wave of British Heavy Metal, is basically split into two sections: the one with Iron Maiden singer Bruce Dickinson and the one without him. Originally going by the he-manly and très beefcakey stage name of "Bruce Bruce," the singer joined forces with the band after their first album, 1979's *Survivors*. The lineup on this album consisted of guitarist Paul Samson, who also handled vocal duties; bassist Chris Aylmer; and drummer Barry "Thunderstick" Graham, who performed in a leather mask and was kept caged, if their music videos are a reliable representation of their concerts. Samson's first album with Dickinson, *Head On*, is generally regarded as the band's high-water mark, with all of the members playing at both their individual and collective peaks. The album caught the attention of many metal fans upon its 1980 release, not the

least of who were the members of Iron Maiden, who used them as an opening act on numerous occasions. Ultimately, this relationship resulted in Maiden poaching Dickinson after that group's original vocalist, Paul Di'Anno, was excused from microphonic duties. Dickinson's departure in 1982 precipitated Thunderstick's escape from his cage and exit from the band, an act that one assumes was committed on all fours while emitting feral grunts that signaled an insatiable hunger for live human flesh. Aylmer was the next one out the door, and Paul Samson, now the only original member, drafted a new lineup in 1990 and changed the band's sound to a bluesier and more straightforward one than that which had won them their admirers. The band reunited in 1999 for some live shows, since apparently Thunderstick had been successfully located deep inside his jungle habitat and tranquilized for uneventful shipping back to England. Sadly, in 2002, the group was dealt a crippling blow when Paul Samson passed away from cancer. Bassist Chris Aylmer succumbed to the disease in 2007.

Chris Aylmer: bass (*Head On* through *Don't Get Mad Get Even*, *Samson*); Bruce "Bruce Bruce" Dickinson: vocals (*Head On*, *Shock Tactics*) (see also Iron Maiden); Mervyn Goldsworthy: bass (*Thank You* and *Goodnight*, *Refugee*) (see also Diamond Head); Barry "Thunderstick" Graham: drums (*Survivors*, *Shock Tactics*); Pete Jupp: drums (*Before the Storm*, *Don't Get Mad Get Even*; *Thank You and Goodnight* through *Samson*); John McCoy: bass (*Survivors*); Nicky Moore: vocals (*Before the Storm* through *Refugee*); Paul Samson: guitars/vocals

Discography: *Survivors* (Thunderbolt, 1979); *Head On* (RCA, 1980); *Shock Tactics* (RCA, 1981); *Before the Storm* (Polydor, 1982); *Don't Get Mad Get Even* (Polydor, 1984); *Mr. Rock'n'Roll* (Thunderbolt, 1984); *Thank You and Goodnight* (Polydor, 1985); *Head Tactics* (Capitol, 1986); *Refugee* (Maze/Kraze, 1990); *Live at Reading '81* (Grand Slamm, 1991); *Samson* (Progressive, 1993); *Joint Forces* (Magnum America, 1996); *Live in London* (Zoom, 2001)

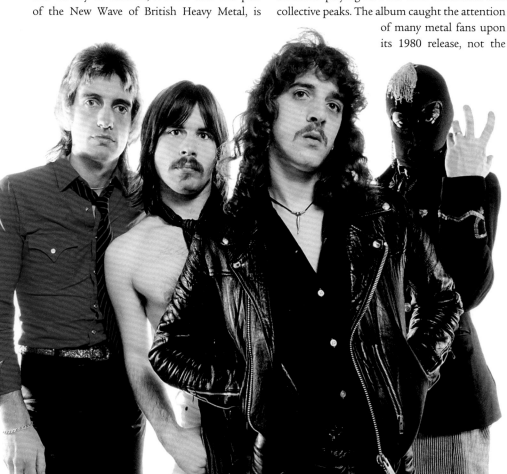

LEFT: Before Bruce Dickinson left for Iron Maiden, he was the front man for Samson. Left to right: Chris Aylmer, Bruce "Bruce Bruce" Dickinson, Paul Samson, and Barry "Thundersticks" Graham.

JOE SATRIANI

YEARS ACTIVE: 1978–PRESENT

To say that Joe Satriani is one of the most gifted rock guitarists in the world is to sell him short. His teaching credentials alone should be more than enough to distinguish him, as his students have included such highly respected six-string luminaries as Metallica's Kirk Hammett, Primus' Larry LaLonde, and, perhaps most impressive, virtuoso guitarist Steve Vai. Anyone who can truthfully claim, as Satriani can, that he taught Steve Vai everything he knows cannot be considered a slouch, to say the very least. Aside from his impressive teaching résumé, however, he is also an accomplished solo artist, has collaborated with a wide variety of musicians, and has cultivated an endless catalog of session jobs over the years.

As a guitar prodigy, Joe Satriani has no problems playing with his eyes closed.

Originally a drummer, Satriani began playing the guitar as a teenager in Long Island, New York, and by the time he had left his adolescence behind him in the early 1980s he was in Berkeley, California, doing session work. He issued his own self-financed and self-released EP in 1984, and although it didn't do much for his career, there were other, more influential forces at work in the universe, forces that proved indispensable to the achievement of his celebrity. In 1986, after David Lee Roth's less than amicable split with Van Halen, the singer formed his own band featuring on guitar none other than Satriani student Vai, who offered his highest praise to his former instructor in every major guitarists' magazine on the planet. That Satriani's major-label debut, *Not of This Earth*, was released almost simultaneously didn't exactly hurt, and the album sold well in the musicians' community, where Satriani quickly gained a reputation as a guitar player's guitar player. His 1987 album, *Surfing with the Alien*, went gold, an unusual accomplishment for an album as instrumentally focused as this one.

In the 1990s, as the musician continued to release albums, the Ibanez corporation released the JS Joe Satriani line of guitars, a dream that most guitarists would love to see fulfilled. Satriani was also hired by a terminally troubled Deep Purple to fill in for Ritchie Blackmore on that band's 1994 tour, after Blackmore left the group because of his chronic personal differences with singer Ian Gillan. Satriani was offered the spot on a permanent basis, but he turned it down in order to return to his very successful solo career. Since then, he has formed the touring unit G3, a tech-head guitarist's ultimate dream band, which features Satriani, Vai, and Eric Johnson, another player of virtuoso proportions. In 2008 he sued Coldplay for copyright infringement when he alleged that their song "Viva la Vida" cribbed whole sections of his 2004 song "If I Could Fly." In 2009 he joined Chickenfoot, the band consisting of Red Hot Chili Peppers drummer Chad Smith and former Van Halen members Sammy Hagar and Michael Anthony.

Discography: *Not of This Earth* (Epic, 1986); *Surfing with the Alien* (Epic, 1987); *Flying in a Blue Dream* (Epic, 1989); *The Extremist* (Epic, 1992); *Time Machine* (Sony, 1993); *Joe Satriani* (Relativity, 1995); *G3: Live in Concert* (Sony, 1997); *Crystal Planet* (Epic, 1998); *Engines of Creation* (Epic, 2000); *Live in San Francisco* (Sony, 2001); *Strange Beautiful Music* (Epic, 2002); *Is There Love in Space?* (Epic, 2004); *Super Colossal* (Epic, 2006); *Satriani Live!* (Red Ink, 2006); *Professor Satchafunkilus and the Musterion of Rock* (Epic, 2008); *Live in Paris: I Just Wanna Rock* (Sony, 2010); *Black Swans and Wormhole Wizards* (Epic, 2010).

SAVATAGE

YEARS ACTIVE: 1978–2002

The members of Florida's Savatage have a history spanning over twenty years, during which time they've crafted superlative heavy metal that has

In the 1980s, Savatage yell and grimace on stage as well as off. Left to right: Steve Wachholz, Criss Oliva, Jon Oliva, and Johnny Lee Middleton.

to do anything further. Oliva and Pitrelli are both members of Trans-Siberian Orchestra, a symphonic power metal ensemble that comes together every Christmas to combine the worst aspects of Cirque de Soleil and John Tesh, and who have sold more copies of their first album than Savatage sold in their entire career.

Chris Caffery: guitars (*Dead Winter Dead* and later); **Keith Collins**: bass (*Sirens* through *Power of the Night*); **Johnny Lee Middleton**: bass (*Fight for the Rock* and later); **Criss Oliva**: guitars (*Sirens* through *Edge of Thorns*); **Jon Oliva**: keyboards/vocals (*Sirens* through *Edge of Thorns*; *Dead Winter Dead* and later); **Al Pitrelli**: guitars (*Dead Winter Dead* and later) (see also Megadeth); **Jeff Plate**: drums (*Dead Winter Dead* and later); **Alex Skolnick**: guitars (*Handful of Rain*) (see also Testament); **Zachary Stevens**: vocals (*Handful of Rain* through *The Wake of Magellan*); **Steve Wachholz**: drums (*Sirens* through *Handful of Rain*)

Discography: *Sirens* (Par, 1983); *Power of the Night* (Atlantic, 1985); *Fight for the Rock* (Atlantic, 1986); *Hall of the Mountain King* (Atlantic, 1987); *Gutter Ballet* (Atlantic, 1989); *Streets: A Rock Opera* (Atlantic, 1991); *Edge of Thorns* (Atlantic, 1993); *Handful of Rain* (Atlantic, 1994); *Dead Winter Dead* (Atlantic, 1995); *Final Bell/Ghost in the Ruins* (SPV, 1995); *From the Gutter to the Stage* (Atlantic, 1996); *The Wake of Magellan* (Atlantic, 1997); *Poets and Madmen* (Nuclear Blast, 2001)

YEARS ACTIVE: 1976–PRESENT

satisfied their loyal following. Originally called Avatar, the band was founded by brothers Jon Oliva, on vocals and keyboards, and Criss Oliva, on guitar. After a name change in 1983, they released their first album, *Sirens*, a power metal classic that drew heavily on the influence of bands like Iron Maiden and Judas Priest and didn't fail to deliver the goods, thanks to the highly accomplished musicianship of the Oliva brothers. However, the band truly broke through in 1989, when they added a second guitarist, Chris Caffery, to their lineup and released the *Gutter Ballet* album, which displayed the band members' flair for progressive structures and skill with melodic writing.

Sadly, Savatage was dealt a severe blow three years later when Criss Oliva was killed in a car accident. Despite the loss of a founding member, to say nothing of the fact that he was the lead singer's brother, the band chose to continue, drafting former Testament guitarist Alex Skolnick and vocalist Zachary Stevens, who stood in for a grieving Jon Oliva. This lineup was short-lived, however. Jon returned to the band for Savatage's 1995 offering, *Dead Winter Dead*, which also saw Al Pitrelli replace Skolnick, who had apparently been a major mismatch for the band. The band's last album was 2001's *Poets and Madmen*, and although the band has never officially broken up, they're unlikely

Along with Def Leppard and Iron Maiden, Saxon was at one time considered a band at the forefront of the New Wave of British Heavy Metal movement. Originally called Son of a Bitch, the band formed in 1977 and

experienced their share of difficulties in finding a deal. It was, after all, the middle of the punk revolution, and metal was almost as unhip as it would be in the 1990s. They finally won a deal with a French label, Carrere, which released their production-deficient self-titled debut. The anemic sound of the record didn't exactly help matters, but any negative effects it might have had were negligible, as the band made a name for itself based on its live performances, most notably opening for Motörhead on one

OPPOSITE: Heavy metal fashion plates, Saxon adds a visor to their exquisite wardrobe. Left to right: Paul Quinn, Graham Oliver, Biff Byford, Nigel Glockner, and Steve Dawson.

ABOVE: The members of Saxon appear to have borrowed some clothes from Huey Lewis and the News. Left to right: Graham Oliver, Biff Byford, Steve Dawson, Paul Quinn, and a dutiful bouncer yanking off an adoring fan.

of that group's many British tours. Saxon built upon this early buzz when they released their 1980 album *Wheels of Steel*, a fully fleshed-out effort that showcased the band in all their brash, confrontational glory and ultimately contributed to their status as giants of the New Wave of British Heavy Metal movement, a status they retained throughout the early 1980s. All of their albums until 1983's *Power and the Glory* were hungrily snatched up by rabid fans, who to this day consider those early releases to be the embodiment of the band's classic output.

Saxon's glory days came to an end in the middle of the decade, as the band tried to court stateside fan hysteria. Their first stab at fame came in 1985 with *Innocence Is No Excuse*, which possessed unprecedentedly slick produc-

tion values that proved to be more than fans of the band's rawer and more aggressive material could handle. Bassist and main songwriter Steve Dawson decided to cut his losses at this point and walked out the door, leaving the band to continue their quest for a commercial breakthrough in America without him. He was thus spared the band's feeble and much-loathed attempts at pop-metal, which were not popular with American audiences. In addition, Saxon succeeded in alienating their original European fan base, who had loved the band for their unpolished, blue-collar metal approach. Finally seeing the writing on the wall, in 1993 the band released *Forever Free*, an exhilarating, full-fledged return to their true metal roots. Saxon has wisely kept to this style for all of their subsequent releases.

There was a legal battle between founding members Steve Dawson and Graham Oliver, and the band's current incarnation, which includes Biff Byford and Paul Quinn. Dawson and Oliver formed their own band, which they had originally christened Son of a Bitch, a gesture that was perhaps meant to symbolize their new band's return to Saxon's pure metal roots. After a while, however, they realized they would get further using the Saxon name, and for a time there were actually two Saxons operating. The two sides reached a settlement, and as of 2000 the parties that had been sued go by the somewhat awkward name of Oliver/Dawson Saxon and still play regularly, while the other Saxon does the same. The other Saxon, known as Saxon, released the acclaimed album *The Inner Sanctum* in 2007 and *Call to Arms* in 2011.

Biff Byford: vocals; **Nibbs Carter**: bass (*Rock'n'Roll Gypsies*; *Lionheart*); **Steve Dawson**: bass (*Saxon* through *Innocence Is No Excuse*); **Nigel Durham**: drums (*Destiny*); **Pete Gill**: drums (*Saxon* through *Denim and Leather*) (see also Motörhead); **Nigel Glockler**: drums (*The Eagle Has Landed* through *Unleash the Beast*; *The Inner Sanctum* and later); **Paul Johnson**: bass (*Rock the Nations*, *Destiny*); **Jörg Michael**: drums (*Lionheart*); **Graham Oliver**: guitars (*Saxon* through *Dogs of War*); **Paul Quinn**: guitars; **Fritz Randow**: drums (*Metalhead*); **Doug Scarratt**: guitars (*The Eagle Has Landed II* and later); **Matthias Ulmer**: keyboards (*Into the Labyrinth*)

Discography: *Saxon* (Carrere, 1979); *Wheels of Steel* (Carrere, 1980); *Strong Arm of the Law* (Carrere, 1980); *Denim and Leather* (Carrere, 1981); *The Eagle Has Landed* (Carrere, 1982); *Power and the Glory* (Carrere, 1983); *Crusader* (Carrere, 1984); *Innocence Is No Excuse* (EMI, 1985); *Rock the Nations* (Capitol, 1986); *Destiny* (Enigma, 1988); *Rock'n'Roll Gypsies* (Enigma, 1990); *Solid Ball of Rock* (Charisma, 1991); *Greatest Hits Live!* (Grand Slamm, 1991); *Forever Free* (Mayhem, 1993); *The Best of Saxon* (Griffin, 1994); *Dogs of War* (Mayhem, 1995); *The Eagle Has Landed II* (CBH, 1996); *Unleash the Beast* (Virgin, 1997); *Metalhead* (Steamhammer, 1999); *Killing Ground* (Steamhammer, 2001); *Lionheart*

(SPV/Steamhammer, 2004); *The Inner Sanctum* (SPV/Steamhammer, 2007); *Into the Labyrinth* (SPV/Steamhammer, 2009); *Call to Arms* (EMI, 2011)

THE SCORPIONS

YEARS ACTIVE: 1965–PRESENT

While the German band the Scorpions unquestionably became the worldwide megastars that they did as the result of their 1980s hits, such as "No One Like You" and their signature song, "Rock You Like a Hurricane," they actually have some highly impressive pure metal albums to their credit that, sadly, their more commercial work has hopelessly overshadowed. The difference, for the most part, lies in whether or not guitarist extraordinaire Ulrich Roth has been a part of the lineup. With the exception of their debut, *Lonesome Crow* (which flirts with psychedelia and at times resembles classic Jethro Tull), the band's first few albums feature Roth's Hendrix-inspired guitar playing, which is so impressive and powerful that it almost completely casts the rest of the band off to the side, Klaus Meine's splendid, smoky vocals notwithstanding. The lineup with Roth produced five of the band's six RCA albums, *Fly to the Rainbow*, *In Trance*, *Virgin Killer*, *Taken by Force*, and the live album *Tokyo Tapes*, which served as a fine document of Roth's final tour with the band. The child pornography on *Virgin Killer*'s cover aside, these albums serve as a severe shock to anyone who is familiar only with the band's later work. This shock is mainly due to the fact that many Americans are simply not aware that these albums exist even though they were popular in Europe and Japan at the time of their releases. In any event, the albums are all classic slices of 1970s guitar-dominated metal that are truly worth seeking out for even the most casual metal fans, with *In Trance* and *Virgin Killer* being the two strongest.

Roth left the band in 1977 and was replaced by Michael Schenker, who had been the lead guitarist on *Lonesome Crow*. Schenker had originally left the Scorpions to join U.F.O., but he was kicked out for reasons pertaining to that old standby, substance abuse. Schenker cut *Lovedrive* with his new/old band in 1979, and the album was the first in a long string of successful releases for the Scorpions' new label, Polydor Records. Unfortunately, Schenker's problems with alcoholic refreshments had not abated any, and he regularly missed tour dates, forcing the band to bring in Matthias Jabs to replace Schenker on nights when he was face-down in his own vomit somewhere in a Hanover back alley. At the tour's end, Schenker was shown the door and Jabs took over guitar duty full-time. This lineup released *Animal Magnetism* in 1980, the band's first album to make a significant dent in the American mar-

Assuming that the members of the Scorpions, in 1989, color coordinated their outfits for a Valentine's Day performance, they did a swell job. Left to right: Francis Buchholz, Rudolf Schenker, Matthias Jabs, and Klaus Meine.

ketplace. They followed it up in 1982 with *Blackout*, an album whose sales were bolstered thanks to the then-new medium of MTV. The band had a video for the single "No One Like You," which earned heavy rotation simply on the basis of being one of the few videos available to the network during its infancy. The

video pushed the album to platinum status, making the band as successful as they had hoped to be in the United States. Then their 1984 album, *Love at First Sting*, pushed them to arena-headliner status, propelled by the single "Rock You Like a Hurricane" and its outrageous video, which featured partially

nude women with a rabid sexual proclivity for balding German forty-year-olds. For the rest of the decade, the Scorpions remained a popular attraction all over the world, and in 1990 the group released *Crazy World*, which, on the strength of its single, "Wind of Change," became their best-selling album. That was

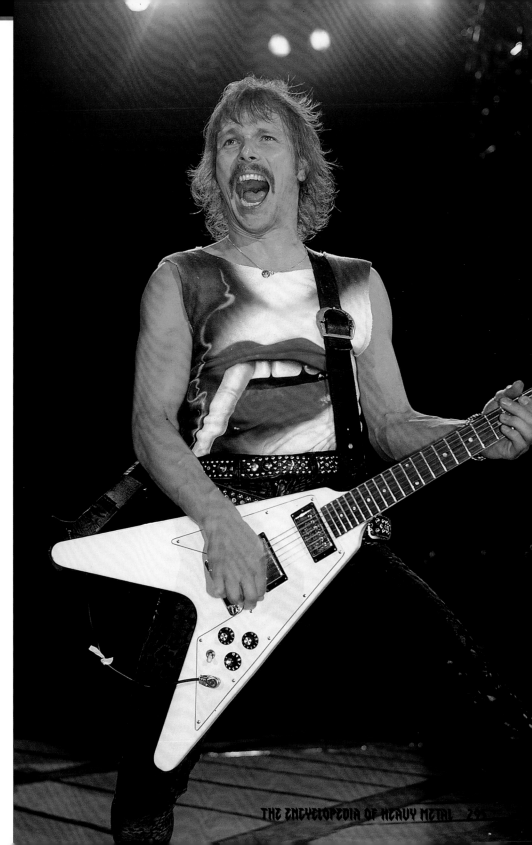

pretty much the end of the ride, though.

Although they always sold records well enough to keep them in Wiener schnitzels, they never again achieved that level of success. After a failed bid at electronica on the atrocious 1999 album *Eye II Eye*, the band recorded with the Berlin Philharmonic Orchestra in 2000 for *Moment of Glory*, which, sadly, did not lay to rest the long-burning question of what an orchestral arrangement of "Another Piece of Meat" would sound like. This was followed in 2001 with the *Acoustica* album, which saw the band playing their numerous light rock anthems in an "unplugged" setting, and even breaking it down for a moving rendition of Kansas' "Dust in the Wind." How wonderful it would be if this was not true. In 2003, the Scorpions plugged their instruments back in and toured North America with Whitesnake and Dokken. After 2004's *Unbreakable* and 2007's *Humanity: Hour I*, the band announced that their next album, 2010's *Sting in the Tail*, would be their last. However, this turned out to be a dirty, dirty lie, and they released *Comeblack* in 2011.

Francis Buchholz: bass (*Fly to the Rainbow* through *Crazy World*); **Curt Cress**: drums (*Pure Instinct*); **Wolfgang Dziony**: drums (*Lonesome Crow*); **Lothar Heinburg**: bass (*Lonesome Crow*); **Matthias Jabs**: guitars (*Lovedrive* and later); **James Kottak**: drums (*Eye II Eye*; *Unbreakable*); **Rudy Lenners**: drums (*In Trance*, *Virgin Killer*); **Pawel Maciwoda**: bass (*Unbreakable* and later); **Klaus Meine**: vocals; **Herman Rarebell**: drums (*Taken by Force* through *Live Bites*); **Ralph Rieckermann**: bass (*Face the Heat* through *Acoustica*); **Jürgen Rosenthal**: drums (*Fly to the Rainbow*); **Uli Jon Roth**: guitars (*Fly to the Rainbow* through *Tokyo Tapes*); **Michael Schenker**: guitars (*Lonesome Crow*, *Lovedrive*) (see also U.F.O.); **Rudolf Schenker**: guitars

OPPOSITE: Lacking a sixth member to complete their pyramid, the members of the Scorpions offer up Rudolf Schenker's guitar. Left to right: Francis Buchholz, Matthias Jabs, Rudolf Schenker, Klaus Meine, and Herman Rarebell.

RIGHT: Rudolf Schenker bolsters his reputation as a cheesy doofus in this highly attractive photograph.

Discography:
Lonesome Crow (RCA, 1972); *Fly to the Rainbow* (RCA, 1974); *In Trance* (RCA, 1975); *Virgin Killer* (RCA, 1976); *Taken by Force* (RCA, 1977); *Tokyo Tapes* (RCA, 1978); *Lovedrive* (Polydor, 1979); *Animal Magnetism* (Polydor, 1980); *Blackout* (Polydor, 1982); *Love at First Sting* (Polydor, 1984); *World Wide Live* (Polydor, 1985); *Savage Amusement* (Polydor, 1988); *Crazy World* (Polydor, 1990); *Face the Heat* (Polydor, 1993); *Live Bites* (Polydor, 1995); *Pure Instinct* (Atlantic, 1996); *Eye II Eye* (Atlantic, 1999); *Moment of Glory* (Atlantic, 2000); *Acoustica* (EastWest, 2001); *Unbreakable* (BMG, 2004); *Humanity: Hour 1* (BMG, 2007); *Sting in the Tail* (Sony, 2010); *Comeblack* (Sony, 2011); *Live 2011: Get Your Sting & Blackout* (Sony, 2011)

Ten years after the Scorpions first formed, they still look as youthful as ever in this 1982 photograph.

GERMANY

Germany has always been a friendly market for heavy metal bands, regardless of what kind of trends happen to be going on in popular music elsewhere in the world. For American metal bands who found themselves suddenly without an audience when grunge and alternative rock exploded, the German market was there to ensure that a lot of these guys held onto their careers. One need look no further for proof than the annual Wacken Open Air festival, which hosts every kind of heavy metal band imaginable and has been going strong for over twenty years. During the lean years of the 1990s, only Wacken offered prominent slots to such bands as Fates Warning, Solitude Aeturnus, and Overkill, none of whom could even get arrested much less a booking back home in the States.

German heavy metal is mostly synonymous with power metal, and with the popularity of bands like Helloween and Blind Guardian that seems unlikely to change anytime soon. But don't despair, Germany has had plenty of other types of metal bands as well, including death metal bands like Necrophagist and Morgoth, thrash bands like Nocturnal, and black metal bands like Moonblood. Germany is also home to the mighty Tankard, a speed metal band dating back to the 1980s which has sung almost exclusively about beer. You could do worse.

Heavy metal is in Germany's DNA, and although they haven't always gotten credit for it, its *volk* was making its own contributions to the music when it was still a nascent movement. The list of bands which were playing proto-metal in Germany in the early 1970s is very long, and sadly most of these bands never escaped obscurity. These blips on the metal radar include Lucifer's Friend, whose 1970 debut LP is the best album Rainbow never made, and Blackwater Park, which made enough of a mark with their sole album to have their name used as the title of an Opeth album. Special mention has to go to the Second Battle label, which has been reissuing the extremely hard to find music of such early German proto-metal bands as Weed, Birth Control, Night Sun, Wind, and Virus, among many others. Without them, a lot of this music might have been lost forever. Rock on, Deutchsland.

SEPULTURA

YEARS ACTIVE: 1984–PRESENT

Aside from being the most popular heavy metal band ever to hail from South America, Sepultura is one of the most popular death metal bands in the world. Their brutally aggressive style won them an international audience that even accepted them through times of musical experimentation—an unpopular move in the death metal fan community. While it is difficult enough for any band in this genre to achieve even modest mainstream commercial acceptance, Sepultura's case is all the more remarkable when one takes into account the considerable obstacles the band had to overcome simply to gain even the slightest shred of recognition. The band was formed in Belo Horizonte in 1985 just as their Brazilian homeland was emerging from the grip of a long-standing totalitarian regime that had isolated the country from the rest of the world. This isolation made it difficult for the country's newly freed citizens to procure basic goods, to say nothing of CDs. So it was truly no small feat for singer and guitarist Max Cavalera and his drummer brother, Igor, to locate heavy metal albums, which in almost all cases were expensive imports that were extremely difficult to come by. But through the dogged persistence that is characteristic of metal fans, the Cavaleras were able to track down albums that influenced them greatly, in particular those of Celtic Frost, Metallica, and Slayer. Just like others who had been moved by these bands, the Cavaleras decided to try their hand at this music themselves and drafted a second guitarist and bassist to fill their ranks.

In 1985, they coughed up the dough themselves to record the extremely raw *Bestial Devastation* album, which was released through the small Brazilian label Cogumelo. The label's legwork helped the band gain some attention

Cleveland, Ohio's own Derrick Green smiles gleefully at his good fortune at becoming Sepultura's new singer.

SEPULTURA

Hell, Purgatory, Paradise... and back! Brazilian thrash masters **SEPULTURA** return with the epic new album, **DANTE XXI**, featuring the single 'Convicted In Life'

"Now Sepultura have ascended the mountain."
— Ian Christe, Metal Maniacs

in local metal circles, which was capitalized upon with Sepultura's *Morbid Visions* album. Realizing that they needed to move to larger and more urbane environs if they wanted to get anywhere, they moved to São Paulo, Brazil's largest city. In addition to putting Sepultura in a better position geographically, the move also provided the group with lead guitarist Andreas Kisser, a technically accomplished musician whose fearsome chops beat the rest of the band into shape in a fashion that was as humiliating as it was quick. They now possessed the musical ability to match their creative vision, and their 1987 release, *Schizophrenia*, was light years ahead of anything in their canon up to that point. It garnered the attention of Roadrunner Records, which was able to distribute the album to a considerably wider audience. Now signed to a label with worldwide distribution, Sepultura recorded *Beneath the Remains*, the album that truly transformed the band into an international phenomenon.

The next few albums saw the band both cement and build upon their reputation as a first-class death metal force of nature. The 1991 release *Arise* achieved platinum status, necessitating Roadrunner's brokerage of a deal with Epic Records to handle the massive distribution demands for the band's next album. It was a smart move, considering that 1993's *Chaos A.D.* ended up selling even more copies than its predecessor, and in more corners of the earth than ever before. But while the bruising, uncompromising album was an artistic success in its own

Sepultura pose for one last photograph in 1989 before front man Max Cavalera leaves the band. Left to right: Max Cavalera, Paulo Jr., Igor Cavalera, and Andreas Kisser.

right, nothing could have prepared anyone for what the band was going to do next. In 1996, they released *Roots*, whose down-tuned death metal aggression was tempered by the incorporation of Brazilian musical and percussion instruments, an idea that, it is safe to assume, nobody had ever considered before. The sheer nerve it took to pull this off instantly put Sepultura in death metal's highest ranks, and it seemed a foregone conclusion that the band was poised to achieve the most dizzying heights imaginable.

But just at this time, Max Cavalera's wife, Gloria, who also managed the band, was struck by tragedy when her son (from a previous marriage) was killed in a car accident. Max and his wife immediately flew home, a complicated situation since this occurred when the band was literally minutes from taking the stage at England's Monsters of Rock Festival. The rest of the band played anyway, performing as a trio. Perhaps concerned that a grieving manager is an unreliable one, Sepultura soon after told Max that they felt it prudent to dump his wife and hire new management. Max understandably hit the roof upon hearing this and immediately quit the band, a move that most people believed spelled the end of Sepultura—Max had been the band's front man and main songwriter, after all. The 1997 release of *Blood-Rooted*, a compilation album, seemed to indicate that the band was, indeed, cleaning out the closet and getting ready to pack it in. To the surprise of many, however, the band replaced him with Cleveland-born vocalist Derrick Greene, with whom they released *Against*. The album sold well enough, although it certainly was not the commercial hit that most people had expected after the success of *Roots*. By comparison, Soulfly, the band that Max Cavalera formed after leaving Sepultura, sold twice as many copies of their debut as his old band had sold of their current album. The moral of the story: if you're in a band, your front man is married to your manager, and her son dies, keep your damn mouth shut about finding new management. In 2007, Igor Cavalera left the group to reunite with his brother Max in a

Lajon Witherspoon does some sensitive crooning for Sevendust.

new band, Cavalera Conspiracy. The now 100% Cavalera-free band released *A-Lex* in 2009. Even though bassist Paulo, Jr. was now the only original member left in the band, you wouldn't have known it from the many very positive reviews the album received. The band's last album was 2011's *Kairos*.

Igor Cavalera: drums (*Bestial Devastation* through *Dante XXI*); **Max Cavalera**: guitars/vocals (*Bestial Devastation* through *Roots*); **Jean Dolabella**: drums (*A-Lex* and later); **Derrick Green**: vocals (*Against* and later); **Andreas Kisser**: guitars (*Schizophrenia* and later); **Paulo Jr.**: bass; **Jairo T.**: guitars (*Bestial Devastation*, *Morbid Visions*)

Discography: *Bestial Devastation* (Cogumelo, 1985); *Morbid Visions* (Cogumelo, 1986); *Schizophrenia* (Roadrunner, 1987); *Beneath the Remains* (Roadrunner, 1989); *Arise* (Roadrunner, 1991); *Chaos A.D.* (Roadrunner, 1993); *Roots* (Roadrunner, 1996); *Against* (Roadrunner, 1998); *Nation* (Roadrunner, 2001); *Under a Pale Grey Sky* (Roadrunner, 2002); *Roorback* (SPV/Steamhammer, 2003); *Dante XXI* (Steamhammer, 2006); *A-Lex* (Steamhammer, 2009); *Kairos* (Nuclear Blast, 2011)

YEARS ACTIVE: 1994–PRESENT

If 1990s metal can be said to have its own sound, a good case can be made that Sevendust was among its primary practitioners. Aggressive, down-tuned, groove-oriented, and soulful, the group included guitarist John Connolly, bassist

Vince Hornsby, guitarist Clint Lowery, and drummer Morgan Rose. There was also singer Lajon Witherspoon. His above-average delivery set the band apart from those who trafficked in similar sounds with a fraction of the talent (cough, cough—Creed—cough, cough).

Sevendust began life as Crawlspace, and got their song "My Ruin" onto the compilation album *Mortal Kombat: More Kombat*, one of those deals where it's an album "inspired by" a movie or video game without any material that actually appeared in either. Where most fledgling bands would view this as their ticket to superstardom and flog that baby into paste, the band made the odd move to change their name instead. Now recording as Sevendust, they released their self-titled debut in 1997. Next came *Home* in 1999, and it was with this album that they really arrived, playing high-profile tours and even appearing at the arson-a-riffic Woodstock '99 festival.

After 2001's *Animosity* and 2003's *Seasons*, Lowery left and was replaced by Sonny Mayo of the elegantly named band Snot. After two albums, Sevendust announced that they would be shitcanning Mayo and reinstating Lowery, which had to kind of suck for the Snot guy. As if that weren't bad enough, they then took the unforgiveable step of allowing *American Idol*'s Chris Daughtry to perform guest vocals on 2008's *Chapter VII: Hope and Sorrow*. Despite this wrongdoing, the band was permitted to release *Cold Day Memory* in 2010. Maybe William Hung can be on the next one?

John Connolly: guitar (*Sevendust*); **Vince Hornsby**: bass (*Sevendust*); **Clint Lowery**: guitar (*Sevendust* through *Seasons*; *Cold Day Memory*); **Sonny Mayo** (*Next*); **Morgan Rose**: drums (*Sevendust*); **Lajon Witherspoon**: vocals (*Sevendust*)

Discography: *Sevendust* (TVT, 1997); *Home* (TVT, 1999); *Animosity* (TVT, 2001); *Seasons* (TVT, 2003); *Next* (Winedark, 2005); *Alpha* (Asylum, 2007); *Chapter VII: Hope & Sorrow* (Asylum, 2008); *Cold Day Memory* (Asylum, 2010)

SIR LORD BALTIMORE

YEARS ACTIVE: 1968–1976; 2006–PRESENT

Sir Lord Baltimore occupies the seemingly endless list of unjustly overlooked proto-metal bands of the early 1970s. The Brooklyn, New York, band would probably never have won even the small shred of footnote space that has been thrown their way if not for the wondrous, heavenly lead vocals of drummer John Garner, whose gravel-throated singing was too good to be hidden behind a drum kit. As far as the band itself, Sir Lord Baltimore functioned as a strong unit, specializing in heavy rock with a predilection for progressive structures and the odd multichapter epic, such as the eleven-minute "Man from Manhattan." Sadly, the band never escaped from the obscurity to which the fates had restricted them, and they broke up after just two albums. However, Sir Lord Baltimore managed to remain a band of interest to both record collectors and fans alike, and their albums, which have been reissued on compact disc from time to time, are worth seeking out by fans of early 1970s hard rock and heavy metal. The band reunited in 2006 and self-released *Sir Lord Baltimore III Raw*, which contained songs originally written for a 1976 album that never happened. It was available through mail order only, via the band's official website.

Joey Dambra: guitar/vocals (*Sir Lord Baltimore*); **Louis Dambra**: guitar/vocals; **Tony Franklin**: bass (*Sir Lord Baltimore III*); **John Garner**: vocals/drums; **Gary Justin**: bass/vocals (*Kingdom Come* through *Sir Lord Baltimore*)

Discography: *Kingdom Come* (Mercury, 1970); *Sir Lord Baltimore* (Mercury, 1971); *Sir Lord Baltimore III Raw* (JG, 2006)

SIX FEET UNDER

YEARS ACTIVE: 1993-PRESENT

If there's one thing you can't accuse death metal bands of, it's of having too few side projects that sound similar to their main gigs. Six Feet Under formed as just such a proposition, although

Oopsy daisy! Chris Barnes of Six Feet Under accidentally hits his thumb with a hammer.

guest vocal appearances by Ice T on "One Bullet Left" and Karyn Crisis on "Sick and Twisted."

After 2003's *Bringer of Blood*, the group went back to the covers trough for 2004's *Graveyard Classics 2*. It is worthwhile noting where the previous outing had contained just one AC/DC song, "TNT," *Graveyard Classics 2* was literally a cover of AC/DC's entire *Back in Black* album. In sequence, no less.

Six Feet Under retained a mostly stable lineup throughout their existence, a remarkable accomplishment for a band in the famously turnover-happy genre of death metal. Sadly, this streak came to an end after their third covers album, *Graveyard Classics 3*, which was the last album to feature Butler and Gall. As of November 2011, the band had a new lineup in place, which included Rob Arnold and Matt Devries of Chimaira.

Chris Barnes: vocals; **Terry Butler**: bass; Greg Gall: drums; **Steven Swanson**: guitar (*Maximum Violence* and later); **Allen West**: guitar (*Haunted* through *Warpath*)

Discography: *Haunted* (Metal Blade, 1995); *Warpath* (Metal Blade, 1997); *Maximum Violence* (Metal Blade, 1999); *Graveyard Classics* (Metal Blade, 2000); *True Carnage* (Metal Blade, 2001); *Double Dead* (Metal Blade, 2002); *Bringer of Blood* (Metal Blade, 2003); *Graveyard Classics 2* (Metal Blade, 2004); *13* (Metal Blade, 2005); *Commandment* (Metal Blade, 2007); *Death Rituals* (Metal Blade, 2008); *Graveyard Classics 3* (Metal Blade, 2010)

they have generally avoided guitar solos and blast beats, preferring a more groove-oriented, riff-based sound instead.

Founded by the vocal pioneer of the Cookie Monster sound Chris Barnes of Cannibal Corpse and Obituary guitarist Allen West, the duo snapped up Death bassist Terry Butler and his drummer brother-in-law Greg Gall. This lineup issued the 1995 debut, *Haunted*, on Metal Blade. Barnes had been at odds with the other members of Cannibal Corpse, so when Six Feet Under took off, he left his old band and made Six Feet Under his regular, full-time gig.

After 1996's half-live stopgap EP *Alive and Dead*, they released their second full-length album, 1997's *Warpath*. West left the band at this point to rejoin Obituary and was replaced by Steve Swanson, who made his debut on 1999's *Maximum Violence*. Six Feet Under then took a break from writing their own material by releasing the covers album *Graveyard Classics* in 2000. Featuring interpretations of both metal classics like Black Sabbath's "Sweet Leaf" and less obvious fare, like "Stepping Stone" by Paul Revere and the Raiders, the group followed it up with 2001's *True Carnage*, which featured

Skid Row, pride of the Garden State.

YEARS ACTIVE: 1986–PRESENT

New Jersey's Skid Row arrived on the scene at the tail end of the glam metal movement. Although the band is probably best remembered for its controversial singer as well as for its power ballads, such as "18 and Life" and "I Remember You," its members displayed genuine talent and versatility. Regrettably, these qualities went largely untapped because of the simple fact of Skid Row's short shelf life. The group was founded in 1986 by bassist Rachel Bolan and guitarist Dave "the Snake" Sabo. They paid their dues by working the East Coast club circuit for three years before Sabo's old band mate Jon Bon Jovi arranged for the Atlantic label to sign the band in 1989. Their self-titled debut benefited greatly from the timing of its release, as power ballads were the order of the day, and Skid Row was sending theirs directly into heavy rotation wherever there was a broadcast media outlet to play them.

Marring Skid Row's success, however, was singer Sebastian Bach's Irritating Front Man Syndrome, which he regularly displayed in behavior that ranged from violent to just plain ignorant. At a concert appearance, Bach was nearly hit in the head by a bottle that an audience member had thrown, and the singer indiscriminately launched it back into the crowd, pelting an innocent female bystander. At around this time, Bach also became embroiled in a publicity discomfiture when he was photographed wearing a T-shirt bearing the words "AIDS: KILLS FAGS DEAD." The singer appeared at a press conference for the ostensible purpose of publicly apologizing for his insensitivity. But he simply made matters worse for himself by stammering through a monologue that was as pathetic as it was physically painful to hear, wherein he conceded that, as his grand-

Skid Row vocalist Sebastian Bach, whose "AIDS: KILLS FAGS DEAD" T-shirt was in no way a form of hetero-male overcompensation, honest.

mother had recently succumbed to cancer, he would have been upset had he spied someone wearing a T-shirt that said "CANCER: KILLS GRANDMAS DEAD." Apparently, this idiotic statement was the only hint of an apology anybody was going to get, and eventually attention turned away from his choice of outerwear to the weightier matters of the world.

In 1991, the band returned with a new album, *Slave to the Grind*, which was approximately fifty times heavier than their debut and served as a huge shock to both their fans and their detractors by receiving favorable reviews in the press. Unfortunately, the joys of having a platinum-selling album dissipated the following year when grunge broke and bands like Skid Row fell out of favor. The band decided to wait out the trend, tossing out the *B-Sides Ourselves* compilation to buy some time, but in 1995 they could apparently wait no longer, releasing *Subhuman Race* to sales figures that were actually better than expected, even though the days of the platinum-selling Skid Row album were unquestionably over. The band broke up soon after, and Bach briefly joined forces with former Smashing Pumpkins drummer Jimmy Chamberlain for the extremely short-lived band Last Hard Men. Skid Row opened for KISS in 2000, on what was supposed to be the latter band's farewell tour. They have since gone on to record two more albums, and in both cases sales and reviews were underwhelming. Meanwhile, Bach took the main role in the Broadway musical production of *Jekyll and Hyde*. At the end of his run, he handed it over into the capable German superstar hands of David Hasselhoff.

Rob Affuso: guitar (*Skid Row* through *Subhuman Race*) ; **Sebastian Bach**: vocals (*Skid Row* through *Subhuman Race*); **Rachel Bolan**: bass; **Dave Gara**: drums (*Revolutions Per Minute*); **Scotti Hill**: drums, guitar; **Dave "the Snake" Sabo**: guitar; **Johnny Solinger**: vocals (*Thickskin* and later); **Phil Varon**: drums (*Thickskin*)

Discography: *Skid Row* (Atlantic, 1989); *Slave to the Grind* (Atlantic, 1991); *B-Sides Ourselves* (Atlantic, 1992); *Subhuman Race* (Atlantic, 1995); *Forty Seasons: The Best of Skid Row* (Atlantic, 1998); *Thickskin* (Blind Man, 2003); *Revolutions Per Minute* (SPV, 2006)

Slade prepares to duel Quiet Riot for back royalties. Left to right: Don Powell, Jim Lea, Noddy Holder, and Dave Hill.

SLADE

Almost without exception, the very small number of Americans who have heard of the British glam band Slade are in possession of this awareness due to Quiet Riot's cover of their song "Cum On Feel the Noize." As we all know, the song gave Quiet Riot its breakthrough hit and made the members of that group heavy metal superstars for a brief period. Slade, however, had existed for almost fifteen years, issued countless albums, and had several Top 10 hits in its native land all a full decade before every home in the United States of America (and its territories, including Puerto Rico, Guam, and American Samoa) that possessed a teenager contained a copy of Quiet Riot's *Metal Health*. Slade's roots go back to the mid-1960s, when, for a few years, the band frequently changed their name, look, and style as they searched for an identity to settle on. At one point during this period, the group was managed by ex-Animals bassist Chas Chandler, who had also managed Jimi Hendrix early in his recording career. Chandler suggested Slade, the name that finally stuck. He also suggested that the band shave their heads and adopt a skinhead look, which they politely declined, instead choosing to grow out their hair and eschew Dr. Martens' reliable and sturdy footwear products for platform shoes with eight-inch heels. They dressed in the new glam style that their fellow countrymen Marc Bolan and David Bowie were sporting, and they also settled upon glam as a musical direction, pursuing a take on it that was less unicorn-centric than T. Rex and more upbeat than Bowie. One could use the term party anthem to describe their sound. As if to underscore the leisure activity–oriented nature of their music, the members of Slade were in the habit of misspelling their song titles, as evidenced by "Cum On Feel the Noize." Other examples include "Mama Weer All Crazee

Now," "Skweeze Me, Pleeze Me," and "Merry Xmas Everybody," which for several years after its initial release entered and reentered the British singles chart during the Christmas season.

Despite their popularity in the United Kingdom, they hardly made a dent in America, and eventually glam gave way to punk and Slade fell out of favor with the masses, although they still retained a sizable hardcore fan base and still appeared on the charts, albeit with less frequency than they had when they were in their prime. The band members finally received their stateside due in 1983 thanks to the Quiet Riot cover, which led to one of the band's 1984 releases, the curiously titled *Keep Your Hands Off My Power Supply*, finally hitting the lower depths of the American Top 40, with two singles to its credit, "Run Runaway" and "My Oh My," both of which charted respectably. But the band was unable to hang on to their success in the United States, and their popularity began to wane at home, too, until eventually they had more or less faded from sight. The group re-formed in the 1990s, without front man Noddy Holder or bassist Jim Lea and going by the name Slade II. In 2002, they went back to calling themselves simply Slade.

Dave Hill: guitar; **Noddy Holder**: vocals/guitar; **Jim Lea**: bass; **Don Powell**: drums

Discography: *Ballzy* (Fontana, 1969); *Play It Loud* (Cotillion, 1970); *Slade Alive!* (Polydor, 1972); *Slayed?* (Polydor, 1972); *Stomp Your Hands, Clap Your Feet* (Warner Bros., 1974); *Slade in Flame* (Warner Bros., 1974); *Nobody's Fools* (Polydor, 1976); *Whatever Happened to Slade* (Polydor, 1977); *Alive, Vol. 2* (Barn, 1978); *Return to Base* (Barn, 1979); *We'll Bring the House Down* (Cheapskate, 1981); *Till Deaf Do Us Part* (RCA, 1981); *On Stage* (RCA, 1982); *The Amazing Kamikaze Syndrome* (RCA, 1983); *Keep Your Hands Off My Power Supply* (Epic, 1984); *Rogues Gallery*(CBS, 1985); *Crackers: The Christmas Party Album* (Telstar, 1985); *You Boyz Make Big Noize* (Columbia,1987)

SLAYER

There can be no substantive discussion of the music of Slayer that does not first state the simple fact that *Reign in Blood* is without question the greatest thrash metal album of all time. While it could be argued that the honor should go to Metallica's *Master of Puppets*, this assertion would hold a lot more water if one of the people heaping this prestigious accolade upon *Reign in Blood* was not Metallica drummer Lars Ulrich. Nobody has ever topped this album—not any of Slayer's contemporaries, not any of the bands it influenced, and not even the band itself. Before making the album with superstar producer Rick Rubin, Slayer was already widely acknowledged as thrash's harshest, fastest, and most aggressive outfit. However, by the mid-1980s, many of the genre's major bands, including Metallica and Megadeth, had begun to entertain fantasies of somehow rehabilitating metal by imbuing it with thought-provoking lyrics and a down-to-earth attitude. Slayer, on the other hand, harbored no such desires. Rather, the band reveled in all of metal's sick, twisted glory and championed the exact attributes that their contemporaries with loftier ambitions sought to downplay. In this regard, *Reign in Blood* can be considered Slayer's mission statement. It possessed all of the band's most infamous hallmarks in extremis: their trademark speed, brutality, and ugliness were pushed to the absolute breaking point, and the lyrics avidly depicted every violent act on God's green earth in sickening detail, with a little satanism and Nazism thrown in to ensure mainstream rejection. The album was over in a blindingly fast twenty-eight minutes after the needle dropped, before you even knew what hit you. Rubin had wisely limited the number of songs to ten, condensing the Slayer magic for maximum effectiveness; even just one more track would have compromised the album's controlled burst of fury. The ultimate collective effect of the album was truly chilling, and as a result, the band won legions of slavering, psychotically dedicated fans whose services Slayer has retained to this day. More significant, however, is that *Reign in Blood* influenced metal as a whole to a degree beyond estimation. It is hard to imagine that either black metal or death metal, for example, would even exist without them.

Originally formed in the Los Angeles area in 1982, Slayer started out in none-too-serious fashion, mainly playing Judas Priest covers and drinking beer. The band eventually began to craft their own material, which won them immediate attention on

the basis of its cartoonishly exaggerated satanic subject matter and high-velocity tempos. After the obligatory appearance on the *Metal Massacre III* compilation, the band was signed to Metal Blade and released their first album, *Show No Mercy*, in 1983. Even at this early stage in their career, they already possessed considerable instrumental prowess—guitarists Kerry King and Jeff Hanneman's violent, chaotic lead styles were already in place, and God of All Drumming Dave Lombardo was already gaining recognition as thrash metal's most accom-

plished percussionist, which is not an exaggeration by any means. Over the next couple of years, the band members fine-tuned their style, and in 1985 they offered up *Hell Awaits*. From its opening grooves, which commanded the listener to "Join Us!" in backward tongues, to its final note, the album heralded Slayer as the most evil band on the face of the earth, supplanting all the mere mortals who had come before. By this time, Slayer commanded a very loyal following, and consequently it was not

OPPOSITE: Slayer's ferocity is lost in the photographer's studio. Left to right: Tom Araya, Jeff Hanneman, Kerry King, and Dave Lombardo. ABOVE: Slayer, shown here live in 1986, is the baddest band in the land.

long before the major labels took notice. Rick Rubin was really only known for the rap acts on his label, Def Jam, so it was quite a surprise when he turned out to be a Slayer fan. More surprising, however, was when he signed Slayer to his label, making them labelmates with Run-DMC and the Beastie Boys. His bone-dry production work on *Reign in Blood* provided Slayer with its first clear, well-expressed recording, which highlighted all of the band's strengths. The hyperspeed tempos were now completely articulate, and bassist and vocalist Tom Araya's deeply disturbing lyrics were now completely intelligible, even on a song like "Necrophobic,"

which is next to impossible to sing along with, even with the benefit of a lyric sheet. But the polishing act worked a little too well. Perhaps fearing the damnation of their eternal souls to hell, the executives at CBS, the company that had originally agreed to distribute the album, backed out of the deal upon hearing its gleeful descriptions of decapitation, diabolical anthropomorphism, and sadistic medical experiments performed without the benefit of either local or general anesthetic. Eventually, Geffen agreed to distribute the album, and an undisputed classic was born.

Naturally, after the requisite tours and

hysteria had wound down, Slayer was faced with the unenviable "What do you do for an encore?" question. While a lot of bands would have simply offered up more of the same (which probably would have been just fine with a lot of Slayer's fans), the band very wisely chose to pursue a less obvious path. *South of Heaven*, while still very clearly a Slayer album, was a much doomier, more atmospheric affair than anyone was expecting. This was particularly evident on the title track, which leads off the album. It built up slowly from an ominous, almost cinematically epic guitar motif. It was quite a contrast to their previous album, which practically

burst out of the gate. Of course, *South of Heaven* featured more than its fair share of blindingly fast, all-out thrash, but some fans were disappointed by the changes. The crestfallen didn't stay that way for long, however, and came out in droves when the band toured to support the album. Slayer was received by audiences who, without exception, went completely crazy, starting elatedly violent mosh pits even in venues that had columns of seats. The highly industrious fans at New York City's Felt Forum went even further, tearing the seats out from the floor and using them as projectiles, which bounced back and forth above the crowd's heads sort of like inflatable beach balls, albeit ones with metal surfaces and sharp, exposed bolts. Lead singer Araya, ever the pacifist, petitioned the audience to calm down, only to have a flying seat cushion pelt him in the head. Needless to say, the tour cemented Slayer's reputation as a live band whose ability to whip audiences into a seething mob was both feared and admired.

After the 1990 release *Seasons in the Abyss*, the band went on what turned out to be a four-year hiatus from recording and touring. Drummer Lombardo had already left Slayer once, after the South of Heaven tour, because of personal differences with his bandmates, but he returned for the next album and tour. However, he left again in 1993, presumably for good, and formed his own band, Grip, Inc. At this point, Slayer released *Decade of Aggression*, a live compilation, as a stopgap measure whose purpose was to buy time while the band members tried to figure out their next move. They eventually hired Paul Bostaph, formerly of Forbidden, and he made his maiden voyage in 1994 on *Divine Intervention*. By this time, the musical climate had changed considerably, but that didn't seem to affect

Slayer's sales. If anything, the band was in a better position commercially speaking than it had been in the 1980s, what with death metal becoming a bona fide movement, of which Slayer was considered its elder statesmen.

Fans of happenstance were given an interesting scenario to ponder when Slayer released *God Hates Us All*, whose street date was September 11, 2001, the day of the terrorist attacks on New York City and Washington, D.C., a creepy little coincidence indeed. Lombardo returned to the fold in 2002, and he remains to

this day, which is as it should be. In 2003 the band embarked on the Still Reigning Tour, in which they played the entire *Reign in Blood* album from start to finish, and climaxed with a torrential downpour of fake blood precipitating upon them from above. In 2011, after the band had released *Christ Illusion* and *World Painted Blood*, Hanneman was forced to sit out a tour when he developed necrotizing fasciitis. This condition is more commonly known as the flesh-eating bacteria, so if Hanneman was going to miss a tour, at least it was because he had contracted the most metal disease in the world.

Tom Araya: vocals/bass; **Paul Bostaph**: drums (*Divine Intervention, Diabolus in Musica* and later) (see also Testament); **Jon Dette**: drums (*Undisputed Attitude*) (see also Testament); **Jeff Hanneman**: guitars; **Kerry King**: guitars; **Dave Lombardo**: drums (*Show No Mercy* through *Decade of Aggression*) (see also Testament)

Discography: *Show No Mercy* (Metal Blade, 1983); *Hell Awaits* (Metal Blade, 1985); *Live Undead* (Metal Blade, 1985); *Reign in Blood* (Def Jam, 1986); *South of Heaven* (Def Jam, 1988); *Seasons in the Abyss* (Def American, 1990); *Decade of Aggression* (American, 1993); *Divine Intervention* (American, 1994); *Undisputed Attitude* (American., 1996); *Diabolus in Musica* (American, 1998); *God Hates Us All* (American, 2001); *Christ Illusion* (American, 2006); *World Painted Blood* (American, 2009)

SLEEP

Years active: 1990-1998; 2009–present

For a band that basically had only one single solitary effective album to its credit while it was active, Sleep had an influence on the doom movement that can be described only by using superlative adjectives. The band's first release, *Volume One*, was completely ignored and made no impact, because in all honesty, it simply didn't deliver. However, their second album, *Sleep's Holy Mountain*, was a different story altogether. While their debut had a strong Black Sabbath influence, the 1992 album sounded as if it was in fact the Great Lost Black Sabbath Record, copyright 1972. Perhaps it had been unearthed from a tomb, plucked from the vile clutches of the walking undead? Actually, Earache, a label that was almost exclusively known for grind-core bands, released Sleep's *Holy Mountain*. Anyone who bought the album based on its label affiliation was surely disappointed when they got home and found exactly zero blast beats on it. Rather, the album was chock-full of stunted, monolithic riffs and chaotic, slow-motion drumming that came across like Ginger Baker playing underwater. The lyrics were almost all about smoking marijuana, and those that weren't contained enough references to clerics and druids to

Upon Sleep's breakup, guitarist Matt Pike would go on to form High on Fire.

render even Ronnie James Dio violently nauseous. It was completely unoriginal, at times verging on outright plagiarism. It was also one of the most influential stoner doom albums ever made, easily standing right alongside anything Kyuss or Monster Magnet ever released. It's also just plain awesome and a total joy to listen to.

London Records came calling and offered the band a huge record deal, despite the fact that Sleep's *Holy Mountain* had really only sold enough copies to indicate that Sleep had a decent-size cult following. In any event, the band decided that their major-label debut should be something special, and they spent a full two years tweaking their new material, an amount of time that was in no way indicative of a band that was spending most of their advance via the wonderful and innovative consumer products created by the Graphix corporation. When they were finally finished, they handed in a single song exceeding sixty minutes with the sure-to-please working title of *Dopesmoker*. One can almost imagine the A&R suits at the record company claiming that, yes, the joke was very funny, but could they have the real album now. Despite the possibility of going down in history as releasing the world's longest single, London Records considered the album unreleasable and put it on hold indefinitely. After a miniature eternity of legal wrangling, Sleep broke up. Years later, the album was acquired by Music Cartel and released in 1999 under the new title *Jerusalem* and edited down to a radio-friendly fifty minutes. After its release, guitarist Matt Pike went on to form the violently heavy High on Fire. In 2003, the full original version of *Dopesmoker* was released by the good people at Tee Pee Records, and bassist Al Cisneros and drummer Chris Hakius formed the trance-inducing duo Om.

Al Cisneros: bass/vocals; **Chris Hakius**: drums; **Justin Marler**: guitars (*Volume One*); **Matt Pike**: guitars

Discography: *Volume One* (Tupelo, 1991); *Sleep's Holy Mountain* (Earache, 1992); *Jerusalem* (Music Cartel, 1999); *Dopesmoker* (Tee Pee, 2003)

SLIPKNOT

YEARS ACTIVE: 1995–PRESENT

Slipknot is among the first generation of bands to be influenced by still relatively new rap-metal groups like the Deftones and Korn. However, these Iowans infuse their music with death metal influences, making them hit quite a bit harder than their predecessors, and they also work the shock-rock angle, which has gone largely untapped in this particular sweatpants-friendly genre. Rather than use their names, all the members of the band have taken on a number from zero to eight, and they wear ghoulish masks that recall something one might find while rummaging through a box in psychotic killer Ed Gein's attic. Aside from their visual presentation, their relentless touring and furious stage shows have been the key elements responsible for Slipknot's success—the band's sheer brutal energy in a live setting has been the stuff of legend since their 1995 formation. Slipknot's self-titled debut for Roadrunner Records was released four years later, and it coincided with the band's first appearance at Ozzfest, which exposed them to a wide and highly enthusiastic audience. Subsequently, Slipknot went platinum, the first album in the history of their label to do so. Their 2001 offering, *Iowa*, debuted at number three on the *Billboard* charts, and they followed it up with yet more touring and another appearance at Ozzfest, this time in a slot that was significantly higher on the food chain than their previous slot. Afterward, the band took some time off, and fans busied themselves by sending a sexually explicit and profanity-laden e-mail to another Slipknot, a British crocheting club that has since changed its domain name. In 2005 the band won a Best Metal Performance Grammy for the song "Before I Forget."

The band members of Iowa's Slipknot conceal their identities so they're not recognized on their weekly visits to the bridges of Madison County. Left to right: Chris Fehn (3), Mic Thompson (7), and Joey Jordinson (1).

In 2010, bassist Paul Gray was found dead in a hotel room near Des Moines. An autopsy revealed that he had died from an overdose of morphine and fentanyl. His death understandably destabilized the group, and in the case of vocalist Corey Taylor, it simply took the wind out of his sails. He publicly speculated as to whether or not it was even appropriate for the group to continue without Gray. The different band members have since issued conflicting statements as to the status of the group, and their future remains up in the air at the time of this writing.

Josh Brainard: guitars (*Mate. Feed. Kill. Repeat.*, *Slipknot*); **Anders Colsefni**: vocals (*Mate. Feed. Kill. Repeat.*); **Shawn Crahan (6)**: percussion; **Chris Fehn (3)**: percussion (*Slipknot* and later); **Paul Gray (2)**: bass; **Craig Jones (5)**: samples (*Slipknot* and later); **Joey Jordison (1)**: drums; **James Root (4)**: guitars (*Slipknot* and later); **Donnie Steele**: guitars (*Mate. Feed. Kill. Repeat.*); **Corey Taylor (8)**: vocals (*Slipknot* and later); **Mick Thompson (7)**: guitars (*Slipknot* and later); **Sid Wilson (0)**: DJ (*Slipknot* and later)

Discography: *Mate. Feed. Kill. Repeat.* (self-released, 1996); *Slipknot* (Roadrunner, 1999); *Iowa* (Roadrunner, 2001); *Vol. 3 (The Subliminal Verses)* (Roadrunner, 2004); *All Hope is Gone* (Roadrunner, 2008)

SLOW HORSE

Years active: 1997–2003

Formed in New York City in 1997, Slow Horse specialized in the traditionally slow, oppressive doom metal played by bands such as Saint Vitus and, of course, Black Sabbath. Slow Horse's six-song debut was released in 1999, clocking in at forty minutes. The lyrical preoccupation of the album was singing guitarist (and author of this book) Daniel Bukszpan's troubles with the ladies, and it is probably the first ever doom metal breakup album. At long last, doom metal had its own Sebadoh. The centerpiece of the album is the band's cover of Chris Isaak's "Wicked Game," which is transformed into a plodding, slovenly dirge that bears almost no resemblance to the original, except possibly at the chorus. Unfortunately, the rhythm section left the band in 1999 before the album was released, and Bukszpan spent a full year trying to find suitable replacements. Two years later, the search ended with bassist Ernest Anderson and drummer Scott Sanfratello, and Slow Horse immediately set about working on its next album. Released in 2001, *Slow Horse II* marked improvements all around. The hopelessly toilet bowl–quality "production" of the debut, which kind and charitable critics referred to as lo-fi, was left in the dust by the engineering genius of Martin Bisi, who had previously worked with Helmet, Sonic Youth, and Cop Shoot Cop, among many others. The album also marked a major expansion in terms of the stylistic vocabulary of the band, from pop vocal harmonies to Middle Eastern textures to noise rock. The album also introduced elements of Bukszpan's much-beloved "slow core" music, with the influence of bands like the Swans, Codeine, Idaho, and particularly Low sitting side by side with the album's slowest, sludgiest wall of doom. Slow Horse was quite possibly the world's first slow core–doom band, or at least one of a handful so small as to be considered nearly microscopic.

Ernest Anderson: bass (*Slow Horse II*); **Daniel Bukszpan**: guitars/vocals; **Rick Fiorio**: drums (*Slow Horse*); **Jeff Mackey**: bass (*Slow Horse*); **Scott Sanfratello**: drums (*Slow Horse II*)

Discography: *Slow Horse* (Freebird, 1999); *Slow Horse II* (Berserker, 2001)

SODOM

Years active: 1981–present

Along with Destruction and Kreator, Sodom is generally acknowledged as one of the pivotal German thrash bands of the 1980s as well as a huge influence on the black metal bands that the following decade produced. The band began in typically sloppy fashion, churning out murky proto-thrash that was similar to bands like Venom or Mercyful Fate sans King Diamond's infectious yodeling. Sodom's original lineup consisted of drummer Witchhunter, guitarist Aggressor, and bassist and vocalist Angelripper, who functions as the leader of the Christ-disliking Teutons. Before they even squeezed out their first album, there was already trouble in paradise, as Aggressor quit the band before recording sessions were scheduled to begin. He was replaced by Grave Violator, who performed six-string duties on the band's infamous 1984 debut, *In the Sign of Evil*. Mr. Violator's tenure was short-lived, however, and he was replaced for the next album, *Obsessed by Cruelty*, by Destructor, who was in turn replaced by Blackfire, et cetera. In a disappointing turn of events, when Witchhunter gave up the drummer's throne after the 1992 release *Tapping the Vein*, the guy who eventually ended up winning the spot on a permanent basis was named simply Bobby. Couldn't he at least change it to something a little more sinister, like Last Potato Chip Eater or Toilet Seat Leaver Upper? In any event, the band has weathered lineup changes of Ritchie Blackmore's Rainbow proportions and enjoys a rabid cult following to this day. Sadly, Chris "Witchhunter" Dudek died in 2008 from liver failure after a long illness.

Tom Angelripper: bass/vocals; **Atomic Steif**: drums (*Aber Bitte Mit Sahne* through *Masquerade in Blood*); **Bernemann**: guitars (*To Death Do Us Unite* and later); **Blackfire**: guitars (*Expurse of Sodomy* through *Ausgebombt*); **Bobby**: drums (*To Death Do Us Unite* and later); **Andy Brings**: guitars (*Tapping the Vein* through *Marooned Live*); **Destructor**: guitars (*Obsessed by Cruelty*); **Grave Violator**: guitars (*In the Sign of Evil*; *Sodom*); **Michael Hoffman**: guitars (*Better Off*

Dead, *The Saw Is the Law*); **Strahli**: guitars (*Masquerade in Blood*); **Witchhunter**: drums (*In the Sign of Evil* through *Tapping the Vein*)

Discography: *Obsessed by Cruelty* (Steamhammer, 1986); *Expurse of Sodomy* (Steamhammer, 1987); *Persecution Mania* (Steamhammer, 1987); *Mortal Way of Live* (Steamhammer, 1988); *Agent Orange* (Steamhammer, 1989); *Better Off Dead* (Steamhammer, 1990); *Tapping the Vein* (Steamhammer, 1992); *Get What You Deserve* (Steamhammer, 1994); *Marooned Live* (Steamhammer, 1994); *Masquerade in Blood* (Steamhammer, 1995); *Til Death Do Us Unite* (GUN, 1997); *Code Red* (Drakkar, 1999); *M-16* (Steamhammer, 2001); *Sodom* (Steamhammer, 2006); *The Final Sign of Evil* (Steamhammer, 2007); *In War and Pieces* (Steamhammer, 2010)

SOLITUDE AETURNUS

YEARS ACTIVE: 1987–PRESENT

Solitude Aeturnus dates to 1987, when Dallas-area guitarist John Perez, inspired by the music of bands like Candlemass and Fates Warning, decided that he wanted to have a go at it his own self. As a result, his band displayed the epic plod of the former and the progressive bent of the latter. What really set his band apart, however, was the unbelievably fantastic vocals of front man Robert Lowe, who has no doubt had to endure much St. Elmo's Fire–related ribbing. On their first two albums, *Into the Depths of Sorrow* and *Beyond the Crimson Horizon*, released in 1991 and 1992, respectively, the band members struggled with their style a little bit, and both albums saw the band meandering to some degree. But by the 1994 release *Through the Darkest Hour*, Solitude Aeturnus had found exactly the right balance for themselves, and the resulting album was quite simply a doom metal masterpiece of epic proportions. This period saw the band achieve their greatest successes, culminating in a 1994 tour with their personal gods, Mercyful Fate. In 1998, they released *Adagio*, which contains a cover of Black Sabbath's "Heaven and Hell," the only Sabbath cover in recorded history to

capture even a fraction of the original's spirit. Afterward, Perez and company put the band on indefinite hold, while the guitarist focused his energy on his label, Brainticket Records. Perez had, however, hinted strongly that the band would reconvene for a new album, and they made good on that when they released 2006's *Alone*. Lowe has since joined Sweden's Candlemass.

John Covington: drums (*Into the Depths of Sorrow* through *Adagio*); **Robert Lowe**: vocals; **James Martin**: bass (*Alone*); **Steve Moseley**: bass (*Adagio*); **Steve Nichols**: drums (*Alone*); **John Perez**: guitars; **Edgar Rivera**: guitars; **Lyle Steadham**: bass (*Into the Depths of Sorrow* through *Downfall*)

Discography: *Into the Depths of Sorrow* (Roadrunner, 1991); *Beyond the Crimson Horizon* (Roadrunner, 1992); *Through the Darkest Hour* (Pavement, 1994); *Downfall* (Pavement, 1996); *Adagio* (Massacre, 1998); *Alone* (Massacre, 2006)

SOUNDGARDEN

YEARS ACTIVE: 1984–1997; 2010–PRESENT

Soundgarden was simply awesome, one of the few bands of the 1990s who actually deserved their success. While the band members hailed from Seattle and reached their greatest commercial peak at the same time as their Washingtonian cohorts Mudhoney and Nirvana, they never fell prey to the negative implications of grunge, as they had won over metal audiences first by playing opening slots with bands such as Danzig and Voivod. Their 1990 album, *Louder Than Love*, had already been out for two years before the grunge movement got under way in earnest, and by then the band's metal credentials were already well established among the general public. By the same token, Soundgarden was also partially responsible for the introduction of devil music to the nation's alternative rock fans. Soundgarden was, after all, on Sub

Pop, a modest little indie label, and as a result most likely brought about the introduction of the first Black Sabbath albums to the R.E.M.-laden CD racks of the nation's hipsters.

Formed in 1984 by guitarist Kim Thayil and bassist Hiro Yamamoto, Soundgarden added the divinely gifted singer (and Yamamoto's roommate) Chris Cornell to its ranks in short order, and after the addition of drummer Matt Cameron in 1986, the band's lineup was complete. In 1987, Bruce Pavitt, who had been a friend of the band for years, signed them to his new label, Sub Pop, for which they released a single and two EPs. Although Soundgarden was already gaining significant attention from major labels at this point, the band signed instead with SST, another indie, home to Black Flag and Firehose, among others. Soundgarden's only release for the label, *Ultramega OK*, was released in 1988 to nearly universal raves in both alternative and metal circles, certainly the first time both camps agreed on anything. The band finally gave in and signed with a major label, choosing A&M for *Louder Than Love*. It earned typically strong reviews and almost cracked *Billboard*'s Top 100. After its release, Yamamoto quit the band to go back to college, and he was briefly replaced by former Nirvana guitarist Jason Everman. For reasons that are shrouded in a veil of mystery, Everman didn't last long, and the slot was eventually and permanently filled by Ben Shepherd in 1990.

The band began work on their next album, and the pressure was intense–not only from the label, which had high expectations, but also from fans of both alternative rock and metal, who universally predicted that Soundgarden's next major-label album would disappoint beyond measure. Much to everyone's amazement, the 1991 release *Badmotorfinger* was arguably the band's finest hour. It truly had everything, from its progressive rock time shifting to the plaintive beauty of songs like "Mind Riot" to its sheer

ten-ton heaviness. The only people who were disappointed were those at A&M, who were expecting an immediate, major hit album. While it did crack the Top 40 charts, it was overshadowed by Nirvana's *Nevermind*, released at almost exactly the same time. Regardless, Soundgarden had their best-selling album yet, and they went on tour with Guns N' Roses to support it. As much as the tour brought them to new audiences, it was the nascent grunge movement that really put the band in the spotlight. Serendipitously, Cornell and Cameron had collaborated with members of Pearl Jam for a project called Temple of the Dog, whose album of the same name was a tribute to Andrew Wood, the singer for a fellow Seattle band, Mother Love Bone, who had died

of a heroin overdose. By the time of the album's release, it was 1992 and Pearl Jam was selling like crazy, which meant that Temple of the Dog was, too. This introduced Soundgarden to still more record buyers, many of whom must have wondered about the identity of the singer who was regularly blowing Pearl Jam singer Eddie Vedder out of the water.

Soundgarden finally hit the big time in 1994 with *Superunknown*. The album debuted at number one and featured real, honest-to-god radio hits in the form of "Spoonman" and "Black Hole Sun." The chart success came almost in spite of the band, which had lost none of its trademark heaviness and certainly none of its originality. In many ways, the album was even more far afield

than *Badmotorfinger*, featuring such unusual and unclassifiable material as "Head Down" and "Limo Wreck," as well as "Like Suicide," which took on new meaning when, a few weeks after the album's release, Nirvana front man and friend of Soundgarden Kurt Cobain took his own life. Ultimately, the album went platinum three times over. However, they couldn't replicate this success on their next album, *Down*

It doesn't get much heavier than Soundgarden, live in concert. Left to right: Kim Thayil, Chris Cornell, and Matt Cameron (buried behind the drums).

OPPOSITE: Soundgarden wades in a pond full of lily pads—just don't ask. Left to right: Chris Cornell, Hiro Yamamoto, Matt Cameron, Kim Thayil.

on the Upside. Released in the summer of 1996, it charted high and eventually went platinum, but it was clear that bands that were associated with the grunge movement, whether it was a fair association or not, were now experiencing the downward slide of the ride. The members of Soundgarden decided to go out while they still had their dignity and were still on top, and after touring to support the album, they disbanded in 1997 with little fanfare.

In 1999, Cornell released a solo album, the brilliant *Euphoria Morning*, and he was a member of Audioslave, which was basically Rage Against the Machine without singer Zach de la Rocha. That band lasted from 2002 to 2007, and when it ended, Cornell went back to his solo career. He released *Carry On* that year, which featured an ill-advised cover of Michael Jackson's "Billie Jean" and "You Know My Name," which appeared in the 2006 James Bond movie *Casino Royale*. Cornell then chose to work with rapper and producer Timbaland on his 2009 solo album *Scream*. The album's electronic pop and R&B stylings were considered a travesty, and it cost the singer much of his fan base, as well as his credibility. Trent Reznor of Nine Inch Nails took to Twitter, in fact, to opine "You know that feeling you get when somebody embarrasses themselves so badly YOU feel uncomfortable? Heard Chris Cornell's record? Jesus."

Cameron joined Pearl Jam in 1998 and recorded four albums with them, and Shepherd played with Mark Lanegan and a solo Tony Iommi. Thayil kept a low profile, for the most part. However, in 2009, Thayil, Shepherd, and Cameron joined Tad Doyle of TAD onstage at Seattle's Crocodile Café and played three songs, including "Spoonman." This marked the first time that as much as 75% of Soundgarden had played together since 1997, and it was hard not to speculate that this performance was the catalyst for the full reunion that they announced in 2010. Later that year the band released the *Telephantasm* compilation and in 2011 they

Soundgarden's Chris Cornell and Ben Shepherd rock the stadium in 1992.

Spinal Tap caught in a moment of levity in between exploding drummers. Left to right: David St. Hubbins, Nigel Tufnel, and Derek Smalls.

released *Live on I-5*, which documented their 1996 tour. The band is reported to be working on a new studio album for 2012.

Matt Cameron: drums; **Chris Cornell**: vocals; **Ben Shepherd**: bass (*Badmotorfinger* and later); **Kim Thayil**: guitars; **Hiro Yamamoto**: bass (*Screaming Life* through *Louder Than Love*)

Discography: *Screaming Life* (Sub Pop, 1987); *Fopp* (Sub Pop, 1988); *Ultramega OK* (SST, 1988); *Louder Than Love* (A&M, 1990); *Badmotorfinger* (A&M, 1991); *Superunknown* (A&M, 1994); *Down on the Upside* (A&M, 1996); *A-Sides* (A&M, 1997); *Live on I-5* (A&M, 2011)

SPINAL TAP

YEARS ACTIVE: 1984–PRESENT

In 1984, Rob "Meathead" Reiner directed *This Is Spinal Tap*, a fictional documentary, or "mockumentary," that follows the members of a 1970s heavy metal band as they desperately cling to what few scraps remain of their rapidly diminishing popularity, a phenomenon that during the Reagan decade was in depressingly bountiful abundance. While the film is itself a brilliant satire of the documentary style (in particular that of Martin Scorsese's *The Last Waltz*), its greatest success is as a portrayal of the rock-star lifestyle, since it depicts every ill-advised creative choice ever made in the name of heavy metal with wounding accuracy and to scathing effect. The film was a modest success during its initial theatrical run, but it really took on a life of its own on home video. *This Is Spinal Tap* has become required viewing

LEFT: What's wrong with being sexy? Spinal Tap performs what is almost certainly "Big Bottom."

ABOVE: Spinal Tap wants you to be its drummer. Left to right: Derek Smalls, David St. Hubbins, and Nigel Tufnel.

for musicians of every stripe, from the most obscure to the internationally renowned, all of whom can relate to virtually any of the events portrayed therein. More significantly, the film has actually exerted a powerful influence on musician culture. It held up a mirror to the rock-star community for the first time, and in so doing it showed established rock stars the idiocy of their behavior, acting as a permanent buzzkill. It also functioned as a cautionary tale to up-and-coming musicians by showing them how not to behave.

The film depicts Spinal Tap as a band made up of opportunist hacks with a revolving string of drummers (who die under mysterious circumstances). They begin their career in the mid-1960s by churning out generic Yardbirds-style white R&B regurgitations, only to shift to by-the-numbers flower-child music the moment it becomes trendy to do so. The band finally settles on heavy metal in the early 1970s, which earns them a decade in the spotlight, a period that they are desperately clinging to on their 1982 tour to promote their fictional album *Smell the Glove*. The tour is an unmitigated disaster, rife with cancellations and distinguished by a disturbing trend in which the venues just get smaller and smaller. While events of this kind were no doubt experienced by many bands whose popularity diminished in the 1980s, the only group at whom the film takes a direct swipe is Black Sabbath, which had just released *Born Again* in 1983. The album featured former Deep Purple singer Ian Gillan, who had been brought in to replace Ronnie James Dio, marking the band's third lineup change in as many years. Apart from the usual battery of dry ice and other stage accoutrements, Black Sabbath's stage show also featured a life-size replica of Stonehenge. While the film depicts Spinal Tap with an eighteen-inch model, which is "in danger of being crushed by a dwarf" dressed in some kind of court jester getup, the real-life Sabbath experience was much more embarrassing, as the band's gigantic model had to be left in parking lots as the tour went on and the venues got progressively smaller thanks to their rapidly thinning fan base. While this is the film's only obvious jab at a specific band, one can easily recognize that there are many, many artists being depicted in as unforgiving a fashion, including Jethro Tull, Led Zeppelin, Deep Purple, Hawkwind, Ted Nugent, Queen—the list goes on and on.

Surprisingly, there have been bands post–*This Is Spinal Tap* who have engaged in behavior that was depicted in the film. The most obvious example is Metallica's self-titled 1991 album, which, just like Spinal Tap's *Smell the Glove*, was packaged in a completely black outer sleeve, which Metallica didn't seem to realize made them look a bit goofy. The only area in which the Spinal Tap project misstepped was when someone believed that there was an actual consumer demand for more product, and in 1992 the "band" reconvened for *Break Like the Wind*. Although it had a few bright spots and celebrity appearances from luminaries such as Joe Satriani and Guns N' Roses' Slash, it was surely that year's least-bidden return to the marketplace. However, they didn't learn their lesson and they released another album, *Back from the Dead*, in 2009.

Derek Smalls: bass; **David St. Hubbins**: guitar/vocals; **Nigel Tufnel**: guitar/vocals

Discography: *This Is Spinal Tap* (Polydor, 1984); *Break Like the Wind* (MCA, 1992); *Back from the Dead* (Polymer, 2009)

SPIRIT CARAVAN

YEARS ACTIVE: 1996–2002

The doom metal genre is not exactly known for its celebrities, but the closest thing to that would have to be Scott "Wino" Weinrich. The singer and guitarist has played in such influential doom bands as the Obsessed, and Saint Vitus, and from 1996 to 2002 he led Spirit Caravan. Weinrich started out in the early 1980s in the Obsessed in the Washington, D.C., area, where he grew up, but he moved to Los Angeles in 1985 to join Saint Vitus. After a few years, he left that band to re-form the Obsessed, which had apparently been handed the keys to the kingdom in the form of a major-label deal with Columbia. Unfortunately, the Obsessed's sole album for the label, *The Church Within*, simply didn't sell. It was at this point that Weinrich withdrew from the music scene altogether to figure out what his next move was going to be.

In 1996 he was coaxed out of retirement by bassist Dave Sherman and former Iron Man drummer Gary Isom, both of whom had been friends of Weinrich's for many years. Originally called Shine, their new band released an EP but later rechristened themselves Spirit Caravan when they found out, via a cease-and-desist order, that there was already another Shine. The newly titled band released their first album, *Jug Fulla Sun*, in 1999. Its release was met by all-out hysteria in the doom metal community, which could not have been happier to see their idols return to the studio. Unfortunately, Spirit Caravan had only a few years in them, and after the *Dreamwheel* EP and another full-length album, the band broke up in 2002. After that, Weinrich joined Place of Skulls, a Christian doom band fronted by his good friend and former Pentagram band member Victor Griffin. The result of this collaboration was released to the public in 2003 in the form of the *With Vision* album, but Weinrich left the band afterwards to focus on a new group, The Hidden Hand.

Gary Isom: drums (see also Iron Man); **Dave Sherman**: bass; **Scott "Wino" Weinrich**: vocals/guitars (see also the Obsessed, Saint Vitus)

Discography: *Jug Fulla Sun* (Tolotta, 1999); *Dreamwheel* (Meteor City, 1999); *Elusive Truth* (Tolotta, 2001)

STARZ

YEARS ACTIVE: 1978–1979, OCCASIONAL REUNION TOURS

Starz was a band just slightly ahead of their own time, though not by much. Had they gone into business just half a decade later than they did, they might have seen some success. But in the mid-1970s, people just weren't ready for them. Starz had the tunes, which melded the pop sense of Cheap Trick and the oomph of vintage Aerosmith, and they had KISS' manager, Bill Aucoin. But sadly, none of this got them as much as a pot to piss in.

Starz formed in New Jersey out of the ashes of Looking Glass, a band who had scored a number one hit in 1972 with the yacht rock epic "Brandy (You're a Fine Girl)." That group lasted just four years and two albums before breaking up, but drummer Jeff Grob and bassist Peter Sweval decided to stay together. Grob then changed his name to Joe X. Dube for reasons best known to him, and then the pair joined forces with the dual-guitar team of Brendan Harkin and Richie Ranno, and singer Michael Lee Smith. The singer was the brother of 1970s teen heartthrob Rex Smith, who is best remembered for breaking the heart of poor, naïve Vikki Stubing on an episode of *The Love Boat*.

The band had the look, the tunes and the pyro-heavy stage show, so Capitol Records got dollar signs in their eyes and promptly signed them, releasing the band's self-titled debut in 1976. Nobody bought it. Next came *Violation* in 1977. The album produced "Cherry Baby," their sole top 40 hit, but otherwise, not much else happened for them. *Attention Shoppers!* came next in 1978, and *Coliseum Rock* emerged in 1979. No matter how hard they tried, Starz simply didn't sell records, and after finishing a run of East Coast club dates, the band broke up.

As is often the case with these things, it turned out a few people were listening after all, and those people formed their own bands. The members of Bon Jovi were never shy about their love of the band, and Poison not only took clear inspiration from the Starz song "Fallen Angel" but even wrote their own, unrelated song called "Fallen Angel." Mötley Crüe and Twisted Sister have been vocal about their affection for the band as well. Starz didn't reunite to capitalize on the 1980s glam metal movement, but they have gotten back together every now and again for the odd reunion concert, and continue to do so to this day. For that we thank them.

Orville Davis: bass (*Coliseum Rock*); **Joe X. Dube**: drums (*Starz*); **Brendan Harkin**: guitar (*Starz* through *Attention Shoppers!*); **Bobby Messano**: guitar (*Coliseum Rock*); **Richie Ranno**: guitars (*Starz*); **Michael Lee Smith**: vocals (*Starz*); **Pieter Sweval**: drums (*Starz* through *Attention Shoppers!*)

Discography: *Starz* (Capitol, 1976); *Violation* (Capitol, 1977); *Attention Shoppers!* (Capitol, 1978); *Live in Action* (Capitol, 1978); *Coliseum Rock* (Capitol, 1979); *Greatest Hits Live* (Capitol, 2004)

The Garden State's own Starz looks to the heavens to send them a manager who can make them sell records.

STORMTROOPERS OF DEATH

YEARS ACTIVE: 1985–2007

Stormtroopers of Death, or S.O.D., as most people refer to them, released a single album in 1985, *Speak English or Die*, which was basically a joke and was created under the most unexceptional circumstances imaginable. To the shock of just about everyone involved, the album became an overnight sensation in the thrash metal community, and it is still considered a classic today. As legend has it, there was a brief lull in Anthrax's punishing touring and recording schedule, and guitarist Scott Ian and drummer Charlie Benante decided that it would be a swell idea to fill the downtime with some type of recreational activity. With the bungee-jumping craze still a few years off and roller disco a thing of the past, they decided that it would be good fun to throw a hardcore album together. Nuclear Assault bassist Danny Lilker, a former member of Anthrax himself, was brought into the project, and Anthrax roadie Billy Milano was handed a microphone. The resulting album,

Speak English or Die, was recorded in three days, and it quickly gained as much notoriety for its humor as for its aggressive, brutal approach. The album reached classic status straightaway, thanks to songs like "Kill Yourself," "Douche Crew," "The Ballad of Jimi Hendrix," and the title track, which is surely a favorite of Pat Buchanan.

While it may have been possible to turn the band into a more serious proposition, the musicians involved saw the project for what it was—a joke—and consequently there were no tours or any other attendant efforts to promote the album, with the exception of a few gigs here and there. Soon after, everyone went back to their respective bands, and Milano used his newfound notoriety to form his own group, Method of Destruction, also known as M.O.D., who mainly made really dumb crossover speed metal that made S.O.D.'s music sound like Rush by comparison. Stormtroopers of Death released a live album in 1992, *Live at Budokan*, which documented their recent reunion (which did not take place in Japan, in case you were

Stormtroopers of Death almost squeeze out a smile for the camera before a 1999 performance. Left to right: Danny Lilker, Scott Ian, Billy Milano, and Charlie Benante.

Stormtroopers of Death, Scott Ian (left) and Billy Milano wow the crowd.

wondering), and they got together yet again in 1999 for a new studio album, *Bigger Than the Devil*. They also released another album, *Rise of the Infidels*, in 2007. However, as is often the case, the joke was only funny once, and the newer albums faded into obscurity while the original masterpiece remains a popular classic to this day.

Charlie Benante: drums (see also Anthrax); **Scott Ian**: guitars (see also Anthrax); **Danny Lilker**: bass (see also Anthrax, Nuclear Assault); **Billy Milano**: vocals

Discography: *Speak English or Die* (Megaforce, 1985); *Live at Budokan* (Megaforce, 1992); *Bigger Than the Devil* (Nuclear Blast, 1999); *Rise of the Infidels* (Nuclear Blast, 2007)

STRATOVARIUS

YEARS ACTIVE: 1984–PRESENT

Finland's Stratovarius is one of the leading lights of symphonic power metal. They often receive credit along with Gamma Ray and Helloween for popularizing the genre, but unlike those bands they had a longer road to mass acceptance. Formed in 1982 by drummer Tuomo Lassila, it took a full seven years for the band to get its shit together and get their debut album, 1989's *Fright Night*, into stores. Things didn't really start happening until 1992's *Twilight Time*, and then only in Japan, the one place on earth where they were able to start building a fan base.

Matias Kupiainen and Lauri Porra of Stratovarius in the middle of minute sixteen of some Roman-numeralled multi-chapter epic.

Most bands would have become discouraged enough at that point to pack it in, but Stratovarius stuck with it and focused on the Japanese market. They toured the Land of the Rising Sun extensively in 1994 to promote their album *Dreamspace*, which features a backing orchestra. The band members were for the most part pleased with the way things were going, but Lassila wasn't one of them. The orchestral sound that the band ultimately became known for wasn't what Lassila had intended when he founded the group, and when he left he took keyboard player Antti Ikonen with him. A bummer, to be sure, but once the departing members had been replaced by drummer Jörg Michael and keyboard player Jens Johansson, the lineup stabilized.

The band finally saw one of their albums get a U.S. release in 1997 when *Visions* was released on Noise Records. This was followed by a U.S. reissue campaign of their back catalog, alongside the 2000 release of *Infinite*. After releasing *Elements, Pt. 1* and *Elements Pt. 2* simultaneously in 2003, the band went on hiatus. Shortly afterwards, guitarist and principal songwriter Timo Tolkki suffered a nervous breakdown and was diagnosed with bipolar disorder. After Tolkki recovered from his initial break with reality, the band reunited and released a self-titled album in 2005.

As nice as it was to have the band back, their audience hated the new album. Stratovarius was a band whose fans wanted less modesty and more epics, and the new album was uncharacteristically stripped-down. It was like Liberace releasing a record of drum solos. Tolkki, like the band's fans, was publicly critical of the album, and the already fragile relationship between the band members hit the skids again. There was an attempt to record a new album despite the internal strife in 2006, but the situation within the band was so miserable by that point that Tolkki broke up the group. He did eventually sign over the rights to the band's name to the other members, leaving them free and clear to continue as Stratovarius without him.

Matias Kupiainen replaced Tolkki, and the group got busy working on their next album. By this time, more than three years had passed since their much-mailgned last album. There was a lot riding on the new one, particularly since it featured a total of exactly no original members. In 2009, the wait came to an end and they released *Polaris*. It was viewed as a bombastic return to form by fans, and all was forgiven. The band's most recent album release was 2011's *Elysium*.

Antti Ikonen: keyboards (*Fright Night* through *Fourth Dimension*); **Jens Johansson**: keyboards (*Episode* and later); **Jari Kainulainen**: bass (*Dreamspace* through *Stratovarius*); **Timo Kotipelto**: vocals (*Fourth Dimension* and later); **Matias Kupiainen**: guitar (*Polaris* and later); **Tuomo Lassila**: drums (*Fright Night* through *Fourth Dimension*); **Jyrki Lentonen**: bass (*Fright Night*); **Jörg Michael**: drums (*Episode* and later); **Lauri Porra**: bass (*Polaris* and later); **Timo Tolkki**: guitar, vocals (*Fright Night* through *Stratovarius*)

Discography: *Fright Night* (Columbia, 1989); *Twilight Time* (Bluelight, 1992), *Dreamspace* (Noise, 1994); *Fourth Dimension* (Noise, 1995); *Episode* (Noise, 1996); *Visions* (Noise, 1997); *Destiny* (Noise, 1998); *Infinite* (Nuclear Blast, 2000); *Intermission* (Nuclear Blast, 2001); *Elements, Pt. 1* (Nuclear Blast, 2003); *Elements, Pt. 2* (Nuclear Blast, 2003); *Stratovarius* (Sanctuary, 2005); *Polaris* (Edel Records, 2009); *Elysium* (EAR Music, 2011)

FINLAND

For a small, remote country with a population smaller than that of Manhattan, Finland has made an impressive mark on heavy metal. But unlike Norway or Germany, Finland isn't strictly identified with one particular subgenre to the exclusion of all others. In fact, if there's any noticeable trend among Finnish metal bands, it's an urge to do things a little differently than everyone else. This is, after all, the country that spawned Apocalyptica, a band consisting of cellists playing Metallica covers.

Extreme metal has been well represented by Finnish bands, and the genres they fall into run the gamut. Black metal is represented by Behexen and Sargeist, but there are also bands that mix up their black metal with other elements, such as Thy Serpent, which imbues it with doom and symphonic elements. There's also Impaled Nazarene, which adds elements of punk and grindcore. Xysma is among the best known Finnish death metal bands, and doom metal has been the province of Swallow the Sun, Thergothon, and Reverend Bizarre. Those last two should be singled out for making music so slow and depressing it makes Candlemass sound like the Monkees (Davy Jones, R.I.P.)

Finland has been home to several influential metal bands, but the two that Finnish bands themselves normally single out for praise are Tarot and Stone. The power metal band Tarot formed in the 1980s and is led by Marco Hietala, bassist for Nightwish. Even though Nightwish keeps Hietala's calendar full, Tarot never broke up, and still plays for the benefit of the Finnish cult audience that has been following them for decades. Stone, on the other hand, was a thrash metal band and unlike Tarot had a very short career that ended in 1991. Nonetheless, they remain influential today, and Children of Bodom' Alexi Laiho has singled them out for particular praise.

Power metal is represented in Finland by Sonata Arctica, the late Crystal Blaze, and Sinergy, which is actually led by an American, Kimberly Goss. In addition to Sinergy, Goss has also sung and played keyboards for other metal bands, including Dimmu Borgir, Therion, and Children of Bodom.

Perhaps unsurprisingly, Finland has also been fertile ground for the genre known as folk metal. As the name implies, this is metal with a strong attachment to traditional Northern European music. In Finland's case, that music is known as *humppa*, which sounds remarkably similar to the music one might hear in Germany during Oktoberfest whilst downing the contents of a particularly large beer stein. Folk metal's most visible Finnish practitioners are Korpiklaani, who sing bouncy songs about the woods and alcohol, and Finntroll, who sing bouncy songs about, you guessed it, trolls.

STRYPER

YEARS ACTIVE: 1983–1993; 2003–PRESENT

Stryper was a Christian heavy metal band that formed in the early 1980s, when the term "Christian heavy metal band" was more than paradoxical enough to spark the average person's curiosity, much like "gay Republican." At that time, heavy metal was a massive youth movement that, with a few exceptions, was synonymous with devil worship and earthly vices no matter how nonthreatening its practitioners might have been. So when the band released their 1984 debut, *The Yellow and Black Attack*, the sheer novelty alone was enough to shift units. In the live setting, the band dressed in yellow-and-black horizontally striped outfits that suggested John Belushi in his killer bee costume, and they threw Bibles at the audience. Stryper hit their commercial peak in 1986, when the album *To Hell with*

This 1988 photograph of Stryper is just wrong on so many levels. Left to right: Tim Gaines, Michael Sweet, Robert Sweet, and Oz Fox.

the Devil went gold, but it was all downhill after that, and after a brief flirtation with plain old secular metal, they broke up in 1993 after releasing *Reason for the Season*. Ten years later, they recorded two new songs to add to a greatest hits compilation, and the experience was positive enough to warrant a new album in 2005, *Reborn*. However, the newfound momentum disappeared when the wife of frontman Michael Sweet was diagnosed with cancer. After attending to his wife, he joined Boston and toured with them in 2007 and 2008. The next Stryper album, *Murder by Pride*, finally came out in 2009. Their last album was 2011's *The Covering*, which featured, you guessed it, covers.

Tracy Ferrie: bass (*Reborn* and later); **Oz Fox**: guitar; **Tim Gaines**: bass (*The Yellow and Black Attack* through *Reason for the Season*); **Michael Sweet**: vocals; **Robert Sweet**: drums (*The Yellow and Black Attack* through *Reborn*; *The Covering*)

Discography: *The Yellow and Black Attack* (Hollywood, 1984); *Soldiers Under Command* (Hollywood, 1985); *To Hell with the Devil* (Hollywood, 1986); *In God We Trust* (Hollywood, 1988); *Reach Out* (Enigma, 1990); *Together As One* (Enigma, 1990); *Against the Law* (Hollywood, 1990); *Reason for the Season* (Enigma, 1993); *Reborn* (Big 3, 2005); *Murder by Pride* (Big 3, 2009); *The Covering* (Big 3, 2011)

SUICIDAL TENDENCIES

YEARS ACTIVE: 1981–1995; 1997–PRESENT

Suicidal Tendencies started out as one of the most well-known bands in the Los Angeles hardcore scene. Their self-titled 1983 debut was a classic of the genre, and it contained what is still their best-known song, "Institutionalized." In fact, their punk credentials were so thoroughly without question that the song appeared on the soundtrack to *Repo Man*, and

their popularity with skater punks of the day made them the unofficial musical mascots of the subculture. They appeared to have a bright future in that particular scene, but they ran into years of label problems that prevented them from following up on their initial success. By the time they finally landed a new deal with Caroline Records, it was 1987. Four years had passed, and half of the band's lineup was long gone—only bassist Louis Mayorga and vocalist Mike Muir remained. The band's sound had changed considerably as well, from the pure hardcore of their debut to a speed metal crossover style that former hardcore bands like D.R.I. had since taken up. Suicidal Tendencies' new album, *Join the Army*, contained the skater

anthem "Possessed to Skate," and the band managed against all odds to retain a sizable portion of their original fan base, which had neither seen nor heard from them in years. Based on the band's considerable following, Epic Records offered them a deal, and their debut for the label, *How Will I Laugh Tomorrow When I Can't Even Smile Today*, was their most popular album to date. Stylistically, it marked a total commitment to the heavy metal sound, which they no longer tempered with even the slightest hardcore tendencies.

After offering *Controlled By Hatred/Feel Like Shit... Deja Vu*, a reissue of two of the band's EPs in 1989, they released *Lights, Camera, Revolution* the following year. The album featured new bassist Robert Trujillo, an extremely talented funk musician whose predisposition for slapping and popping was well matched to the spirit of the times, which saw bands like the Red Hot Chili Peppers gaining popularity and influencing many metal bands to experiment with funk, making for a dark time in heavy metal history. To further explore their new funk bent, Trujillo and Muir started a side project in 1992 called Infectious Grooves while simultaneously playing with Suicidal Tendencies. But it may have eventually proven too much to keep both bands afloat, because in 1994, after the release of *Suicidal for Life*, Suicidal Tendencies broke up, and Muir and Trujillo began to work on Infectious Grooves exclusively. The bassist was also hired by Ozzy Osbourne as part of his touring band and has since appeared on Ozzy's 2001 album *Down to Earth* and on the 2002 reissues of *Blizzard of Ozz* and *Diary of a Madman*, whose original bass and drum tracks were erased in favor of new ones performed by Trujillo and former Faith No More drummer Mike Bordin. Trujillo joined Metallica in 2003. In the meantime, Muir has re-formed Suicidal Tendencies, and also recorded solo material under the alias Cyco Miko. A new Suicidal Tendencies album has been rumored since 2006, but several official, confirmed release dates have come and gone since then with no product in sight.

Mike Clark: guitars (*How Will I Laugh Tomorrow When I Can't Even Smile Today* and later); **Jimmy DeGrasso**: drums (*Suicidal for Life*) (see also Megadeth, Y&T); **Grant Estes**: guitars (*Suicidal Tendencies*); **Josh Freese**: drums (*The Art of Rebellion, Still Cyco After All These Years*); **Rocky George**: guitars (*Join the Army* through *Suicidal for Life*); **Bob Heathcote**: bass (*How Will I Laugh Tomorrow When I Can't Even Smile Today*); **R. J. Herrera**: drums (*Join the Army* through *Lights, Camera; Revolution*); **Louis Mayorga**: bass (*Suicidal Tendencies, Join the Army*); **Mike Muir**: vocals; **Josh Paul**: bass (*Prime Cuts: The Best of Suicidal Tendencies* and later); **Dean Pleasants**: guitars (*Prime Cuts: The Best of Suicidal Tendencies* and later); **Amery Smith**: drums (*Suicidal Tendencies*); **Stymee**: bass (*Controlled by Hatred/Feel Like Shit... Deja Vu*); **Robert**

Los vatos locos are Suicidal Tendencies. Left to right: Robert Trujillo, Mike Clark, Mike Muir, and Rocky George.

Trujillo: bass (*Lights, Camera, Revolution* through *Suicidal for Life*); **Brooks Wackerman**: drums (*Prime Cuts: The Best of Suicidal Tendencies* and later)

Discography: *Suicidal Tendencies* (Frontier, 1983); *Join the Army* (Caroline, 1987); *How Will I Laugh Tomorrow When I Can't Even Smile Today* (Epic, 1988); *Lights, Camera, Revolution* (Epic, 1990); *The Art of Rebellion* (Epic, 1992); *Suicidal for Life* (Epic, 1994); *Prime Cuts: The Best of Suicidal Tendencies* (Epic, 1997); *Friends and Family* (Suicidal, 1998); *Freedumb* (Suicidal, 1999); *Free Your Soul and Save My Mind* (Suicidal, 2000); *Friends and Family, Vol. 2* (XIII Bis, 2001)

YEARS ACTIVE: 1968–1982

Along with T. Rex and Mott the Hoople, the Sweet was the exemplary 1970s British glam rock band. They used heavy guitar sounds to distract listeners from their very obvious bubblegum inclinations—melodically speaking, they were easily in the same league as the Bay City Rollers, and the fact that they are considered a glam band or a metal band is more of a testament to the deftness of their tailors than to their musicianship. In any event, whatever the Sweet's formula was, it worked; the band sold equally well on both sides of the Atlantic, quite a rarity among British glam bands. A lot of the credit for this goes to the independent songwriting team of Mike Chapman and Nicky Chinn, who wrote the group's material when the Sweet was initially signed to RCA in 1971. Among the songs for which the pair was responsible were "Funny Funny," "Little Willy," and "Wigwam Bang," all of which were Top 40 hits. In contrast, the actual band members of the Sweet were allowed to write songs only for use as B-sides and album filler, and the material they wrote was significantly harder-edged than the stuff that was done for them. This prompted Chapman and Chinn to try their hand at writing music for the Sweet that was more appropriate and imitative of the band's own lyrics. Their first

The Sweet performs for the BBC television show *Top of the Pops*. Left to right: Mick Tucker, Steve Priest, Brian Connolly, and Andy Scott.

no shortage of newly repackaged greatest-hits albums, so there must be some kind of ongoing demand for their music.

Brian Connolly: vocals (*Funny How Sweet Coco Can Be* and later); **Gary Moberley**: keyboards (*Waters Edge*); **Steve Priest**: bass; **Andy Scott**: guitar; **Frank Torpey**: guitar; **Mick Tucker**: drums/vocals

Discography: *Funny How Sweet Co-Co Can Be* (RCA, 1971); *Sweet Fanny Adams* (RCA, 1974); *Desolation Boulevard* (Capitol, 1974); *Strung Up* (RCA, 1975); *Give Us a Wink* (Capitol, 1976); *Off the Record* (Capitol, 1977); *Level Headed* (One Way, 1978); *Cut Above the Rest* (Capitol, 1979); *Waters Edge* (Capitol, 1980); *Identity Crisis* (Polydor, 1982);

THE TEA PARTY

YEARS ACTIVE: 1990–2005; 2011–PRESENT

While incredibly overlooked in the United States, the Tea Party does just fine in its native Canada. The fact that the band hails from anywhere other than Morocco or Turkey, however, must have come as a surprise to anyone whose first exposure to them was through their 1995 album, *The Edges of Twilight*, which came the closest of any of their releases to bringing them to a wide audience in the United States. While they had certainly displayed undeniable exotic leanings on their 1993 debut, *Splendor Solis*, that album drew heavily on 1970s album-oriented rock, resulting in a sound that was basically identical to Led Zeppelin with Jim Morrison singing. The voice of singer Jeff Martin is a dead ringer to that of the Lizard King, and Martin's remarkable guitar playing suggests that he could have been stranded for twenty years on a desert island with nothing but Jimmy Page tablature books. *The Edges of Twilight*, on the other hand, while still obviously indebted to Zeppelin and the like, saw the band augment their power-trio sound with a dizzying array of authentic Middle Eastern instruments. The band also covered other musical territory, capably handling straightforward blues-rock material, Celt-

such effort, the aptly titled "Blockbuster," shot to number one in the United Kingdom, and was followed in similar fashion by a succession of hit singles, one of which, "Ballroom Blitz," remains the Sweet's best-known song.

Alas, in 1974 the Sweet decided that it was time to crawl out from under the iron heel of the Chapman/Chinn songwriting team and strike out on its own. Surely it was a mere coincidence that their first album without the duo, *Sweet Fanny Adams*, was 100 percent hit-free. The following year, however, the band bounced

back with "Fox on the Run," which charted in the Top 10, but by this time they were moving more and more toward album-oriented rock, a decision that was proving less and less successful for them with every release. They had one more hit in 1978, with "Love Is Like Oxygen," but that was it—they never again had another song reach the Top 10. They slugged it out for another couple of years, finally deciding to hang it up in 1982. The band has since reformed a few times for the odd reunion tour, and as their discography shows, there has been

Jeff Martin does double duty as the Tea Party singer and guitarist.

of two things—that the band hasn't sold the domain name, and that the site features "No politics . . . Just Rock and Roll."

Jeff Burrows: drums; **Stuart Chatwood**: bass; **Jeff Martin**: vocals/guitar

Discography: *Splendor Solis* (Chrysalis, 1993); *The Edges of Twilight* (EMI, 1995); *Transmission* (Atlantic, 1997); *Triptych* (EMI Canada, 1999); *The Interzone Mantras* (EMI Canada, 2001); *Seven Circles* (EMI, 2004)

TERRA FIRMA

YEARS ACTIVE: 1999–2002

Hailing from Sweden, Terra Firma boasted guitarist Freddie Eugene of the death metal band Unleashed and singer Christian "Lord Chritus" Lindersson, formerly of Count Raven and the legendary Saint Vitus. The band's self-titled ten-song debut, which was over much too quickly at forty minutes, was one of the best metal albums of 1999. It is aggressive and inventive and just downright swings, a trait not too many doom albums are famous for. In 2001, Terra Firma released the excellent *Harm's Way*, which expanded upon the band's already evident strengths and possessed production values that were light years ahead of the debut's somewhat shrill and tinny sound. The band never gained much recognition outside of the doom metal fan dungeon, and they broke up after their second album.

Freddie Eugene: guitars; **Izmo Ledderfejs**: drums; **Christian "Lord Chritus" Lindersson**: vocals (see also Saint Vitus); **Nico Moosebeach**: bass

Discography: *Terra Firma* (Music Cartel, 1999); *Harm's Way* (SPV, 2001)

influenced folk guitar, and their own unique brand of songwriting, which sometimes, as in the case of their single "The Bazaar," sounded like an Iranian folk song as performed by Living Colour. It was pretty heady stuff, to be sure, which is probably why it didn't catch on as well as it would have in a perfect universe, where talent is rewarded. In 1997, the band released *Transmission*, another brilliant album, which added techno beats and tape loops to their sound. It probably sold about ten copies in the United States, thanks to the nonexistent push from their label, which did them the courtesy of dropping them shortly thereafter. The band made three albums for EMI Music Canada and then broke up in 2005. They reunited in 2011, just in time for the right wing U.S. anti-tax Tea Party movement to make overtures to buy their domain name, TeaParty. com. Currently, visitors to the site are informed

TESLA

California's Tesla is unfairly lumped with the 1980s glam metal movement, pretty much because of the time period in which they operated. The band simply produced straightforward hard rock, and their popularity during the 1980s was less the product of their affiliation with any scene than with a curious phenomenon, wherein people who liked Tesla's music bought it. Yes, it's true; every so often, bands sell records because people like the music, not because there's some MTV mandate. Tesla started out in Sacramento in 1982, finally winning a contract with Geffen Records, which released the band's 1986 debut, *Mechanical Resonance*. It went platinum on the strength of the single "Modern Day Cowboy." This set the stage for the band's breakthrough album, *The Great Radio Controversy*, which was released in 1989 and got a huge push from the Top 10 single "Love Song." The next logical step was, of course, for the band to try to come up with a follow-up that would cynically cash in on all the attributes that had made the previous album a hit, but instead they followed in 1990 with *Five Man Acoustical Jam*, which featured the band in a live acoustic setting, a decision that the programming executives at MTV surely took to heart, to which the spate of *MTV Unplugged* albums that the 1990s produced will attest.

Tesla managed to survive into the middle of the grunge revolution pretty much unscathed. Even though the band was no longer the platinum-selling juggernaut it had been just a few years prior, their 1994 album, *Bust a Nut*, went gold, a remarkable achievement given that it received no promotion whatsoever. Unfortunately, guitarist Tommy Skeoch had been nursing drug problems for some time, and in 1995 he was given the axe. Rather than replace him, the band chose to continue as a quartet, with remaining guitarist Frank

Tesla's members loaf around in an unassuming fashion. Left to right: Tommy Skeoch, Troy Luccketta, Jeff Keith, Brian Wheat, and Frank Hannon.

Hannon capably handling all the six-string duties. But things just weren't the same without their recovering comrade, with whom they had struggled and built up the band over all those years, and they decided to disband in 1996. In 2000, with Skeoch well enough to take part, Tesla mounted a small reunion tour, and in 2001 the band released *Replugged Live*, an album culled from those performances. This was followed in 2002 with *Standing Room Only*, another live album. Rather than continue to release nothing but live albums with nearly identical track listings on an annual basis for the remainder of its career, Tesla finally released a new studio album, *Into the Now*, in 2004. Despite the band's terminal unhipness and long drought of new product, the album debuted in the Top 40. Their audience had never given up on them, even if popular culture had. Unfortunately, Skeoch's drug problems resurfaced, and the band replaced him with new guitarist Dave Rude. Their first album with this lineup was the 2007 covers album *Real to Reel*, which they followed in 2008 with *Forever More*.

Frank Hannon: guitar; **Jeff Keith**: vocals; **Troy Luccketta**: drums; **Dave Rude**: guitar (*Real to Reel* and later); **Tommy Skeoch**: guitar; **Brian Wheat**: bass

Discography: *Mechanical Resonance* (Geffen, 1986); *The Great Radio Controversy* (Geffen, 1989); *Five Man Acoustical Jam* (Geffen, 1990); *Psychotic Supper* (Geffen, 1991); *Bust a Nut* (Geffen, 1994); *Replugged Live* (Sanctuary, 2001); *Standing Room Only* (Sanctuary, 2002); *Into the Now* (Sanctuary, 2004); *Real to Reel* (Ryko, 2007); *Real to Reel Vol. 2* (Ryko, 2007); *Forever More* (Ryko, 2008)

TESTAMENT

Testament is one of the most influential Bay Area thrash bands, right alongside Exodus and that other band that does those Diamond Head covers (also known as Metallica). Testament also boasts many, many musicians who went on to other well-known bands, such as

After fifteen years in the business, the members of Testament still are not allowed to smile. Left to right: Louie Clemente, Alex Skolnick, Greg Christian, Eric Peterson, and Chuck Billy.

Slayer drummer Paul Bostaph, White Zombie drummer John Tempesta, and Death guitarist James Murphy, to name but a few. While the band has never achieved the top-tier status of groups like Megadeth or Anthrax, they retain a sizable following and are still going strong.

Testament formed in 1983 and started hitting the clubs, finally attracting the attention of Megaforce Records in 1986. Vocalist Souza left the group to join Exodus at this time, a turn of events that could have proven disastrous because the charismatic Souza was generally regarded as an irreplaceable element of the band. However, his replacement was the very large Chuck Billy, who ended up being a much better and more versatile singer, and between his vocals and the lead guitar mastery of Alex Skolnick, the band now had a sound that was accomplished enough to set them apart from the rest of the pack. While they compromised none of their speed or their massive crunch, they possessed a melodic sensibility and musicianship that most of their peers lacked. Their Megaforce debut, *The Legacy* (the title was taken from the band's original name), was immediately assigned classic status by thrash fans. A subsequent tour with Anthrax significantly increased their profile within this community of fans, who snatched up their 1988 sophomore effort, *The New Order*, and 1989's *Practice What You Preach*, their most successful effort yet. A massive yearlong tour followed, which was accompanied by regular airplay on MTV's *Headbanger's Ball*. Clearly, Testament was about to become huge. But it didn't happen.

The band was permanently derailed from

Testament singer Chuck Billy belts it out.

been jamming with jazz guitarists with alarming frequency, left the band, citing artistic frustration. Then drummer Louie Clemente also said his good-byes to Testament. Finally, after *Return to the Apocalyptic City*, a live EP, and the band's almost death metal–sounding *Low* album, their label dropped them in 1994. This combination of factors would have spelled certain death for most bands, but it actually served as a catalyst for new beginnings.

Apparently, while Skolnick had felt artistically limited within the band's thrash confines, the other members had felt that their music was being compromised in order to accommodate his jazzier and more melodic propensities. With Skolnick out of the way and infamous death metal guitarist James Murphy in his place, the band made up for lost time by crafting the most brutal records they could, even enlisting the incalculable talents of Slayer skin basher Dave Lombardo on their 1999 album, *The Gathering*. Soon after its release, Murphy was diagnosed with a brain tumor, and Billy was diagnosed with a rare form of cancer. Had it not been for the generosity of the heavy metal community, who held fundraisers and benefit shows to get treatment for the uninsured musicians, it's unlikely that either of them would be alive today. However, both of them were treated successfully, and with all that bullshit out of the way the band released 2008's *The Formation of Damnation*, their first new studio album in nine years. In the meantime, Testament is still going strong, and if the past is any indication, there isn't much out there with the power to stop them.

Glen Alvelais: guitars (*Return to the Apocalyptic City* through *Demonic*); **Chuck Billy**: vocals; **Paul Bostaph**: drums (*Return to the Apocalyptic City*; *The Formation of Damnation*) (see also Slayer); **Greg Christian**: bass (*The Legacy* through *Live at the Fillmore*; *The Formation of Damnation*); **Louie Clemente**: drums (*The Legacy* through *The Ritual*); **Jon Dette**: drums

what seemed like a sure road to the top of the heap, mostly because of a few bad decisions and just plain bad luck. The first misstep occurred in 1990 with the release of the *Souls of Black* album, which simply didn't live up to the standards that had been set by the band's previous output. They lost quite a bit of their hard-won credibility, something they had a very hard time winning back. The 1992 album *The Ritual* was a step in the right direction, but it couldn't have been released at a worse time. Had it come out one year earlier, it might have stood a chance, but in the face of the grunge revolution there was not much a metal band that was not Metallica could do to get their records into buyers' hands. Next, guitarist extraordinaire Skolnick, who in the previous few months had

(*Live at the Fillmore*) (see also Slayer); **Steve DiGiorgio**: bass (*The Gathering* and later) (see also Death, Iced Earth); **Gene Hoglan**: drums (*Demonic*) (see also Dark Angel, Death); **Dave Lombardo**: drums (*The Gathering*) (see also Slayer); **James Murphy**: guitars (*Low*, *Live at the Fillmore*, *The Gathering*) (see also Death, Obituary); **Eric Peterson**: guitars; **Derek Ramirez**: bass (*Demonic*); **Alex Skolnick**: guitars (*The Legacy* through *The Ritual*; *First Strike Still Deadly* and later) (see also Savatage); **John Tempesta**: drums (*Low*, *First Strike Still Deadly*) (see also Exodus, White Zombie)

Discography: *The Legacy* (Megaforce, 1987); *The New Order* (Atlantic, 1988); *Practice What You Preach* (Atlantic, 1989); *Souls of Black* (Atlantic, 1990); *The Ritual* (Atlantic, 1992); *Return to the Apocalyptic City* (Atlantic, 1993); *Low* (Atlantic, 1994); *Live at the Fillmore* (Burnt Offerings, 1995); *Demonic* (Burnt Offerings, 1997); *The Gathering* (Spitfire, 1999); *The Formation of Damnation* (Nuclear Blast, 2008)

THERAPY!

YEARS ACTIVE: 1989–PRESENT

Therapy? had the good fortune to be active during the early 1990s, benefiting greatly from the alternative rock movement, without which the group likely never would have gained the relatively high level of recognition that they enjoyed at their commercial peak. Their metal leanings were tempered by a distinct postpunk sensibility that recalled bands like Sonic Youth, whose influence on this Irish band was easily as strong as that of Black Sabbath. As a result, the band occupied a gray area between metal and alternative rock that was ambiguous enough to ingratiate them to both audiences. The band started their career in an inauspicious fashion, independently releasing the single "Meat Abstract." The legendary BBC disc jockey John Peel was a big fan of the song and regularly played the single on his show. For many bands, the John Peel Stamp of Approval meant the difference between obscurity and notoriety, and indeed in the case of Therapy?, it went a long way toward putting them on the map. They eventually gained enough recognition to warrant a compilation of all of their singles and EPs, and the resulting 1992 collection, *Caucasian Psychosis*, gained the attention of the major labels. The band ended up signing to A&M, which, it should be said, displayed better taste during the alternative rock signing frenzy than a lot of its contemporaries.

Therapy?'s first A&M release, *Nurse*, was issued in 1993, and the subsequent *Hats Off to the Insane* EP saw the band developing a slightly less noisy sound that focused more on melody than their previous output did. These releases sound as if Therapy? was struggling a little bit to find a good balance between its influences. But it all came together by 1994 with *Troublegum*, which brought the band as close as they were ever going to get to mainstream

Andy Cairns plays a friendly game of hide-and-seek during a Therapy? concert.

The Irish MacDaddies of Therapy? know a thing or two about pimping. Left to right: Michael McKeegan, Graham Hopkins, and Martin McCarrick.

popularity. Although the album featured a strong single, "Screamager," and was their most melodically focused effort to date, the band was simply too harsh-sounding and negative for mainstream audiences, while at the same time they were too poplike for fans of grating noise rock. For a while, however, there were enough people in the middle to keep Therapy? in the spotlight.

Unfortunately, in 1998, several major labels were gobbled up by the media giant Seagram's, which immediately went about the business of downsizing its operation by firing employees on a massive scale and dropping bands left and right that were not major-league sellers—the

term "bloodbath" was regularly used to describe this particular chapter in the history of corporate culture. Therapy? was a textbook example of the kind of band Seagram's was very enthusiastic about kicking off its roster; seeing no need to waste its time with a band that was not going to sell in Janet Jackson numbers, the company dropped the cranky Celts faster than you can say Erin go bragh. Happily, though, the label merger phenomenon had inadvertently created an inverse and opposite reaction, wherein hundreds of independent labels cropped up with the sole intention of providing new homes for the recent casualties of corporate downsizing. So Therapy? wasn't homeless for very long—Miles Copeland signed the band to his Ark 21 label, for which they issued 2001's *Shameless*. Their last album, *A Brief Crack of Light*, was released on Valentine's Day of 2012, so forgo the roses and chocolates and buy your sweetheart the 13th studio album by Therapy? instead.

Andy Cairns: vocals/guitar; **Neil Cooper**: drums (*High Anxiety* and later); **Fyfe Ewing**: drums (*Caucasian Psychosis* through *Suicide Pact: You First*); **Graham Hopkins**: drums (*Shameless*); **Martin McCarrick**: guitar (*Caucasian Psychosis* through *Never Apologise Never Explain*); **Michael McKeegan**: bass

Discography: *Caucasian Psychosis* (Quarterstick, 1992); *Nurse* (A&M, 1993); *Troublegum* (A&M, 1994); *Infernal Love* (A&M, 1995); *Semi-Detached* (A&M, 1998); *Suicide Pact: You First* (Ark 21, 2000); *So Much for the Ten Year Plan* (Ark 21, 2000); *Shameless* (Ark 21, 2001); *High Anxiety* (Spitfire, 2003); *Never Apologise Never Explain*

(Spitfire, 2004); *Once Cure Fits All* (Spitfire, 2006); *Crooked Timber* (Demolition, 2009); *A Brief Crack of Light* (Blast, 2012)

YEARS ACTIVE: 1987–PRESENT

When Sweden's Therion formed in the 1980s, it was supposed to be a death metal band, with strong elements of Celtic Frost worship. But their sound shifted and mutated over the years, and ultimately it became something else that was totally unique. Therion was put together by vocalist and guitarist Christofer Johnsson, and to this day he has remained the only constant member. He alone has guided the band through permutation after permutation. Even though a dizzying number of musicians have come and gone, Johnsson deserves the lion's share of the credit for making the band what it is today.

Therion's original lineup was Johnsson, bassist Erik Gustafsson, guitarist Peter Hansson, and drummer Oskar Forss, and this foursome appears on the 1990 debut, *Of Darkness . . .* That version of the group was already a thing of the past by the time they released their next album, 1991's *Beyond Sanctorum*, which was recorded without the services of Gustafsson. By their 1993 album *Symphony Masses: Ho Drakon Ho Megas*, Johnsson was the only original member left.

Throughout these lineup changes, the sound of Therion shifted considerably. Classical instrumentation and choral elements had been introduced, while the overtly death metal tendencies were getting progressively downplayed. Anyone who hoped that the symphonic elements were just an experiment was out of luck. By 1996's *Theli*, the bombast had almost completely taken over, and Therion simply was not the same band any more. Nor would it ever be again. The album may have contained a nod to the past by featuring the song "To Mega

Therion," the title of the second Celtic Frost album, but that was about it. The growling vocals and demo-quality production were long gone, and Therion was now a fully symphonic metal band.

Therion continued in this vein throughout the next decade. After 2000's *Deggial*, they released 2001's *Secret of the Runes*, their most heavily orchestrated offering yet. It also featured a cover of ABBA's "Summer Night City" as a bonus track, which must be heard to be believed. In 2004 they planned to release two albums simultaneously, *Lemuria* and *Sirius B*, but in the end they released them together as a two-disc set. It featured the use of over 170 different musicians, including a 32-member choir. The end result was so grandiloquent and pompous that it suggested Wagner's Ring cycle, minus the four intermissions. The 2007 album

Gothic Kabbalah marked the 20th anniversary of the band, and their most recent album was 2010's *Sitra Ahra*. In 2011, the group released a board game, "011."

Magnus Barthelsson: guitar (*Symphony Masses: Ho Drakon Ho Megas*); **Tommy Eriksson**: guitar (*Vovin* through *Crowning of Atlantis*); **Oskar Forss**: drums (*Of Darkness . . .* through *Beyond Sanctorum*); **Kimberly Goss**: vocals (*Vovin* through *Crowning of Atlantis*); **Erik Gustafsson**: bass (*Of Darkness . . .*); **Peter Hansson**: guitar (*Of Darkness . . .* through *Beyond Sanctorum*); **Fredrik Isaksson**: bass (*Lepaca Kliffoth*); **Christofer Johnsson**: guitar, keyboards; **Petter Karlsson**: drums (*Gothic Kabbalah*); **Sami Karppinen**: drums (*Deggial* through *Secret of the Runes*); **Jan Kazda**: bass (*Vovin* through *Crowning of Atlantis*); **Jonas Mellberg**: guitar (*Theli* through *A'arab Zaraq—Lucid Dreaming*); **Johan Niemann**: bass (*Deggial* through *Gothic Kabbalah*); **Kristian Niemann**: (*Deggial* through *Gothic Kabbalah*); **Nalle Pahlsson**: bass (2009–present); **Lars Rosenberg** (*Theli* through

Thomas Vikström of Therion can always star in a production of *Phantom of the Opera* if this whole symphonic metal thing doesn't work out.

A'arab Zaraq—Lucid Dreaming); **Wolf Simon**: drums (*Vovin* through *Crowning of Atlantis*); **Christian Vidal**: guitar (*Sitra Ahra*); **Thomas Vikström**: vocals (*Sitra Ahra*); **Andreas Wallan Wahl**: bass (*Symphony Masses: Ho Drakon Ho Megas*); **Piotr Wawrzeniuk**: drums (*Symphony Masses: Ho Drakon Ho Megas* through *A'arab Zaraq—Lucid Dreaming*)

Discography: *Of Darkness* (Nuclear Blast, 1990); *Beyond Sanctorum* (Nuclear Blast, 1991); *Symphony Masses: Ho Drakon Ho Megas* (Nuclear Blast, 1993); *Theli* (Nuclear Blast, 1997); *A'arab Zaraq—Lucid Dreaming* (Nuclear Blast, 1997); *Vovin* (Nuclear Blast, 1998); *Crowning of Atlantis* (Nuclear Blast, 1999); *Deggial* (Nuclear Blast, 2000); *Secrets of the Runes* (Nuclear Blast, 2001); *Lemuria/Sirius B* (Nuclear Blast, 2004); *Gothic Kabbalah* (Nuclear Blast, 2007)

NORWAY

Norway is a small country in the Scandinavian peninsula. Its politics are liberal and its people are nice. A lot of them even speak English! Perhaps as a reaction to this predominantly genial demeanor, it's also the home to countless black metal bands, some of whom have gone a bit overboard to demonstrate how badass they are. These bands have had members who have burned down churches and committed murder. But hey, they were just keeping it real.

Not every metal band in Norway is a black metal band, but it would be accurate to say that the country has indeed produced a shitload of them. A lot of this actually comes down to the fact that its black metal scene is pretty incestuous. A member of band X has probably at some point been in band Y and band Z, as well as done a side project with the drummer from band W. One of the best examples of this phenomenon is probably Gorgoroth. Based in Bergen and founded in 1992 by guitarist and sole remaining original member Infernus, the band's drummer, Goat Pervertor (yes, really, Goat Pervertor), stayed with the band for about two years, making him a veteran.

One of the better-known members of the group is former vocalist Gaahl, who was also in Gaahlskagg and Trelldom. He and former Gorgoroth bassist King ov Hell would eventually leave to form their own band, God Seed. In a move out of left field, Gaahl left that group and the music business entirely behind to become a clothing designer in 2009. This left King ov Hell to form a new black metal band, Ov Hell. Gaahl and King ov Hell have also been involved in projects outside of black metal. Gaahl was involved in a dark ambient folk project called Wardruna, and King ov Hell is a member of the heavy rock band Sahg, who at times sounds downright commercial.

Hailing from Bergen, Borknagar is a black metal band that utilizes elements of folk metal and progressive rock. Oslo's Tsjuder formed in 1993 and gained attention for the brutality of their music, which was extreme even by black metal standards. Ulver released their first album, *Bergtatt—Et Eeventyr I 5 Capitler* in 1995, a black metal effort with folk metal overtones. They abandoned that approach pretty quickly and have since adopted an experimental approach that's hard to pin down as part of any particular genre. Keep of Kalessin also started out in the black metal scene, but over time their approach became more melodic and experimental, while still extreme. Guitarist, keyboardist, and Keep of Kalessin founder Obsidian C also played in Satyricon, which has been playing black metal mixed with medieval music since 1991. Other Norwegian black metal bands include Strid, founded in 1993, and Taake, which released its first album, *Nattestid Ser Porten Vid*, in 1999. Taake got into a bit of hot water during a 2007 concert in Essen, Germany, when their vocalist, Høst, took to the stage with a swastika drawn on his chest, costing them all of their remaining German tour dates. Germans, apparently, are a little sensitive about that swastika business. Smooth move, Ex-Lax!!

Now, not every band in Norway is a Christ-hating, torch-bearing black metal entity in cloaks and corpsepaint. It's lonely, but the bands are out there. Among them are Devil, a doom metal band whose debut album, *Time to Repent*, was released in 2011, Dodheimsgard, who abandoned black metal for industrial, and Kvelertak, who abandoned it for a rowdy take on metal bordering on punk. TNT is a glam band, and they've been going strong since 1982 thanks to the ongoing efforts of founding guitarist Ronni Le Tekrø. TNT also saw some brief chart action in the U.S., which is more than you can say for that Goat Pervertor dude. Going back to the early 1970s, there's Aunt Mary, which made three excellent albums of progressive proto-metal in the early 1970s, with 1972's *Loaded* being particularly tasty. Finally, there's Lucifer Was, a 1970s heavy prog band with dueling flutes which took over 20 years to finally make its debut album, 1997's *Underground and Beyond*. If you like Jethro Tull, but feel like they don't have enough flutes, this is the band for you.

SWEDEN

Sweden's neighbor Norway is on the Scandinavian peninsula, and even though it's similar in some ways to that country, the people, culture, and music are very different. Sweden's primary contribution to modern heavy metal has been its death metal bands, such as Entombed, Arch Enemy, and In Flames. The country also made numerous contributions to the stoner rock genre with such bands as Dozer and the Hellacopters. But there's more than just death metal and stoner rock to the land that gave us "Dancing Queen" by ABBA and "The Final Countdown" by Europe, and the bands occupy the full spectrum of metal and beyond.

Sweden made important contributions to early metal in the 1970s. November was formed in 1969 and was one of the earliest examples of heavy acid rock to emerge from that country. Clearly influenced by bands like Cream and Mountain, the group featured standout musicians, particularly drummer Björn Inge. They made only three studio albums, 1970's *En Ny Tid Är Här*, 1971's *2:a* and 1972's *6:e*, which can still be found on CD if you Google them relentlessly. They are worth the effort. Another Swedish band of this vintage is Heavy Load, sometimes hailed as the country's first true heavy metal band. They frequently invoked the imagery of their Viking forefathers, as in "Heathens from the North" and "Might for Right," a full decade or more before the black metal hordes picked up the mantle.

Joining Hammer-Fall in the Swedish power metal genre is Sabaton, whose lyrics serve primarily as seminars on various wars through-

JANUS/Aunt Mary

out history. Sweden has made some contributions to the black metal genre too, such as Dissection, Watain, and Abruptum. Abruptum was formed in 1989 by midget vocalist (or "little person" if you prefer) Tony Särkkä, better known as IT. He was not named IT because he was an information technology consultant, but because he was "too evil to have a human name," according to the 1998 book *Lords of Chaos*. Abruptum was signed to the Deathlike Silence Productions label, founded by the late Euronymous of Mayhem. Stockholm's Tiamat formed in 1988 as a black metal band, but they abandoned the style after their debut, slowing the music down and adding keyboard textures that wouldn't be out of place on Pink Floyd's *Meddle*.

If you prefer not to acknowledge any music created after 1980, there have been plenty of Swedish bands willing to perpetuate the illusion for you. Among them are the very heavy sludge rock retro band Grand Magus, whose self-titled debut came out in 2001, and whose two best albums, *Monument* and *Wolf's Return*, came out in 2003 and 2005 respectively. Spiritual Beggars, meanwhile, have been releasing quality retro-stoner metal since being founded in 1994 by Michael Amott of Carcass. They broke through to a larger audience with 2000's excellent *Ad Astra*, which is heavy on the Hammond organ, praise Jesus. Newer retro metal bands include Witchcraft, whose self-titled album is pure 1970s plod, and Ghost, whose debut, *Opus Eponymous*, was released in 2010 to rave reviews. Sadly, their stage act, which involves the singer wearing a skeleton mask and a pointy pope hat, is a put-on, just like their mock-Satanic lyrics, but that doesn't seem to be a problem for anybody besides this writer. Rounding out the throwback posse is In Solitude, which wields a wholly classic sound reminiscent of such New Wave of British Heavy Metal bands as Judas Priest and Iron Maiden.

While diversity is nice, it still wouldn't be Sweden without death metal. Some of the noteworthy bands include Amon Amarth, the on-again-off-again At The Gates, whom many people believe were instrumental in the creation of the Gothenburg death metal sound, and Repugnant, whose sole album, *Epitome of Darkness*, is considered a classic of the genre despite not seeing release until after the band had already broken up. Dismember, who only recently broke up in 2011, debuted in 1991 with *Like an Ever Flowing Stream*, which is also considered an essential pillar of the Swedish death metal movement. Finally, there's Soilwork, founded in 1996 and still going strong today.

witchcraft
— THE ALCHEMIST —

THIN LIZZY

That Thin Lizzy ever got famous is nothing short of a miracle when one considers the many daunting obstacles that stood in their way. For one thing, they had the distinction of being the first hard rock band from Ireland to gain any kind of significant recognition outside their country, so they had to break into completely new markets in order to be heard. Second, their bassist and lead singer, Phil Lynott, was black, and while it is still a rarity for heavy metal bands today to have black members much less front men, it was nearly unheard-of in the 1970s. As such, Thin Lizzy had two major cultural walls to break through, to say nothing of the massive effort that normally accompanies getting a band off the ground even under the most ideal circumstances. However, anyone who was able to look past the superficial bullshit saw a band of immense talent and originality. They had a unique and distinct musical style, exemplified by a double harmonized lead guitar sound that influenced bands like Iron Maiden and Metallica. The band also had Lynott's world-class singing voice and intelligent lyrics going for them. Although the word *poet* is regularly abused and bandied about in discussions of lyricists of even the most dubious skill, in Lynott's case it really did apply. He showed genuine mastery over the form, and whether he was engaged in simple wordplay or expressing the most esoteric concepts, he always articulated himself in a manner that was simultaneously gritty and romantic. He also managed to carve out his own niche in this area as far as subject matter was concerned—his lyrics rejected the mystical preoccupations of most heavy metal songs in favor of romanticized meditations on day-to-day life among the poor and working class; many of the songs would not have sounded out of place on a Steve Earle album.

The group took a few tries before they really set their approach in stone and a few more after that before they hit the big time. In fact, it wasn't until 1976, with their seventh studio album, *Jailbreak*, that they achieved widespread recognition. The album contained "The Boys Are Back in Town," which was their biggest hit and is certainly their most well-known song today. While the ode to blue-collar average Joes blowing off some steam is to blame for the subsequent proliferation of terrible songs with this theme (check out Loverboy's "Working for the Weekend"), at the time it was an unusual topic for a heavy metal song, and the fact that it became the unutterable cliché that it is today is more a testament to its groundbreaking popularity than to any inherently loathsome qualities that it might possess. The single's popularity and the subsequent popularity of *Jailbreak* created a demand for Thin Lizzy all over the world, to which the band responded with endless touring, which increased their popularity even more.

In addition to the band's aforementioned talents, they were also a stellar live unit, coming across onstage with a ferocity that was not even remotely hinted at in their studio work. Although they never again achieved the level of success that they enjoyed with *Jailbreak*, they continued to tour and record nonstop, and they managed to hold on to their loyal fan base for the remainder of their career, long after all the trend-hoppers had gotten off the bus when "The Boys Are Back in Town" ceased to be a hit song. It all came to an end in 1983, however, after the release of *Thunder and Lightning*, when everyone in the band decided that they had had a good run and the time to pack their bags was nigh. Sadly, three years later, Lynott succumbed to his drug and alcohol vices, dying in 1986 at the age of thirty-five—the life and brilliant career of one of heavy metal's true giants was over, and so was Thin Lizzy. After all, Lynott *was* Thin Lizzy, and going on without him was as ludicrous a proposition as Rush going on without Geddy Lee.

Thin Lizzy, seen here in 1977, finally broke through after recording seven albums. Left to right: Brian Robertson, Phil Lynott, Brian Downey, and Scott Gorham.

Since Lynott's death, the band was resurrected on a few occasions for charity events, and it was always made very clear from the outset that there was no intention of it going any further than that. That changed in 1996 when guitarist John Sykes reunited the band, billing it as a tribute to the front man. The effort lasted for several years and yielded a live album, 2000's *One Night Only*, but concerts became increasingly sporadic and ultimately petered out. However, in 2009, guitarist Scott Gorham put together a new lineup of the band which this time included original drummer Brian Downey. His presence lent the new-look band additional credibility, and this lineup kicked off a major world tour in 2011. At the same time, remixed and remastered versions of the band's back catalog were reissued, an effort that had been desperately needed for a very long time. Not long into the tour, Gorham told Billboard.com that the band was thinking about the possibility of making a new studio album, something that would have been considered blasphemy not too long before. They had already blasphemed by touring under the Thin Lizzy name, so what harm could there be in smashing the last remaining taboo?

Eric Bell: guitars (*Thin Lizzy* through *Vagabonds of the Western World*); **Brian Downey**: drums; **Scott Gorham**: guitars (*Nightlife* and later); **Phil Lynott**: bass/vocals; **Gary Moore**: guitars (*Nightlife, Black Rose: A Rock Legend*); **Brian Robertson**: guitars (*Nightlife* through *Live and Dangerous*) (see also Motörhead); **John Sykes**: guitars (*Thunder and Lightning*) (see also Tygers of Pan Tang, Whitesnake); **Darren Wharton**: keyboards (*Thunder and Lightning*); **Snowy White**: guitars (*Chinatown, Renegade*)

Discography: *Thin Lizzy* (Decca, 1971); *New Day* (Decca, 1971); *Shades of a Blue Orphanage* (Decca, 1972); *Vagabonds of the Western World* (Decca, 1973); *Nightlife* (Vertigo, 1974); *Fighting* (Vertigo, 1975); *Jailbreak* (Vertigo, 1976); *Remembering: Part 1* (Decca, 1976); *Johnny the Fox* (Vertigo, 1976); *Bad Reputation* (Vertigo, 1977); *Live and Dangerous* (Vertigo, 1978); *Black Rose: A Rock Legend* (Vertigo, 1979); *Chinatown* (Vertigo, 1980); *Renegade* (Vertigo, 1981); *Thunder and Lightning* (Vertigo, 1983); *Life: Live* (Warner Bros., 1983); *BBC Radio 1 Live in Concert* (Windsong, 1994);

The Peel Sessions (Strange Fruit, 1994); *The Boys Are Back in Town: Live in Australia* (Nipon, 1999); *One Night Only* (CMC, 2000); *UK Tour '75* (RSK, 2008); *Still Dangerous: Live At the Tower Theatre Philadelphia 1977* (VH1 Classic, 2009); *Thin Lizzy At the BBC* (Universal, 2011); *Live in London 2011* (Plastic Head, 2011); *Live at High Voltage 2011* (101 Distribution, 2011)

YEARS ACTIVE: 1990–PRESENT

Tool was one of the true originals to emerge from the 1990s alternative rock movement. In truth, the band was equal parts alternative rock, progressive rock, heavy metal, punk, and other influences too obscure to identify. This is to say nothing of the fact that they brought a genuinely dark and creative atmosphere to the music charts, which are not renowned for rewarding the purveyors of these attributes with high positions. Good timing was certainly a factor. Tool emerged when grunge did, and even if the group's complicated and technical music wasn't a perfect fit with the style of the times, their deeply pained, angst-ridden subject matter was. This allowed them to sneak into the mainstream through the back door, and they have managed to stay there, against all odds, ever since.

Although they already had an EP, 1992's *Opiate*, to their credit, Tool truly broke through in 1993, simultaneously appearing at Lollapalooza and releasing *Undertow*, their first full-length album, which went platinum despite edited radio singles and album artwork that appeared to have been culled from the pages of *BUF* magazine. Their 1996 follow-up, *Aenima*, was a similar success, although its recep-

tion was somewhat dampened by the death of the alternative rock movement. Fortunately, the band had established themselves among metal fans and within the musicians' community, two of the most rabidly loyal fan bases in existence, which made it unnecessary for Tool to rely upon widespread mainstream acceptance. Their 1997 tour with Korn was a great success, and when it was all over in 1998, Tool went on a well-earned hiatus. During this time, vocalist Maynard James Keenan formed a side project, A Perfect Circle, whose 2000 album, *Mer de Noms*, sold well on the merits of its Tool affiliation.

Tool reconvened in 2001 to release *Lateralus*, which debuted at number one and went on to become the band's most successful album. After extensive touring, which included ten dates with King Crimson, the band came off the road at the end of 2002 and didn't release another album until 2006's *10,000 Days*. Writing for the next album didn't start in earnest until 2011, and if a statement made by singer Maynard Keenan is any indication, it's going to be a while before the band produces anything. "When it's done everyone will know," he told *Loudwire*. "But I haven't done anything yet." In the meantime, Keenan has been busying himself with the side project Puscifer.

Danny Carey: drums; **Justin Chancellor**: bass (*Aenima* and later); **Paul D'Amour**: bass (*Opiate, Undertow*); **Adam Jones**: guitars; **Maynard James Keenan**: vocals

Discography: *Opiate* (Zoo, 1992); *Undertow* (Zoo, 1993); *Aenima* (Zoo, 1996); *Lateralus* (Zoo, 2001); *10,000 Days* (Volcano, 2006)

Tool's Maynard James Keenan defies convention with regard to music and appearances.

TROUBLE

YEARS ACTIVE: 1979–1995; 2006–PRESENT

Along with Saint Vitus and Candlemass, Chicago's Trouble is another influential doom band of the 1980s. Like its down-tuned brethren, the group never found acceptance outside its loyal cult following because of doom metal's consistent rejection by the mainstream. The band's experience was also consistent with that of their depressed contemporaries in that everyone who ever had a favorable opinion of them went on to form their own doom metal bands. Trouble caught some flak every now and again on the basis of its deeply spiritual Christian lyrics, which caused the band to be labeled as "white metal," one of the sillier subcategory names that heavy metal fans have produced. But Trouble stuck to its guns, and besides, everyone knows that Christian iconography is a perfect visual complement to heavy doom music. Apparently, the people at Metal Blade agreed, as they signed Trouble in 1984 despite the fact that the overwhelming majority of the bands on Metal Blade's imprint espoused satanic viewpoints, whether they meant it or not.

Trouble's first two albums, 1984's *Psalm 9* and 1985's *The Skull*, are now regarded as classic albums of the doom metal subgenre, in particular *The Skull*, which possesses an extremely dark atmosphere and depressing subject matter. This was for good reason—at the time, singer Eric Wagner was in the grip of serious drug problems, and the band was slowly but surely tearing itself apart thanks to internal personal tensions. When it was all over, bassist Sean McAllister and drummer Jeff Olson left the band (rumors exist that Olson eventually went on to become a preacher), to be replaced by Ron Holzner and Dennis Lesh, respectively. Although their first effort in this configuration, the 1987 album *Run to the Light*, was not as well received as their previous albums, the band was picked up by producer Rick Rubin, who signed them to his Def American label and oversaw their new, self-titled album.

Released in 1990, *Trouble* was a revelation to fans of the band's more straightforward early work; it flirted with a psychedelic sound that didn't compromise their gargantuan crunch one iota. The album gained them critical accolades and expanded their audience. After getting off the road from the ensuing tour, they immediately marched back into the studio, vowing to make the album that would break them wide open even if it killed them. In 1992, they emerged with *Manic Frustration*, an elaborate, ambitious album that, creatively speaking, was everything the band could possibly have hoped for. However, it didn't accomplish the goal of expanding their audience. If anything,

people seemed even less interested now that grunge was all the rage and metal was as welcome as a case of anal fissures. They soon found themselves dropped by their label, and after one more album in 1995, *Plastic Green Head*, they disbanded, obviously weary of a continuous uphill battle that seemed to yield few results. However, they reunited and released *Simple Mind Condition* in 2007, and when singer Eric Wagner left the following year, he was replaced by Kory Clarke of Warrior Soul.

Bruce Franklin: guitars; **Ron Holzner**: bass (*Run to the Light* and later); **Dennis Lesh**: drums (*Run to the Light*); **Sean McAllister**: bass (*Psalm 9*, *The Skull*); **Jeff Olson**: drums (*Psalm 9*, *The Skull*, *Plastic Green Head* and later); **Chuck Robinson**: bass (*Simple Mind Con-*

dition); **Barry Stern**: drums (*Trouble, Manic Frustration*); **Eric Wagner**: vocals; **Rick Wartell**: guitars

Discography: *Psalm 9* (Metal Blade, 1984); *The Skull* (Metal Blade, 1985); *Run to the Light* (Metal Blade, 1987); *Trouble* (Def American, 1990); *Manic Frustration* (Def American, 1992); *Plastic Green Head* (Bullet, 1995); *Simple Mind Condition* (Escapi, 2007)

In this 1995 photograph, Trouble avoids causing havoc while standing about. Left to right: Ron Holzner, Bruce Franklin, Jeff Olson, Rick Wartell, and Eric Wagner.

TWISTED SISTER

YEARS ACTIVE: 1972–1987; 2001–PRESENT

In most people's minds, New York's Twisted Sister was a product of the 1980s hair metal movement. However, the band's roots actually go back to 1972, more than a decade before they had any of their signature hit songs. Founded by guitarist J. J. French, the band was heavily influenced by glam rock, which makes sense considering that he had once been in a band with future KISS members Gene Simmons and Paul Stanley, who had themselves originally modeled their band after the New York Dolls. Twisted Sister went through a cornucopia of personnel changes until 1976, when the band's knight in shining armor, Dee Snider, joined as the lead singer. With his powerful voice, huge and imposing stage presence, and domineering personality, Snider easily worked his way up to the position of band leader, writing almost all of their material and helping to gain an audience through his undeniable charisma as a front man. Musically, he brought a harder, metal sensibility to the band's glam sound, and by the time ex-Dictators bassist Mark "the Animal" Mendoza joined, Twisted Sister's journey to the metal side was complete.

As the 1980s began, the band was still struggling for recognition, but in 1981 the tiny independent label Secret Records decided to take a chance on them. A full nine years after their initial formation, they finally had a deal. The band recorded *Under the Blade* for the label, which quickly became a surprise hit among underground metal fans. Twisted Sister's popularity eventually became significant enough for Atlantic Records to step in, and the band was finally on its way to the big time after years and years of paying their dues. In 1983 they released their Atlantic debut, *You Can't Stop Rock and Roll*, which didn't exactly sell like crazy but certainly helped the band to develop a growing

Based on this 1985 photograph, it's not hard to imagine why someone might throw human excrement at Twisted Sister—an event that happened during a performance in the U.K. Left to right: Mark "the Animal" Mendoza, J. J. French, and Eddie "Fingers" Ojeda.

audience and set the stage for their 1984 album, *Stay Hungry*, which as we all know became a big hit with the kids. The album contained songs that were tailor-made for the musical climate of the time, chief among these being "I Wanna Rock" and "We're Not Gonna Take It." While the radio-friendliness of these songs is beyond estimation, it was the videos that truly put them on the map, both of which featured Mark Metcalf, otherwise known as the guy who played Neidermeyer in *Animal House*, as an overbearing authority figure (a teacher in "I Wanna Rock" and a strict disciplinarian father in "We're Not Gonna Take It") who suffers a series of violent and humiliating mishaps, à la Wile E. Coyote, either at the hands of the band or via his own reckless quest for power over the young and disenfranchised. Needless to say, these videos found a great deal of favor with teenagers across America, and the ensuing hysteria pushed *Stay Hungry* to platinum status many times over. It would not have been an exaggeration to characterize the band as a cultural phenomenon at this point in their career, a phenomenon that, strangely, was key to their eventual undoing.

Things turned against Twisted Sister very quickly. Overexposure was part of the problem. The band's music and videos were quite simply played to death, and their image, which had once been synonymous with dangerous heavy metal biker trash, was now synonymous with the MTV Video Music Awards and appearances on *Late Night with David Letterman*. Next up was the 1985 *Come Out*

and Play album, which for the most part was designed to shift units and didn't have much in the way of decent music to recommend it. The group's core fan base, which had already been made uncomfortable by the pop sheen of *Stay Hungry*, was permanently alienated at this point, and mainstream music fans weren't buying the album, either. Atlantic, however, had expected the album to sell in greater numbers than its predecessor, and consequently *Come Out and Play* was a huge commercial disappointment. In the hopes of winning back the band's initial fan base, Atlantic tried to patch things up by reissuing *Under the Blade*, but it was too late—fans just weren't going for it. Snider remained in the media spotlight in 1985 when he appeared with Frank Zappa and John Denver in front of a Senate committee at the Parents Music Resource Center hearings, but once that all died down, Twisted Sister was officially out of favor with both the media and the fans. With external problems weighing on them, the band members started tearing themselves apart from the inside, with interpersonal animosity among members reaching an all-time high. They squeezed off one more album, 1987's *Love Is for Suckers*, which didn't sell enough to even qualify for zinc certification, and the band broke up shortly thereafter.

Since then, there were the standard greatest-

hits packages and live albums, and Snider kept himself busy with a variety of musical projects. French, on the other hand, turned in his guitar and began his own management company, one of whose more high-profile clients is the band Sevendust. However, the band reunited in 2001 to perform at the New York Steel benefit concert for the families of the New York City police and fire department who had died in the September 11, 2001 terrorist attacks. It was the first time Twisted Sister had graced a stage in 14 years, and they were suddenly deluged with requests to play other dates as well. They hit the live circuit, and in 2004 they released *Still Hungry*. Despite the multiplatinum status of *Stay Hungry* and everything it had done for the band in the 1980s, they had never been happy with its sound, so the new album was their attempt to avenge the injustice by rerecording it. Two years later they released *A Twisted Christmas*, a joyous Noel album that finally answered the question that had long been burning on so many people's minds—what would it sound like if the band that performed "I Wanna Rock" were to reunite 22 years later and perform "I Saw Mommy Kissing Santa Claus"?

Joey "Seven" Franco: drums (*Love Is for Suckers*); **J. J. French**: guitar; **Mark "the Animal" Mendoza**: bass; **Eddie "Fingers" Ojeda**: guitar; **A. J. Pero**: drums (*Ruff Cutts* through *Come Out and Play, Club Daze: The Studio Sessions, Vol. 1, Noble Savage* and later); **Tony Petri**: drums (*Live at Hammersmith, Early Works, Never Say Never: Club Daze, Vol. 2*); **Dee Snider**: vocals

Discography: *Ruff Cutts* (Secret, 1982); *Under the Blade* (Secret, 1982); *You Can't Stop Rock and Roll* (Atlantic, 1983); *Stay Hungry* (Atlantic, 1984); *Come Out and Play* (Atlantic, 1985); *Love Is for Suckers* (Atlantic, 1987); *Live at Hammersmith* (CMC, 1994); *Early Works* (Spitfire, 1999); *Club Daze: The Studio Sessions, Vol. 1* (Spitfire, 1999); *Never Say Never: Club Daze, Vol. 2* (Spitfire, 2001); *Noble Savage* (Recall, 2002); *Club Daze Volume II: Live in the Bars* (Spitfire, 2002); *Still Hungry* (Spitfire, 2004); *A Twisted Christmas* (Razor & Tie, 2006)

TYGERS OF PAN TANG

YEARS ACTIVE: 1978–PRESENT

Tygers of Pan Tang got its name from a novel called *Stormbringer*, by an author with the unfortunate name of Michael Moorcock. Formed in 1978, the band was one of the best and the brightest of the New Wave of British Heavy Metal, forging a sound on their first couple of releases that can be described only as classic. They took the standard New Wave of British Heavy Metal approach of crafting songs that owed a stylistic debt to metal's giants, like Led Zeppelin and Deep Purple, and blended it with punk, whose influence could be seen both in the raw aggression of the music and in the band's attitude toward the fun and excitement of the music business. They had regularly recorded demos at a studio owned by Neat Records, which issued their first single, "Don't Touch Me There." Rather than send out the single to win a recording contract, the band chose to hit the road instead, where they both opened for established bands and played with those who were of their movement, such as a little up-and-coming outfit called Iron Maiden. MCA Records eventually signed Tygers of Pan Tang, as much for the single they had released as for the fan base that they had built up while on tour. They released their debut, *Wild Cat*, in 1980, which charted high in the United Kingdom and won the band a slot at that year's Reading Festival, a gig that is about as high-profile as you can imagine, to say nothing of its effect on a bunch of very green British musicians in their early twenties who had just released their first album. Perhaps feeling that it was all a little too much for him, singer Jess Cox quit the band soon after. He was replaced by Jon Deverill, and between the new vocalist and the recent addition of John Sykes on second guitar, the band was poised for greatness. The injection of new blood gave them renewed enthusiasm and a new lease on life, which was reflected on 1981's excellent *Spellbound* album, which many fans consider the band's best.

Tygers of Pan Tang capitalized on the album's

Even though they lack spandex, Tygers of Pan Tang manage to look nice and shiny.

success by touring relentlessly to support it. Stupidly, however, their record company rushed the band back into the studio, forcing them to make a new record and giving them exactly three weeks in which to do it from scratch. Released seven months after *Spellbound*, the album with which they emerged, *Crazy Nights*, was pretty good when one considers the ridiculous demands placed on them, but it certainly wasn't a worthy follow-up to *Spellbound*. Between that pressure-

cooker situation and the added stress of the subsequent tour, Sykes flew the coop, going on to join the relatively sane environs of Thin Lizzy. He was replaced by Fred Purser, and the band was rushed back into the studio again, emerging in 1982 with *The Cage*, yet another album that circumstance rendered substandard. Its pop-metal tendencies not only failed to expand their audience but rubbed the band's fans very much the wrong way. By this time, the adversity began coming at the band fast and furious, culminating in their management dropping them on the eve of a major Japanese tour. The band tried their hand at managing themselves for about five minutes before breaking up.

In 1985, Deverill and drummer Brian Dick re-formed the band with new members, releasing *The Wreck-Age*, an unspirited, half-baked attempt to cash in on the new glam metal movement. Adding insult to injury was the 1986 release of *First Kill*, a collection of the band's original demos from Neat Records that was so much better than the "comeback" album that it could only be described as degrading. After 1987's *Burning in the Shade* failed to catch on, the recently re-formed band finally gave up on the reunion, presumably closing the book for good on a very talented and classy band that deserved a lot better than it got. Still, interest in the band has remained strong through the years, as evidenced by the ongoing trade in live recordings from the band's classic era, such as *Live at Nottingham Rock City '81*, and in 1999 the band reunited for a series of concerts and a new album, *Mystical*, which was released in 2001. Their last album was 2008's *Animal Instinct*.

Jess Cox: vocals (*Wild Cat, First Kill*); **Jon Deverill**: vocals (*Spellbound* through *Live at Nottingham Rock City '81*); **Brian Dick**: drums (*Wild Cat* through *Live at Nottingham Rock City '81*); **Craig Ellis**: drums (*Mystical* and later); **Steve Lamb**: guitars (*The Cage, The Wreck-age, Burning in the Shade*); **Tony Liddell**: vocals (*Mystical*); **Jacopo Meille**: vocals (*Animal Instinct*); **Fred Purser**: guitars (*The Cage*); **Deano Robertson**: guitars (*Mystical* and later); **Rocky**: bass (*Spellbound, Crazy Nights, Live at Nottingham Rock City '81*); **Neil Sheppard**: guitars (*The Wreck-age*); **John Sykes**: guitars (*Spellbound, Crazy Nights, Live at Nottingham Rock City '81*) (see also Thin Lizzy, Whitesnake); **Robb Weir**: guitars (*Wild Cat* through *The Cage*; *First Kill, Live at Nottingham Rock City '81, Mystical* and later); **Brian West**: bass (*Mystical* and later)

Discography: *Wild Cat* (MCA, 1980); *Spellbound* (MCA, 1981); *Crazy Nights* (MCA, 1981); *The Cage* (MCA, 1982); *The Wreck-Age* (Music for Nations, 1985); *First Kill* (Neat, 1986); *Burning in the Shade* (Zebra, 1987); *Live at Nottingham Rock City '81* (Neat, 2001); *Live at Wacken '99* (Spitfire, 2001); *Mystical* (Z, 2001); *Animal Instinct* (Cargo, 2008)

TYPE O NEGATIVE

YEARS ACTIVE: 1989–2010

After the dissolution of Brooklyn's Carnivore in 1987, many fans wondered what the very tall bassist, vocalist, and songwriter Peter Steele would come up with next. The second and final Carnivore album had covered every type of offensive subject matter conceivable, ranging from hatred of Catholics and the impending race war to advocacy of violent sexual assault and everything else in between. That it was all meant to be an ironic joke was surely lost on many of the band's fans and was absolutely, unquestionably lost on their detractors, who regularly painted Steele as a misogynist Nazi who actively endeavored toward the death of the entire human race or, even worse, the New York hardcore scene. In any event, few could deny Steele's talent both as a songwriter and as a musician, and the wait for him to come up with something new took nearly an unbearable four years. Finally, in 1991 the wait ended, and his new band, Type O Negative, released *Slow, Deep and Hard*, a positively hateful album whose seven songs clocked in at one hour,

Apparently, lead singer Peter Steele was inspired by an advertisement for a blood bank in the phone book when he came up with the name Type O Negative. Left to right: Josh Silver, Peter Steele, Kenny Hickey, and Johnny Kelly.

songs stretching well past the twelve-minute mark. This was partially because Steele had fallen under the spell of the Swans, and consequently he was now incorporating tempos into his songs that were so slow that a single riff could take up the better part of a full minute. He had employed time-consuming cadences with Carnivore, but only sporadically. In comparison, on *Slow, Deep and Hard*, they were a primary songwriting element, and at times the tempos were so extremely, painfully slow that they could almost be described as idle. Lyrically, however, Steele threw a bit of a curveball in that the songs were almost entirely about girl trouble, a heretofore new area for the former sanitation worker. The typically hostile lyrics now made people add the phrase "bloodthirsty rapist" to Steele's long list of offenses, and anyone reading the lyric sheet could likely have been led to this same conclusion. "Unsuccessfully Coping with the Natural Beauty of Infidelity," for example, contained such charming couplets as "You had cock on your mind and cum on your breath/ Inserted that diaphragm before you left." The song's chorus was a James Brown–esque call-and-response shout of "I know you're fucking someone else." This was, by the way, the most accessible song on the album; the rest featured Steele threatening, in rhyme no less, to use a pickax to kill a lover who had spurned him, a veritable bargain when compared with the fate of the woman he threatens to rape with a jackhammer, an act whose sound is enacted for the listener's benefit at the end of "Prelude to Agony." All in all, Carnivore fans were more than pleased, and they looked forward to a lifetime of similar work from Steele.

After *Origin of the Feces* in 1992, a pointless album of rerecorded songs from *Slow, Deep and Hard* with fake audience noise, the band released

Bloody Kisses in 1993, an album that surely had Carnivore fans in a state of utter shock. Steele's hardcore-influenced macho screaming was gone, replaced by a smooth, extreme baritone vocal that suggested Lurch from *The Addams Family*. The album wallowed in the same territory as its predecessor and was certainly, for the most part, agonizingly slow, but the songwriting took on much more epic proportions and added layers of melody and harmony that, apart from signifying a downright skilled practitioner, came as a complete surprise to listeners. Steele's lyrics had also been toned down, and he now seemed merely upset as opposed to sadistically homicidal. However, the album's crowning achievement was a cover of Seals & Crofts' "Summer Breeze," which the band had managed to imbue with a plodding dreariness that was utterly jaw-dropping. In all, Type O Negative had managed to reinvent itself as a goth metal band, to thoroughly convincing effect. The band followed in 1996 with *October Rust*, which pushed the goth elements even further and was more of a keyboard-driven album than anything the band had released. Unfortunately, this sapped some of the album's power, and it ended up being a little too poplike for some fans' tastes, despite the presence of some very strong material, such as "Wolf Moon" and "Love You to Death." Steele also posed for Playgirl magazine around this time, confirming a popularly held theory regarding the size of his hands. In 1999, the band released *World Coming Down*, a much heavier and more guitar riff–oriented album than its predecessor. The follow-up was 2003's *Life Is Killing Me*, distinguished by such material as

"I Don't Wanna Be Me" and "Todd's Ship Gods (Above All Things)."

In 2005, there was trouble in Type O land when Steele was incarcerated. He had served a 30-day sentence at Riker's Island for assaulting another man whom he believed to be a love rival. According to Blabbermouth.net, he had been abusing cocaine for years, and it had caught up with him at the time of the assault. "I was suffering from drug-induced psychosis, and I was doing some pretty insane things, like putting cameras in light switches and in shower heads," he admitted. "All the paranoia was because of all the cocaine I was doing." After leaving prison, he checked into a rehabilitation facility, and he eventually returned to the music scene in 2007 with *Dead Again*. It would be the last Type O Negative studio album. On April 14, 2010, Steele died of heart failure at the age of 48. According to a statement on the band's official website, "Peter had been enjoying a long period of sobriety and improved health," making his death all the more painful. The surviving band members confirmed in 2010 that there was no possibility of going on without him, and Type O Negative had officially and permanently broken up.

Sal Abruscato: drums (*Slow, Deep and Hard* through *Bloody Kisses*); **Kenny Hickey**: guitars; **Johnny Kelly**: drums (*October Rust* and later); **Josh Silver**: keyboards; **Peter Steele**: vocals/bass (see also Carnivore)

Discography: *Slow, Deep and Hard* (Roadrunner, 1991); *Origin of the Feces* (Roadrunner, 1992); *Bloody Kisses* (Roadrunner, 1993); *October Rust* (Roadrunner, 1996); *World Coming Down* (Roadrunner, 1999); *Life is Killing Me* (Roadrunner, 2003); *Dead Again* (SPV/Steamhammer, 2007)

The members of U.F.O. take a break from their 1995 Walk on Water tour to pose for a publicity photograph. Left to right: Simon Wright, Michael Schenker, Pete Way, Phil Mogg, and Paul Raymond.

U.F.O.

YEARS ACTIVE: 1969–1986; 1995–PRESENT

U.F.O. was one of the truly great British metal bands of the 1970s. They were mainly distinguished because they counted legendary guitarist Michael Schenker—brother of the Scorpions' Rudolf Schenker—among their ranks, although his place in the band has been somewhat erratic over the years (he has left and rejoined a number of times). Originally formed in 1969 by guitarist Mick Bolton, singer Phil Mogg, drummer Andy Parker, and bassist Pete Way, the band found success initially in foreign markets such as

Germany and Japan. Bolton quit the band in 1974, but the timing was fortuitous. Schenker had just left the Scorpions after recording that band's *Lonesome Crow* album, and with Bolton gone, he was able to join U.F.O. His entrance resulted in what many consider the band's classic lineup. Schenker's considerable heavy metal chops beefed up their sound considerably, as evidenced in 1974 on *Phenomenon*, the first album to feature him. The albums that followed, from 1975's *Force It* through 1978's *Obsession*, comprise a string of classic material generally regarded as the band's finest output.

Unfortunately, Schenker quit after *Obsession* to rejoin the Scorpions, and he seemed to take the band's success with him—

the subsequent Scorpions album, *Lovedrive*, was that group's best seller up to then, while U.F.O.'s first post-Schenker album, *No Place to Run*, was a disappointment. The band had one more brief moment of glory in 1982, when the single off their *Mechanix* album, "The Writer," made it to number twenty-three on the *Billboard* charts, but this was followed by the departure of founding member Way, a crippling blow to the rest of the band. After the 1983 album *Making Contact*, they disbanded, although they reunited two years later for *Misdemeanor*, after which they, like, really disbanded. In 1993, the classic lineup of Mogg, Parker, Schenker, Way, and Lights Out keyboard player Paul Raymond reunited, releasing *Walk on Water* in 1995 and reunited, releasing *Walk on Water* in 1995 and embarking on a successful tour. The band recorded two more studio albums after that, but was constantly plagued by instability in its ranks, particularly on the part of the chronically quitting and rejoining Schenker. In 2004 the band replaced him with Vinnie Moore, who remains in the band today. The band's last album was 2009's *The Visitor*.

Laurence Archer: guitars (*Lights Out in Tokyo, High Stakes and Dangerous Men*); **Mick Bolton**: guitars (*U.F.O. 1* through *Live in Japan*); **Jason Bonham**: drums (*You Are Here*); **Neil Carter**: keyboards (*Obsession; The Wild the Willing and the Innocent* through *Making Contact*); **Paul Chapman**: guitars (*No Place to Run* through *Making Contact*); **Aynsley Dunbar**: drums (*Covenant* through *Sharks*); **Clive Edwards**: drums (*High Stakes and Dangerous Men, Lights Out in Tokyo*); **Paul Gray**: bass (*Misdemeanor, Ain't Misbehavin'*); **Tommy McClendon**: guitars (*Misdemeanor, Ain't Misbehavin'*); **Phil Mogg**: vocals; **Vinnie Moore**: guitar (*You Are Here* and later); **Andy Parker**: drums (*U.F.O. 1* through *Making Contact, Walk on Water, The Monkey Puzzle*); **Danny Peyronel**: keyboards (*No Heavy Petting*); **Paul Raymond**: keyboards (*Lights Out* through *No Place to Run; Misdemeanor, Walk on Water; You Are Here* and later); **Michael Schenker**: guitars (*Phenomenon* through *Strangers in the Night; Walk on Water* through *Sharks*) (see also the Scorpions); **Jim Simpson**: drums (*Misdemeanor, Ain't Misbehavin'*); **Pete Way**: bass (*U.F.O. 1* through *Mechanix; High Stakes and Dangerous Men* and later) (see also Fastway)

Discography: *U.F.O. 1* (AKA, 1970); *Flying* (AKA, 1973); *Live in Japan* (AKA, 1973); *Phenomenon* (Chrysalis, 1974); *Force It* (Chrysalis, 1975); *No Heavy Petting* (Chrysalis, 1976); *Lights Out* (Chrysalis, 1977); *Obsession* (Chrysalis, 1978); *Strangers in the Night* (Chrysalis, 1978); *No Place to Run* (Chrysalis, 1979); *The Wild the Willing and the Innocent* (Chrysalis, 1981); *Mechanix* (Chrysalis, 1982); *Making Contact* (Chrysalis, 1983); *Misdemeanor* (Chrysalis, 1985); *Ain't Misbehavin'* (FM, 1988); *Lights Out in Tokyo* (Victor, 1992); *High Stakes and Dangerous Men* (Castle, 1992); *Walk on Water* (Zero, 1995); *Covenant* (Shrapnel, 2000); *Sharks* (Shrapnel, 2002); *Live on Earth* (Zoom Club, 2003); *You Are Here* (SPV/Steamhammer, 2004); *The Monkey Puzzle* (SPV/Steamhammer, 2006); *The Visitor* (SPV/Steamhammer, 2009)

RIGHT: This photograph documents the seventh iteration of Uriah Heep, with David Byron (left) on vocals and John Wetton on bass.

UNORTHODOX

YEARS ACTIVE: 1987–PRESENT

Unorthodox was one of the Washington, D.C.–area bands from the 1990s doom metal scene, and was also part of the first generation of groups to be influenced by 1980s doom bands such as Pentagram and the Obsessed. However, unlike many of its Black Sabbath–cloning contemporaries, Unorthodox stood apart from the pack by adding elements of thrash, psychedelia, and prog rock to its doom, resulting in a highly unique sound. The band released two albums on Hellhound before the label went bankrupt, after which time Unorthodox completely disappeared from sight. In 2000, vocalist and guitarist Dale Flood reemerged with a new lineup, and in 2008 they finally released their third album, *Awaken*, a solid 13 years after their sophomore effort. They always say the third album's the toughest.

Mark Ammen: bass (*Awaken*); **Dale Flood**: guitars/vocals; **Josh Hart**: bass (*Balance of Power*); **Greg Isom**: drums (*Awaken*); **Ronnie Kalimon**: drums (see also Iron Man); **Jeff Parsons**: bass (*Asylum*)

Discography: *Asylum* (Hellhound, 1993); *Balance of Power* (Hellhound, 1995); *Awaken* (The Church Within, 2008)

URIAH HEEP

YEARS ACTIVE: 1969–PRESENT

Although they were never a favorite of the critics during the 1970s—and that alone should convince you to go out and buy all of their albums—the British band Uriah Heep has consistently delivered high-quality progressive heavy metal to the masses since their 1970 debut. Originally called Spice, the band was based around singer David Byron and guitarist Mick Box, who decided to form a new group after the one they were in together fell apart. The pair guided Uriah Heep through the usual whirlwind of personnel changes, which was no small feat when one considers that no fewer than thirty musicians have been in the band, a considerable portion of whom never even made it to the first album. They released their self-titled debut in 1970 (which was titled *. . . Very 'eavy . . . Very 'umble* in the United Kingdom), but even that didn't slow down the attrition rate, particularly when it came to drummers. Nevertheless, the band's

Uriah Heep guitarist Mick Box yells "Mine!"

1971 album *Salisbury* was an ambitious leap forward from the debut, with a title track that was a sixteen-minute-long epic recorded with a twenty-six-piece orchestra. More important, the album put the band on the top of the prog rock heap, relatively new heap that it was.

After releasing *Look at Yourself* later that year, Uriah Heep experienced still more personnel strife, but when it was all over, the band found themselves with a stable lineup for the first time in their turbulent history. This configuration—featuring Byron and Box along with keyboard player Ken Hensley, drummer Lee Kerslake, and bassist Gary Thain—proved to be more than just stable, as the output by this group is regarded by many fans as the band's best. Starting in 1972 with *Demons and Wizards*, which contained the hit "Easy Living," the band finally made it onto American charts, and they released a string of high-quality albums over the next few years. After the 1974 release *Wonderworld*, Thain was excused from further bassmanship duties, thanks to drug problems that, sadly, claimed his life within a year's time. He was replaced by John Wetton, who was out of a job after the demise of King Crimson. Wetton played on 1975's *Return to Fantasy* and 1976's *High and Mighty*, but was out the door shortly thereafter, and the band was soon besieged yet again by the kind of personnel traumas that had dogged them at the start of their career. Perhaps as a result, Hensley and Byron turned against each other, with Byron eventually exiting the band for good, leaving his former colleagues to salvage Uriah Heep. Hensley and Box replaced Byron with former Lucifer's Friend singer John Lawton and Wetton with former David Bowie bassist Trevor Bolder, and soldiered on. The band seemed to be doing all right, but after 1980's *Conquest*, Hensley quit, leaving Box, the only remaining original member, with the unenviable task of keeping the band going—which he did like a trouper. While the band continued to suffer lineup change upon lineup change, they were rewarded for sticking it out on various occasions, most notably in 1987, when they gained the distinction of becoming the first Western heavy metal band ever to play in Moscow. Unbelievably, the band still exists after four decades, still records, and still tours to this very day, and we can probably expect them to keep it up for as long as Mick Box still cares to.

Keith Baker: drums (*Uriah Heep, Salisbury*); **Trevor Bolder**: bass (*Innocent Victim* through *Conquest, Equator* and later); **Mick Box**: guitar; **David Byron**: vocals (*Uriah Heep* through *High and Mighty*); **Ian Clarke**: drums (*Look at Yourself*); **Bob Daisley**: bass (*Abominog, Head First*) (see also Rainbow); **Russell Gilbrook**: drums (*Wake the Sleeper* and later); **Peter Goalby**: vocals (*Abominog* through *Equator*); **Ken Hensley**: keyboards/vocals (*Uriah Heep* through *Conquest; Live January 1973*); **Lee Kerslake**: drums (*Demons and Wizards* through *Electrically Driven*); **Phil Lanzon**: keyboards (*Live in Moscow* through *Acoustically Driven; Into the Wild*); John Lawton: vocals (*Firefly* through *Fallen Angel; Live in Europe 1979*); **Paul Newton**: bass (*Uriah Heep* through *Look at Yourself*); **Nigel Olsson**: drums (*Uriah Heep*); **Bernard Shaw**: vocals (*Live in Moscow* and later); **John Sinclair**: keyboards (*Abominog* through *Equator*); **Chris Slade**: drums (*Conquest*); **John Sloman**: vocals (*Conquest*); **Gary Thain**: bass (*Demons and Wizards* through *Wonderworld*); **John Wetton**: bass (*Return to Fantasy, High and Mighty*)

Discography: *Uriah Heep* (Mercury, 1970); *Salisbury* (Mercury, 1971); *Look at Yourself* (Mercury, 1971); *Demons and Wizards* (Mercury, 1972); *The Magician's Birthday* (Mercury, 1972); *Uriah Heep Live* (Mercury, 1973); *Sweet Freedom* (Roadrunner, 1973); *Wonderworld* (Sanctuary, 1974); *Return to Fantasy* (Sanctuary, 1975); *High and Mighty* (Sanctuary, 1976); *Firefly* (Sanctuary, 1977); *Innocent Victim* (Sanctuary, 1977); *Fallen Angel* (Castle, 1978); *Conquest* (Castle, 1980); *Abominog* (Castle, 1982); *Head First* (Castle, 1983); *Equator* (Portrait, 1985); *Live in Moscow* (World of Hurt, 1988); *Raging Silence* (Enigma, 1989); *Different World* (Griffin, 1994); *Still 'eavy Still Proud* (Griffin, 1994); *Two Decades* (Castle, 1994); *Rarities from the Bronze Age* (Sequel, 1994); *Sea of Light* (HTD, 1995); *Live January 1973* (Castle, 1996); *King Biscuit Flower Hour Presents in Concert* (King Biscuit, 1997); *Sonic Origami* (Spitfire, 1998); *Spellbinder* (Spitfire, 1999); *Future Echoes of the Past* (Phantom, 2001); *Acoustically Driven* (Import, 2001); *Electrically Driven* (Import, 2001); *Live in Europe 1979* (Sanctuary, 2001); *Live* (Castle, 2001); *The Ballads* (Castle/Windson, 2001); *Rarities* (Castle/Windson, 2001); *20th Century Masters* (Mercury, 2001); *Between Two Worlds* (Navarre, 2002); *Wake the Sleeper* (Sanctuary, 2008); *Celebration* (Sanctuary, 2009); *Into the Wild* (Frontiers, 2011)

YEARS ACTIVE: 1980–PRESENT

While Eddie Van Halen and Yngwie Malmsteen may have been the greater celebrities, Steve Vai was easily as accomplished a guitar player as either of them, if not more so, and he raised the bar for supertechnical lead guitar playing among aspiring musicians of the 1980s. When he was a freshman in high school, Vai took lessons from none other than Joe Satriani, whose influence on that decade's guitar players was equally great. Vai showed an aptitude for the instrument and attended Boston's prestigious Berklee School of Music at the age of eighteen to study full-time. Vai was a huge Frank Zappa fan, and while he was at Berklee he took it upon himself to transcribe some of Zappa's insanely complicated compositions for the guitar, even sending a transcription to the man himself. Much to Vai's surprise, Zappa responded by inviting him to join his band, an offer Vai gleefully and unhesitatingly accepted. Suddenly, he was filling the much-needed slots of "Little Italian Virtuoso," "Strat Abuse," or "Stunt Guitarist," depending on the particular demands of the recording. He appeared on several Zappa albums in the early 1980s, including *Ship Arriving Too Late to Save a Drowning Witch*, which featured "Valley Girl," the closest Zappa ever got to a hit single.

By 1984, Vai had decided that it was time to go it alone, and he released his first album, *Flex-Able*, that year. He was not, however, above appearing in bands or on other people's albums, and throughout the late 1980s he could be found on several records at a time. He replaced Yngwie Malmsteen in Graham Bonnett's Alcatrazz, appearing on its 1985 album *Disturbing the Peace*, while also appearing in the 1985 movie *Crossroads*, playing a guitarist who has sold his soul to the devil. (In an interesting paradox, the movie shows Ralph Macchio defeating Vai's character

OPPOSITE: Steve Vai learns a painful but valuable lesson in the proper grounding of onstage electrical sockets.

in a guitar-playing competition by reeling off some lightning-fast classical arpeggios on what is obviously sped-up film; in reality, the guitar parts that Macchio mimed were performed by none other than—you guessed it—Steve Vai.) The following year, Vai won the lead guitarist's spot in David Lee Roth's solo band after the singer left Van Halen. This turn of events increased Vai's profile considerably, particularly when the band's videos showed him playing a triple-necked heart-shaped pink guitar.

Vai left Roth's band in 1988 to work on another solo album but also accepted an offer to join Whitesnake, as that group tried to one-up their self-titled hit album from 1987. The Whitesnake album on which he appeared, *Slip of the Tongue*, was surely nothing that fans of Vai's hyperspeed technical guitar playing were interested in, and apparently it didn't particularly appeal to him, either, as it was both the first and the last Whitesnake album that he ever appeared on. He chose to make another solo album, *Passion and Warfare*, which was released in 1990 and went gold, not bad for an album of nothing but thirty-second-note arpeggios and sweep-picking. He also created a guitar for Ibanez at this time, which a lot of buyers balked on buying because it had seven strings. Since then, Vai has continued to release solo albums, and he partakes in his annual G3 tour with former instructor Satriani. He also continues to do session work, as he has done

Steve Vai plays a guitar with practical applications that number in the thousands.

for most of his professional career, appearing on albums by artists as diverse as Alice Cooper, Al DiMeola, and Billy Sheehan, and he appeared, in an extremely odd move, on Public Image Ltd.'s 1986 release, *Album*. Fans who are interested in his work with Zappa will be happy to know that there is a veritable treasure trove of material from Vai's tenure in Zappa's band, much of which can be found on the *You Can't Do That on Stage Anymore* music series. His last solo album was 2005's *Real Illusions: Reflections*. Discography: *Flex-Able* (Epic, 1984); *Passion and Warfare* (Epic, 1990); *Sex and Religion* (Epic, 1993); *Alien Love Secrets* (Epic, 1995); *Fire Garden* (Epic, 1996); *Flex-Able Leftovers* (Epic, 1998); *The Ultra Zone* (Epic, 1999); *The 7th Song: Enchanting Guitar Melodies* (Sony, 2000); *Alive in an Ultra World* (Sony, 2001); *The Elusive Light and Sound, Vol. 1* (Favored, 2002); *Real Illusions: Reflections* (Epic, 2005)

YEARS ACTIVE: 1972–PRESENT

Eddie Van Halen is inarguably the most significant heavy metal guitarist of the 1980s, and that's only part of the story. He is also the most significant electric guitarist of any genre since

Van Halen in their very, very early years look fresh as spring colts. Left to right: Alex Van Halen, Michael Anthony, David Lee Roth, and Eddie Van Halen.

Jimi Hendrix. He is, after all, the last guy to create a style so revolutionary that it rendered obsolete any popular notions of what the instrument is supposed to sound like. Eventually, someone will come along with a completely new technique that relegates Eddie to the dustbin, but it hasn't happened yet, and you probably shouldn't hold your breath. Eddie and his older brother, Alex, the sons of a bandleader, grew up in a musical household. The family relocated from Holland to southern California when Alex was fourteen and Eddie was twelve, and both of them were expected to continue their classical piano lessons. But popular American influences seeped in, and soon enough Alex was playing guitar and Eddie was playing drums. Perhaps sensing that such a move might make them extremely popular one day, they switched instruments, which most heavy metal fans would probably concede was the right choice. Alex, an accomplished and unique drummer, recalls having something akin to a social life as a teenager. This is not so with Eddie, who spent his adolescence in his bedroom for hours on end playing records from front to back and learning all the guitar solos verbatim. Eventually, he grew beyond the influence of players like Eric Clapton and Jimmy Page and developed his own technique, one that was rife with all kinds of tricks and goodies that were previously unheard-of from a guitar. Eventually, the brothers decided to form their own heavy metal band, initially going by the name Mammoth. They played around the Pasadena area, where they had grown up, eventually gaining the attention of an aspiring singer named David Lee Roth, who signed on in 1974. The singer later claimed that from the outset he was absolutely floored by the pair's musicianship, particularly that of Eddie, whose trademark pyrotechnic style was already on full display.

Mammoth teamed up with bassist Michael Anthony, and later that year they changed the group's name to Van Halen. The band played the Los Angeles club circuit for three years, finally gaining the attention of KISS' Gene Simmons in 1977. Simmons had seen them perform at a Los Angeles club and had been so impressed with them that he offered to finance a demo and help them secure a recording contract. With Simmons' help, Van Halen won a deal with Warner Bros., which released the band's self-titled debut in 1978 to major success. The band was a huge hit on all fronts, gaining strong support from both radio stations and fans, who were positively won over by the band's live presentation. The considerable musicianship of the Van Halen brothers aside, Roth was a master showman who compensated for whatever technical shortcomings he may have had with his undeniable charisma and stage persona, equal parts rock god and used-car salesman.

It all conspired to bring the band's debut to platinum status six times over. It didn't hurt that the album was chock-full of strong material, such as "Runnin' with the Devil," "Jamie's Cryin'," and "Eruption," whose tablature sales during the late 1970s and early 1980s probably put their publishers' children through law school. The band followed it up quickly with *Van Halen II* in 1979, a hugely successful album whose sales replicated those of their first album. Even their lowest-selling album of the Roth era, 1981's *Fair Warning*, was still a Top 10 hit, and had plenty of classic material on it, such as "Unchained," which is alone worth the purchase price.

However, it was *1984* that turned Van Halen from a mere band into a force of nature. While Roth had originally opposed the use of the synthesizer that Eddie was tinkering with on a now-constant basis, he couldn't deny its powerful influence in the marketplace, so he kept his mouth shut and watched *1984* become the biggest album of the band's career, spurred by the hit single "Jump." The album also featured plenty of guitar-dominated heavy metal, such as "Hot for Teacher" and "Panama," which became hits in their own right. However, it was "Jump" that transformed Van Halen from a very popular heavy metal band to one of the most popular bands in the world.

Things did not stay too happy for too long. Roth had opposed not only the use of synthesizer on their album but also Eddie's appearance on Michael Jackson's "Beat It," perhaps fearing that it might alienate some of their more hardcore heavy metal fans. But it was Roth who was truly the odd man out. While he may have groused at certain artistic choices that the band was making, what his mates were really tiring of was his Robert-Plant-as-Catskills-comedian shtick. Finally, they fired the singer, replacing him with former Montrose front man Sammy Hagar. It seemed an odd decision; here was a band that had just had the biggest hit record of their career, and they were throwing the opportunity away by firing their most visible member. Furthermore, they were replacing him with a singer whose celebrity was dubious at best, which was the real issue. Regardless of who was technically the more capable singer, Roth was hands down the greater celebrity, and many people felt that in firing him the rest of Van Halen had truly shot themselves in the foot.

Along with strong studio recordings, Van Halen's live concerts—like this one from 1982—rocketed the band into superstardom.

David Lee Roth shows off his gymnastic talents while Michael Anthony rocks on. OPPOSITE: At this 1983 concert, Eddie Van Halen nonchalantly discourages a stadium full of aspiring guitar players with his prowess.

Much to the surprise of many, Hagar's first album with Van Halen, *5150*, was a monstrous hit. It expanded upon the new musical textures that the band had explored on *1984* and gave them a glossy sheen that was tailor-made for the stadiums of North America. They followed it up in 1988 with *OU812*, another smash. In short order, Hagar became completely accepted by the fans as a fully ingrained member, and as the string of hits continued well into the 1990s, it seemed that his status would never again be questioned. But Hagar eventually fell out of favor with the band for reasons that are difficult to pin down. The singer's side of the story completely contradicts the band's,

with each side citing the other as wholly responsible for the rift that ultimately caused Hagar's exit. Both sides do agree that everything came to a head when the band was asked to contribute a song to the soundtrack of the movie *Twister*. Whatever the specific problems may have been, at the end of the day Hagar was out, and there has yet to be a consensus as to whether he was fired or he quit. To make matters worse, the other members had recorded tracks for two new songs to be included on an upcoming greatest-hits compilation (itself a source of disagreement between Hagar and the rest of the band) and had enlisted none other than Roth to sing on them. This, of course,

set off a firestorm of speculation, as fans and entertainment news sources alike tried to sort out what was actually going on. For one brief, shining moment, it appeared to the general public that Van Halen had reunited with its original singer, that in the topsy-turvy world of 1996, with its Marilyn Mansons and its No Doubts and its Courtney Loves, at least Van Halen would come back with David Lee Roth, returning some small semblance of normalcy and happiness to a wounded heavy metal consciousness. This hope was reinforced when the band appeared at the MTV Video Music Awards with Roth in tow. However, the band parted ways with the singer mere days after

In 1993, it was all smiles for Eddie Van Halen (left) and Sammy Hagar. In three years these two would hate each other.
OPPOSITE: Eddie Van Halen is one of the blessed few who actually deserves to own one of these little guitars.

the MTV appearance, dashing the dreams of millions of armchair music journalist Gen-Xers across the globe. Roth eventually went on to say that he had been out-and-out lied to by the Van Halen camp, who had told him that he would be returning on a permanent basis but were really interested only in utilizing his services for the two new songs. Then the Van Halen camp announced that, after an exhaustive search, they had finally found a new singer: Extreme's Gary Cherone. Somewhere, Sammy Hagar was laughing very hard. In all seriousness, though, Cherone was put in an impossible position, and when his debut album with the group, 1998's *Van Halen III*, simply didn't sell, he was unfairly blamed for the downturn in the band's fortunes, as

opposed to the fact that the band had been engaged in an extremely ugly and public airing of their dirty laundry for a full two years. Whatever the reason, the album ended up being the lowest-selling in the band's career, and Cherone was soon shown the door. This of course sparked the rumor mill, particularly since hopeful fans were being teased yet again by the possibility of another reunion with Roth. This seemed like an eventuality when Roth announced that he had recorded several new songs with the band at the beginning of 2000, although he had not heard from the band since. Considering that the announcement was made in 2001, he should probably have taken it as a sign not to expect much. Indeed, Eddie Van Halen finally appeared

on MTV stating that although the band had recorded enough material to fill three albums, they still had not chosen a replacement for Cherone, but one thing was for sure: it wasn't going to be Roth. Shortly thereafter, the band made the decision to part ways with Warner Bros., which had been their label of twenty-three years. To make Van Halen look even more like chumps, Roth and Hagar went on tour together in what they called "The Sam and Dave Tour." All the while, time passed . . . and passed . . . and passed . . . and the Van Halen camp produced nothing but silence.

In 2004, Van Halen released *The Best of Both Worlds*, a compilation featuring three new songs with Hagar on vocals. Strangely, the songs were credited to "Hagar/Van Halen/Van

Halen," with Anthony's name conspicuously excluded. The bassist later revealed that he had been specifically barred from the sessions, and the guitarist had cut the bass parts himself. The Hagar-fronted band went on tour, with Anthony in tow, but reviews started out mediocre and became outright hostile as it progressed. Anthony and Hagar later alleged that this was because the guitarist, who had a long history behind him of supposedly resolved problems with the bottle, had begun drinking again, and it had accelerated as the tour progressed. Fan-shot videos of the guitarist royally fucking up his trademark fleet-fingered runs made their way to the Internet, and seemed to corroborate this. Anthony also revealed to the Japanese heavy metal magazine *Burrn!* that the Van Halen brothers never wanted him on the tour in the first place, and only took him because Hagar had insisted on it as a precondition for rejoining. He also claimed that he was given a reduced royalty rate, and when the tour was over he was required to end all association with the band. Additionally, he was legally barred from using their name to promote himself.

In 2007, both the Van Halen camp and Roth confirmed that they would embark on a North American tour. Filling the bass slot would be none other than Eddie Van Halen's 17-year-old son, Wolfgang. In 2009, the guitarist was forced to undergo surgery on his fretting hand, which had been bothering him during the previous tour. Then, in 2011, they entered the studio to begin recording their first new album since 1998, and their first with Roth since the *1984* album. The new recording, *A Different Kind of Truth*, was released in February 2012, and in spite of all the years of interpersonal bullshit and shenanigans that had gone on, the reviews were almost uniformly positive. A reviewer named Skid at Sleazeroxx.com perhaps put it best when he or she said "Regardless of how much bad blood has been spilled over the years, of how insane Roth and the Van Halen brothers can act, one thing is certain—when they get together magic happens."

Michael Anthony: bass; **Gary Cherone**: vocals (*Van Halen III*) (see also Extreme); **Sammy Hagar**: vocals (*5150* through *Balance*); **David Lee Roth**: vocals (*Van Halen* through *1984*; *A Different Kind of Truth*); **Alex Van Halen**: drums; **Eddie Van Halen**: guitar; **Wolfgang Van Halen**: bass (*A Different Kind of Truth*)

Discography: *Van Halen* (Warner Bros., 1978); *Van Halen II* (Warner Bros., 1979); *Women and Children First* (Warner Bros., 1980); *Fair Warning* (Warner Bros., 1981); *Diver Down* (Warner Bros., 1982); *1984* (Warner Bros., 1984); *5150* (Warner Bros., 1986); *OU812* (Warner Bros., 1988); *For Unlawful Carnal Knowledge* (Warner Bros., 1991); *Van Halen Live: Right Here, Right Now* (Warner Bros., 1993); *Balance* (Warner Bros., 1995); *Van Halen III* (Warner Bros., 1998); *The Best of Both Worlds* (Warner Bros., 2004); *A Different Kind of Truth* (Interscope, 2012)

VENOM

YEARS ACTIVE: 1979–1993; 1996–PRESENT

Venom is the best band in the world to ever claim in song that they drank the vomit of a priest. As if that is not enough, they are one of the most infamous bands in heavy metal. The trio combined the showmanship of KISS with the raw fury of Motörhead, inventing an early prototype of black metal in the process. Actually, for the way the members of KISS dressed, they certainly should have sounded like Motörhead, so it was nice of Venom to take care of that little inequity. Formed during the late 1970s in England, the band was contemporaneous with the New Wave of British Heavy Metal, but nobody would have mistaken them for Diamond Head, not even for one second. Rather, Venom favored a raw, violent sound and a deeply satanic image. Although the band claimed repeatedly and unambiguously that their allegiance to the Horned One was not even the slightest bit sincere (they may have used the term "marketing gimmick"), it certainly was taken seriously by their fans, many of whom even used the title of Venom's second album, *Black Metal*, as a term with which to describe their favorite soundtrack to setting church fires.

OPPOSITE: Here's yet another example of Venom's exaggerated efforts to appear formidable. Left to right: Tony "Abaddon" Bray, Conrad "Cronos" Lant, and Jeff "Mantas" Dunn.

Most of the band's fans feel that their first four albums, starting with *Welcome to Hell* and ending with *Possessed*, represent their best and most relevant output. This argument is particularly compelling given the fact that these albums were followed by a lengthy period of turmoil marked by a deeply, profoundly confusing series of lineup changes that even the most devoted fan would be hard-pressed to keep up with. In 1996, however, the three original members reunited, and released *Cast in Stone* in 1997. Sadly, the reunion proved short-lived, and by 2002 Conrad "Cronos" Lant was again the sole original member. However, the band is still together, and most recently they released *Fallen Angels* in 2011.

Al Barnes: rhythm guitar (*Prime Evil* through *Temples of Ice*); **Tony "Abaddon" Bray**: drums (*Welcome to Hell* through *Cast in Stone*); **Jimmy Clare**: guitars (*Calm Before the Storm*); **Tony Dolan**: vocals/bass (*Prime Evil* through *Black Reign*); **Jeff "Mantas" Dunn**: guitars (*Welcome to Hell* through *Eine Kleine Nachtmusik*, *Prime Evil* and later); **Mike "Mykvs" Hickey**: guitars (*Calm Before the Storm*); **Anthony "Antton" Lant**: drums (*Resurrection* and later); **Conrad "Cronos" Lant**: bass (*Welcome to Hell* through *Calm Before the Storm*; *Cast in Stone*; *Metal Black* and later); **Danny "Dante" Needham**: drums (*Fallen Angels*); **Rage**: guitar (*Hell*); **V.X.S.**: keyboards (*Temples of Ice*, *The Waste Lands*); **Steve "War Maniac" White**: guitars (*Temples of Ice*, *The Waste Lands*)

Discography: *Welcome to Hell* (Neat, 1981); *Black Metal* (Neat, 1982); *At War with Satan* (Neat, 1984); *Possessed* (Neat, 1985); *Calm Before the Storm* (Under One Flag, 1987); *Prime Evil* (Under One Flag, 1989); *Temples of Ice* (Under One Flag, 1991); *The Waste Lands* (Under One Flag, 1992); *Cast in Stone* (Receiver, 1997); *Resurrection* (SPV, 2000); *Metal Black* (Castle, 2006); *Hell* (Universal, 2008); *Fallen Angels* (Universal, 2011)

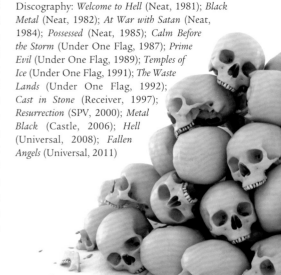

VIXEN

YEARS ACTIVE: 1980–PRESENT

Can a band with three albums, only one of which was ever actually purchased by anyone, release two greatest-hits compilations? This is the intriguing question presented by the recorded canon of the band Vixen, an all-female glam metal group from Los Angeles. To the outsider, Vixen probably seemed like a band that was cynically thrown together at the last minute to cash in on the glam fad, but in reality they had existed since 1981—seven years before their debut album was released—and had absolutely, without question paid their dues in the Los Angeles club scene. One can only imagine what this all-female band in the uniformly male field of heavy metal had had to put up with by the time EMI decided to grace them with a recording contract. Their self-titled debut was released in 1988 and went multiplatinum,

mainly on the strength of the hit single and video "Edge of a Broken Heart." Unfortunately, this success didn't repeat itself on their second album, 1990's *Rev It Up*, and before too long the band was dropped from their label, falling completely out of sight until 1998, when they released a reunion album, *Tangerine*, for CMC International. *Live and Learn* was released in 2006, and *Reloaded* was released in 2011.

Janet Gardner: vocals (*Vixen* through *Tangerine*); **Kat Kraft**: drums (*Live & Learn*, 2006); **Jan Kuehnemund**: guitar; **Lynn Louise Lowrey**: bass (*Live & Learn*); **Share Pedersen**: bass (*Vixen* through *Tangerine*); **Roxy Petrucci**: drums (*Vixen* through *Tangerine*); **Jenna Sanz-Agero**: vocals (*Live & Learn*)

Discography: *Vixen* (EMI, 1988); *Rev It Up* (EMI, 1990); *Tangerine* (CMC, 1998); *The Best of Vixen: Full Throttle* (Razor & Tie, 1999); *Live & Learn* (Demolition, 2006); *Reloaded* (self-released, 2011)

The women of Vixen—despite their gender—don't look half as effeminate as Poison. Left to right: Share Pedersen, Jan Kuehnemund, Roxy Petrucci, and Janet Gardner.

VOIVOD

YEARS ACTIVE: 1982–PRESENT

Hailing from northern Quebec, Voivod was one of the first Canadian thrash bands to reach a wide international audience. The group's first two albums, *War and Pain* (released in 1984) and *Rrröööaaarrr!* (released in 1986), were basic, noisy thrash albums with the occasional weird overtone, but their 1987 release, *Killing Technology*, marked the band's arrival. In retrospect, it's amazing that this album was even made, much less released or bought. It was by far one of the weirdest albums that the thrash movement had yet to offer up. From the opening pod-bay-door beeps of its first song to its final salvo at the end of "This Is Not an Exercise," the album had more in common with the art-punk of bands like Die Kreuzen, or even Chrome, than with anything in the Exodus catalog. The songs were all extremely dark, minor-key excursions into every bizarre time signature that drummer Michel "Away" Langevin could hammer out and every grating diminished chord that guitarist Denis "Piggy" D'Amour could summon to counteract the burping bass lines of Jean-Yves "Blacky" Theriault, whose sound and style were a dead ringer for those of Yes bassist Chris Squire. Clearly, this was not your average Noise Records band. They didn't even play their fast thrash beats like anyone else. While most speed metal bands of the day were mainly inspired by Slayer's *Reign in Blood* and were consequently trying to win the World's Fastest Drummer sweepstakes, Voivod actually reeled in their fast tempos a bit, cruising along at an almost relaxed clip that suggested Tin Pan Alley jazz or western swing. The only bands that Voivod could really be compared to were Rush in its most technical moments and King Crimson

OPPOSITE: In this 1993 photograph, the members of Voivod look just as broken down as the truck they lean on. Clockwise from top left: Michel "Away" Langevin, Denis "Snake" Belanger, and Denis "Piggy" D'Amour.

circa *Red*. Otherwise, the niche that Voivod had carved out for themselves was so unique that no one dared copy it. It was all virgin territory. The band had quite a few things going for them, not the least of which was D'Amour's exceptional guitar playing. While most thrash guitarists played their rhythm parts on the absolute lowest note of the absolute lowest string and their leads at the absolute highest fret of the guitar neck, D'Amour was aware that there were actually several other frets and as many as four other strings that he could manipulate, and he made use of them all, easily outpacing his peers and distinguishing himself as the most creative and colorful musician in thrash. As a lad he had studied classical violin, and now, as a guitarist, he used everything that he had learned. The band also had a brilliant lyricist in Denis "Snake" Belanger. From *Killing Technology* through the release of *Nothingface* in 1989, their records were all concept albums that followed the science fiction adventures of the Voivod, some kind of sentient creature, as he traveled through the universe. This would have been a major ten-car pileup of a disaster in the hands of a lesser lyricist, but Belanger was able to get it all across without relying either on clichés or the even more popular crutch of irony. The singer also developed over the course of the next few albums into one of thrash's most melodic vocalists, graduating from a typical speed metal screamer to a highly unique balladeer with a voice so distinctive that it was instantly recognizable. Basically, if there was an area in which the band did not excel, they presented an alternative so bizarre that the sheer nerve displayed in pulling it off rendered moot the issue of its technical execution.

Despite its extremely left-field approach, *Killing Technology* struck a chord with an overwhelming number of thrash fans, most of whom were simply fascinated by the album's

Voivod is pictured here in 1990, when it was on top of the world and could do no wrong in the universe. Clockwise from left: Jean-Yves "Blacky" Theriault, Denis "Snake" Belanger, Denis "Piggy" D'Amour, and Michel "Away" Langevin.

unpredictability and originality. Buoyed by its success, Voivod came roaring back in 1988 with *Dimension Hatross*, which was, inconceivably, even stranger than its predecessor. It was also more unique and more musically accomplished, as the band used it as a vehicle to break away from thrash into an area that truly was all their own. With a few exceptions, the band had removed the thrash tempos from their repertoire, replacing them with viciously swaying grooves and a shockingly exotic sense of melody. With such excellent material as "Tribal Convictions," "Brain Scan," and the utterly brilliant "Chaosmongers," the album achieved classic status among thrash fans and eventually gained the attention of the major labels, which had run out of glam bands to sign and were offering contracts to the most commercially successful thrash bands they could sniff out. Against all odds, Voivod fulfilled this criterion and was soon signed to Mechanic, the metal subsidiary of MCA, for which the band made *Nothingface*. The 1989 release was easily the most progressive album the band had ever done, yet it also proved to be their most commercially successful, thanks to MTV regularly airing the video for "Astronomy Domine." The song, originally recorded by Pink Floyd in their Syd Barrett days, was the sole nod to conventional music that the album possessed, and thus it became the single by default. The rest of the album, however, was a commercially hopeless and utterly unclassifiable mixture of odd time signatures, musical textures, and melodic motifs that sounded like nothing that had ever come before, metal or otherwise. While the last two albums had seen the band breaking away from thrash, on *Nothingface* Voivod broke almost entirely away from any conventionally held notions of what music should sound like. There were moments here and there that briefly touched the earth, but those lasted only a few measures before some monstrosity of an oddly metered, melodically irregular motif barged in and swept it away, only to be replaced by yet another section that seemed to have been grafted on, second evil head–like, from another song. It was truly an album like no other, and it heralded the band's most successful period, which at its height saw them headline above Faith No More and Soundgarden on the Bands All Over tour of 1990.

Naturally, expectations were high for Voivod's 1991 follow-up, *Angel Rat*, and the band certainly seemed poised to be put over the top. However, the album was a complete 180-degree turnaround from *Nothingface*, as it possessed very few odd time signatures or terrifying diminished chords from Monsieur D'Amour. Instead, it was a straightforward—one might even say conventional—album of classic-sounding prog rock songs, and it caught the band's fans completely off guard. Their admirers had spent the previous year wondering how far Voivod would push it this time and were certainly not expecting the album that they got. Helmed by longtime Rush producer Terry Brown, it actually had a lot in common with Rush's output circa *Moving Pictures* or *Signals* in some respects, particularly melodically. Ultimately, though, *Angel Rat* proved to be the start of a major downturn for Voivod. Theriault was absent from the album artwork, a red flag that surely signaled some kind of trouble in paradise. As it turned out, he had left the band as soon as his tracks were recorded, which spoke volumes about what he thought of their new direction. Fans were for the most part put off by what appeared to be Voivod, the weirdest band on earth, selling out. Today, when one listens to the album, it's obvious that this was absolutely not the case at all. The band crafted an album that was, in a sense, a tribute to the classic progressive rock that had influenced all of their work, and it, too, was utterly unlike anything released at the time or since. But its straightforward sound was misinterpreted as a cynical attempt to cash in, leading to vicious fan criticism. The album didn't sell at all, hampered as much by disillusioned fans as by the grunge revolution that was under way. It was truly remarkable that so much could go so wrong so quickly. Voivod had gone from being thrash's next big thing to yesterday's news in a single year, and you couldn't go to a used-CD store in 1991 without seeing multiple copies of *Angel Rat* priced to move at $2.99. This was an utter tragedy, as the album was an absolutely brilliant classic that more than holds its own today, particularly when removed from the context of the time in which it was released.

The band returned in 1993 with *The Outer Limits*, which combined the approach of *Angel Rat* with that of the band's previous weirdo-jazz output, but the situation had become pretty grim. Although the album was easily as strong as anything the band had done before and was in many ways even more adventurous than the thrash albums that had won Voivod their fan base, it was not promoted in any way, and it contained another Pink Floyd cover, this time of "The Nile Song," which even the most sympathetic fans could see only as the band desperately trying to replicate their *Nothingface*-era glory. More depressing still was the supporting tour, which started with the band headlining and playing to mostly empty clubs and then ended in a decidedly downscaled fashion, with Voivod opening for such lesser bands as Carcass. That the band's fortunes had turned so drastically in four years was nothing short of bewildering, and after the tour, Belanger decided not to stick around any longer, perhaps

CANADA

Canada's contributions to metal music have formed some of the essential pillars of the genre. Since the 1980s, Voivod have proudly carried the torch, even when their sole rewards for doing so were poverty and ridicule. And of course there's Rush, not a heavy metal band in its purest sense, but one whose music has been so essential to metal that they have lifetime club membership. Their seminal status is so well established that Rush even remained in the club when they were making techno-synth garbage during the 1980s.

Canada has been well represented by the thrash genre. Besides Anvil and Exciter, there's Annihilator and Razor, both of whom have been going strong since 1984. There are also notable Canadian black metal groups such as Blasphemy and Revenge, the latter forming from the ashes of a 1990s black metal group called Conqueror. There's also Iskra, who play a mix of crust punk and black metal which the band refers to as "blackened crust." Tasty.

Canadian metal also features bands whose whole raison d'être is to glorify the past. Cauldron is a traditional metal band that formed in 2006, but whose sound is pure, vintage 1982 through and through. There's also the stoner doom band Sheavy, whose throwback sound is so convincing, and whose singer, Steve Hennessey, does such a spot-on Ozzy impression, that their 1997 song "Electric Sleep" was mistakenly identified as a lost Black Sabbath song. Both the mistake and the mp3 went viral until Joe Siegler, webmaster of Black-Sabbath.com, personally disabused visitors to the site of this fantasy. Sad for fans, perhaps, but well done Hennessey!

feeling that he had already experienced enough of the humiliating downward spiral. This left D'Amour and Langevin as the only members, and many people must have felt that this was surely the end of the line for Voivod. Its journey had come to an end. It had broken up upon reentering earth's atmosphere. H.A.L. would no longer open the pod bay door. The Romulans had vaporized the members. They couldn't repel firepower of the Death Star's magnitude. But much to the surprise of the metal community, Voivod hired Eric Forrest, a vocalist and bassist, and soldiered on as a power trio.

The group negotiated a new deal with Mausoleum Records, secure in the knowledge that their old label MCA could not care less whether they lived or died, and emerged with *Negatron* in 1995. The album signaled a full-fledged return to the band's thrash glory days, although it rejected their progressive inclinations for the most part. The group was once again covering territory that was new to them and doing it their own way. Their fan base returned, albeit to a smaller degree, and they settled comfortably into a role at the top of the underground-metal mountain. The band finally seemed to be back on track, until 1998, when Forrest was in a major car accident while on tour with the band and was sidelined indefinitely. To make matters worse, he brought legal action against the band to get them to cover his medical expenses. This was the official last straw, and D'Amour and Langevin decided that it was time to split up the band. But just a few months later, they reunited with Belanger, and they enlisted the services of recently departed Metallica bassist and lifelong Voivod fan Jason Newsted to fill the still-vacant four-string slot.

Voivod released a self-titled album in 2003 which picked up in roughly the same stylistic territory as where *The Outer Limits* had left off. The repetitive, overcompensating thrash of the Eric Forrest years was gone, and in its place was an odd tunefulness and paranoid lyrics that suited the George W. Bush era all too well, particularly on the opener "Gasmask Revival." The album increased the band's profile significantly and

helped them regain much of the ground that they lost in the latter days of the MCA Records debacle.

In 2005, D'Amour was diagnosed with inoperable colon cancer. With very little time left, he told Langevin that he had stored a treasure trove of completed guitar tracks on his laptop. Not long after passing his work on to the drummer, he slipped into a coma and died. His bandmates now had the task before them of salvaging the recordings and turning them into fully realized songs. D'Amour hadn't played to a click track or a metronome, so the tempo wavered throughout the tracks, but Langevin nonetheless recorded drums that fit in seamlessly with the guitars. Newsted and Belanger finished their parts next, and the final product was released in 2006 as *Katorz*. The band had used only half of the tracks that D'Amour had recorded, and the rest were used for the 2009 album *Infini*, which was recorded the same way.

The remaining band members decided to promote the albums by performing live. Theriault returned to the group for the concerts, and the guitar parts were handled by Dan Mongrain of Martyr. This lineup toured to support both albums, and fans accepted the new lineup. Voivod had earned their fair share of good will over the years, and audiences wanted to see them thrive. The band released the live recording *Warriors of Ice* in 2011, and Langevin confirmed in an interview that the band would record a new studio album.

Denis "Snake" Belanger: vocals (*War and Pain* through *The Outer Limits*; *Voivod* and later); **Denis "Piggy" D'Amour**: guitars; **Eric Forrest**: vocals/bass (*Negatron* through *Phobos*); **Michel "Away" Langevin**: drums; **Jason "Jasonic" Newsted**: bass (*Voivod* and later); **Jean-Yves "Blacky" Theriault**: bass (*War and Pain* through *Angel Rat*)

Discography: *War and Pain* (Metal Blade, 1984); *Rrröööaaarrr!* (Noise, 1986); *Killing Technology* (Noise, 1987); *Dimension Hatröss* (Noise, 1988); *Nothingface* (Mechanic, 1989); *Angel Rat* (MCA, 1991); *The Outer Limits* (MCA, 1993); *Negatron* (Mausoleum, 1995); *Phobos* (Hypnotic, 1997); *Voivod Lives* (Century Media, 2000); *Voivod* (Chophouse, 2003); *Katorz* (Nuclear Blast, 2006); *Infini* (Relapse, 2009); *Warriors of Ice* (Sonic Unyon, 2011)

WARHORSE

YEARS ACTIVE: 1996–2005

Scientists have observed that human beings, when exposed to an extremely low sound frequency, will involuntarily move their bowels. Well, Warhorse was the best thing to happen to bowel evacuation since Metamucil's invention. The Massachusetts doom metal band (not to be confused with the other Warhorse, formed by that ex–Deep Purple bassist in the 1970s) was easily one of the heaviest bands that the genre produced, giving groups in other heavy metal genres a run for their money. The usual doom metal ingredients of extremely slow tempos and extremely low tunings are apparent here, but Warhorse exaggerated them and pushed them to an absurdly surpassing degree, such that it is difficult to conceive of what the group could possibly have done to top themselves. Originally formed by drummer Mike Hubbard and bassist Jerry Orne, the band had a strong background in death metal before falling under the influence of doom and shifting styles accordingly. Their self-titled debut was independently released in 1998, with Krista Van Guilder on guitar and vocals. Her voice was somewhere between alto and soprano, providing a stark contrast to the low-end churn of the band. But she didn't hang around for too long and was eventually replaced

Warhorse bassist and vocalist Jerry Orne projects the blackest seething hatred toward all humanity.

by guitarist Todd Laskowski. After Orne took up the microphone that Van Guilder had vacated, the lineup was complete, and in 2001 the band produced *As Heaven Turns to Ash*, without question that year's heaviest album. Warhorse toured extensively with the likes of Electric Wizard and was one of the likeliest contenders for total doom supremacy in the United States. However, after the prophetically titled 2002 *I Am Dying* EP, the band broke up.

Mike Hubbard: drums/backing vocals; **Todd Laskowski**: guitars (*As Heaven Turns to Ash*); **Jerry Orne**: bass/vocals; **Krista Van Guilder**: guitars/vocals (*Warhorse*)

Discography: *Warhorse* (self-released, 1998); *As Heaven Turns to Ash* (Southern Lord, 2001); *I Am Dying* (Southern Lord, 2002)

WARLOCK

YEARS ACTIVE: 1982–1988

The German band Warlock is mainly recognized today as the band that gave singer and former model Doro Pesch her start, although the group was certainly a solid power

metal unit in its own right. Formed in 1983, Warlock produced European power metal that was influenced by the usual suspects: Iron Maiden and Judas Priest. The difference was that Warlock was fronted by a woman, a rarity in the testosterone-dominated heavy metal field. There had already been plenty of female rock stars, even heavy metal rock stars such as Girlschool and Heart, but Pesch sang about the same kinds of demons-and-wizards topics as Ronnie James Dio and just as forcefully, separating her from the pack in a decisive manner. Warlock was eventually picked up by the independent Mausoleum label, which released the group's debut, *Burning the Witches*, in 1984. Their next three albums all saw the band grow musically but didn't do much for them commercially. They had always retained an enthusiastic cult following but weren't able to expand upon it in any significant way, even after touring with Dio and Megadeth. In 1989, the band called it quits, and Pesch went on to start her career as Doro, solo artist, releasing albums that were less heavy metal and more hard rock than those she had made with Warlock.

Nico Arvanitis: guitars (*True As Steel* and later); **Tommy Bolan**: guitars (*Triumph and Agony*); **Michael Eurich**: drums; **Rudy Graf**: guitars (*Burning the Witches, Hellbound*); **Tommy Henriksen**: bass (*Triumph and Agony*); **Doro Pesch**: vocals; **Frank Rittel**: bass (*True As Steel*); **Peter Szigeti**: guitars (*True As Steel* and later)

Discography: *Burning the Witches* (Mausoleum, 1984); *Hellbound* (Polydor, 1985); *True As Steel* (Phonogram, 1986); *Triumph and Agony* (Phonogram, 1987)

YEARS ACTIVE: 1980–1986; 2002

Warlord was one of the classic power metal bands of the 1980s, but its members were

OPPOSITE: Warlock had a good run with singer Doro Pesch front and center. Left to right: Rudy Graf, Peter Szigeti, Doro Pesch, Frank Rittel, and Michael Eurich.

unjustly overlooked during their short career, during which they released only enough material to fill a single compact disc. In fact, the curious can learn everything there is to know about the Los Angeles band by purchasing the 1993 release *The Best of Warlord*, which contains virtually all the material from their one full-length album and two EPs. However, quantity isn't everything, and the band-released material signified great songwriting talent and musicianship. As a bonus, Warlord was also extremely resourceful when it came to stage aliases. When original singer Jack "Damien King I" Rucker quit the band after the *Deliver Us* EP, his replacement, Rick Cunningham, was anointed with the stage name "Damien King II," a move that should overjoy conservationists the world over. The band reunited in 2002 and recorded *Rising Out of the Ashes*.

Diane "Sentinel" Arens: keyboards; **Joacim Cans**: vocals (*Rising Out of the Ashes*); **Rick "Damien King II" Cunningham**: vocals (*And the Cannons of Destruction* through *Thy Kingdom Come*); **Jack "Damien King I" Rucker**: vocals (*Deliver Us*); **Bill "Destroyer" Tsamis**: guitars; **Dave "Archangel" Waltry**: bass (*Deliver Us* through *Thy Kingdom Come*); **Mark "Thunder Child" Zonder**: drums (see also Fates Warning)

Discography: *Deliver Us* (Metal Blade, 1983); *And the Cannons of Destruction* (Metal Blade, 1984); *Thy Kingdom Come* (Metal Blade, 1986); *Rising Out of the Ashes* (Drakkar, 2002)

YEARS ACTIVE: 1984–PRESENT

Warrant was one of the most popular glam metal bands of the movement's tail end. Although in retrospect they got there only in time for the death rattle, their timing initially appeared as though it couldn't have been better. Their debut album, *Dirty Rotten Filthy Stinking Rich*, was released in 1989 and

quickly became a hit, climbing into the Top 10 just months after its release, remarkable for a debut. The music was exactly what the general public wanted at the time, and the album was supported to a considerable degree by the hit singles "Down Boys" and "Heaven," which enjoyed perpetual rotation on MTV. The songs even had enough crossover appeal not to be limited to the *Headbanger's Ball*—they could be found on the network at any time of the day. Their next album, *Cherry Pie*, released in 1990, was an even bigger hit, as was the title track, which reached the Top 10 on the singles charts. Unfortunately, it was all downhill after that. Their 1992 album, *Dog Eat Dog*, sold only a fraction of what its predecessors had (despite the fact that the rap-metal band Dog Eat Dog returned the favor by calling its debut album *Warrant*), and 1995's *Ultraphobic* didn't sell even marginally, a fate that many of their glam compatriots suffered right along with them. However, Warrant stayed together, and in 2001 the band issued *Under the Influence*, a covers album. Singer and principal songwriter Jani Lane, who had briefly left the band in 1994, left again in 2004. The group replaced him with former Black N' Blue vocalist Jaime St. James and released *Born Again* in 2006. Lane was supposed to return to the band in 2008 for a tour with Cinderella, but the situation didn't pan out and he never worked with them again. Warrant's last album was 2011's *Rockaholic*, and just a few months after its

Singer Jani Lane prays that Warrant's fifteen minutes of fame will last long enough for him to make his last Camaro payment. Left to right: Joey Allen, Jerry Dixon, Jani Lane, Erik Turner, and Steven Sweet.

release, Lane was found dead of acute alcohol poisoning in a Comfort Inn in Woodland Hills, California.

Joey Allen: guitar; **Jerry Dixon**: bass; **Jaime St. James**: vocals (*Born Again*); **Jani Lane**: vocals (*Dirty Rotten Filthy Stinking Rich* through *Under the Influence*); **Robert Mason**: vocals (*Rockaholic*); **Steven Sweet**: drums; **Erik Turner**: guitar

Discography: *Dirty Rotten Filthy Stinking Rich* (Columbia, 1989); *Cherry Pie* (Columbia, 1990); *Dog Eat Dog* (Columbia, 1992); *Ultraphobic* (CMC, 1995); *Rocking Tall* (Sony Music, 1996); *Warrant Live 1986–1997* (CMC, 1997); *Greatest and Latest* (Dead Line, 1999); *Under the Influence* (Perris, 2001); *Born Again* (Deadline, 2006); *Rockaholic* (Frontiers, 2011)

W.A.S.P.

YEARS ACTIVE: 1982–PRESENT

While Alice Cooper spent the 1980s attending to his angry and toxic liver in rehab, it seemed that his most likely heir to the shock rock throne would be Blackie Lawless of the Los Angeles band W.A.S.P. The singer/guitarist/bassist and his cohorts gained an infamous reputation virtually overnight based on their live performances, during which they partook in such ridiculously hokey sensationalism as the binding and torture of scantily clad female victims and the distribution of raw meat into the audience in chunky, wet, projectile form. Although these antics alone would have been enough to give any artist his or her fifteen minutes of spotlight time, W.A.S.P. also incidentally was composed of talented songwriters who crafted canny, memorable, KISS-like hooks and choruses. Earning the band more notoriety was the flap caused by one of their choruses, "I fuck like a beast," which caught the attention of the Parents Music

Dude, nobody wants to see that: W.A.S.P.'s Blackie Lawless.

Resource Center (PMRC). This, of course, inadvertently made the band more popular than ever. Even though Capitol Records had signed and released W.A.S.P.'s self-titled debut in 1984, it wasn't until a year later that the PMRC focused attention on the band's *Animal (F**k Like a Beast)* EP, the cover of which featured a close-up shot of a crotch fully equipped with a circular saw blade in place of private parts.

The attention proved to be a little too much for the band, and their musical output began to suffer as a result—the media scrutiny was so intense that it had them constantly looking over their shoulders. As a result, the next couple of albums were mediocre at best. Matters were not helped when guitarist Chris Holmes appeared in the 1988 movie *Decline of Western Civilization Part II: The Metal Years*; one scene of which showed Holmes in a raging alcoholic stupor in his mother's swimming pool while she sat silently embarassed at poolside with a please-kill-me-now look on her face. The band soldiered on and suffered a number of lineup changes, even breaking up briefly, but the relentlessly persistent Lawless stuck with it no matter what, and the band remains together today.

Frankie Banali: drums (*The Headless Children* through *Still Not Black Enough*) (see also Quiet Riot); **Doug Blair**: guitar (*Dominator* and later); **Mike Duda**: bass (*Kill, Fuck, Die* and later); **Mike Dupke**: drums (*Dominator* and later); **Chris Holmes**: guitars (*W.A.S.P.* through *The Headless Children*, *Kill, Fuck, Die* and later); **Stet Howland**: drums (*The Crimson Idol* through *The Neon God: Part 2—The Demise*); **Mark Josephson**: violin (*Still Not Black Enough*); **Bob Kulick**: guitars (*The Crimson Idol* through *Still Not Black Enough*); **Blackie Lawless**: vocals/guitars/bass; **Randy Piper**: guitars (*W.A.S.P.*, *The Last Command*); **Tony Richards**: drums (*W.A.S.P.*); **Steve Riley**: drums (*Inside the Electric Circus*, *Live . . . in the Raw*) (see also L.A. Guns); **Darrell Roberts**: guitar (*Dominator*); **Johnny Rod**: bass (*Inside the Electric Circus* through *The Headless Children*)

Discography: *Animal (F**k Like a Beast)* (Restless, 1983); *W.A.S.P.* (Capitol, 1984); *The Last Command* (Capitol, 1985); *Inside the Electric Circus* (Capitol, 1986); *Live . . . in the Raw* (Capitol, 1987); *The Headless* *Children* (Capitol, 1989); *The Crimson Idol* (Capitol, 1992); *Still Not Black Enough* (Castle, 1995); *Kill, Fuck, Die* (Castle, 1997); *Double Live Assassins* (CMC, 1998); *Helldorado* (CMC, 1999); *The Sting* (Snapper, 2000); *Unholy Terror* (Metal-Is, 2001); *Dying for the World* (Metal-Is, 2002); *The Neon God: Part 1—The Rise* (Sanctuary, 2004); *The Neon God: Part 2—The Demise* (Sanctuary, 2004); *Dominator* (Demolition, 2007); *Babylon* (Demolition, 2009).

WHITESNAKE

YEARS ACTIVE: 1978–1991; 1997–PRESENT

While Whitesnake is regarded today as one of the most popular bands of the hair metal explosion, its history actually dates back to 1978, almost ten years before the band stormed up the charts. What is equally surprising is that the band was originally made up of well-respected musicians from the classic rock era. Whitesnake is the brainchild of David Coverdale, who formed the band fresh off his first experience with fame in Deep Purple. Coverdale had replaced the departing Ian Gillan right when Purple was about to reach the peak of its popularity.

With the impressive distinction of having "former Deep Purple singer" to add to his résumé, Coverdale encountered little resistance when he decided to form his own band, and Whitesnake was born. The band had to their credit some of the day's most highly respected musicians, including ex-Juicy Lucy guitarists Mick Moody and Bernie Marsden, to say nothing of one of Coverdale's former Deep Purple bandmates, the godly and awe-inspiring drummer Ian Paice. This incarnation of Whitesnake played straight-ahead hard rock with pronounced blues influences, much of which came courtesy of Marsden, who deserves credit for cowriting a great deal of the band's early material. Marsden can be credited as well for

some of the band's later commercial success, as he and Coverdale wrote a little ditty called "Here I Go Again," which made quite a few people in the 1980s decide that they'd like their own personal copy of the song. But despite his influence on what would become the band's biggest hit song, Marsden was already becoming deeply disturbed by the more commercial sound that Coverdale wanted to pursue, and he left the band in 1983 (although he would reappear briefly to contribute some guitar tracks to the band's 1987 album).

It was around this time that the singer's

OPPOSITE: You can almost hear W.A.S.P. growl "Aaarrrgh!!! Graaahhh!!! Raarrrhhh!!!"

THE ENCYCLOPEDIA OF HEAVY METAL 375

daughter fell ill, so a sabbatical seemed appropriate, and for a while Whitesnake was relegated to the back burner.

When Coverdale decided to return to action, it was 1984, and the band was signed that year to Geffen, which issued *Slide It In*. The album was a hit on both sides of the Atlantic, but the glory was brief. Coverdale was diagnosed with a sinus condition that sidelined him indefinitely and presented the strong possibility that he might never sing again. However, he eventually overcame the illness, and in 1987 the band released their second, self-titled album for Geffen, which simply exploded. Despite the fact that the band's original lineup had completely changed and their first single, "Still of the Night," was the most blatant Led Zeppelin rip-off in human history, the album sold like crazy, eventually moving ten million copies. Suddenly, there was huge demand for more, more, more Whitesnake, and Geffen responded by reissuing all of the band's earlier material, which no doubt confused many record buyers, most of whom believed Whitesnake was a new band.

In 1989, Whitesnake, now featuring virtuoso guitarist Steve Vai, issued its follow-up, *Slip of the Tongue*, which was doomed to failure right from the start. Whitesnake had sold a ridiculous, unprecedented number of copies, and if the new album did anything but triple the sales figures of its predecessor, it would have been considered a commercial disappointment. In fact, *Slip of the Tongue* went platinum, which constituted a mere 10 percent of what the last album had sold. After the indignity and humiliation of having an album that achieved merely platinum certification, Coverdale disbanded Whitesnake and wasn't heard from until 1993, when he and Jimmy Page released an album together, arching

BELOW: This photograph documents six-piece Whitesnake in its early blues-rock incarnation.
OPPOSITE: By the 1980s, Whitesnake's transformation from straight-ahead blues rockers to big-haired arena rockers was complete.

the eyebrows of Led Zeppelin fans the world over, many of whom considered Coverdale to be nothing but a mere rip-off artist who had usurped Zeppelin singer Robert Plant's stage persona lock, stock, and barrel, such that he was often referred to in the metal press as "David Cover Version." Coverdale eventually re-formed Whitesnake in 1997 with all-new members, except for guitarist Adrian Vandenberg, the sole returnee. This iteration of Whitesnake released *Restless Heart* through EMI, except in the United States, where it wasn't issued at all. The band released one more album, *Starkers in Tokyo*, which was basically Whitesnake unplugged and featured only Coverdale and Vandenberg. By this time, it was clear that Whitesnake was simply running on fumes, and Coverdale took it off life support not long after, choosing to focus on his solo career instead. Apparently, that didn't go so well either, because in 2008, Whitesnake returned and released *Good to Be Bad*, their first studio album in 11 years. It was followed in 2011 by *Forevermore*.

Don Airey: keyboards (*Whitesnake, Slip of the Tongue*) (see also Rainbow); **Doug Aldrich**: guitars (*Good to Be Bad* and later); **Reb Beach**: guitars (*Good to Be Bad* and later); **David Coverdale**: vocals (see also Deep Purple); **Michael Devin**: bass (*Forevermore*); **David Dowle**: drums (*Snakebite* through *Live at Hammersmith*; *Whitesnake*); **Timothy Drury**: keyboards (*Good to Be Bad*); **Uriah Duffy**: bass (*Good to Be Bad*); **Chris Frazier**: drums (*Good to Be Bad*); **Jon Lord**: keyboards (*Trouble* through *Slide It In*) (see also Deep Purple); **Bernie Marsden**: guitar (*Snakebite* through *Whitesnake*); **Micky Moody**: guitar (*Snakebite* through *Whitesnake*); **Neil Murray**: bass (*Snakebite* through *Whitesnake*); **Ian Paice**: drums (*Snakebite* through *Whitesnake*) (see also Deep Purple); **Rudy Sarzo**: bass (*Slip of the Tongue*); **John Sykes**: guitar (*Slide It In, Whitesnake*) (see also Thin Lizzy, Tygers of Pan Tang); **Brian Tichy**: drums (*Forevermore*); **Steve Vai**: guitar (*Slip of the Tongue*); **Adrian Vandenberg**: guitar (*Whitesnake* through *Restless Heart*)

Discography: *Trouble* (Geffen, 1978); *Lovehunter* (Geffen, 1979); *Live in the Heart of the City* (Geffen, 1980); *Live at Hammersmith* (Sunburst, 1980); *Ready an' Willing* (EMI, 1980); *Come an' Get It* (Geffen, 1981); *Saints and Sinners* (Geffen, 1982); *Slide It In* (Geffen, 1984); *Whitesnake* (Geffen, 1987); *Slip of the Tongue* (Geffen, 1989); *Restless Heart* (EMI, 1998); *Starkers in Tokyo* (EMI, 1998); *20th Century Masters* (Geffen, 2000); *Good to Be Bad* (SPV/Steamhammer, 2008); *Forevermore* (Frontiers, 2011)

WHITE ZOMBIE

YEARS ACTIVE: 1985–1998

In 1985 vocalist Rob Zombie and bassist Sean Yseult formed White Zombie in New York City. Although the band eventually became widely commercially successful, their cynical take on metal was not immediately appreciated, as mid-1980s metal was not a genre in which irony could be found in abundant supply. Between their tongue-in-cheek humor and the crushing heaviness of their early releases, the band was not an early favorite, but as their sound developed from one of utter darkness to one that mixed its metal with psychedelic influences, industrial overtones, and the unmistakable aura of schlock horror movies, the public began to warm up to them. Their 1992 Geffen debut, *La Sexorcisto: Devil Music, Vol. 1*, seemed at first to catch on slowly in a manner consistent with their previous releases, but the following year, their video for "Thunder Kiss '65" went into heavy rotation, particularly on *Beavis & Butthead*, and the album wouldn't stay on record-store shelves for long ever again. The band replicated the album's formula with similar results for their 1995 release, *Astro Creep: 2000—Songs of Love, Destruction and Other Synthetic Delusions of the Electric Head*, but after 1996's *Supersexy Swingin' Sounds*, an album of remixes, White Zombie disappeared from sight. Finally it was revealed that they had in fact broken up, and Rob Zombie has since gone on to have a successful career as a solo artist and a director of horror films.

Ivan de Prume: drums (*Pig Heaven* through *God of Thunder*); **Tom Guay**: guitars (*Psych-Head Blowout, Soul Crusher*);

Tim Jeffs: guitars (*Pig Heaven*); **Ena Kostabi**: guitars (*Gods on Voodoo Moon*); **Peter Landau**: drums (*Gods on Voodoo Moon*); **John Ricci**: guitars (*Make Them Die Slowly*); **John Tempesta**: drums (*La Sexorcisto: Devil Music, Vol. 1* and later) (see also Exodus, Testament); **Sean Yseult**: bass; **Jay Noel Yuenger**: guitars (*God of Thunder* and later); **Rob Zombie**: vocals

Discography: *Soul-Crusher* (Caroline, 1987); *Make Them Die Slowly* (Caroline, 1989); *La Sexorcisto: Devil Music, Vol. 1* (Geffen, 1992); *Astro Creep: 2000—Songs of Love, Destruction and Other Synthetic Delusions of the Electric Head* (Geffen, 1995); *Supersexy Swingin' Sounds* (Geffen, 1996)

White Zombie in Chicago during its 1992 commercial peak.

JAPAN

Just like Germany, Japan has offered a consistent home to metal bands from all over the world, regardless of the music's popularity elsewhere. "We're big in Japan" may be shorthand for "Our band's not popular here in the States," but it's also offered consolation to metal bands for whom the Western hemisphere's tit has dried up, and will offer sustenance no longer. The phrase also provided Alphaville with fodder for their first single, but that's another story. The message for metal bands in search of an audience is: Go east, young men, go east.

Japan is similar to Germany in that it's not only embraced American bands, but has been cranking out its own metal even before metal was metal. Blues Creation was among the first of the country's psychedelic blues bands to crank up their amps and unleash torrents of sludge upon an unsuspecting nation. They were joined by Strawberry Path, who lost two members to Flied Egg, and Foodbrain, which lost exceptional guitarist Shinki Chen to Speed, Glue & Shinki.

When metal became an entrenched style, Japan had bands at the ready. Bow Wow was Japan's answer to Aerosmith, forming in 1975 with a sound that wouldn't have been out of place on American FM radio. They went in a poppier direction as the years passed and changed their name to Vow Wow, gaining Whitesnake bassist Neil Murray in the process. EZO, meanwhile, formed in 1982 in Sapporo, and they're considered a classic band. They came to the U.S. at the behest of one Gene Simmons, who produced their self-titled U.S. debut in 1987. There was also Anthem, which was a contemporary of EZO, and Earthshaker, which date back to 1978.

As commercial 1980s metal began to fade, more underground genres took hold of the market. Sabbat formed in the 1980s as a thrash band, and their style eventually shifted to black metal. Sex Machineguns are a thrash band formed in 1983 that emphasizes crazed, high-speed instrumental soloing and quirky lyrics. Double Dealer, Concerto Moon, and Galneryus are all power-metal bands. Galneryus also adds a strong neoclassical element to their sound. Onmyouza, another serious player that formed in 1999, means "the gathering of yin and yang," although you wouldn't know it to listen to their music, which is pure, traditional heavy metal.

Dir En Grey formed in 1997, originally intending to be a visual kei band. Visual kei is usually described as Japan's answer to glam metal, and while the bands definitely wear makeup, use hairspray, and dress in over-the-top finery, the music tends to have elements of punk rock mixed in with the glam. Mainly, however, visual kei bands dress funny, and one such band is Nightmare, which formed in 2000 and whose members also all play in the side project, Sendai Kamotsu. X Japan is also a visual kei band, and they are considered the genre's godfathers, in part due to their insistence on wearing gigantic hairstyles. Sort of like the B-52s of metal.

If Japanese metal of the 2000s and the 2010s can be said to have a "sound," it's the sound of a band starting in an established style and then pushing it as far into bizarro-land territory as it will go. Boris, Corrupted, and Sigh all began their careers fitting into an established genre—sludge in the case of Boris, extreme doom in the case of Corrupted, and black metal in the case of Sigh. No matter what their origins were, Boris and Sigh went on to radically change their styles.

Sigh had originally been signed to the Deathlike Silence Productions label run by Oystein Aarseth, better known as the late Euronymous of Mayhem. That gave them all the black metal cred they could possibly have asked for, and they promptly abandoned it to pursue an experimental, psychedelic direction. As for Boris, it left the sludge behind, shifting into an avant-garde, ambient drone band. Only Corrupted has kept it real, and can still be described as an extreme doom band. In fact, their 2005 *El Mundo Frio* album consists of exactly one song, which clocks in at 72 minutes.

Other current Japanese bands have not even bothered to abandon an established style, making up their own new genres. Zeni Geva, a band led by KK Null of Yb02, fuses death metal with elements of punk, noise, and torturously complicated math rock, and Ruins is a duo consisting of just bass and drums. Describing itself as a "Zeuhl" band in the tradition of Magma, its music is unbelievably intricate and almost totally inaccessible to anyone but the most determined listeners. Good luck.

Winter's influence in the doom-death metal field is rather notable considering that the band has only one full-length album and an EP to its credit. Hailing from New York City, Winter was among the first to combine the growling vocals of death metal with the slow tempos of doom, and did so to devastating effect. Even though there are countless bands who utilize this approach today, Winter did it first and deserves the credit for influencing, if not inventing, the genre to which bands as diverse as Evoken and Burning Witch owe their sound. The band's two releases, 1992's *Into Darkness* and 1994's *Eternal Frost*, were thoughtfully reissued on a single disc so that the listener lying in the bathtub crying his or her eyes out will not have to get up to change CDs.

John Alman: vocals/bass; **Stephen Flam**: guitars; **Joe Gonclaves**: drums

Discography: *Into Darkness* (Nuclear Blast, 1992); *Eternal Frost* (Nuclear Blast, 1994); *Into Darkness/ Eternal Frost* (Nuclear Blast, 2000)

YEARS ACTIVE: 1979–1984; 2006–PRESENT

Although Witchfinder General was originally associated with the New Wave of British Heavy Metal, this was more a function of the band's 1980s pedigree than its sound. The band was 100 percent pure doom metal, which was actually a style that many metal bands were trying to break away from at the time as they tried to embrace a more aggressive, almost punk-influenced sound. Because of this, Witchfinder General didn't find much success during their extremely brief existence, but they have become a major influence on the current doom metal scene. The band also achieved some notoriety for their extremely stupid album covers, which featured the band members torturing topless women in cemeteries and in front of castles, no doubt providing the inspiration for certain Mentors album covers. Sleeve "art" notwithstanding, both of the group's albums are classic, quality doom metal and are more than worth seeking out. The group reunited in 2006 and released their third full-length album, *Resurrected*, in 2008.

Zak Bajjon: bass (*Death Penalty*); **Phil Cope**: guitars; **Graham Ditchfield**: drums (*Friends of Hell*); **Rod Hawkes**: bass (*Friends of Hell*); **Gary Martin**: vocals (*Resurrected*); **Kid Nimble**: drums (*Death Penalty*); **Zeeb Parkes**: vocals; **Dermot Redmond**: drums (*Resurrected*)

Discography: *Death Penalty* (Heavy Metal, 1982); *Friends of Hell* (Heavy Metal, 1983); *Resurrected* (Buried in Time and Dust, 2008)

YEARS ACTIVE: 2000–PRESENT

The Australian power trio Wolfmother formed in 2000. Consisting of drummer Myles Heskett, bassist and keyboard player Chris Ross, and singer and guitarist Andrew Stockdale, the band took their cues from newer retro bands like Kyuss and older masters like Black Sabbath. After two EP releases on the local Australian label Modular Recordings, they secured an international distribution deal through Interscope and released a self-titled debut album in 2005. In 2006, Wolfmother's retro bona fides were validated when the surviving members of Led Zeppelin asked the band to perform "Communication Breakdown" at the metal godfathers' induction into the U.K. Music Hall of Fame. If they didn't all faint from shock and gratitude, they should have.

After winning a Grammy in 2007 for Best Hard Rock Performance for the song "Woman," both Heskett and Ross left the group citing

Andrew Stockdale of Wolfmother shows how limber he is after just a few Pilates classes.

musical differences and leaving Stockdale to fend for himself. He enlisted a new crew, consisting of drummer Dave Atkins, guitarist Aidan Nemeth and bassist and keyboard tickler Ian Peres. This lineup released *Cosmic Egg* in 2009, whose name is inspired by a yoga pose. Go figure. In 2011 the band announced that it had begun work on its next album, and expected it to be released sometime in 2012.

Dave Atkins: drums; **Myles Heskett**: drums (*Wolfmother*); **Aidan Nemeth** (*Cosmic Egg*); **Ian Peres**: bass, keyboards (*Cosmic Egg*); **Chris Ross**: bass (*Wolfmother*); **Andrew Stockdale**: vocals

Discography: *Wolfmother* (Interscope, 2006); *Cosmic Egg* (Interscope, 2009)

Y&T

Years active: 1974–1991; 1995–present

One of the thousands of heavy metal bands from the 1970s and 1980s, Y&T was never able to achieve the type of top-tier stardom that its members sought, despite their best efforts and considerable talent. The band was formed in San Francisco in 1973 and was originally called Yesterday and Today, inspired by a Beatles album. They slowly built a following by playing gigs locally, at times opening for prominent local bands, such as Journey in its pre–Steve Perry jam band days. However, their first two albums, issued under the name Yesterday and Today and through London Records, didn't sell particularly well, and the band began to seek out a new deal, which they eventually found in 1981. They signed to A&M and, perhaps influenced by their new label's name, shortened theirs to Y&T. Their new label did a much better job of marketing them, and the band, whose hard rock and heavy metal tendencies had now become front and center, released *Earthshaker*, their first album to sell in significant numbers. Their new high profile won them gigs opening for hard rock heavyweights such as AC/DC and KISS, and it appeared as though they were finally on the fast track. Regrettably, though, their best days were already behind them. *Black Tiger*, their follow-up to *Earthshaker*, was expected to be a huge smash, but it bombed, as did the next album, 1983's *Mean Streak*, whose failure was mitigated only by the fact that it produced "Midnight in Tokyo," an unexpected and unrepeated international hit. The band made three more albums for A&M, but after satisfying its contractual album-count obligations with the release of a greatest-hits compilation, the label dropped Y&T.

Geffen decided to give the band a new home, but Y&T committed a major blunder by opting for a new, glam rock image and by firing longtime drummer Leonard Haze in order to replace him with Jimmy DeGrasso, the skin basher with poster-boy good looks. Their first album for Geffen was 1987's *Contagious*, which sold about as well as the albums that had caused them to get dropped from A&M—that is, not at all. Guitarist Joey Alves left the band at this point and was replaced, and the new lineup released the consumer-repelling *Ten* in 1990. Once vocalist Dave Meniketti and bassist Phil Kennemore also decided to call it a day, the remaining members had no band left to quit, and Y&T appeared to have been all done. However, unbelievably, after the 1991 postmortem release of a live album, which was sure to be the band's last, Y&T got back together in 1995 to release *Musically Incorrect* to massive indifference, a reaction that was replicated in 1997 with *Endangered Species*. The band's lineup continued to shuffle and its status kept switching back and forth from "over for good" to "triumphant

Y&T guitarist Dave Meniketti squeezes that high note over a lucky audience.

After four years of releasing Y&T's records, A&M dropped the band in 1985—the year this photograph was taken. Left to right: Joey Alves, Leonard Haze, Dave Meniketti, and Phil Kennemore.

reunion" numerous times until 2010, when the band released *Facemelter*, their first studio album in 13 years. Sadly, Kennemore died early in 2011 after being diagnosed with lung cancer.

Joey Alves: rhythm guitar (*Yesterday and Today* through *Contagious*); **Stef Burns**: rhythm guitar (*Ten* through *Endangered Species*); **Jimmy DeGrasso**: drums (*Contagious* through *Endangered Species*) (see also Megadeth, Suicidal Tendencies); **Leonard Haze**: drums (*Yesterday and Today* through *Down for the Count*); **Phil Kennemore**: bass/vocals; **Dave Meniketti**: vocals/lead guitar; **John Nymann**: guitar, vocals (*Facemelter*); **Mike Vanderhule**: drums (*Facemelter*)

Discography: *Yesterday and Today* (London, 1976); *Struck Down* (London, 1978); *Earthshaker* (A&M, 1981); *Black Tiger* (A&M, 1982); *Mean Streak* (A&M, 1983); *In Rock We Trust* (A&M, 1984); *Open Fire* (A&M, 1985); *Down for the Count* (A&M, 1985); *Contagious* (Geffen, 1987); *Ten* (Geffen, 1990); *Yesterday and Today: Live* (Metal Blade, 1991); *Musically Incorrect* (D-Rock, 1995); *Endangered Species* (D-Rock, 1997); *Ultimate Collection* (Hip-O, 2001); *Facemelter* (Frontiers, 2010)

Guitarist Randy Jackson performs at a Zebra show after the band signed with Atlantic Records in 1983.

YEARS ACTIVE: 1975–1990; 2002–PRESENT

Zebra came to life in 1975 in New Orleans. During a night of on-the-town alcohol consumption, the members of the band overcame their double vision, their knocking over of items, and their yelling of "I love this guy!" for long enough to spy a 1922 *Vogue* magazine cover on the wall of a tavern. The image depicted a woman astride a zebra, and in a manner typical of pie-eyed drunks, they believed that the deeply profound image had been placed in their pathway by the swirling eddy of fate, leaving them little choice but to embrace their collective destinies and take the name of the striped quadruped as their own. However, even though the Big Easy is a world-famous music town and even though there was no shortage of places to play, the band wanted to break out of the local market, choosing to split gigs between their hometown and Long Island, New York, which at the time had a very active and fertile club scene. Eventually, Zebra permanently relocated there and made a name for itself in short order, receiving a significant shot in the arm from local radio stations, which played the band's demo tapes with a frequency not normally associated with unsigned bands. Eventually, the group won a deal with Atlantic Records, which released their self-titled debut in 1983. The album soon won the distinction of being the fastest-selling debut in the history of the record company, and it enjoyed an eight-month stay on the charts, thanks in part to the classic single "Who's Behind the Door?" That's not bad for a band that many rock magazines of the day, including *Rolling Stone*, refused to even review within their hallowed pages.

After the success of the debut and Zebra's subsequent tour, expectations were high for the band's follow-up. But the 1984 release, *No Tellin' Lies*, failed to live up to them, both artistically and commercially. The album was an attempt at a more adventurous style than that of the Zeppelin-referencing debut, and although the second album was somewhat successful in that respect, many viewed the band's new direction as a watering-down of their previous work as opposed to an expansion upon it. The band has since conceded that the album was, in retrospect, a rushed affair that they themselves were not 100 percent confident about. They experienced something of an upswing with their 1986 album, *3.V*; the band really came into their own on this one, and many die-hard fans consider it their best. Unfortunately, that didn't translate to sales, and Atlantic dropped Zebra after a poorly attended tour, eventually squeezing off *Live* in 1990 as a contract-fulfilling last gasp. The band members went their separate ways after that, but reunited in 1997 and released *Zebra IV* in 2003. In 2010 they were inducted into the Louisiana Music Hall of Fame.

Guy Gelso: drums; **Felix Hanemann**: bass/keyboards; **Randy Jackson**: vocals/guitar

Discography: *Zebra* (Atlantic, 1983); *No Tellin' Lies* (Atlantic, 1984); *3.V* (Atlantic, 1986); *Live* (Atlantic, 1990); *The Best of Zebra: In Black and White* (Mayhem, 1998); *King Biscuit Flower Hour* (King Biscuit, 1999); *Zebra IV* (Mayhem, 2003)

HEAVY METAL TIMELINE

MEMORABLE MOMENTS IN HEAVY METAL HISTORY

1964

The Kinks and the Who stretch rock-and-roll boundaries with "You Really Got Me" and "My Generation" respectively, creating primitive versions of heavy metal in the process.

1969

Jimi Hendrix gives his famous electric guitar-feedback rendition of "The Star-Spangled Banner" at Woodstock.

Led Zeppelin releases its self-titled debut album.

1971

Led Zeppelin IV is released, and it contains the all-time most requested song in the history of radio, "Stairway to Heaven." The album itself goes on to become the highest-selling heavy metal album of all time.

1976

Two major events mark the emergence of the New Wave of British Heavy Metal movement: Iron Maiden is formed by bassist Steve Harris, and Judas Priest releases *Sad Wings of Destiny*, now considered a British Metal classic.

1979

KISS goes disco with "I Was Made for Loving You." A wounded nation grieves.

1981

Ozzy Osbourne bites the head off a dove in front of executives at his new record label.

Joan Jett releases *I Love Rock 'n' Roll* and becomes the first female role model of heavy metal.

1968

Inspired by a phrase in a William S. Burroughs novel, Steppenwolf becomes the first band to use the term "heavy metal," with the lyric "I like smoke and lightning/ heavy metal thunder" in the classic song "Born to Be Wild."

Two albums are released that would prove massively influential in the transition from acid rock to heavy metal: Blue Cheer's *Vincebus Eruptum* and Iron Butterfly's *In-A-Gadda-Da-Vida*.

Alice Cooper introduces shock-rock performance art to the rock and roll stage. It is not well received. That, of course, would soon change.

1970

On Friday, February 13th, Black Sabbath releases its eponymous debut album, establishing the band as the pioneer of doom metal.

1972

Deep Purple's *Machine Head* is released, containing the FM radio staple "Smoke on the Water."

1980

Rather than replace John Bonham and continue milking the cash cow that would no doubt have rewarded such a decision, Led Zeppelin instead chooses to disband after the alcohol-induced death of its drummer.

AC/DC singer Bon Scott dies of alcohol poisoning in February. Later that same year, the band releases *Back in Black*, their most popular album and the second highest-selling heavy metal album of all time.

1984

Tragedy strikes the hugely popular Def Leppard during the recording of their much anticipated fourth album, when drummer Rick Allen loses his left arm in a car accident.

This Is Spinal Tap is released. The movie pokes fun at rock star extravagances, to sometimes uncomfortable effect.

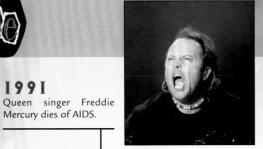

Mötley Crüe

1987
Mötley Crüe releases its fourth album, *Girls, Girls, Girls*, to much success. Bassist Nikki Sixx decides to celebrate with a heroin overdose that leaves him legally dead for several minutes. The doctors revive him, a happy miracle that Sixx celebrates by doing some more heroin.

1985
At a Parents' Music Resource Center hearing, Tennessee Senator and future Vice President Al Gore recites the Mentors' lyric "Bend up and smell my anal vapor/ Your face will be my toilet paper" in front of the U.S. Senate.

1991
Queen singer Freddie Mercury dies of AIDS.

1990
Judas Priest is accused of inciting two fans to commit suicide through alleged subliminal commands in their song "Better By You, Better Than Me."

1999
Metallica files suit against Victoria's Secret for copyright infringement when the band discovers a lip pencil hue called Metallica. The following year, they enter into a long-term legal battle against the file-sharing service Napster.

2007
Led Zeppelin reunite for a one-off concert in London, with Jason Bonham taking his father's place at the drummer's throne.

2003
A Great White performance at the Station nightclub in Warwick, Rhode Island ends in tragedy when the band's pyrotechnics set fire to the club. One hundred people are killed, including Great White guitarist Ty Longley.

1986
Slayer's *Reign in Blood* is released, and is widely considered the best thrash metal album of all time, a distinction that still stands.

Run-D.M.C. collaborates with Aerosmith on a cover of the Boston heavy metal band's classic song "Walk This Way." This becomes the first ever commercially successful merger of rap and heavy metal.

1995
The introduction of Marilyn Manson via its MTV hit cover of the Eurythmics' "Sweet Dreams" ignites a flurry of protests over the use of satanic imagery (à la Black Sabbath and Alice Cooper) and the transgender front man.

2002
The MTV reality series *The Osbournes*, starring Ozzy Osbourne, his wife, Sharon, and two of their three children, Kelly and Jack, becomes the network's most successful program, with eight million viewers.

2004
Former Pantera guitarist "Dimebag" Darrell Abbott is murdered onstage on December 8 by Nathan Gale while performing in Columbus, Ohio.

2010
Singer Ronnie James Dio dies of stomach cancer at age 67.

THE BEST OF...

TOP 15 BEST-SELLING METAL ALBUMS⚡

Heavy metal is the music of the disenfranchised, the powerless, and all those who seek to bang their heads. However, one of the other reasons it's still around despite many shifts in public tastes can be summed up with one word: greenbacks. Here are the fifteen albums that have sold the most copies, and in so doing have earned the most of the aforementioned.

1 LED ZEPPELIN
Led Zeppelin IV
(Atlantic, 1971)
23 million copies sold

2 AC/DC
Back in Black
(Atco, 1980)
22 million copies sold

3 GUNS N' ROSES
Appetite for Destruction
(Geffen, 1987)
18 million copies sold

4 LED ZEPPELIN
Physical Graffiti
(Swan Song, 1975)
16 million copies sold

5 METALLICA
Metallica
(Elektra, 1991)
15 million copies sold

6 BON JOVI
Slippery When Wet
(Mercury, 1986)
12 million copies sold

7 DEF LEPPARD
Hysteria
(Mercury, 1987)
12 million copies sold

8 LED ZEPPELIN
Led Zeppelin II
(Atlantic, 1969)
12 million copies sold

9 AEROSMITH
Greatest Hits
(Columbia, 1980)
11 million copies sold

10 LED ZEPPELIN
Houses of the Holy
(Atlantic, 1973)
11 million copies sold

11 LED ZEPPELIN
Led Zeppelin I
(Atlantic, 1969)
10 million copies sold

12 VAN HALEN
1984
(Warner Bros., 1984)
10 million copies sold

13 VAN HALEN
Van Halen
(Warner Bros., 1978)
10 million copies sold

14 DEF LEPPARD
Pyromania
(Mercury, 1990)
10 million copies sold

15 WHITESNAKE
Whitesnake
(Geffen/Warner Bros., 1987)
9 million copies sold

⚡ According to the Recording Industry Association of America, as of July 1, 2011

TOP 10 BEST-SELLING METAL ARTISTS EVER*

This is a listing of the heavy metal artists who have sold the highest total number of records. The ranking is slightly misleading, in that not all of the artists have released the same number of albums; for example, Guns N' Roses, who have only six albums to their credit, rank lower than Van Halen, whose catalog is more than twice that amount, and whose life span as a commercially successful entity predates GN'R by an entire decade. This means that Van Halen have actually, on average, sold fewer units per album than Axl and his outfit. Three cheers to the bottom line.

1. Led Zeppelin—111.5 million units certified sold
2. AC/DC—71 million units certified sold
3. Aerosmith—66.5 million units certified sold
4. Metallica—60 million units certified sold
5. Van Halen—56.5 million units certified sold
6. Guns N' Roses—44.5 million units certified sold
7. Bon Jovi—35 million units certified sold
8. Def Leppard—35 million units certified sold
9. Queen—32.5 million units certified sold
10. Ozzy Osbourne—28.75 million units certified sold

* According to the Recording Industry Association of America, as of July 1, 2011

TOP 10 BEST LIVE ALBUMS

The live album is an inherently flawed proposition. The chances of having a good soundboard mix, a responsive audience, and a band playing in top form, all while tapes are rolling, are slim indeed. When it all works out, however, the live heavy metal album is a powerful document. Here are the cases when it all clicked.

1. Deep Purple: *Made in Japan* (Warner Bros., 1972)
2. Jimi Hendrix: *Band of Gypsys* (Capitol, 1970)
3. AC/DC: *If You Want Blood You've Got It* (Atco, 1978)
4. Iron Maiden: *Live After Death* (EMI, 1985)
5. KISS: *Alive!* (Casablanca, 1975)
6. Candlemass: *Live* (Metal Blade, 1990)
7. Rush: *Exit...Stage Left* (Mercury, 1981)
8. Slayer: *Decade of Aggression* (American, 1993)
9. Judas Priest: *Unleashed in the East* (Live in Japan) (Columbia, 1979)
10. Grand Funk Railroad: *Live Album* (Capitol, 1970)

TOP 10 MOST ESSENTIAL METAL ALBUMS

These albums represent the heavy metal genre in virtually all of its various permutations, in the broadest manner possible. If you have been in a monastery for the last thirty-five years, and/or you want to get a quick overview of what all this heavy metal foolishness is about, listening to the following ten albums is the best place to start.

1. Black Sabbath *Heaven and Hell* (Warner Bros., 1980)

2. Slayer *Reign in Blood* (Def Jam, 1986)

3. Metallica *Master of Puppets* (Elektra, 1986)

4. Iron Maiden *Powerslave* (EMI, 1984)

5. Judas Priest *Screaming for Vengeance* (Columbia/Legacy, 1982)

6. Deep Purple *Made in Japan* (Warner Bros., 1972)

7. Black Sabbath *Paranoid* (Warner Bros., 1970)

8. Led Zeppelin *Led Zeppelin IV* (Atlantic, 1971)

9. Rainbow *Rising* (Polydor, 1976)

10. AC/DC *Back in Black* (Atco, 1980)

TOP 10 MOST UNDERRATED BANDS

In a genre as big and overpopulated as heavy metal, there are bound to be a greater number of bands who fall through the cracks than who receive their due. Below are bands that through bad timing, mismanagement, bad decisions, or countless other snafus have not received a fraction of the success they deserve.

1. King's X
2. Voivod
3. Kyuss
4. Candlemass
5. The Tea Party
6. Dust
7. Carnivore
8. Atomic Rooster
9. Granicus
10. Sir Lord Baltimore

TOP 10 MOST CONTROVERSIAL ALBUM COVERS

With respect to its sound and fury, heavy metal continually pushes the envelope. Sometimes though, instead of gaining new fans, a band's extreme approach backfires, especially when various large retail chains, such as WalMart, have a policy of not stocking albums with parental advisory stickers. Needless to say, if chain stores won't sell an album based on what's inside the packaging, imagine the fate of an album that features an illustration of a bloody circular chain saw ripping through a man's groin. For this reason, album covers that are deemed offensive often necessitate a second, family-friendly jacket, a fate that befell several of the selections below.

1. The Scorpions: *Virgin Killer* (RCA, 1976)
2. Carcass: *Reek of Putrefaction* (Earache, 1988)
3. W.A.S.P.: *Animal (F**k Like a Beast)* (Restless, 1983)
4. Guns N' Roses: *Appetite for Destruction* (Geffen, 1987)
5. The Scorpions: *Lovedrive* (Polydor, 1979)
6. Jane's Addiction: *Ritual de lo Habitual* (Warner Bros., 1990)
7. The Scorpions: *Love at First Sting* (Polydor, 1984)
8. Jane's Addiction: *Nothing's Shocking* (Warner Bros., 1988)
9. Tool: *Undertow* (Zoo, 1993)
10. Marilyn Manson: *Holy Wood (In the Valley of the Shadow of Death)* (Nothing/Interscope, 2000)

TOP 10 BEST METAL ALBUMS THAT ARE NOT METAL ALBUMS

Whether they realize it or not, many non-metal artists often stray into stylistic territory that could be unhesitatingly described as metal. Most of these musicians would deny it to the grave. Unfortunately for these highfalutin, self-styled hipsters, any artist who performs a song featuring heavy guitars and pounding drums is flirting with this most unhip of genres. Add a few downer melodies, odd meters, lengthy guitar solos, or screaming vocals, and you've got heavy metal, like it or not. The albums below satisfy these criteria, and could sit comfortably alongside the recorded output of many of the artists mentioned in this book.

1. Andrew Lloyd Webber: *Jesus Christ Superstar* (Decca, 1971)
2. King Crimson: *Red* (Atlantic, 1974)
3. The Beatles: *White Album* (Parlophone, 1968)
4. Mahavishnu Orchestra: *The Inner Mounting Flame* (Columbia, 1971)
5. Buddy Guy: *Sweet Tea* (Jive, 2001)
6. Yes: *Fragile* (Atlantic, 1972)
7. Bob Mould: *Black Sheets of Rain* (Virgin, 1990)
8. Swans: *Filth* (Young God, 1983)
9. Pink Floyd: *Meddle* (Capitol, 1971)
10. Lynyrd Skynyrd: *One More From The Road* (MCA, 1976)

TOP 10 BEST METAL ARTISTS THAT ARE NOT METAL ARTISTS

One of the most complicated tasks befalling any ethnomusicologist is distinguishing where hard rock ends and heavy metal begins. In most cases, the bands listed below remain in the hard rock camp due to a mellow hippie vibe that prevents them from qualifying as bona fide heavy metal acts. However, they also possess a darkness, instrumental prowess, or musical sophistication that makes their heavy metal credentials hard to ignore.

1. King Crimson
2. Lynyrd Skynyrd
3. Yes
4. Neil Young and Crazy Horse
5. Jethro Tull
6. The Doors
7. Stevie Ray Vaughan and Double Trouble
8. The Who
9. Magma
10. ZZ Top

TOP 10 BANDS WITH THE MOST RABID FAN BASES

If you value your life, you are hereby advised to keep your mouth shut when in the presence of anybody wearing a T-shirt bearing the name of the bands on this list. In the case of Rush, for example, you should know that not only are you putting yourself in physical danger by disparaging them, but their fans make it their personal mission to turn Rush-dislikers into Rush fans. So unless you want an army of Hessians stalking you at all hours, dummy up.

1. Manowar
2. Rush
3. Slayer
4. Iron Maiden
5. Dio
6. Emperor
7. King Diamond
8. Carnivore
9. King's X
10. Iced Earth

TOP 10 GOOFIEST/MOST AWESOME SONGS

In heavy metal parlance, goofy and awesome often relay the same sentiment. Manowar was ineligible for inclusion in this list, as a band's entire catalog does not qualify for individual ranking.

1. "Cygnus X-1" by Rush: *A Farewell to Kings* (Mercury, 1977)
2. "Altar of Sacrifice" by Slayer: *Reign in Blood* (Def Jam, 1986)
3. "Flash's Theme" by Queen: *Flash Gordon* (Elektra, 1981)
4. "Kill the King" by Rainbow: *Long Live Rock'n'Roll* (Polydor, 1978)
5. "Rime of the Ancient Mariner" by Iron Maiden: *Powerslave* (EMI, 1984)
6. "Immigrant Song" by Led Zeppelin: *Led Zeppelin III* (Atlantic, 1970)
7. "Jawbreaker" by Judas Priest: *Defenders of the Faith* (Columbia, 1984)
8. "Male Supremacy" by Carnivore: *Carnivore* (Roadracer, 1986)

9. "Metal Militia" by Metallica: *Kill 'Em All* (Megaforce, 1983)
10. "Shout at the Devil" by Mötley Crüe: *Shout at the Devil* (Elektra, 1983)

TOP 10 SONGS ABOUT DEPRESSION

Believe it or not, some of the people who have created the relentlessly minor-key, nihilistic music known as heavy metal have been without sunny dispositions. Go figure. Here are the most irretrievably bleak examples of their craft, almost all of which, unsurprisingly, predate Zoloft.

1. "Over and Over" by Black Sabbath: *Mob Rules* (Warner Bros., 1981)
2. "Solitude" by Candlemass: *Epicus Doomicus Metallicus* (Leviathan, 1986)
3. "Nutshell" by Alice in Chains: *Jar of Flies* (Columbia, 1994)
4. "Paranoid" by Black Sabbath: *Paranoid* (Warner Bros., 1971)
5. "No One Wants You When You're Down" by Slow Horse: *Slow Horse* (Freebird, 1999)
6. "Fade to Black" by Metallica: *Ride the Lightning* (Elektra, 1984)
7. "Banstead" by Atomic Rooster: *Atomic Rooster* (Elektra, 1970)
8. "Falling Off the Edge of the World" by Black Sabbath: *Mob Rules* (Warner Bros., 1981)
9. "Suicide" by Dust: *Hard Attack* (Kama Sutra, 1972)
10. "Solitude" by Black Sabbath: *Master of Reality* (Warner Bros., 1971)

TOP 10 MOST BORING SONGS

A note to musicians, both professional and amateur: no matter how good you are, unaccompanied solos are horrible. Just stop. Thank you.

1. "In-A-Gadda-Da-Vida" by Iron Butterfly: *In-A-Gadda-Da-Vida* (Atco, 1968)
2. "The Frayed Ends of Sanity" by Metallica: *. . . And Justice for All* (Elektra, 1988)
3. "Moby Dick" by Led Zeppelin: *The Song Remains the Same* (Warner Bros., 1976)
4. "The Mule" by Deep Purple: *Made in Japan* (Warner Bros., 1972)
5. "Warning" by Black Sabbath: *Black Sabbath* (Warner Bros., 1970)

6. "Brainstorm" by Monster Magnet: *Superjudge* (A&M, 1993)
7. "The Prophet's Song" by Queen: *A Night at the Opera* (Elektra, 1975)
8. "November Rain" by Guns N' Roses: *Use Your Illusion I* (Geffen, 1991)
9. "The Thing That Should Not Be" by Metallica: *Master of Puppets* (Elektra, 1986)
10. "Whole Lotta Love" by Led Zeppelin: *Led Zeppelin II* (Atlantic, 1969)

TOP 10 GREATEST HEAVY METAL SINGERS

Heavy metal is different from many other popular rock'n'roll subgenres in that its audience holds the singer of a band up to an operatically high standard. Naturally, a high level of musicianship is expected from all band members, but it is up to the singer to really sell the package. Here are the ones who hard-sell their respective bands, in many cases overshadowing everyone else who has the misfortune to be on stage with them.

1. Ronnie James Dio (Black Sabbath, Dio, Rainbow)
2. Freddie Mercury (Queen)
3. Bruce Dickinson (Iron Maiden)
4. Rob Halford (Judas Priest, Fight, Halford)
5. Tarja Turunen (Nightwish)
6. Chris Cornell (Soundgarden)
7. Doug Pinnick (King's X)
8. John Garcia (Kyuss)
9. Messiah Marcolin (Candlemass, Memento Mori)
10. Klaus Meine (Scorpions)

TOP 10 GREATEST HEAVY METAL GUITARISTS

The guitar is heavy metal's most potent instrument, and as such heavy metal guitarists are expected to display a high degree of manual dexterity. What follows is a list of guitarists who not only had the fastest fingers but whose originality and sense of style put them in a class of their own.

1. Jimi Hendrix
2. Eddie Van Halen (Van Halen)
3. Ritchie Blackmore (Deep Purple, Rainbow)
4. Vernon Reid (Living Colour)
5. Brian May (Queen)
6. Denis D'Amour (Voivod)

7. Ty Tabor (King's X)
8. Uli Jon Roth (The Scorpions)
9. Tony Iommi (Black Sabbath)
10. Angus Young (AC/DC)

TOP 10 GREATEST HEAVY METAL BASSISTS

Bassists are the unsung heroes of most rock bands, but there is no genre that disrespects them with more frequency than heavy metal. They're almost always buried in the mix, when they're even heard at all. Therefore, a lot of heavy metal bassists have had to be aggressive and put themselves front and center, either through the purchase of very loud equipment or by being pushy jerks. What follows is a list of bassists who muscled their way to the forefront through technique, skill, and creativity.

1. Geddy Lee (Rush)
2. Steve Harris (Iron Maiden)
3. Geezer Butler (Black Sabbath)
4. Glenn Hughes (Deep Purple)
5. Kenny Aaronson (Dust)
6. Roger Glover (Deep Purple, Rainbow)
7. John Paul Jones (Led Zeppelin)
8. Scott Reeder (Kyuss, The Obsessed)
9. Jean-Yves Theriault (Voivod)
10. Danny Lilker (Anthrax, Nuclear Assault, S.O.D.)

TOP 10 GREATEST HEAVY METAL DRUMMERS

Drummers are the athletes of heavy metal bands. Apart from having the greatest quantity of equipment to haul around, they are expected to pound and smash for the duration of a two-hour set, all while keeping clocklike time and enduring the disrespect of the guitar player. The following drummers do all this and more; in several cases their skill alone distinguishes an unbelievable band from a mediocre band.

1. Neil Peart (Rush)
2. Ian Paice (Deep Purple, Whitesnake)
3. Dave Lombardo (Slayer)
4. Reed St. Mark (Celtic Frost)
5. John Bonham (Led Zeppelin)
6. Vinnie Appice (Black Sabbath, Dio)
7. Matt Cameron (Soundgarden)
8. Bill Ward (Black Sabbath)
9. Dale Crover (The Melvins)
10. Tommy Lee (Mötley Crüe)

BIBLIOGRAPHY

BOOKS

Charlesworth, Cris. *Deep Purple: The Illustrated Biography*. London: Omnibus, 1998.

Davis, Stephen. *Hammer of the Gods*. Berkeley, California: Berkley Publishing Group, 2001.

Luerssen, John D. *Mouthing Off: A Book of Rock and Roll Quotes*. Brooklyn, New York: Telegraph Company, 2002.

Marsh, Dave (editor). *Black Sabbath: An Oral History*. New York: Harper Entertainment, 1998.

Moynihan, Michael and Didrik Soderlind. *Lords of Chaos: The Bloody Rise of the Satanic Metal Underground*. Venice, California: Feral House, 1998.

Rosen, Steven. *Black Sabbath*. Berlin: Sanctuary Publishing, 2002.

Wall, Mick. *Paranoid: Black Days With Sabbath and Other Horror Stories*. Edinburgh: Mainstream Publishing, 2001.

WEBSITES

All Movie Guide: http://www.allmovie.com
All Music Guide: http://www.allmusic.com
American Nihilist Underground Society: http://www.anus.com
Blabbermouth.net: http://www.roadrunnerrecords.com/blabbermouth.net/
BNR Metal Pages, The: http://www.bnrmetal.com
Brief History of Banned Music in the United States: http://ericnuzum.com/banned/index.html
Brutal Metal: http://brutalmetal.com
Dark Legions Archive: http://www.anus.com/metal

Denim & Leather: http://www.sundin.net/denim
Doom-metal.com: http://www.doom-metal.com
Encyclopaedia Metallum: The Metal Archives: http://www.metal-archives.com
Evil Music: http://www.evilmusic.com
The Gauntlet: http://www.thegauntlet.com
German Metal: http://www.germanmetal.com
"Hair Metal Look," Yesterdayland Fashion: http://www.yesterdayland.com/popopedia/shows/fashion/fa2144.php
Heavy Metal Parking Lot Official Website: http://www.heavymetalparkinglot.net
Hessian Cultural Library: http://www.anus.com/hsc/hcl
Mega's Metal Asylum: http://www.lut.fi/~mega/music.html
The Metal Gospel: http://www.metalgospel.com
The Metal Reference: http://www.metal-reference.com
Metal Roots: http://metalroots.orcon.net.nz
Metal-Rules.com: http://www.metal-rules.com
Norwegian Metal Band List: http://liquid2k.com/normetal
The Pit: http://www.avmdev.com/thepit/index.htm
Rock Wisdom.com: http://rockwisdom.com/mainpage.htm

FILMS

Decline of Western Civilization Part II: The Metal Years (Penelope Spheeris, 1988).

This is Spinal Tap (Rob Reiner, 1984).

The publisher would like to thank Herb Friedrich of Herb's Hut, P.O. Box 18412, San Antonio, TX 78218. (hutstuff@webtv.net) for providing most of the heavy metal memorabilia that appears in this book. Herb allowed us access to his amazing collection which included patches, posters, pins, ticket stubs, and other items.

NORWAY
Borknagar
Darkthrone
Devil
Dodheimsgard
Emperor
God Seed
Gorgoroth
Immortal
Keep of Kalessin
Kvelertak
Lucifer Was
Mayhem
Ov Hell
Sahg
Satyricon
Strid
Taake
TNT
Tsjuder
Ulver
Veles
Wardruna

CANADA
Annihilator
Anvil
Blasphemy
Cauldron
Conqueror
Exciter
Iskra
Revenge
Razor
Rush
Sheavy
Tea Party
Voivod

SCOTLAND
Holocaust
Nazareth

DENMARK
King Diamond
Mercyful Fate

ENGLAND
Anathema
Atomic Rooster
Bad Company
Black Sabbath
Budgie
Carcass
Cradle of Filth
Cream
The Darkness
Deep Purple
Def Leppard
Diamond Head
Electric Wizard
Fastway
Free
Girlschool
Godflesh
Grim Reaper
Humble Pie
Iron Maiden
Judas Priest
Led Zeppelin
Motörhead
My Dying Bride
Napalm Death
Ozzy Osbourne
Paradise Lost
Queen
Rainbow
Raven
Samson
Saxon
Slade
Sweet
Tygers of Pan Tang
U.F.O.
Uriah Heep
Venom
Whitesnake
Witchfinder General

IRELAND
Therapy?
Thin Lizzy

UNITED STATES
Abigail Williams
Aerosmith
Alice In Chains
Angel
Anthrax
Argus
Armored Saint
Biohazard
Black Dahlia Murder
Blue Cheer
Blue Öyster Cult
Bon Jovi
Cactus
Cannibal Corpse
Carnivore
Cinderella
Cirith Ungol
Confessor
Alice Cooper
Corrosion of Conformity
Danzig
Dark Angel
Darkest Hour
Death (Detroit)
Death (Florida)
Deftones
Deicide
Dio
Dokken
Down
Dream Theater
D.R.I.
Dust
Dying Fetus
Exodus
EyeHateGod
Faith No More
Faster Pussycat
Fates Warning
Fear Factory
Flotsam & Jetsam
Lita Ford
Fu Manchu
Goatsnake
Grand Funk Railroad
Granicus
Guns n' Roses
GWAR
Hallow's Eve
Hatebreed
Helmet
Jimi Hendrix
Hidden Hand
High On Fire
Iced Earth
Iron Butterfly
Isis
Jag Panzer
Jane's Addiction
Joan Jett
Jex Thoth
Killswitch Engage
King's X
KISS
Kylesa
Kyuss
L7
L.A. Guns
Lamb of God
Legs Diamond
Living Colour
Manilla Road
Manowar
Mastodon
Megadeth
Melvins
Mentors
Metal Church
Metallica
Monster Magnet
Morbid Angel
Mötley Crüe
Mountain
Municipal Waste
Nebula
Neurosis
Nuclear Assault
Obituary
The Obsessed
Overkill
Pantera
Penance
Pentagram
Place of Skulls
Poison
Possessed
Prong
Queens of the Stone Age
Queensrÿche
Quiet Riot
Rage Against the Machine
Ratt
Riot
Rwake
Sacred Reich
Saigon Kick
Saint Vitus
Joe Satriani
Savatage
Sevendust
Sir Lord Baltimore
Six Feet Under
Skid Row
Slayer
Sleep
Slow Horse
Solace
Solitude Aeturnus
Soundgarden
Spirit Caravan
Starz
Stormtroopers of Death
Stryper
Suffocation
Suicidal Tendencies
Tesla
Testament
Tool
Trouble
Twisted Sister
Type O Negative
Unorthodox
Steve Vai
Van Halen
Vixen
Warhorse
Warlord
Warrant
Warpig
W.A.S.P.
White Zombie
Winter
Wolves in the Throne Room
Y&T
Zebra

NETHERLANDS
Asphx
Atheist
Legion of the Damned
Pestilence

FRANCE
Antaeus
Gojira
Mutilation
Vlad Tepes

SWITZERLAND
Celtic Frost
Coroner
Krokus
Samael

ITALY
Paul Chain
Death SS
Lacuna Coil
Mortuary Drape
Rhapsody of Fire

CZECH REPUBLIC
Arakain
Debustrol
Root
Silent Stream of Godless Elegy
Törr

COLOMBIA
Inquisition

BRAZIL
Sarcofago
Sepultura

ARGENTINA
Los Natas

SOUTH AFRICA
Mind Assault

SWEDEN
Abruptum
Arch Enemy
At the Gates
Aunt Mary
Candlemass
Dark Tranquility
Dissection
Dismember
Entombed
Ghost
Grand Magus
Hammerfall
In Flames
In Solitude
Katatonia
Yngwie Malmsteen
Memento Mori
November
Opeth
Repugnant
Sabaton
Soilwork
Spiritual Beggars
Terra Firma
Therion
Watain
Witchcraft

FINLAND
Amorphis
Apocalyptica
Behexen
Children of Bodom
Finntroll
Hanoi Rocks
Impaled Nazarene
Korpiklaani
Nightwish
Sargeist
Sentenced
Stone
Stratovarius
Swallow the Sun
Synergy
Tarot
Xysma

GERMANY
Accept
Ascension
Belphegor
Birth Control
Blackwater Park
Blind Guardian
Destruction
Grave Digger
Helloween
Hell
Kreator
Lucifer's Friend
Moonblood
Morgoth
Necrophagist
Night Sun
Nocturnal
Rammstein
Running Wild
Scorpions
Sodom
Tankard
Toad
Virus
Warlock
Weed
Wind

RUSSIA
Aria
Cherniy Obelisk
Gorky Park
Korrozia Metalla
Master
Master's Hammer
Mgla
Old Wainds

HUNGARY
Karthago

POLAND
Behemoth
Decapitated
Hate
KAT
Niemen
TSA
Vader
Vesania

EGYPT
Scarab

JAPAN
Acid Mothers Temple
Boris
Corrupted
Flower Travellin' Band
Fushitsusha
Ground Zero
Haino Keiji
High Rise
Loudness
Merzbow
KK Null
Ruins
Sigh
Strawberry Path
Ybo2

GREECE
Rotting Christ
Varathron

ZAMBIA
Ngozi Family

BOTSWANA
Wrust

AUSTRALIA
AC/DC
Adorior
Airbourne
Buffalo
Destroyer
Mournful Congregation
Rose Tattoo
Wolfmother

N

MAP OF METAL